WELCOME TO PARIS

Paris is one of the most beautiful cities on earth, a truth easily appreciated on a stroll that could yield one stunning vista after another, from the epic Eiffel Tower to the regal Jardin des Tuileries to the petite cafés bursting onto the sidewalks. Beyond the city's visual appeal, the cultural riches of the French capital are unsurpassed. Whether you opt to explore the historic, fashion-conscious, bourgeois, or bohemian and arty sides of Paris, one thing is certain: the City of Light will always enthrall.

TOP REASONS TO GO

★ **Iconic Landmarks:** From the Eiffel Tower to the Arc de Triomphe, Paris dazzles.

★ **Chic Shopping:** The Champs-Élysées and Rue St-Honoré are the ultimate shopaholic high.

★ **Heavenly Food:** Whether it's haute cuisine or baguettes, locals know how to eat.

★ **The Seine:** The river's bridges and islands reward exploration by foot or boat.

★ **Grand Museums:** From the mammoth Louvre to the petite Musée Rodin, art abounds.

★ **Majestic Churches:** Notre-Dame and Sacré-Coeur boldly mark the city's skyline.

Fodor's PARIS 2015

Publisher: Amanda D'Acierno, *Senior Vice President*

Editorial: Arabella Bowen, *Editor in Chief*; Linda Cabasin, *Editorial Director*

Design: Fabrizio La Rocca, *Vice President, Creative Director*; Tina Malaney, *Associate Art Director*; Chie Ushio, *Senior Designer*; Ann McBride, *Production Designer*

Photography: Melanie Marin, *Associate Director of Photography*; Jessica Parkhill and Jennifer Romains, *Researchers*

Maps: Rebecca Baer, *Senior Map Editor*; Mark Stroud, Henry Colomb, and David Lindroth, *Cartographers*

Production: Linda Schmidt, *Managing Editor*; Evangelos Vasilakis, *Associate Managing Editor*; Angela L. McLean, *Senior Production Manager*

Sales: Jacqueline Lebow, *Sales Director*

Marketing & Publicity: Heather Dalton, *Marketing Director*; Katherine Punia, *Senior Publicist*

Business & Operations: Susan Livingston, *Vice President, Strategic Business Planning*; Sue Daulton, *Vice President, Operations*

Fodors.com: Megan Bell, *Executive Director, Revenue & Business Development*; Yasmin Marinaro, *Senior Director, Marketing & Partnerships*

Copyright © 2015 by Fodor's Travel, a division of Random House LLC

Writers: Jennifer Ditsler-Ladonne, Linda Hervieux, Nancy Heslin, Victoria Tang, Jack Vermee

Editors: Susan MacCallum-Whitcomb, Mark Sullivan

Production Editor: Carolyn Roth

ISBN 978-0-8041-4256-4

ISSN 0149–1288

All details in this book are based on information supplied to us at press time. Always confirm information when it matters, especially if you're making a detour to visit a specific place. Fodor's expressly disclaims any liability, loss, or risk, personal or otherwise, that is incurred as a consequence of the use of any of the contents of this book.

SPECIAL SALES

This book is available at special discounts for bulk purchases for sales promotions or premiums. For more information, e-mail specialmarkets@randomhouse.com

PRINTED IN THE UNITED STATES OF AMERICA

10 9 8 7 6 5 4 3 2 1

Fodor's 2015

PARIS

CONTENTS

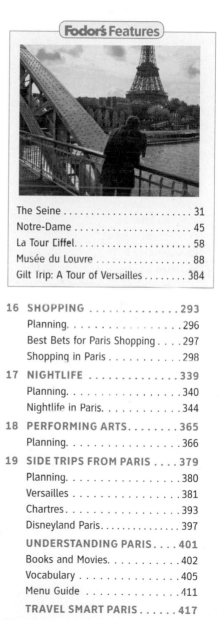

Fodor's Features

CONTENTS

ABOUT THIS GUIDE

Fodor's Recommendations
Everything in this guide is worth doing—we don't cover what isn't—but exceptional sights, hotels, and restaurants are recognized with additional accolades. **Fodor's**Choice ★ indicates our top recommendations; and **Best Bets** call attention to notable hotels and restaurants in various categories. Care to nominate a new place? Visit Fodors.com/contact-us.

Trip Costs
We list prices wherever possible to help you budget well. Hotel and restaurant price categories from $ to $$$$ are noted alongside each recommendation. For hotels, we include the lowest cost of a standard double room in high season. For restaurants, we cite the average price of a main course at dinner or, if dinner isn't served, at lunch. For attractions, we always list adult admission fees; discounts are usually available for children, students, and senior citizens.

Hotels
Our local writers vet every hotel to recommend the best overnights in each price category, from budget to expensive. Unless otherwise specified, you can expect private bath, phone, and TV in your room. For expanded hotel reviews, facilities, and deals visit Fodors.com.

Top Picks	Hotels & Restaurants
★ **Fodor's**Choice	🏨 Hotel
Listings	🛏 Number of rooms
✉ Address	🍴 Meal plans
✉ Branch address	✕ Restaurant
☎ Telephone	🥢 Reservations
🖷 Fax	👔 Dress code
🌐 Website	▭ No credit cards
✉ E-mail	$ Price
🎫 Admission fee	**Other**
⊙ Open/closed times	⇨ See also
Ⓜ Subway	☞ Take note
✛ Directions or Map coordinates	🏌 Golf facilities

Restaurants
Unless we state otherwise, restaurants are open for lunch and dinner daily. We mention dress code only when there's a specific requirement and reservations only when they're essential or not accepted. To make restaurant reservations, visit Fodors.com.

Credit Cards
The hotels and restaurants in this guide typically accept credit cards. If not, we'll say so.

EXPERIENCE PARIS

1

PARIS TODAY

Bienvenue à Paris! Or, welcome to Paris! Although it may seem as if time stands still in this city—with its romantic buildings and elegant parks and squares—there's an undercurrent of small but significant changes happening here that might not be immediately obvious.

Today's Paris . . .

. . . is greener. Parisians are breathing a little easier today as the city moves toward a more eco-friendly lifestyle. Emission-free buses and the city's first completely electric riverboat made the capital a little more eco-friendly in 2013. And although the image of intellectuals sitting in a café, cigarette in hand, has largely disappeared since a smoking ban was instituted in 2008, the city is now encouraging locals to trash their butts in 10,000 specially designed trash cans. The city is also cutting down on smog with its popular Vélib' municipal bikes and AutoLib' car-sharing service. In addition to the gradual replacement of paved streets with more aesthetically pleasing cobblestones and widening the tree-lined sidewalks, the city is slowly implementing an ambitious project to permanently pedestrianize the expressways along the Seine, following the success of Paris Plage, the yearly beach party along

the river. Even rooftops are going green with gardens and solar panels popping up in several arrondissements.

. . . is healthier. Paris is a gastronomic capital, so you'll always be able to find *macarons* and foie gras (despite a poll confirming that 29% of the population forgo the latter delicacy for "ethical reasons"). But Parisians are opening up to more diverse dining options and healthier lifestyles. Gluten-free visitors can indulge in a traditional French pastry at Helmut Newcake, France's first gluten-free bakery. Lactose intolerant gelato lovers can swoon at the dairy-free options at Amorino. Parisians are also moving their bodies. Ever-expanding gym facilities and yoga studios are also making exercising more culturally acceptable than ever before—not that the French had a huge weight problem to begin with.

. . . is friendlier. In an attempt to woo more travelers, the Paris Chamber of Commerce and Industry and the Regional Tourism Committee jointly issued a pamphlet called "Do You Speak Touriste?" in 2013. The publication highlights how to treat 11 different visiting nationalities. What do they say about American tourists? They expect speedy service and a

WHAT'S HOT

Place de la République kicked cars to the curb with a €35 million overhaul in 2014. While the bronze statue of Marianne still dominates the square, it's now a kid-friendly zone (complete with a wading pool) and a serene place to sneak a peek at the locals lounging

beneath the 150 newly planted trees.

By the end of 2014, Guy Savoy will have relocated his award-winning Monnaie de Paris to an 18th-century palace at Quai de Conti. Savoy will launch a second restaurant, Metal Café, an outdoor brasserie where

five pedestrian streets will create a shortcut between the Louvre and Odéon.

Costing a cool €30 million, Les Berges, a waterfront walk along the Left Bank between the Eiffel Tower and the Louvre, is open for business—if your business is sipping

proficiency in English, for starters. They also "demand Wi-Fi and prefer to have dinner at 6 pm."

...is tech-savvy. New gadgets and gizmos are popping up everywhere since an ongoing government program began encouraging innovation. The result? Centers like the Gaîté Lyrique mix technology with art on a daily basis. Google opened the Google Cultural Institute in late 2013 (an event shunned by the country's cultural minister), which includes a permanent exhibit at the Pavillon de l'Arsenal. Versailles enlists the latest technology to engage visitors, and the Louvre uses Nintendo 3DS systems as their audioguides. Even bakeries are giving a nod to the future by letting you pay directly at an automated machine.

...is swankier. Did somebody say there's a recession? If so, the hospitality industry has been too busy building new luxury palace hotels in Paris to have heard the news. The glamorous Ritz Hotel in Place Vendôme is scheduled to reopen by early 2015 after undergoing a €140 million facelift. That's pennies compared to The Peninsula Paris, whose renovation of a century-old building near the Arc de Triomphe cost a whopping €338 million.

...is artistic. In 2014, the city was abuzz about the hugely anticipated reopening of the Musée Picasso. After extensive renovation work, including bulletproof windows at €12,000 a pop, the museum will occupy the entire Hôtel Salé, vastly increasing its original size. Le BAL LAB in Montmartre is a new independent center for documentary images, and the historic Gaîté Lyrique reopened as a digital arts center in 2011.

...is open on Sunday. Since the fall of 2013, "Yes Weekend" demonstrations by Parisian workers have encouraged the government to further relax laws banning stores from opening on Sunday. Change has come gradually, with shops in tourist areas already exempt. The Marais, the Avenue des Champs-Élysées, and St-Germain des-Prés are among the liveliest places to go on weekends, but other neighborhoods aren't the ghost towns they once were. As recently as five years ago, Paris was still largely deserted in August when the locals fled to the countryside and beaches, leaving a wake of closed shops and restaurants. Today the city is very much alive throughout the summer, with outdoor music festivals, the beach along the Seine that is Paris Plage.

rosé at Faust Terrace, playing backgammon at the Centipede, or working off that baguette gut at nine fitness stations. Hang out with real Parisians at the scattering of cafés and restaurants, or grab a seat at the amphitheater near the Musée d'Orsay.

Once described by Hemingway as being "full of nocturnal pleasure-seekers," Paris was named the "European capital of boredom" by the newspaper *Le Monde* a few years ago. To help prevent Paris from turning into the City of Lights Out, the city elected its first "Nightlife

Mayor" in late 2013. Clement Léon, 31, promises a club scene to rival such European hotspots as Berlin, London, and Barcelona. Said Léon: "We can't afford to become the laughing stock of Europe."

WHAT'S WHERE

These numbers refer to chapters.

2 The Islands. Although they're just a few quick steps from the "mainland," the Ile de la Cité and Ile St-Louis are the heart of Paris. This is where you can find Notre-Dame and Sainte-Chapelle.

3 Around the Eiffel Tower. With the Champs de Mars, Les Invalides, and the Seine nearby, many lovely strolls give you striking views of Paris's ultimate monument.

4 Champs-Élysées. The Champs-Élysées and Arc de Triomphe attract the tourists, but there are also several excellent museums here, well worth checking out.

5 Around the Louvre. The Faubourg St-Honoré, with its well-established shops and cafés, has always been chic, and probably always will be. Les Halles, the city's food market, just finished its €500 million renovation.

6 The Grands Boulevards with the Opéra Garnier. Use the Opéra Garnier as your landmark and set out to do some power shopping. There are some good, small museums in the area, too.

7 Montmartre. Like a small village within a big city, Montmartre feels distinctly separate from the rest of

Paris—but it's prime tourist territory, with Sacré-Coeur as its main attraction.

8 Marais. The Marais, which used to be Paris's Jewish neighborhood, is now one of the city's hippest destinations. While away the afternoon at Place des Vosges or shop to your heart's content.

9 Eastern Paris. If it's new and happening in Paris, you'll find it out here in neighborhoods like Canal St-Martin, Bastille, Oberkampf, and République. The area is filled with trendy restaurants, funky galleries, and cutting-edge boutiques.

10 The Latin Quarter. Leave yourself lots of time to wander the Latin Quarter, known for its vibrant student life.

11 St-Germain-des-Prés. Fabulous cafés and the Musée d'Orsay are here, but make sure you leave time to wander the Jardin du Luxembourg.

12 Montparnasse. Once the haunt of artists and writers—Picasso and Hemingway included—this neighborhood is now known for its contemporary-art scene, as well as the Catacombs.

13 Western Paris. The Bois de Boulogne and the Musée Marmottan Monet are two great reasons to trek out here.

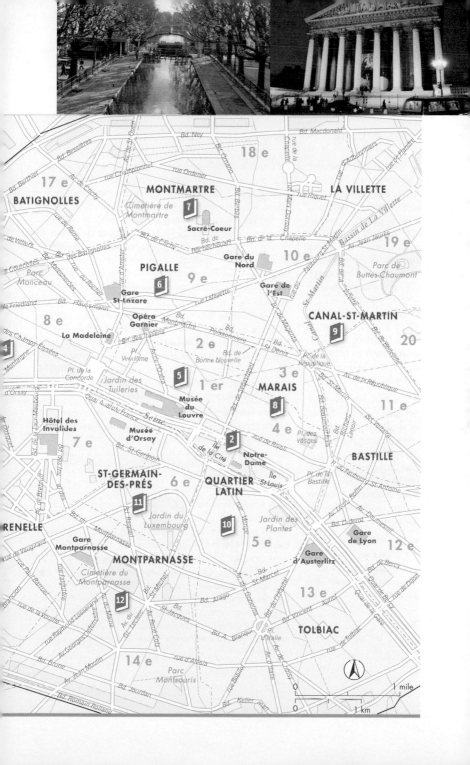

17 e BATIGNOLLES

18 e

Bd. Ney

Bd. Bessières

Bd. Berthier

Av. de Clichy

rue Championnet

rue Ordener

Bd. d'Ornano

rue de la Chapelle

Bd. Macdonald

rue de Flandre

rue d'Aubervilliers

LA VILLETTE

de Villiers

de Rome

rue de Rome

Bd. de Courcelles

Bd. Haussmann

Parc Monceau

Bd. des Batignolles

MONTMARTRE

7

Cimetière de Montmartre

Sacré-Coeur

Bd. de Clichy

Bd. de Rochechouart

Bd. de la Chapelle

Gare du Nord

10 e

Bassin de La Villette

Av. Jean Jaurès

19 e

Parc de Buttes-Chaumont

20

8 e

La Madeleine

PIGALLE

6

9 e

Gare St-Lazare

Opéra Garnier

Gare de l'Est

rue Lafayette

Bd. Montmartre

rue Poissonnière

Bd. de Magenta

Canal St-Martin

CANAL-ST-MARTIN

9

Pl. de la République

11 e

de Courcelles Élysées

4

Montaigne

d'Orsay

Pl. de la Concorde

Jardin des Tuileries

Pl. Vendôme

Bd. des Italiens

2 e

Bd. de Bonne Nouvelle

St-Denis

1 er

5

Musée du Louvre

3 e

MARAIS

8

4 e

Pl. des Vosges

Av. de la République

Bd. Voltaire

Hôtel des Invalides

7 e

Musée d'Orsay

Bd. St-Germain

Seine

Île de la Cité

2

Notre-Dame

rue de Rivoli

Île St-Louis

Pl. de la Bastille

BASTILLE

Pl. du Faubourg St-Antoine

GRENELLE

ST-GERMAIN-DES-PRÉS

6 e

11

Jardin du Luxembourg

QUARTIER LATIN

10

rue Monge

Jardin des Plantes

5 e

Gare de Lyon

12 e

rue de Vaugirard

Gare Montparnasse

MONTPARNASSE

Bd. du Montparnasse

Cimetière du Montparnasse

12

Bd. St-Michel

Bd. Arago

Bd. St-Marcel

Gare d'Austerlitz

13 e

Bd. de Bercy

Av. Jean Moulin

Bd. Brune

Bd. Jourdan

Bd. Romain Rolland

14 e

Parc Montsouris

rue d'Alésia

Pl. d'Italie

TOLBIAC

0   1 mile

0   1 km

PARIS PLANNER

Getting Around

Paris is without question best explored on foot, and thanks to Baron Haussmann's mid-19th-century redesign, the City of Light is a compact wonder of wide boulevards, gracious parks, and leafy squares. When you want a lift, though, public transportation is easy and inexpensive. The *métro* (subway) goes just about everywhere you're going for €1.70 a ride (a *carnet*, or "pack" of 10 tickets, is €13.70); tickets also work on buses and trams and the RER train line within Paris.

Paris is divided into 20 *arrondissements* (neighborhoods) spiraling out from the center of the city. The numbers reveal the neighborhood's location and its age, the 1er arrondissement at the city's heart being the oldest. The arrondissements in central Paris—the 1er to 8e—are the most visited.

It's worth picking up a copy of *Paris Pratique Par Arrondissement*, the essential map guide, available at newsstands and bookstores.

Saving Time and Money

Paris is one of the world's most visited cities—with crowds to prove it—so it pays to be prepared. Buy tickets online when you can: most cultural centers and museums offer advance-ticket sales, and the small service fee you'll pay is worth the time saved waiting in line. Investigate alternative entrances at popular sites (there are three at the Louvre, for example), and check when rates are reduced, often during once-a-week late openings. Also, national museums are free the first Sunday of each month. There are many within Paris, including the Louvre, Musée d'Orsay, and Centre Pompidou.

A Paris Museum Pass (⊕ www.parismuseumpass.com) can save you money if you're planning serious sightseeing, but it might be even more valuable because it allows you to bypass the lines. It's sold at the destinations it covers and at airports, major métro stations, and the tourism office in the Carrousel du Louvre. The two-, four-, and six-day passes are €39, €54, and €69, respectively.

Stick to the omnipresent ATMs for the best exchange rates; exchanging cash at your hotel or in a store is never going to be to your advantage.

Hours

Paris is by no means a 24/7 city, so planning your days beforehand can save you aggravation. Museums are closed one day a week, usually Tuesday, and most stay open late at least one night each week, which is also the least crowded time to visit. Store hours are generally 10 am to 7 pm, though smaller shops may not open until 11 am, only to close for several hours during the afternoon. Retailers now have the option of doing business on Sunday, although your best bets are department stores, the shops along the Champs-Élysées, the Carrousel du Louvre, and around the Marais where most boutiques open around 2 pm.

Eating Out

Restaurants follow French mealtimes, serving lunch from noon to 2:30 pm and dinner from 7:30 or 8 pm. Some cafés serve food all day long. Always reserve a table for dinner, as top restaurants book up months in advance. When it comes to the check, you must ask for it (it's considered rude to bring it unbidden). In cafés you'll get a register receipt with your order. *Servis* (gratuity) is always included in the bill, but it's good form to leave something extra if you're satisfied with the service: a few cents for drinks, €1 for lunch, €3 at dinner. Leave 5% of the bill only in higher-end restaurants.

What to Wear

When it comes to clothing, the standard French look is dressier than the American equivalent. Athletic clothes are reserved for sports. Sneakers are not usually worn by adults, but if you pack yours, keep them for daytime only. Neat jeans are acceptable everywhere except at higher-end restaurants; check to see whether there's a dress code.

When to Go

The City of Light is magical all year round, but it's particularly gorgeous in June, when the long days (the sun doesn't set until 10 pm) stretch sightseeing hours and make it ideal to linger in the cafés.

Winter can be dark and chilly, but it's also the best time to find cheap airfares and hotel deals.

April in Paris, despite what the song says, is often rainy.

Summer is the most popular (and expensive) season. Keep in mind that, as in many other European cities, some shops and restaurants close in August for several weeks, though there are still plenty of fun things to do, like free open-air movies and concerts, and the popular Paris Plage, the "beach" on the Right Bank of the Seine.

September is gorgeous, with temperate weather, saner airfares, and cultural events timed for the *rentrée* (or return), signifying the end of summer vacation. In the third weekend in September, scores of national buildings that are normally closed to the public open for visits during the annual Journées du Patrimoine (Patrimony Days).

Paris Etiquette

The Parisian reputation for rudeness is undeserved. In fact, Parisians are sticklers for politesse and exchanging formal greetings is the rule. Informal American-style manners are considered impolite. Beginning an exchange with a simple "Do you speak English?" will get you on the right foot. Learning a few key French words will take you far. Offer a hearty *bonjour* (bohn-zhoor) when walking into a shop or café and an *au revoir* (o ruh-vwahr) when leaving, even if nobody seems to be listening (a chorus may reply). When speaking to a woman over age 16, use *madame* (ma-dam), literally "my lady." For a young woman or girl, use *mademoiselle* (mad-mwa-zel). A man of any age goes by *monsieur* (murh-syur). Always say please, *s'il vous plaît* (seel-voo-play), and thank you, *merci* (mehr-see).

Paris Temps

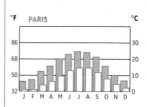

PARIS
TOP ATTRACTIONS

Eiffel Tower

(A) Originally built as a temporary exhibition for the 1889 World's Fair, today there's no other monument that symbolizes Paris better than Gustave Eiffel's world-famous Iron Lady. It's breathtaking, whether you see it sparkling from your hotel window after dark or join the millions of annual visitors to brave the glass-elevator trip to the top.

Notre-Dame

(B) It took almost 200 years to finish this 12th-century Gothic masterpiece, immortalized by Victor Hugo and his fictional hunchback. In 2013 the Dame celebrated her 850th birthday with a bang—or at least a clang: nine new bells now reproduce the sounds of yesteryear.

Jardin du Luxembourg

(C) This is one of the prime leisure spots on the Left Bank for urban-weary Parisians. Relax in a reclining park chair with a picnic lunch or a book, watch a game of *boules* while the kids enjoy a marionette show, or visit an exhibition at the Musée du Luxembourg in a wing of the 17th-century Palais de Luxembourg, now home to the Paris Senate.

Jardin des Tuileries

(D) The 17th-century formal French landscape of these gardens behind the Louvre is punctuated by contemporary sculptures, a café, and two noteworthy museums: the Jeu de Paume and the Musée de l'Orangerie. In summer there's a small amusement park and Ferris wheel.

Arc de Triomphe

(E) The 164-foot-tall Arc de Triomphe has served as the backdrop for official military parades since its completion in 1836. Use the underground passageway to reach the monument, where you can visit the Tomb of the Unknown Soldier beneath the arch or climb the stairs for amazing panoramic views of the city.

Musée d'Orsay

(F) What started out as a train station constructed for the 1900 World's Fair became this beautiful Belle Époque building filled with Art Nouveau objects, Impressionist paintings, vintage photography, and realist sculptures. Don't miss the scale model of the Opéra Garnier or the views of the Seine from the grand ballroom, now housing the museum's restaurant.

Opéra Garnier

(G) Opulent, stunning, and magnificently over the top, Charles Garnier's opera house is one of the outstanding jewels of the Second Empire. Its illustrious marble staircase and ruby-red box seats have been featured in films from *Dangerous Liaisons* to *Marie-Antoinette,* and its backstage corridors are famously haunted by the Phantom of the Opera.

Centre Pompidou

(H) The Centre Pompidou's groundbreaking "inside-out" design is still visually shocking (it opened in 1977). This is also the top destination for modern-art lovers in Paris.

Sacré-Coeur

(I) This wedding-cake white basilica dominates Montmartre's hilltop. Most visitors are content with the views overlooking the city from the basilica stairs, but ambitious sight seekers can climb to the bell tower for an even higher vantage point.

Musée du Louvre

(J) The grandest museum in the world was just a humble fortress in the 12th century, but grew in size and prestige as a sumptuous royal palace until the French Revolution gave it a new lease on life as home to the Republic's art collection. Don't miss the big three—*Mona Lisa, Winged Victory,* and *Venus de Milo.*

PARIS LIKE A LOCAL

To appreciate the City of Light as the locals do, you can start by learning some of the daily rituals of Paris life. These simple, fun pleasures will quickly get you into the swing of being Parisian.

Shop Like a Parisian

Parisians prefer the boisterous atmosphere of bustling street markets to the drab *supermarchés*. Even if you're just buying picnic fixings, you can follow suit. For a full listing of Paris's markets, check out the city's website at ⊕ *www.paris.fr/ english*, but these are some of our faves.

Le Marché d'Aligre, just off Rue du Faubourg St-Antoine beyond the Opéra Bastille, dates back to the 18th century. Open Tuesday through Sunday, the market has fruit, vegetables, cheese, meat, fish, and poultry, as well as a host of other products. The best selection is on the weekend (Tuesday to Saturday 9 to 1 and 4 to 7, Sunday 9 to 1:30, métro: Ledru-Rollin). Le Marché Mouffetard, between the Panthéon and the Jardin des Plantes, is a combination of stands and food shops spilling out onto a cobbled pedestrian Rue Mouffetard (a marketplace of its own with restaurants, cafés, and shops). Olive oil, chocolates, books, and wine are available, in addition to produce, cheese, and meats (Tuesday to Saturday 9 am to 6 pm, Sunday 9 am to 1 pm, métro: Censier-Dubenton).

If flea markets are your thing, Paris has three that can satisfy any bargain hunter. **Les Puces des Vanves** (weekends, 7 am to 7:30 pm, métro: Porte de Vanves; Avenue de le Porte de Vanves and Avenue Marc Sangnier) is two in one: in the morning, collectors revel among old furniture, stamps, postcards, and everything else; in the afternoon, merchants of new and vintage clothing take over. **Les Puces de St-Ouen** (Saturday 9 am to 6 pm, Sunday 10 am to 6 pm, and Monday 10 am to 5 pm, métro: Porte de Clignancourt), otherwise known as the Clignancourt flea market, is a little more expensive, but a real treasure trove. Bypass the noisy stands near the métro in favor of the buildings beyond the elevated highway, where antiques dealers and vintage-clothing boutiques set up. You might not *need* to buy flowers, but the flower markets are lovely for wandering. Try one of **Les Marchés aux Fleurs**: at Place de la Madeleine (Monday to Saturday, 8 am to 7:30 pm), Place des Ternes (Tuesday to Sunday, 8 am to 7:30 pm), or Place Lépine on the Ile de la Cité (daily 8 am to 7:30 pm, with the bird market Sunday morning).

Drink Coffee Like a Parisian

Le café in Paris isn't simply a drink that begins the day: it's a way of life. Though Parisians do stop at the counter to order a quick *café expresse, bien serré, s'il vous plaît* ("good and strong, please"), more often people treat the café as an extension of their apartments, with laptops precariously balanced, cell phones ringing, and business being done; in Paris the café is the place to work, read, and chat with friends any time of the day. Think of Simone de Beauvoir, who spent more time at **Café de Flore** (✉ *172 bd. St-Germain*, 6e ☎ *01–45–48–55–26*) than in her chilly apartment. Choose a café with a patio or good windows for people-watching, or pause at the nearest counter, and you're in for a dose of Parisian café culture. Most locals have their own favorites, and we've listed some of our top choices on the neighborhood Getting Oriented pages; you're bound to find your own preferred haunt(s).

Walk Like a Parisian

Paris was made for wandering, and the French have coined a lovely word for a person who wanders the streets: *le flâneur,* one who strolls or loiters, usually without a destination. In Paris the streets beckon, leading you past monuments, down narrow alleyways, through arches, and into hidden squares. As a flâneur, you can become attuned to the city's rhythm and, no matter how aimlessly you stroll, chances are you'll end up somewhere magical. Some of our suggestions for wandering are along the Seine, into the poetic streets of **St-Germain**, or into the tangled lanes around the **Bastille** and **Canal St-Martin**. Strolling is a favorite Sunday pastime for locals—but you're on vacation, so you can be a flâneur any day of the week.

Eat Baguettes Like a Parisian

The Tour Eiffel might be the most famous symbol of Paris, but perhaps the true banner of France is the baguette, the long, caramel-color bread brandished at every meal. Locals take inordinate pride at finding the best baguette in the neighborhood. To find a worthy *boulangerie*—a bakery that specializes in bread, as opposed to a pâtisserie, specializing in pastries—look for a line outside on weekend mornings. Three faves in Paris are **Arnaud Delmontel** (⌧ *39 rue des Martys, 9e* ☎ *01–48–78–29–33*), **Jean-Pierre Cohier** (⌧ *270 rue du Faubourg St-Honoré, 8e* ☎ *01–42–27–45–26*), and **Boulanger de Monge** (⌧ *123 rue Monge, 5e* ☎ *01–43–37–54–20*). True Parisians know that all baguettes are not created equal and will order one *bien cuit* (well-done) to get the crispiest of the litter. Also look for places labeled *boulangerie* and *artisan* to ensure that you're getting the real thing and not a less-tasty industrial version. (If you see little raised dots on the underside of a baguette, that means it was made by a machine, not by hand.) As you're leaving the bakery, do as many Parisians do—nibble the end of the crust to taste the bread while it's still warm.

Eat Pastries Like a Parisian

High prices are making luxury all the more elusive in Paris, but there's one indulgence most people can still afford, at least occasionally—fine pastries. As you can see when you stop in at any of Paris's extraordinary pâtisseries (pastry shops), a wonderful array of French treats awaits. Tops on our list are the deliciously airy and intense *macarons*—nothing in common with the heavy American shredded-coconut macaroons you might be familiar with. **Ladurée** (⌧ *16 rue Royale, 8e* ☎ *01–42–60–21–79*) claims to have invented these ganache-filled cookies, but two Left Bank pâtisseries also have particularly devoted fans of their *macarons*: the flavors at **Gérard Mulot** (⌧ *76 rue de Seine, 6e* ☎ *01–43–26–85–77*) include pistachio, caramel, and terrific orange-cinnamon, and **Pierre Hermé** (⌧ *72 rue Bonaparte, 6e* ☎ *01–43–54–47–77*) has exotic ones like white truffle and roasted slivers of hazelnuts. The classic opera pastry—almond cake layered with chocolate and coffee cream—can be found at **Lenôtre** (⌧ *61 rue Lecourbe, 15e* ☎ *01–42–73–20–97*), but devotees also flock to the fine-food emporium **Fauchon** (⌧ *26 pl. de la Madeleine, 8e* ☎ *01–70–39–38–02*). Another traditional pastry is the *mont-blanc*, a mini-mountain of chestnut puree capped with whipped cream, best rendered by **Jean-Paul Hévin** (⌧ *3 rue Vavin, 6e* ☎ *01–43–54–09–85*). And those really in the know watch for anything from the Tokyo-born **Sadaharu Aoki** (⌧ *35 rue Vaugirard, 6e* ☎ *01–45–44–48–90*); look for his green-tea madeleines and black-sesame éclairs.

PARIS WITH KIDS

Paris is often promoted as an adult destination, but there's no shortage of children's activities to keep the young 'uns busy, not to mention that many of the city's top attractions have carousels parked outside them in summer. Make sure to buy a *Pariscope* (found at most newsstands) and check the *enfants* section for current children's events. In addition to what's below, sites of particular interest to children are marked with a family icon.

Museums

Paris has a number of museums that cater to the young and the young at heart. They're a great place to occupy restless minds, especially if the weather is bad. The **Cité des Sciences et de l'Industrie** (the Museum of Science and Industry), at the Parc de la Villette, is an enormous science center, and the children's area is divided into two main sections: one for children from 2 to 7 years of age; another for those from 5 to 12. Interactive exhibits allow kids to do everything from building a house and comparing their body to that of a favorite animal, to learning about communications systems throughout history, from the Tom Tom to the satellite. The **Musée de la Poupée** (the Doll Museum) is a cozy museum in the heart of the Marais, with a collection of more than 500 dolls dating back to the 1800s, complete with costumes, furniture, and accessories. Labels might be in French, but they're not really the point anyway, and the museum features a "Doll Hospital," where "sick" dolls and plush toys come to be repaired; the doctor (*restauratrice*) is in two Thursdays a month, but free estimates are offered throughout the week. The **Palais de la Découverte** (the Palace of Discovery) has high-definition, 3-D exhibits covering everything from chemistry, biology, and physics to the weather,

so there's bound to be some interesting dinner conversation when the day is done. Many of the displays are in French, but that doesn't stop most kids from having a blast; hands down, the choice between this and the Louvre is a no-brainer.

Sites and Shows

A zoo is usually a good bet to get the kids' attention—although you might want to keep in mind that most European zoos aren't as spacious as American zoos. The **Ménagerie** at the Jardin des Plantes is an urban zoo dating from 1794 and home to more than 240 mammals, 400 birds, 270 reptiles, and a number of insects. The renovated **Parc Zoologique**, in the Bois de Vincennes, reopened in 2014. The **Musée de la Chasse et de la Nature**, run by the François Sommer Foundation in the Marais, is another place to get up close and personal with ferocious lions, tigers, and one in-your-face polar bear—these animals just aren't alive. An impressive collection of taxidermy trophies takes children on a safari to discover man's relationship with animals through art, stuffed animals, and hunting gizmos. When it comes to spectacles, what child would pass up the circus? There are several in the city, and the **Cirque de Paris** has a special feature called a "Day at the Circus"—your kids (and you) can learn some basics like juggling and tightrope walking, then you can lunch with the artists and see a performance in the afternoon. Less interactive are **Les Guignols**, French puppet shows: the original Guignol was a marionette character created by Laurent Mourguet, supposedly in his own likeness, celebrating life, love, and wine. Today the shows are primarily aimed at children, and are found in open-air theaters throughout the city in the warmer months. Check out the Champs-Élysées, Parc Montsouris, Parc

des Buttes-Chaumont, Jardin du Luxembourg, and the Parc Floral in the Bois de Vincennes. Even if they don't understand French, kids are usually riveted. Of course, the best sight in Paris is the city itself, and a **boat ride** on the Seine is a must for everyone. It's the perfect way to see the sights, rest weary feet, and, depending on which option you choose, lunch or dinner may be part of the treat.

Expending Energy
Most kids are thrilled (at least more than the grown-ups) at the prospect of climbing innumerable stairs to be rewarded with cool views: the **Eiffel Tower** is the quintessential Paris climb, but **Notre-Dame** gets extra points for the gargoyles, and the **Arc de Triomphe** is a good bet, since it's at the end of the Champs-Élysées. When it comes to open spaces for running around, Paris has lots of park options, with extra attractions in summer when kids can work off steam on the trampolines or ride ponies at the **Jardin des Tuileries**. The **Jardin du Luxembourg** has a playground and a pond where kids can rent miniature boats, and the **Bois de Boulogne** has a zoo, rowboats, bumper cars, and lots of wide-open spaces. Ice-skating is seasonal but always a thrill, and from mid-December through February several outdoor Paris sites are turned into spectacular ice-skating rinks with Christmas lights, music, and instructors. The rinks are free to the public; skate rental for adults costs €5. The main rink is at **Place de l'Hôtel de Ville**, the square in front of City Hall.

Underground Paris
There's something about exploring underground that seems to fascinate kids, at least the older ones. **Les Égouts**, the Paris sewer system, has a certain gross factor but isn't actually that disgusting. Keep in mind, though, that the smell is definitely ranker in the summer months. At the **Catacombs**, in Montparnasse, dark tunnels filled with bones are spookily titillating—at least for those not prone to nightmares. For some cheap underground entertainment without the ick factor, the **métro** itself can be its own sort of adventure, complete with fascinating station art such as the submarine decor at Arts-et-Metiers, the colorful Parisian timeline murals at Tuileries, or the Egyptian statues of the Louvre–Rivoli station. A good tip: métro lines 1 and 14 feature driverless trains that let you sit at the very front; kids love the zooming sensation that they're driving.

And for Treats
All that fun will no doubt bring on an appetite, and there's no shortage of special places to stop for a snack in Paris. **La Charlotte de l'Isle** (✉ *24 rue St-Louis-en-l'Ile*), on the Ile Saint Louis, is a whimsically decorated tearoom known for its hot chocolate—deliciously thick and yummy, unlike what American children are usually used to. Just down the street is **Berthillon**, renowned for its decadent ice cream—though the **Amorino** gelaterias give it a run for its money. And when in need, a pâtisserie selling chocolate croissants is never hard to find. French children adore the pastel clouds of meringue (which resemble hardened whipped-cream puffs) that decorate almost every bakery's window, and there are all sorts of cookies to tempt a smile from a tired tot.

GREAT WALK: ARTISTS AND WRITERS OF THE LEFT BANK

Some of the greatest artists and writers of the 20th century were attracted to the winding streets and bustling boulevards of Paris's Left Bank between the end of WWI and the social upheavals of the 1960s.

Winding Streets of the Quartier Latin

The streets around **Place de la Contrescarpe** have hardly changed since they were immortalized in Hemingway's *Moveable Feast*. He lived at 74 rue du Cardinal Lemoine (down the street from James Joyce at No. 71) and worked at 39 rue Descartes. George Orwell lived nearby, at 6 rue Pot de Fer, while writing *Down and Out in Paris and London*. The famous bookshop **Shakespeare & Co.** lost its owner, George Whitman, in 2011, but his daughter Sylvia continues his legacy in a medieval house at 37 rue de la Bûcherie; many of the Beat Generation writers who frequented it in the '60s, like Burroughs, Ginsberg, and Kerouac, stayed in the **Hôtel du Vieux Paris,** aka the "Beat Hotel," at 9 rue Gît-le-Coeur. Pablo Picasso perfected his cubist style at 7 rue des Grands Augustins from 1936 to 1955.

The Heyday of St-Germain-des-Prés

Follow Rue St-André-des-Arts and Rue de Seine to Rue Jacob, home to American writers like Djuna Barnes, who stayed at the Hôtel d'Angleterre at No. 44. On the corner of Rue Bonaparte is **Le Pré aux Clercs,** where Hemingway and Fitzgerald shared many a drink. Henry Miller lived up the street at 24 rue Bonaparte and later at No. 36. Pass the home of Jean-Paul Sartre at No. 42 to the square that now bears his and Simone de Beauvoir's names. Along noisy Boulevard St-Germain are the **Deux Magots, Café de Flore,** and **Brasserie Lipp,** legendary establishments frequented by the couple as well as by Faulkner, Camus, Apollinaire, André Gide, Giacometti, Cocteau, Duras, Hemingway, Fitzgerald, and André Breton. Bookshops like **La Hune** still give the area intellectual character despite the proliferation of fashion boutiques.

Odéon and Luxembourg Gardens

At 12 rue de l'Odéon, a plaque commemorating Sylvia Beach's publication of James Joyce's *Ulysses* marks the original location of Shakespeare & Co., which closed in 1944. On Rue de Vaugirard, Faulkner lived at No. 42 and Fitzgerald and his wife Zelda at No. 58. Man Ray's studio is still intact at No. 2 bis, rue Ferou. Hemingway lived at No. 6 for a year, writing often about the **Luxembourg Gardens.**

Montparnasse

Leaving the Luxembourg Gardens, follow Rue du Fleurus, where Gertrude Stein and Alice B. Toklas lived at No. 27, entertaining artists and writers such as Picasso, Matisse, Erik Satie, and *New Yorker* correspondent Janet Flanner. Stein's friends Ezra Pound and Hemingway—who moved a lot—lived nearby on Rue Notre-Dame des Champs (at No. 70 and No. 113, respectively), near Boulevard du Montparnasse, the expat epicenter a decade before St-Germain held that distinction. Some of the establishments still here are **Closerie des Lilas** (No. 171), **Le Sélect** (No. 99), **Le Dôme** (No. 108), **La Rotonde** (No. 105), and **La Coupole** (No. 102), where Modigliani, Dalí, Samuel Beckett, Colette, and Miró rubbed shoulders. Rue Delambre leads to the **Cimetière du Montparnasse,** the final resting place for many of the illustrious names of the Left Bank, including publishers Hachette and Larousse; artists Man Ray, Kiki de Montparnasse, Brancusi, and Brassaï; and writers like Baudelaire, Ionesco, Sartre et Beauvoir, Beckett, and Duras.

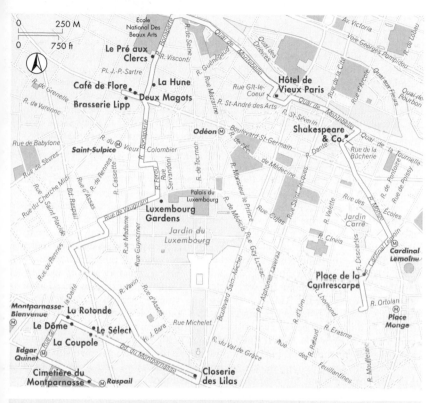

Highlights	The historic decor of La Coupole, the picturesque winding streets of the Quartier Latin, the storied charm of Shakespeare & Co.
Where to Start	Place de la Contrescarpe, at the top of the Montaigne St-Geneviève; take métro 10 to Cardinal Lemoine or métro 7 to Place Monge for a less steep incline.
Length	5¼ km (3.2 miles); duration approximately 2½–3 hours without stops.
Where to End	At the Cimetière du Montparnasse, just east of the Tour du Montparnasse, next to métro Edgar Quinet (Line 6) and métro Raspail (Lines 4, 6).
Best Time to Go	Any time of day when you can see all of the sights in daylight.
Worst Time to Go	Being entirely outside, it's not a good idea to do when it's raining or very cold.
Editor's Choice	Artistic detour to the Musée du Montparnasse (⊠ 21 av. du Maine Ⓜ Montparnasse or Falguière), the Musée Zadkine (⊠ 100 bis, rue d'Assas Ⓜ Notre-Dame-des-Champs), or the Musée du Luxembourg (⊠ 19 rue de Vaugirard Ⓜ Odéon or St-Sulpice).

GREAT ITINERARIES

Paris is a treasure of neighborhoods and history, and a visit to this glorious city is never quite as simple as a quick look at a few landmarks. These one-day itineraries are mix and match: follow the ones that intrigue you—and leave yourself time to just walk and explore.

Monumental Paris

Begin your day at the Trocadéro métro, where you can get the best views of the Tour Eiffel from the esplanade of the Palais de Chaillot. If you absolutely must ride to the top, now is the best time to get in line. Otherwise, get a Seine-side view of the city's other noteworthy monuments from the Bateaux Parisiens, moored below the Pont d'Iéna. Hour-long cruises loop around the Ile de la Cité, with multilingual commentary on the sights along the way. Afterward you can take the RER to the Musée d'Orsay for lunch in the museum's Belle Époque dining room before tackling the late-19th-century works of art. Then it's a short walk to the imposing Hôtel des Invalides, the French military museum built as a retirement home for wounded soldiers under Louis XIV. The emperor Napoléon Bonaparte rests beneath the golden dome. If the weather's nice, have tea next door in the sculpture gardens of the Musée Rodin (entrance to the gardens €1). If your feet are still happy, cross the gilded Pont Tsar Alexandre III to the Champs-Élysées, passing the Belle Époque art palaces known as the Grand Palais and Petit Palais. You can take Bus 73 from the Assemblée Nationale across the bridge to Place de la Concorde and all the way up Avenue des Champs-Élysées to the Arc de Triomphe. Open until 10:30 pm (11 pm from May to September), its panoramic viewing platform is ideal for admiring the City of Light.

Alternative: Instead of the traditional Seine cruise, try the Batobus, which allows you to hop on and hop off throughout the day with one ticket. The eight Batobus ports include the Eiffel Tower, Champs-Élysées, Notre-Dame, Hôtel de Ville, Louvre Museum, and Musée d'Orsay. Note that there's no commentary on these tours.

Old Paris

Start at Pont Neuf for excellent views off the western tip of the Ile de la Cité, then explore the island's magnificent architectural heritage, including the Conciergerie, Sainte-Chapelle, and Notre-Dame. The brave can climb the corkscrew staircase to the towers for a gargoyle's-eye view of the city. Then detour to the neighboring Ile St-Louis for lunch before heading into the medieval labyrinth of the Quartier Latin: its most valuable treasures are preserved in the Musée de Cluny, including the reconstructed ruins of 2nd-century Gallo-Roman steam baths. At the summit of the hill above the Sorbonne university is the imposing Panthéon, a monument (and mausoleum) of French heroes. Don't miss the exquisite Église St-Etienne-du-Mont next door, where the relics of the city's patron Saint Geneviève are displayed and where iconic scenes in *Midnight in Paris* were filmed on its stairs. Follow Rue Descartes to Rue Mouffetard for a *café crème* on one of the oldest market streets in Paris. If the sun's still shining, visit the Gallo-Roman Arènes de Lutèce.

Alternative: A different look at the Quartier Latin can include a visit to the sleek Institute du Monde Arabe, then a relaxing afternoon at the authentic steam baths and tearoom of the nearby Mosquée de Paris.

Royal Paris

Begin at Place de la Concorde, where an Egyptian obelisk replaces the guillotine where Louis XVI and Marie-Antoinette met their bloody fate during the French Revolution, then escape the traffic in the formal Jardin des Tuileries, which once belonged to the 16th-century Tuileries Palace, destroyed during the Paris Commune of 1871. Pass through the small Arc du Carrousel to the modern glass pyramid that serves as the main entrance to the Louvre, the world's grandest museum, once a 12th-century fortress. When you've built up an appetite, cross the street to the peaceful gardens of the Palais Royal for lunch at a café beneath the stone arcades. From here take métro Line 1 to station St-Paul. To the south you can find the Hôtel de Sens, home to King Henry IV's feisty ex-wife Queen Marguerite, and one of the few surviving examples of late-medieval architecture. Around the corner on Rue Charlemagne is a preserved section of the city's 12th-century fortifications built by King Philippe-Augustus. Cross busy Rue St-Antoine to Le Marais and enter the Hôtel de Sully, a fine example of the elegant private mansions built here by aristocrats in the early 17th century. Pass through the gardens to the doorway on the right, which leads to the lovely symmetrical town houses of Place des Vosges, designed by King Henry IV. Many of the old aristocratic mansions in Le Marais have been turned into museums, including the Musée Carnavalet and the Musée Picasso.

Power-Shopping Paris

Get an early start to avoid crowds at Au Printemps and Galeries Lafayette, two of the city's grandest historic department stores conveniently side by side behind the Opéra Garnier. Refuel at Place de la Madeleine, where gourmet food boutiques such as Hédiard and Fauchon offer light deli foods for shoppers on the move. If the luxury boutiques on Rue Royale aren't rich enough for you, head down Rue du Faubourg St-Honoré and Avenue Montaigne (via Avenue Matignon), where you pass the exclusive couture houses of Chanel, Dior, Hermès, and Yves St-Laurent. Department stores are closed on Sunday, but open late on Thursday. Most small boutiques are closed Sunday and Monday. Le Marais and the Champs-Élysées are the best bets for Sunday shopping. ■ TIP→ Beginning in 2014, if you spend more than €175 in one store the retailer should give you a computer-generated Value-Added Tax (V.A.T) refund form. To make sure you get your rebate, make sure you scan the form using handy machines at the airport before you check in for your flight.

Alternative: For a more genteel shopping experience, head to the Left Bank's chic Bon Marché department store, then work your way through the fashion and home decor boutiques around Église St-Sulpice and St-Germain-des-Prés. Shops get less expensive between métro Odéon and the Quartier Latin.

FREE AND ALMOST FREE

It's easy to break the bank in Paris, but those acquainted with the city know where to find the free (or almost free) stuff. Here are some tips.

Free Art

Thanks to the City of Paris's dedication to promoting culture, access to the permanent collections in the city's municipal museums is free, so you can learn about the city's rich history, the characters who contribute to its aura of romance, and the warriors who fought for France's liberation—all without dropping a cent. Setting the example, the **Hôtel de Ville** (City Hall) in Le Marais regularly runs several expositions at a time, most of which focus on French artists. Past expos have included the "Life of Edith Piaf" and the works of photographers Wally Ronis and Robert Doisneau. The **Maison Européene de la Photographie**, also in Le Marais, is a favorite among flashbulb-poppers and amateur photography buffs alike—and every Wednesday evening, from 5 to 8, this museum opens its doors free of charge. Expositions can cover everything from the history of the camera and the evolution of printing to selections from some of the world's most famous photographers. It's a perfect prelude to cocktail hour. The **Musée Carnavalet**—yup, this is in Le Marais also, near Place des Vosges—puts Paris's history on display with a collection of old signs, relics from bars and cafés, paintings of what the city looked like before it was fully developed (Montmartre was all farmland!), and old keepsakes and letters. It's an excellent place to get a feel for Paris past and present. More free art throughout the year can be found at **Maison de Balzac, Maison de Victor Hugo, Musée d'Art Moderne de la Ville de Paris,** and the **Petit Palais,** also known as **Musée des Beaux-Arts de la Ville de Paris.**

Free Music

For free classical music in an ethereal setting, many of Paris's churches host free or almost-free concerts at lunchtime and in the evening. Flyers are posted around the city and outside the churches, or check weekly events listings. There are free organ recitals on Sunday at **Notre-Dame** (4:30 pm) and **Église St-Eustache** (5:30 pm). **Radio France** sponsors about 200 free concerts throughout the year (usually at 12:30 on Saturday, with tickets given out 30 minutes beforehand) at the Petit Palais and various locations across the city. In summer and fall there are free concerts in the city's parks, including the **Jardin des Luxembourg** (classical music), the **Parc de la Villette** (world music and jazz), and the **Parc Floral** in the Bois de Vincennes (classical and jazz). During **Paris Plage,** in late summer, there are free nightly pop and rock concerts on the quays of the Seine. When the weather's nice you're also likely to find would-be, wannabe, and even a few real musicians along the quai of the **Canal St-Martin,** or in **Place des Vosges,** guitars in hand for spontaneous song.

Free Serenity

If the hustle and bustle of Paris is getting to you, opt for a free session of qi gong at the **Parc des Buttes-Chaumont** in the 19e arrondissement. Every day at 9 am instructor Thoi Tin Cau leads classes, free of charge, at 7 rue Botzaris, métro Botzaris, on the patch of grass in the middle of the park. Parisians also like to recharge their batteries with an afternoon catnap in one of the handy reclined chairs scattered throughout the city's gardens. This is the cheapest option for relaxation, reading, and postcard writing—just make sure your possessions are secure if you're actually going to grab some shut-eye. Perennial favorites for parking yourself,

La Dernière Goutte

or weary companions, are the **Jardin des Luxembourg** and the **Jardin du Tuileries**, but one of the most serene venues, buffered from the traffic by the arcaded shops, is the garden at the **Palais Royal**, not far from the Louvre. Any perch along the Seine will also do in a pinch if the busy streets are getting to you: it's amazing how serene a spot by the water can be, so close to the frenetic workings of the city, especially if you find yourself on the incomparably charming **Ile de la Cité**.

Cheap Souvenirs

Perfect for yourself or friends back home, what souvenir retails for just about €0.10 each? The postcard, of course. Go retro (snail mail!) and send some quintessential scenery home with a "J'aime Paris" scribbled on the back, or just bring back a little packet of choice images. For the best prices, check out the news kiosks along Rue de Rivoli and the Grands Boulevards, or visit a location of the bookstore **Mona Lisait** (✉ *9 rue St-Martin, 4e* ☎ *01–42–74–03–02*). Keep an eye out for vintage postcards, too, sold by the *bouquinistes* along the Seine and by collectors inside Passage des Panoramas. You can buy stamps at any *tabac* as well as at post offices.

(Almost) Free Sightseeing Tours

Imagine passing the Louvre as part of your daily commute. Some of the city's public bus routes are fantastically scenic; hop on the right one and you can get a great tour for just €1.70—sans squawking commentary. The **No. 29** route reaches from Gare St-Lazare, past the Opéra Garnier, to the heart of Le Marais, crossing Place des Vosges before ending up at the Bastille. This is one of the few lines that runs primarily on small streets, not major arteries. Hop the **No. 69** bus at Champ de Mars (by the Tour Eiffel) and ride through

parts of the Quartier Latin, across the bridge to the Rive Droite near the Louvre, and on to the Bastille. The **No. 72** bus follows the Seine from the Hôtel de Ville west past the Louvre and most of the big-name Rive Droite sights, also giving you views of the Rive Gauche, including the Tour Eiffel. Bus **No. 73** is the only line that goes along Avenue des Champs-Élysées, from the Arc de Triomphe through Place de la Condorde and ending at Musée d'Orsay. You can also take free (though tips are appreciated) walking tours with the enthusiastic guides from **Sandemans** (⊕ *www.newparistours.com*) or **City Free Tour** (⊕ *www.cityfreetour.com*).

Free Wine (Tastings)

Here's a tip for getting tipsy: wine stores sometimes offer free or inexpensive wine tastings, generally on the weekends. Check out **La Dernière Goutte** (✉ *6 rue de Bourbon le Château, 6e* ☎ *01–43–29–11–62*) and the prestigious **Caves Taillevent** (✉ *199 rue du Faubourg St-Honore, 8e* ☎ *01–45–61–14–09*) on Saturday afternoon. **La Cave du Panthéon** (✉ *174 rue Saint-Jacques, 5e* ☎ *01–46–33–90–35*), touted for its conviviality, is another destination where wine lovers congregate on Saturday afternoon to learn about—and indulge in—their favorite beverage. If you're lucky, the winemaker hailing from the featured winery of the day may be among those taking part in the tasting.

PARIS MUSEUMS, AN OVERVIEW

There's no shortage of museums in Paris, so it's a good idea to make a plan. This overview includes all the museums listed elsewhere in the book; check the index for full listings.

Major Museums

Ambitious art goers will focus on the Big Three—the **Louvre**, the **Musée d'Orsay**, and **Centre Georges Pompidou**. The Louvre's collection spans from about 7000 BC until 1848, and has its own Big Three: the *Mona Lisa*, the *Venus de Milo*, and *Winged Victory*. The d'Orsay's collection picks up where the Louvre's leaves off, and continues until 1914. The Pompidou has art from the early 20th century to the present.

One-Man Shows

Three major must-sees are **Musée Rodin**, with its lovely sculpture garden; **Musée Picasso** (which recently underwent a massive renovation); and **Musée Marmottan Monet**. There are also **Musée Delacroix**, **Musée Gustave Moreau**, **Musée Zadkine**, and **Musée Maillol**. Dalí enthusiasts will appreciate **Espace Dalí**, while French chanson fans shouldn't miss the tiny **Edith Piaf Museum**.

House Museums

A house museum is two treats in one: the art and the house itself. **Maison de Victor Hugo** and **Maison de Balzac** are the former homes of writers. **Musée Jacquemart-André** has an intriguing collection of Italian art, and **Musée Nissim de Camondo** has decorative art, mostly from the 18th century. **Musée de la Vie Romantique,** dedicated to the novelist George Sand, was the elegant town house of Dutch-born painter Ary Scheffer, and **Musée Cognacq-Jay** was the home of Ernest Cognacq, founder of the now closed *La Samaritaine* department store. The **Palais Galliera** opens for exhibits on costume and clothing design. The small **Musée Baccarat** has some Baccarat masterpieces in a Philippe Starck–designed, surrealist building.

Contemporary Art

Excellent venues for modern art include the **Palais de Tokyo** and **Musée d'Art Moderne de la Ville de Paris**. There's also **Fondation Cartier pour l'art contemporain** for emerging artists' work, and **La Maison Rouge**, which shows private collections. The **Pinacothèque de Paris** is a private museum dedicated solely to temporary exhibits, while **Halle St. Pierre** has exhibits of outsider and folk art. **Le 104** is an offbeat art space with artist studios, boutiques, and performance spaces.

French History

Musée de Cluny has the well-known tapestry *Lady and the Unicorn*. **Musée d'Art et d'Histoire du Judaïsme** documents Jewish history in France. For Parisian history, don't miss **Musée Carnevalet**. Montmartre has its own museum, **Musée de Montmartre**. The new **Cité de l'Architecture et du Patrimoine** presents a history of French architecture, and maritime history is the subject of the **Musée National de la Marine** (both are in the Palais Chaillot). The **Musée de la Légion d'Honneur** is an exploration of French and foreign military decoration, and the **Musée de l'Armée,** at the Hotel des Invalides, is a phenomenal military museum. There's also the **Musée Jean Moulin** in the Jardin Atlantique, focusing on the life of the famous leader of the French Resistance. Architecture buffs might appreciate Google's permanent exhibit in association with **Pavillon de l'Arsenal**, which traces the entire history of the city, as well as its future.

Best for Kids

Kids love the hands-on science and technology displays at **Cité des Sciences et de l'Industrie** and **Musée de la Musique,** both in Parc de la Villette. The **Grande Galerie de l'Evolution** and **Musée de la Chasse et de la Nature** have stuffed animals in natural surroundings. The **Palais de la Découverte,** a planetarium, and **Musée Grévin,** a wax museum, are perennial faves. The fabulous **Musée des Art et Metiers** has neat scientific instruments and inventions. For doll lovers, there's the **Musée de la Poupée.** For chocolate lovers of all ages, check out **Choco-Story,** the museum of chocolate.

Art and Design

For a mix of photographs from different artists, your best bet is the **Maison Européenne de la Photographie. Fondation Henri Cartier-Bresson** features works by the well-known French photographer in a building that was also his atelier. The **Jeu de Paume,** in the Tuileries, showcases modern photography exhibits. For modern design, the **Fondation Le Corbusier** is well worth the trip to the western edge of the city. The **Fondation Pierre Bergé-Yves Saint Laurent** is the designer's atelier as well as an archive and gallery of his work. For those interested in urban planning, visit the free **Pavillion de l'Arsenal** to see the miniature models of Paris neighborhoods. The **Musée des Arts Decoratifs** inside **Les Arts Décoratifs** (which includes the **Musée de la Publicité** and **Mode et Textile**) has one of the world's greatest decorative-art collections. The **Manufacture des Gobelins** traces the history of weaving and tapestry. The **Palais Galliera,** which reopened after renovations in 2013, hosts temporary exhibits about fashion in an incredibly ornate palace.

African, Asian, and Islamic Art

There are two places in town to see Asian art: **Musée Guimet** is not to be missed, and **Musée Cernuschi** is a small house museum that holds the personal Asian art collection of Enrico Cernuschi. For Arab and Islamic art and architecture, visit the impressive **Institut du Monde Arabe,** and for African art, try **Musée Dapper.** The **Musée du Quai Branly** features African, Asian, and Oceanic art.

Etc.

Some museums aren't easily classified. The **Musée de l'Erotisme** is a seven-story building dedicated to everything associated with erotic fantasy. The **Musée du Vin** is a history of wine making that also has wine tastings; the **Musée du Parfum** on Rue Scribe is dedicated to the art of perfume. **La Musée de la Prefecture de Police** is, you guessed it, a museum of the Paris police. The **Musée de l'Orangerie** is a stunning setting for Monet's *Water Lilies.*

Art Galleries

The city's hottest avant-garde art scene is on and around Rue Vieille du Temple in the north Marais. Around St-Germain and Place des Vosges the galleries are more traditional; works by old masters and established modern artists dominate the galleries around Rue du Faubourg St-Honoré and Avenue Matignon. Carré Rive Gauche, around Rue du Bac in St-Germain, has dozens of art and antiques galleries on its narrow streets.

The **Association des Galeries** (⊕ *www.associationdesgaleries.org*) lists exhibits in more than 125 galleries through the city. **Paris-art.com** (⊕ *www.paris-art.com*) focuses on contemporary art, with reviews, exhibition calendars, and interviews, in French only.

BICYCLING IN PARIS

You've seen those 1930s photographs of Paris—men in berets bicycling the streets, a baguette tucked under one arm; elegant women in billowing skirts gliding past the Eiffel Tower on two wheels. Until recently, though, it was difficult for visitors to the City of Lights to do the same without signing up for a bike tour. That changed when Paris introduced a bike-rental program called **Vélib'** (📞 *01–30–79–79–30* ⊕ *www.velib.paris.fr*), whose odd-sounding name is an amalgam of *vélo* (bike) and *liberté* (liberty).

Even if cycling across the French countryside is your dream, taking to the streets of Paris can seems like a nightmare, with motorcycles weaving in and out of traffic, delivery vans double parked, pedestrians texting while walking—you get the picture. But the resounding success of Vélib' has meant that dedicated bike lanes have been popping up in the center of the city to accommodate all the new cyclists.

You'll encounter several different types of bike lanes in Paris: bike-only lanes completely separated from vehicular traffic (these are well worth seeking out); lanes divided from traffic by white lines (you can easily be cut off by turning cars or buses making a stop); lanes shared by buses, taxis, and bike; and lanes where you'll pedal against the flow of traffic. There are also lanes running adjacent to sidewalks (watch out for crossing pedestrians).

There's always safety in numbers, and many seasoned cyclists opt to join the group **Paris Rando Vélo** (⊕ *www.paris randovelo.fr*) every Friday evening for a free ride through the streets of Paris. Rendez-vous at 9:30 pm at l'Hôtel de Ville. On the third Sunday of each month there's also a morning ride at 10:30 am.

Take to the streets

So you're ready to rent a Vélib' bike? You can't miss the silver-and-purple cycles at more than 1,800 docking stations—with additional locations every year—spread around the city, from the Champs Élysées to Montmarte to the Louvre. Logging more than 60 million trips, they are showing some wear and tear, so check yours over thoroughly before hopping onto the saddle, especially to ensure that the bell is fully functional.

There are several stands near the Eiffel Tower, four of which form a not-quite-symmetrical square around the landmark: one on Quai Branly at Avenue de la Bourdonnais, another on Avenue Rapp near the corner of Bourdonnais, a third on Rue de Suffren off Avenue Joseph Bouvard, and the last on Avenue Octave Gréard where it intersects with Avenue de Suffren. This neighborhood is ideal for cycling: the roads are wide, there are several dedicated bike lanes, and most important, the terrain is gloriously flat. Try a relaxing ride across the Champs de Mars, along Rue St-Dominique, and around the Invalides.

You'll pay €1.70 a day—or €8 for a seven-day pass—to use Vélib'. If you ride for less than 30 minutes at a time, there's no additional fee (you get a code to use throughout the day, which allows you to take out a bike whenever you want one). If you keep it for more than 30 minutes you pay an additional €1, then €2 for the next 30 minutes, and €4 for each half hour on top of that. If you're spending a lot of time in Paris, opt for the €29 annual pass. A combination métro/bike pass is also available. The system accepts debit or credit cards that contain an electronic chip that can be read by the French system.

THE SEINE

No matter how you approach Paris — historically, geographically, or emotionally — the Seine flows through its heart, dividing the City of Light into two banks, the *Rive Droite* (Right Bank) and the *Rive Gauche* (Left Bank).

The Seine has long been used as a means for transportation and commerce and although there are no longer any factories along its banks, all manner of boats still ply the water. You'll see tugboats, fire and police boats, the occasional bobbing houseboat, and many kinds of tour boats; it might sound hokey, but there's really no better introduction to the City of Light than a boat cruise, and there are several options, depending on whether you want commentary on the sights or not. Many of the city's most famous attractions can be seen from the river, and are especially spectacular at dusk, as those celebrated lights of Paris glint against the sky.

FROM ILE DES CYGNES TO THE LOUVRE

Musée d'Orsay clock

Petit Palais

Pont de l'Alma

Grand Palais

Assemblée Nationale

Pont Alexandre III

Bir Hakeim Bridge

Eiffel Tower

Ile des Cygnes

The **Zouave of the Pont de l'Alma**, sole survivor of the bridge's four original stone soldiers, is used by Parisians to judge water levels.

Whether you hop on a boat cruise or stroll the quays at your own pace, the Seine comes alive when you get off the busy streets of Paris. At the western edge of the city on the **Ile des Cygnes** (literally the Isle of Swans), a small version of the Statue of Liberty stands guard. Auguste Bartholdi designed the original statue, given as a gift from France to America in 1886, and in 1889 a group of Americans living in Paris installed this ¼ scale bronze replica—it's 37 feet, 8 inches tall.

You can get to the Ile des Cygnes via the **Bir Hakeim** bridge named for the 1942 Free French battle in Libya—whose lacy architecture horizontally echoes the nearby **Eiffel Tower**. You might recognize the view of the bridge from the movie *Last Tango in Paris*.

As you make your way downstream you can drool in envy at the houseboats docked near the bronze lamp–lined Pont Alexandre III. No other bridge over the Seine epitomizes the fin-de-siècle frivolity of the Belle Epoque: It seems as much created of cake frosting and sugar sculptures as of stone and iron, and makes quite the backdrop for fashion shoots and weddings. The elaborate decorations include Art Nouveau lamps, cherubs, nymphs, and winged horses at either end. The bridge was built, like the Grand Palais and Petit Palais nearby, for the 1900 World's Fair.

Along the banks of the Seine   *Bouquinistes*

The average depth of the Seine within Paris city limits is 8 m (about 26 feet).

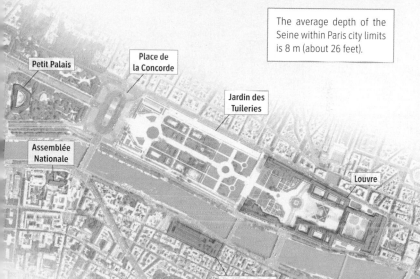

Petit Palais

Place de la Concorde

Jardin des Tuileries

Assemblée Nationale

Louvre

Musée d'Orsay

Past the dome of the Église du Dôme is the 18th-century neoclassical façade of the **Assemblée Nationale**, the palace that houses the French Parliament. Across the river stands the **Place de la Concorde.** Also look for the great railway station clocks of the Musée d'Orsay that once allowed writer Anaïs Nin to co ordinate her lovers' visits to her houseboat, moored below the Tuileries. The palatial **Louvre** museum, on the Right Bank, seems to go on and on as you continue up the Seine.

PERFECT PICNIC PLACES

Paris abounds with romantic spots to pause for a picnic or a bottle of wine, but the Seine has some of the best.

Try scouting out a place on the point of Ile St-Louis; at sunset you can watch the sun slip beneath receding arches of stone bridges.

The long, low quays of the Left Bank, with its public sculpture work, are perfect for an alfresco lunch.

FROM PONT DES ARTS TO JARDIN DES PLANTES

At the water's edge.

Pont des Arts

Pont Neuf

Châtelet Theatres

Hotel de Ville

Institut de France

Ile de la Cité

Conciergerie

Notre-Dame

The Institut de France

Parisians love to linger on the elegant **Pont des Arts** footbridge that streches between the palatial Louvre museum and the Institut de France. Napoléon commissioned the original cast-iron bridge with nine arches; it was rebuilt in 1984 with seven arches.

Five carved stone arches of the **Pont Neuf**—the name means "new bridge" but it actually dates from 1605 and is the oldest bridge in Paris—connect the Left Bank to the Ile de la Cité. Another seven arches connect the Ile and the Right Bank. The pale gray curv-

ing balustrades include a row of stone heads; some say they're caricatures of King Henry IV's ministers, glaring down at the river.

On the Right Bank at the end of the Ile de la Cité is the **Hôtel de Ville (City Hall)**—this area was once the main port of Paris, crowded with boats delivering everything from wood and produce to visitors and slaves.

Medieval turrets rise up from **Ile de la Cité,** part of the original royal palace; the section facing the Right Bank includes the **Conciergerie**, where Marie Antoinette was imprisoned in 1793 before her execution.

PARIS PLAGE

Paris Plage, literally Paris Beach, is Mayor Bertrand Delanoë's summer gift to Parisians and visitors. In August the roads along the Seine are closed, tons of sand are brought in and decorated with palm trees, and a slew of activities are organized, from free early-morning yoga classes to evening samba and swimming (not in the Seine, but in the fabulous Josephine Baker swimming pool). Going topless is discouraged, but hammocks, kids' playgrounds, rock-climbing, and cafés keep everyone entertained.

View of the Seine and the Pont des Arts

Paris Plage

Notre-Dame

Also on the Ile de la Cité is the cathedral of **Notre-Dame,** a stunning sight from the water. From the side it looks almost like a great boat sailing down the Seine.

As you pass the end of the island, you'll notice a small grated window: this is the evocative Deportation Memorial.

Next to the Ile de la Cite is the lovely residential **Ile St-Louis**; keep an eye out for the "proper" depth measuring stick on Ile St-Louis, near the Tour d'Argent restaurant.

Sightseeing boats turn near the public sculpture garden at the **Jardin des Plantes**, where you'll get a view of the huge national library, **Bibliothèque François Mitterrand** the four towers look like opened books. Moored in the Seine near the bibliothèque is the Josephine Baker swimming pool with its retractable roof. Paris used to have several floating pools, including the elaborate Piscine Deligny, which was used in the Paris Olympics in 1924; it inexplicably sank in 1993.

Ile St-Louis

Jardin des Plantes

Bibliothèque Francois Mitterand

PLANNING A BOAT TOUR ON THE SEINE

■ Most boat tours last about an hour; in the winter, even the interior of the boats can be cool, so take an extra scarf or sweater.

■ It never hurts to book ahead since schedules vary with the season and the (unpredictable) height and mood of the Seine.

■ As you float along, consider that Parisians used similar boats as a form of public transportation until the 1930s. Not really like Venice; more like the Staten Island ferry.

■ For optimal Seine enjoyment, combine a boat tour with a stroll—walk around Ile St-Louis, stroll along the Left Bank quays near the Pont Neuf, or start at the quay below the Louvre and walk to the Eiffel Tower, past the fabulous private houseboats.

WHICH BOAT IS FOR YOU?

If you want... lots of information	☎ 01–42–25–96–10 ⊕ www.bateaux-mouches.fr ✉ €12.50 Ⓜ Alma-Marceau	
	The massive, double-decker **Bateaux Mouches,** literally "fly boats," offer prerecorded commentary in seven languages.	Departs from the Pont de l'Alma (Right Bank) daily April to September: every 20, 30, or 45 min., from 10:15 AM to 10:30 PM; daily: October through March approximately every hour from 11 AM to 9 PM.
If you want... to do your own thing	☎ 08–25–05–01–01 ⊕ www.batobus.com ✉ €15, €18 *for 2 consecutive days*	
	The commentary-free **Batobus** boat-bus service allows you to hop on and off at any of the eight stops along the river. The company also runs an eco-friendly, 100% electric riverboat.	Departs from 8 locations: Eiffel Tower, Champs Elysées, Musée d'Orsay, Louvre, St. Germain-des-Pres, Notre-Dame, Hotel de Ville, and Jardin des Plantes.
If you want... to impress a date or client	☎ 01–44–54–14–70 ⊕ www.yachtsdeparis.fr ✉ €198–249 *for dinner cruise* Ⓜ Bastille	
	The **Yachts de Paris** specialize in gorgeous boats—expensive, yes, but glamorous as all get-out, with surprisingly good meals.	Dinner cruises leave from Port Henri IV (near Bastille).
If you want... the Seine, with music	☎ 01–43–54–50–04 ⊕ www.calife.com ✉ €67 *and up for dinner cruise* Ⓜ Louvre-Rivoli	
	Le Calife is the Aladdin's lamp of the Seine, moored across from the Louvre. Jazz, piano music, and evenings devoted to French song makes this a quirky and charming choice.	Departs from the Port des Saints-Pères, at Quai Malaquais, opposite the Louvre and under the Pont des Arts footbridge.

THE ISLANDS

Ile St-Louis and Ile de la Cité

GETTING ORIENTED

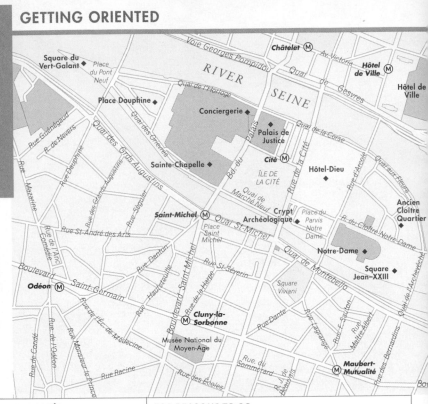

BEST CAFÉS

La Charlotte de l'Isle. Sip tea and sample tasty cakes at this atmospheric salon. ✉ *24 rue St-Louis-en-l'Ile, Ile St-Louis* ☎ *01–43–54–25–83* ⊕ *www. lacharlottedelisle.fr* ⏱ *Tues. and Wed. 2–8 pm, Thurs.–Sun. 11–7 pm* Ⓜ *Pont Marie.*

Le Saint Régis. Wondering where locals take their coffee on touristy Ile St-Louis? Try this old-timer (cheerier now after an extensive reno). It's a good option for lunch, too. ✉ *6 rue Jean de Bellay, Ile St-Louis* ☎ *01–43–54–59–41* ⊕ *www. cafesaintregisparis.com* ⏱ *Mon.– Sun. 7 am–2 am* Ⓜ *Pont Marie.*

TOP REASONS TO GO

Notre-Dame. This gorgeous Gothic cathedral has welcomed visitors to Paris for centuries. Gaze at its famed rose windows, climb the bell tower to mingle with gargoyles, or amble around back to contemplate the awe-inspiring flying buttresses from Square Jean-XXIII. At the end of the plaza in front of the cathedral, down the stairs, is the interesting Crypte Archéologique, a museum that showcases the city's Roman ruins.

Sainte-Chapelle. Visit on a sunny day to best appreciate the exquisite stained glass in this 13th-century chapel built for King Louis IX.

Strolling the islands. Ile de la Cité is where Paris began. Start with the city's oldest bridge, the Pont Neuf (incongruously called the "new bridge") and give a nod to the statue of Henry IV, who once proudly said, "I make love, I make war, and I build." From here, cross to Place Dauphine and make your way to Ile St-Louis, one of the city's most exclusive enclaves.

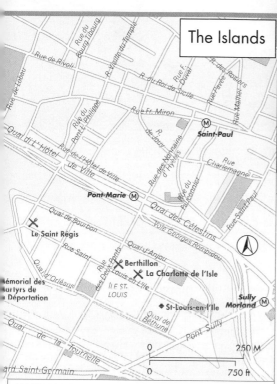

The Islands

ICE CREAM VS. GELATO

Amorino. Popping up all over—and winning converts faster than you can finish a double scoop—is the Amorino chain of gelaterias, which serves inventive frozen concoctions in the shape of a flower blossom. Popular flavors include rich *bacio* (dark chocolate with hazelnuts) and mascarpone with figs. The Ile St-Louis location (one of 25 in Paris) is open noon to midnight daily from March to November. ✉ *47 rue St-Louis-en-l'Ile, Ile St-Louis* ☎ *01–44–07–48–08* ⊕ *www. amorino.com* Ⓜ *Pont-Marie.*

Berthillon. Parisian ice cream is served at cafés all over town, but it's worth making a pilgrimage to the mecca of artisanal *glacé* to understand what all the fuss is about. The family-owned Berthillon shop features more than 30 flavors that change with the seasons, from mouth-puckering *cassis* (black currant) in summer to nutty *marron* (candied chestnut) in winter. Expect to wait in a lengthy line for a tiny scoop. ✉ *31 rue St-Louis-en-l'Ile, Ile St-Louis* ☎ *01–43–54–31–61* ⊕ *www. berthillon.fr* Ⓜ *Pont-Marie.*

MAKING THE MOST OF YOUR TIME

This little area of Paris is easily walkable and packed with sights and stunning views, so give yourself as much time as possible to explore. With Notre-Dame, the Conciergerie, and Sainte-Chapelle, you could spend a day wandering but the islands are easily combined with the St-Germain quarter. On warmer days, Rue de Buci is an ideal place to pick up a picnic lunch to enjoy in leafy Square du Vert-Galant at the tip of Ile de la Cité. If you have limited time in the area, make sure you visit Notre-Dame and go for a stroll.

GETTING HERE

Ile de la Cité and Ile St-Louis are in the 1er and 4e arrondissements (Boulevard du Palais is the dividing line between the 1er and 4e arrondissements on Ile de la Cité). If you're too far away to get here on foot, take the métro to St-Michel station or La Cité.

Sightseeing
★★★★
Dining
★★
Lodging
★★★
Shopping
★★
Nightlife
★

At the heart of Paris, linked to the banks of the Seine by a series of bridges, are two small islands: Ile St-Louis and Ile de la Cité. They're the perfect places to begin your visit, with postcard-worthy views all around. The Ile de la Cité is anchored by mighty Notre-Dame; farther east, the atmospheric Ile St-Louis is dotted with charming hotels, cozy restaurants, and small specialty shops.

Updated by
Victoria Tang

At the western tip of Ile de la Cité is regal **Place Dauphine,** one of Paris's oldest squares. The impressive Palais de Justice (courthouse) sits between **Sainte-Chapelle,** the exquisite medieval chapel of saintly King Louis IX, and the **Conciergerie,** the prison where Marie-Antoinette and other bluebloods awaited their slice of history at the guillotine.

The Gothic powerhouse that is **Notre-Dame** originally loomed over a medieval huddle of buildings that were later ordered razed by Baron Georges-Eugène Haussmann, the 19th-century urban planner who transformed Paris into the city we see today. In front of the cathedral is now Place du Parvis, the point from which all roads in France are measured. On the north side of the square is the **Hôtel-Dieu** (roughly translated as "general hospital"): it was immortalized by Balzac as the squalid last stop for the city's most unfortunate but today houses a modern hospital. Just behind the cathedral lies Rue du Cloître-Notre-Dame, which cuts through the **Ancien Cloître Quartier,** on whose narrow streets you can imagine the medieval quarter as it once was, densely packed and teeming with activity. At 9–11 quai aux Fleurs, a plaque commemorates the abode that was the setting of the tragic, 12th-century love affair between the philosopher Peter Abélard and his young conquest, Héloïse.

At the farthest eastern tip of Ile de la Cité is the **Mémorial des Martyrs de la Déportation,** all but hidden in a pocket-size park. A set of stairs leads down to the impressive and moving memorial to the more than 200,000 French citizens who died in Nazi concentration camps.

Nearby Pont St-Louis, which always seems to be occupied by street performers, leads to the Ile St-Louis, one of the city's best places to wander. There are no cultural hot spots, just a few narrow streets that comprise one of the most privileged areas in the city. Small hotels, eateries, art galleries, and shops selling everything from chocolate and cheese to silk scarves line the main street, Rue St-Louis-en-L'Ile. There were once two islands here, Ile Notre-Dame and Ile aux Vaches ("Cow Island," an erstwhile grazing pasture), both owned by the Church. Speculators bought the islands, joined them, and sold the plots to builders who created what is today some of the city's most elegant and expensive real estate. Baroque architect Louis Le Vau (who later worked on Versailles) designed fabulous private mansions for aristocrats, including the majestic Hôtel de Lauzun on lovely Quai d'Anjou.

MONSIEUR GUILLOTIN

Beheading by means of an ax or sword was a popular means of punishment long before the French Revolution, but it was Dr. Joseph-Ignace Guillotin who suggested there was a more humane way of decapitating prisoners. Not surprisingly, Dr. Guillotin's descendants changed their surname.

2

TOP ATTRACTIONS

FAMILY **Conciergerie.** Most of Ile de la Cité's medieval structures fell victim to wunderkind urban planner Baron Haussmann's ambitious rebuilding program of the 1860s. Among the rare survivors are the jewel like Sainte-Chapelle, a vision of shimmering stained glass, and the Conciergerie, the cavernous former prison where Marie-Antoinette and other victims of the French Revolution spent their final days.

Constructed by Philip IV in the late 13th and early 14th centuries, the Conciergerie—which takes its name from the building's concierge or keeper—was part of the original palace of the kings of France before the royals moved into the Louvre around 1364. In 1391, it became a prison. During the French Revolution, Marie-Antoinette languished 76 days here awaiting her date with the guillotine. There is a re-creation of the doomed queen's sad little cell—plus others that are far smaller—complete with wax figures behind bars. In the chapel, stained glass, commissioned after the queen's death by her daughter, is emblazoned with the initials M. A. Outside you can see the small courtyard where women prisoners took meals and washed their clothes in the fountain (men enjoyed no similar respite). Well-done temporary exhibitions on the ground floor aim to please kids and adults alike; previous themes have included enchanted forests and Gothic castles. There are free guided tours (in French only) most days at 11 and 3. ⊠ *2 bd. du Palais, Ile de la Cité* ☎ *01–53–40–60–80* ⊕ *www.conciergerie.monuments-nationaux. fr* ⊠ *€8.50; joint ticket with Sainte-Chapelle €12.50* ⊘ *Daily 9:30–6 (ticket window closes at 5:30)* Ⓜ *Cité.*

Mémorial des Martyrs de la Déportation (*Memorial of the Deportation*). On the eastern tip of Ile de la Cité lies this stark monument to the more than 200,000 French men, women, and children who died in Nazi concentration camps during World War II. The evocative memorial, inaugurated by Charles de Gaulle in 1962, was intentionally designed to be claustrophobic. Concrete blocks mark the narrow entrance to the crypt, which contains the tomb of an unknown deportee killed at the Neustadt camp. A dimly lit narrow gallery studded with 200,000 pieces of glass symbolizes the lives lost; while urns at the lateral ends contain ashes from the camps. ⊠ *Ile de la Cité* ◻ *Free* ☉ *Mar.–Oct., daily 10–5; Apr.–Sept., daily 10–7* Ⓜ *Maubert Mutualité, Pont Marie.*

> ## THE FLOWER MARKET
>
> Every day of the week except Monday, you can find the Marché aux Fleurs (flower market) facing the entrance to the imposing Palais de Justice on Boulevard du Palais. It's a fragrant detour from the Ile de la Cité, and the Guimard-designed entrance to the Cité métro station seems to blend beautifully with the potted plants on display in open-air and covered pavilions. On Sunday, the place is chirping with birds and other small pets for sale.

FodorśChoice
★ **Notre-Dame**
See the highlighted listing in this chapter.

FodorśChoice
★ **Sainte-Chapelle**
See the highlighted listing in this chapter.

WORTH NOTING

FodorśChoice
★ **Ancien Cloître Quartier.** Hidden in the shadows of Notre-Dame is this evocative, often-overlooked tangle of medieval streets. Through the years lucky folks, including Ludwig Bemelmans (who created the beloved *Madeleine* books) and the Aga Khan have called this area home, but back in the Middle Ages it was the domain of cathedral seminary students. One of them was the celebrated Peter Abélard (1079–1142)— philosopher, questioner of the faith, and renowned declaimer of love poems. Abélard boarded with Notre-Dame's clergyman, Fulbert, whose 17-year-old niece, Héloïse, was seduced by the compelling Abélard, 39 years her senior. She became pregnant and the vengeful clergyman had Abélard castrated; amazingly, he survived and fled to a monastery, while Héloïse took refuge in a nunnery. The poetic, passionate letters between the two cemented their fame as thwarted lovers, and their story inspired a devoted following during the romantic 19th century. They still draw admirers to the Père Lachaise Cemetery, where they're interred *ensemble*. The clergyman's house at 10 rue Chanoinesse was redone in 1849; a plaque at the back of the building at 9–11 quai aux Fleurs commemorates the lovers. ⊠ *Rue du Cloître-Notre-Dame north to Quai des Fleurs, Ile de la Cité* Ⓜ *Cité.*

Palais de Justice. This 19th-century neoclassical courthouse complex occupies the site of the former royal palace of St-Louis that later housed Parliament until the French Revolution. It is recognizable from afar with the tower of Sainte-Chapelle, tucked inside the courtyard, peeking out. Some 4000 magistrates, lawyers, state *fonctionnaires*, and police officials work on the property. ■ TIP→ Black-frocked judges can often

SAINTE-CHAPELLE

✉ *4 bd. du Palais, Ile de la Cité* ☎ *01–53–40–60–97* ⊕ *www.sainte-chapelle. monuments-nationaux.fr* 🎫 *€8.50; joint ticket with Conciergerie €12.50* ⊘ *Mar.– Oct., daily 9:30–6; Nov.–Feb., daily 9–5 (ticket window closes 30 min before closing)* Ⓜ *Cité.*

2

TIPS

■ Sunset is the optimal time to see the rose window; however, to avoid waiting in killer lines, plan your visit for a weekday morning, the earlier the better.

■ Come on a sunny day to appreciate the full effect of the light filtering through all of that glorious stained glass.

■ You can buy a joint ticket with the Conciergerie: lines are shorter if you purchase it there or online, though you'll still have to go through a longish metal detector line to get into Sainte-Chapelle itself.

■ Sights aside, the chapel makes a divine setting for classical concerts; check the schedule at www.infoconcert. com.

Built by the obsessively pious Louis IX (1226–70), this Gothic jewel is home to the oldest stained-glass windows in Paris. The chapel was constructed over three years, at phenomenal expense, to house the king's collection of relics acquired from the impoverished emperor of Constantinople. These included Christ's Crown of Thorns, fragments of the Cross, and drops of Christ's blood—though even in Louis's time these were considered of questionable authenticity. Some of the relics have survived and can be seen in the treasury of Notre Dame, but most were lost during the Revolution.

Highlights

The narrow spiral staircase by the entrance takes you to the upper chapel where the famed beauty of Sainte-Chapelle comes alive: 6,458 square feet of stained glass is delicately supported by painted stonework that seems to disappear in the colorful light streaming through the windows. Deep reds and blues dominate the background, noticeably different from later, lighter medieval styles such as those of Notre-Dame's rose windows.

The chapel is essentially an enormous magic lantern illuminating 1,130 biblical figures. Its 15 windows— each 50-feet high—were dismantled and cleaned with laser technology during a 40-year restoration, completed in 2014 to coincide with the 800th anniversary of St. Louis's birth. Besides the dazzling glass, observe the detailed carvings on the columns and the statues of the apostles. The lower chapel is gloomy and plain, but take note of the low, vaulted ceiling decorated with fleurs-de-lis and cleverly arranged Ls for Louis.

be spotted taking a cigarette break on the majestic rear staircase facing Rue du Harlay. ⊠ *4 bd. du Palais, Ile de la Cité* ⊕ *www.ca-paris. justice.fr* Ⓜ *Cité.*

Place Dauphine. The Surrealists called Place Dauphine "le sexe de Paris" because of its suggestive V shape; however, its origins were much more proper. The pretty square on the western side of Pont Neuf was built by Henry IV, who named it as an homage to his son the crown prince (or dauphin) who became Louis XIII when Henry was assassinated. ■ **TIP→** In warmer weather, treat yourself to a romantic meal on a restaurant terrace here—the square is one of the best places in Paris to dine en plein air. ⊠ *Ile de la Cité* Ⓜ *Cité.*

Square du Vert-Galant. The equestrian statue of the Vert Galant himself— amorous adventurer Henry IV—keeps a vigilant watch over this leafy square at the western end of the Ile de la Cité while his real head, rediscovered in 2010, sits in a bank vault. The dashing but ruthless Henry, king of France from 1589 until his assassination in 1610, was a stern upholder of the absolute rights of monarchy and a notorious womanizer. He is probably best remembered for his cynical remark that "*Paris vaut bien une messe*" ("Paris is worth a mass"), a reference to his readiness to renounce Protestantism to gain the throne of predominantly Catholic France. To ease his conscience, he issued the Edict of Nantes in 1598, according French Protestants (almost) equal rights with their Catholic countrymen. ■ **TIP→** The square is a great place for a quai-side picnic. It's also the departure point for Vedette Pont Neuf tour boats (at the bottom of the steps to the right). ⊠ *Ile de la Cité* Ⓜ *Pont Neuf.*

St-Louis-en-L'Ile. You can't miss the unusual lacy spire of this church as you approach the Ile St-Louis; it's the only church on the island and there are no other steeples to compete with it. It was built from 1652 to 1765 according to the Baroque designs of architect François Le Vau, brother of the more famous Louis, who designed several mansions nearby—as well as the Palace of Versailles. St-Louis's interior was essentially stripped during the Revolution, as were so many French churches, but look for the odd outdoor iron clock, which dates from 1741. ■ **TIP→** Check the church website for upcoming classical music events. ⊠ *19 bis, rue St-Louis-en-L'Ile, Ile St-Louis* ☎ *01–46–34–11–60* ⊕ *www.saintlouisenlile.catholique.fr* Ⓜ *Pont Marie.*

NOTRE-DAME

Notre-Dame is the symbolic heart of Paris and, for many, of France itself. Napoléon was crowned here, and kings and queens exchanged marriage vows before its altar. There are a few things worth seeing inside the Gothic cathedral, but the real highlights are the exterior architectural details and the unforgettable view of Paris, framed by stone gargoyles, from the top of the south tower.

THE STONE GARGOYLES

Notre-Dame's gargoyles were designed by Eugène Viollet-le-Duc, the architect who oversaw the cathedral's 19th-century renovations. Technically they're chimeras, not gargoyles, as they're purely ornamental; a true "gargoyle" is a carved sculpture that functions as a waterspout.

OUTSIDE NOTRE-DAME

Begun in 1163, completed in 1345, badly damaged during the Revolution, and restored by the architect Eugène Viollet-le-Duc in the 19th century, Notre-Dame may not be France's oldest or largest cathedral, but in beauty and architectural harmony it has few peers. The front entranceways seem like hands joined in prayer, the sculpted kings on the facade form a noble procession, and the west (front) rose window gleams with what seems like divine light.

The most dramatic approach to Notre-Dame is from the Rive Gauche, crossing at the Pont au Double from quai de Montebello, at the St-Michel métro or RER stop. This bridge will take you to the open square, place du Parvis, in front of the cathedral. (The more direct metro stop is Cité.)

THE WEST (FRONT) FACADE

The three front entrances are, left to right: the Portal of the Virgin, the Portal of the Last Judgment (above), and the Portal of St. Anne, the oldest of the three. Above the three front entrances are the 28 restored statues of the kings of Israel, the Galerie des Rois.

INSIDE THE CATHEDRAL

TIMELINE

1160 Notre-Dame is conceived by Bishop Maurice de Sully, the bishop of Paris.

1163 Construction begins.

1182 Choir is completed; the main altar is consecrated.

1196 Bishop de Sully dies.

c. 1200 The western facade
-1245 and towers are completed.

1208 The Nave is completed.

1235 A series of chapels
-1250 are added to the nave.

1250 The High Gothic–style
-1270 north and south Rose windows are installed.

1296- A series of chapels are
1330 added to the apse.

1345 Construction of the original cathedral is completed.

1699 The original Gothic
-1723 choir is replaced with a Baroque one.

c 1790 The church is plundered during the Revolution.

1845 Viollet-le-Duc's restoration begins, lasting 23 years.

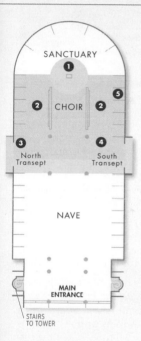

❶ **The Pietà,** behind the choir, represents the Virgin Mary mourning over the dead body of Christ.

❷ **The biblical scenes** on the north and south screens of the choir represent the life of Christ and the apparitions of Christ after the Resurrection.

❸ **The north rose window** is one of the cathedral's original stained-glass panels; at the center is an image of Mary holding a young Jesus.

❹ At the south (right) entrance to the choir, you'll glimpse the haunting 12th-century statue of **Notre-Dame de Paris,** "Our Lady of Paris," the Virgin, for whom the cathedral is named.

❺ **The treasury,** on the south side of the choir, holds a small collection of religious garments, reliquaries, and silver- and gold-plate.

MAKING THE CLIMB A separate entrance, to the left of the front facade if you're facing it, leads to the 387 stone steps of the south tower. These steps take you to the bell of Notre-Dame (as tolled by the fictional Quasimodo). Looking out from the tower, you can see how Paris—like the trunk of a tree developing new rings—has grown outward from the Ile de la Cité. To the north is Montmartre; to the west is the Arc de Triomphe, at the top of the Champs-Elysées; and to the south are the towers of St-Sulpice.

Place du Parvis

Detail of the Gallery of Kings, over the front entrance.

Notre-Dame was one of the first Gothic cathedrals in Europe and one of the first buildings to make use of **flying buttresses**—exterior supports that spread out the weight of the building and roof. At first people thought they looked like scaffolding that the builders forgot to remove. ■ TIP→ **The most tranquil place to appreciate the architecture of Notre-Dame is from the lovely garden behind the cathedral, Square Jean-XXIII. By night, take a boat ride on the Seine for the best view—the lights at night are magnificent.**

Place du Parvis is *kilomètre zéro*, the spot from which all distances to and from the city are officially measured. A polished brass circle set in the ground, about 20 yards from the cathedral's main entrance, marks the exact spot.

The Crypt Archéologique (entrance down the stairs in front of the cathedral) offers a fascinating subterranean view of this busy area from the 1st century when Paris was a Roman city called Lutetia, with ruins of houses, baths and even a quay, through medieval times when the former rue Neuve-Notre-Dame that passed through here was packed with houses and shops. A 2012 renovation cleaned the remains and added 3-D video touch screen panels that bring the ruins to life.

☎ 01–42–34–56–10

⊕ www.notredame deparis.fr

✆ Cathedral free. Towers: €8.50. Crypt €5. Treasury €3.

⊙ Cathedral daily 8–6:45 and 7:15 on weekends. Towers Apr.– June and Sept., daily 10 AM–6:30; July and Aug., weekdays 10 AM–6:30, weekends 10 AM–11 PM; Oct.–Mar., daily 10–5:30. Note: towers close early when overcrowded. Treasury weekdays 9:30– 6 PM, Sat. 9:30–6:30, Sun. 1:30–6:30. Crypt Tues.– Sun. 10–6.

■ TIP→ The best time to visit Notre-Dame is early in the morning, when the cathedral is at its brightest and least crowded.

■ TIP→ There are free guided tours in English several times a week; check website for times.

SOMETHING TO PONDER

Do Notre-Dame's hunchback and its gargoyles have anything in common other than bad posture? Quasimodo was created by Victor Hugo in the novel *Notre-Dame de Paris*, published in 1831. The incredible popularity of the book made Parisians finally take notice of the cathedral's state of disrepair and spurred Viollet-le-Duc's renovations. These included the addition of the gargoyles, among other things, and resulted in the structure we see today.

AROUND THE EIFFEL TOWER

with Invalides

GETTING ORIENTED

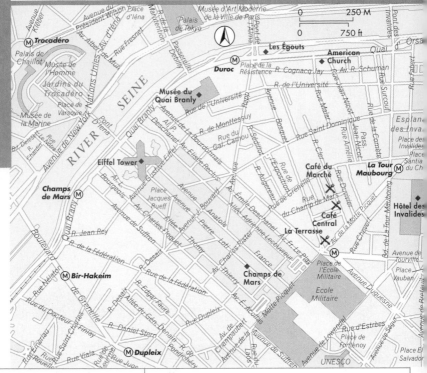

GETTING HERE

The most romantic way to reach the Eiffel Tower is by boat. Alternately, you can head for RER C: Champs de Mars/Tour Eiffel. For the best view, get off at the Trocadéro station (métro Line 9 or 6) and make the short walk over the Pont (bridge) d'Iéna to the tower. For the Musée Rodin, get off at Varenne (Line 13). Use this stop, or La Tour Maubourg (Line 8), for Napoléon's Tomb and Hôtel des Invalides. For the Musée Rodin, get off at Varenne (Line 13). Use this stop or La Tour Maubourg (Line 8) for Napoléon's Tomb and Hôtel des Invalides.

TOP REASONS TO GO

Eiffel Tower. No question: The ultimate symbol of France is worth a visit at least once in your life.

Musée Rodin. A must-see for fans of the master sculptor, this magnificent 18th-century *hôtel particulier* (private mansion) was Rodin's former workshop. The manicured garden is a perfect setting for his timeless works.

Napoléon's Tomb. The golden-domed Hôtel des Invalides is a fitting place for Napoléon's remains. Military history buffs will appreciate the impressive display of weaponry and armor in the adjoining Musée de l'Armée.

A boat ride. Whether you choose a guided Bateaux Mouche tour or a Batobus (water taxi) trip, cruising the Seine is a relaxing way to see city highlights without traffic or crowds. Book a ride after dark when all of Paris is aglow.

Around the Eiffel Tower

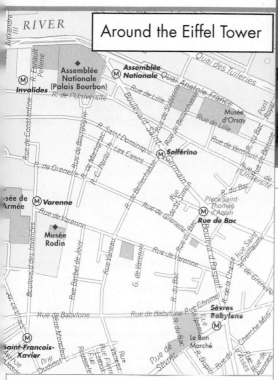

Map labels:

Alexandre III
R. Esnault Pellerie
Assemblée Nationale (M) Invalides (Palais Bourbon)
R. de l'Université
Assemblée Nationale (M)
Quai Anatole France
Quai des Tuileries
Boulevard Saint-Germain
Rue de Lille
Rue de Bellechasse
Musée d'Orsay
Rue de Lille
Pont Royal
R. de Constantine
R. Saint-Dominique
Les Cases
R. de Bourgogne
Solférino (M)
Rue de Varenne
Rue de Verneuil
R. de l'Université
R. de Grenelle
sée de Armée (M) Varenne
Musée Rodin
R. du Bac
Place Saint-Thomas d'Aquin (M)
Rue de Bac
Rue de Varenne
Boulevard des Invalides
Boulevard de Raspail
Bd Saint-Germain
Rue de la Chaise
Rue du Bac
Rue de Grenelle
Rue du Bac
Rue Saint-Guillaume
Rue de Babylone
Rue de Babylone
Rue du Cherche-Midi
Sèvres Babylone (M)
Rue de Sèvres
Saint-François-Xavier (M)
Rue Dupin
Le Bon Marché
Rue du Bac
Rue de Babylone

MAKING THE MOST OF YOUR TIME

This neighborhood is home to one of the world's most iconic sites, the Eiffel Tower. Depending on the time of year, you can wait hours to ascend La Tour (it helps to buy your ticket online or come at night, when lines are shorter), but even if you stay firmly on the ground, it's worth a trip to see this landmark up close. Afterward, explore Rue St-Dominique's shops, bakeries, and restaurants. If you're up for a picnic, grab fixings on Rue Cler (between Rue de Grenelle and Avenue de La Motte Piquet), a pedestrian-only market street; then head back to the park at the foot of the tower.

If you have a day to spare, visit the Musée Rodin. If you're pressed for time, do a quick tour of the garden, where some of the best-known sculptures can be seen. From here it's a short walk to Napoléon's over-the-top tomb at the Hôtel des Invalides, which also houses the Musée de l'Armée devoted to military history. To appreciate art from Asia, Africa, and Oceania, devote an hour to the Musée du Quai Branly.

BEST CAFÉS

Café Central. If it's aperitif time, this is the place to be. With soft lighting, loungy music, plus a generous selection of cocktails, Café Central makes an ideal spot for an end-of-the-afternoon drink. ✉ *40 rue Cler, Tour Eiffel/Invalides* ☎ *01–47–05–00–53* ⊕ *www.cafecentralparis.com* Ⓜ *École Militaire.*

Café du Marché. On the quaint Rue Cler, this small but busy café is popular with residents. Savor your morning café and croissant here, or enjoy Paris after hours—it is one of the few establishments to stay open late. ✉ *38 rue Cler, Tour Eiffel/Invalides* ☎ *01–47–05–51–27* Ⓜ *La Tour-Maubourg, École Militaire.*

Carette. Serving chic Parisians since 1927, this Art Deco tea salon on Place du Trocadéro is a hot spot for lunch or afternoon tea. Relish a *salade composée* of mixed leaves with warm goat cheese, or a sublime slice of raspberry charlotte. ✉ *4 pl. du Trocadero, Trocadéro/Tour Eiffel* ☎ *01–47–27–98–85* Ⓜ *Trocadéro.*

Sightseeing
★★★★★
Dining
★★★
Lodging
★★★★★
Shopping
★★★★
Nightlife
★★★

One of Paris's most upscale neighborhoods, the posh 7e arrondissement (where nearly every block affords a view of La Tour Eiffel) is home to the French *bourgeoisie* and well-heeled expats. Commanding the southwestern end of Paris, the Eiffel Tower was considered an iron-latticed monstrosity when it opened in 1889. Today it is a beloved icon, especially at night when thousands of twinkling lights sparkle at the top of every hour.

Updated by
Victoria Tang

There are other monumental sights here, too, notably **Hôtel des Invalides,** a sprawling Baroque complex with a towering golden dome under which lies the enormous tomb of the pint-size dictator, Napoléon. Along the river, the **Palais Bourbon,** seat of the French Parliament, is an 18th-century homage to ancient Greek architecture. Nearby is the modern **Musée du Quai Branly,** built by star architect Jean Nouvel. Don't miss the **Musée Rodin,** where the master's sculptures ooze sensuality both outside in the garden and inside the elegant Hôtel Biron.

From the Eiffel Tower east, the walkway along the Seine will take you past **Les Égouts** (where you can embark on a subterranean tour of actual working sewers) and the **American Church.** For one of the best views in Paris, cross **Pont Alexandre III,** the city's most ornate bridge spanning the Seine from Invalides to the Grand Palais. Named for the Russian czar to celebrate Franco-Russian friendship, it was built between 1896 and 1900, and is bedecked with gilded sculptures, cherubs, and Art Nouveau lamps.

TOP ATTRACTIONS

Fodor's Choice
★

Eiffel Tower.
See the highlighted listing in this chapter.

Fodor's Choice
★

Hôtel des Invalides. The Baroque complex known as Les Invalides (pronounced *lehz-ahn-vah-leed*) is the eternal home of Napoléon Bonaparte

DID YOU KNOW?

For the 200th anniversary of the French Revolution, in 1989, the dome of Les Hôtel des Invalides was regilded using more than half a million gold leaves—that's the equivalent of 20-plus pounds of gold.

(1769–1821) or, more precisely, the little dictator's remains, which lie entombed under the towering golden dome.

Louis XIV ordered the facility built in 1670 to house disabled soldiers (hence the name), and at one time 4,000 military men lived here. Today, a portion of it still serves as a veterans' residence and hospital. The Musée de l'Armée, containing an exhaustive collection of military artifacts from antique armor to weapons, is also here.

If you see only a single sight, make it the Église du Dome (one of Les Invalides' two churches) at the back of the complex. Napoléon's tomb was moved here in 1840 from the island of Saint Helena, where he died in forced exile. The emperor's body is protected by a series of no fewer than six coffins—one set inside the next, sort of like a Russian nesting doll—which is then encased in a sarcophagus of red quartzite. The bombastic tribute is ringed by statues symbolizing Napoléon's campaigns of conquest. To see more Napoléoniana, check out the collection in the Musée de l'Armée featuring his trademark gray frock coat and huge bicorne hat. Look for the figurines reenacting the famous coronation scene when Napoléon crowns his empress, Josephine. You can see a grander version of this scene hanging in the Louvre by the painter David.

The Esplanade des Invalides, the great lawns in front of the building, are favorite spots for pickup soccer, Frisbee games, sunbathing, and dog walking—despite signs asking you to stay off the grass. ■TIP→ The best entrance to use is at the southern end, on Place Vauban (Avenue de Tourville). The ticket office is here, as is Napoléon's Tomb. There are automatic ticket machines at the main entrance on the Place des Invalides. ⊠ *Pl. des Invalides, Tour Eiffel, Paris* ☎ *01–44–42–38–77* ⊕ *www.invalides.org* 🎫 *€9.50* ⊙ *Église du Dôme and museums Apr.–Oct., daily 10–6; Nov.–Mar., daily 10–5 (ticket window closes 30 mins before museum); closed 1st Mon. of every month Oct.–June* Ⓜ *La Tour-Maubourg/Invalides.*

FAMILY **Musée du Quai Branly.** This eye-catching museum overlooking the Seine was built by star architect Jean Nouvel to house the state-owned collection of "non-Western" art, culled from the Musée National des Arts d'Afrique et d'Océanie and the Musée de l'Homme. Exhibits mix artifacts from antiquity to the modern age, such as funeral masks from Melanesia, Siberian shaman drums, Indonesian textiles, and African statuary. A corkscrew ramp leads from the lobby to a cavernous exhibition space, which is color coded to designate sections from Asia, Africa, and Oceania. The lighting is dim—sometimes too dim to read the information panels (which makes investing in the €5 audioguide a good idea).

Renowned for his bold modern designs, Nouvel has said he wanted the museum to follow no rules; however, many critics gave his vision a thumbs down when it was unveiled in 2006. The exterior resembles a massive rust-color rectangle suspended on stilts, with geometric shapes cantilevered to the facade facing the Seine and louvered panels on the opposite side. The colors (dark reds, oranges, and yellows) are meant to evoke the tribal art within. A "living wall" comprised of some 150 species of exotic plants grows on the exterior, which is surrounded by a wild jungle garden with swampy patches—an impressive sight after dark when scores of cylindrical colored lights are illuminated. ■TIP➜The trendy Les Ombres restaurant on the museum's fifth floor (separate entrance)

WORD OF MOUTH

"You should visit the Rodin in good weather. The gardens are marvelous, both for the greenery and the sculptures scattered among it." —Eurocentric

has premier views of the Tour Eiffel—and prices to match. The budget-conscious can enjoy the garden at Le Café Branly on the ground floor. ✉ 37 quai Branly, Trocadéro/Tour Eiffel ☎ 01–56–61–70–00 ⊕ www. quaibranly.fr 🎫 €8.50; €10 with temporary exhibits ⊙ Tues., Wed., and Sun. 11–7; Thurs.–Sat. 11–9 (ticket office closes 1 hr before museum); closed Mon. Ⓜ Alma-Marceau.

Fodor's Choice **Musée Rodin.**
★ See the highlighted listing in this chapter.

OFF THE BEATEN PATH

Paris's most ornate Art Nouveau front door can be found at **29 av. Rapp,** a few minutes' walk from the Pont de l'Alma. The six-story hôtel particulier to which it's attached was built in 1901 by Jules Lavirotte, who used brick, stone, and ceramics to create whimsical motifs inspired by nature. The historical plaque in front of the building notes that the architect's rebellious style added a "breath of youth and fantasy." Notice the expressions of the pair of nude sculptures: she with a smirk and a jaunty hand on hip; he with a hand cupped to his mouth, calling out to someone. The house was owned by ceramics expert Alexandre Bigot, who frequently teamed up with Lavirotte. The door is the most intriguing feature: carved wood with large oval windows resembling an owl's eyes. The metal handle takes the shape of a curled lizard, its head arching back. Twisting leaves and vines curl around the stone door frame; a woman's head (possibly the architect's wife) is centered at the top, a furry critter crawling down her neck, its pointed nose suspended just above the door. Walk around the corner to 3 square Rapp to see the house Lavirotte later built for himself.

WORTH NOTING

American Church. Not to be confused with the American Cathedral, across the river at 23 avenue George V, this pretty neo-Gothic church built in 1927-31 features a pair of Tiffany stained-glass windows—a rare find in Europe. Besides ecumenical Protestant services, it hosts architectural tours, free classical and acoustic concerts, plus popular exercise classes (including yoga). ■TIP➜ You can check event listings and download a self-guided PDF tour at the church website. ✉ 65 quai d'Orsay, Trocadéro/Tour Eiffel ☎ 01–40–62–05–00 ⊕ www.acparis. org ⊙ Mon.–Sat. 9–noon and 1–10:30, Sun. 3–7:30 Ⓜ Alma-Marceau; RER: Pont de l'Alma.

Champ de Mars. Flanked by tree-lined paths, this long expanse of grass lies between the Eiffel Tower and École Militaire. It was previously used as a parade ground and was the site of the world exhibitions in

Continued on page 60

MUSÉE RODIN

✉ *79 rue de Varenne, Troca-déro/Tour Eiffel* ☎ *01–44–18–61–10* ⊕ *www.musee-rodin. fr* 🎟 *€9; €1 gardens only; free 1st Sun. of month* ⊙ *Tues.– Sun. 10–5:45 (Wed. until 8:45); closed Mon.* Ⓜ *Varenne.*

TIPS

■ For €1 you can enjoy the seven acres of gardens.

■ If you want to linger, the Café du Musée Rodin serves meals and snacks in the shade of the garden's linden trees.

■ As you enter, a gallery on the right houses temporary exhibitions.

■ An English audioguide (€6) is available for the permanent collection and for temporary exhibitions. Buy your ticket online for priority access (€1.80 extra fee).

Auguste Rodin (1840–1917) briefly made his home and studio in the Hôtel Biron, a grand 18th-century mansion that now houses a museum dedicated to his work. He died rich and famous, but many of the sculptures that earned him a place in art history were originally greeted with contempt by the general public, which was unprepared for his powerful brand of sexuality and raw physicality. During a much-needed, multiyear renovation that has closed parts of the Hôtel Biron (it's set to finish in late 2014), the museum is showcasing a pared-down, "greatest hits" selection of Rodin's works.

Highlights

Most of his best-known sculptures are in the gardens. The front garden is dominated by *The Gates of Hell* (circa 1880). Inspired by the monumental bronze doors of Italian Renaissance churches, Rodin set out to illustrate stories from Dante's *Divine Comedy*. He worked on the sculpture for more than 30 years, and it served as a "sketch pad" for many of his later works. Look carefully and you can see miniature versions of *The Kiss* (bottom right), *The Thinker* (top center), and *The Three Shades* (top center).

Inside the museum, look for *The Bronze Age*, which was inspired by the sculptures of Michelangelo: this piece was so realistic that critics accused Rodin of having cast a real body in plaster. There's also a room (condensed during the renovation) of works by Camille Claudel (1864–1943), Rodin's student and longtime mistress, who was a remarkable sculptor in her own right. Her torturous relationship with Rodin eventually drove her out of his studio—and out of her mind. In 1913 she was packed off to an asylum, where she remained until her death.

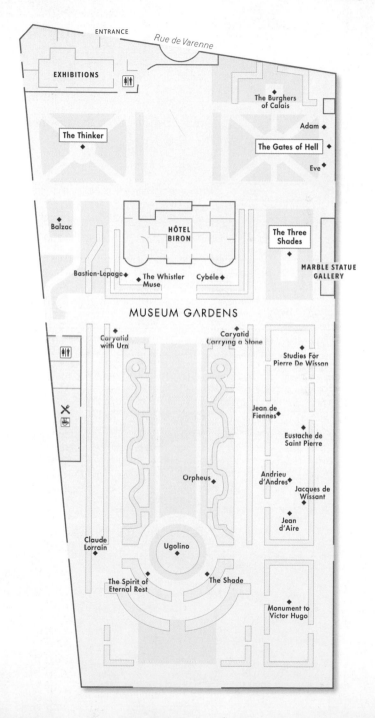

ENTRANCE
Rue de Varenne

EXHIBITIONS

The Burghers
of Calais

Adam ♦

The Thinker
♦

The Gates of Hell ♦

Eve ♦

Balzac
♦

HÔTEL
BIRON

The Three
Shades
♦

MARBLE STATUE
GALLERY

Bastien-Lepage ♦   ♦ Cybéle
          ♦ The Whistler
          Muse

MUSEUM GARDENS

Caryatid
with Urn ♦

Caryatid
Carrying a Stone ♦

Studies For
Pierre De Wissan ♦

Jean de
Fiennes ♦

Eustache de
Saint Pierre ♦

Orpheus ♦

Andrieu
d'Andres ♦

Jacques de
Wissant ♦

Jean
d'Aire ♦

Claude
Lorrain ♦

Ugolino ♦

The Spirit of
Eternal Rest ♦

The Shade ♦

Monument to
Victor Hugo ♦

3

New York has the Statue of Liberty, London has Big Ben—and Paris has the Eiffel Tower. This symbol of Paris, recognized the world over, did not, however, begin life as the beloved icon it is today. Engineer Gustave Eiffel's iron creation for the 1889 World's Fair was greeted with disgust by Parisians, who dubbed it the Giant Asparagus. French author Guy de Maupassant supposedly hated the tower so much that he often ate lunch there, explaining that it was the only place in the city where he could avoid seeing it. Parisians eventually warmed to the tower, an inescapable part of the landscape that has captured the minds and hearts of generations.

———— Total height: 1,063 feet ————

■ More than 250 million visitors have gone to the top since 1889.

■ To get to the first viewing platform, Gustave Eiffel originally used avant-garde

■ Every 7 years the tower is repainted. The job takes 15 months and uses 60 tons of "Tour Eiffel Brown" paint in three shades—lightest on top, darkest at the bottom.

LA TOUR EIFFEL

hydraulic cable elevators designed by American Elisha Otis for two of the curved base legs of the tower. French elevators with a chain-drive system were used in the other two legs. During the 1989 renovation, all the elevators were rebuilt by the Otis company.

■ An expensive way to beat the queue is to reserve a table at **Le Jules Verne**, the restaurant on the 2nd level, which has a private elevator. Taken over by star chef Alain Ducasse, count on a dinner bill of €175 to €210 per person, without drinks, though there's a €90 prix-fixe weekday menu at lunch (without wine). ⊕ *www.lejulesverne-paris.com* ☎ 01-45-55-61-44.

■ If you're in good shape, you can take the stairs to the 2nd level. If you want to go to the top you have to take the elevator.

■ The tower nearly became a giant heap of scrap in 1909, when its concession expired, but its use as a radio antenna saved the day.

■ The tower is most breathtaking at night, when the girders are illuminated. The light show, conceived to celebrate the turn of the millennium, was so popular that the 20,000 lights were reinstalled for permanent use in 2003. It does its electric shimmy for 5 minutes every hour on the hour (cut from 10 to save energy) until 1 am.

NEED A BITE?

58 Tour Eiffel, the restaurant on the first level, serves a good-value, self-service lunch. There is table service at dinner.

Le Café Branly, in the nearby Musée du Quai Branly (⊠ *27 Quai Branley, Trocadéro/Tour Eiffel* ☎ *01-47-53-68-01*) is a good choice for lunch or a late-afternoon snack.

The base formed by the tower's feet is 410 by 410 feet.

☎ 08-92-70-12-39 (€.34 per minute)

⊕ www.tour-eiffel.fr

🎫 By elevator: 1st and 2nd levels €9, top €15; By stairs: 1st and 2nd levels only, €5

⊙ mid June through Aug., daily 9 AM–12:45 AM

(11 PM for summit); Sept.–May, daily 9 AM–11 PM (10:30 PM for summit); Stairs close at 6 PM in winter

Ⓜ Bir-Hakeim, Trocadéro, Ecole Militaire; RER Champ de Mars

■ **TIP→** Beat the crush by reserving your tickets online.

1867, 1889 (when the tower was built), and 1900. Today the park, landscaped at the start of the 20th century, is a great spot for temporary art exhibits, picnics, pickup soccer games, and outdoor concerts. You can also just sprawl on the center span of grass, which is unusual for Paris. There's a playground where kids can let off steam. ■ TIP→ **Visiting during Bastille Day? If you can brave the crowds, arrive early to get a prime viewing position for the spectacular July 14th fireworks display, with the Eiffel Tower as a backdrop. Be vigilant at night.** ⊠ *Trocadéro/ Tour Eiffel* Ⓜ *École Militaire; RER: Champ de Mars.*

FAMILY **Les Égouts** (*The Sewers*). Leave it to the French to make even sewers seem romantic. Part exhibit but mostly, well, sewer, this 1,650-foot stretch of tunnels provides a fascinating—and not too smelly—look at the underbelly of Paris. Visitors can stroll the so-called galleries of this city beneath the city, which comes complete with street signs mirroring those above ground. Walkways flank tunnels of whooshing waste water wide enough to allow narrow barges to dredge sand and sediment. Lighted panels, photos, and explanations in English detail the workings of the system. Immortalized as the escape routes of the Phantom of the Opera and Jean Valjean in *Les Misérables*, the 19th-century sewers have a florid real-life history. Since Napoléon ordered the underground network built to clean up the squalid streets, they have played a role in every war, secreting revolutionaries and spies and their stockpiles of weapons. Grenades from World War II were recovered not far from where the gift shop now sits. The display cases of stuffed toy rats and "Eau de Paris" glass carafes fold into the walls when the water rises after heavy rains. ■ TIP→ **Buy your ticket at the kiosk on the Left Bank side of the Pont de l'Alma. Guided 1-hour tours by friendly égoutiers (sewer workers) are available in French only; call or email ahead for details.** ⊠ *Opposite 93 quai d'Orsay, Trocadéro/ Tour Eiffel* ☎ *01-53-68-27-81* ✎ *visite-des-egouts@paris.fr* ⊕ *www. paris.fr* ⊟ *€4.30* ☽ *May–Sept., Sat.–Wed. 11–5; Oct.–Apr., Sat.–Wed. 11–4; closed Thurs., Fri., and 2 wks in Jan.* Ⓜ *Alma-Marceau; RER: Pont de l'Alma.*

Palais Bourbon. The most prominent feature of the Palais Bourbon—home of the Assemblée Nationale (or French Parliament) since 1798—is its colonnaded facade, commissioned by Napoléon to match that of the Madeleine, across the Seine. Jean-Pierre Cortot's sculpted pediment portrays France holding the tablets of Law, flanked by Force and Justice. Inside is an exquisite library with a soaring ceiling of cupolas painted by Delacroix. Visits are by guided tour only (free, in French with an English audioguide); reservations, which are essential, can be made by phone or online. ■ TIP→ **Security is tight. When visiting, bring your passport as proof of identity.** ⊠ *33 quai d'Orsay, Trocadéro/Tour Eiffel* ☎ *01-40-63-56-00* ⊕ *www.assemblee-nationale.fr* ☽ *Tours Mon.–Sat. 9:30, 10:30, 2, and 3; Sat. only when Parliament is in session* Ⓜ *Assemblée Nationale.*

THE CHAMPS-ÉLYSÉES

GETTING ORIENTED

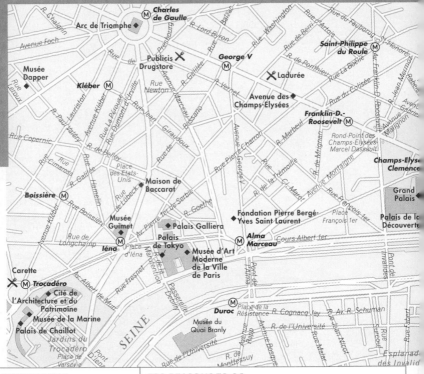

GETTING HERE

This neighborhood includes the 8e and 16e arrondissements. For the top of the Champs-Élysées/Arc de Triomphe, take métro Line 1, 2, or 6, or the RER A, to Charles-de-Gaulle–Étoile. For the bottom of the avenue, near the Grand Palais, go to the Champs-Élysées–Clemenceau métro station (Line 1). For the Palais de Chaillot, use the Trocadéro métro station on lines 6 and 9.

TOP REASONS TO GO

Avenue Champs-Élysées. Splurge in the upscale boutiques on and around this fabled avenue, or simply practice the fine art of lèche-vitrines (literally "window licking," the French term for window shopping).

Palais de Chaillot. A favorite of fashion photographers, this statue-lined plaza-terrace at Place du Trocadéro boasts the city's best view of the Eiffel Tower.

Musée Guimet. One of Paris's finest smaller museums has a world-class collection of art from all over Asia. Don't miss the rare Khmer sculptures from Cambodia.

Macarons from Ladurée. Is it worth lining up for 30 minutes to get a little taste of heaven? You decide. But rest assured: the round meringue cookies made by this famous pâtissier since 1862 are as scrumptious as ever.

The Champs-Élysées

Café La Belle Férronnière. A favorite of Parisians for morning *noisettes*, business lunches, and after-work *apéros*, this popular spot is a short walk from the Champs-Élysées. Settle in at a sidewalk table or retreat to the quieter interior. The enigmatic painting for which the café is named—da Vinci's *Portrait of an Unknown Woman*—hangs in the Louvre. ⊠ 53 rue Pierre Charron, Champs-Élysées ☏ 01–42–25–03–82 Ⓜ George V.

Ladurée. With 40-plus locations worldwide, the most opulent branch of the Ladurée tea salon empire is worth the splurge. Reserve a table upstairs or grab a bite in the Art Nouveau bar in the back. The menu promises generous salads and flavorful *plats du jour*. Sweets are a house specialty. In addition to more than a dozen flavors of *macaron*, it has assorted cakes, pastries, and beautifully boxed treats ideal for gift-giving. ⊠ 75 av. des Champs-Élysées, Champs-Élysées ☏ 01–40–75–08–75 ⊕ www.laduree.com Ⓜ George V.

MAKING THE MOST OF YOUR TIME

This neighborhood is an essential stop for every first-time visitor to Paris, and returning travelers will find plenty to do, too. Leave yourself a full day to tour some of the museums around Place du Trocadéro before heading to the Champs-Élysées, worth a walk from end to end. Stop for lunch or dessert at one of the cafés or tea salons en route; then detour down Avenue Montaigne, Paris's answer to Rodeo Drive. If your time is limited, you can just come for a stroll at night, when the Champs is alight: there are bars and nightclubs for all tastes, plus movie houses showing French films and English-language blockbusters (look for v.o., for *version originale*) if you prefer something more low-key.

Sightseeing
★★★★★
Dining
★★★
Lodging
★★★★★
Shopping
★★★★
Nightlife
★★★★★

Make no mistake: the Champs-Élysées, while ceding some of its elegance in recent times, remains the most famous avenue in Paris—and, perhaps, the world. Like New York's Times Square or London's Piccadilly Circus, it is a mecca for travelers and locals alike. Some Parisians complain that fast-food joints and chain stores have cheapened Avenue des Champs-Élysées, but others are more philosophical, noting that there is something here for everyone. If you can't afford lunch at Ladurée, there's always McDonald's (and the view from its second floor is terrific).

Updated by
Victoria Tang

Anchoring the Champs is the **Arc de Triomphe,** Napoléon's monument to himself. At the other end, the exquisitely restored **Grand Palais** plays host to some of the city's grandest art exhibitions. Across the street, the permanent art collection is free at the **Petit Palais,** and there's also a quiet garden café. Between here and **Place du Trocadéro,** a busy traffic circle, you can find several museums housed in some of Paris's most impressive buildings: at the **Palais de Chaillot** complex is the **Cité de l'Architecture et du Patrimoine,** a must for architecture buffs, and across the plaza is the charming nautical-theme **Musée National de la Marine.** Farther on, the **Musée Guimet** has a superlative Asian art collection. The **Musée d'Art Moderne de la Ville de Paris,** on Avenue du Président Wilson, contains a free permanent collection of 20th-century pieces. Contemporary art lovers should also check out what's showing next door at the trendy **Palais de Tokyo.** These twin Art Nouveau buildings, constructed for the 1937 World's Fair, are notable for their monumental facades. Across the street is the **Palais Galliera:** framed by a lovely garden outside, it has a museum inside that focuses on fashion.

DID YOU KNOW?

The magnificent Grand Palais, with its enormous glass dome, is known for provocative and crowd-pleasing temporary art exhibits.

TOP ATTRACTIONS

Fodor's Choice   Arc de Triomphe

★   *See the highlighted listing in this chapter.*

FAMILY   **Avenue des Champs-Élysées.** Marcel Proust lovingly described the genteel elegance of the storied Champs-Élysées (pronounced chahnz-*eleezay*, with an "n" sound instead of "m" and no "p") during its Belle Époque heyday, when its cobblestones resounded with the clatter of horses and carriages. Today, despite unrelenting traffic and the intrusion of chain stores and fast-food franchises, the avenue still sparkles. There's always something happening here: stores are open late (and many are open on Sunday, a rarity in Paris); nightclubs remain top destinations; and cafés offer prime people-watching, though you'll pay for the privilege—after all, this is Europe's most expensive piece of real estate. Along the 2-km (1-mile) stretch, you can find marquee names in French luxury, like Cartier, Guerlain, and Louis Vuitton. Car manufacturers lure international visitors with space-age showrooms. Old stalwarts, meanwhile, are still going strong—including the Lido cabaret and Fouquet's, whose celebrity clientele extends back to James Joyce. The avenue is also the setting for the last leg of the Tour de France bicycle race (the third or fourth Sunday in July), as well as Bastille Day (July 14) and Armistice Day (November 11) ceremonies. The Champs-Élysées, which translates to "Elysian Fields" (the resting place of the blessed in Greek mythology), began life as a cow pasture and in 1666 was transformed into a park by the royal landscape architect André Le Nôtre. Traces of its green origins are visible towards the Concorde, where elegant 19th-century park pavilions house the historic restaurants Ledoyen, Laurent, and the more recent Le Nôtre. ⊠ *Champs-Élysée* Ⓜ *Champs-Élysées–Clemenceau, Franklin D. Roosevelt, George V, Étoile.*

▮ NEED A BREAK?   **Publicis Drugstore.** A stone's throw from the Arc de Triomphe, this trendy spot—part mini-department store, part brasserie—is stocked with an ever-changing array of upscale wares from designer handbags and diamond bracelets to fine wine and cigars. When you're done browsing, enjoy a quick bite at the on-site eatery (a prix-fixe menu is available) or stop by the bakery for food to take away. ⊠ *133 av. des Champs-Élysées, Champs-Élysées* ☎ *01–44–43–77–64* ⊕ *www.publicisdrugstore.com* Ⓜ *Charles de Gaulle–Étoile.*

Cité de l'Architecture et du Patrimoine. The greatest gems of French architecture are represented at the City of Architecture and Heritage, which bills itself as the largest architectural museum in the world. Reopened in 2007 after an €84-million renovation, the former French Monuments Museum contains some 350 plaster-cast reproductions spread out over 86,000 square feet. While it may seem odd to see a collection comprised entirely of copies, these are no ordinary ones: they include partial facades from some of the most important Gothic churches, a gallery of frescoes and windows (among them a stained-glass stunner from the famous Chartres cathedral), plus an assembly of gargoyles practically leaping off the back wall of the soaring first-floor gallery. Video

ARC DE TRIOMPHE

✉ *Pl. Charles-de-Gaulle, Champs-Élysées* ☎ *01–55–37–73–77* ⊕ *arc-de-triomphe. monuments-nationaux.fr* 🎟 *€8* ⏱ *Apr.–Sept., daily 10 am–11 pm; Oct.–Mar., daily 10 am–10:30 pm* Ⓜ *Métro or RER: Étoile.*

4

TIPS

■ France's Unknown Soldier is buried beneath the arch, and a commemorative flame is rekindled every evening at 6:30. That's the most atmospheric time to visit, but, to beat the crowds, come early in the morning or buy your ticket online (€1.60 service fee).

■ Be wary of the traffic circle that surrounds the arch. It's infamous for accidents—including one several years ago that involved the French transport minister. Always use the underground passage from the northeast corner of Avenue des Champs-Élysées.

Inspired by Rome's Arch of Titus, this colossal, 164-foot triumphal arch was ordered by Napoléon—who liked to consider himself the heir to Roman emperors—to celebrate his military successes. Unfortunately, Napoléon's strategic and architectural visions were not entirely on the same plane, and the Arc de Triomphe proved something of an embarrassment. Although the emperor wanted the monument completed in time for an 1810 parade in honor of his new bride, Marie-Louise, it was still only a few feet high, and a dummy arch of painted canvas was strung up to save face. Empires come and go, but Napoléon's had been gone for more than 20 years before the Arc was finally finished in 1836. A small museum halfway up recounts its history.

Highlights

The Arc de Triomphe is notable for magnificent sculptures by François Rude, including *The Departure of the Volunteers in 1792*, better known as *La Marseillaise*, to the right of the arch when viewed from the Champs-Élysées. Names of Napoléon's generals are inscribed on the stone facades—the underlined names identify the hallowed figures who fell in battle.

The traffic circle around the Arc is named for Charles de Gaulle, but it's known to Parisians as "L'Étoile," or the Star—a reference to the streets that fan out from it. Climb the stairs to the top of the arch and you can see the star effect of the 12 radiating avenues and the vista down the Champs-Élysées toward Place de la Concorde and the distant Musée du Louvre.

monitors with joysticks allow a 360-degree view of some of the grandest cathedrals. The upper-floor gallery is devoted to architecture since 1851, with a life-size replica of a postwar apartment in Marseille designed by the urban-planning pioneer Le Corbusier. It's worth springing for the €3 English audiovisual guide. ■TIP➔ The museum's small café offers a great view of the Eiffel Tower. ⊠ 1 pl. du Trocadéro, Trocadéro/Tour Eiffel ☎ 01–58–51–52–00 ⊕ www. citechaillot.fr 🖼️ €8; €10 with temporary exhibits ⊙ Fri.–Mon. and Wed. 11–7, Thurs. 11–9; closed Tues. Ⓜ Trocadéro.

Grand Palais. With its curved-glass roof and gorgeously restored Belle Époque ornamentation, you can't miss the Grand Palais whether you're approaching from the Seine or the Champs-Élysées. It forms an elegant duo with the Petit Palais across Avenue Winston Churchill: both stone buildings, adorned with mosaics and sculpted friezes, were built for the 1900 World's Fair, and, like the Eiffel Tower, were not intended to be permanent. The exquisite main exhibition space called le Nef (or nave) plays host to large-scale shows that might focus on anything from jewelry to cars. The art-oriented shows staged here are some of the hottest tickets in town. Previous must-sees included an Edward Hopper retrospective, "Marie-Antoinette," and "Picasso and the Masters." ■TIP➔ To skip the long queue, book an advance ticket online for an extra euro. ⊠ Av. Winston Churchill, Champs-Élysées ☎ 01–44–13–17–17 ⊕ www.grandpalais.fr, www.rmn.fr for reservations 🖼️ €12 (can vary) ⊙ Wed.–Mon. 10–8 or 10–10, depending on exhibit; closed Tues. Ⓜ Champs-Élysées–Clemenceau.

Musée d'Art Moderne de la Ville de Paris (Paris Museum of Modern Art). Although the city's modern art museum hasn't generated a buzz comparable to that of the Centre Georges Pompidou, visiting can be a more pleasant experience because it draws fewer crowds. The Art Nouveau building reopened after a long renovation in 2006, and its vast, white-walled galleries make an ideal backdrop for temporary exhibitions of 20th-century art and postmodern installation projects. The permanent collection on the lower floor takes over where the Musée d'Orsay leaves off, chronologically speaking: among the earliest works are Fauvist paintings by Maurice Vlaminck and André Derain, followed by Pablo Picasso's early experiments in Cubism. Other highlights include works by Robert and Sonia Delaunay, Chagall, Matisse, Rothko, and Modigliani. ⊠ 11 av. du Président Wilson, Trocadéro/Tour Eiffel ☎ 01–53–67–40–00 ⊕ www.mam.paris.fr 🖼️ Permanent collection free, temporary exhibitions €5–€12 ⊙ Tues.–Sun. 10–6, Thurs. until 10 for temporary exhibits Ⓜ Alma Marceau, Iéna.

Fodor's Choice ★ **Musée Guimet.** The outstanding Musée Guimet boasts the western world's biggest collection of Asian art, thanks to the 19th-century wanderings of Lyonnaise industrialist Émile Guimet. Exhibits, enriched by the state's vast holdings, are laid out geographically in airy, light-filled rooms. Just past the entry, you can find the largest assemblage of Khmer sculpture outside Cambodia. The second floor has statuary and masks from Nepal, ritual funerary art from Tibet, and jewelry and fabrics from India. Peek into the library rotunda, where Monsieur Guimet once entertained the city's notables under the gaze of eight caryatids atop ionic columns; Mata Hari danced here in 1905. The much-heralded Chinese collection, made up of 20,000-odd objects, covers seven millennia. Pick up a free English language audioguide and brochure at the entrance. If you need a pick-me-up, stop at the Salon des Porcelaines café on the lower level for a ginger milk shake. ■TIP→ Don't miss the Guimet's impressive Buddhist Pantheon, with two floors of Buddhas from China and Japan, and a Japanese garden. Admission is free and it's just up the street at 19 avenue d'Iéna. ⊠ 6 pl. d'Iéna, Trocadéro/Tour Eiffel ☎ 01–56–52–53–00 ⊕ www.guimet.fr ☜ €7.50; €9.50 with temporary exhibition ⓥ Wed.–Mon. 10–6; closed Tues. Ⓜ Iéna, Boissiére.

4

FAMILY **Palais de Chaillot.** This honey-color Art Deco cultural center on Place du Trocadéro was built in the 1930s to replace a Moorish-style building constructed for the 1878 World's Fair. Its esplanade is a top draw for camera-toting visitors intent on snapping the perfect shot of the Eiffel Tower. In the building to the left is the Cité de l'Architecture et du Patrimoine—an excellent architecture museum—and the Théâtre National de Chaillot, which occasionally stages plays in English. Also here is the Institut Français d'Architecture, an organization and school. The twin building to the right contains the Musée National de la Marine, a charming small museum showcasing nautical history; and the Musée de l'Homme, a natural history museum that's closed for renovation until late 2015. Sculptures and fountains adorn the garden leading to the Seine. ⊠ Pl. du Trocadéro, Trocadéro/Tour Eiffel Ⓜ Trocadéro.

Palais de Tokyo. The go-to address for some of the city's funkiest exhibitions, the Palais de Tokyo is a stripped-down venue that spotlights provocative, ambitious contemporary art. There is no permanent collection: instead, cutting-edge temporary shows are staged in a cavernous space reminiscent of a light-filled industrial loft. The programming extends to performance art, concerts, readings, and fashion shows. Night owls will appreciate the midnight closing. ■TIP→ The museum's Tokyo Eat

Hemingway's Paris

There is a saying: "Everyone has two countries, his or her own—and France." For the Lost Generation after World War I, these words rang particularly true. Lured by favorable exchange rates, free-flowing alcohol, and a booming arts scene, many American writers, composers, and painters moved to Paris in the 1920s and 1930s, Ernest Hemingway among them. He arrived in Paris with his first wife, Hadley, in December 1921 and headed for the Rive Gauche—the Hôtel de l'Angleterre, to be exact (still operating at 44 rue Jacob). To celebrate their arrival the couple went to the Café de la Paix for a meal they nearly couldn't afford.

Hemingway worked as a journalist and quickly made friends with expat writers such as Gertrude Stein and Ezra Pound. In 1922 the Hemingways moved to 74 rue du Cardinal Lemoine, a bare-bones apartment with no running water (his writing studio was around the corner, on the top floor of 39 rue Descartes). Then, in 1924, they and their baby son settled at 113 rue Notre-Dame des Champs. Much of *The Sun Also Rises*, Hemingway's first serious novel, was written at nearby café La Closerie des Lilas. These were the years in which he forged his writing style, paring his sentences down to the pith—as he noted in *A Moveable Feast*, "hunger was good discipline." There were

some especially hungry months when Hemingway gave up journalism for short-story writing, and the family was "very poor and very happy."

They weren't happy for long: in 1926, as *The Sun Also Rises* made him famous, Hemingway left Hadley. The next year, he wed his mistress, Pauline Pfeiffer, and moved to 6 rue Férou, near the Musée du Luxembourg.

For gossip and books, and to pick up his mail, Papa would visit Shakespeare & Co. (then at 12 rue de l'Odéon). For cash and cocktails, Hemingway usually headed to the upscale Rive Droite. He collected the former at the Guaranty Trust Company, at 1 rue des Italiens. He found the latter, when he was flush, at the bar of the landmark Hôtel de Crillon, on Place de la Concorde next to the American Embassy, or, when poor, at the Caves Mura, at 19 rue d'Antin, or Harry's Bar, still in brisk business at 5 rue Daunou. Hemingway's loyal and legendary association with the Hôtel Ritz was sealed during the Liberation in 1944, when he strode in at the head of his platoon and "liberated" the joint by ordering martinis all around. Here Hemingway asked Mary Welsh to become his fourth wife, and here also, the story goes, a trunk full of notes regarding his first years in Paris turned up in the 1950s, giving him the raw material for writing *A Moveable Feast*.

restaurant—serving an affordable French-Asian fusion menu—is a haunt of hip locals, especially at lunch. Visit the offbeat gift shop for souvenirs that are as edgy and subversive as the exhibits. ⊠ *13 av. du Président Wilson, Trocadéro/Tour Eiffel* ☎ *01–81–97–35–88* ⊕ *www.palaisdetokyo. com* ⊠ *€10* ⊗ *Wed.–Mon. noon–midnight; closed Tues.* Ⓜ *Iéna.*

Fodor's Choice **Palais Galliera, Musée de la Mode.** The city's Museum of Fashion occupies a
★ suitably fashionable mansion—the 19th-century residence of Marie Brignole-Sale, Duchess of Galliera; and, having emerged from an extensive

makeover in September 2013, it is now more stylish than ever. Inside, temporary exhibitions focus on costume and clothing design (a reopening retrospective, for instance, honored the visionary Azzedine Alaïa). Covering key moments in fashion history and showcasing iconic French designers, the museum's collection includes 100,000 dresses and accessories that run the gamut from basic streetwear to haute couture. Details on shows (there are no permanent displays) are available on the museum website. ■TIP→ Don't miss the lovely 19th-century garden that encircles the palace. ✉ *10 av. Pierre-1er-de-Serbie, Trocadéro/Tour Eiffel* ☎ *01–56–52–86–00* ⊕ *palaisgalliera.paris.fr* ✆ *€8, admission varies* ⏱ *Tues.–Sun. 10–6 (Thurs. until 9); closed Mon.* Ⓜ *Iéna.*

> ### WORD OF MOUTH
>
> "The Cité de l'Architecture et du Patrimoine is off the tourist track, since it is a huge national museum that you can see all by yourself instead of being trampled by the crowds. I also recommend it to people who just can't see everything in France during their visit, or are looking for things to go and see in person during their next visit. I know that the idea that everything in this museum is a copy is what is most off-putting, but you really have to see it for yourself to understand its importance. So please give the Cité de l'Architecture et du Patrimoine a chance next time you are at Place du Trocadéro." —kerouac

Petit Palais, Musée des Beaux-Arts de la Ville de Paris. The "little" palace has a small, overlooked collection of excellent painting, sculpture, and objets d'art, with works by Monet, Gauguin, and Courbet, among others. Temporary exhibitions, beefed up in recent years (and often free), are particularly good—especially those dedicated to photography. The building, like the Grand Palais across the street, is an architectural marvel of marble, glass, and gilt built for the 1900 World's Fair, with impressive entry doors and huge windows overlooking the river. Search directly above the main galleries for 16 plaster busts set into the wall representing famous artists. Outside, note two eye-catching sculptures: French WWI hero Georges Clemenceau faces the Champs-Élysées, while a resolute Winston Churchill faces the Seine. ■TIP→ In warmer weather, head to the garden café with terrace seating. ✉ *Av. Winston Churchill, Champs-Élysées* ☎ *01–53–43–40–00* ⊕ *www.petitpalais. paris.fr* ✆ *Permanent collection free; temporary exhibit entry fees vary* ⏱ *Tues.–Sun. 10–6, Thurs. until 8 for temporary exhibits; closed Mon.* Ⓜ *Champs-Élysées–Clemenceau.*

NEED A BREAK?

Le Jardin du Petit Palais. The quiet little café hidden in the lush garden of the Petit Palais is one of this quarter's best-kept secrets. ✉ *Av. Winston Churchill, Champs-Élysées* ☎ *01–53–43–40–00* ⊕ *www.petitpalais.paris. fr* ⏱ *Tues.–Sun. 10–5:15 (7:30 Thurs. during temporary exhibitions); closed Mon.* Ⓜ *Champs-Élysées–Clemenceau.*

WORTH NOTING

FAMILY **Aquarium de Paris.** An aquarium and cinema may seem like a strange combination but the two coexist nicely in this attractive space beneath the Trocadéro gardens. In addition to 10,000 fish and a giant tank of small sharks, it promises puppet and magic shows, along with workshops for children in animation, art, and dance (these are offered in French but the staff speaks English). There are also kid-oriented films showing on one big screen and, for the grown-ups, feature films showing on a second. Check the website for times and activities. ■TIP➔ **Book tickets online to avoid lines.** ⊠ *5 av. Albert De Mun, Champs-Élysées* ☎ *01–40–69–23–23* ⊕ *www.cineaqua.com* ☎ *€19.50; €15.50 ages 13–17; €12.90 ages 3–12; free under 3* ⊙ *Daily 10–7 (last entry 1 hr before closing)* Ⓜ *Trocadéro.*

> **DID YOU KNOW?**
>
> Did you know that the former residents of the Baccarat Museum financed Luis Buñuel's first movie, *L'Age d'Or?* Marie-Laure, Vicomtesse de Noailles (nicknamed "Countess Bizarre"), and her husband lived in the magnificent mansion that is now the Baccarat showroom. Marie-Laure was a great supporter and friend of the Surrealists, including Buñuel, Man Ray, and Jean Cocteau (whom she considered marrying).

Fondation Pierre Bergé–Yves Saint Laurent. With his business partner, Pierre Bergé, the late fashion designer Yves Saint Laurent reopened his former atelier as a gallery and archive of his work in 2004. Unfortunately, YSL's private collection of dresses can be viewed only on private group tours booked in advance. What you can see here are exhibitions staged twice annually. Themes include painting, photography and, of course, fashion—such as a retrospective on couture maven Nan Kempner. Check the website to see what's on. ⊠ *3 rue Léonce Reynaud, Trocadéro/Tour Eiffel* ☎ *01–44–31–64–31* ⊕ *www.fondation-pb-ysl.net* ☎ *€7* ⊙ *Tues.– Sun. 11–6 (last entry at 5:15)* Ⓜ *Alma-Marceau.*

Maison de Baccarat. Designer Philippe Starck brought an irreverent *Alice in Wonderland* approach to the HQ and museum of the venerable Baccarat crystal firm. Relocated to the 16e arrondissement in 2003, Starck played on the building's surrealist legacy: Cocteau, Dalí, Buñuel, and Man Ray were all frequent guests of the mansion's onetime owner, Countess Marie-Laure de Noailles. At the entrance, talking heads are projected onto giant crystal urns, and a lighted chandelier is submerged in an aquarium. Upstairs, the museum features masterworks created by Baccarat since 1764, including soaring candlesticks made for Czar Nicholas II and the perfume flacon Dalí designed for Schiaparelli. Don't miss the rotunda's "Alchemy" section by Gérard Garouste showcasing the technical history of cutting, wheel-engraving, enameling, and gilding. If you're in the mood for shopping, contemporary crystal by top-name designers, as well as stemware, vases, tableware, jewelry, chandeliers, and even furniture is sold in the on-site shop. ■TIP➔ **Set aside a few moments to enjoy the little park just outside in Place des États-Unis with impressive statues of Washington and Lafayette.** ⊠ *11*

The Musée Guimet features Asian art and an auditorium for concerts and other events.

pl. des États-Unis, Trocadéro/Tour Eiffel ☎ *01–40–22–11–00* ⊕ *www. baccarat.fr* 🔲 *€5* ⊘ *Mon. and Wed.–Sat. 10–6:30* Ⓜ *Iéna.*

Musée Dapper. Dedicated to the art of Africa and the African diaspora, the Dapper Museum showcases an ever-changing selection of impressive temporary exhibitions, ranging from elaborate masks, traditional sculptures, and ceremonial jewelry to contemporary African designs. Opened in 1986 as a museum and cultural space by Christiane Falgayrettes-Leveau (a native of French Guyana) and her husband, Michel Leveau, the museum relocated to its current modern-design building in 2000. A visit to the Dapper makes a good pairing with a stop at the nearby Musée Guimet. Most of the visitor information is in French, but the website has English descriptions of current exhibitions. There is no permanent collection. ⊠ *35 bis, rue Paul Valéry, Champs-Élysées* ☎ *01–45–00–91–75* ⊕ *www.dapper.com.fr* 🔲 *€6* ⊘ *Wed. and Fri.– Mon. 11–7; closed Tues. and Thurs.; open during exhibitions only.* Ⓜ *Charles-de-Gaulle–Étoile.*

FAMILY **Musée National de la Marine** (*Maritime Museum*). Perfect for naval and history buffs, this underrated museum in the southwest wing of Palais Chaillot has a treasure trove of art and artifacts documenting maritime development pertinent to France over the centuries. It's one of five national museums dedicated to all things nautical (other locations are in Brest, Port-Louis, Rochefort, and Toulon). Inside you'll see impressive models of vessels from 17th-century flagships to modern warships. Kids can climb a step to get a closer look at a model aircraft carrier, cut in half to expose its decks. The main gallery features several figureheads recovered from sunken ships, including a giant Henri IV, with hand on heart, miraculously saved from a shipwreck in 1854 during the Crimean War. Another enormous representation of Napoléon, in his favored guise as a Roman emperor, was taken from the prow of the frigate *Iéna* in 1846. There is also a metal diving suit from 1882 and the menu from a 1935 voyage of the SS *Normandie* cruise ship. ■**TIP→** Free English audioguides are available. ⊠ *17 pl. du Trocadéro, Trocadéro/ Tour Eiffel* ☎ *01–53–65–69–53* ⊕ *www.musee-marine.fr* ⊠ *€7 permanent collection; €10 with temporary exhibits* ☉ *Mon. and Wed.–Fri. 11–6, weekends 11–7; closed Tues.* Ⓜ *Trocadéro.*

FAMILY **Palais de la Découverte** (*Palace of Discovery*). The Palace of Discovery, a popular science museum in the rear of the Grand Palais complex, has a wide variety of exhibits spread out over two floors under an elegant glass-and-iron roof. Subjects include astronomy, chemistry, biology, physics, and earth sciences. Although most information is in French, there are plenty of buttons and levers to press and pull to keep little (and not so little) hands busy. This fun facility—a smaller cousin of the Cité des Sciences et de l'Industrie in Parc de la Villette— also features regularly scheduled demos and 3-D films, along with daily planetarium shows (in French only). ⊠ *Av. Franklin D. Roosevelt, Champs-Élysées* ☎ *01–56–43–20–25* ⊕ *www.palais-decouverte. fr* ⊠ *€8; €11 with planetarium* ☉ *Tues.–Sat. 9:30–6, Sun. 10–7; closed Mon.* Ⓜ *Champs-Élysées–Clemenceau.*

AROUND THE LOUVRE

with Les Halles and Faubourg St-Honoré

GETTING ORIENTED

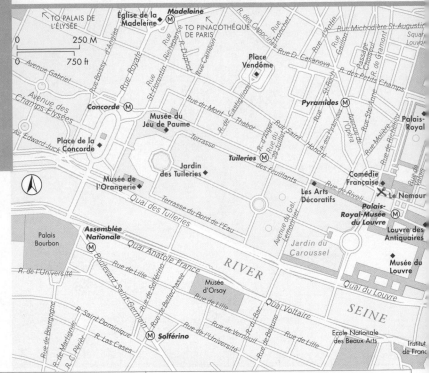

GETTING HERE

The neighborhoods in the Around the Louvre chapter include the 1er and 2e arrondissements, from the Faubourg St-Honoré to Les Halles. If you're heading to the Louvre, take the métro Line 1 to the Louvre/Rivoli or Palais-Royal/Musée du Louvre stop. For the Tuileries, use the Tuileries stop on the same line. For Place de la Concorde, use the Concorde stop on Line 1, 8, or 12. This is a good starting point for a walk on Rue St-Honoré. If you're going to Les Halles, take Line 4 to Les Halles or Line 1 to Châtelet.

TOP REASONS TO GO

Musée du Louvre. The world's first great art museum—which displays such renowned works as the serenely smirking *Mona Lisa* and the statuesque *Venus de Milo*—deserves a long visit.

Tuileries to Place de la Concorde. For centuries, Parisians and visitors alike have strolled the length of this magnificent garden to the gold-tipped obelisk at Place de la Concorde.

Galerie Vivienne. The prettiest 19th-century glass-roofed shopping arcade left in Paris, this *passage* is worth a stop for shopping, lunch, or afternoon tea.

Palais-Royal. Visit these arcades and the romantic garden to understand why the French writer Colette called the view from her window "a little corner of the country."

Rue Montorgueil. This historic market street, fringed with food shops and cafés, is at the heart of one of the city's trendiest neighborhoods.

Around the Louvre

BEST CAFÉS

Au Rocher de Cancale. As its impressive facade attests, this café is something special. It opened in 1846, when Balzac was a regular and Rue Montorgueil was *the* place to buy oysters. There's a sunny terrace that invites lunchtime lingering. ✉ *78 rue Montorgueil. Beaubourg/Les Halles* ☎ *01–42–33–50–29* Ⓜ *Les Halles.*

Le Fumoir. Equal parts café, bar, and restaurant, Le Fumoir is a timelessly popular place to sip coffee and read the paper, or enjoy an after-dinner drink. Reservations are recommended for dinner and Sunday brunch. ✉ *Pl. du Louvre, 6 rue de l'Amiral-Coligny, Louvre/Tuileries* ☎ *01–42–92–00–24* Ⓜ *Louvre.*

Le Nemours. Plan your day over a croissant and a *café crème* at this classic café with two long rows of tables overlooking lively Place Colette, just steps from the Palais Royal and the Louvre. ✉ *2 pl. Colette, Louvre/Tuileries* ☎ *01–42–61–34–14* Ⓜ *Palais-Royal.*

MAKING THE MOST OF YOUR TIME

Try to devote two days or more—one alone for the Louvre—to these vastly different neighborhoods. The narrow sidewalks of the Faubourg St-Honoré are lined with some of the finest Parisian boutiques. Place de la Concorde is the gateway to the Tuileries garden. At the eastern end, Les Halles (the old market district) is booming with shops and eateries popping up around cobbled Rue Montorgueil, where traffic is mercifully restricted.

If you're headed to the mammoth Musée du Louvre, it's best to have a game plan in mind. First step: avoid the lines at the main entrance under the pyramid by using the underground entrance in the Carrousel du Louvre, 99 rue de Rivoli. Buy your ticket at one of the machines.

Sightseeing
★★★★
Dining
★★
Lodging
★★★★
Shopping
★★★★★
Nightlife
★★

Updated by
Linda Hervieux

The neighborhoods in this chapter—from the très chic Faubourg St-Honoré to trendy Les Halles—are a study in contrasts, with the Louvre in the midst of the bustle.

The impossibly posh **Rue Faubourg St-Honoré,** once the stomping ground of kings and queens, is now home to the French president and assorted foreign ambassadors. Beloved by fashionistas for three centuries, it is as popular today as it was when royal mistresses shopped here—which explains the plethora of high-end stores (almost every luxury brand is represented). Not surprisingly, ritzy restaurants and haute hotels are located here as well. To the east, **Les Halles** (pronounced leh-*ahl*) has risen from its roots as a down-and-out market district to become one of the city's hottest, hippest neighborhoods. Vermin-infested cobbled streets have given way to trendy shops, cafés, and bars, centered on Rue Montorgueil; and a sweeping multiyear renovation of the former wholesale food market (which closed in 1969) is giving a much-needed facelift to the plaza above ground and the vast shopping mall below.

Between Faubourg St-Honoré and Les Halles, you can find some of Paris's top draws—namely the mighty **Musée du Louvre** and, next door, the majestic **Jardin des Tuileries.** The garden is home to the **Musée de l'Orangerie,** with its curved galleries showcasing Monet's *Water Lilies,* while nearby **Les Arts Décoratifs** is a must for design buffs. In Place Colette, the stately theater, the **Comédie Française,** is still going strong after 400 years, and at the edge of the square is the psychedelic sculpture—doubling as a métro entrance—of the *kiosque des noctambules* (kiosk of the night-crawlers), designed by artist Jean-Michel Othoniel. Hidden just off Place Colette is the **Palais-Royal,** a romantic garden ringed by arcades with boutiques selling everything from old-fashioned music boxes to fashion-forward frocks. A stone's throw away is **Galerie Vivienne,** an exquisitely restored 19th-century shopping arcade.

TOP ATTRACTIONS

Galerie Véro-Dodat. A lovely 19th-century passage, gorgeously restored, the Véro-Dodat has a dozen artsy boutiques selling objets d'art, textiles, furniture, and accessories. The headliner tenant is Christian Louboutin, at Rue Jean-Jacques Rousseau, whose red-soled stilettos are favored by Angelina, Madonna and other members of the red-carpet set. On the opposite end, at the Rue du Bouloi entrance, star cosmetics maker Terry De Gunzburg has a boutique, By Terry. ⊠ *19 rue Jean-Jacques Rousseau, Louvre/Tuileries* Ⓜ *Palais-Royal.*

Galerie Vivienne. Considered the grande dame of Paris's 19th-century *passages couverts*—the world's first shopping malls—this graceful covered arcade evokes an age of gaslights and horse-drawn carriages. Once Parisians came to passages like this one to tred tiled floors instead of muddy streets, and to see and be seen browsing boutiques under the glass-and-iron roofs. Today, the Galerie Vivienne still attracts top-flight retailers such as Jean-Paul Gaultier (6 rue Vivienne) and the high-quality secondhand clothes seller La Marelle (No. 21), as well as shops selling accessories, housewares, and fine wine. ∎TIP➡ Place des Victoires, a few steps away, is one of Paris's most picturesque squares. In the center is a statue of an outsized Louis XIV (1643–1715), the Sun King, who appears almost as large as his horse. ⊠ *Main entrance at 4 rue des Petits-Champs, Louvre/Tuileries* Ⓜ *Palais-Royal/Bourse.*

5

NEED A BREAK? **A Priori Thé.** American Peggy Hancock opened A Priori Thé in 1980. She— and her delicious scones and cakes—have been comforting travelers ever since. Come for lunch, afternoon tea, or weekend brunch. ⊠ *35 Galerie Vivienne, Louvre/Tuileries* ☎ *01–42–97–48–75* Ⓜ *Bourse.*

FAMILY

Fodor'sChoice
★

Jardin des Tuileries.
See the highlighted listing in this chapter.

Les Arts Décoratifs. Sharing a wing of the Musée du Louvre, but with a separate entrance and admission charge, Les Arts Décoratifs is actually three museums in one. Spread across nine floors, it showcases a stellar array of decorative arts, design and fashion, and graphics. The collection includes altarpieces from the Middle Ages and furnishings from the Italian Renaissance to the present day. There are period rooms reflecting the ages, such as the early 1820s salon of the Duchesse de Berry (who actually lived in the building), plus several rooms reproduced from designer Jeanne Lanvin's 1920s apartment. Don't miss the gilt-and–green velvet bed of the Parisian courtesan who inspired the boudoir in Émile Zola's novel *Nana.* You can hear Zola's description of it on the free English audioguide, which is highly recommended. The second-floor jewelry gallery is a must-see, and special events are often staged in the Nef (nave).

The center is also home to an exceptional collection of textiles, advertising posters, films, and related objects that are shown in rotating temporary exhibitions. Before leaving, take a break at Le Saut du Loup restaurant: its outdoor terrace is an ideal spot for lunch or afternoon tea. Shoppers should also browse through the tempting on-site store (107 Rivoli), which carries books, jewelry, paper products, toys, tableware, and items inspired by the past but with an up-to-date design. ∎TIP➡ If you're combining a visit here with the Musée du Louvre, note that the two close on different days, so don't come on Monday or Tuesday. If you're pairing it with the exquisite Nissim de Camondo (a partner museum), joint tickets are available. ⊠ *107 rue de Rivoli, Louvre/*

DID YOU KNOW?

La Fontaine des Mers (the Fountain of the Seas) is one of two fountains flanking the towering stone obelisk on Place de la Concorde.

Tuileries 🕾 *01–44–55–57–50* 🌐 *www.lesartsdecoratifs.fr* 🕮 *€9.50; €13.50 with Nef temporary exhibits; €12 joint ticket with Musée Nissim de Camondo* ☉ *Tues.–Sun. 11–6 (Thurs. until 9 during exhibits); closed Mon.* Ⓜ *Palais-Royal.*

Les Halles. For 800 years, Paris was fed by the acres of food halls overflowing with meats, fish, and vegetables that made up this district. Sensuously described in Émile Zola's novel *The Belly of Paris*, Les Halles was teeming with life—though not all of it good. Hucksters and homeless shared these streets with prostitutes (who still ply their trade in diminishing numbers on nearby Rue St-Denis); and the plague of cat-size rats didn't cease until the market moved to the suburbs in 1969. Today, you can still see stuffed pests hanging by their tails in the windows of the circa-1872 shop Julien Aurouze (8 rue des Halles) whose sign, *Destruction des Animaux Nuisibles* (in other words, vermin extermination), says it all. All that remains of the 19th-century iron-and-glass market buildings, designed by architect Victor Baltard, is a portion of the superstructure on the southern edge of the Jardins des Halles. The Fontaine des Innocents, from 1550, at rues Berger and Pierre Lescot, marks the site of what was once a vast cemetery before the bones were moved to the Catacombs.

After years of delays, Les Halles is undergoing one of the city's most ambitious public works projects: a sweeping €500 million renovation that will transform the plaza, and the much-maligned underground concrete mall called the Forum des Halles, into a place where Parisians actually want to go. While the project was not without opponents, most Parisians are happy about the prospect of a prettier Les Halles—even if they have to wait until 2016 for the end of it. In an echo of the past, a 18-foot iron-and-glass canopy will cover the entrance to the mall in 2015, flooding light into the stores below. Aboveground, the renamed Jardin Nelson Mandela has already transformed a once down-and-out patch into a verdant 10-acre space dotted with trees, decorative pools, and play areas for kids. On the northern end, a redesigned Place René Cassin is surrounded by tiered steps centered around a newly scrubbed *L'Ecoute,* the giant head and hand sculpture by Henri de Miller. Looming behind is the magnificent church of St-Eustache, a Gothic gem. Film buffs with time to spare can stop by the Forum des Images, with some 7,000 films available for viewing on individual screens. To find it, enter the mall on the side of the church at the Porte St-Eustache.

The streets surrounding Les Halles have boomed in recent years with boutiques, bars, and restaurants galore that have sent rents skyrocketing. Historic Rue Montorgueil is home to food shops and cafés. Running parallel, Rue Montmartre, near the church, still has a few specialty shops selling foie gras and other delicacies, though these merchants, like the butchers and bakers before them, are slowly being pushed out by trendy clothing boutiques. ✉ *Garden entrances on rues Coquillière, Berger, and Rambuteau. Mall entrances on rues Pierre Lescot, Berger, and Rambuteau, Beaubourg/Les Halles* 🌐 *www.forum-des-halles.com* ☉ *Mall Mon.–Sat. 10–8* Ⓜ *Les Halles; RER: Châtelet Les Halles.*

JARDIN DES TUILERIES

✉ *Bordered by Quai des Tuileries, Pl. de la Concorde, Rue de Rivoli, and the Louvre, Louvre/Tuileries* ☎ *01–40–20–90–43* 🎫 *Free* ⊙ *June–Aug., daily 7 am–11 pm; Apr., May, and Sept., daily 7:30 am–9 pm; Oct.–Mar., daily 7:30–7:30* Ⓜ *Tuileries or Concorde.*

TIPS

■ Garden buffs will enjoy the small bookstore at the Place de la Concorde entrance, open 10 am to 7 pm. Aside from volumes on gardening and plants (including some titles in English), it has gift items, knickknacks, and toys for the junior gardener.

■ The Tuileries is one of the best places in Paris to take kids if they're itching to run around. There's a carousel (€2.50), trampolines (€2) and, in summer, an amusement park.

■ If you're hungry, look for carts serving gelato from Amorino or sandwiches from the chain bakery Paul. Also, there are four cafés with terraces in the center of the garden. One of the two closer to Place de la Concorde—Le Médicis—serves fare that's a bit more upscale.

The quintessential French garden, with its verdant lawns, manicured rows of trees, and gravel paths, was designed by André Le Nôtre for Louis XIV. After the king moved his court to Versailles in 1682, the Tuileries became *the* place for stylish Parisians to stroll. (Ironically, the name derives from the decidedly unstylish factories which once occupied this area: they produced *tuiles*, or roof tiles, fired in kilns called *tuileries*.) Monet and Renoir captured the garden with paint and brush, and it's no wonder the Impressionists loved it—the gray, austere light of Paris's famously overcast days make the green trees appear even greener.

Highlights

The garden still serves as a setting for one of the city's loveliest walks. Laid out before you is a vista of must-see monuments, with the Louvre at one end and Place de la Concorde at the other. The Eiffel Tower is on the Seine side, along with the Musée d'Orsay, reachable across a footbridge in the center of the garden. A good place to begin is at the Louvre end, at the Arc du Carrousel, a stone-and-marble arch ordered by Napoléon to showcase the bronze horses he stole from St. Mark's Cathedral in Venice. The horses were eventually returned and replaced here with a statue of a *quadriga*, a four-horse chariot. On the Place de la Concorde end, twin buildings bookend the garden. On the Seine side, the former royal greenhouse is now the exceptional Musée de l'Orangerie, home to the largest display of Monet's lovely *Water Lilies* series, as well as a sizable collection of early-20th-century paintings. On the opposite end is the Jeu de Paume, which has some of the city's best temporary photography exhibits.

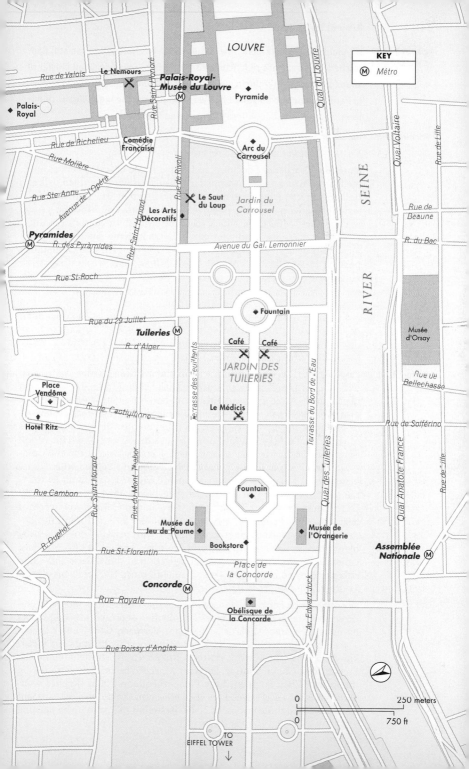

LOUVRE

Rue de Valois

Le Nemours

Palais-Royal-
Musée du Louvre Ⓜ

Pyramide

Palais-
Royal

Rue Saint-Honoré

Rue de Richelieu

Comédie
Française

Rue Molière

Arc du
Carrousel

Rue de Rivoli

Rue Ste-Anne

Avenue de l'Opéra

Le Saut
du Loup

Les Arts
Décoratifs

Jardin du
Carrousel

SEINE

Quai du Louvre

Quai Voltaire

Rue de Lille

Rue de
Beaune

Pyramides Ⓜ

R. des Pyramides

Rue Saint-Honoré

Avenue du Gal. Lemonnier

R. du Bac

Rue St-Roch

RIVER

Rue du 29 Juillet

Fountain

Tuileries Ⓜ

R. d'Alger

Café

Café

Musée
d'Orsay

Place
Vendôme

R. de Castiglione

JARDIN DES
TUILERIES

Terrasse des Feuillants

Le Médicis

Terrasse du Bord de l'Eau

Rue de
Bellechasse

Rue de Solférino

Hotel Ritz

Rue Cambon

Rue Saint-Honoré

Rue du Mont-Thabor

Fountain

Quai des Tuileries

Quai Anatole France

Rue de Lille

R. Duphot

Musée du
Jeu de Paume

Bookstore

Musée de
l'Orangerie

Assemblée
Nationale Ⓜ

Rue St-Florentin

Place de
la Concorde

Concorde Ⓜ

Rue Royale

Obélisque de
la Concorde

Av. Edward Tuck

Rue Boissy d'Anglas

0   250 meters

0   750 ft

TO
EIFFEL TOWER
↓

Although the mojito crowd now dominates in Les Halles, you can still find traces of this quarter's rich history as a food hub. There's a small cluster of shops stocking everything a well-dressed kitchen needs. During her years in Paris, American chef Julia Child was a regular at the legendary E. Dehillerin, at 18–20 rue Coquillière (⊕ *www.e-dehillerin.fr*).

Fodor's Choice ★ **Musée de Louvre.**
See the highlighted listing in this chapter.

Musée de l'Orangerie. The lines can be long to see Claude Monet's huge, meditative *Water Lilies (Nymphéas)*, displayed in two curved galleries designed in 1914 by the master himself. But they are well worth the wait. These works are the highlight of the Orangerie Museum's small but excellent collection, which includes early-20th-century paintings by Renoir, Cézanne, and Matisse. Many hail from the private holdings of art dealer Paul Guillaume (1891–1934), including Guillaume's portrait by Modigliani entitled *Novo Pilota,* or new pilot, signaling Guillaume's status as an important presence in the arts world. Built in 1852 to shelter orange trees, the museum reopened in 2006 after a long renovation that unearthed a portion of the city's 16th-century wall (you can see remnants on the lower floor). ⊠ *Jardin des Tuileries at pl. de la Concorde, Louvre/Tuileries* ☎ *01–44–77–80–07* ⊕ *www.musee-orangerie.fr* ⊠ *€9; €16 joint ticket with Musée d'Orsay* ⊗ *Wed.–Mon. 9–6; closed Tues.* Ⓜ *Concorde.*

Fodor's Choice ★ **Palais-Royal.** The quietest, most romantic Parisian garden is enclosed within the former home of Cardinal Richelieu (1585–1642). It's an ideal spot to while away an afternoon, cuddling with your sweetheart on a bench under the trees, soaking up the sunshine beside the fountain, or browsing the 400-year-old arcades that are now home to boutiques ranging from quirky (picture Anna Joliet's music boxes) to chic (think designs by Stella McCartney and Marc Jacobs). One of the city's oldest restaurants is here, the haute-cuisine Le Grand Véfour, where brass plaques recall regulars like Napoléon and Victor Hugo. Built in 1629, the *palais* became royal when Richelieu bequeathed it to Louis XIII. Other famous residents include Jean Cocteau and Colette, who wrote of her pleasurable "country" view of the *province à Paris.* Today, the garden often plays host to giant-size temporary art installations sponsored by another tenant, the Ministry of Culture. The courtyard off Place Colette is outfitted with an unusual collection of short black-and-white columns created in 1986 by artist Daniel Buren. ⊠ *Pl. du Palais-Royal, Louvre/Palais-Royal* Ⓜ *Palais-Royal.*

Pinacothèque de Paris. The Pinacothèque, one of the city's most original art spaces, stages a steadily rotating calendar of crowd-pleasing shows by marquee names such as Van Gogh, Vermeer, Goya, and Munch. The exhibitions are often eclectic, bringing together masters and lesser-known artists whose work shares a link, such as Modigliani and the French artist Chaïm Soutine. Director Marc Restellini is used to stirring things up. When he opened the Pinacothèque in 2003, skeptics wondered whether Paris needed another museum: the crowds massing out front answered those critics. In 2011, Restellini followed up by opening

Pincothèque 2 at 8 rue Vignon, just steps away from the main venue behind the Église de la Madeleine. It hosts temporary exhibitions and has a small but notable permanent collection that blends periods and styles (imagine a Rembrandt paired with a Pollack). ■ TIP➔ For popular shows, pay an extra €1.50 to buy your ticket online and cut the

queue. ⊠ 28 pl. de la Madeleine, Opéra ☎ 01–42–68–02–01 ⊕ www. pinacotheque.com ☎ €8.30–€12 one show; €18 two shows; €23 all shows ⊙ Daily 10:30–6:30 (Wed. and Fri. until 9) Ⓜ Madeleine.

Place de la Concorde. This square at the foot of the Champs-Élysées was originally named after Louis XV. It later became Place de la Révolution, where crowds cheered as Louis XVI, Marie-Antoinette, and some 2,500 others lost their heads to the guillotine. Renamed Concorde in 1836, it got a new centerpiece: the 75-foot granite Obelisk of Luxor, a gift from Egypt quarried in the 8th century BC. Among the handsome 18th-century buildings facing the square is the Hôtel Crillon, which was originally built as a private home by Gabriel, the architect of Versailles's Petit Trianon. ⊠ Champs-Élysées Ⓜ Concorde.

Place Vendôme. Jules-Hardouin Mansart, an architect of Versailles Palace, designed this perfectly proportioned octagonal plaza near the Tuileries in 1702; and, to maintain a uniform appearance, he gave the surrounding *hôtels particuliers* (private mansions) identical facades. It was originally called Place des Conquêtes to extoll the military conquests of Louis XIV, whose statue on horseback graced the center until Revolutionaries destroyed it in 1792. Later, Napoléon ordered his likeness erected atop a 144 foot column modestly modeled after Rome's Trajan Column. But that, too, was toppled in 1871 by painter Gustave Courbet and his band of radicals. The Third Republic raised a new column and sent Courbet the bill, though he died in exile before paying it. Chopin lived and died at No. 12, which is also where Napoléon III enjoyed trysts with his mistress; since 1902 it has been home to the high-end jeweler Chaumet. The Hotel Ritz at No. 15 and its famous Hemingway Bar—closed in 2012 for a top-to-bottom renovation—is slated to reopen in late 2014 or early 2015. ⊠ Louvre/Tuileries Ⓜ Tuileries.

Fodor's Choice ★ **Rue Montorgueil.** Rue Montorgueil was once the gritty oyster hub of Les Halles. Now lined with food shops and cafés, the cobbled street whose name translates to Mount Pride is the heart of one of the city's trendiest neighborhoods. History runs deep here. Monet captured the scene in 1878 when Montorgueil was ablaze with tricolor flags during the World's Fair (see it in the Musée d'Orsay). Honoré de Balzac and his 19th-century band of scribes frequented Au Rocher de Cancale at No. 78, whose famously crumbling facade has been painstakingly restored with gilt panache. Other addresses have been around for centuries: Stohrer at No. 58 has been baking elaborate *tartes* since 1730; and L'Escargot Montorgueil at No. 38, a favorite of Charlie Chaplin, is still graced by a giant golden snail. Relative newcomers include the luxury

Nuxe spa at Nos. 32 and 34. Browse the boutiques on Rue Montmartre, which runs parallel, or shop for cookware at Julia Child's old haunt, E. Dehillerin, still in business at 18-20 rue Coquillière. Rue Tiquetonne is rife with bistros, and previously sleepy Rue Saint-Sauveur became a destination when the Experimental (No. 37) cocktail lounge moved in. Even Rue St-Denis, once a scruffy red-light district, is now a hipster fave with bar-restaurants like Le Pas Sage at the entrance of the lovely covered arcade, Passage du Grand Cerf. Ⓜ *Sentier, Les Halles.*

St-Eustache. Built as the market neighborhood's answer to Notre-Dame, this massive church is decidedly squeezed into its surroundings. Constructed between 1532 and 1640 with foundations dating to 1200, the church mixes a Gothic exterior, complete with impressive flying buttresses, and a Renaissance interior. On the east end (Rue Montmartre), Dutch master Rubens' *Pilgrims of Emmaus* (1611) hangs in a small chapel. Two chapels to the left is Keith Haring's *The Life of Christ*, a triptych in bronze and white-gold patina: it was given to the church after the artist's death in 1990, in recognition of the parish's efforts to help victims of AIDS. On the Rue Montmartre side of the church, look for the small door to Saint Agnes's crypt, topped with a stone plaque noting the date, 1213, below a curled fish, an indication the patron made his fortune in fish. ✉ *2 impasse St-Eustache, Beaubourg/Les Halles* ⊕ *www. saint-eustache.org for concert info* ☉ *Weekdays 9:30–7, weekends 9–7* Ⓜ *Les Halles; RER: Châtelet Les Halles.*

WORTH NOTING

Bibliothèque Nationale Richelieu. Superseded by the Bibliothèque Nationale François-Mitterand, France's longtime national library now hosts well-done temporary exhibits, often featuring photography from its vast collection of legends such as Cartier-Bresson and Man Ray. The library remains open (though some portions are off-limits) during a multiyear renovation that's set to end in 2017. ✉ *58 rue de Richelieu, Opéra/ Grands Boulevards* ☎ *01–53–79–59–59* ⊕ *www.bnf.fr* 🎫 *Free–€7, depending on show* ☉ *Tues.–Sat. 10–7, Sun. 1–7* Ⓜ *Bourse.*

Bourse du Commerce. Best approached from the rear, the old Commerce Exchange looks like a giant spaceship. Now home to the Paris Chamber of Commerce, it's worth a stop inside to see the beautifully restored iron-and-glass dome, which Victor Hugo dismissively likened to a jockey's cap. Built in 1809, this was the first iron structure in France. Behind it, the 100-foot-tall Colonne Medicis is a remnant of a mansion constructed in 1572 for Catherine de Medici. The column, which miraculously escaped destruction through the ages, was used as a platform for stargazing by her powerful astrologer, Cosimo Ruggieri. Legend has it that on stormy nights, a silhouetted figure can be seen in the metal cage at the top. ▪TIP➜ **To learn more about the building of the dome, check out the short video of its construction in the Musée des Arts and Métiers.** ✉ *2 rue de Viarmes, Les Halles* Ⓜ *Métro or RER: Les Halles.*

Comédie Française. Refined productions by Molière and Racine are staged regularly (though only in French) at the vintage venue where actress Sarah Bernhardt began her career. Founded in 1680 by Louis

XIV, the theater finally opened its doors to the public in 1799. It nearly burned to the ground a hundred years later. The current building dates from 1900 and underwent an extensive renovation in 2012. ✉ *1 pl. Colette, Louvre/Tuileries* ☎ *08–25–10–16–80 €0.15 per minute* ⊕ *www.comedie-francaise. fr* Ⓜ *Palais-Royal.*

Église de la Madeleine. With its rows of uncompromising columns, this enormous neoclassical edifice in the center of Place de la Madeleine was consecrated as a church in 1842,

nearly 78 years after construction began. Initially planned as a Baroque building, it was later razed and begun anew by an architect who had the Roman Pantheon in mind. Interrupted by the Revolution, the site was razed yet again when Napoléon decided to make it into a Greek temple dedicated to the glory of his army. Those plans changed when the army was defeated and the emperor deposed. Other ideas for the building included making it into a train station, a market, and a library. Finally, Louis XVIII decided to make it a church, which it still is today. Classical concerts are held here regularly, some of them free. ✉ *Pl. de la Madeleine, Faubourg* ☎ *01–44–51–69–00* ⊕ *www.eglise-lamadeleine. com* ◷ *Daily 9:30–7* Ⓜ *Madeleine.*

NEED A BREAK?

Foyer de la Madeleine. A cheap meal in the Madeleine? Even most Parisians don't know it's possible to find one in this posh *place*, yet a reasonable option awaits in the basement of the eponymous Église. On the Rue de Surène side of the church is the entrance to the Foyer, where friendly church ladies provide a three-course lunch for €13 (€8 plus €5 for a one-year membership card). The fare—served buffet style on weekdays, from 11:45 to 2—is solid, if not gourmet, and the wine is a great deal at €7 a bottle. Best to go early when the food is freshest. ✉ *14 rue de Surène, Madeleine* ☎ *01–47–42–39–84* Ⓜ *Madeleine.*

Église St-Germain-l'Auxerrois. Founded in 500 AD, this grand church across from the Louvre's eastern end is one of the city's oldest. It was destroyed during the Norman seige in 885–886, rebuilt in the 11th century, and subsequently expanded until the current edifice was finished in 1580. The bell, named Marie, dates from 1527. ✉ *2 pl. du Louvre, Louvre/Tuileries* ☎ *01–42–60–13–96* ⊕ *www.saintgermainauxerrois. cef.fr* ◷ *Weekdays 8–7, weekends 9–8* Ⓜ *Louvre/Rivoli.*

Jeu de Paume. This Napoleon III-era building at the north entrance of the Jardin des Tuileries began life in 1861 as a place to play *jeu de paume* (or "palm game"), a forerunner of tennis. It later served as a transfer point for art looted by the Germans during World War II. Today, it's been given another lease on life as an ultramodern, white-walled

Continued on page 100

MUSÉE DU LOUVRE

Try to wrap your mind around this: The Louvre has more than 37,000 pieces of art in its collection, representing nearly every civilization on earth, and more than 675,000 square feet of exhibition space. It's gone through countless cycles of construction and demolition, expansion and renovation, starting as a medieval fortress, then becoming a royal residence before opening its doors as the Museum Central des Arts at the end of the 18th century.

Left: Michelangelo's *Dying Slave*

Below: The Louvre's iconic *Pyramide*, designed by I. M. Pei.

Don't make the mistake of thinking that you'll be able to see the Louvre's entire collection in one visit and still enjoy—or remember—what you've seen. The three most popular artworks here are, of course, the *Mona Lisa*, the *Venus de Milo,* and *Winged Victory*. Beyond these must-sees, your best bet is to focus on highlights that interest you the most—and don't worry about getting lost because you're bound to stumble upon something interesting. Stop by the information desk for a free color-coded map. For help navigating the collection, rent an excellent Nintendo 3DS multimedia guide (€5), or take a guided tour (€9) in English at 11 or 2 daily. The Louvre has three wings—the Richelieu, the Sully, and the Denon—arranged like a horseshoe, with I.M. Pei's striking *Pyramide* nestled outside in the middle.

HISTORY OF THE LOUVRE

Evolution of the Building

1527. François I (left) expands the palace, demolishing many original buildings and rebuilding in the new Renaissance style.

1655-58. The Queen Mother, Anne of Austria, orders up private apartments and imports Italian artists to decorate it.

1672. Sun King Louis XIV moves the royal court to Versailles and the Louvre is abandoned.

1756. Louis XV (right) resumes construction. After a century, the Cour Carrée finally gets a roof.

12TH C.	13TH C.	14TH C.	15TH C.	16TH CENTURY	17TH CENTURY	18TH CENTURY
FORTRESS		▲		ROYAL PALACE		▲ ROYAL ARTS ACADEMY

1190. Philippe Auguste builds a fortress to protect Paris.

1364. Charles V converts it into a royal palace.

Henry IV adds the Grand Gallery and begins the passage to the adjacent Tuileries Palace. Work halts upon his death in 1610.

1660. Architect **Louis LeVau** is hired to finish the Louvre. Erasing all medieval traces, he adds pavilions, rebuilds facades, and doubles the palace's width.

1699. Royal Academy of Painting and Sculpture stages first exhibition.

1791. Revolutionary government declares the Louvre a national museum.

1793. Doors open to the public. Admission is free.

Acquisition of Art

17TH CENTURY
18TH CENTURY

Mona Lisa
Leonardo da Vinci, 1503-06.

Purchased by Francois I under unknown circumstances. It later adorned Napoléon I's bedroom wall.

The Slaves
Michelangelo 1513-1515.

From François I's collection. **Entered the Louvre in 1794.**

Pilgrimage to Cythera
1717, Watteau.

Acquired in 1793.

Coronation of Napoléon
1806-07, Jacques Louis David.

Commissioned by Napoléon, whose collection fell into state hands after his defeat in 1815.

Venus de Milo (Aphrodite)
Late 2nd century BC.

Found on the Greek island of Milos in 1820 and purchased by the French ambassador to Turkey, who presented it to Louis XVIII. **Placed in the Louvre in 1821.**

The Raft of the Medusa
1819, Géricault.

Purchased after the artist's death, 1824.

18TH CENTURY
19TH CENTURY

1803. Renamed Musée Napoléon and stocked with booty from the emperor's many conquests.

1852. Napoléon III (right) lays the cornerstone of the New Louvre.

1939. Artwork is hidden as World War II erupts.
1940. Near-empty museum reopens.

1989. I.M. Pei's controversial glass *Pyramide* rises over the new entrance in the Cour Napoléon.
1993. Renovated Richelieu Wing reopens.

19TH CENTURY | **20TH CENTURY** | **21ST CENTURY**

NATIONAL MUSEUM

1815. Artworks plundered by **Napoléon** returned to their native countries after his defeat.

1852-1861. Collection expands with works acquired from Egypt, Spain, and Mexico. Cour Napoléon completed.

1871. Mob sets fire to Tuileries Palace. Louvre is damaged.

1945. Asian collection sent to the new Musée Guimet.

1981. President François Mitterrand (above) kicks off Grand Louvre project to expand and modernize the museum.

2000. Non-French works destined for the future Musée de Quai Branly shown at Louvre.

2012. New 30,000-square-foot Arts of Islam wing opens in the Cour Visconti.

Louis XV's Coronation Crown
1793. Apollo Gallery

Acquired in 1852. Original stones replaced with paste in 1729.

Seated Scribe
Around 2500 BC.

Discovered in Saqqara, Egypt in 1850. **Given to France by the Egyptian government in 1854.**

The Lacemaker
Vermeer, 1669-70.

Purchased at auction in Paris, 1870.

The Turkish Bath
Ingres, 1862.

Gift to the Louvre, 1911. Commissioned by Napoléon but deemed too shocking to display. Revealed to the public in 1905.

Winged Victory of Samothrace
Around 190 BC.

Discovered on the Greek island of Samothrace in 1863 by a French archaeologist who sent the pieces to be reassembled at the Louvre. Her right hand (in nearby glass case) was discovered in 1950.

Gabrielle d'Estrées and One of Her Sisters
Unknown artist, 1594.

Purchased in 1937. This (nipple-pinching) scene could represent sisterly teasing related to the pregnancy of Gabrielle, the favorite mistress of Henri IV.

19TH CENTURY | 20TH CENTURY

20TH CENTURY | 21ST CENTURY

RICHELIEU WING

COLLECTIONS
Near East Antiquities
French Painting
French Sculpture
Northern Schools
Decorative Arts

Below Ground & Ground Floor. Entering from the Pyramide, head upstairs to the sculpture courtyards, Cour Marly and Cour Puget. In Cour Marly you'll find the **Marley Horses** (see right). Salle 2 has fragments from Cluny, the powerful Romanesque abbey in Burgundy that dominated 11th-century French Catholicism. Salles 4–6 follows the evolution of French sculpture, and in Salles 7–10 you'll find funerary art. In Cour Puget, products from the Académie Royale, the art school of 18th-century France, fill Salles 25–33. Behind this is the Near East Antiquities Collection. Salle 3's centerpiece is the Codex of Hammurabi, an 18th-century BC black-diorite stela containing the world's oldest written code of laws. In Salle 4, you'll find **Lamassu** (see right).

First Floor. Head straight through Decorative Arts to see the magnificently restored **Royal Apartments of Napoléon III** (see right).

Second Floor. Much of this floor is dedicated to French and Northern School paintings. At the entrance is a 14th-century painting of John the Good—the oldest-known individual portrait from the north of Italy. In Salle 4 hangs *The Madonna of Chancellor Rolin*, by the 15th-century Early Netherlandish master Jan van Eyck (late 14th century–1441). Peter Paul Rubens's (1577–1640) the *Disembarkation of Marie de' Medici at the Port of Marseille* is in Salle 18. In Salle 31 are several paintings by Rembrandt van Rijn (1606–69), including **Bathsheba**, his largest nude. The masterpiece of the Dutch collection is Vermeer's *The Lacemaker* (see right).

TIPS

■ The 25 paintings by Rubens commisioned by Marie de Medici for the Luxembourg Palace in Salle 18 on the second floor each mark an event in the queen's life.

■ To see what's on the minds of the museum staff, check out the Painting of the Month in Salle 17, French section, on the 2nd floor.

■ Take a hot chocolate break in the Café Richelieu on the first floor, run by the upscale *confiseur* Angelina. There is an outdoor terrace in summer and a tempting lunch menu.

■ Save your ticket and duck out for lunch via the Porte Richelieu, an entry point for ticket-holders and groups.

DON'T MISS

LAMASSU, 8TH CENTURY   SALLE 4

With their fierce beards and gentle eyes, these massive winged beasts are benevolent guardians straight from the dreamworld. Magical for children and adults, the strangely lifelike sculptures are located in the Near Eastern antiquities collection. The winged bull demigods are part of the Cour Khorsabad, a re-creation of the temple erected by Assyrian king Sargon II. ✛ *Richelieu, ground floor*

Lamassu

THE LACEMAKER, 1669–1671   SALLE 38

This is a small but justifiably famous gem of Dutch optical accuracy (and a must-see for fans of the movie and book, *Girl With a Pearl Earring*, to see how his style evolved over a 5-year period.) Here, Jan Vermeer (1632–75) painted the red thread in the foreground as a slightly blurred jumble, just as one would actually see it if focusing on the girl. The lacemaker's industriousness represents domestic virtue, but the personal focus of the painting is far more engaging than a simple morality tale. ✛ *Richelieu, second floor*

The Lacemaker

MARLY HORSES, 1699–1740   COUR MARLY

During the dramatic 1989 reorganization of the Louvre, two courtyards were elegantly glassed over to match the entrance pyramid. The dramatic glass-roofed Marly sculpture court houses several sculptures from Louis XIV's garden at Marly, including two magnificent winged horses by Antoine Coysevox. Later, the artist's nephew Guillaume Coustou created two accompanying earthbound horse sculptures for Louis XV; their fame was such that, during the Revolution, these sculptures were moved to the Tuileries gardens for public viewing. Now the four original horses greet visitors to the Richelieu Wing, ready to gallop off into the museum; replicas stand guard in the Tuileries. ✛ *Richelieu, lower ground floor*

The Marly Horses

ROYAL APARTMENTS
OF NAPOLÉON III, 1860s   SALLE 87

These dozen reception rooms, hung with crystal chandeliers, elaborate mirrors, and imperial velour, are a gilt-covered reminder that the Louvre was a palace for centuries, regally designed to impress. En route, you'll pass decorative items like the solid-crystal Restoration dressing table (Salle 77) that prepare you for the eye-popping luxury of the Second Empire. ✛ *Richelieu, first floor*

Royal Apartments of Napoléon

SULLY WING

Below Ground & Ground Floor. Start your visit with a journey to the roots of the Louvre—literally. From the *Pyramide* entrance, tour the 13th-century foundations of the original fortress and the Medieval Moat. In Salle 12 you'll find towering Ramses II. Check out the mummies in Salles 14 and 15, along with rare examples of Egyptian funerary art.

Upstairs, the north galleries of the Sully continue the ancient Iranian collection begun in the Richelieu Wing. Salle 16 has the 2nd-century BC **Venus de Milo** (see right), anchoring the Greek collection of Salles 7–17.

First Floor. The northern galleries of the first floor continue with the Decorative Arts collection including works from all over Europe, and connect with the Napoléon III apartments. American Cy Twombly's contemporary ceiling in Salle 32 was unveiled in 2010.

Second Floor. Sully picks up French painting in the 17th century where the Richelieu leaves off. The Académiciens are best exemplified by Nicolas Poussin (1594–1665, Salle 19), the first international painting star from France. The antithesis of this style was the candlelit modest work by outsider Georges de La Tour (Salle 28), as in his *Magdalene of Night Light*.

The Académie Royale defined the standards of painting through revolution, republic, and empire. Exoticism wafted in during the Napoleonic empire, as in the **Turkish Bath** (see right) painting of Jean-Auguste-Dominique Ingres (1780–1867). Fresh energy crackled into French painting in the 18th century. Antoine Watteau (1684–1721), was known for his theatrical scenes and *fêtes galantes*, portrayals of well-dressed figures in bucolic settings. In *Pilgrimage to the Island of Cythera* (Salle 36), he used delicate brushstrokes and soft tones to convey the court set, here depicted arriving on (or departing from) Cythera, the mythical isle of love.

TIPS

■ There is a little-known collection with Monet, Renoir, and Cezanne in Salle C on the second floor, the only Impressionist works in the Louvre.

■ There's a surprise in Salle 17 on the ground floor—the *Sleeping Hermaphrodite* by the entrance.

■ Be sure to look up as you make your way up Escalier Henri II. It took four years to complete this 16th-century vaulted ceiling.

■ Need a bathroom? There are some tucked between Salles 22 and 23 on the 1st floor. (And admire the colorful, 4,000-year-old Seated Scribe in Salle 22.)

■ For a breather, head to the bench in Salle 33 on the first floor and enjoy the sedate three-part ceiling by Georges Braque (1955) called *Les Oiseux* (The Birds).

DON'T MISS

RAMSES II, APPROX. 1200 BC   **SALLE 12**

The sphinx-guarded Egyptian Wing is the biggest display of Egyptian antiquities in the world after the Cairo museum—not surprising, considering that Egyptology as a Western concept was invented by a Frenchman, Champollion, founder of the Louvre's Egypt collection and translator of the hieroglyphics on the Rosetta Stone. This statue from the site of Tanis, presumed to be Ramses II, never fails to stop visitors' breath with its gleaming stone, beatific expression, and perfect proportions. ✛ *Sully, ground floor*

Ramses II

VENUS DE MILO, APPROX. 120 BC   **SALLE 16**

After countless photographs and bad reproductions, the original Aphrodite continues to dazzle. The armless statue, one of the most reproduced and recognizable works of art in the world, is actually as beautiful as they say—and even lovelier after a 6-month cleaning and rehab in 2010 that took place afer hours and on Tuesdays, when the museum is closed. She was unearthed on the Greek island of Milos in the 19th century and sold for 6,000 francs to the French ambassador in Constantinople, who presented her to King Louis XVIII. ✛ *Sully, ground floor*

Venus de Milo

MEDIEVAL MOAT, 13TH CENTURY   **MEDIEVAL LOUVRE**

Wander around the perimeter of the solidly built original moat to reach the remarkable Salle Saint-Louis with its elegant columns and medieval artifacts. Keep an eye out for the parade helmet of Charles VI, which was dug up in 169 fragments and astonishingly reassembled. ✛ *Sully, lower ground floor*

Medieval Moat

THE TURKISH BATH, 1862   **SALLE 60**

Though Jean-August-Dominique Ingres' (1780–1867) long-limbed women hardly look Turkish, they are singularly elegant and his polished immaculate style was imitated by an entire generation of French painters. This painting is a prime example of Orientalism, where Western artists played out fantasies of the Orient in their work. Popular as a society portrait painter, Ingres returned repeatedly to langorous nudes—compare the women of the *Turkish Bath* with the slinky figure in his *La Grande Odalisque*, in the Denon Wing. ✛ *Sully, second floor*

The Turkish Bath

5

IN FOCUS THE LOUVRE

THE DENON WING

COLLECTIONS
Ancient Egypt
Greek, Roman, & Etruscan
Antiquities
French Painting
Italian & Spanish Painting
Graphic Arts
Italian, Spanish, &
Northern Sculpture
African, Asian, Oceanic, &
American Arts
Arts of Islam

Below Ground & Ground Floor. The Stunning Arts of Islam wing opened in late 2012 with 30,000 square feet of gallery space built into the Cour Visconti and topped with an undulating glass roof meant to evoke a floating head scarf. Here you'll find Europe's largest collection of treasures from across the Islamic world, including the Ottoman Empire. On the lower level, don't miss the Baptistery of Saint Louis, a 14th-century sculpted golden basin. The galleries to the south and east of the *Pyramide* entrance display early Renaissance Italian sculpture, including a 15th-century *Madonna and Child* by Florentine Dontallo (1386–1466). Drift upstairs to the Italian sculptures on the ground level, where you'll find the exquisite Michelangelo's *Slaves* (1513–15) in Salle 4.

First Floor. Walk up the marble Escalier Daru to discover the sublime **Winged Victory of Samothrace** (see right), cleaned in 2014. Then head to the stunning Galerie d'Apollon (Apollo Gallery). Built in 1661 but not finished until 1851, the hall was a model for Versailles's Hall of Mirrors.

Back out and into Paintings, you'll find four by Leonardo da Vinci (1452–1519). His enigmatic, androgynous St-John the Baptist hangs here, along with more overtly religious works such as the 1483 Virgin of the Rocks. Take a close look at the pretty portrait of La Belle Ferronnière, which Leonardo painted a decade before the **Mona Lisa** (see right); it will give you something to compare with Mona when you finally get to meet her in the Salle des Etats, near Salles 5 and 6. Head across to Salle 75 for an artistic 180°: the gleaming pomp and circumstance of a new empire with the **Coronation of Napoléon** (see right) by French classicist Jacques-Louis David (1748–1825).

In Salle 77 is the graphic 1819 **The Raft of the Medusa**, (see right) by Théodore Géricault (1791–1824).

TIPS

■ Don't skip the coat check on the ground floor tucked behind the stairs. Much of the museum is hot and stuffy.

■ Don't miss the glass case near *Winged Victory of Samothrace* on the first floor. It contains her two-fingered hand.

■ Need a bathroom? There are some tucked away at the end of the wing on the first floor near Salle 13.

DON'T MISS

MONA LISA, 1503   SALLE 7

The most famous painting in the world, *La Gioconda* (*La Joconde* in French) is tougher than she looks: the canvas was stolen from the Louvre by an Italian nationalist in 1911, recovered from a Florentine hotel, and survived an acid attack in 1956. She is believed to be the wife of Francesco del Giocondo, a Florentine millionaire, and was probably 24 when she sat for this painting; some historians believe the portrait was actually painted after her death. Either way, she has become immortal through da Vinci's ingenious "sfumato" technique, which combines glowing detail with soft, depth-filled brushwork. ⚜ *Denon, first floor*

Mona Lisa

THE RAFT OF THE MEDUSA, 1819   SALLE 77

Théodore Géricault was inspired by the grim news report that survivors of a wrecked French merchant ship were left adrift on a raft without supplies. Géricault interviewed survivors, visited the morgue to draw corpses, and turned his painting of the disaster into a strong indictment of authority, the first time an epic historical painting had taken on current events in this way. Note the desperate energy from the pyramid construction of bodies on the raft and the manipulation of greenish light. ⚜ *Denon, first floor*

The Raft of the Medusa

WINGED VICTORY OF SAMOTHRACE, 305 BC   STAIRS

Poised for flight at the top of the Escalier Daru, this exhilarating statue was found on a tiny Greek island in the northern Aegean. Depicted in the act of descending from Olympus, *Winged Victory*, or Nike, to the Ancient Greeks, was carved to commemorate the naval victory of Demetrius Poliorcetes over the Persians. ⚜ *Denon, first floor*

Winged Victory of Samothrace

CORONATION OF NAPOLÉON, 1805   SALLE 75

Classicist Jacques-Louis David (1748–1825) was the ultimate painter-survivor: he began his career under the protection of the King, became official designer of the Revolutionary government, endured two rounds of exile, and became one of the greatest of Napoléon's painters. Here, David avoided the politically fraught moment of December 2, 1804—when Napoléon snatched the crown from the hands of Pope Pius VII to place it upon his own head—choosing instead the romantic moment when the new emperor turned to crown Joséphine. ⚜ *Denon, first floor*

Detail from the Coronation of Napoléon

PLANNING YOUR VISIT

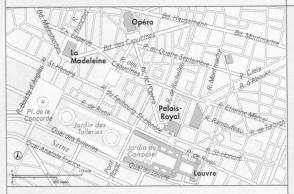

TOURS

Pick up a slick Nintendo 3DS multimedia guide at the entrance to each wing; €5 buys you information on 250 artworks, four self-guided tours, and a GPS function so you can get your bearings.

There are 90-minute guided tours (€15) in English daily at 11 and 2. The meeting point is at "Accueil des Groups" under the pyramid. There are also free thematic leaflets to self-guide through a particular trail—some designed especially for kids. The Louvre has a phenomenal program of courses and workshops (mostly in French); see website for details.

ACCESSIBILITY

Wheelchair visitors or those with strollers can skip the long entry line and use the marvelous cylinder lift inside the entrance pyramid.

WITH KIDS

Begin your tour in the Sully Wing at the Medieval moat, which leads enticingly to the sphinx-guarded entrance of the Egyptian Wing, a must for mummy enthusiasts. For a more in-depth visit, you can reserve private kid-centric family tours such as the Paris Muse Clues (www.parismuse.com) Don't forget the Tuileries is right next door (with carnival rides in summer).

ENTRY TIPS

Online ticket sales were expected to arrive in late 2014. Until then, those in the know head straight for the entrance in the underground mall, the Carrousel du Louvre (99 rue de Rivoli), which has automatic ticket machines. There are more machines under the pyramid entrance. Be sure to hold onto your ticket; you can come and go as often as you like in the same day. The shortest entry lines tend to be at 9:30 AM and 1 PM. Crowds are also thinner on late-night Wednesday and Friday openings. Be sure to check the website for room closings; renovations are always taking place. Remember the Louvre is closed on Tuesday.

A WHIRLWIND TOUR

If you've come to Paris and feel you must go to the Louvre to see the Big Three—**Venus de Milo, Winged Victory,** and **Mona Lisa**—even though you'd rather be strolling along the Champs-Elysees, it can be done in an hour or less if you plan well. Start in Denon and head upstairs through Estruscan and Greek antiquities, walking down the long hall of sculptures until you see the Winged Victory in front of you. Take a right and head up the staircase through French painting to the Mona Lisa. Then go back down under the Pyramid to Sully to see the Venus de Milo.

✉ Palais du Louvre, Louvre/ Tuileries

☎ 01-40-20-53-17 (information)

🌐 www.louvre.fr

🎟 €12; Free 1st Sun. of month, under 18 (anytime); €13 for Napoléon Hall exhibitions; €16 with all temporary exhibits and same day entry to the Musée Eugène Delacroix

🕐 Mon., Thurs., and weekends 9–6; Wed. and Fri. 9 AM– 9:30 PM; closed Tues.

Ⓜ Palais-Royal / Musée du Louvre

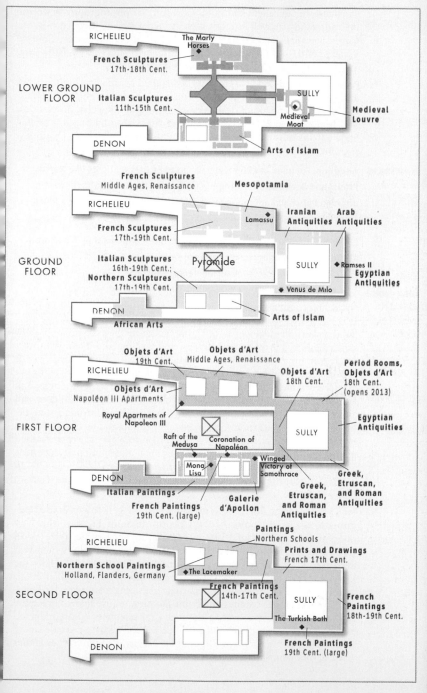

showcase for excellent temporary exhibits of photography featuring up-and-comers as well as icons such as Diane Arbus, Richard Avedon, Cindy Sherman, and Robert Frank. ⊠ *1 pl. de la Concorde, Louvre/ Tuileries* 🕾 *01–47–03–12–50* ⊕ *www.jeudepaume.org* 🎫 *€8.50* ☼ *Tues. 11–9, Wed.–Sun. 11–7; closed Mon.* Ⓜ *Concorde.*

Passage du Grand-Cerf. This pretty glass-roofed arcade was built in 1825 and expertly renovated in 1988. Today it's home to about 20 retailers, many of them small designers selling original jewelry, accessories, and housewares. ■TIP➔ If it's aperitif time, stop by popular Le Pas Sage bar-restaurant at the entrance at Rue St-Denis. ⊠ *8 rue Dussoubs, Beaubourg/Les Halles* Ⓜ *Étienne Marcel.*

NEED A BREAK?

Angélina. Founded in 1903 and patronized by literary lights like Marcel Proust and Gertrude Stein, Angélina is famous for its *chocolat l'Africain*, ultrarich hot chocolate topped with whipped cream. ⊠ *226 rue de Rivoli, Louvre/Tuileries* 🕾 *01–42–60–82–00* ⊕ *www.angelina-paris.fr* Ⓜ *Tuileries.*

Ladurée. There are few delicacies in Paris more enticing than a *macaron* at Ladurée, the elegant bakery and tea salon. ⊠ *16 rue Royal* 🕾 *01–42–60–21–79* ⊕ *www.laduree.com* Ⓜ *Madeleine, Concorde.*

OFF THE BEATEN PATH

Tour Jean Sans Peur. This fascinating little tower is the only remnant of a sprawling complex built on the edge of the original city walls in 1369. It is named for Jean Sans Peur (John the Fearless), the Duke of Burgundy, who gained power in 1407 after ordering the assassination of his rival, the king's brother. In 1409, as civil war raged, he had the tower erected and put his bedroom on a high floor with a bird's-eye view of approaching enemies. Carved into the vaulted second-floor ceiling—a masterwork of medieval architecture—is an ornate sculpture of an oak tree entwined with plants representing the duke's family. Children will enjoy the climb up to see the restored red velvet–lined latrine, a state-of-the-art comfort in its time. Costumed mannequins and medieval-themed exhibits covering subjects from food to furniture give the tower added kid appeal. ■TIP➔ Be sure to ask for English information at the entry. ⊠ *20 rue Etienne Marcel, Beaubourg/Les Halles* 🕾 *01–40–26–20–28* ⊕ *www.tourjeansanspeur.com* 🎫 *€5* ☼ *Apr.–Oct., Wed.–Sun. 1:30–6; Nov.–Mar., Wed., Sat., and Sun. 1:30–6* Ⓜ *Étienne Marcel.*

Tour Saint-Jacques. For centuries, this 170-foot bell tower guided pilgrims to a starting point of the Chemin de Saint Jacques (the Way of Saint James). Built in 1508 in the Flamboyant Gothic style, it's all that remains of the Église Saint-Jacques-de-la-Boucherie, which was destroyed in the French Revolution. Purchased by the city in 1836, the tower languished until a three-year renovation, completed in 2009, restored 660 tons of stone and statues, including the gargoyles hanging from the upper reaches and Saint Jacques, whose figures grace the top. Blaise Pascal was among the medieval scientists who conducted experiments here (his involved gravity), which is why his statue sits at the base. ⊠ *Rue de Rivoli at Rue Nicolas Flamel, Beaubourg/Les Halles* ⊕ *www.tour-saint-jacques-paris.com* Ⓜ *Chatelet.*

LES GRANDS BOULEVARDS

with the Opéra Garnier

GETTING ORIENTED

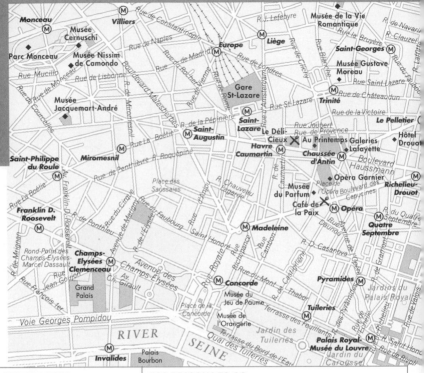

GETTING HERE

This neighborhood covers parts of the 2e, 3e, 8e, and 9e arrondissements. Take the métro to the Opéra station, named for the opulent opera house. Just behind it, you can find the department stores Galeries Lafayette and Au Printemps, each with three buildings (women's, men's, home) along Baron Haussmann's wide avenues known as the Grands Boulevards. If you're planning to visit the numerous small museums, take the métro to Parc Monceau.

TOP REASONS TO GO

Les Grands Magasins. Sample a new perfume under the magnificent dome at Galeries Lafayette; update your look, wander the sumptuous food halls, or gaze at Parisian rooftops from the outdoor café at Au Printemps.

Opéra Garnier. It may not be haunted by the Phantom, but this 19th-century opera house still dazzles. Enjoy a ballet or an opera, take the guided tour, or simply ogle the halls bedecked in marble and gold leaf.

Musée Jacquemart-André. Peruse the private collection of Italian Renaissance masterpieces and admire the elegant furnishings in one of the city's grandest mansions.

Parc Monceau. Join the well-dressed children of well-heeled Parisians and frolic on some of the prettiest lawns in the city.

Les Passages Couverts. Stroll the passages Jouffroy, Verdeau, and Panoramas to experience what the original shopping malls were like 200 years ago.

Les Grands Boulevards

BEST CAFÉS

Café de la Paix. Once described as the "center of the civilized world," this grand café was a meeting place for the glitterati of the Belle Époque. It's an elegant place to enjoy a drink overlooking the Opéra Garnier. The terrace serves simpler fare. ✉ 5 pl. de l'Opéra, Opéra/Grands Boulevards ☎ 01–40–07–36–36 ⊕ www.cafedelapaix.fr Ⓜ Havre Caumartin, Opéra.

Delaville Café. This edgy café is a favorite with locals. Open until 2 am, it's best for an evening aperitif and snack. A DJ spins tunes at night, Thursday through Saturday. ✉ 34 bd. de Bonne Nouvelle, Opéra/Grands Boulevards ☎ 01–48–24–48–09 ⊕ www.delavillecafe.com Ⓜ Bonne Nouvelle.

Le Déli-Cieux. Perched on the top floor of Printemps Beauté/Maison store, Déli-Cieux serves sandwiches, salads, and burgers. It's not expensive, and the view from the outdoor terrace is priceless. ✉ Bd. Haussmann and Rue du Havre, 9th fl., Opéra/Grands Boulevards ☎ 01–42–82–62–76 Ⓜ Havre-Caumartin, Opéra.

MAKING THE MOST OF YOUR TIME

If you're a serious shopper, plan on a daylong visit to this neighborhood, beginning with the department stores near the Opéra métro stop. Nearly every French chain has a shop dotting the boulevard, which changes names several times (Boulevard Haussmann, Montmartre, Poissonnière, de Bonne Nouvelle, etc.) as it plods its way from west to east. If shopping isn't your bag, plan on a long afternoon's visit: tour the Opéra Garnier and one or two museums, or bring a picnic lunch to lovely Parc Monceau on the western edge.

Sightseeing
★★★
Dining
★★★
Lodging
★★★★★
Shopping
★★★★★
Nightlife
★★★★★

In Belle Époque Paris, the Grands Boulevards were the place to see and be seen: in the cafés, at the opera, or in the ornate *passages couverts* (glass-roofed arcades that served as the world's first malls). If you close your eyes, you can almost imagine the Grands Boulevards immortalized on canvas by the Impressionists, with well-attired Parisians strolling wide avenues dotted with shops, cafés, and horse-drawn carriages—all set against a backdrop of stately Haussmannian buildings. Today, despite the chain stores, sidewalk vendors, and fast-food joints, the Grands Boulevards remain the city's shopping epicenter, home to the most popular department stores, Galeries Lafayette and Au Printemps, near Place de l'Opéra.

Updated by
Jack Vermee

Shopping aside, the Grands Boulevards are a cultural destination anchored by the magnificent **Opéra Garnier**, commissioned by Napoléon III. The neighborhood is also home to some of the city's best small museums, all former private collections housed in 19th-century *hôtels particuliers* (or mansions) that alone are worth the trip. The exquisite **Musée Jacquemart-André** displays an impressive collection of Italian Renaissance art, while the jewel-box **Musée Nissim de Camondo** remembers one family's tragic end. The **Musée Cernuschi** has an impressive collection of Asian art, and the **Musée National Gustave-Moreau** is an offbeat tribute to the Symbolist master.

TOP ATTRACTIONS

Au Printemps. Spread across three buildings, this vast upscale department store has been luring shoppers since 1865. Besides the clothes, shoes, and everything else, there are appealing lunch options here. You can admire the Belle Époque green-and-gold dome in Brasserie Printemps on the sixth floor of the main store; Le World Bar on the fifth floor of the men's store is a cozy pub with a cool vibe; and Le Déli-Cieux, the ninth-floor cafeteria-style restaurant at Printemps Beauté/Maison, has a large outdoor terrace with a great view. ⊠ *64 bd. Haussmann, Opéra/Grands Boulevards* ☎ *01–42–82–50–00* ⊕ *www.printemps. com* ⊙ *Mon.–Wed., Fri., and Sat. 9:35–8, Thurs. 9:35 am–10 pm; closed Sun.* Ⓜ *Havre Caumartin, Opéra.*

> ### SUPER SHOPPING TIP
>
> Both Galeries Lafayette and Au Printemps offer 10% discount cards to foreign visitors. Some items, usually designer clothing and sale items, are excluded. To get one, go to the welcome desk on the main floor of either store. Remember to bring a passport or driver's license.

FAMILY **Chocostory: Le Musée Gourmand du Chocolat.** Considering that a daily dose of chocolate is practically obligatory in Paris, it's hard to believe that this spot (opened in 2010) is the city's first museum dedicated to the sweet stuff. Exhibits on three floors tell the story of chocolate from the earliest traces of the "divine nectar" in Mayan and Aztec cultures, through to its introduction in Europe by the Spanish, who added milk and sugar to the spicy dark brew and launched a continental craze. There are detailed explanations in English, with many for the kids. While the production of chocolate is a major topic, there is also a respectable collection of some 1,000 chocolate related artifacts, such as terra-cotta Mayan sipping vessels (they blew into straws to create foam) and delicate chocolate pots in fine porcelain that were favored by the French royal court. ■ **TIP→ Frequent chocolate-making demonstrations finish with a free tasting.** ⊠ *28 bd. de Bonne Nouvelle, Opéra/Grands Boulevards* ☎ *01–42–29–68–60* ⊕ *www.museeduchocolat.fr* ⊟ *€9* ⊙ *Daily 10–6 (last entry at 5)* Ⓜ *Bonne-Nouvelle, Strasbourg, St-Denis.*

Galeries Lafayette. The stunning Byzantine glass *coupole* (dome) of the city's most famous department store is not to be missed. Amble to the center of the main store, amid the perfumes and cosmetics, and look up. If you're not in the mood for shopping, sip a glass of champagne at the Bar à Bulles at the top of the first-floor escalator. Or have lunch at one of the restaurants, including a rooftop café in the main store (open in spring and summer). On your way down, the top floor of the main store is a good place to pick up interesting Parisian souvenirs. Next door, the excellent Lafayette Gourmet food hall, on the second floor of the men's store, has one of the city's best selections of delicacies. Try a green tea éclair from Japanese–French baker Sadaharu Aoki. ⊠ *40 bd. Haussmann, Opéra/Grands Boulevards* ☎ *01–42–82–34–56* ⊕ *www. galerieslafayette.com* ⊙ *Mon.–Wed., Fri., and Sat. 9:30–7:30, Thurs. 9:30–9; closed Sun.* Ⓜ *Chaussée d'Antin, Opéra; RER A: Auber.*

Fodor's Choice ★ **Musée Cernuschi.** Wealthy Milanese banker and patriot Enrico (Henri) Cernuschi fled to Paris in 1850 after the new Italian government collapsed, only to be arrested during the 1871 Paris Commune. He subsequently decided to wait out the unrest by traveling and collecting Asian art. Upon his return 18 months later, he had a special mansion built

6

on the edge of Parc Monceau to house his treasures, notably a two-story bronze Buddha from Japan. Today, this well-appointed museum contains France's second-most important collection of Asian art, after the Musée Guimet. Cernuschi had an eye not only for the bronze pieces he adored but also for Neolithic pottery (8,000 BC), *mingqi* tomb figures (300–900 AD), and an impressive array of terra-cotta figures from various dynasties. A collection highlight is *La Tigresse,* a bronze wine vessel in the shape of a roaring feline (11th century BC) purchased after Cernuschi's death. Although the museum is free, there is a charge for temporary exhibitions: previous shows have featured Japanese drawings, Iranian sculpture, and Imperial Chinese bronzes. ✉ *7 av. Velasquez, Parc Monceau* ☎ *01–53–96–21–50* ⊕ *www.cernuschi.paris.fr* ✉ *Free; temporary exhibitions €7* ☾ *Tues.–Sun. 10–6; closed Mon.* Ⓜ *Monceau.*

> **DID YOU KNOW?**
>
> The inspiration for the mysterious lake underneath the Opéra Garnier in *The Phantom of the Opera* occurred when construction of the building was delayed while the marshy site was drained. Rumors of an underground river began to circulate, and from there it was a small leap for Gaston Leroux to invent the Phantom sailing on a subterranean waterway. In the movie version, a vengeful Phantom sent the opera's chandelier crashing into the audience, an idea also drawn from real life: in 1896 one of the counterweights of the 8-ton crystal chandelier fell, crushing a woman in her red velvet seat.

Fodor's Choice ★ **Musée Jacquemart-André.** Perhaps the city's best small museum, the opulent Musée Jacquemart-André is home to a huge collection of art and furnishings lovingly assembled in the late 19th century by banking heir Edouard André and his artist wife, Nélie Jacquemart. Their midlife marriage in 1881 raised eyebrows—he was a dashing bachelor and a Protestant, and she, no great beauty, hailed from a modest Catholic family. Still, theirs was a happy union fused by a common passion for art. For six months every year, the couple traveled, most often to Italy, where they hunted works from the Renaissance, their preferred period. Their collection also includes French painters Fragonard, Jacques-Louis David, and François Boucher, and Dutch masters Van Dyke and Rembrandt. The Belle Époque mansion itself is a major attraction. The elegant ballroom, equipped with collapsible walls operated by then-state-of-the-art hydraulics, could hold 1,000 guests. The winter garden was a wonder of its day, spilling into the *fumoir,* where the dashing André would share cigars with the *grands hommes* (important men) of the day. You can tour the separate bedrooms—his in dusty pink, hers in pale yellow. The former dining room, now an elegant café, features a ceiling by Tiepolo. Don't forget to pick up the free audioguide in English, and do inquire about the current temporary exhibition (two per year), which is usually top-notch. ■TIP➔ Plan on a Sunday visit and enjoy the popular brunch (€28.50) in the café from 11 to 3. Reservations are not accepted, so come early or late to avoid waiting in line. ✉ *158 bd. Haussmann, Parc Monceau* ☎ *01–45–62–11–59* ⊕ *www.*

CLOSE UP

Paris's Covered Arcades

Before there were the *grands magas-ins,* there were the *passages couverts,* covered arcades that offered the early-19th-century Parisian shopper a hodgepodge of shops under one roof, and a respite from the mud and grit of streets that did not have sidewalks. Until the rise of the department stores in the latter part of the century, they would rule as the top places to wander, as well as shop. Technical and architectural wonders of the time, the vaulting structures of iron and frosted glass inspired artists and writers such as Émile Zola.

Of the 150 arcades built around Paris in the early 1800s, only about a dozen are still in business today, mostly in the 2e and 9e arrondisse-ments. Two arcades still going strong are the fabulously restored Galerie Vivienne (⊠ *4 rue Petits Champs, 2e*) and the Galerie Véro-Dodat (⊠ *19 rue Jean-Jacques Rousseau, 1er*), both lined with glamorous boutiques such as Jean-Paul Gaultier and Christian Louboutin *(see Chapter 5: Around the Louvre).*

Three other modest passages enjoying a renaissance can be found end to end off the Grands Boulevards, east of Place de l'Opéra. Begin with the most refined, the **Passage Jouffroy** (⊠ *10 bd. Montmartre, 9e*), which is home to the Musée Grevin and the well-regarded budget Hotel Chopin. There's an eclectic array of shops such as M.G.W. Segas at No. 34, where the three Segas brothers sell a wildly eccentric collection of furnishings and canes capped with animal heads and whatnot. You can outfit your dollhouse at Pain d'épices (No. 29), which stocks thousands of minia-tures. Pop out at the northern end of Passage Jouffroy and cross Rue de la Grange-Batelière into the **Passage Verdeau** (9e), where you can pick up some antique candlesticks—or a cow skull—at the quirky red-walled Valence gallery at No. 22. On the southern end of the Passage Jouffroy, across Boulevard Montmartre, is the **Passage des Panoramas** (2e). The granddaddy of the arcades, built in 1800, became the first public space in Paris equipped with gaslights in 1817. A few philatelist shops remain, though the arcade is now dominated by restaurants, including two popular wine bar/bistros (Racines at No. 8 and Coinstot at No. 26 bis), as well as Paris's original gluten-free restaurant (Noglu, at No. 16).

6

---

musee-jacquemart-andre.com ⊠ *€11* ⊙ *Daily 10–6 (until 8:30 Mon. and Sat. during exhibitions)* Ⓜ *St-Philippe-du-Roule, Miromesnil.*

OFF THE
BEATEN
PATH **Musée National Gustave-Moreau.** Visiting the quirky town house and stu-dio of painter Gustave Moreau (1826–98) is well worth your time. With an eye on his legacy, Moreau—a high priest of the Symbolist movement—created a light-flooded gallery on the two top floors to showcase his dark paintings. Some of the works appear unfinished, such as *Unicorns (No. 213)* inspired by the medieval tapestries in the Musée de Cluny: Moreau refused to work on it further, spurning the wishes of a wealthy would-be patron. His interpretation of Biblical scenes and Greek mythology combine flights of fantasy with a keen use of color, shadow, and tracings influenced by Persian and Indian miniatures.

There are wax sculptures and cupboards with sliding vertical doors containing small-format paintings. The Symbolists loved objects, and Moreau was no different. His cramped private apartment on the second floor is jam-packed with bric-a-brac, and artworks cover every inch of the walls. Note that the home's top three stories are newly renovated; work on the ground floor, which will include six rooms that have been closed to the public for more than a decade, is set to finish in late 2014. ⊠ *14 rue de la Rochefoucauld, Opéra/ Grands Boulevards* ☎ *01–48–74–38–50* ⊕ *www.musee-moreau.fr* ⊠ *€5* ⊙ *Mon., Wed., and Thurs. 10–12:45 and 2–5:15, Fri–Sun. 10–5:15; closed Tues.* Ⓜ *Trinité.*

> **DID YOU KNOW?**
>
> Around the corner from the Musée Jacquemart-André, at 45 rue de Courcelles, is the former apartment of French writer Marcel Proust, whose epic *Remembrance of Things Past* was reputedly inspired by the smell of a madeleine cookie. You can buy your own delicious madeleines at Fauchon in Place de la Madeleine (although the address has nothing to do with the cookie).

Fodor'sChoice
★

Opéra Garnier. Haunt of the Phantom of the Opera and the real-life inspiration for Edgar Degas's dancer paintings, the gorgeous Opéra Garnier is one of two homes of the National Opera of Paris. The building, the Palais Garnier, was begun in 1860 by then-unknown architect Charles Garnier, who finished his masterwork 15 long years later, way over budget. Festooned with (real) gold leaf, colored marble, paintings, and sculpture from the top artists of the day, the opera house was about as subtle as Versailles and sparked controversy in post-Revolutionary France. The sweeping marble staircase, in particular, drew criticism from a public skeptical of its extravagance. But Garnier, determined to make a landmark that would last forever, spared no expense. The magnificent grand foyer is one of the most exquisite salons in France. In its heyday, the cream of Paris society strolled all 59 yards of the vast hall at intermission, admiring themselves in the towering mirrors. To see the opera house, buy a ticket for an unguided visit, which allows access to most parts of the building, including a peek into the auditorium. There is also a small ballet museum with a few works by Degas and the tutu worn by prima ballerina Anna Pavlova when she danced her epic Dying Swan in 1905. To get to it, pass through the unfinished entrance built for Napoléon III and his carriage (construction was abruptly halted when the emperor abdicated in 1870). On the upper level, you can see a sample of the auditorium's original classical ceiling, which was later replaced with a modern version by an octogenarian Mark Chagall. His trademark willowy figures encircling the dazzling crystal chandelier—today the world's third largest—shocked an unappreciative public upon its debut in 1964. Critics who fret that Chagall's masterpiece clashes with the fussy crimson-and-gilt decor can take some comfort in knowing that the original ceiling is preserved underneath, encased in a plastic dome.

The Opéra Garnier plays host to the Paris Ballet as well as a few operas each season (most are performed at the Opéra Bastille). If you're planning to see a performance, tickets cost €10–€195 and should be reserved as soon as they go on sale—typically a month ahead at the box office, earlier by phone or online; otherwise, try your luck last minute. ■**TIP→ To learn about the building's history, and get a taste of aristocratic life during the Second Empire, take an entertaining English-language tour. They're offered most months at 11:30 and 2:30 on Wednesday, Saturday, and Sunday; same times daily in summer. To complete the experience, dine at L'Opéra, the contemporary on-site restaurant run by star chef Christophe Aribert; or browse through the Palais Garnier gift shop for ballet-inspired wares, along with fine Bernardaud porcelain depicting the famous Chagall ceiling, and an exceptional selection of themed DVDs and books.** ⊠ *Pl. de l'Opéra, Opéra/Grands Boulevards* ☎ *08–92–89–90–90 €0.34 per min* ⊕ *www. operadeparis.fr* ⊠ *€10; €12.50 for tours* ☉ *Daily 10–5 (until 6 mid-July–Aug.)* Ⓜ *Opéra.*

FAMILY **Parc Monceau.** This exquisitely landscaped park began in 1778 as the Duc de Chartres's private garden. Though some of the land was sold off under the Second Empire (creating the exclusive real estate that now borders the park), the refined atmosphere and some of the fanciful faux ruins have survived. Immaculately dressed children play under the watchful eye of their nannies, while lovers cuddle on the benches. In 1797 André Garnerin, the world's first-recorded parachutist, staged a landing in the park. The rotunda—known as the Chartres Pavilion—is surely the city's grandest public restroom: it started life as a tollhouse. ⊠ *Entrances on Bd. de Courcelles, Av. Velasquez, Av. Ruysdaël, Av. van Dyck, Parc Monceau* Ⓜ *Monceau.*

WORTH NOTING

Hôtel Drouot. Hidden away in a small antiques district, not far from the Opéra Garnier, is Paris's central auction house. With everything from old clothes to haute couture gowns and from tchotchkes to ornate Chinese lacquered boxes, rare books, and wine, Drouot sells it all. Anyone can attend the sales and viewings, which draw a mix of art dealers, ladies who lunch, and art amateurs hoping to discover an unknown masterpiece. Check the website to see what's on the block. ■**TIP→ Don't miss the small galleries and antiques dealers in the Quartier Drouot, a warren of small streets around the auction house, notably on rues Rossini and de la Grange-Batelière.** ⊠ *9 rue Drouot, Opéra/Grands Boulevards* ☎ *01–48–00–20–20* ⊕ *www.drouot.com* ☉ *Viewings of merchandise Mon.–Sat. 11–6; auctions begin at 2* Ⓜ *Richelieu Drouot.*

NEED A BREAK?

J'go. Steps from the Drouot auction house, J'go, one of two Paris outposts of the Toulouse wine bar/restaurant, is perfect for an aperitif or light dinner. The cozy bar serves impressive *grignotages* (tapas) from France's southwest. ⊠ *4 rue Drouot, Grands Boulevards* ☎ *01–40–22–09–09* ⊕ *www. lejgo.com* Ⓜ *Richelieu-Drouot.*

Musée de la Vie Romantique. A visit to the charming Museum of the Romantic Life, dedicated to novelist George Sand (1804–76), will transport you to the countryside. Occupying a pretty 1830s mansion in a tree-lined courtyard, the small permanent collection features drawings by Delacroix and Ingres, among others, though Sand is the undisputed star. Displays include glass cases stuffed with her jewelry and even a mold of the hand of composer Frédéric Chopin—one of her many lovers. The museum, about a five-minute walk from the Musée National Gustave-Moreau, is in a picturesque neighborhood once called New Athens, a reflection of the architectural tastes of the writers and artists who lived there. There is usually an interesting temporary exhibit here, too. ■ TIP→ The garden café (open March to October) is a lovely spot for lunch or afternoon tea. ⊠ *16 rue Chaptal, Opéra/Grands Boulevards* ☎ *01–55–31–95–67* ⊕ *www.vie-romantique.paris.fr* ✉ *Free; €7 temporary exhibits* ☉ *Tues.–Sun. 10–6; closed Mon.* Ⓜ *Blanche, Pigalle, St-Georges.*

Musée du Parfum. More of a showroom than a museum, the small exhibit run by *parfumier* Fragonard above its boutique on Rue Scribe is heavy on decorative objects associated with perfume, including crystal bottles, gloves, and assorted bibelots. The shop is a good place to find gifts, like the €14 honey body lotion, myriad soaps, and, of course, perfume. There's another mini-museum in the Fragonard shop nearby at 39 boulevard des Capucines. ⊠ *9 rue Scribe, Opéra* ☎ *01–47–42–04–56* ⊕ *www.fragonard.com* ✉ *Free* ☉ *Mon.–Sat. 9–6, Sun. 9–5* Ⓜ *Opéra.*

FAMILY **Musée Grévin.** If you like wax museums, this one founded in 1882 ranks among the best. Pay the steep entry price and ascend a grand Phantom-of-the-Opera–like staircase into the Palais des Mirages, a mirrored salon from the 1900 Paris Exposition that transforms into a hokey light-and-sound show the kids will love (it was a childhood favorite of designer Jean-Paul Gaultier). From there, get set for a cavalcade of nearly 300 statues, from Elvis to Ernest Hemingway, Picasso to Barack Obama. Every king of France is here, along with Michael Jackson and George Clooney, plus scores of French singers and celebrities. ⊠ *10 bd. Montmartre, Opéra/Grands Boulevards* ☎ *01–47–70–85–05* ⊕ *www.grevin.com* ✉ *€23.50 adults; €16.50 children 6–14* ☉ *Weekdays 10–6:30, weekends 10–7* Ⓜ *Grands Boulevards.*

Musée Nissim de Camondo. The story of the Camondo family is steeped in tragedy, and it's all recorded within the walls of this superb museum. Patriarch Moïse de Camondo, born in Istanbul to a successful banking family, built his showpiece mansion in 1911 in the style of the Petit Trianon at Versailles, and stocked it with some of the most exquisite furniture, wainscoting, and bibelots of the mid- to late 18th century. Despite his vast wealth and purported charm, his wife left him five years after their marriage. Then his son, Nissim, was killed in World War I. Upon Moïse's death in 1935, the house and its contents were left to the state as a museum named for his lost son. A few years later, daughter Béatrice, her husband, and two children were murdered at Auschwitz. No heirs remained and the Camondo name died out. Today, the house remains an impeccable tribute to Moïse's life, from the gleaming salons to the refined private rooms. ⊠ *63 rue de Monceau, Parc Monceau* ☎ *01–53–89–06–50* ⊕ *www.lesartsdecoratifs.fr* ✉ *€7.50; €12 joint ticket with Les Arts Décoratifs* ☉ *Wed.–Sun. 10–5:30; closed Mon. and Tues.* Ⓜ *Villiers or Monceau.*

MONTMARTRE

7

Visit Fodors.com for advice, updates, and bookings

GETTING ORIENTED

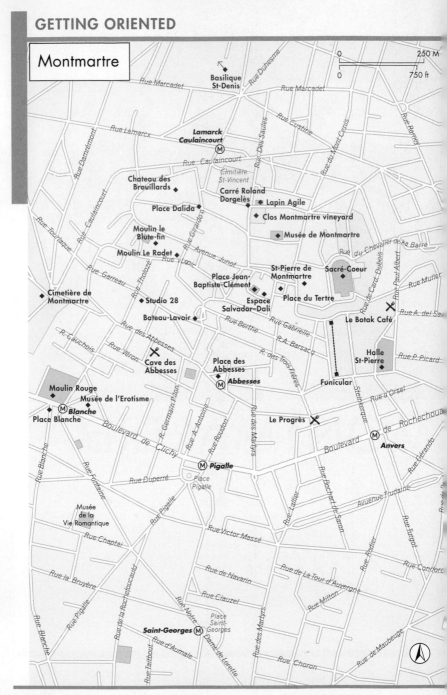

Montmartre

Rue Marcadet

Basilique
St-Denis

Rue Marcadet

Rue Duhesme

Rue Custine

Rue Ramey

0   250 M

0   750 ft

Rue Lamarck

Rue Damrémont

Rue Lamarck

Lamarck
Caulaincourt
Ⓜ

Rue Caulaincourt

Rue Des Saules

Rue du Mont-Cenis

Cimetière
St-Vincent

Chateau des
Brouillards

Carré Roland
Dorgelès

Lapin Agile

Place Dalida

Clos Montmartre vineyard

Moulin le
Blute-fin

Musée de Montmartre

Rue Caulaincourt

Rue Tourlaque

Rue Girardon

Avenue Junot

Moulin Le Radet

Rue Lepic

Rue du Chevalier de la Barre

Rue Garreau

Rue Thérèze

St-Pierre de
Montmartre

Sacré-Coeur

Rue de Cato. Dubois

Rue Paul Albert

Rue Muller

Place Jean-
Baptiste-Clément

Cimetière de
Montmartre

Studio 28

Espace
Salvador-Dali

Place du Tertre

✕

Le Botak Café

Rue A. del Sa

Bateau-Lavoir

Rue Berthe

Rue Gabrielle

R. Cauchois

Rue des Abbesses

Rue Veron

R.A. Barsacq

R. des Trois Frères

Halle
St-Pierre

Rue P. Picard

Cave des
Abbesses

Place des
Abbesses

Ⓜ Abbesses

Funicular

Steinkerque

Moulin Rouge

Musée de l'Erotisme

Rue J.-B. Germain-Pilon

Rue A.-Antoine

Rue Houdon

Rue des Martyrs

Le Progrès ✕

Rue d'Orsel

Ⓜ Blanche

Place Blanche

Boulevard de Clichy

Boulevard de Rochechoua

Ⓜ Anvers

Rue Blanche

Rue Fontaine

Rue Pigalle

Rue Duperré

Ⓜ Pigalle

Place
Pigalle

Rue Laffitte

Rue Bochart-de-Seron

Rue Gérando

Avenue Trudaine

Rue Turgot

Rue Condor

Musée
de la
Vie Romantique

Rue Chaptal

Rue Victor Massé

Rue Rodier

Rue la Bruyère

Rue de Navarin

Rue de La Tour-d'Auvergne

Rue Milton

Rue Pigalle

Rue de la Rochefoucauld

Rue Clauzel

Rue Blanche

Saint-Georges Ⓜ

Place
Saint-
Georges

Rue Notre-Dame-de-Lorette

Rue des Martyrs

Rue Choron

Rue de Maubeuge

Rue Taitbout

Rue d'Aumale

TOP REASONS TO GO

Sacré-Coeur. The best view of Paris is worth the climb—or the funicular ride—especially at twilight when the city lights create a magnificent panorama below the hill of Montmartre.

Place du Tertre. This bustling square behind Sacré-Coeur teems with crowds of tourists and hordes of street artists clamoring to paint them.

Place des Abbesses. Capture the village ambience that makes Montmartre special by exploring the tiny streets branching out from this picturesque square.

Carré Roland Dorgelès. Bring your camera to this little square overlooking a pair of classic Montmartre sights: the city's only vineyard and the famous Au Lapin Agile cabaret.

MAKING THE MOST OF YOUR TIME

Devote a day to this neighborhood if you want to see more than the obligatory Sacré-Coeur basilica. If possible, avoid weekends, when the narrow—and extremely hilly—streets are jam-packed.

GETTING HERE

Montmartre is in the 18e arrondissement. Take Line 2 to Anvers métro station, and then take the funicular (costs one métro ticket) up to Sacré-Coeur. Or take Line 12 to Abbesses station and take your time wandering the cobbled streets and staircases that lead up to the basilica. For a scenic tour, hop the public bus, Montmartrobus (costs one métro ticket). An easy starting point is the métro station Jules-Joffrin (Line 12): the bus winds up the hilly streets, with a convenient stop at Sacré-Coeur. Alternatively, pile the kids onto Le Petit Train de Montmartre, a bus disguised as a minitrain that runs a circuit every 30 minutes from Place Blanche (€4–€6.50).

BEST CAFÉS

Le Progrès. This photo op-ready corner café draws a quirky mix of hipsters, artists, and discriminating tourists. The food is good, with classics like steak tartare. Try the menu du jour (€17 for two courses). If you're craving a taste of home, the excellent cheeseburger comes with a heap of crispy fries. ⊠ *7 rue des Trois Frères, Montmartre* ☎ *01–42–64–07–37* Ⓜ *Abbesses.*

Cave des Abbesses. Locals head to this charming retro-looking *caviste* (wine shop) and wine bar for a glass of something special with a side of oysters, or perhaps La Grande Mixte, a platter of charcuterie, terrine, and cheese (€13). ⊠ *43 rue des Abbesses, Montmartre* ☎ *01–42–52–81–54* Ⓜ *Abbesses.*

Le Botak Café. On the eastern side of Sacré-Coeur, at the bottom of the stairs, you'll find the leafy Square Louise Marie and this little café, which serves a small, ever-changing menu of French home cooking like *saumon au pistou* (salmon in pesto) and *poulet botak* (roasted chicken with garlic and mashed potatoes). The daily lunch specials (about €14) are a great deal, but service can sometimes be slow when it's busy. ⊠ *1 rue Paul Albert, Montmartre* ☎ *01–46–06–98–30* Ⓜ *Anvers, Château Rouge.*

7

Sightseeing
★★★★

Dining
★★★

Lodging
★★

Shopping
★★★

Nightlife
★

Montmartre has become almost too charming for its own good. Yes, it feels like a village (if you wander off the beaten path); yes, there are working artists here (though far fewer than there used to be); and yes, the best view of Paris is yours for free from the top of the hill (if there's no haze). That's why on any weekend day, year-round, you can find scores of visitors crowding these cobbled alleys, scaling the staircases that pass for streets, and queuing to see Sacré-Coeur, the "sculpted cloud," at the summit.

Updated by
Jack Vermee

If you're lucky enough to have a little corner of Montmartre to yourself, you'll understand why locals love it so. Come at nonpeak times, on a weekday, or in the morning or later in the evening. Stroll around **Place des Abbesses,** where the rustic houses and narrow streets escaped the heavy hand of urban planner Baron Haussmann. Until 1860 the area was in fact a separate village, dotted with windmills. Always a draw for bohemians and artists, many of whom had studios at what is now the **Musée de Montmartre** and **Bateau-Lavoir,** Montmartre has been home to such painters as Suzanne Valadon and her son Maurice Utrillo, Picasso, van Gogh, Géricault, Renoir, and, of course, Henri de Toulouse-Lautrec, whose iconic paintings of the cancan dancers at the **Moulin Rouge** are now souvenir-shop fixtures. While you can still see shows at the Moulin Rouge in **Place Blanche** and the pocket-size cabaret **Au Lapin Agile** *(see the Nightlife chapter),* much of the entertainment here is on the seedier side—the area around Pigalle is the city's largest red-light district, though it's far tamer than it used to be. **Boulevard de Clichy** was virtually an artists' highway at the turn of the 20th century: Degas lived and died at No. 6, and Picasso lived at No. 11. The *quartier* is a favorite of filmmakers (the blockbuster *Moulin Rouge* was inspired by it), and visitors still seek out Café des Deux Moulins at 15 rue Lepic, the real-life café (unfortunately with a remodeled look) where Audrey

Tautou waited tables in 2001's *Amélie*. In 1928 **Studio 28** opened as the world's first cinema for experimental films.

TOP ATTRACTIONS

Bateau-Lavoir (*Wash-barge*). The birthplace of Cubism isn't open to the public, but a display in the front window details this unimposing spot's rich history. Montmartre poet Max Jacob coined the name (it means "wash barge") because the original structure here reminded him of the laundry boats that used to float in the Seine, and he joked that the warren of paint-splattered artists' studios needed a good hosing down (wishful thinking, since the building had only one water tap). It was in the Bateau-Lavoir that, early in the 20th century, Pablo Picasso, Georges Braque, and Juan Gris made their first bold stabs at Cubism, and Picasso painted the groundbreaking *Les Demoiselles d'Avignon* in 1906–07. The experimental works of the artists weren't met with open arms, even in liberal Montmartre. All but the facade was rebuilt after a fire in 1970. Like the original building, though, the current incarnation houses artists and their studios. ✉ *13 pl. Émile-Goudeau, Montmartre* Ⓜ *Abbesses.*

Carré Roland Dorgelès. This unassuming square is a perfect place to take in two of Montmartre's most photographed sites: the pink-and-green Au Lapin Agile cabaret and Clos Montmartre, Paris's only working vineyard. While the former, famously painted by Camille Pissarro, still welcomes revelers after 150 years, the latter is closed to visits except during the annual Fête de Jardins (Garden Festival) weekend in September. The stone wall on the northwestern edge of the square borders the peaceful Cimetière Saint-Vincent, one of the neighborhood's three atmospheric cemeteries. ✉ *Corner of Rue des Saulnes and Rue St-Vincent, Montmartre* Ⓜ *Lamarck-Caulaincourt.*

Halle St-Pierre. This elegant iron-and-glass 19th-century market hall at the foot of Sacré-Coeur stages dynamic exhibitions of *art brut* (raw art), or outsider and folk art. The international artists featured are contemporary in style and out of the mainstream. There's also a good bookstore and a café serving light, well-prepared dishes, such as savory tarts and quiches with salad on the side, plus homemade desserts. ✉ *2 rue Ronsard, Montmartre* ☎ *01–42–58–72–89* ⊕ *www.hallesaintpierre. org* 🎟 *Museum €8* ☉ *Weekdays 11–6, Sat. 11–7, Sun. 12–6; closed weekends in Aug.* Ⓜ *Anvers.*

Moulin de la Galette. Of the 14 windmills (*moulins*) that used to sit atop this hill, only two remain. They're known collectively as Moulin de la Galette—the name being taken from the bread that the owners used to produce. The more storied of the two is Le Blute-fin. In the late 1800s there was a dance hall on the site, famously captured by Renoir (you can see the painting in the Musée d'Orsay). A facelift restored the windmill to its 19th-century glory; however, it is on private land and can't be visited. Down the street is the other moulin, Le Radet. ✉ *Le Blute-fin, corner of Rue Lepic and Rue Tholozé, Montmartre* Ⓜ *Abbesses.*

Place des Abbesses. This triangular square is typical of the countrified style that has made Montmartre famous. Now a hub for shopping and people-watching, the *place* is surrounded by hip boutiques, sidewalk cafés, and shabby-chic restaurants—a prime habitat for the young, neo-bohemian crowd and a sprinkling of expats. Trendy streets like Rue Houdon and Rue des Martyrs have attracted small designers, an international beer seller, and even a cupcake shop. Some retailers remain open on Sunday afternoon. ⊠ *Intersection of Rue des Abbesses and Rue la Vieuville, Montmartre* Ⓜ *Abbesses.*

Place du Tertre. Artists have peddled their wares in this square for centuries. Though busloads of tourists have changed the atmosphere, if you come off-season—when the air is chilly and the streets are bare—you can almost feel what is was like when up-and-coming Picassos lived in the houses, which today are given over to souvenir shops and cafés. ⊠ *East end of Rue Norvin, Place du Tertre, Montmartre* Ⓜ *Abbesses.*

Fodor's Choice **Sacré-Coeur.** *See the highlighted listing in this chapter.*
★

WORTH NOTING

OFF THE
BEATEN
PATH

Basilique de St-Denis. Built between 1136 and 1286, St-Denis Basilica is one of the most important Gothic churches in France. It was here, under dynamic prelate Abbé Suger, that Gothic architecture (typified by pointed arches and rib vaults) was said to have made its first appearance. The kings of France soon chose St-Denis as their final resting place, and their richly sculpted tombs—along with what remains of Suger's church—can be seen in the choir area at the east end. The basilica was battered during the Revolution; afterward, however, Louis XVIII reestablished it as the royal burial site by moving the remains of Louis XVI and Marie-Antoinette here to join centuries' worth of monarchial bones. The vast 13th-century nave is a brilliant example of structural logic; its columns, capitals, and vault are a model of architectural harmony. The facade, retaining the rounded arches of the Romanesque that preceded the Gothic period, is set off by a small rose window, reputedly the oldest in France. ■TIP→ **Check out the extensive archaeological finds, such as a Merovingian queen's grave goods. Guided tours in English are available by reservation.** ⊠ *1 rue de la Légion d'Honneur, St-Denis* ☎ *01–48–09–83–54* ⊕ *www.saint-denis.monuments-nationaux. fr* ⊠ *Basilica €4.50 with audioguide; choir and tombs €7.50* ⊙ *Apr.–Sept., Mon.–Sat. 10–6:15, Sun. noon–6:15; Oct.–Mar., Mon.–Sat. 10–5, Sun. noon–5:15* Ⓜ *St-Denis Basilica.*

Cimetière de Montmartre. Overshadowed by better-known Père-Lachaise, this cemetery is just as picturesque. It's the final resting place of a host of luminaries, including painters Degas and Fragonard; Adolphe Sax, inventor of the saxophone; dancer Vaslav Nijinsky; filmmaker François Truffaut; and composers Hector Berlioz and Jacques Offenbach. The Art Nouveau tomb of novelist Émile Zola (1840–1902) lords over a lawn near the entrance—though Zola's remains were removed to the Panthéon in 1908. ⊠ *20 av. Rachel, Montmartre* ⊙ *Mar. 16–Nov. 5, weekdays 8–6, Sat. 8:30–5:30, Sun. 9–6; Nov. 6–Mar. 15, weekdays 8–5:30, Sat. 8:30–5:30, Sun. 9–5:30* Ⓜ *Blanche.*

Espace Salvador-Dalí (*Dalí Center*). One of several museums dedicated to the Surrealist master, the collection in this black-walled exhibition space

DID YOU KNOW?

Like many of the "streets" in Montmartre, Rue du Calvaire, off Place du Terte, is actually a staircase, and a scenic way down from the top of the hill.

includes about 300 works, mostly etchings and lithographs. Among the two-dozen sculptures are several versions of Dalí's melting bronze clock and variations on the *Venus de Milo*. Since he was a multimedia pioneer ahead of his time, there are videos with Dalí's voice, and temporary exhibits have included the mustachioed man's foray into holograms. There's plenty of information in English. ⊠ *11 rue Poulbot, Montmartre* ☎ *01–42–64–40–10* ⊕ *www.daliparis.com* 🖃 *€6* ⊙ *Daily 10–6 (until 8 in July and Aug.)* Ⓜ *Abbesses.*

Moulin Rouge. When this world-famous cabaret opened in 1889, aristocrats, professionals, and the working classes all flocked in to ogle the scandalous performers (the cancan was considerably more kinky in Toulouse-Lautrec's day, when girls kicked off their knickers). There's not much to see from the outside except for tourist buses and sex shops, but this square—called Place Blanche—takes its name from the chalky haze once churned up by carts carrying plaster of Paris down from the quarries. Souvenir seekers should check out the Moulin Rouge gift shop (around the corner at 11 rue Lepic), which sells better-quality official merchandise, from jewelry to sculpture, by reputable French makers. *(⇨ See the Nightlife chapter.)* ⊠ *82 bd. de Clichy, Montmartre* ☎ *01–53–09–82–82* ⊕ *www.moulinrouge.fr* Ⓜ *Blanche.*

Musée de l'Érotisme. What better place for the Museum of Erotic Art than smack in the heart of the city's red-light district? Though the subject matter is rather limited, the collection features a respectable mix of world art (think carvings from Africa, Indonesia, and Peru, plus Chinese ivories and Japanese prints). It also has racy cartoons by Robert Crumb and photographs of Pigalle prostitutes and bordellos, some quite chic, from the 1930s and 1940s. Three floors are dedicated to temporary exhibits by contemporary artists and photographers. ⊠ *72 bd. de Clichy, Montmartre* ☎ *01–42–58–28–73* ⊕ *www.musee-erotisme.com* 🖃 *€10; €8 per person or €14 per couple if purchased online* ⊙ *Daily 10 am–2 am* Ⓜ *Blanche.*

Musée de Montmartre. In its turn-of-the-20th-century heyday, the building—now home to Montmartre's historical museum—was a studio block for painters, writers, and cabaret artists. Foremost among them were Renoir (who painted the *Moulin de la Galette,* an archetypal scene of sun-drenched revelers, while he lived here) and Maurice Utrillo. Recapping the area's history, the museum has a charming permanent collection that includes many Toulouse-Lautrec posters and original Eric Satie scores. An ambitious renovation that will double the current museum's space and revitalize its lovely gardens is due to be completed by the end of 2014. The museum remains open in the meantime. ⊠ *12 rue Cortot, Montmartre* ☎ *01–49–25–89–37* ⊕ *www.museedemontmartre.fr* 🖃 *€9* ⊙ *Daily 10–6* Ⓜ *Lamarck Caulaincourt.*

Place Jean-Baptiste-Clément. Monsieur Clément, a singer, was "Mayor of Montmartre" during the heady 70 days of the 1871 Commune, when this area actually seceded from Paris. Painter Amedeo Modigliani (1884–1920) had a studio at No. 7, and Picasso lived around the corner at 49 rue Gabrielle. Look for the octagonal tower at the north end of the square. It's all that's left of Montmartre's first water tower,

CLOSE UP

A Scenic Walk in Montmartre

One of Paris's most charming walks begins at the Abbesses métro station (Line 12), which has one of only two remaining iron-and-glass Art Nouveau canopies designed by famed architect Hector Guimard. Explore the streets ringing **Place des Abbesses,** or begin the walk immediately by heading west along Rue des Abbesses. Turn right on Rue Tholozé and note the historic movie house, **Studio 28,** at No. 10. At the top of the street is **Le Blute-fin,** a windmill portrayed in a well-known work by Renoir. A right on Rue Lepic takes you past the only other windmill still standing, **Le Radet.** Take a left here onto Rue Girardon, to **Place Dalida,** marked with a voluptuous bust of the beloved French singer who popularized disco. (Yolanda Gigliotti, aka Dalida, lived until her death in 1987 at 11 bis, rue d'Orchampt, one of the city's narrowest streets, opposite Le Radet.)

The stone house behind Dalida's bust is the 18th-century **Château des Brouillards,** whose name, Castle of the Mists, is taken from the light fog that used to cloak this former farmland. Detour down the romantic alley of the same name. Renoir is said to have lived in the château before moving to the small house across the way at No. 8. From Place Dalida, head down the winding Rue de l'Abreuvoir, one of the most-photographed streets in Paris. Residents used to walk their horses to the *abreuvoir,* or watering trough, at No. 15. Pissarro kept a pied-à-terre at No. 12. The stone-and-wood-beamed house at No. 4 was once home to a historian of the Napoleonic wars whose family symbol was an eagle. Notice the wooden sundial with a rooster and the

inscription: "When you chime, I'll sing." At the pink-and-green **Maison Rose** restaurant, committed to canvas by resident artist Maurice Utrillo, turn left on Rue des Saules where you'll find Paris's only working vineyard, **Clos de Montmartre.**

Across the street is the famous cabaret **Au Lapin Agile,** still going strong. On the opposite corner, a stone wall rings the **Cimetière Saint-Vincent,** one of the city's smallest cemeteries, where Utrillo is buried (to see it, walk west along Rue St-Vincent, take a right, then another quick right). Backtrack up Rue des Saules and take the first left onto Rue Cortot to the **Musée de Montmartre,** once home to a bevy of artists. Renoir rented a studio here to store his painting of Le Blute-fin. A few doors down, at No. 6, the composer Erik Satie, piano player at Le Chat Noir nightclub, lived during a penniless period in a 6-by-4-foot flat with a 9-foot ceiling (plus skylight). At the corner of Rue Mont-Cenis, the white water tower Château d'Eau still services the neighborhood. Turn right to reach **Place du Tertre,** a lively square packed with tourists and street artists. Easily overlooked is **St-Pierre de Montmartre,** one of the city's oldest churches, founded in 1147. End your walk at the basilica **Sacré-Coeur,** and enjoy one of the best views of Paris from the city's highest point. This *butte,* or hilltop, has been famous since the 3rd century: St-Denis (the first bishop of Paris) was martyred here, and after his decapitation he was said to have walked miles while holding his own head. For an easy descent, take the funicular, which has been ferrying people up and down since 1900.

7

DID YOU KNOW?

The views *of* majestic Sacré-Coeur might be as lovely as the views *from* Sacré-Coeur, especially as the sun is setting or rising.

SACRÉ-COEUR

✉ *Pl. du Parvis-du-Sacré-Coeur, Montmartre* ☎ *01–53–41–89–00* ⊕ *www.sacre-coeur-montmartre.com* 💳 *Basilica free; dome €6, crypte €3, combined ticket €8* ⊙ *Basilica daily 6 am–10:30 pm; dome Oct.–Apr., daily 9–5; May.–Sept., daily 8:30–8; crypt Thurs.–Mon. 10–5* Ⓜ *Anvers, plus funicular; Jules Joffrin, plus Montmartrobus.*

TIPS

■ The best time to visit Sacré-Coeur is early morning or early evening, and preferably not on a Sunday, when the crowds are thick. If you're coming to worship, there are daily masses.

■ Photographers angling for the perfect shot of the church should aim for a clear blue-sky day or arrive at dusk, when the pink sky plays nicely with the lights of the basilica.

■ To avoid the steps, take the funicular, which costs one métro ticket each way.

It's hard to not feel as though you're climbing up to heaven when you visit Sacred Heart Basilica, the white castle in the sky, perched atop Montmartre. The French government commissioned it in 1873 to symbolize the return of self-confidence after the devastating years of the Commune and Franco-Prussian War; and architect Paul Abadie employed elements from Romanesque and Byzantine styles when designing it—a mélange many critics dismissed as gaudy. Construction lasted until World War I, and the church was finally consecrated in 1919.

Highlights

Many people come to Sacré-Coeur to admire the superlative view from the top of its 271-foot-high dome. If you opt to skip the climb up the spiral staircase, the view from the front steps is still ample compensation for the trip.

Inside, expect another visual treat—namely the massive golden mosaic set high above the choir. Created in 1922 by Luc-Olivier Merson, *Christ in Majesty* depicts Christ with a golden heart and outstretched arms, surrounded by various figures, including the Virgin Mary and Joan of Arc. It remains one of the largest mosaics of its kind. Also worth noting are the seemingly endless vaulted arches in the basilica's crypt; the portico's bronze doors, decorated with biblical scenes; and the stained-glass windows, which were installed in 1922, destroyed by a bombing during World War II (there were miraculously no deaths), and later rebuilt in 1946. In the basilica's 262 foot-high campanile hangs La Savoyarde, one of the world's heaviest bells, weighing about 19 tons.

built around 1840 to boost the area's feeble water supply. ⊠ *Top of Rue Lepic, just before it intersects with Rue Norvins, Montmartre* Ⓜ *Abbesses.*

Saint Jean L'Evangéliste de Montmartre. This eye-catching church was the first modern house of worship built in Paris (1897–1904) and the first to be constructed of reinforced cement. Architect Anatole de Bau-

dot's revolutionary technique defied the accepted rules at the time with its use of unsupported masonry. Critics, who failed to stop construction, feared the building would crumble under its own weight. Today the church attracts a steady flow of visitors curious about its unusual Moorish-inspired facade of redbrick and curved arches. Note the tiny clock at the top left of the bell tower. The compact Art Nouveau interior features impressive stained-glass windows. There are free concerts and art exhibitions from time to time. ⊠ *19 rue des Abbesses, Montmartre* ☎ *01–46–06–43–96* ⊕ *www.saintjeandemontmartre.com* ⊗ *Mon.–Sat. 9–7, Sun. 9:30–6 (7 in summer)* Ⓜ *Abbesses.*

St-Pierre de Montmartre. Tucked in the shadow of mighty Sacré-Coeur is one of the oldest churches in Paris. Built in 1147 on the site of a 5th-century temple to the god Mars, this small sanctuary with its impressive sculpted metal doors was once part of a substantial Benedictine abbey. Besides the church, all that remains is a small cemetery, now closed (you can see it through the ornate metal door on the left as you enter the courtyard). Renovated multiple times through the ages, St-Pierre combines various styles. Interior elements, such as the columns in the nave, are medieval; the facade dates to the 18th century, with renovations in the 19th century; and the impressive stained-glass windows are 20th century. Maurice Utrillo's 1914 painting of the titular saint hangs in the Musée de l'Orangerie. ⊠ *2 rue du Mont Cenis, off Pl. du Tertre, Montmartre* ☎ *01–46–06–57–63* ⊕ *www.saintpierredemontmartre.net* ⊗ *Daily 9–7* Ⓜ *Anvers.*

Studio 28. This little movie house has a distinguished history: when it opened in 1928, it was the first theater in the world purposely built for *art et essai*, or experimental film (Luis Bruñel and Salvador Dali's *L'age d'or* caused a riot when it premiered here). Through the years artists and writers came to see "seventh art" creations by directors such as Jean Cocteau, François Truffaut, and Orson Welles. Today it's a repertory cinema, showing first-runs, just-runs, and previews—usually in their original language. In the back of the movie house is a cozy bar and café that has a quiet outdoor terrace decorated with murals of film stars. Oh, and those charmingly bizarre chandeliers in the *salle*? Cocteau designed them. ⊠ *10 rue Tholozé, Montmartre* ☎ *01–46–06–36–07* ⊕ *www.cinemastudio28.com* Ⓜ *Abbesses.*

THE MARAIS

GETTING ORIENTED

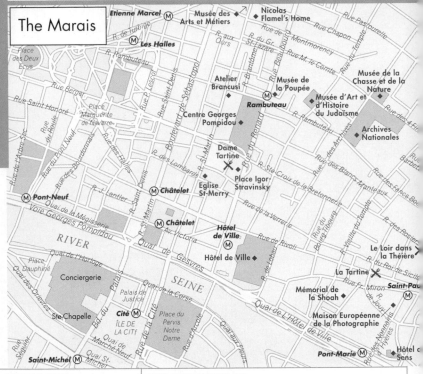

The Marais

Etienne Marcel Ⓜ
Rue de Turbigo
Ⓜ Les Halles
R. Rambuteau
R. Berger
Place des Deux Écus
Rue Saint Honoré
R. du Pont Neuf
R. de l'Arbre Sec
Place Marguerite de Navarre
R. de l'Essol
Boulevard de Sébastopol
Rue Saint Denis
R. des Halles
R. des Bourdonnais
R. de la Monnaie
Ⓜ Pont-Neuf
Quai de la Mégisserie
Voie Georges Pompidou
R. J. Lantier
R. St-Martin
Ⓜ Châtelet
Av. Victoria
Ⓜ Châtelet
RIVER
Quai de l'Horloge
Quai de Gesvres
Place Dauphine
Conciergerie
Palais de Justice
Quai des Orfèvres
Bd. du Palais
Quai de la Corse
SEINE
Ste-Chapelle
Cité Ⓜ
ÎLE DE LA CITÉ
Place du Parvis Notre Dame
Rue de la Cité
Quai Saint-Michel
Rue de Marché-Neuf
Ⓜ Saint-Michel
Quai St-Michel
R. St-Martin
Musée des Arts et Métiers ◆
Nicolas Flamel's Home ◆
Rue de St-Montmorency
Rue M-le-Comte
R. aux Ours
R. du Gr. St-Lazare
R. Beaubourg
R. Brantôme
Rue Chapon
Rue du Temple
Rue Pastourelle
Atelier Brancusi ◆
Musée de la Poupée
Ⓜ Rambuteau
Centre Georges Pompidou ◆
R. du Renard
R. Rambuteau
Musée de la Chasse et de la Nature
Musée d'Art et d'Histoire du Judaïsme ◆
Archives Nationales ◆
Rue des Archives
Rue Vieille du Temple
Rue des 4 Fils
Rue Barbet
Dame Tartine ✕
R. des Lombards
Eglise St-Merry
Place Igor Stravinsky
R. Ste-Croix de la Bretonnerie
Rue des Blancs Manteaux
Rue des Francs Bourgeois
Hôtel de Ville
Rue de la Verrerie
Rue de Rivoli
Rue du Bourg Tibourg
Vieille du Temple
Rue des Rosiers
Le Loir dans la Thèière
Hôtel de Ville ◆
R. de Lobau
La Tartine
R. du Roi de Sicile
Saint-Paul Ⓜ
Mémorial de la Shoah ◆
Rue Fr. Miron
R. de Jouy
R. Ar.
Quai de L'Hôtel de Ville
Maison Européenne de la Photographie
Rue des Nonnains d'Hyères
Pont-Marie Ⓜ
Hôtel de Sens
Place des Deux Écus

| GETTING HERE | TOP REASONS TO GO |

The Marais includes the 3e and 4e arrondissements. It's a pleasant walk from the Beaubourg—the area around Centre Pompidou—into the heart of the Marais. Rue Rambuteau turns into Rue des Francs Bourgeois, which runs right into Place des Vosges. If you're going by métro, the most central stop is St-Paul on Line 1. If you're going to the Pompidou, take Line 11 to Rambuteau. For the Musée Picasso, the closest stop is St-Sébastien Froissart on Line 8. For the 3e arrondissement, get off at Arts et Métiers on Line 3 or 11, or Filles du Calvaire on Line 8.

Centre Pompidou. The city's leading modern art museum is also a vast arts center presenting films, theater, and dance performances.

Place des Vosges. Paris's prettiest square surrounds a manicured park whose inviting patches of grass are—unusual for Paris—accessible to those needing a siesta.

Musée Picasso. This is a must-stop for fans of the Spanish master, who painted some of his best work while living in the French capital.

Jewish history tour. The historic Jewish quarter has two world-class sites: Mémorial de la Shoah (the Holocaust Memorial) and the Musée d'Art et d'Histoire du Judaïsme, with fascinating artwork and cultural artifacts.

No reason at all. Lose yourself in this neighborhood. Explore the tiny streets near the Centre Pompidou, grab a falafel sandwich on Rue des Rosiers, or people-watch in a café on Rue Vieille du Temple.

BEST CAFÉS

Dame Tartine. Cafés abound around the Centre Pompidou, but this one—overlooking the Stravinsky fountain, with its colorful sculptures—is a good choice. You won't go wrong with one of their many *tartines*, toasts topped with delicious ingredients. ⊠ *2 rue Brisemiche, Marais* ☎ *01–42–77–32–22* Ⓜ *Rambuteau.*

La Tartine. This calm café on busy Rue de Rivoli is a local favorite with an impressive wine list. Try the €8 French onion soup or indulge in classic French dishes like *steak frites* or even escargots. ⊠ *24 rue de Rivoli, Marais* ☎ *01–42–72–76–85* Ⓜ *St-Paul.*

Le Loir dans la Théière. Sink into a comfortable shabby armchair at this popular tearoom, whose name translates to the Dormouse in the Teapot (from *Alice in Wonderland*). The savory tarts are stellar, but the real stars are desserts like the decadent chocolate crumble tart. ⊠ *3 rue des Rosiers, Marais* ☎ *01–42–72–90–61* Ⓜ *St-Paul.*

MAKING THE MOST OF YOUR TIME

The Marais has something for everyone, and how much time you spend here depends on how much time you have in Paris. One day seems painfully short, but it would allow you to take a do-it-yourself walking tour, peeking into private courtyards and picnicking in the Place des Vosges as you proceed. Leave at least two days if your itinerary includes the Centre Pompidou and the Musée Picasso. In three days you could cover some of the smaller museums, which are well worth visiting as many are housed in exquisite mansions. If time permits, wander to the 3e arrondissement to see the charming streets, away from the crowds, or drop into the quirky science-centric Musée des Arts et Métiers. Sunday afternoon is a lively time to come because many shops are open, notably on Rue des Francs-Bourgeois. This neighborhood thrives after dark as well; business is brisk at cafés and bars—particularly those aimed at the gay community.

Sightseeing
★★★★★
Dining
★★★★
Lodging
★★★★
Shopping
★★★★★
Nightlife
★★★★

From swampy to swanky, the Marais has a fascinating history. Like an aging pop star, the *quartier* has remade itself many times, and today retains several identities. It's the city's epicenter of cool with hip boutiques, designer hotels, and art galleries galore; the hub of Paris's gay community; and, though fading, the nucleus of Jewish life. You could easily spend your entire visit to Paris in this neighborhood—there is that much to do.

Updated by
Jack Vermee

"Marais" means marsh, and that is exactly what this area was until the 12th century, when it was converted to farmland. In 1605 Henri IV began building the Place Royale (today's Place des Vosges, the oldest square in Paris), which touched off a building boom, and the wealthy and fabulous moved in. Despite the odors—the area was one of the city's smelliest—it remained the chic quarter until Louis XIV moved his court to Versailles, trailed by dispirited aristocrats unhappy to decamp to the country. Merchants moved into their exquisite *hôtels particuliers* (private mansions), which are some of the city's best surviving examples of Baroque architecture. Here you can see the hodgepodge of narrow streets that so vexed Louis Napoléon and his sidekick, Baron Haussmann, who feared a redux of the famous *barricades* that Revolutionaries threw up to thwart the monarchy. Haussmann leveled scores of blocks like these, creating the wide, arrow-straight avenues that are a hallmark of modern Paris. Miraculously, the Marais escaped destruction, though much of it fell victim to neglect and ruin. Thanks to restoration efforts over the past half century, the district is enjoying its latest era of greatness, and the apartments here—among the city's oldest—are also the most in demand, with *beaucoup* charm, exposed beams, and steep crooked staircases barely wide enough to fit a supermodel. (Should you be lucky enough to find an elevator, don't expect it to fit your suitcase.) Notice the impressive *portes cochères,* the huge doors built to accommodate aristocratic carriages that today open into many sublime courtyards and hidden gardens.

The 4e arrondissement, the Marais's glitzier half, is sandwiched between two opposite poles—the regal **Place des Vosges** in the east and the eye-teasing modern masterpiece **Centre Pompidou** in the west. Between these points you'll find most of the main sites, including the **Musée Picasso**, the **Maison Européenne de la Photographie**, and the **Musée Carnavalet**, which is the best place to see how the city evolved through the ages. To tour an exquisitely restored 17th-century *hôtel particulier*, visit the excellent **Musée Cognacq-Jay** or wander into the manicured back garden of the magnificent **Hôtel de Sully**. To the north, the quieter 3e arrondissement is a lovely neighborhood to explore. Techies will appreciate a stop at the **Musée des Arts and Métiers**, Europe's oldest science museum.

> ### FREE IN LE MARAIS
>
> The moving displays at the **Mémorial de la Shoah** are always free, as are the engaging permanent collections at the **Maison de Victor Hugo**, the **Musée Carnavalet**, and the **Musée Cognacq-Jay**. Entry fees are also waived daily at the Atelier Brancusi, a small exhibition space in the **Centre Pompidou**, while the center's renowned modern art museum is (like all national museums) free on the first Sunday of the month. The **Maison Européenne de la Photographie** is free on Wednesday after 5, and the **Église St-Merry** hosts free classical music concerts on the weekend.

Paris's **Jewish quarter** has existed here in some form since the 13th century, and still thrives around Rue des Rosiers, even as hip boutiques encroach on the traditional bakeries, delis, and falafel shops. Not far away is the beating heart of the gay Marais, radiating out from Rue Vieille du Temple, along Rue St-Croix de la Bretonnerie to Rue du Temple, where you can find trendy cafés, shops, and cool nightspots aimed at gays but welcoming to all.

The 3e arrondissement half of the Marais, around Rue de Bretagne, has evolved into one of Paris's most in-demand areas to live—and one of the most interesting areas to explore. Here you can find art galleries, boutiques, and funky cafés and bars off the tourist track.

TOP ATTRACTIONS

3e arrondissement. The thick crowds that flock to Place des Vosges rarely venture to the other side of the Marais: the 3e arrondissement, which has morphed into one of the hottest neighborhoods in Paris. Good luck finding an apartment to rent here—most are small walk-ups with exposed wooden beams and lots of charm. But even if you can't move in, you can enjoy this trendy *quartier* like a local. First, head to Rue de Bretagne, the main drag. Stop for lunch at one of the food stalls in the Marché des Enfants Rouges (No. 39, open Tuesday through Sunday): it's the oldest covered market in Paris. Next, explore narrow side streets, like rues Charlot, Debelleyme, and Poitou, lined with art galleries and small boutiques. Stop for a real English scone at the Marais outpost of the popular Rose Bakery (30 rue Debelleyme); try a cup of Joe and a croissant at Poilâne (38 rue Debelleyme); or treat yourself to a gelato at

Mary's (1 rue Charles-Francois Dupuis). Across the street is the 19th-century iron-and-glass Carreau du Temple, which, after a long overdue renovation, will reopen as a locally driven arts and sports community center. This is the site of the former Templar Tower, where Louis XIV and Marie-Antoinette were imprisoned before the king's date with the guillotine (Napoléon later razed it). For your evening aperitif, make a beeline for the buzzy Café Charlot, at 38 rue de Bretagne. If you're in the mood for couscous, try Chez Omar, a neighborhood institution at No. 47. ⊠ *Marais.*

FAMILY
Fodor's Choice
★

Centre Pompidou
See highlighted listing in this chapter.

Église St-Merry. This impressive Gothic church, in the shadow of the Centre Pompidou, was completed in 1550. Notable features include the turret (it contains the oldest bell in Paris, cast in 1331) and an 18th-century pulpit supported on carved palm trees. There are free concerts here Saturday at 8 pm and Sunday at 4 pm. See the website for more information. ⊠ *76 rue de la Verrerie, Beaubourg/Les Halles* ☎ *01–42–71–93–93* ⊕ *www.accueilmusical.fr* Ⓜ *Hôtel de Ville.*

Hôtel de Sully (*Hôtel de Béthune-Sully*). This early Baroque gem, built in 1624, is one of the city's loveliest hôtels particuliers. Like much of the area, it fell into ruin until the 1950s, when it was rescued by the administration of French historic monuments, the Centre des Monuments Nationaux, which is based here. The recently renovated headquarters aren't open to the public; however, you are welcome to enjoy the equally lovely garden. Stroll through it, past the Orangerie, to find a small passage into nearby Place des Vosges: Sully's best buddy, King Henri IV, would have lived there had he not been assassinated in 1610. ■ TIP→ **An onsite bookstore (with a 17th-century ceiling of exposed wooden beams) stocks specialized Paris guides in English.** ⊠ *62 rue St-Antoine, Marais* ☎ *01–44–61–21–50* ⊕ *www.sully.monuments-nationaux.fr* ☉ *Daily 9–7* Ⓜ *St-Paul.*

Hôtel de Ville. Overlooking the Seine, City Hall contains the residence and offices of the mayor. Reconstructed in 1873 after an attack by rioting crowds, it is one of the city's most stunning buildings, made all the more dramatic by elaborate nighttime lighting. There are frequent free exhibits celebrating famous photographers like Doisneau or Atget and their notable subjects, often the city of Paris herself—the entrance is on the side across from the department store BHV. Alas, the impressive interior, with lavish reception halls, is open only for public visits during Patrimony Weekend in September, but the grand public square out front is always lively, playing host to events and temporary exhibitions. There's a carousel and a beach volleyball court (or similar) in summer, and an ice-skating rink (with skate rental available) in winter. ⊠ *Pl. de l'Hôtel-de-Ville, Marais* Ⓜ *Hôtel de Ville.*

La Gaîté Lyrique. One of Paris's newest contemporary art venues combines innovative exhibits with live musical performances and a multimedia space that features a library, movies, and free video games. Think of it as a smaller, more interactive Centre Pompidou. La Gaîté Lyrique occupies three floors of a 19th-century theater—remnants of which are visible in the café upstairs. ⊠ *3 bis rue Papin, Marais* ☎ *01–53–01–52–00* ⊕ *www.gaite-lyrique.net* ⊠ *Free; €5–€7 for temporary exhibitions; concerts prices vary* ☉ *Tues. 2–10, Wed.–Sat. 2–8, Sun. 2–7; closed Mon.* Ⓜ *Réaumur–Sébastopol.*

Maison de Victor Hugo. France's most famous scribe lived in this house on the northeast corner of Place des Vosges between 1832 and 1848. It's now a museum dedicated to the multitalented author of *Les Misérables*. In Hugo's apartment on the second floor, you can see the tall desk, next to the short bed, where he began writing his masterwork *Les Miz* (as always, standing up). There are manuscripts and early editions of the novel on display, as well as others such as *The Hunchback of Notre Dame*. You can see illustrations of Hugo's writings by other artists, including Bayard's rendering of the impish Cosette holding her giant broom (which has graced countless *Les Miz* T-shirts). The collection includes many of Hugo's own, sometimes macabre, ink drawings (he was a fine artist) and furniture from several of his homes. Particularly impressive is the room of carved and painted Chinese-style wooden panels that Hugo designed for the house of his mistress, Juliet Drouet, on the island of Guernsey, when he was exiled there for agitating against Napoléon III. Try to spot the intertwined Vs and Js. (Hint: Look for the angel's trumpet in the left corner.) The first floor is dedicated to temporary exhibitions that often have modern ties to Hugo's work. ⊠ *6 pl. des Vosges, Marais* ☎ *01–42–72–10–16* ⊕ *www.musee-hugo.paris.fr* ⊠ *Free; €5–€7 for temporary exhibitions* ☉ *Tues.–Sun. 10–6; closed Mon.* Ⓜ *St-Paul.*

Maison Européenne de la Photographie (*Center for European Photography*). Much of the credit for the city's ascendancy as a hub of international photography goes to MEP and its director, Jean-Luc Montcrosso, who also founded Paris's hugely successful Mois de la Photo festival (a biennial event held in November of even-numbered years). The MEP hosts up to four simultaneous exhibitions, changing about every three months. Shows feature the work of an international crop of photographers and video artists. Works by superstar Annie Leibovitz or designer-photographer Karl Lagerfeld may overlap with a collection of self-portraits by an up-and-coming Japanese artist. MEP often stages retrospectives of the classics (by Doisneau, Cartier-Bresson, Man Ray, and others) from its vast private collection. ■TIP➜ **Programs are available in English and English-language tours are sometimes given; check the website for details.** ⊠ *5 rue de Fourcy, Marais* ☎ *01–44–78–75–00* ⊕ *www.mep-fr.org* ⊠ *€8, free Wed. after 5* ☉ *Wed.–Sun. 11–8; closed Mon.–Tues.* Ⓜ *St-Paul.*

Mémorial de la Shoah (*Memorial to the Holocaust*). The first installation in this compelling memorial and museum is the deeply moving Wall of Names, tall plinths honoring the 76,000 French Jews deported from France to Nazi concentration camps, of whom only 2,500 survived. Opened in 2005, the center has an archive on the victims, a library, and a gallery hosting temporary exhibitions. The permanent collection includes riveting artifacts and photographs from the camps, along with video testimony from survivors. The children's memorial is particularly

CENTRE POMPIDOU

✉ Pl. Georges-Pompidou, Beaubourg/Les Halles ☎ 01–44–78–12–33 ⊕ www. centrepompidou.fr 🖳 Museum and exhibitions €11–€13 (free first Sun. of month); Atelier Brancusi free ⊙ Museum and exhibitions Wed.–Mon. 11–9 (extended hrs Thurs. during temporary exhibitions); Atelier Brancusi Wed.–Mon. 2–6; closed Tues. Ⓜ Rambuteau.

TIPS

■ The Pompidou's permanent collection takes up a relatively small amount of the space when you consider this massive building's other features: temporary exhibition galleries, with a special wing for design and architecture; a highly regarded free reference library (there's often a queue of university students on Rue Renard waiting to get in); and the basement, which includes two cinemas, a theater, a dance space, and a small, free exhibition space.

■ On your way up the escalator, you'll have spectacular views of Paris, ranging from the Tour Montparnasse, to the left, around to the hilltop Sacré-Coeur on the right.

■ The trendy rooftop restaurant, Georges (wwww. beaumarly.com/en/georges/ home), is a romantic spot for dinner. Be sure to reserve a table near the window.

■ There are public toilets on the lower level without the long lines of those on the ground floor.

Love it or hate it, the Pompidou is certainly the city's most unique-looking building. Most Parisians have warmed to the industrial, Lego-like exterior that caused a scandal when it opened in 1977. Named after French president Georges Pompidou (1911–74), it was designed by then-unknowns Renzo Piano and Richard Rogers. The architects' claim to fame was putting the building's guts on the outside and color-coding them: water pipes are green, air ducts are blue, electrics are yellow, and things like elevators and escalators are red. Art from the 20th century to the present day is what you can find inside.

Highlights

The Musée National d'Art Moderne (Modern Art Museum, entrance on Level 4) occupies the top two levels. Level 5 is devoted to modern art from 1905 to 1960, including major works by Matisse, Modigliani, Marcel Duchamp, and Picasso; Level 4 is dedicated to contemporary art from the '60s on, including video installations. The Galerie d'Enfants (Children's Gallery) on the mezzanine level has interactive exhibits designed to keep the kids busy. Outside, next to the museum's sloping plaza—where throngs of teenagers hang out (and where there's free Wi-Fi)—is the Atelier Brancusi. This small, airy museum contains four rooms reconstituting Brancusi's Montparnasse studios with works from all periods of his career. On the opposite side, in the Place Igor-Stravinsky, is the Stravinsky fountain, which has 16 gyrating mechanical figures in primary colors, including a giant pair of ruby red lips. On the opposite side of Rue Rambuteau, on the wall at the corner of Rue Clairvaux and Passage Brantôme, is the appealingly bizarre mechanical brass-and-steel clock, Le Défenseur de Temps.

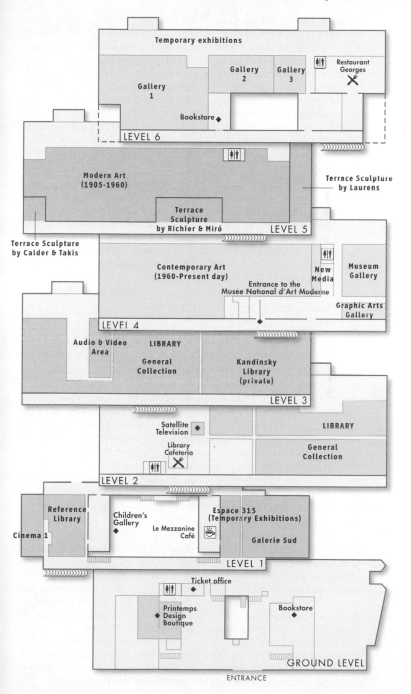

Temporary exhibitions

Gallery 2

Gallery 3

Restaurant Georges

Gallery 1

Bookstore

LEVEL 6

Modern Art (1905-1960)

Terrace Sculpture by Laurens

Terrace Sculpture by Richier & Miró

LEVEL 5

Terrace Sculpture by Calder & Takis

Contemporary Art (1960-Present day)

New Media

Museum Gallery

Entrance to the Musee National d'Art Moderne

Graphic Arts Gallery

LEVEL 4

Audio & Video Area

LIBRARY

General Collection

Kandinsky Library (private)

LEVEL 3

8

Satellite Television

LIBRARY

Library Cafeteria

General Collection

LEVEL 2

Reference Library

Children's Gallery

Espace 315 (Temporary Exhibitions)

Cinema 1

Le Mezzanine Café

Galerie Sud

LEVEL 1

Ticket office

Printemps Design Boutique

Bookstore

GROUND LEVEL

ENTRANCE

poignant and not for the faint of heart—scores of back-lighted photographs show the faces of many of the 11,000 murdered French children. The crypt, a giant black marble Star of David, contains ashes recovered from the camps and the Warsaw ghetto. You can see the orderly drawers containing small files on Jews kept by the French police. (France only officially acknowledged the Vichy government's role in 1995.) The history of anti-Semitic persecution in the world is revisited as well as the rebounding state of Jewry today. ■**TIP➔ There is a free guided tour in English the second Sunday of every month at 3 pm.** ☒ *17 rue Geoffroy l'Asnier, Marais* ☎ *01–42–77–44–72* ⊕ *www.memorialdelashoah.org* ☞ *Free* ☉ *Sun.–Fri. 10–6 (Thurs. until 10); closed Sat.* Ⓜ *Pont Marie or St-Paul.*

Fodor's Choice
★

Musée Carnavalet. If it has to do with Parisian history, it's here. A fascinating hodgepodge of artifacts and art, the collection ranges from the prehistoric canoes used by Parisii tribes to the furniture of the cork-lined bedroom where Marcel Proust labored over his evocative novels. Thanks to scores of paintings, nowhere else in Paris can you get such a precise picture of the city's evolution through the ages. The museum fills two adjacent mansions, the Hôtel Le Peletier de St-Fargeau and the Hôtel Carnavalet. The latter is a Renaissance jewel that in the mid-1600s became the home of writer Madame de Sévigné. Throughout her long life, Sévigné wrote hundreds of frank and funny letters to her daughter, giving an incomparable view of both public and private life during the time of Louis XIV. The museum offers a glimpse into her world, but the collection covers far more than just the 17th century. The exhibits on the Revolution are especially interesting, with scale models of guillotines and a replica of the Bastille prison carved from one of its stones. Louis XVI's prison cell is reconstructed along with mementos of his life, even medallions containing locks of his family's hair. Other impressive interiors are reconstructed from the Middle Ages through the Rococo period and into Art Nouveau—showstoppers include the Fouquet jewelry shop and the Café de Paris's original furnishings. The sculpted garden at 16 rue des Francs Bourgeois is open from April to the end of October. Extensive renovations, begun in 2013, may be ongoing; be prepared for room closures. ☒ *23 rue de Sévigné, Marais* ☎ *01–44–59–58–58* ⊕ *www.carnavalet.paris.fr* ☞ *Free; around €7 for temporary exhibitions* ☉ *Tues.–Sun. 10–6; closed Mon.* Ⓜ *St-Paul.*

Musée Cognacq-Jay. One of the loveliest museums in Paris, this 16th-century Rococo-style mansion contains an outstanding collection of mostly 18th-century artwork in its rooms of *boiserie* (intricately carved wood paneling). A tour through them allows a rare glimpse into the lifestyle of wealthy 19th-century Parisians. Ernest Cognacq, founder of the now closed department store La Samaritaine, and his wife, Louise Jay, amassed furniture, porcelain, and paintings—notably by Fragonard, Watteau, François Boucher, and Tiepolo—to create one of the world's finest private collections of this period. Some of the best displays are also the smallest, like the tiny enamel medallion portraits showcased on the second floor; or, on the third floor, the glass cases filled with exquisite inlaid snuff boxes, sewing cases, pocket watches, perfume bottles, and cigar cutters. ■**TIP➔ Exhibits are labeled in French only, but free**

pamphlets and €5 audioguides are available in English. ☒ *8 rue Elzévir, Marais* ☎ *01–40–27–07–21* ⊕ *www.cognacq-jay.paris.fr* ☜ *Free; €5
for temporary exhibitions* ⊘ *Tues.–Sun. 10–6; closed Mon.* Ⓜ *St-Paul.*

Musée d'Art et d'Histoire du Judaïsme. This excellent museum traces the
tempestuous history of French and European Jews through art and
history. Opened in 1998 in the refined 17th-century Hôtel St-Aignan,
exhibits have good explanatory texts in English, and the free English
audioguide is a must; guided tours in English are also available on
request. Highlights include 13th-century tombstones excavated in Paris;
a wooden model of a destroyed Eastern European synagogue; a roomful
of early paintings by Marc Chagall; and Christian Boltanski's stark, two-
part tribute to Shoah (Holocaust) victims in the form of plaques on an
outer wall naming the (mainly Jewish) inhabitants of the Hôtel St-Aignan in 1939, and canvas hangings with the personal data of the 13 residents who were deported and died in concentration camps. ■**TIP→** The
rear-facing windows offer a view of the Jardin Anne Frank. To visit it, use
the entrance on Impasse Berthaud, off Rue Beaubourg, just north of Rue
Rambuteau. ☒ *71 rue du Temple, Marais* ☎ *01–53–01–86–60* ⊕ *www.
mahj.org* ☜ *€8; €10 with temporary exhibitions* ⊘ *Weekdays 11–6, Sun.
10–6; closed Sat.* Ⓜ *Rambuteau or Hôtel de Ville.*

FAMILY **Musée des Arts et Métiers.** Science buffs should not miss this cavernous
museum, Europe's oldest dedicated to invention and technology. It's a
treasure trove of wonkiness with 80,000 instruments, machines, and
gadgets—including 16th-century astrolabes, Pascal's first mechanical
calculator, and film-camera prototypes by the Frères Lumière. You can
watch video simulations of groundbreaking architectural achievements,
like the cast-iron dome, or see how Jacquard's machine revolutionized
cloth-making. Kids will love the flying machines (among them the first
plane to cross the English Channel), and the impressive display of old
automobiles in the high-ceilinged chapel of St-Martin-des-Champs. Also
in the chapel is a copy of Foucault's Pendulum, which proved to the
world in 1851 that the Earth rotated (demonstrations are staged daily
at noon and 5). The building, built between the 11th and 13th centuries, was a church and priory. It was confiscated during the Revolution,
and after incarnations as a school and a weapons factory, became a
museum in 1799. Most displays have information in English, but having an English audioguide (€5) helps. There is a quiet café on the first
floor. ■**TIP→** If you're taking the subway here, check out the platform
of métro Line 11 in the Arts and Métiers station—one of the city's most
elaborate—made to look like the inside of a machine, complete with
rust-color metal walls, giant bolts, and faux gears. ☒ *60 rue Réaumur,
Opéra/Grands Boulevards* ☎ *01–53–01–82–00* ⊕ *www.arts-et-metiers.
net* ☜ *€6.50; €7.50 with temporary exhibitions* ⊘ *Tues., Wed., and
Fri.–Sun. 10–6, Thurs. 10–9:30; closed Mon.* Ⓜ *Arts et Métiers.*

FodorśChoice **Musée Picasso**
★   *See highlighted listing in this chapter.*

8

MUSÉE PICASSO

✉ *5 rue de Thorigny, Marais*
☎ *01–42–71–25–21* ⊕ *www.*
musee-picasso.fr ✉ *Admission to be determined when opened* Ⓜ *St-Sébastien.*

TIPS

■ The reopening date remains subject to change, so check the website for updates or call before you go in case of further delays.

To the chagrin of Picasso fans everywhere, this immensely popular museum in the regal 17th-century Hôtel Salé closed for a top-to-bottom overhaul in 2009, and delays have pushed back the reopening date to late 2014. (About 200 works from the permanent collection have been on the road in the United States and elsewhere in the interim.) The good news is that the museum will emerge from its €52 million makeover thoroughly transformed, with more than double the dedicated public space. The exhibition area's 34 rooms will cover almost 41,000 square feet; and a sprawling new building in the back garden, dedicated to temporary exhibitions and other programs, will open when the final stage of renovations wraps up.

Highlights

The collection of more than 100,000 paintings, sculptures, drawings, documents, and other archival materials (much of it given to the government by Picasso's heirs to settle a hefty tax bill following his death in 1973) spans the artist's entire career; and while it doesn't include his most recognizable works it does contain many of the paintings and sculptures treasured most by Picasso himself—among them pieces from his personal collection created by friends and influences such as Matisse, Braque, Cézanne, and Rousseau.

NEED A
BREAK?

Jardin Francs-Bourgeois-Rosiers. Tucked behind the Maison de l'Europe, the Jardin Francs-Bourgeois-Rosiers is a Zen gem in the heart of the bustling Marais. Bring a snack to enjoy in this quiet garden amid the roses and little trees. Open daily from 2 to 5:15 in winter, 2 to 7 in summer. ✉ *35–37 rue des Francs Bourgeois, Marais.*

FAMILY
Fodor's Choice
★

Place des Vosges

See highlighted listing in this chapter.

WORTH NOTING

Agoudas Hakehilos Synagogue. Art Nouveau genius Hector Guimard built this unique synagogue (also called Synagogue de la Rue Pavée) in 1913 for a Polish-Russian Orthodox association. The facade resembles an open book: Guimard used the motif of the Ten Commandments to inspire the building's shape and its interior, which can only rarely be visited. Knock on the door and see if the caretaker will let you upstairs to the balcony, where you can admire Guimard's well-preserved decor. Like other Parisian synagogues, the front door of this address was dynamited by Nazis on Yom Kippur, 1941. The Star of David over the door was added after the building was restored. ✉ *10 rue Pavé, Marais* ☎ *01–48–87–21–54* Ⓜ *St-Paul.*

NEED A
BREAK?

L'As du Falafel. Jewish food is tops in the Marais, where you can get a falafel sandwich to go, loaded with salad and sauce, for €5.50. You'll find one of the best versions here. ✉ *34 rue des Rosiers, Marais* ☎ *01–48–87–63–60* ⊘ *Closed Fri. at sundown and Sat.*

Sacha Finkelsztajn–La Boutique Jaune. Order a Yiddish sandwich (a poppy seed roll stacked with meats) or baba ghanoush (eggplant puree) at Sacha Finkelsztajn's—a family-run favorite since 1946. It also sells delicious cakes and pastries like apple strudel. ✉ *27 rue des Rosiers, Marais* ☎ *01–42–72–78–91* ⊕ *www.laboutiquejaune.com* ⊘ *Closed Tues. and mid-July–mid-Aug.*

Schwartz's Deli. Schwartz's Deli—a taste of New York's Lower East Side—serves matzo ball soup, piled-high pastrami sandwiches, and strawberry cheesecake. You'll find other locations around Place du Trocadéro and Place des Ternes. ✉ *16 rue des Ecouffes, Marais* ☎ *01–48–87–31–29* ⊕ *www.schwartzsdeli.fr* ⊘ *Weekdays noon–3 and 7:30–11, Sat. noon–5 and 7–11:30, Sun. noon–5 and 7–11.*

Archives Nationales. Thousands of important historical documents are preserved inside Hôtel de Soubise and Hôtel de Rohan—a pair of spectacular buildings built in 1705 as private homes. Fans of the decorative arts will appreciate a visit to the former, where the well-preserved private apartments of the Prince and Princess de Soubise are among the first examples of the Rococo style, which preceded the more somber Baroque opulence of Louis XIV. Hôtel de Soubise also has a museum

8

that displays documents dating from 625 to the 20th century. High-lights include the Edict of Nantes (1598), the Treaty of Westphalia (1648), the wills of Louis XIV and Napoléon, and the Declaration of Human Rights (1789). Louis XVI's diary is also here, containing his sadly clueless entry for July 14, 1789—the day the Bastille was stormed and the French Revolution was launched. The Hôtel de Rohan, open to the public only during Patrimony weekend in September, was built for Soubise's son, Cardinal Rohan. Before you leave, notice the medieval turrets in the courtyard: this is the Porte de Clisson, all that remains of a stately 14th-century mansion. ⊠ *60 rue des Francs-Bourgeois, Marais* 🕾 *01–40–27–60–96* ⊕ *www.archives-nationales.culture.gouv.fr* 🎫 *€3 (free first Sun. of month); €6 temporary exhibitions* ☉ *Mon. and Wed.– Fri. 10–5:30, weekends 2–5:30; closed Tues.* Ⓜ *Rambuteau.*

Hôtel de Sens. One of the few remaining structures in Paris from the Middles Ages, this little castle was most famously the home of Queen Margot, who took up residence here in 1605 after her marriage to Henry IV was annulled. Margot was known for her many lovers (she supposedly wore wigs made from locks of their hair) and reputedly ordered a servant beheaded in the courtyard after he ridiculed one of her companions. The street is said to be named after a fig tree she ordered cut down because it was inconveniencing her carriage. Perhaps for that reason there's a fig tree planted in the elegant rear garden, which is open to the public. Notice the cannonball lodged in the front facade com-memorating a battle here during the three-day revolution in July 1830. Built for Archbishop of Sens in 1475, the castle was extensively reno-vated in the 20th century and is today home to the Bibliothèque Forney, a library that also stages temporary exhibitions drawn from its extensive collection of fine and graphic arts. ⊠ *1 rue du Figuier, Marais* 🕾 *01– 42–78–14–60* ⊕ *equipement.paris.fr/bibliotheque-forney-18* 🎫 *Library free; €6 for exhibitions* ☉ *Library Tues., Fri., and Sat. 1–7:30, Wed. and Thurs. 10–7:30; exhibitions Tues.–Sat. 1–7* Ⓜ *Pont Marie.*

FAMILY **Musée de la Chasse et de la Nature.** Mark this down as one of Paris's most bizarre—and fascinating—collections. The museum, housed in the gor-geous 17th-century Hôtel de Guénégaud, features lavishly appointed rooms stocked with animal- and hunt-theme art by the likes of Rubens and Gentileschi, plus antique weaponry and taxidermy animals. In a tribute to Art Nouveau, the decor includes chandeliers curled like ant-lers and matching railings. Older kids will appreciate the jaw-dropping Trophy Room with an impressive menagerie of beasts, not to mention the huge polar bear stationed outside. There is a lovely multimedia exhibit on the myth of the unicorn; as well as an interactive display of bird calls. Temporary exhibits and silent auctions take place on the first floor. ⊠ *62 rue des Archives, Marais* 🕾 *01–53–01–92–40* ⊕ *www. chassenature.org* 🎫 *€8* ☉ *Tues.–Sun. 11–6 (Wed. until 9:30); closed Mon.* Ⓜ *Rambuteau.*

FAMILY **Musée de la Poupée** (*Doll Museum*). Providing an impressive overview of dolls through the ages, this charming museum is a little girl's dream. Here you'll see dolls made from Bisque porcelain, sturdy wood, soft cotton, delicate papier mâché, plus the first plastic dolls from the early 20th century. Some play music, others make tea. Cases lining the walls

PLACE DES VOSGES

✉ *Off Rue des Francs Bourgeois, near Rue de Turenne, Marais* Ⓜ *Bastille, St-Paul.*

TIPS

■ One of the best things about this park is that you're actually allowed to sit—or snooze or snack—on the grass during spring and summer.

■ There is no better spot in the Marais for a picnic: you can pick up fixings at the nearby street market on Thursday and Saturday mornings (it's on Boulevard Richard Lenoir between rues Amelot and St-Sabin).

■ The most likely approach to Place des Vosges is from Rue de Francs Bourgeois, the main shopping street. However, for a grander entrance walk along Rue St-Antoine until you get to Rue de Birague, which leads directly into the square.

The oldest square in Paris and—dare we say it?—the most beautiful, Place des Vosges represents an early stab at urban planning. The precise proportions offer a placid symmetry, but things weren't always so calm here. Four centuries ago this was the site of the Palais des Tournelles, home to King Henry II and Queen Catherine de Medici. The couple staged regular jousting tournaments, and during one of them, in 1559, Henry was fatally lanced in the eye. Catherine fled for the Louvre, abandoning her palace and ordering it destroyed. In 1612 it became Place Royal on the occasion of Louis XIII's engagement to Anne of Austria. Napoléon renamed it Place des Vosges to honor the northeast region of Vosges, the first in the country to pony up taxes to the Revolutionary government.

Highlights

At the base of the 36 redbrick-and-stone houses—nine on each side of the square—is an arcaded, covered walkway lined with art galleries, shops, and cafés. There's also an elementary school, a synagogue (whose barrel roof was designed by Gustav Eiffel), and several chic hotels. The formal, gated garden's perimeter is lined with chestnut trees; inside are a children's play area and a fountain.

Aside from hanging out in the park, people come here to see the house of the man who once lived at No. 6—Victor Hugo, the author of *Les Misérables* and *Notre-Dame de Paris* (aka *The Hunchback of Notre-Dame*).

8

are stocked with baby dolls, minidolls (*mignonettes*), and grown-up lady dolls in satin dresses—the foremothers of Barbie. There are also antique toy prams, high chairs, and tattered teddy bears in need of a hug. Too extensive to show at one time, the permanent collection changes frequently and can be arranged by period or theme. Temporary exhibitions might focus on Barbie's evolution or offer a classic look at postwar French dolls. Workshops allow kids to make a doll to take home (they're in French but the mostly bilingual staff is happy to speak English; check the website for details). There's also a doll hospital and a well-stocked gift shop on-site. ⊠ *Impasse Berthaud, Marais* ☎ *01–42–72–73–11* ⊕ *www.museedelapoupeeparis.com* ⊠ *€8; €4 ages 3–11 or €14 with workshop* ⊙ *Tues.–Sat. 1–6; closed Sun. and Mon.* Ⓜ *Rambuteau.*

OFF THE BEATEN PATH

Nicolas Flamel's Home. Built in 1407 and reputed to be the oldest house in Paris (though other buildings claim that title), this abode has a mystical history. Harry Potter fans should take note: this was the real-life residence of Nicolas Flamel, the alchemist whose sorcerer's stone is the source of immortality in the popular book series. A wealthy scribe, merchant, and dabbler in the mystical arts, Flamel willed his home to the city as a dormitory for the poor, on the condition that boarders pray daily for his soul. Today, the building contains apartments and a restaurant. ⊠ *51 rue Montmorency, Marais* Ⓜ *Rambuteau.*

St-Paul–St-Louis. The leading Baroque church in the Marais, its dome rising 180 feet above the crossing, was begun in 1627 by the Jesuits, who modeled it after their Gesù church in Rome. Recently cleaned on the outside but dark and brooding inside, it contains Delacroix's *Christ on the Mount of Olives* in the transept and a shell-shape holy-water font at the entrance, which was donated by Victor Hugo. Hugo lived in nearby Place des Vosges, and his beloved daughter Léopoldine was married here in 1843—though she met a tragic end less than seven months later, when she fell into the Seine and drowned, along with her husband Charles, who tried to save her. ⊠ *99 rue St-Antoine, Marais* ☎ *01–42–72–30–32* ⊕ *www.saintpaulsaintlouis.com* Ⓜ *St-Paul.*

EASTERN PARIS

with Bastille, Canal St-Martin, République,
Oberkampf, and Belleville

GETTING ORIENTED

Eastern Paris

TOP REASONS TO GO

Canal St-Martin. This scenic canal is now one of the city's hottest, hippest hangouts—it's great for strolling, with plenty of galleries, shops, and cafés en route.

Place de la Bastille. The flashpoint of the French Revolution still draws agitators and their frequent noisy demonstrations today. It's also a nightlife hub and home to the Opéra Bastille.

Cimetière du Père-Lachaise. Fans of celebrities, from Frédéric Chopin to Oscar Wilde to Jim Morrison, come to pay tribute at their final resting place.

Parc de la Villette. As the site of the city's well-regarded science museum and planetarium, this is a good place to take the kids or grown-up science buffs.

Viaduc des Arts/Promenade Plantée. An abandoned rail line has been turned into a tree-fringed walkway perched atop a brick viaduct that's bursting with design-oriented boutiques.

BEST CAFÉS

Café A. The Maison de l'architecture—a center for architectural advancement and an international artists' residence, just a short walk from the Canal St-Martin—occupies a one-time monastery. Inside the elegant Renaissance building's courtyard, Café A offers a seasonal menu at prices that are reasonable for this ever-gentrifying neighborhood. In warm weather, you can join trendy locals as they soak up some sun with a glass of wine or a cold beer in the enclosed garden. As an added bonus, the café is open late (Tues.–Sat. 10 am–midnight). ⊠ *148 rue du Faubourg St-Martin, République* ☎ *09–81–29–83–38* Ⓜ *Gare de l'Est.*

Merci. This sweet little café works wonders with a small menu of mostly organic, high-quality ingredients. Come for lunch, tea, or a freshly squeezed juice and watch a classic film projected on the wall. ⊠ *111 bd. Beaumarchais, Bastille* ☎ *01–42–77–79–46* Ⓜ *St-Sébastien Froissart.*

GETTING HERE

Canal St-Martin, Bastille, and Oberkampf include the 10e, 11e, 12e, 19e, and 20e arrondissements. The Bastille métro stop, on lines 1, 5, and 8, is a good place to start. For Canal St-Martin, use the Place de la République stop (lines 3, 5, 8, 9, 11) and walk along Rue Faubourg du Temple, or go to Gare de l'Est stop (lines 4, 5, 7) and walk along Rue des Récollets to the canal. For Oberkampf, go to the Parmentier stop on Line 3 or the Oberkampf stop on Line 9. For the Cimetière du Père-Lachaise, take Line 2 or 3 to the eponymous stop.

MAKING THE MOST OF YOUR TIME

The Canal St-Martin is one of the city's most popular destinations, particularly on Sunday afternoon, when the streets are closed to cars. Have lunch in a café, grab a Vélib' rental bike, and head to Parc de la Villette, or take a canal boat tour. A Sunday-morning stop at the picturesque Marché d'Aligre is also recommended, even if you're not buying. The heaps of fresh produce and colorful flowers hawked by excited vendors are worth seeing. On any day Place de la Bastille is a lively place to stop for drinks or lunch; if time is limited, reserve this neighborhood for after dark, when the streets around Place de la Bastille and Oberkampf really come to life.

9

Sightseeing
★★
Dining
★★★★
Lodging
★★
Shopping
★★★★
Nightlife
★★★★★

The Bastille used to be the star of this area, and a stop here—at the epicenter of the French Revolution—was a must. The small streets forking off Place de la Bastille still buzz at night, thanks to bars, music clubs, and the top-flight Opéra Bastille. But today the neighborhoods farther afield are the real draw, having evolved into some of Paris's top destinations. The Canal St-Martin, once the down-and-out cousin on the northeastern border, is now trend-spotting central, brimming with funky bars, cafés, art galleries, and boutiques. The scene is similar to the south, on rues Oberkampf, St-Maur, and Jean-Pierre-Timbaud, where artists and small designers have set up shop, and where a substantial slice of the city's *bobo* (bourgeois-bohemian) contingent is buying up the no-longer-so-affordable apartments.

Updated by
Jack Vermee

The areas to the north and east of the canal are also flourishing, around the rougher streets near **Ménilmontant** and **Belleville,** home to a small Chinatown (watch your purse and avoid wearing attention-getting jewelry). The city's largest cemetery, **Père Lachaise,** is here, with a roster of famous tenants. Not far away is the impressively wild **Parc Buttes-Chaumont,** with grassy fields, a small Greek-style temple, and sweeping hilltop views of Paris. It's the perfect place to eat a picnic lunch and let museum-weary kids work off some steam. There is a pair of other notable parks to the east: **Parc de la Villette,** where you'll find the city's science museum, and the **Bois de Vincennes.**

Not far from the Bastille opera house, the **Viaduc des Arts** is a much-admired urban-renewal project that transformed an old elevated rail line into arcaded design-focused studios and shops. Along the top, the **Promenade Plantée** makes for a lovely stroll through the 12e arrondissement, a nice middle-class neighborhood with stately apartment buildings and the pretty **Square Trousseau,** gateway to the **Marché d'Aligre** (one of the city's best covered markets). Come on Sunday morning with a shopping basket—or just your camera—when the vendors spill over into neighboring streets.

To the south of **Bastille,** the old wine warehouses at **Bercy** have become a veritable village of shops and restaurants bordering Park de Bercy. Directly across the Seine is the **Bibliothèque National François Mitterand,** the National Library of France, a sprawling complex of modern glass towers opened in 1998.

TOP ATTRACTIONS

FAMILY **Bercy.** Tucked away south of the Gare de Lyon in the 12e arrondissement, blocks of stone warehouses that once stored wine are now home to Bercy Village, a collection of shops and restaurants that stay open unusually late for Paris (shops until 9 pm, Monday to Saturday; restaurants until 2 am daily). You can still see the old train tracks used to transport the wine barrels from the provinces. Adjacent to the shops is the tranquil Parc de Bercy, with lawns, ponds, and flower beds crisscrossed by gravel paths, and the Jardin Yitzhak Rabin, a garden named for the late Nobel Peace Prize winner. On the western edge of the park, near the Bercy métro stop, is the Palais Omnisports, a venue for concerts and sports. Nearby, at 51 rue de Bercy, a cubist building by Frank Gehry houses the Cinémathèque Française, a film buff's paradise showing classic films, many in English. There are frequent homages to directors and actors, plus a cinema library and museum (⇨ *see the listing in Chapter 18, Performing Arts).* ⊠ *Bercy Village, 28 rue François Truffaut, Bercy/Tolbiac* ⊕ *www.bercyvillage.com* ⊙ *Daily 11–9* Ⓜ *Cour St-Emilion, Bercy.*

NEED A BREAK? **Pink Flamingo.** Pink Flamingo is an American-owned pizzeria that will deliver your pie directly to the banks of the canal—they spot you thanks to the pink balloon you're holding. ⊠ *67 rue Bichat, Canal St-Martin* ☎ *01–42–02–31–70* ⊕ *www.pinkflamingopizza.com* Ⓜ *Jacques Bonsergent, Colonel Fabien.*

Fodor's Choice ★ **Canal St-Martin.** This once-forgotten canal has morphed into one of the city's trendiest places to wander. A good time to come is Sunday afternoon, when the Quai de Valmy is closed to cars and some of the shops are open. Rent a bike at any of the many Vélib' stations, stroll along the banks, or go native and cuddle quai-side in the sunshine with someone special.

In 1802 Napoléon ordered the 4.3-km (2.7-mile) canal dug as a source of clean drinking water after cholera and other epidemics swept the city. When it finally opened 23 years later, it stretched north from the Seine at Place de la Bastille to the Canal de l'Ourcq, near La Villette. Baron Haussmann later covered a 1.6-km (1-mile) stretch of it, along today's Boulevard Richard Lenoir. It nearly became a highway in the 1970s, before the city's urban planners regained their senses. These days you

9

can take a boat tour from end to end through the canal's nine locks: along the way, the bridges swing or lift open. The drawbridge with four giant pulleys at Rue de Crimée, near La Villette, was a technological marvel when it opened in 1885.

In recent years gentrification has swept the once-dodgy canal, with artists taking over former industrial spaces and creating studios and galleries. The bar and restaurant scene is hipster central, and small designers have arrived, fleeing expensive rents in Le Marais. To explore this evolving *quartier,* set out on foot: Start on the Quai de Valmy at Rue Faubourg du Temple (use the République métro stop). Here, at Square Frédéric Lemaître facing north, there is a good view of one of the locks (behind you the canal disappears underground). As you head north, detour onto side streets like Rue Beaurepaire, a fashionista destination with several "stock" (or surplus) shops for popular brands, some open on Sunday. Rues Lancry and Vinaigriers are lined with bars, restaurants, and small shops.

A swing bridge across the canal connects Lancry to Rue de la Grange aux Belles, where you'll find the entrance to the massive Hôpital Saint-Louis, built in 1607 to accommodate plague victims and still a working hospital today. In front of you is the entrance to the chapel, which held its first Mass in July 1610, two months after the assassination of the hospital's patron, Henry IV. Stroll the grounds, flanked by the original brick-and-stone buildings with steeply sloping roofs. The peaceful courtyard garden is a neighborhood secret.

Back on Quai Valmy, browse more shops near Rue des Récollets. Nearby is the Jardin Villemin, the 10e arrondissement's largest park (4½ acres) on the former site of another hospital. The nighttime scene, especially in summer, is hopping with twenty-somethings spilling out of cafés and bars and onto the canal banks. If you've made it this far, reward yourself with a fresh taco or burrito at the tiny and authentically Mexican El Nopal taqueria at 3 rue Eugène Varlin. Further up, just past Place Stalingrad, is the Rotonde de la Villette, a lively square with restaurants and twin MK2 cinemas on either side of the canal, with a boat to ferry ticket holders across. **Canauxrama** (⊕ *www.canauxrama. com*) offers 2½-hour boat cruises through the locks (€16 adults; low-season weekday specials are often offered). Embarkation is at each end of the canal: at Bassin de la Villette (*13 quai de la Loire, La Villette*) or Marina Arsenal (*50 bd. de la Bastille, Bastille*). ⊠ *Canal St-Martin* Ⓜ *Jaurès (northern end) or Bastille (southern end).*

NEED A BREAK?   **Hôtel du Nord.** With a retro white facade, the Hôtel du Nord looks like a movie set—in fact, it was famously used by Marcel Carné in his 1938 namesake film. The star, actress-icon Arletty, claimed to be unmoved by the romantic canal-side setting, uttering the memorable line "Atmosphere, atmosphere, I've had it with atmosphere!" Today the restaurant, beautifully restored, is a hipster favorite, though the food is not as fabulous as the ambience. ⊠ *102 quai de Jemmappes, République* ☎ *01–40–40–78–78* ⊕ *www.hoteldunord.org* Ⓜ *Jacques Bonsergent.*

DID YOU KNOW?

Many people take boat rides on the Seine but there are also several companies that offer trips along the Canal St-Martin. Check out ⊕ *en. pariscanal.com* or ⊕ *www. canauxrama.com* for more information.

CANAUXRAMA

CIMETIÈRE DU PÈRE-LACHAISE

✉ *Entrances on Rue des Rondeaux, Bd. de Ménilmontant, and Rue de la Réunion, Père Lachaise* ☎ *01–55–25–82–10* ⊕ *www.pere-lachaise.com* ⊘ *Daily 8–6, 5:30 in winter (opens 8:30 Sat. and 9 Sun.)* Ⓜ *Gambetta, Philippe-Auguste, Père-Lachaise.*

TIPS

■ Pinpoint grave sites on the website before you come, but buy a map anyway outside the entrances—you'll still get lost, but that's part of the fun.

■ One of the best days to visit is on All Saints' Day (November 1), when Parisians bring flowers to adorn the graves of loved ones or favorite celebrities.

Bring a red rose for "the Little Sparrow" Edith Piaf when you visit the cobblestone avenues and towering trees that make this 118-acre oasis of green perhaps the world's most famous cemetery. Named for Père François de la Chaise, Louis XIV's confessor, Père-Lachaise is more than just a who's who of celebrities. The Paris Commune's final battle took place here on May 28, 1871, when 147 rebels were lined up and shot against the Mur des Fédérés (Federalists' Wall) in the southeast corner.

Highlights

Aside from the sheer aesthetic beauty of the cemetery, the main attraction is what (or who, more accurately) is belowground.

Two of the biggest draws are Jim Morrison's grave (with its own guard to keep Doors fans under control) and the life-size bronze figure of French journalist Victor Noir, whose alleged fertility-enhancing power accounts for the patches rubbed smooth by hopeful hands. Other significant grave sites include those of 12th-century French philosopher Pierre Abélard and his lover Héloïse; French writers Colette, Honoré de Balzac, and Marcel Proust; American writers Richard Wright, Gertrude Stein, and Alice B. Toklas; Irish writer Oscar Wilde; French actress Sarah Bernhardt; French composer Georges Bizet; Greek-American opera singer Maria Callas; Franco-Polish composer Frédéric Chopin; painters of various nationalities including Georges-Pierre Seurat, Camille Pissaro, Jean Auguste Dominique Ingres, Jacques-Louis David, Eugène Delacroix, Théodore Géricault, Amedeo Clemente Modigliani, and Max Ernst; French jazz violinist Stephane Grappelli; French civic planner Baron Haussmann; French playwright and actor Molière; and French singer Edith Piaf.

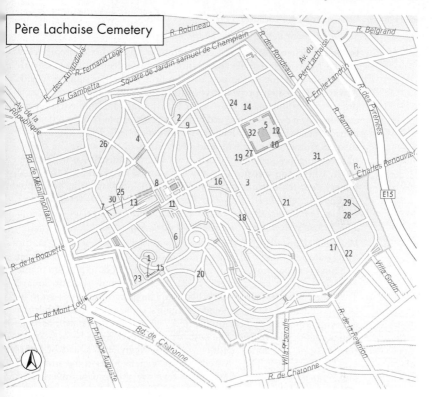

Père Lachaise Cemetery

Pierre Abélard **1**

Honoré de Balzac **2**

Sarah Bernhardt **3**

Georges Bizet **4**

Maria Callas **5**

Frédéric Chopin **6**

Sidonie-Gabrielle Colette ... **7**

Jacques-Louis David **8**

Eugène Delacroix **9**

Max Ernst **10**

Théodore Géricault **11**

Stéphane Grappelli **12**

Baron Haussmann **13**

Sedegh Hedayat **14**

Héloïse **15**

Jean-Auguste-
Dominique Ingres **16**

Amedeo Clemente
Modigliani **17**

Molière (Jean-Baptiste
Poquelina) **18**

Yves Montand **19**

Jim Morrison **20**

Victor Noir **21**

Edith Piaf **22**

Camille Pissarro **23**

Marcel Proust **24**

Giaocchino Rossini **25**

Georges-Pierre Seurat **26**

Simone Signoret **27**

Gertrude Stein **28**

Alice B. Toklas **29**

Louis Visconti **30**

Oscar Wilde **31**

Richard Wright **32**

9

Fodor's Choice   **Cimetière du Père-Lachaise**
★   *See highlighted listing in this chapter.*

La Maison Rouge. One of the city's premier spaces for contemporary art, La Maison Rouge art foundation was established by former gallery owner Antoine de Galbert to fill a hole in the Parisian art world. Always edgy, often provocative, the foundation stages several temporary exhibitions each year in a cleverly renovated industrial space anchored by a central courtyard building that's painted bright red on the outside (hence the name). Past shows have included "Tous Cannibales," themed around cannibalism, and "Memories of the Future," a death-obsessed display featuring artists from Hieronymus Bosch to Damien Hirst. Check the website to see what's on. ■TIP→ **Stop by the Rose Bakery near the entrance: it's the latest Parisian outpost of the popular English café.** ⊠ *10 bd. de la Bastille, Bastille* ☎ *01–40–01–08–81* ⊕ *www.lamaisonrouge.org* ⊠ *€8* ⊘ *Wed. and Fri.–Sun. 11–7, Thurs. 11–9; closed Mon. and Tues.* Ⓜ *Quai de la Rapée/Bastille.*

Marché d'Aligre. Place d'Aligre boasts two of Paris's best markets: the lively outdoor Marché d'Aligre and the covered Marché Beauvau. Open at 8 am every day but Monday, both are great places to pick up picnic essentials, which you can enjoy nearby in the small park at Square Trousseau or on the Promenade Plantée. The picturesque outdoor market has dozens of excitable vendors, their stands laden with fresh fruits and vegetables, flower bouquets, and regional products such as jam, honey, and dried sausage. The best bargains are had just before closing time at 1 pm, and many vendors are happy to give you a taste of whatever they're selling. The covered market, which closes in the afternoon and reopens from 4 to 7:30 pm, stocks everything from meats and cheeses to Belgian beer. Sunday morning is the liveliest time to visit. Don't forget your camera. ■TIP→ **Stop for a plate of saucisse (sausage) and a glass of rouge (even Sunday morning) at one of the city's quirkiest wine bars, Le Baron Rouge, 1 rue Théophile Roussel.** ⊠ *Pl. d'Aligre, Bastille* ⊕ *www.marchedaligre.free.fr* Ⓜ *Ledru-Rollin/Bastille.*

Opéra de la Bastille. Paris's main opera house opened its doors on July 14, 1989, to mark the bicentennial of the French Revolution. The fabulous acoustics of the steeply sloping, stylish auditorium have earned more plaudits than the modern facade designed by Uruguay-born architect Carlos Ott. If you want to see a show, reserve your seat well in advance, or take your chances on the same day, when any unclaimed seats (at all price levels) are released 45 minutes before showtime. There are also 32 standing-room-only tickets available 90 minutes before each show for €5. Same-day seats are much in demand, so be sure to line up two hours or more before the curtain. ■TIP→ **Tickets for a 75-minute guided tour cost €12.** ⊠ *Pl. de la Bastille, Bastille/Nation* ☎ *08–92–89–90–90 for tickets (€0.34 per minute), 01–71–25–24–23 from outside of France* ⊕ *www.operadeparis.fr* Ⓜ *Bastille.*

FAMILY   **Parc de la Villette.** This former abattoir is now a 130-acre ultramodern park. With lawns and play areas, an excellent science museum, a music complex, and a cinema, it's also the perfect place to entertain sightseeing-weary kids. You could easily spend a whole day here.

The park itself was designed in the 1980s by postmodern architecture star Bernard Tschumi, who melded industrial elements, children's games (don't miss the dragon slide), ample green spaces, and funky sculptures along the canal into one vast yet unified playground. Loved by picnickers, the lawns also attract rehearsing samba bands and pickup soccer players. In summer there are outdoor festivals and a free open-air cinema, where people gather at dusk to watch movies on a huge inflatable screen.

In cold weather you can visit an authentic submarine and the Espace Chapiteaux (a circus tent featuring contemporary acrobatic theater performances) before hitting the museums. The hands-on one at the **Cité des Sciences et de l'Industrie** is a favorite stop for families and a must for science fans (⇨ *below*). Its 3-D Omnimax cinema—La Géode—is housed in a giant silver ball. The postmodern **Cité de la Musique** is a music academy designed by noted urban architect Christian de Portz-amparc. It has a state-of-the-art concert hall and houses the excellent **Musée de la Musique** (⇨ *below*). The park will have even more in store for music lovers in 2015, when the curtain rises on a striking 2,400-seat philharmonic concert hall designed by Jean Nouvel.

As for the abattoir that once stood here, all that's left of the slaughter-house is La Grande Halle, a magnificent iron-and-glass building now used for exhibitions, performances, and trade shows. ⊠ *Parc de la Villette, 211 av. Jean Jaurès* ☎ *01–40 03–75–17* ⊕ *www.villette.com.*

Cité des Sciences et de l'Industrie (*Museum of Science and Industry*). This ambitious science museum, in a colorful three-story industrial space that recalls the Pompidou Center, is packed with things to do—all of them accessible to English speakers. Scores of exhibits focus on subjects like space, transportation, and technology. Hands-on workshops keep the kids entertained and the planetarium is invariably a hit. Temporary exhibitions, like a recent exploration of the human voice, are always multilingual and usually interactive. ⊠ *30 av. Corentin-Cariou, La Villette* ☎ *01 40–05–70–00* ⊕ *www.cite-sciences.fr* ⊠ *€8; €11 with planetarium or temporary exhibits* ⊙ *Tues.–Sat. 10–6; Sun. 10–7; closed Mon.* Ⓜ *Porte de la Villette.*

Musée de la Musique. The music museum inside the Cité de la Musique contains four centuries'-worth of instruments from around the world—about 1,000 in total, many of them exquisite works of art. Their sounds and story are evoked on numerous video screens and via commentary you can follow on headphones (ask for a free audioguide in English). Leave time for the excellent temporary exhibitions, like 2013's show about the marriage between cinema and music. ⊠ *221 av. Jean-Jaurès, La Villette* ☎ *01–44–84–44–84* ⊕ *www.cite-musique. fr* ⊠ *€7 permanent collection; €9 with temporary exhibits* ⊙ *Tues.–Sat. noon–6, Sun. 10–6; closed Mon.* Ⓜ *Porte de Pantin.*

Café de la Musique. Across the plaza, the outdoor terrace at Café de la Musique is an inviting place to have a drink on a sunny day. ⊠ *213 av. Jean-Jaurès, La Villette* ☎ *01–48–03–15–91* Ⓜ *Porte de Pantin.*

FAMILY **Parc des Buttes-Chaumont.** If you're tired of perfectly manicured Parisian parks with lawns that are off-limits to your weary feet, this place

9

is for you. The lovely 61-acre hill-top expanse in the untouristy 19e arrondissement has grassy fields, shady walkways, waterfalls, and a picturesque lake dotted with swans. Rising from the lake is a rocky cliff you can climb to find a mini Greek-style temple and a commanding view of Sacré-Coeur Basilica. A favorite of families, the park also has pony rides and an open-air puppet theater—Guignol de Paris (€4; shows at 4 pm Wednesday and at 4 pm and 5 pm weekends, year-round)—not far from the entrance at Buttes-Chaumont métro stop. Built in 1863 on abandoned gypsum quarries and a former gallows, this was northern Paris's first park,

part of Napoléon III's planned greening of Paris (the emperor had spent years in exile in London, where he fell in love with the public parks). Major renovation work through 2016 will mean some unsightly construction, but it will remain open. ■TIP➜ Grab a snack at café Rosa Bonheur (⊕ www.rosabonheur.fr) or reserve a table for weekend lunch at Le Pavillon du Lac restaurant (⊕ www.lepavillondulac.fr). ✉ *Entrances on Rue Botzaris or Rue Manin, Buttes-Chaumont* Ⓜ *Buttes-Chaumont, Botzaris, Laumière.*

Place de la Bastille. Almost nothing remains of the infamous Bastille prison, destroyed more than 200 years ago, though tourists still ask bemused Parisians where to find it. Until the late 1980s, there was little more to see here than a busy traffic circle ringing the Colonne de Juillet (July Column), a memorial to the victims of later uprisings in 1830 and 1848. The opening of the Opéra Bastille in 1989 rejuvenated the area, however, drawing art galleries, bars, and restaurants to the narrow streets, notably along Rue de Lappe—once a haunt of Edith Piaf—and Rue de la Roquette.

Before it became a prison, the Bastille St-Antoine was a defensive fortress with eight immense towers and a wide moat. It was built by Charles V in the late 14th century and transformed into a prison during the reign of Louis XIII (1610–43). Famous occupants included Voltaire, the Marquis de Sade, and the Man in the Iron Mask. On July 14, 1789, it was stormed by an angry mob that dramatically freed all of the remaining prisoners (there were only seven, including one lunatic), thereby launching the French Revolution. The roots of the revolt ran deep. Resentment toward Louis XVI and Marie-Antoinette had been building amid a severe financial crisis. There was a crippling bread shortage, and the free-spending monarch was blamed. When the king dismissed the popular finance minister, Jacques Necker, enraged Parisians took to the streets. They marched to Les Invalides, helping themselves to stocks of arms, then continued on to the Bastille. A few months later, what was left of the prison was razed—and 83 of its stones were carved into miniature Bastilles and sent to the provinces as a memento (you can see one of them in the Musée Carnavalet). The key to the prison was given to George Washington by Lafayette and has remained at Mount Vernon ever since. Today, nearly every major street demonstration in Paris—and there are many—passes through this square. ✉ *Bastille* Ⓜ *Bastille*.

Viaduc des Arts/Promenade Plantée (*La Coulée Verte*). Once a train line from the Paris suburbs to Bastille, this redbrick viaduct is now

BASTILLE AT NIGHT

From Place de la Bastille, take Rue de la Roquette and turn right onto Rue de Lappe, Paris's answer to Bourbon Street. Once a haunt of artists and writers like Henry Miller, its many bars and eateries draw a mostly young crowd today *(see Chapter 17, Nightlife)*; however, there is something for everyone. In recent years these tangled streets have added shops, theaters, and galleries to the constantly evolving lineup.

the green heart of the unpretentious 12e arrondissement. The rails have been transformed into a 4.5-km (2.8-mile) walkway lined with trees, bamboo, and flowers, offering a bird's-eye view of the stately Haussmanian buildings along Avenue Daumesnil. Below, the *voûtes* (arcades) have been transformed by the city into artisan boutiques, many focused on decor and design. All tenants are hand-picked. There are also temporary galleries showcasing art and photography. The Promenade, which gained fame as a setting in the 2004 film *Before Sunset*, was the inspiration for New York's High Line. It ends at the Jardin de Reuilly. From here you can continue your walk to the Bois de Vincennes. ■TIP➔ **If you're hungry, grab a bite at L'Arrosoir, a cozy café under the viaduct at 75 avenue Daumesnil.** ✉ *Av. Daumesnil, Bastille* ⊕ *www.leviaducdesarts.com* Ⓜ *Bastille, Gare de Lyon*.

9

WORTH NOTING

Bibliothéque National François Mitterand. The National Library of France, across the sleek Simone de Beauvoir footbridge from Bercy Park, is a stark complex comprised of four 22-story L-shaped buildings representing open books. Commissioned by President Mitterrand, the €1-billion library was said to be the world's most modern when it opened in 1998—a reputation quickly sullied when it was discovered that miles of books and rare documents were baking in the glass towers, unprotected from the sun (movable shutters were eventually installed). Some of the most important printed treasures of France are stored here, though the majority of them are available only to researchers. Visitors can see the impressive 17th-century Globes of Coronelli, a pair of two-ton orbs made for Louis XIV. There's a sunken center garden with tall trees (open to the public the first weekend in June) ringed by low-ceilinged reading rooms, which are nothing special. A first-floor gallery hosts popular temporary exhibitions on subjects such as the life of Casanova. Enter through the easternmost tower. ✉ *Quai François Mauriac, Bibliothèque* ☎ *01–53–79–59–59* ⊕ *www.bnf.fr* ⊡ *Globes gallery* *free; reading rooms €3.50; exhibitions €7 ⊙ Tues.–Sat. 10–8, Sun. 1–7; closed Mon.* Ⓜ *Bibliothèque, Quai de la Gare.*

FAMILY **Bois de Vincennes.** Like the Bois de Boulogne to the west, this much-loved retreat on the city's eastern border was landscaped by Napoléon III. Its roots, however, reach back to the 13th century, when Philippe Auguste created a hunting preserve in the shadow of the royal **Château de Vincennes,** which once ranked as the largest château in Europe *(⇨ below).* In 1731 Louis XV created a public park here, and the bois (or wood) now features lush lawns, a flower garden, and summertime jazz concerts. Rowboats are for hire at a pair of lakes: Lac Daumesnil, which has two islands, and Lac des Minimes, which has three. There's also a **Parc Zoologique** *(⇨ below),* a racetrack (the **Hippodrome de Vincennes**), two cafés, and, in spring, an amusement park. You can rent a bike at the Château de Vincennes métro stop. To reach the park, use the Château de Vincennes stop (Line 1) or Porte Dorée (Line 8). ⊠ *Bois de Vincennes.*

Château de Vincennes. The imposing high-walled Château de Vincennes, on the northern edge of the Bois, was France's medieval answer to Versailles. Built and expanded by various kings between the 12th and 14th centuries, it is now surrounded by a dry moat and dominated by a 170-foot keep (the last of nine original towers). The royal residence eventually became a prison holding convicts, notably of both sexes—and "the doors did not always remain closed between them," as one tour guide coyly put it. Inmates included the philosopher Diderot and the Marquis de Sade. Both the château and its cathedral, **Sainte-Chapelle** (designed in the style of the Paris church of the same name), have undergone a spectacular restoration, returning them to their previous glory. If you speak French, the free 90-minute tour is worthwhile. ⊠ *Av. de Paris, Bois de Vincennes* ☎ *01–48–08–31–20* ⊕ *www.chateau-vincennes.fr* ✎ *€8.50* ⊙ *Mid-May–mid-Sept., daily 10–6; mid-Sept.–mid-May, daily 10–5* Ⓜ *Château de Vincennes.*

Parc Floral de Paris. A lake, a butterfly garden, and seasonal displays of blooms make the Bois de Vincennes's 70-acre floral park a lovely place to spend a summer afternoon. Kids will also enjoy the miniature train, paddleboats, ponies, pool, and game area, among other attractions (most of which cost extra). The park hosts jazz concerts most weekends from April to October, but other months many attractions are closed. ⊠ *Rte. de la Pyramide, Bois de Vincennes* ✎ *€5.50 Wed. and weekends, June–Sept.; free other days in season and every day off-season* ⊙ *Apr.–Sept., daily 9:30–8, Oct.–Mar., daily 9:30–5* Ⓜ *Château de Vincennes.*

Parc Zoologique. The 35-acre Parc Zoologique is France's largest zoo and, thanks to a major renovation, now promises a more hands-on experience. Its 1,000 animals are housed in newly designed environments (aka "biozones") that mix species as Mother Nature intended: these include a free-range aviary you can walk through and a greenhouse that re-creates a slice of the rain forest. ⊠ *Entrance at intersection of Av. Daumesnil and Rte. de Ceinture du Lac Daumesnil, 53 av. de St-Maurice, Bois de Vincennes* ☎ *01–44–75–20–00* ⊕ *www.*

parczoologiquedeparis.fr €22; €14 children 3–11 ⊙ Mid-Mar.–mid-Oct., Mon–Fri. 10–6, Sat.–Sun. 9:30–7:30; mid-Oct.–mid-Mar. daily 10–5 Ⓜ *Porte Dorée.*

Palais de la Porte Dorée & Tropical Aquarium. One of the best examples of Art Deco architecture in Paris, this stunning building is home to an immigration museum and a tropical aquarium. It's worth a visit just to see the Palais, built for the 1931 Colonial Exhibition (entry to the ground floor is free). The ornate facade features bas-relief sculptures representing France's erstwhile empire. Inside, the elaborate marble, ornate metal work, and original lighting are all beautifully maintained. On either end of the ground floor are furnished salons, one representing Asia, the other Africa (a Gucci commercial was filmed in the latter). Peek into the central room, called the Forum, where restored Africa-inspired mosaics line the walls. The upper floors are occupied by the **Cité Nationale de l'Historie de l'Immigration,** a well-executed modern museum tracing the history of immigration in France. There are usually similarly themed temporary exhibitions. The basement contains **L'Aquarium Tropical,** an aquarium with a pair of alligators from Mississippi. There is little information available in English. ✉ *293 av. Daumesnil, Bois de Vincennes* ☎ *01-53-59-58-60* ⊕ *www.histoire-immigration.fr; www.aquarium-portedoree.fr* €4.50 museum; €5 aquarium; €8 combined ticket; prices vary during special exhibitions* ⊙ *Tues.–Fri. 10–5 :30, weekends 10–7; closed Mon.* Ⓜ *Porte Dorée.*

OFF THE
BEATEN
PATH

Le 104. Le Cent Quatre takes its name from its address in a rough-around-the-edges corner of the 19e arrondissement, not far from the top of the Canal St-Martin. The former site of the city morgue, this cavernous art hub is home to an offbeat collection of performance venues, shops, and studios (artists of all genres compete for free studio space, and sometimes you can get a sneak peak of them at work). Contemporary art exhibits, some of which charge admission fees, are staged here, as are concerts. On-site you'll also find a restaurant, a café, a bookstore, a natural clothing boutique, a secondhand shop, and a play area for children. Check the website's schedule before going to see what's on. ✉ *104 rue d'Aubervilliers, alternate entry at 5 rue Curial, Stalingrad* ☎ *01-53-35-50-01* ⊕ *www.104.fr* Free; prices for exhibits and concerts vary* ⊙ *Tues.–Fri. 12–7, weekends 11–7; closed Mon.* Ⓜ *Stalingrad.*

OFF THE
BEATEN
PATH

Musée Edith Piaf. Devotees will appreciate the tiny two-room apartment where the "little sparrow" lived for a year, when she was 28-years old and sang in the working-class cafés on Rue Oberkampf. The flat was obtained by Les Amis d'Edith Piaf in 1978 and is now a shrine to the petite crooner, whose life-size photo (she was just 4 feet, 9 inches tall) greets visitors at the door. The red walls are covered with portraits of Piaf done by her many artist friends, and her personal letters are framed. Her books and handbags are displayed, as well as a few dresses, her size 4 shoes, and a touching pair of old boxing gloves belonging to one of her great loves—champion pugilist Marcel Cerdan. ✉ *5 rue Crespin du Gast, Oberkampf* ☎ *01-43-55-52-72* Free, donations strongly encouraged* ⊙ *Mon.–Wed. 1–6, by reservation only (no English spoken); closed Thurs.–Sun. and all of June and Sept.* Ⓜ *Ménilmontant.*

FAMILY **Pavillon de l'Arsenal.** If your knowledge of Paris history is *nul* (nil), stop here for an entertaining free explainer. Built in 1879 as a private museum, the Pavillion today is a restored structure of glass-and-iron that showcases the city's urban development through the ages. A giant model of Paris traces its evolution (with information in English). There are photos, maps, and videos, plus a giant digital interactive model detailing what Paris is predicted to look like in 2020. The standout, created in partnership with Google, is a floor mosaic made up of 48 LED screens that allows visitors at stationary consoles to explore the city via Google Maps. There are frequent architecture-theme temporary exhibits, plus a café and bookstore. ⊠ *21 bd. Morland, Bastille* ☎ *01–42–76–33–97* ⊕ *www.pavillon-arsenal.com* ⊠ *Free* ⊘ *Tues.–Sat. 10:30–6:30, Sun. 11–7; closed Mon.* Ⓜ *Sully-Morland, Bastille.*

FAMILY **Piscine Josephine Baker.** This modern floating aquatic center, named after the much-beloved American entertainer, features a pool with a retractable glass roof, two solariums, a steam room, Jacuzzis, and a gym. Check the opening hours and schedule of classes online. ⊠ *Porte de la Gare, 21 quai François Mauriac, Bibliothèque* ☎ *01–56–61–96–50* ⊕ *www.carilis.fr/centre/piscine-josephine-baker* ⊠ *€3 for pool; fees may apply for other activities* ⊘ *Mon., Wed., and Fri. 7–8:30 am and 1–9 pm, Tues. and Thurs. 1–11, Sat. 11–8, Sun. 10–8; extended hrs during school vacations* Ⓜ *Quai de la Gare, Bibilothèque François Mitterrand.*

THE LATIN QUARTER

GETTING ORIENTED

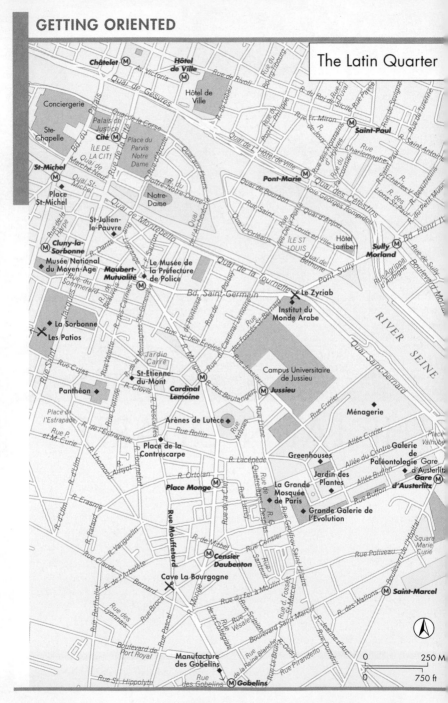

The Latin Quarter

TOP REASONS TO GO

Musée de Cluny. On the site of an ancient Roman bath, this former abbey is home to the famous *Lady and the Unicorn* tapestries; the building, tranquil garden, and extensive collection have the hush of a medieval monastery.

Shakespeare & Co. This legendary English-language bookstore is more than a shopping destination; it's a meeting place for young expats and curious travelers alike.

Rue Mouffetard. Whether you're a gastronome or just plain hungry, you'll be enthralled by the array of characteristically French edibles sold on this winding market street.

Jardin des Plantes. This is a great spot to enjoy a picnic or to rest your tired feet on one of the many shaded benches.

La Grande Mosquée de Paris. Relax with a little glass of mint tea in the leafy courtyard café at Paris's most beautiful mosque.

MAKING THE MOST OF YOUR TIME

The Quartier Latin is the perfect place to wander sans itinerary, though there is no shortage of sites worth seeing. Shopping here is generally more affordable (but less original) than in other neighborhoods, and there are lots of new- and used-book stores, many of which stock English-language titles. Pick up picnic supplies in the food shops along Rue Mouffetard (mostly closed Monday) or the open-air market at Place Monge (Wednesday, Friday, and Sunday morning), then savor your booty on a bench at the Jardin des Plantes. Sip mint tea at the lovely Grande Mosquée (Mosque) de Paris or take in a terrific view from the roof of the Institut du Monde Arabe (closed Monday). Stroll the hilly streets around the Panthéon on your way to see the treasures at the Musée de Cluny (closed Tuesday). Finish with a sunset aperitif on one of the barge cafés (open spring to fall) along the Seine, across from Notre-Dame.

GETTING HERE

The Quartier Latin is in the 5e arrondissement. Take métro Line 4 to St-Michel to start exploring at the Lucifer-slaying fountain near Shakespeare & Co., across the Seine from Notre-Dame. Go to the Cluny stop on Line 10 if you're heading to the Musée de Cluny. The Place Monge stop on Line 7 puts you near the Panthéon and Rue Mouffetard, the Mosquée de Paris, and the Jardin des Plantes. Les Gobelins neighborhood straddles the 5e, 13e, and 14e arrondissements, but is considered part of the 5e because of the Manufacture des Gobelins.

BEST CAFÉS

Cave La Bourgogne. Settle in on the terrace of this old-school bistro for lunch, or join the locals at the zinc bar. ✉ *144 rue Mouffetard, Latin Quarter* ☎ *01–47–07–82–80* Ⓜ *Censier Daubenton.*

Les Patios. If you're young— or young at heart—come here to hang with the Sorbonne crowd. It's in the square across from the university. ✉ *5 pl. de la Sorbonne, Latin Quarter* ☎ *01–43–54–34–43* Ⓜ *Cluny– La Sorbonne.*

Le Zyriab. This café–outdoor terrace on the top floor of the Institut du Monde Arabe has a fantastic view. ✉ *Institut du Monde Arabe, 1 rue des Fossés-St-Bernard, Latin Quarter* ☎ *01– 55–42–55–42* ⊕ *www.imarabe. org/restaurants* Ⓜ *Jussieu.*

10

Sightseeing
★★★★
Dining
★★★
Lodging
★★★★
Shopping
★★★
Nightlife
★★★

The Quartier Latin is the heart of student Paris—and has been for more than 800 years. France's oldest university, La Sorbonne, was founded here in 1257, and the neighborhood takes its name from the fact that Latin was the common language of the students, who came from all over Europe. Today the area is full of cheap and cheerful cafés, bars, and shops.

Updated by
Jack Vermee

The main drag, **Boulevard St-Michel,** is a busy street where bookshops have given way to chain clothing stores and fast-food joints—but don't let that stop you! There are (almost) as many French people wandering the streets here as there are tourists. At **Place St-Michel,** the symbolic gateway to the *quarter,* notice the 19th-century fountain depicting Saint Michael slaying the "great dragon," Satan—a symbolic warning to rebellious locals from Napoléon III. Today the fountain serves as a meeting spot and makes a rather fine metaphor for the boulevard it anchors: a bit grimy but extremely popular.

When you've had enough of the crowds, turn off the boulevard and explore the side streets, where you can find quirky boutiques and intimate bistros. Or stop for a demi (a half pint of draft beer) at one of the cafés on **Place de la Sorbonne,** ground zero for students (and their many noisy demonstrations). Around the winding streets behind the **Panthéon,** where French luminaries are laid to rest, you can still find plenty of academics arguing philosophy while sipping espresso, but today the 5e arrondissement is also one of Paris's most charming and sought-after (read: expensive) places to live.

Shop along **Rue Mouffetard** as Parisians do—all the while complaining about the high prices—for one of the best selections of runny cheeses, fresh breads, and charcuterie. Grab a seat in a bustling café—or follow the locals' lead and stand at the bar, where drinks are always cheaper. Film buffs won't have to look far to find one of the small cinema revival houses showing old American films in English (look for v.o., for *version originale*). Not far from le Mouffe is the gorgeous white **Grande**

Mosquée de Paris with its impressive minaret. Just beyond the mosque is the **Jardin des Plantes**—a large, if somewhat bland, botanical garden that is home to three natural-history museums, most notably the **Grande Galerie de l'Évolution**. Inside, kids can marvel at enormous whale skeletons, along with all sorts of taxidermy. Some of Paris's most intriguing sites are in this neighborhood, including the **Musée de Cluny** and the innovative **Institut du Monde Arabe**. See ancient history mingle with modern life at the **Arènes de Lutèce,** a Roman amphitheater and favorite soccer pitch for neighborhood kids.

> **DID YOU KNOW?**
>
> French architect Jean Nouvel made news when the Quai Branly museum opened in 2006, but in 1987 he was already wowing Parisians with the Institut du Monde Arabe, an intriguing fusion of Arabian and French styles. His new Orchestra Hall in Parc de la Villette is sure to get attention, too, when it opens in 2015. Nouvel was awarded the Pritzker Architecture Prize in 2008.

TOP ATTRACTIONS

FAMILY **Grande Galerie de l'Évolution** (*Great Hall of Evolution*). With a parade of taxidermied animals ranging from the tiniest dung beetle to the tallest giraffe, this four-story natural history museum in the Jardin des Plantes will perk up otherwise museum-weary kids. The flagship of three natural-history museums in the garden, this restored 1889 building has a ceiling that changes color to suggest storms, twilight, or the hot savanna sun. Other must-sees are the gigantic skeleton of a blue whale and the stuffed royal rhino (he came from the menagerie at Versailles, where he was a pet of Louis XV). Kids 6 to 12 will enjoy La Galerie d'Enfants (The Children's Gallery): opened in 2010, it has bilingual interactive exhibits about the natural world. A lab stocked with microscopes often offers free workshops, and most of the staff speaks some English. ■TIP➜ Hang on to your ticket; it will get you a discount at the other museums within the Jardin des Plantes. ⊠ *36 rue Geoffroy-St-Hilaire, Latin Quarter* ☎ *01–40–79–54–79* ⊕ *www.mnhn.fr* 🎫 *€7* ⊙ *Wed.–Mon. 10–6; closed Tues.* Ⓜ *Pl. Monge, Jussieu.*

Institut du Monde Arabe. This eye-catching metal-and-glass tower by architect Jean Nouvel cleverly uses metal diaphragms in the shape of square Arabic-style screens to work like a camera lens, opening and closing to control the flow of sunlight. The vast cultural center's layout is intended to reinterpret the traditional enclosed Arab courtyard. Inside, there are various spaces—among them a museum, inaugurated in 2012, that explores the culture and religion of the 22 Arab League member nations. With the addition of elements from the Louvre's holdings and private donors, the museum's impressive collection includes Islamic art, artifacts, ceramics, and textiles, which are displayed on four floors. There is also a performance space, a sound-and-image center, a library, and a bookstore. Temporary exhibitions usually have information and an audioguide in English. ■TIP➜ Glass elevators whisk you to the ninth floor, where you can sip mint tea in the rooftop café, Le

CLOSE UP

Literary Lion

This English-language **Shakespeare & Company** (✉ *37 rue de la Bûcherie* ☎ *01-43-25-40-93* 🌐 *www.shakespeareandcompany. com*) is one of Paris's most eccentric and lovable literary institutions. Founded by George Whitman, the maze of new and used books has offered a sense of community (and often a bed) to wandering writers since the 1950s. The store takes its name from Sylvia Beach's original Shakespeare & Co., which opened in 1919 at 12 rue d'Odéon, welcoming the likes of Ernest Hemingway, James Baldwin, and James Joyce. Beach famously bucked the system when she published Joyce's *Ulysses* in 1922, but her original store closed in 1941. After the war Whitman picked up the gauntlet, naming his own bookstore after its famous predecessor.

When Whitman passed away in December 2011, heavy-hearted locals left candles and flowers in front of his iconic storefront. He is buried in the literati-laden Père Lachaise cemetery. His legacy lives on through his daughter Sylvia who runs the shop and welcomes a new generation of Paris dreamers. Walk up the almost impossibly narrow stairs to the second floor and you'll still see laptop computers and sleeping bags tucked between the aging volumes and under dusty daybeds; it's sort of like a hippie commune. A revolving cast of characters helps out in the shop or cooks meals for fellow residents. They're in good company; Henry Miller, Samuel Beckett, and William Burroughs are among the famous writers to benefit from the Whitman family hospitality.

Zyriab, while feasting on one of the best views in Paris. ✉ *1 rue des Fossés-St-Bernard, Latin Quarter* ☎ *01-40-51-38-38* 🌐 *www.imarabe. org* 🎫 *€8* 🕐 *Tues.–Thurs. 10–6, Fri. 10–9:30, weekends 10–7; closed Mon.* Ⓜ *Cardinal Lemoine.*

FAMILY **Jardin des Plantes** (*Botanical Gardens*). Opened in 1640 and once known as the Jardin du Roi (or King's Garden), this sprawling patch of greenery is a neighborhood gem. It's home to several gardens and various museums, all housed in 19th-century buildings whose original architecture blends glass with ornate ironwork. If you have kids, take them to the excellent Grande Galerie de l'Évolution (⇨ *see entry above*) or one of the other natural-history museums here: the Galerie de Paléontologie, stocked with dinosaur and other skeletons, and the rock-laden Galerie de Minéralogie (which will welcome visitors again in late 2014 after a makeover). The botanical and rose gardens are impressive, and plant lovers won't want to miss the towering greenhouses (*serre* in French). After a five-year renovation, they reopened in 2010 and are filled with one of the world's most extensive collections of tropical and desert flora. If the kids prefer fauna, visit the Ménagerie, a small zoo founded in 1795 whose animals once fed Parisians during the 1870 Prussian siege. The star attractions are Nénette, the grande-dame orangutan from Borneo, and her swinging friends in the monkey and ape house. ■TIP➔ If you need a break, there are three kiosk cafés in the Jardin. ✉ *Entrances on Rue Geoffroy-St-Hilaire, Rue Cuvier, Rue de Buffon, and Quai*

10

St-Bernard, Latin Quarter 📞 *01–40–79–54–79* ⊕ *www.mnhn.fr* 🖥 *Museums and zoo €4–€11 (free, 3 and under); greenhouses €6* ☉ *Museums Wed.–Mon. 10–5 or 6; zoo daily 9–5; gardens daily 8–7 (hrs vary by season)* Ⓜ *Gare d'Austerlitz, Jussieu.*

Fodor's Choice ★ **Musée de Cluny** (*Musée National du Moyen-Age [National Museum of the Middle Ages]*). Built on the ruins of Roman baths, the Hôtel de Cluny has been a museum since medievalist Alexandre Du Sommerard established his collection here in 1844. The ornate 15th-century mansion was created for the abbot of Cluny, leader of the mightiest monastery in France. Symbols of the abbot's power surround the building, from the crenellated walls that proclaimed his independence from the king, to the carved Burgundian grapes twining up the entrance that symbolize his valuable vineyards. The scallop shells (*coquilles St-Jacques*) covering the facade are a symbol of religious pilgrimage, another important source of income for the abbot; the well-traveled pilgrimage route to Spain once ran around the corner along Rue St-Jacques. The highlight of the museum's collection is the world-famous *Dame à la Licorne* (*Lady and the Unicorn*) tapestry series, woven in the 16th century, probably in Belgium, and now presented in newly refurbished surroundings. The vermillion tapestries (Room 13) are an allegorical representation of the five senses. In each, a unicorn and a lion surround an elegant young woman against an elaborate *millefleur* (literally, 1,000 flowers) background. The enigmatic sixth tapestry is thought to be either a tribute to a sixth sense, perhaps intelligence, or a renouncement of the other senses. "To my only desire" is inscribed at the top. The collection also includes the original sculpted heads of the *Kings of Israel and Judah* from Notre-Dame, decapitated during the Revolution and discovered in 1977 in the basement of a French bank. The *frigidarium* (Room 9) is a stunning reminder of the city's cold-water Roman baths; the soaring space, painstakingly renovated in 2009, houses temporary exhibits. Also notable is the pocket-size chapel (Room 20) with its elaborate Gothic ceiling. Outside, in the Place Paul Painlevé, is a charming medieval-style garden with flora depicted in the unicorn tapestries. ■**TIP**➜ The free audioguide in English is highly recommended. ✉ *6 pl. Paul-Painlevé, Latin Quarter* 📞 *01–53–73–78–00* ⊕ *www.musee-moyenage.fr* 🖥 *€8; €8.50 during temporary exhibitions; free first Sun. of month* ☉ *Wed.–Mon. 9:15–5:45; closed Tues.* Ⓜ *Cluny–La Sorbonne.*

10

NEED A BREAK?

Place de la Contrescarpe. Place de la Contrescarpe is a popular square behind the Panthéon that attracts locals, students, and Hemmingway enthusiasts (he once lived around the corner). The square has a small-town feel during the day and a lively atmosphere after dusk when the cafés and bars fill up. Café Delmas (*2 pl. de la Contrescarpe* 📞 *01–43–26–51–26*) has a large terrace and serves food every day until 2 am, plus it has added a diner-style restaurant next door for more relaxed meals. ✉ *Latin Quarter* Ⓜ *Pl. Monge.*

Panthéon. Rome has St. Peter's, London has St. Paul's, and Paris has the Panthéon, whose enormous dome dominates the Left Bank. Built as the church of Ste-Geneviève, the patron saint of Paris, it was later converted to an all-star mausoleum for some of France's biggest names, including Voltaire, Zola, Dumas, Rousseau, and Hugo. Pierre and Marie Curie were reinterred here together in 1995. Begun in 1764, the building was almost complete when the French Revolution erupted. By then, architect Jacques-German Soufflot had died—supposedly from worrying that the 220-foot-high dome would collapse. He needn't have fretted: the dome was so perfect that Foucault used it in his famous pendulum test to prove the Earth rotates on its axis. Time, however, has taken its toll on the Panthéon and the structure is now in the midst of an extensive, multi-year overhaul. The crypt and nave remain accessible to the public but the dome is expected to be closed until late 2015. ⊠ *Pl. du Panthéon, Latin Quarter* ☎ *01–44–32–18–00* ⊕ *www.pantheon.monuments-nationaux.fr* ⊠ *€7.50* ⊘ *Apr.–Sept., daily 10–6:30; Oct.–Mar., daily 10–6* Ⓜ *Cardinal Lemoine; RER: Luxembourg.*

THE 13E ARRONDISSEMENT

The villagelike neighborhood of La Butte aux Cailles (in the 13e arrondissement, south of Place d'Italie) is a fun destination with a hip crowd, not far from the Quartier Latin if you want a break from the tourists.

Le Temps des Cerises. Fill up on bistro fare at the crowded, fun, and cooperatively run Le Temps des Cerises, whose name recalls a song made famous by the Paris Commune. ⊠ *18–20 rue de la Butte aux Cailles, La Butte aux Cailles* ☎ *01–45–89–69–48* ⊕ *www.letempsdescerisescoop.com* Ⓜ *Corvisart.*

Fodor's Choice **Rue Mouffetard.** This winding cobblestone street is one of the city's oldest ★ and was once a Roman road leading south from Lutetia (the Roman name for Paris) to Italy. The upper half is dotted with restaurants and bars that cater to tourists and students; the lower half is the setting of a lively morning market, Tuesday through Sunday. The highlight of *le Mouffe*, though, is the stretch in between where the shops spill into the street with luscious offerings such as roasting chickens and potatoes, rustic *saucisson*, pâtés, and pungent cheeses, especially at Androuët (No. 134). If you're here in the morning, Le Mouffetard Café (No. 116) is a good place to stop for a continental breakfast (about €10). If it's aperitif time, head to Place des Contrescarpe for a cocktail *(⇨ Need a Break entry)*, or enjoy a glass of wine at Cave La Bourgogne (No. 144). Prefer to just do a little noshing? Sample the chocolates at de Neuville (No. 108) and Mococha (No. 89). For one of the best baguettes in Paris and other delicious organic offerings, detour to nearby Boulanger de Monge, at 123 rue Monge. Note that most shops are closed Monday. ⊠ *Latin Quarter* Ⓜ *Place Monge, Censier-Daubenton.*

WORTH NOTING

FAMILY **Arènes de Lutèce** (*Lutetia Amphitheater*). This Roman amphitheater, designed as a theater and circus, was almost completely destroyed by barbarians in AD 280. The site was rediscovered in 1869, and you can still see part of the stage and tiered seating. Along with the remains of the baths at Cluny, the arena constitutes rare evidence of the powerful Roman city of Lutetia that flourished on the Rive Gauche in the 3rd century. It's a favorite spot for picnicking, pickup soccer, or *boules*. ⊠ *47 rue Monge, or Rue de Navarre, Latin Quarter* ☎ *Free* ⊙ *Daily 8–dusk in winter, 9–dusk in summer* Ⓜ *Pl. Monge, Cardinal Lemoine.*

La Grande Mosquée de Paris. This awe-inspiring white mosque, built between 1922 and 1926, has tranquil arcades and a minaret decorated in the style of Moorish Spain. Enjoy sweet mint tea and an exotic pastry in the charming courtyard tea salon or tuck into some couscous in the restaurant. Prayer rooms are not open to the public. But there are inexpensive—and quite rustic—hammams, or Turkish steam baths, with scrubs and massages on offer (women only; check website for prices). ⊠ *2 bis pl. du Puits de l'Ermite, entrance to tea salon and restaurant at 39 rue Geoffroy Saint-Hillaire, Latin Quarter* ☎ *01–43–31–38–20* ⊕ *www.la-mosquee.com* ⊙ *Sat.–Thurs. 9 am–noon and 2 pm–7 pm (until 6 in winter); closed Fri.* Ⓜ *Pl. Monge.*

La Sorbonne (*Paris IV*). You can't get into the city's most famous university without a student ID, but it's fun to hang out in the area with all the students. Although La Sorbonne remains the soul of the Quartier Latin, it is only one of several campuses that make up the public Université de Paris. ⊠ *1 rue Victor Cousin, Latin Quarter* Ⓜ *Cluny-La Sorbonne.*

OFF THE BEATEN PATH

le Musée de la Préfecture de Police. Crime buffs will enjoy this museum hidden on the second floor of the 5e arrondissement's police station. Although the exhibits are in French only, the photographs, letters, drawings, and memorabilia pertaining to some of the city's most sensational crimes are easy enough to follow. Among the 2,000-odd relics you'll find a guillotine, old uniforms, and remnants of the World War II occupation—including what's left of a firing post, German machine guns, and the star insignias worn by Jews. ⊠ *4 rue de la Montagne Ste-Geneviève, Latin Quarter* ☎ *01–44–41–52–50* ☎ *Free* ⊙ *Weekdays 9–5:30, Sat. 10:30–5:30* Ⓜ *Maubert-Mutualité.*

Manufacture des Gobelins. Tapestries have been woven at this spot in southeastern Paris, on the banks of the long-covered Bièvre River, since 1662. The Galerie des Gobelins stages exhibitions on two light-flooded floors, highlighting tapestries, furnishings, timepieces, and other treasures mostly drawn from the state collection. Guided visits to the Manufacture (in French only) allow a fascinating look at weavers—from students to accomplished veterans—as they work on tapestries and rugs that take years to complete. Also on-site is a highly selective school that teaches weaving, plus a workshop charged with repairing and restoring furnishings belonging to the French government, which are also stored here in a vast concrete warehouse. ⊠ *42 av. des Gobelins, Les Gobelins* ☎ *01–44–08–53–49* ⊕ *www.mobiliernational.culture.gouv. fr* ☎ *€6 temporary exhibits; €9 workshop visit; €11 workshop and exhibits; free last Sun. of month* ⊙ *Galerie, Tues.–Sun. 11–6; workshop, guided tours in French by reservation only, Tues.–Thurs. at 1:15, 2:45, and 3* Ⓜ *Gobelins.*

10

Place St-Michel. This square was named for Gabriel Davioud's grandiose 1860 fountain sculpture of St. Michael vanquishing Satan—a loaded political gesture from Napoléon III's go-to guy, Baron Haussmann, who hoped St-Michel would quell the Revolutionary fervor of the neighborhood. The fountain is often used as a meeting point. ⊠ *Latin Quarter* Ⓜ *Métro or RER: St-Michel.*

St-Étienne-du-Mont. This jewel box of a church has been visited by several popes, owing to the fact that Ste-Geneviève (the patron saint of Paris) was buried here before Revolutionaries burned her remains. Built on the ruins of a first-century abbey founded by Clovis, the first King of the Franks, it has a unique combination of Gothic, Renaissance, and early Baroque elements, which adds a certain warmth that is lacking in other Parisian churches of pure Gothic style. Here you'll find the only rood screen left in the city—an ornate 16th-century masterwork of carved wood spanning the nave like a bridge, with a spiral staircase on either side. Observe the organ (dating from 1631, it is the city's oldest) and the marker in the floor near the entrance that commemorates an archbishop of Paris who was stabbed to death here by a defrocked priest in 1857. ⊠ *30 rue Descartes, Latin Quarter* ☎ *01–43–54–11–79* ⊕ *www.saintetiennedumont.fr* Ⓜ *Cardinal Lemoine.*

St-Julien-le-Pauvre. This tiny shrine in the shadow of Notre-Dame is one of the three oldest churches in Paris. Founded in 1045, it became a meeting place for university students in the 12th century and was Dante's church of choice when he was in town writing his *Divine Comedy.* Today's structure dates mostly from the 1600s, but keep an eye out for older pillars, which crawl with carvings of demons. You can maximize your time inside by attending one of the classical or gospel concerts held here. Alternately, go outside and simply perch on a bench in the garden to relish the view of Notre-Dame. ⊠ *1 rue St-Julien-le-Pauvre, Latin Quarter* ☎ *01–43–54–52–16* ⊕ *www.sjlpmelkites.org; www.concertinparis.com for concert schedule* Ⓜ *St-Michel.*

ST-GERMAIN-DES-PRÉS

GETTING ORIENTED

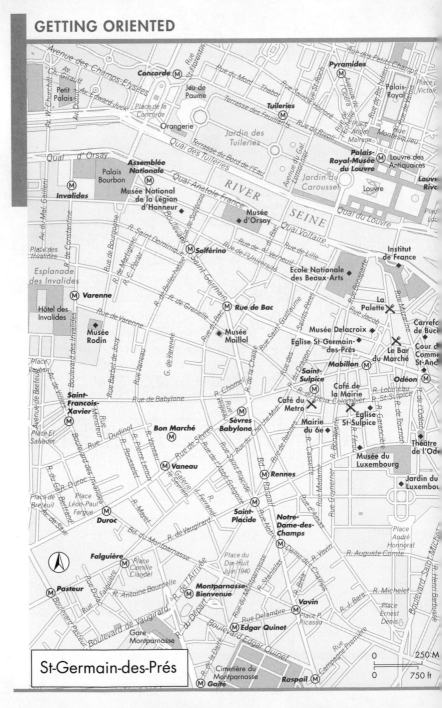

St-Germain-des-Prés

TOP REASONS TO GO

Musée d'Orsay. The magnificent vaulted ceiling and abundant natural light inside this train station–turned–art museum are reminders of why the Impressionist painters thought les gares were the cathedrals of the 19th century.

Jardin du Luxembourg. Take in a puppet show, wander the tree-lined gravel paths, or simply laze by the fountain in one of the city's most elegant gardens.

Boulevard St-Germain. The main artery of this chic neighborhood is edged with shops and galleries. The top boutiques are clustered just off it, around Rue de Rennes.

Café life. This is prime people-watching territory. So pull up a seat at a comfy café, order a coffee, beer, or boisson, and prepare to watch the world go by.

MAKING THE MOST OF YOUR TIME

Aim for an early start—savor a *café crème* at a café along the river and get to the Musée d'Orsay early, when crowds are thinner. Leave some time for window-shopping around Boulevard St-Germain and Rue de Rennes on your way to the Jardin du Luxembourg. You might want to plan your visit on a day other than Monday, when the Orsay, many of the art galleries, and even some shops are closed. The Maillol museum is open every day and late on Friday while the Delacroix is closed Tuesday.

GETTING HERE

The St-Germain neighborhood is in the 6e arrondissement and a bit of the 7e. To get to the heart of this area, take the Line 4 métro to St-Germain-des-Prés. For shopping, use this station or St-Sulpice. It's a short walk to the Jardin du Luxembourg, or take the RER B line to the Luxembourg station. For the Musée d'Orsay, take the Line 12 métro to Solferino or the RER C line to the Musée d'Orsay.

BEST CAFÉS

Café de la Mairie. Overlooking the St-Sulpice church, this slightly shabby café recalls the Latin Quarter of yesteryear before the proliferation of luxury boutiques and trendy eateries. ✉ *8 pl. St-Sulpice, St-Germain-des-Prés* ☎ *01-43-26-67-82* Ⓜ *St-Sulpice.*

Café du Métro. You can refuel at this friendly café-brasserie after an exhausting round of shopping around Rue de Rennes. Main menu items are pricey, but the free Wi-Fi compensates. Closed Sunday. ✉ *67 rue de Rennes, St-Germain-des-Prés* ☎ *01-45-48-58-56* ⊕ *www.cafedumetro.com* Ⓜ *St-Sulpice.*

La Palette. The terrace of this corner café, opened in 1902, is a favorite haunt of local gallery owners and Beaux Arts students. Meals are served at lunch, while lighter fare is available at other times. ✉ *43 rue de Seine, St-Germain-des-Prés* ☎ *01-43-26-68-15* ⊕ *www.cafelapaletteparis.com* Ⓜ *Mabillon or Odéon.*

Le Bar du Marché. Grab a sidewalk table—if you're lucky—or stand at the bar, skip the food, and order an aperitif at this constantly packed little place. The feel is classic French with a splash of kitsch, right down to the waiters in overalls and berets. ✉ *75 rue de Seine, St-Germain-des-Prés* ☎ *01-43-26-55-15* Ⓜ *Mabillon.*

Sightseeing
★★★★★
Dining
★★★
Lodging
★★★★★
Shopping
★★★★★
Nightlife
★★

If you had to choose the most classically Parisian neighborhood, this would be it. St-Germain-des-Prés has it all: genteel blocks lined with upscale art galleries, storied cafés, designer boutiques, atmospheric restaurants, and a fine selection of museums. Cast your eyes upward after dark and you may spy a frescoed ceiling in a tony apartment. These historic streets can get quite crowded, especially in summer, so mind your elbows and plunge in.

Updated by
Victoria Tang

This *quartier* is named for the oldest church in Paris, **St-Germain-des-Prés,** and it's become a prized address for Parisians and expats alike. Despite its pristine facade, though, this wasn't always silver-spoon territory. Claude Monet and Auguste Renoir shared a cramped studio at 20 rue Visconti, and the young Picasso barely eked out an existence in a room on Rue de Seine. By the 1950s St-Germain bars bopped with jazz, and the likes of Albert Camus, Jean-Paul Sartre, and Simone de Beauvoir puffed away on Gauloises while discussing the meaninglessness of life at Café Flore. Nearby in the 7e arrondissement, the star attraction is the **Musée d'Orsay,** home to a world-class collection of Impressionist paintings in a converted Belle Époque railway station on the Seine. It's famous for having some of Paris's longest lines, so a visit to the Orsay should be planned with care. There are also several smaller museums worth a stop, including the impressive **Musée Maillol,** a private collection in an elegant mansion dedicated to the work of sculptor Aristide Maillol. The **Musée Delacroix,** in lovely Place Furstenburg, is home to a small collection of the Romantic master's works. Not far away is the stately **Église St-Sulpice,** where you can see two impressive Delacroix frescoes.

Paris is a city for walking, and St-Germain is one of the most enjoyable places to practice the art of the *flâneur,* or stroller. Make your way to the busy crossroads of **Carrefour de Buci,** dotted with cafés, flower markets, and shops. Rue de l'Ancienne Comédie is so named because it was the first home of the legendary Comédie Française; it cuts through to busy Place de l'Odéon and Rue St-André des Arts. Along the latter you can

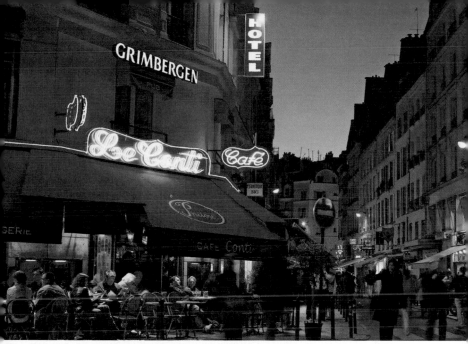

The cafés in St-Germain-des-Prés are perfect for people-watching along with coffee, dinner, or an apéro (cocktail).

find the historic **Cour du Commerce St-André** (opposite No. 66), a charming cobbled passageway filled with cafés—including, halfway down on the left, Paris's oldest, Le Procope.

Make sure you save some energy for the exquisite **Jardin du Luxembourg,** a vintage French garden whose tree-lined paths have attracted fashionable fresh air fans through the ages.

TOP ATTRACTIONS

FAMILY

Fodor's Choice

★

Carrefour de Buci. Just behind the neighborhood's namesake St-Germain church, this colorful crossroads (carrefour means "intersection") was once a notorious Rive Gauche landmark. During the French Revolution, the army enrolled its first volunteers here. It was also here that thousands of royalists and priests lost their heads during the 10-month wave of public executions known as the Reign of Terror. There's certainly nothing sinister about the carrefour today, though; brightly colored flowers are for sale alongside take-out ice cream and other sweet treats. Devotees of the superb, traditional bakery Carton (at 6 rue de Buci) line up for fresh breads and pastries (try their *pain aux raisins, tuiles* cookies, and *tarte de citron*). ⊠ *Intersection of rues Mazarine, Dauphine, and de Buci, St-Germain-des-Prés* Ⓜ *Mabillon.*

Église St-Germain-des-Prés. Paris's oldest church was built to shelter a simple shard of wood, said to be a relic of Jesus's cross brought back from Spain in AD 542. Vikings came down the Seine and sacked the sanctuary, and Revolutionaries used it to store gunpowder. Yet the elegant building has defied history's abuses: its 11th-century Romanesque tower continues to be the central symbol of the neighborhood. The colorful 19th-century frescoes in the nave are by Hippolyte Flandrin, a pupil of the classical master Ingres; and the Saint Benoit chapel contains the tomb of philosopher René Descartes. Step inside for spiritual nourishment, or pause in the square to people-watch—there's usually a street musician tucked against the church wall, out of the wind. ■TIP➡ The church stages superb organ concerts and recitals. See the website for details. ⊠ *Pl. St-Germain-des-Prés, St-Germain-des-Prés* ☎ *01–55–42–81–10* ⊕ *www.eglise-sgp.org* ⊗ *Mon. 2:30–6:45,* Tues.–Fri. 10:30–noon and 2:30–6:45, Sat. 10:30–1; Mass weekdays 12:15 and 7, Sun. 9, 11, 5, and 7 Ⓜ St-Germain-des-Prés.

> **DID YOU KNOW?**
>
> Ste-Catherine Labouré was famed for having been visited twice by the Virgin Mary, who told her to create the "miraculous medal" worn by millions of Catholics. When her body was exhumed in 1933, her eyes were said to be as blue as the day this humble nun died 57 years earlier. You can see her perfectly preserved body in a glass case at Chapelle Notre-Dame de la Médaille Miraculeuse, 140 rue du Bac, just steps from Le Bon Marché.

Fodor'sChoice ★ **Église St-Sulpice.** Dubbed the Cathedral of the Rive Gauche, this enormous 17th-century Baroque church has entertained some unlikely christenings—among them those of the Marquis de Sade and Charles Baudelaire—as well as the nuptials of novelist Victor Hugo. The church's most recent appearance was a supporting role in the best-selling novel *The Da Vinci Code*, and it now draws scores of tourists to its obelisk (part of a *gnomon*, a device used to determine exact time and the equinoxes, built in the 1730s). Other notable features include the exterior's asymmetrical towers and two magnificent Delacroix frescoes, which can be seen in a chapel to the right of the entrance. ■TIP➡ In the square just in front, view Visconti's magnificent 19th-century fountain. It's especially beautiful at night. ⊠ *Pl. St-Sulpice, 2 rue Palatine, St-Germain-des-Prés* ☎ *01–42–34–59–60* ⊕ *www.paris.catholique.fr/saint-sulpice* ⊗ *Daily 7–6:30* Ⓜ *St-Sulpice, Sèvres Babylone, Mabillon.*

QUICK BITES

✕ **Les Editeurs.** Once favored by the Parisian publishing set, Les Editeurs is a casual, occasionally noisy café where you can sip a kir (white wine with black currant syrup) from a perch on the skinny sidewalk or at an inside table shadowed by book-lined walls. The menu offers a modern twist on French classics. Brunch (€26) is served weekends from 11 to 5. ⊠ *4 carrefour de l'Odéon, St-Germain-des-Prés* ☎ *01–43–26–67–76* ⊕ *www. lesediteurs.fr* ⊗ *Daily 8 am–2 am* Ⓜ *Odéon.*

Fodor'sChoice ★ **Jardin du Luxembourg**
See the highlighted listing in this chapter.

Fodor'sChoice ★ **Musée d'Orsay**
See the highlighted listing in this chapter.

11

CLOSE UP

Dueling Cafés

Les Deux Magots (⊠ 6 pl. St-Germain-des-Prés) and the neighboring **Café de Flore** (⊠ 172 bd. St-Germain) have been duking it out on this bustling corner in St-Germain for more than a century. Les Deux Magots, the snootier of the two, is named for the two Chinese figurines, or magots, inside, and has hosted the likes of Oscar Wilde, Hemingway, James Joyce, and Richard Wright. Jean-Paul Sartre and Simone du Beauvoir frequented both establishments, though they are claimed by the Flore. The two cafés remain packed, but these days you're more likely to rub shoulders with tourists than with philosophers. Still, if you're in search of that certain *je ne sais quoi* of the Rive Gauche, you can do no better than to station yourself at one of the sidewalk tables—or at a window table on a wintry day—to watch the passing parade. Stick to a croissant and an overpriced coffee, or enjoy an early-evening aperitif; the food is expensive and nothing special.

NEED A BREAK?

✕ **Brasserie Lipp.** Step through the antique revolving door of this landmark brasserie for a blast from the past. These are the same tables where Hemingway penned pre-war notes, Proust ordered Alsatian beer, and intellectuals like Camus rubbed elbows with artists like Chagall. Maintaining its original 1926 decor (think paneled wood, mirrors, and tiled floors), the eatery serves hearty dishes, such as *choucroute* with sausages and *confit de canard* with sautéed potatoes. Expect a convivial atmosphere and friendly service from traditionally dressed waiters. ■TIP➔ A small outdoor terrace is good for drinks, but go inside to get the full experience. $ *Average main: €35* ⊠ *151 bd. St-Germain, St-Germain-des-Prés* ☎ *01–45–48– 53–91* ⊕ *www.groupe-bertrand.com/lipp.php* ⚭ *Reservations not accepted* ☉ *Daily 9 am–1 am* Ⓜ *St. Germain-des-Pres, St. Sulpice, Mabillon.*

WORTH NOTING

Cour du Commerce St-André. Like an 18th-century engraving come to life, this charming street arcade is a remnant of *ancien* Paris with its uneven cobblestones, antique roofs, and old-world facades. Famed for its rabble-rousing inhabitants—journalist Jean-Paul Marat ran the Revolutionary newspaper *L'Ami du Peuple* at No. 8, and the agitator Georges Danton lived at No. 20—it is also home to Le Procope, Paris's oldest café. The passageway contains a turret from the 12th-century wall of Philippe-Auguste, which is visible through the windows of Un Dimanche à Paris, a chocolate shop-pastry atelier at No. 4. ⊠ *Linking Bd. St-Germain and Rue St-André-des-Arts, St-Germain-des-Prés* Ⓜ *Odéon.*

École Nationale des Beaux-Arts. Occupying three large mansions near the Seine, the national fine arts school—today the breeding ground for painters, sculptors, and architects—was once the site of a convent founded in 1608 by Marguerite de Valois, the first wife of Henri IV. After the

JARDIN DU LUXEMBOURG

✉ Bordered by Bd. St-Michel and rues de Vaugirard, de Medicis, Guynemer, and Auguste-Comte, St-Germain-des-Prés 🎫 Free ⊙ Daily 7:30–dusk (hrs may vary depending on season) Ⓜ Odéon; RER: B Luxembourg.

TIPS

■ If the grass is en repos, a nice way of saying "stay off," feel free to move the green chairs around to create a picnic spot or people-watching perch.

■ If you want to burn off that breakfast pain au chocolat, there's a well-maintained trail around the perimeter that is frequented by gentrified joggers.

■ If you're looking for a familiar face, one of the original (miniature) casts of the Statue of Liberty was installed in the gardens in 1906.

■ Gendarmes regularly walk the grounds to ensure park rules are enforced; follow guidelines posted on entry gates.

Everything that is charming, unique, and befuddling about Parisian parks can be found in the Luxembourg Gardens: cookie-cutter trees, ironed-and-pressed walkways, sculpted flower beds, and immaculate emerald lawns meant for admiring, not necessarily for lounging. The tree- and bench-lined paths are a marvelous reprieve from the bustle of the two neighborhoods it borders: the Quartier Latin and St-Germain-des-Prés. Beautifully austere during the winter months, the garden grows intoxicating as spring brings blooming beds of daffodils, tulips, and hyacinths, and the circular pools teem with boats nudged along by children. The park's northern boundary is dominated by the Palais du Luxembourg and the Sénat (Senate), which is one of two chambers that make up the Parliament.

Highlights

The original inspiration for the gardens came from Marie de Medici, nostalgic for the Boboli Gardens of her native Florence. She is commemorated by the Fontaine de Medicis.

Les Marionettes du Théâtre du Luxembourg is a timeless attraction, where, on weekends at 11 and 3:15 and Wednesday at 3:15 (hours may vary), you can catch classic *guignols* (marionette shows) for €4.70. The wide-eyed kids might be the real attraction—their expressions of utter surprise, despair, and glee have fascinated the likes of Henri Cartier-Bresson and François Truffaut. The park also has a merry-go-round, swings, and pony rides; the bandstand hosts free concerts on summer afternoons.

Check out the rotating photography exhibits hanging on the perimeter fence near the entrance on Boulevard St-Michel and Rue Vaugirard.

R. de l'Odéon

R. R. Racine

R. Monsieur le Prince

Rue de Condé

Rue de Tournon

Rue de Garancière

R. Férou

Théâtre de l'Odéon

Rue de Vaugirard

Senate Library

Petit Luxembourg

Palais du Luxembourg

Musée du Luxembourg

Rue de Vaugirard

Rue de Médicis

Pavillon Guynemer

Orangerie

Fontaine de Medicis

Rue Soufflot

Rue Madame

Rue Guynemer

Place Edmond Rostand

Rue de Fleurus

Shetland Ponies

Grand Bassin

Rue Royer Collard

R. V. Cousin

Théâtre des Marionettes

Jardin du Luxembourg

Carrousel

Rucher du Luxembourg

Place André Honnorat

Rue Vavin

Rue Auguste Comte

Boulevard Saint-Michel

R. de l'Abbé de l'Epée

Rue d'Assas

Rue Michelet

Rue J. Bara

Place Ernest Denis

R. du Val de Grâce

Rue Notre-Dame des Champs

Boulevard du Montparnasse

0   250 meters

0   500 ft

La Closerie des Lilas

R. Henri Barbusse

Rue Pierre Nicole

R. Saint-Jacques

MUSÉE D'ORSAY

✉ 1 rue de la Légion d'Honneur, St-Germain-des-Prés ☎ 01–40–49–48–14 ⊕ www.musee-orsay.fr 🏷 €11; €8.50 after 4:30, except Thurs. after 6 🕐 Tues., Wed., and Fri.–Sun. 9:30–6; Thurs. 9:30 am–9:45 pm; closed Mon. Ⓜ Solférino; RER: Musée d'Orsay.

TIPS

■ Lines here are among the worst in Paris. Book ahead online or buy a Museum Pass; then go directly to entrance C. Otherwise, go early.

■ Thursday evening the museum is open until 9:45 pm and less crowded.

■ The elegant Musée d'Orsay Restaurant once served patrons of the 1900 World's Fair; the Café du Lion offers quick fare on the ground floor by the entrance; there's also a café and a self-service cafeteria on the top floor just after the Cézanne galleries. Don't miss the views of Sacré-Coeur from the balcony—this is the Paris that inspired the Impressionists.

■ The d'Orsay is closed Monday, unlike the Pompidou and the Louvre, which are closed Tuesday.

Opened in 1986, this gorgeously renovated Belle Époque train station displays a world-famous collection of Impressionist and Post-Impressionist paintings on three floors. To visit the exhibits in a roughly chronologic manner, start on the first floor, take the escalators to the top, and end on the second. If you came to see the biggest names here, head straight for the top floor and work your way down. English audioguides and free color-coded museum maps (both available just past the ticket booths) will help you plot your route. Renovations will be ongoing until 2015.

Highlights

Ground floor: Galleries off the main alley feature early works by Manet and Cézanne in addition to pieces by masters such as Delacroix and Ingres. Later works by the likes of Toulouse-Lautrec are found in Salle 10. The Pavillon Amont has Courbet's masterpieces *L'Enterrement à Ornans* and *Un Atelier du Peintre*. Hanging in Salle 14 is Édouard Manet's *Olympia*, a painting which pokes fun at the fashion for all things Greek and Roman (his nubile subject is a 19th-century courtesan, not a classical goddess).

Top floor: Impressionism gets going here, with iconic works by Degas, Pissarro, Sisley, and Renoir. Don't miss Monet's series on the cathedral at Rouen and, of course, samples of his water lilies. Other selections by these artists are housed in galleries on the ground floor.

Second floor: An exquisite collection of sculpture as well as Art Nouveau furniture and decorative objects is housed here. There are rare surviving works by Hector Guimard (designer of the swooping green Paris métro entrances), plus Lalique and Tiffany glassware. Post-Impressionist galleries include work by van Gogh and Gauguin, while Neo-Impressionist galleries highlight Seurat and Signac.

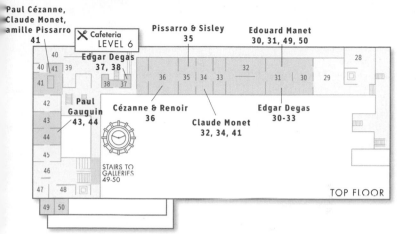

Paul Cézanne, Claude Monet, Camille Pissarro
41

Cafeteria
LEVEL 6

Pissarro & Sisley
35

Edouard Manet
30, 31, 49, 50

Edgar Degas
37, 38

Cézanne & Renoir
36

Paul Gauguin
43, 44

Claude Monet
32, 34, 41

Edgar Degas
30-33

STAIRS TO GALLERIES 49-50

TOP FLOOR

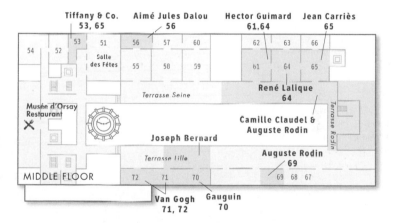

Tiffany & Co.
53, 65

Aimé Jules Dalou
56

Hector Guimard
61,64

Jean Carriès
65

Salle des Fêtes

Musée d'Orsay Restaurant

Terrasse Seine

René Lalique
64

Terrasse Rodin

Camille Claudel & Auguste Rodin

Joseph Bernard

Terrasse Lille

Auguste Rodin
69

MIDDLE FLOOR

Van Gogh
71, 72

Gauguin
70

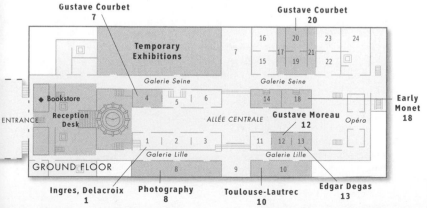

Gustave Courbet
7

Gustave Courbet
20

Temporary Exhibitions

Galerie Seine

Galerie Seine

Bookstore

ENTRANCE

Reception Desk

ALLÉE CENTRALE

Gustave Moreau
12

Opéra

Early Monet
18

Galerie Lille

Galerie Lille

GROUND FLOOR

Ingres, Delacroix
1

Photography
8

Toulouse-Lautrec
10

Edgar Degas
13

Revolution the convent was turned into a museum for works of art salvaged from buildings attacked by the rampaging French mobs. In 1816 the museum was turned into a school. Today its peaceful courtyards host contemporary installations and exhibits. The courtyard and school galleries are accessible on 90-minute guided tours, which can be arranged through Cultival (see ⊕ *www.cultival.fr* for details). ⊠ *14 rue Bonaparte, St-Germain-des-Prés* ☎ *01–47–03–50–00* ⊕ *www.beauxartsparis.com* ⊠ *€13.50* ⊗ *Weekdays 9–8:30; closed weekends* Ⓜ *St-Germain-des-Prés.*

> **WORD OF MOUTH**
>
> "We made our way to Jardin du Luxembourg. WOW!!!! Just WOW!!!! What a stunningly beautiful park. It just so happened that it was a warm, sunny Sunday afternoon by this time, and the park was filled with people. Children were racing their boats in the water, the flowers were still in bloom." —BuffaloGirl

Institut de France. The *Institut* is one of France's most revered cultural institutions, and its golden dome is one of the Rive Gauche's most impressive landmarks. The site was once punctuated by Tour de Nesle (forming part of Philippe-Auguste's medieval fortification wall, the tower had many royal occupants—including Henry V of England). Then, in 1661 wealthy Cardinal Mazarin willed 2-million French *livres* (pounds) for the construction of a college here. It's also home to the Académie Française: protectors of the French language. The edicts issued by this esoteric group of 40 *perpétual* (lifelong) members are happily ignored by the French public, who prefer to send an email rather than the Académie-approved *courriel*. The Institute is off-limits to visitors. ⊠ *Pl. de l'Institut, St-Germain-des-Prés* ⊕ *www.institut-de-france.fr* Ⓜ *Pont Neuf.*

Mairie du 6e. The "town hall" of the 6e arrondissement (as "mairie" is roughly translated) often stages impressive free art exhibitions and other cultural offerings. Stop by the *accueil* (reception desk) on the ground floor to see what's on or to pick up information on other timely happenings around this artsy district. ⊠ *78 rue Bonaparte, St-Germain-des-Prés* ☎ *01–40–46–75–06* ⊕ *www.mairie6.paris.fr* ⊠ *Free* ⊗ *Weekdays 8:30–5 (7:30 on Thurs.); Sat. 9–12:30; hrs can vary based on exhibit; closed Sun.* Ⓜ *Saint-Sulpice.*

Musée Delacroix. The final home of artist Eugène Delacroix (1798–1863) contains only a small collection of his sketches and drawings. But you can check out the lovely studio he had built in the large garden at the back to work on frescoes he created for St-Sulpice Church, where they remain on display today. The museum also plays host to temporary exhibitions, such as Delacroix's experiments with photography. France's foremost Romantic painter had the good luck to live on **Place Furstenberg**, one of the smallest, most romantic squares in Paris: seeing it is reason enough to come. ⊠ *6 rue Furstenberg, St-Germain-des-Prés* ☎ *01–44–41–86–50* ⊕ *www.musee-delacroix.fr* ⊠ *€6; €7.50 with temporary exhibitions; €12 with same-day admission to the Louvre* ⊗ *Weds. –Mon. 9:30–5; closed Tues.* Ⓜ *St-Germain-des-Prés.*

Musée de la Monnaie. Louis XVI transferred the royal mint to this imposing mansion in the late 18th century. It was moved again (to Pessac, near Bordeaux) in 1973; however, weights and measures, medals, and limited-edition coins are still made here, and the site houses a museum devoted to currency. Slated to re-open in late 2014 following a two-year renovation, the Musée de la Monnaie has an extensive collection of coins and related artifacts, plus workshops where you can watch artisans in action as they mint, mold, sculpt, polish, and engrave using century-old techniques. The man behind the museum makeover, renowned urban architect Philippe Prost, will also be adding a concept store and a Zen garden. Refreshed public spaces will host cultural programs and temporary contemporary art exhibitions. ⊠ *11 quai de Conti, St-Germain-des-Prés* ☎ *01–40–46–56–66* ⊕ *www. monnaiedeparis.fr* 🖾 *€8 entry with audioguide; €3 for atelier visit by reservation only (✑ musee@monnaiedeparis.fr); entry prices vary for temporary exhibitions* ⊙ *Tues.–Fri. 11–5:30, weekends noon–5:30; closed Mon.* Ⓜ *Pont Neuf, Odéon.*

Musée Maillol. Bronzes by Art Deco sculptor Aristide Maillol (1861–1944), whose voluptuous, stylized nudes adorn the Tuileries Gardens, can be admired at this handsome mansion lovingly restored by his former model and muse, Dina Vierny. The museum is particularly moving because it's Vierny's personal collection. She met Maillol when she was a teenager and he was already an old man. The stunning life-size drawings upstairs are both erotic and tender—age gazing on youth with fondness and longing. The museum often stages popular temporary exhibits of 20th-century painters such as Jean-Michel Basquiat and Francis Bacon that are worth the wait. ⊠ *61 rue de Grenelle, St-Germain-des-Prés* ☎ *01–42–22–59–58* ⊕ *www.museemaillol.com* 🖾 *€11* ⊙ *Sat.–Thurs. 10:30–7, Fri. 10:30–9:30 (last entry 45 mins before closing)* Ⓜ *Rue du Bac.*

Musée National de la Légion d'Honneur (*Hôtel de Salm*). A must for military-history buffs, the National Museum of the Legion of Honor is dedicated to French and foreign military leaders. Housed in an elegant mansion just across from the Musée d'Orsay, it features a broad collection of military decorations, themed paintings, and video tributes to various luminaries—including U.S. general Dwight Eisenhower, a Légion member who led the Allied liberation of France in 1944. The palatial complex was completed in 1788 and acquired by the Legion of Honor in 1804. ■**TIP➔** Entrance is free and includes an English audioguide. ⊠ *2 rue de la Légion d'Honneur, St-Germain-des-Prés* ☎ *01–40–62–84–25* ⊕ *www.musee-legiondhonneur.fr* 🖾 *Free* ⊙ *Wed.–Sun. 1–6; closed Mon.; Tues. groups only* Ⓜ *Solférino; RER: Musée d'Orsay.*

MONTPARNASSE

Visit Fodors.com for advice, updates, and bookings

GETTING ORIENTED

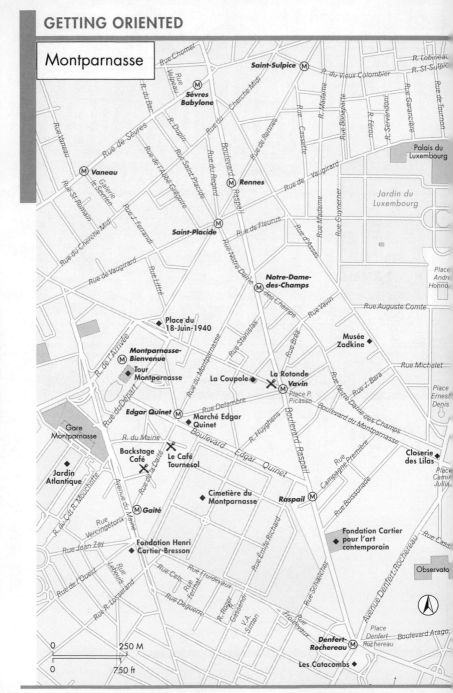

Montparnasse

TOP REASONS TO GO

Catacombs. History buffs, lovers of the macabre, and the just plain curious, can make an unforgettable descent into Paris's underground bastion of bones; claustrophobic folks, however, need not apply.

Fondation Cartier pour l'art contemporain. Connoisseurs of cutting-edge art will appreciate what's on view here. The building itself was designed by Jean Nouvel, the avant-garde darling of Paris architecture.

Fondation Henri Cartier-Bresson. Photography fans shouldn't miss the chance to see Cartier-Bresson's restored atelier, featuring a small collection of his work plus photographs from young artists.

The Tour Montparnasse. Even though this 680-foot black behemoth of a skyscraper is considered one of the biggest eyesores in Paris, its open-air roof terrace is still one of the best spots to see the City of Light.

BEST CAFÉS

Backstage Café. This hot spot is on one of Montparnasse's most lively streets, aptly named Rue de la Gaîté (or "Cheerful Street"). Settle into a comfy chair and order a creation from the extensive cocktail list or choose from a menu of affordable French and international standards. ⊠ *31 bis, rue de la Gaîté, Montparnasse* ☏ *01–43–20–68–59* ⊕ *www.backstagecafe.fr* Ⓜ *Edgar Quinet.*

Le Sélect Café and Brasserie. Isadora Duncan and Hart Crane used to hang out here; now it's a popular place for a postcinema beer, a glass of wine, or a well-made cocktail. Emmentaler cheese lovers should try the *croque madame* with a bowl of French onion soup. ⊠ *99 bd. Montparnasse, Montparnasse* ☏ *01–45–48–38–24* Ⓜ *Vavin.*

GETTING HERE

Montparnasse includes the 14e and 15e arrondissements. Take Line 4, 6, 12, or 13 to Montparnasse–Bienvenue for the Tour Montparnasse; walk along Boulevard du Montparnasse to reach the cafés. Take Line 4 or 6 to the Raspail métro stop for the Cimetière du Montparnasse or the Fondation Henri Cartier-Bresson. To visit the Catacombs, take the 4 or 6 lines to Denfert-Rochereau. Other nearby métro stops include the Edgar Quinet stop on the 6 line and the Gaîté stop on the 13 line.

12

MAKING THE MOST OF YOUR TIME

If you can get to the top of Tour Montparnasse on a clear day, you'll be rewarded with a vista unmatched in all of Paris. The viewing deck is open until 10:30 pm (11:30 on Friday and Saturday), so you can watch the lights sparkle on the Eiffel Tower at the top of the hour. The Catacombs and the Fondation Henri Cartier-Bresson are closed Monday. The Cimetière du Montparnasse is open daily.

Sightseeing
★★★
Dining
★★★
Lodging
★★
Shopping
★
Nightlife
★★

Once a warren of artists' studios and swinging cafés, much of Montparnasse was leveled in the 1960s to make way for a gritty train station and the Tour Montparnasse, Paris's only—and much maligned—skyscraper. Over the years, this neighborhood has evolved into a place where Parisians can find more reasonable rents, well-priced cafés, and the kind of real-life vibe lost in some of the trendier sections of the city.

Updated by
Victoria Tang

Despite its soulless modern architecture, the **Tour Montparnasse** has an upside—after all, the rooftop terrace provides a prime panoramic view of Paris. It's okay to feel smug during your ascent, as you consider yourself savvy for having avoided long lines at Tour Eiffel; afterward, congratulate yourself with a fancy cocktail at Le Bar Américain on the 56th floor.

The other star attraction of Montparnasse is belowground. The labyrinthine tunnels of the Paris **Catacombs** contain the bones of centuries' worth of Parisians, moved here when disease, spread by rotting corpses, threatened the city center.

The café society that flourished in the early 20th century—Picasso, Modigliani, Hemingway, Man Ray, and even Trotsky raised a glass here—is still evident along Boulevard du Montparnasse. The Art Deco interior of **La Coupole** attracts diners seeking piles of golden *choucroute*.

Along Boulevard Raspail you can see today's art stars at the **Fondation Henri Cartier-Bresson** and the **Fondation Cartier pour l'art contemporain,** or pay your respects to Baudelaire, Alfred Dreyfus, or Simone de Beauvoir in the **Cimetière du Montparnasse.**

TOP ATTRACTIONS

Cimetière du Montparnasse. Many of the neighborhood's most illustrious residents rest here, a stone's throw from where they lived and loved: Charles Baudelaire, Frédéric Bartholdi (who designed the Statue of

Liberty), Alfred Dreyfus, Guy de Maupassant, and, more recently, photographer Man Ray, playwright Samuel Beckett, writers Marguerite Duras, Jean-Paul Sartre, and Simone de Beauvoir, actress Jean Seberg, and singer-songwriter Serge Gainsbourg. Opened in 1824 and spread over 47 acres, the ancient farmland is the second largest burial ground in Paris. ✉ *Entrances on Rue Froidevaux and Bd. Edgar Quinet, Montparnasse* ☉ *Mid-Mar.–early Nov., weekdays 8–6, Sat. 8:30–6, Sun. 9–6; early Nov.–mid-Mar., weekdays 8–5:30, Sat. 8:30–5:30, Sun. 9–5:30* Ⓜ *Raspail, Gaîté.*

> ### WORD OF MOUTH
>
> ". . . go down into the Catacombs. They are easily accessible via métro, and won't take a big chunk out of your limited time—and are quite the sight."
> —RaymondLuxuryYacht

12

FAMILY
Fodor's Choice
★

Fondation Cartier pour l'art contemporain. There's no shortage of museums in Paris, but this eye-catching gallery may be the city's premier place to view cutting-edge art. Funded by luxury giant Cartier, the foundation is at once an architectural landmark, a corporate collection, and an exhibition space. Architect Jean Nouvel's 1993 building is a glass house of cards layered seamlessly between the boulevard and the garden. The foundation regularly hosts *Soirées Nomades* (Nomadic Nights) featuring lectures, dance, music, film, or fashion on Thursday evenings. Some are in English. Check the website for times and details. ■TIP➔ Family tours and creative workshops for children 9–13 are available. ✉ *261 bd. Raspail, Montparnasse* ☎ *01–42–18–56–50* ⊕ *www.fondation.cartier. com* ⊡ *€10.50* ☉ *Tues. 11–10, Wed.–Sun. 11–8* Ⓜ *Raspail.*

Fodor's Choice
★

Fondation Henri Cartier-Bresson. Photography has deep roots in Montparnasse, as great experimenters like Louis Daguerre and Man Ray lived and worked here. In keeping with this spirit of innovation, Henri Cartier-Bresson, legendary photographer and creator of the Magnum photo agency, opened the HCB foundation in 2003 with Martine Franck and their daughter Melanie to support contemporary photography. The restored 1913 artists' atelier holds three temporary exhibitions each year. Be sure to go to the top floor to see a small gallery of Cartier-Bresson's own work. ✉ *2 impasse Lebouis, Montparnasse* ☎ *01–56–80–27–00* ⊕ *www.henricartierbresson.org* ⊡ *€7; free on Wed. 6:30 pm–8:30 pm* ☉ *Tues., Thurs., Fri., and Sun. 1–6:30, Wed. 1–8:30, Sat. 11–6* Ⓜ *Gaîté, Edgar Quinet.*

Les Catacombes. This is just the thing for anyone with morbid interests. What you'll see after a descent through dark, clammy passages is Paris's principal ossuary, which also once served as a hideout maze for the French Resistance. Bones from the defunct Cimetière des Innocents were the first to arrive in 1786, when decomposing bodies started seeping into the cellars of the market at Les Halles, drawing swarms of ravenous rats. The legions of bones dumped here are stacked not by owner but by type—rows of skulls, packs of tibias, and piles of spinal disks, often rather artfully arranged. Be prepared for lots of steep stairs and a long underground walk. Wear non-slip shoes, too, as the floor can be damp. The good news is that you won't be shrouded in tomblike darkness since the tunnels are well lighted. Among the nameless 6 million or so are the bones of Madame de Pompadour (1721–64), laid to rest with the riffraff after a lifetime spent as the mistress of Louis XV. Unfortunately, one of the most interesting aspects of the catacombs is one you probably won't see: *cataphiles,* mostly art students, have found alternate entrances into its 300 km (186 miles) of tunnels and here they make art, party, and purportedly raise hell. ■ TIP→ Arrive early as the line can get long and only 200 people can descend at a time. Audioguides are available (€3). Not recommended for claustrophobes or young children. ⊠ *1 ave. du Colonel Henri Roi-Tanguy, Montparnasse* ☎ *01–43–22–47–63* ⊕ *www. catacombes.paris.fr* ⊠ *€8* ⊙ *Tues.–Sun. 10–5 (last entry at 4)* Ⓜ *Métro or RER: Denfert-Rochereau.*

Musée Zadkine. The sculptor Ossip Zadkine spent nearly four decades living in this bucolic retreat near the Jardin du Luxembourg, creating graceful, elongated figures known for their clean lines and simplified features. Zadkine, a Russian-Jewish émigré, moved to Paris in 1910 and fell into a circle of avant-garde artists. His early works, influenced by African, Greek, and Roman art, later took a Cubist turn, no doubt under the influence of his friend, the founder of the Cubist movement: Pablo Picasso. The museum displays a substantial portion of the 400 sculptures and 300 drawings bequeathed to the city by his wife, artist Valentine Prax. It was renovated in 2012 to celebrate its 30th anniversary. There are busts in bronze and stone reflecting the range of Zadkine's style, and an airy back room filled with lithe female nudes in polished wood. The leafy garden is worth the trip alone: it contains a dozen statues nestled in the trees, including *The Destroyed City,* a memorial to the Dutch city of Rotterdam, destroyed by the Germans in 1940. ⊠ *100 bis, rue d'Assas, Montparnasse* ☎ *01–55–42–77–20* ⊕ *www.zadkine.paris. fr* ⊠ *Free; fee (varies) for temporary exhibitions only* ⊙ *Tues.–Sun. 10–6 (last entry 5:40)* Ⓜ *Vavin, Notre-Dame-des-Champs.*

Tour Montparnasse. One of continental Europe's tallest skyscrapers offers visitors a stupendous view of Paris from its 56th-floor observation deck, and the upwardly mobile can climb another three flights to its open-air roof terrace. Completed in 1973, the 680-foot building attracts 800,000 gawkers each year because, on a clear day, you can see for 40 km (25 miles). Well-placed plaques and a glossy brochure, "Paris Vu d'en Haut" ("Paris from on High"), explain what to look for. Have a cocktail as you drink in the view at **Le Bar Américain** on the 56th floor, which also serves light food, or splurge on dinner in **Le Ciel de Paris** restaurant. ■ TIP→ Purchase tickets online to avoid lines. ⊠ *Rue de l'Arrivée, Montparnasse* ☎ *01–45–38–52–56, 01–40–64–77–64 Le Ciel de Paris* ⊕ *www.tourmontparnasse56.com* ⊠ *€14.50* ⊙ *Apr.– Sept., daily 9:30 am–11:30 pm; Oct.–Mar., Sun.–Thurs. 9:30 am–10:30 pm, Fri. and Sat. 9:30 am–11 pm; last elevator 30 min before closing* Ⓜ *Montparnasse Bienvenüe.*

WORTH NOTING

Closerie des Lilas. Now a popular and pricey bar-restaurant, the Closerie remains a staple of all Parisian literary tours. Commemorative plaques are bolted to the bar as if they were still saving seats for their former

Artists, Writers, and Exiles

CLOSE UP

12

Paris became a magnet for the international avant-garde in the mid-1800s and remained Europe's creative capital until the 1950s. It all began south of **Montmartre**, when Romantics, including writers Charles Baudelaire and George Sand (with her lover, Polish composer Frédéric Chopin), moved into the streets below Boulevard de Clichy. Impressionist painters Claude Monet, Edouard Manet, and Mary Cassatt had studios here, near Gare St-Lazare, so they could commute to the countryside. In the 1880s the neighborhood dance halls had a new attraction: the cancan, and in 1889 the **Moulin Rouge** cabaret was opened.

The artistic maelstrom continued through the Belle Époque and beyond. In the early 1900s Picasso and Braque launched Cubism from a ramshackle hillside studio, the **Bateau-Lavoir**, and a similar beehive of activity was established at the south end of the city in a curious studio building called La Ruche (the beehive, at the Convention métro stop). Artists from different disciplines worked together on experimental productions. In 1917 the modernist ballet *Parade* hit the stage, danced by impresario Sergei Diaghilev's Ballets Russes, with music by Erik Satie and costumes by Picasso—everyone involved was hauled off to court, accused of being cultural anarchists.

World War I shattered this creative frenzy, and when peace returned, the artists had moved. The narrow streets of **Montparnasse** had old buildings suitable for studios, and the area hummed with a wide, new, café-filled boulevard. At 27 rue Fleurus, Gertrude Stein held court with her partner, Alice B. Toklas. Picasso drew admirers to **La Rotonde,** and F. Scott Fitzgerald drank at the now-defunct Dingo.

The Spanish Civil War and World War II brought an end to carefree Montparnasse. But the literati reconvened in **St-Germain-des-Prés**. **Café de Flore** and **Deux Magots** had long been popular with an alternative crowd. Expat writers Samuel Beckett and Richard Wright joined existentialists Jean-Paul Sartre, Simone de Beauvoir, and Albert Camus in the neighborhood, drawn into the orbit of literary magazines and publishing houses.

Although Paris can no longer claim to be the epicenter of Western artistic innovation, pockets of outrageous creativity still bubble up. The galleries on Rue Louise Weiss in **Tolbiac** and the open-studio weekends in **Belleville** and **Oberkampf**, for instance, reveal the city's continuing artistic spirit; and the Ménilmontant district, where past arts icons rest in peace at the Père Lachaise Cemetery, is considered a new mecca for creative souls.

clientele: an impressive list of literati including Zola, Baudelaire, Rimbaud, Apollinaire, Beckett, and, of course, Hemingway. ("Papa" wrote pages of *The Sun Also Rises* here and lived around the corner at 115 rue Notre-Dame-des-Champs.) Although the lilacs that once graced the garden—and shaded such habitués as Ingres, Whistler, and Cézanne—are gone, the terrace still opens onto a garden wall of luxuriant foliage. There is live music in the piano bar. ⊠ *171 bd. du Montparnasse, Montparnasse* ☎ *01–40–51–34–50* ⊕ *www.closeriedeslilas.fr* Ⓜ *Vavin; RER: Port Royal.*

Jardin Atlantique. Built above the tracks of Gare Montparnasse, this park nestled among tall modern buildings is named for its assortment of trees and plants typically found in coastal regions near the Atlantic Ocean. At the far end of the garden are small twin museums devoted to World War II: the **Mémorial du Maréchal-Leclerc,** named for the liberator of Paris, and the adjacent **Musée Jean-Moulin,** devoted to the leader of the French Resistance. Both feature memorabilia and share a common second floor showing photos and video footage (with English subtitles) of the final days of the war. Entrance is free, though temporary exhibitions cost a few euros. In the center of the park, what looks like a quirky piece of metallic sculpture is actually a meteorological center, with a battery of flickering lights reflecting temperature, wind speed, and monthly rainfall. ✉ *1 pl. des Cinq-Martyrs-du-Lycée-Buffon, Montparnasse* ☎ *01–40–64–39–44* ⊕ *www.equipement.paris.fr* ⊘ *Jardin weekdays 8–dusk, weekends 9–dusk (hrs vary depending on season); museums Tues.–Sun. 10–6* Ⓜ *Montparnasse Bienvenüe.*

La Coupole. One of Montparnasse's most famous brasseries, La Coupole opened in 1927 and soon became a home-away-from-home for Apollinaire, Cocteau, Satie, Stravinsky, and (again) Hemingway. In the 1980s the brasserie was bought by the Flo chain, which preserved the superb Art Deco interior, including pillars by Chagall and Brancusi. The place retains its hustle and bustle—with scurrying waiters and the overwhelming noise of clinking glasses and clattering silverware. Executive Chef Jean Philippe Bourgueil whips up house specialties, including curried farmhouse lamb (served since 1927) and beef fillet flambéed with Armagnac. ✉ *102 bd. du Montparnasse, Montparnasse* ☎ *01–43–20–14–20* ⊕ *www.lacoupole-paris.com* ⊘ *Tues.–Sat. noon–midnight, Sun.–Mon. noon–11* Ⓜ *Vavin.*

Marché Edgar Quinet. One of the best ways to experience local living, this excellent street market sells everything from fresh fruit to hot crêpes to wool shawls on Wednesday and Saturday. It's a good place to pick up lunch-on-the-go before paying your respects at Cimetière du Montparnasse across the street. ✉ *Bd. du Edgar Quinet at métro Edgar Quinet, Montparnasse* ⊘ *Wed. 8–2:30, Sat. 8–3* Ⓜ *Edgar Quinet.*

Place du 18-Juin-1940. Next to Tour Montparnasse, this square commemorates an impassioned radio broadcast Charles de Gaulle made from London on June 18, 1940. In it he urged the French to resist Nazi occupiers (who'd invaded the month prior), thereby launching the French Resistance Movement. It was also here that German military governor Dietrich von Choltitz surrendered to the Allies in August 1944, ignoring Hitler's orders to destroy the city as he withdrew. ✉ *Montparnasse* Ⓜ *Montparnasse–Bienvenüe.*

WESTERN PARIS

with the Bois de Boulogne

GETTING ORIENTED

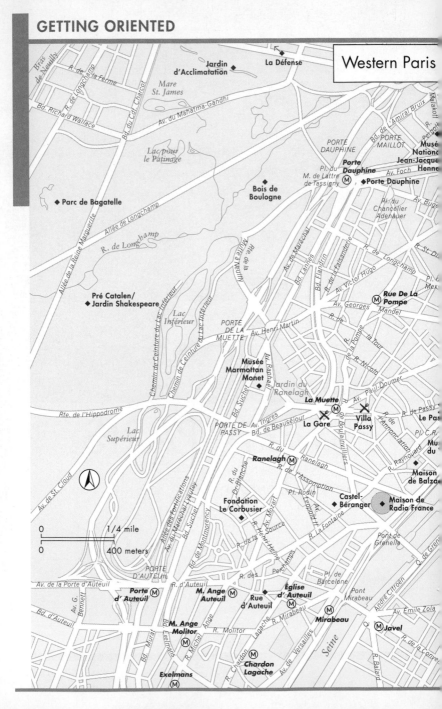

Western Paris

Jardin d'Acclimatation

La Défense

Bras de Neuilly

R. de Longchamp

R. de la Ferme

Mare St. James

Bd. Richard Wallace

Av. du Carl Charcot

Av. du Mahatma-Gandhi

Bd. de l'Amiral Bruix

Malakoff

Perzoix

PORTE DAUPHINE

Bd. de l'Amiral Bruix

PORTE MAILLOT

Musée National Jean-Jacques Henne

Lac pour le Patinage

Porte Dauphine

Pl. du M. de Lattre de Tassigny

Av. Foch

Porte Dauphine

Av. Bug

Bois de Boulogne

Pl. du Chancelier Adenauer

Parc de Bagatelle

Allée de Longchamp

Allée de la Reine Marguerite

R. de Longchamp

Av. de Maréchal

Av. de la Porte de Neuilly

Bd. Lannes

R. de la Faisanderie

Av. Victor Hugo

R. de Longchamp

Pl. St. Di

Pl. de Mex

Av. Georges Mandel

Av. Buge

Pré Catelan/ Jardin Shakespeare

Chemin de Ceinture du Lac Inférieur

Chemin de Ceinture au Lac Inférieur

Lac Inférieur

PORTE DE LA MUETTE

Av. Henri Martin

R. de la Pompe

R. de la Tour

R. de R. Nicolo

Rue De La Pompe

Musée Marmottan Monet

Av. Raphaël

Bd. Suchet

Jardin du Ranelagh

La Muette

Av. Paul-Doumet

R. de Passy

Le Pas

Rte. de l'Hippodrome

PORTE DE PASSY

Av. Ingres

Bd. de Beauséjour

La Gare

Villa Passy

Pl. C.R.

Lac Supérieur

Ranelagh

R. du Dr. Blanche

R. de l'Assomption

Ranelagh

Bd. de Boulainvilliers

R. de l'Annonciation

R. Raynouard

Mu du

Av. de St. Cloud

Allée des fortifications

Av. du Maréchal Lyautey

Bd. Suchet

Fondation Le Corbusier

Pl. Rodin

R. du Dr. Blanche

Av. Th. Gautier

Av. Leopold II

R. La Fontaine

Maison de Balzac

Castel-Béranger

Maison de Radio France

Pont de Grenelle

Q. de Gren

André Citroën

0   1/4 mile

0   400 meters

PORTE D'AUTEUIL

Bd. de Montmorency

R. des Perchamps

Pl. de Barcelone

Pont Mirabeau

Av. de la Porte d'Auteuil

R. d'Auteuil

R. des

Église d'Auteuil

Av. Émile Zola

Porte d'Auteuil

M. Ange Auteuil

Rue d'Auteuil

R. Mirabeau

Mirabeau

Javel

Av. G. Bennett

Bd. d'Auteuil

Bd. Murat

Bd. Exelmans

M. Ange Molitor

R. Michel Ange

R. Molitor

R. Chardon Lagache

R. de la Conve

Seine

R. Balard

Exelmans

Chardon Lagache

Av. de Versailles

13

TOP REASONS TO GO

Musée Marmottan Monet. If you're a fan of Claude Monet, don't miss this gem of a museum tucked away deep in the 16e near the Jardin de Ranelagh.

Bois de Boulogne. Whether you spend your afternoon in a rowboat or wandering gardens filled with foliage, the Bois is a perfect escape from the city.

Jardin d'Acclimatation. There's not a child under the age of five who won't love this amusement park on the northern edge of the Bois de Boulogne.

Fondation Le Corbusier. The Modernist designs of Le Corbusier fill this compelling museum, which the iconic architect designed as a private home.

MAKING THE MOST OF YOUR TIME

If this isn't your first time in Paris, or even if it is and you've had enough of the touristy central part of the city, this neighborhood is a great choice and can be treated like a day trip. Spend the morning admiring the Monets at the uncrowded Musée Marmottan Monet (closed Monday), then take in the Art Nouveau architecture on Rue la Fontaine.

GETTING HERE

Western Paris includes the 16e and 17e arrondissements. Take Line 9 to La Muette métro stop for the Musée Marmottan Monet, or to the Jasmin stop (also Line 9) to explore Rue la Fontaine. Take Line 6 to the Passy stop for the Musée du Vin or to reach the main drag, Rue de Passy; alternately, take Bus 72 from the Hôtel de Ville or 63 from St. Sulpice. For the Bois de Boulogne, take Line 2 to the Porte Dauphine stop or RER C to Avenue Foch. For the Jardin d'Acclimatation, enter the park from the Les Sablons or Porte Maillot métro stops on Line 1. If you're heading out to La Défense, it's the terminus of Line 1.

BEST CAFÉS

La Gare. Housed in a former train station, this restaurant-lounge is frequented by business types and chic youth alike. Sit on the large terrace or descend the wide staircase to a room bathed in natural light by day and warm golden tones at night. ⊠ *19 chausée de la Muette, Western Paris* ☎ *01–42–15–15–31* ⊕ *restaurantlagare.com* Ⓜ *La Muette.*

Le Passy. The plush chestnut-and-cream decor of this café is the work of one of Givenchy's nephews. Cocktails are classy, there's a good variety of beer on tap, and the food (bistro fare such as steaks, fish, and frites) is tasty. In the evening, candlelight makes everyone look that much more glamorous. ⊠ *2 rue de Passy, Passy, Western Paris* ☎ *01–42–88–31–02* Ⓜ *Passy or Trocadéro.*

Villa Passy. The tucked-away courtyard of this bucolic café just off Rue de Passy may make you think you've stumbled into a small village. Sit outside on a cushioned banquette shaded by ivy and order the plat du jour, prepared with fresh market ingredients. ⊠ *4 impasse des Carrières (opposite 31 rue de Passy), Passy, Western Paris* ☎ *01–45–27–68–76* Ⓜ *Passy.*

Sightseeing
★★

Dining
★

Lodging
★

Shopping
★

Nightlife
—

Meet Paris at its most prim and proper. This genteel area is a study in smart urban planning, with classical architecture and newer construction cohabitating as easily as the haute bourgeoisie inhabitants mix with their expat neighbors. There's no shortage of celebrities seeking some peace and quiet here, but you're just as likely to find well-heeled families who decamped from the center of the city in search of a spacious apartment. Passy, once a separate village and home to American ambassadors Benjamin Franklin and Thomas Jefferson, was incorporated into the city in 1860 under Napoléon III.

Updated by
Victoria Tang

A walk along the main avenues gives you a sense of Paris's finest Art Nouveau and Modernist buildings, including **Castel-Béranger,** by Hector Guimard, and the **Fondation Le Corbusier** museum, a prime example of the titular architect's pioneering style (it was one of Corbusier's first Paris commissions). This neighborhood is also home to one of the city's best and most overlooked museums—the **Musée Marmottan Monet**—which has an astonishing collection of Impressionist art. Enjoy a *dégustation* (tasting) at the **Musée du Vin** or simply find a café on Rue de Passy and savor a moment in one of the city's most exclusive enclaves. If it's a leafy landscape you're after, spend an afternoon at the **Bois de Boulogne,** especially if you have kids in tow. At *le Bois,* you can explore the Pré Catelan and peacock-filled Bagatelle gardens, both meticulously landscaped and surrounded by woods. Head to the old-fashioned amusement park at the Jardin d'Acclimatation or take a rowboat out on one of the park's two bucolic lakes. You can also rent a bike and hit 14 km (9 miles) of marked trails.

TOP ATTRACTIONS

FAMILY
Fodor'sChoice
★

Bois de Boulogne

See highlighted listing in this chapter.

Fodor'sChoice
★

Castel-Béranger. It's a shame you can't go inside this house, which is considered the city's first Art Nouveau structure. Dreamed up in 1898 by Hector Guimard, the wild combination of materials and the grimacing grillwork led neighbors to call it Castle *Dérangé* (Deranged). Yet the project catapulted the 27-year-old Guimard into the public eye, leading to his famous métro commission. After ogling the sea-inspired front entrance, go partway down the alley to admire the inventive treatment of the traditional Parisian courtyard, complete with a melting water fountain. Just up the road at No. 60 is the Hotel Mezzara, designed by Guimard in 1911 for textile designer Paul Mezzara. You can trace Guimard's evolution by walking to the subtler Agar complex at the end of the block. Tucked beside the stone entrance at the corner of Rue la Fontaine and Rue Gros is a tiny café-bar with an Art Nouveau glass front and furnishings. ⊠ *14 rue la Fontaine, Passy-Auteuil* Ⓜ *Ranelagh; RER: Maison de Radio France.*

13

QUICK
BITES

Café Antoine. Established in 1911 within an original Hector Guimard building, the charming Café Antoine (named after its original owner) warrants a visit for its Art Nouveau facade, floor tiles, and carved wooden bar. Count on €35 for a meal or about €17 for a shared charcuterie plate. Fresh desserts and friendly service welcome guests. Closed weekends. ⊠ *17 rue Jean de la Fontaine, Passy-Auteuil* ☎ *01–40–50–14–30* ⊙ *Weekdays 8–2:30 and 6:30–10:30* Ⓜ *Ranelagh.*

Fondation Le Corbusier (*Le Corbusier Foundation*). Maison La Roche is a must-see for architecture and design lovers. Built as a private residence in 1923, it's a stellar example of Swiss architect Le Corbusier's innovative construction techniques based on geometric forms, recherché color schemes, and a visionary use of iron and concrete. The sloping ramp that replaces the traditional staircase is one of the most eye-catching features. Hour-long English tours are available at 2 pm every Tuesday and must be reserved online. ⊠ *8–10 sq. du Docteur Blanche, Passy-Auteuil* ☎ *01–42–88–41–53* ⊕ *www.fondationlecorbusier.fr* ☎ *€8* ⊙ *Mon. 1:30–6, Tues.–Sat. 10–6; Closed Sun.* Ⓜ *Jasmin, Michel Ange Auteuil.*

Fodor'sChoice
★

Musée Marmottan Monet. A few years ago the underrated Marmottan tacked "Monet" onto its official name—and justly so, as this is the largest collection of the artist's works anywhere. More than 100 pieces, donated by his son Michel, occupy a specially built basement gallery in an elegant 19th-century mansion, which was once the hunting lodge of the Duke de Valmy. Among them you can find such works as the *Cathédrale de Rouen* series (1892–96) and *Impression: Soleil Levant* (*Impression: Sunrise*, 1872), the painting that helped give the Impressionist movement its name. Other exhibits include letters exchanged by Impressionist painters Berthe Morisot and Mary Cassatt. Upstairs, the mansion still feels like a graciously decorated private home. Empire

BOIS DE BOULOGNE

✉ *Porte Dauphine for main entrance; Porte Maillot or Les Sablons for northern end; Porte d'Auteuil for southern end, Western Paris* ☎ *01–53–64–53–80 Parc de Bagatelle, 01–40–67–90–85 Jardin d'Acclimatation* ⊕ *www.jardindacclimatation.fr* 💶 *Parc de Bagatelle free except during exhibitions, otherwise €5.50; Jardin Shakespeare €1; Jardin d'Acclimatation €3 entry, €2.90 per for rides* ☉ *Daily; hrs vary according to time of yr but are generally around 10–dusk* Ⓜ *Porte Dauphine for main entrance, Porte Maillot for northern end, Porte d'Auteuil for southern end.*

TIPS

■ The main entrance to the Bois is off Avenue Foch near the Porte Dauphine métro stop on the 2 Line; it is best for accessing Pré Catelan and Jardin Shakespeare, both located off the Route de la Grande-Cascade by the lake.

■ For the Jardin d'Acclimatation, off Boulevard Des Sablons, take the 1 Line to Les Sablons or Porte Maillot, where you can walk or ride the petit train to the amusement park.

■ The Parc de Bagatelle, off Route de Sèvres-à-Neuilly, can be accessed from either Porte Dauphine or Porte Maillot, though it's a bit of a hike.

■ You'll want to leave the park by dusk, as the Bois—seedy and potentially dangerous after dark—turns into a distinctly "adult" playground.

When Parisians want to experience the great outdoors without going too far from home, they head to the Bois de Boulogne. Once a royal hunting ground, the Bois is not a park in the traditional sense—more like a vast tamed forest where romantic lakes and wooded paths are complemented by formal gardens and family-friendly amusements. Art lovers flock to the new Frank Gehry–designed exhibition space and cultural center dedicated to contemporary art near the Jardin d'Acclimatation: The Louis Vuitton Foundation for Creation's 65,000-square-foot sculptural glass-and-steel building is expected to be unveiled in late 2014.

Highlights

The Parc de Bagatelle is a floral garden with irises, roses, tulips, water lilies, and roaming peacocks that is at its most colorful between April and June. Pré Catelan contains one of Paris's largest trees: a copper beech more than 200 years old. The romantic Le Pré Catelan restaurant, where *le tout Paris* used to dine on the elegant terrace during the Belle Époque, still draws diners and wedding parties—especially on weekends. The Jardin Shakespeare inside the Pré Catelan has a sampling of the flowers, herbs, and trees mentioned in Shakespeare's plays, and becomes an open-air theater for the Bard's works in spring. The Jardin d'Acclimatation, on the northern edge of the Bois, is an amusement park that attracts seemingly every local preschooler on summer Sunday afternoons. A miniature railway shuttle runs from Porte Maillot on Wednesday and weekends beginning at 1:30 (tickets cost €2.90, round-trip). Boats or bikes can be rented for a few euros at Lac Inférieur. You can row or take a quick "ferry" to the island restaurant Chalet des Iles.

furnishings fill the salons overlooking the Jardin de Ranelagh on one side and the private yard on the other. There's also a captivating room of illuminated medieval manuscripts. ■TIP➜ To best understand the collection's context, buy an English-language catalog in the museum shop on your way in. ⊠ *2 rue Louis-Boilly, Passy-Auteuil* ☎ *01–44–96–50–33* ⊕ *www.marmottan.com* ⊠ *€10* ⊙ *Wed.–Sun. 10–6 (until 8 Thurs.); closed Mon.* Ⓜ *La Muette.*

WORTH NOTING   13

OFF THE
BEATEN
PATH

La Défense. First conceived in 1958, this Modernist suburb just west of Paris was inspired by Le Corbusier's dream of high-rise buildings, pedestrian walkways, and sunken vehicle circulation. Built as an experiment to keep high-rises out of the historic downtown, the Parisian business hub has survived economic uncertainty to become the city's prime financial district. Visiting La Défense gives you a crash course in contemporary skyscraper evolution, from the solid blocks of the 1960s and '70s to the curvy fins of the '90s and beyond. Today 20,000 people live in the suburb, but 180,000 people work here, and many more come to shop in its enormous mall. While riding the métro Line 1 here, you'll get a view of the Seine, then emerge at a pedestrian plaza studded with some great public art, including César's giant thumb, Joan Miro's colorful figures, and one of Calder's great red "stabiles." The Grande Arche de La Défense dominates the area: it was designed as a controversial closure to the historic axis of Paris (an imaginary line that runs through the Arc de Triomphe, the Arc du Carrousel, and the Louvre Pyramid). Glass bubble elevators in a metal-frame tower whisk you a heart-jolting 360 feet to the viewing platform. ■TIP➜ At the end of June, La Défense hosts an annual week-long jazz festival with free concerts and events. See ⊕ ladefensejazzfestival.hauts-de-seine.net for details. ⊠ *Parvis de La Défense, La Défense* ☎ *01–49–07–27–55* ⊕ *www.grandearche.com* ⊠ *Grande Arche €10* ⊙ *Apr.–Aug., daily 10–8; Sept.–Mar., daily 10–7* Ⓜ *Métro or RER: Grande Arche de La Défense.*

Maison de Balzac. Literature aficionados can visit the modest home of the great French 19th-century novelist Honoré de Balzac (1799–1850), which contains exhibits charting his tempestuous yet prolific career. Balzac penned nearly 100 novels and stories known collectively as *The Human Comedy,* many of them set in Paris. You can still feel his presence in his study and pay homage to his favorite coffeepot—his working hours were fueled by a tremendous consumption of the "black ink." He would escape his creditors by exiting the flat through a secret passage that led down to what is now the Musée du Vin. ⊠ *47 rue Raynouard, Passy-Auteuil* ☎ *01–55–74–41–80* ⊕ *www.balzac.paris.fr* ⊠ *Free; temporary exhibitions €4* ⊙ *Tues.–Sun. 10–6 (last entry 5:30); closed Mon.* Ⓜ *Passy, La Muette.*

Musée du Vin. Oenophiles with some spare time will enjoy this quirky museum housed in a 15th-century abbey, a reminder of Passy's roots as a pastoral village. Though hardly exhaustive and geared to beginners, the small collection contains old wine bottles, glassware, and ancient wine-related pottery excavated in Paris. Wine-making paraphernalia shares the grottolike space with hokey figures retired from the city's wax museum, including Napoléon appraising a glass of Burgundy. But you can partake in a thoroughly nonhokey wine tasting, or bring home one of the 200-plus bottles for sale in the tiny gift shop. There's a free English audioguide. Check online for a calendar of wine tastings and classes offered in English. You can book ahead for a casual lunch, too (restaurant open Tuesday through Saturday, noon to 3). ■**TIP**→ This is one of the only places in Paris where you'll find a nondosage (no sugar added) champagne. Children are welcome. ⊠ *Rue des Eaux/5 sq. Charles Dickens, Passy-Auteil* ☎ *01–45–25–63–26* ⊕ *www.museeduvinparis.com* ⌷ *€11.90 with glass of wine; €17 or €27 with 3-wine tastings* ⊙ *Tues.–Sun. 10–6* Ⓜ *Passy.*

Porte Dauphine métro entrance. Visitors come here to snap pictures of the queen of subway entrances—one of the city's two remaining Art Nouveau canopied originals designed by Hector Guimard (the other is at the Abbesses stop on Line 12). A flamboyant scalloped "crown" of patina-painted panels and runaway metal struts adorns this whimsical 1900 creation. ■**TIP**→ Porte Dauphine is the terminus of Line 2. The entrance is on the Bois de Boulogne side of Avenue Foch, so take the Boulevard de l'Amiral Bruix exit. ⊠ *Western Paris* Ⓜ *Porte Dauphine.*

Rue d'Auteuil. This narrow shopping street escaped Haussmann's urban renovations and today still retains the country feel of old Auteuil, a sedate bourgeois enclave. Molière once lived on the site of No. 2, while Racine was on nearby Rue du Buis: the pair met up to clink glasses and exchange drama notes at the Mouton Blanc Inn, now a traditional brasserie, at No. 40. Numbers 19–25 and 29 are an interesting combination of 17th- and 18th-century buildings. At the foot of the street, the scaly dome of the Église Notre Dame d'Auteuil (built in the 1880s) is an unmistakable small-time cousin of the Sacré-Coeur. Rue d'Auteuil is at its liveliest on Wednesday and Saturday mornings, when a much-loved street market crams onto Place Jean-Barraud. ⊠ *Western Paris* Ⓜ *Michel-Ange-Auteuil, Église d'Auteuil.*

FAMILY **Tenniseum.** This sprawling museum, sponsored by the French Tennis Federation, claims to house the world's largest collection of tennis memorabilia. Hidden underneath the Stade Roland Garros (site of the French Open), it also has an archive relating to the sport's 500-year history and hosts themed art and photo exhibits. If you're a serious tennis buff, the museum is worth the short walk from the métro station. Guided stadium tours (€10.50) are available in English on Wednesday and Friday through Sunday at 11 and 3, by appointment only. ⊠ *2 av. Gordon-Bennett, Auteil* ☎ *01–47–43–48–48* ⊕ *www.fft.fr/roland-garros/musee/informations-pratiques* ⌷ *€8; €15.50 with stadium entry* ⊙ *Wed. and Fri.–Sun. 10–6* Ⓜ *Porte d'Auteuil.*

WHERE TO EAT

Updated
by Jennifer
Ditsler-Ladonne

A new wave of culinary confidence has been running through one of the world's great food cities and spilling over both banks of the Seine. Whether cooking up *grand-mère*'s roast chicken and *riz au lait* or placing a whimsical hat of cotton candy atop wild-strawberry-and-rose ice cream, Paris chefs—established and up-and-coming, native and foreign—have been breaking free from the tyranny of tradition and following their passion.

Emblematic of the "bistronomy" movement is the proliferation of "gastrobistros"—often in far-flung or newly chic neighborhoods—helmed by established chefs fleeing the constraints of the star system or passionate young chefs unfettered by overblown expectations. Among the newcomers to the scene are Yannick Alleno, who, in 2010, left behind two Michelin stars at Le Meurice to open his locavore bistro Terroir Parisien and the new Terroir Parisien at the Palais Brogniart; David Toutain at the exceptional new Restaurant David Toutain; sibling chefs Maxime and Romain Teschenko's Le Galopin; and Katsuaki Okiyama's Abri.

But self-expression is not the only driving force behind the current trend. A traditional high-end restaurant can be prohibitively expensive to operate. As a result, more casual bistros and cafés, which reflect the growing allure of less formal dining and often have lower operating costs and higher profit margins, have become attractive opportunities for even top chefs.

For tourists, this development can only be good news, because it makes the cooking of geniuses such as Joël Robuchon, Guy Savoy, Eric Frechon, and Pierre Gagnaire a bit more accessible (even if these star chefs rarely cook in their lower-price restaurants) and opens up a vast range of new possibilities for exciting dining.

Like the chefs themselves, Paris diners are breaking away from tradition with renewed enthusiasm. New restaurants, wine bars, and rapidly multiplying épiceries and sandwich shops recognize that not

BATIGNOLLES

MONTMARTRE
Mix of hip
resto-lounges &
quaint bistros

LA VILLETTE

Bd. de Clichy

Bd. de Rochechouart

Bd. de la Chapelle

Bd. Barbès

Rue Marx Dormoy

Bd. des Batignolles

PIGALLE

8 e

9 e

Rue la Fayette

10 e

Rue du Faubourg Saint-Martin

CHAMPS-ÉLYSÉES
Luxe lane studded
with star-chef
eateries & celebrity
clientele

Bd. Haussmann

OPÉRA

Bd. des Capucines   Bd. des Italiens   Bd. Poissonnière   Bd. de Bonne Nouvelle

Canal Saint-Martin

Bd. de Strasbourg

Bd. de Magenta

CANAL
ST-MARTIN
Boho bistros

Av. des
Champs-Élysées

Rue
Royale

1 er

LOUVRE/
LES HALLES
All-night eats
and boho
bistros

2 e

Rue de Turbigo

3 e

Rue Beaubourg

Boulevard de Sébastopol

Jardin des
Tuileries

Quai des Tuileries

Quai Anatole France

River   Seine

Quai du Louvre

Louvre

Place du
Louvre

Place René
Cassin

Voie Georges
Pompidou

LE MARAIS
Delis, teahouses
and falafel
shops

Bd. Saint-Germain

Quai Voltaire

Quai des Grands Augustins

ÎLE DE
LA CITÉ

THE ISLANDS
Few notable
eateries

Quai de l'Hôtel de ville

Place des
Vosges

7 e

INVALIDES

ST-GERMAIN
Crème of the
café crop

6 e

Bd. Saint-Germain

Quai de
Montebello

ÎLE ST
LOUIS

Quai de la Tournelle

Pont Sully

4 e

Voie Mazas

BASTILLE
Edgy eateries
run by young
chefs

Rue de Sèvres

Bd. Raspail

Palais du
Luxembourg

Jardin du
Luxembourg

Bd. Saint-Michel

Pl. Alphonse Laveran

LATIN
QUARTER
Too many tourist
traps; simple
student cafés

5 e

Rue Monge

Jardin des
Plantes

Av. des Gobelins

Bd. de Vaugirard

Bd. Edgar Quinet

MONTPARNASSE
Pricey brasseries
& oysters
on ice

Av. Denfert-Rochereau

Bd. Saint-Jacques

Av. des Gobelins

Bd. Auriol Vincent

0   500 meters

0   1,500 ft

everyone wants a three-course blowout every time they dine out. And because Parisians are more widely traveled than in the past, many ethnic restaurants—notably the best North African, Vietnamese/Laotian, Chinese, Spanish, and Japanese spots—are making fewer concessions to French tastes, resulting in far better food.

PLANNING

WINE BARS

For tantalizing wines, good food, and great value, look no farther than one of Paris's many wine bars. The past 10 years have seen an explosion of a new kind of *bar à vins,* or, more accurately, *cave à manger*— essentially amplified wineshops with a few tables, which serve a plate or two of regional cheeses or artisanal charcuterie to complement the wines. The new generation of *cavists* stood apart as champions of natural wines, which are unfiltered, contain minimal or no added sulphites, and are often *bio* (organic) or grown biodynamically, that is, according to a specific set of agricultural guidelines. As the natural wine movement dovetailed with the crusade toward simply prepared foods made from quality seasonal ingredients, the contemporary wine bar was born. Indeed, the food in a handful of wine bars now rivals that in the best Paris bistros—and can be a lot more affordable. Whatever the emphasis, the upward trajectory of the wine bar has had a major hand in reinvigorating Paris's wine and food scene.

Wine bars usually keep restaurant hours (noon–2 pm and 7:30–11 pm); some combine with an *épicerie* (gourmet grocer), stay open all day, and close earlier in the evening; others offer a late-night scene. Although casual, most wine bars nowadays require reservations, so call in advance, especially if Sunday brunch is available—still a rarity in Paris. Look for the "wine bar" designation in our restaurant listings.

CHILDREN

Some restaurants provide booster seats, but don't count on them: be sure to ask when you confirm your reservation.

DINING STRATEGY

Where should we eat? With thousands of Paris eateries competing for your attention, it may seem like a daunting question. But fret not—our expert writers and editors have done the legwork. The 120-plus selections here represent the best this city has to offer. Search our "Best Bets" for top recommendations by price, cuisine, and experience; read about local flavors in the neighborhood features; or find a review in the listings, arranged by neighborhood. Delve in, and enjoy!

HOURS

Paris restaurants generally serve food from noon to 2 pm and from 7:30 or 8 pm to about 11 pm. Brasseries have longer hours and often serve all day and late into the evening; some are open 24 hours. Surprisingly, many restaurants close on Saturday as well as Sunday, and Monday closings are also not uncommon. July and August are common months for annual closings, but restaurants may also close for a week in February, around Easter, or at Christmas.

MENUS

All establishments must post menus outside so they're available to look over before you enter. Most have two basic types of menu: à la carte and fixed price (*prix fixe, le menu,* or *la formule*). Although it limits your choices, the prix fixe is usually the best value. If you feel like indulging, the *menu dégustation* (tasting menu), consisting of numerous small courses, lets you sample the chef's offerings. *See the Menu Guide in the Understanding Paris section at the back of this book for guidance with common French menu items.*

14

ORDERING WINE

Most sommeliers are knowledgeable about their lists and can make appropriate suggestions after you've made your tastes and budget known. Simpler spots serve wine in carafes (*en carafe,* or *en pichet*). All restaurants sell wine by the glass, but prices can be steep; be sure to do the math.

SMOKING

Many Parisians are accustomed to smoking before, during, and after meals, but since 2008, the national smoking ban was extended to restaurants, bars, and cafés. Many establishments have compensated by adding covered terraces for smokers, but you'll be happy to know that inside, the air is much clearer.

TIPPING AND TAXES

According to French law, prices must include tax and tip (*service compris* or *prix nets*), but pocket change left on the table in cafés, or an additional 5% in better restaurants, is always appreciated. Beware of bills stamped "Service Not Included" in English or restaurants slyly using American-style credit-card slips, hoping that you'll be confused and add the habitual 15% tip.

WHAT IT COSTS

You'll be lucky to find a good bistro meal for €25 or less, even at lunch, so consider economizing on some meals to have more to spend on the others. Slurping inexpensive Japanese noodles on Rue Ste-Anne, grabbing a sandwich at a casual eatery, or having a picnic in a park will save euros for dinner. And, of course, if you've rented an apartment, you can shop at the city's wonderful markets and cook a few meals at "home." *Prices in the reviews are the average cost of a main course at dinner or, if dinner is not served, at lunch.*

WHAT TO WEAR

Casual dress is acceptable at all but the fanciest restaurants—this usually means stylish sportswear, which might be a bit dressier than in the United States. When in doubt, leave the T-shirts and sneakers behind. If an establishment requires jacket and tie, it's noted in the review.

BEST BETS FOR PARIS DINING

With thousands of restaurants to choose from, how will you decide where to eat? Fodor's writers and editors have selected their favorite restaurants by price, cuisine, and experience below. You can also search by neighborhood for excellent eating experiences—peruse the following pages.

RESTAURANT REVIEWS

In alphabetical order by neighborhood. Use the coordinate (⊕ 1:B2) at the end of each review to locate a property on the corresponding map at the end of the chapter.

THE ISLANDS

ILE ST-LOUIS

$$ BRASSERIE

🍴 **Brasserie de l'Isle Saint-Louis.** With so much going for it, including a dream location on the tip of the Ile Saint-Louis overlooking the Seine and Notre Dame, you'd think this charming brasserie, like so many before it, would have succumbed to its own success. Yet it remains exactly what a decent neighborhood brasserie should be, with an authentic decor, efficiently friendly service, and good brassiere fare—classic leeks vinaigrette, country terrine, and a savory onion tarte à la maison for starters, followed by tender sole meuniere, classic choucroute, or buttered entrecôte. The outdoor terrace simply can't be beat. [$] *Average main: €19* ✉ *55 quai de Bourbon, 4e, Ile St-Louis* ☎ *01–43–54–02–59* 🌐 *www.labrasserie-isl.fr* ✍ *Reservations not accepted* 🕒 *Open noon–11* 🕒 *Closed Wed.* [M] *Pont Marie, Maubert-Mutualité, Sully-Morland* ⊕ *4:E3.*

$$ MODERN FRENCH
Fodor's Choice ★

🍴 **Mon Vieil Ami.** "Modern Alsatian" might sound like an oxymoron, but once you've tasted the food here, you'll understand. The updated medieval dining room—stone walls and dark-wood tables—provides a stylish milieu for the inventive cooking orchestrated by star Alsatian chef Antoine Westermann, which showcases heirloom vegetables (such as yellow carrots and pink-and-white beets) from star producer Joël Thiébault. Pâté *en croûte* (wrapped in pastry) with a knob of foie gras is hard to resist among the starters. Among the mains, red mullet might come in a bouillabaisse sauce with sautéed baby artichokes, and the shoulder of lamb with white beans, preserved lemon, and cilantro has become a classic. This is not necessarily the place for a romantic dinner, since seating is a little tight, but the quality of the food never falters, and the portions are quite generous. [$] *Average main: €24* ✉ *69 rue St-Louis-en-l'Ile, 4e, Ile St-Louis* ☎ *01–40–46–01–35* 🌐 *www.mon-vieil-ami.com* 🕒 *Closed 3 wks in Aug., and 3 wks in Jan.* [M] *Pont Marie* ⊕ *4:E3.*

AROUND THE EIFFEL TOWER

AROUND THE EIFFEL TOWER

$$ BISTRO

🍴 **Afaria.** This otherwise unexciting arrondissement has become home to yet another promising young chef: Ludivine Merlin. Basque cooking is known for its bold flavors and generosity, and the choices at Afaria are no exception: crisp-skinned duck breast with balsamic-fig vinegar (for two) is served dramatically, inside a ceramic roof tile, with the accompanying potato gratin perched on a bed of twigs; and big chunks of spoon-tender slow-cooked pork from Gascony come in an earthenware dish with cubes of roasted celery root. Another signature dish consists of slices of blood sausage layered with apple and topped with grainy mustard. Tapas are served at a high table near the entrance, and there's a large-screen TV for rugby matches. [$] *Average main: €20* ✉ *15 rue Desnouettes, 15e, Around the Eiffel Tower* ☎ *01–48–42–95–90* 🌐 *www.restaurant-afaria.fr* ⊙ *Closed Sun., Mon., 3 wks in Aug.* [M] *Convention* ✥ *3:C6.*

$$$$ BISTRO 🍴 **Au Bon Accueil.** To see what well-heeled Parisians like to eat these days, book a table at this chic little bistro run by Jacques Lacipière as soon as you get to town. The contemporary dining room is unusually comfortable, and the sidewalk tables have an Eiffel Tower view, but it's the excellent, well-priced *cuisine du marché* that has made this spot a hit. Typical of the sophisticated fare from chef Keita Kitamura, who trained at Le Bristol, are Salers beef and green asparagus, roast lobster with mushroom risotto, and game in season. House-made desserts could include citrus terrine with passion-fruit sorbet or caramelized apple mille-feuille with hazelnut ice cream. The €32 prix-fixe menu for lunch or dinner, featuring dishes with a distinct haute-cuisine touch, is one of the city's great bargains. [$] *Average main: €34* ✉ *14 rue de Monttessuy, 7e, Around the Eiffel Tower* ☎ *01–47–05–46–11* 🌐 *www.aubonaccueilparis.com* ✍ *Reservations essential* ⊙ *Closed weekends and 3 wks in Aug.* [M] *Métro or RER: Pont de l'Alma* ✥ *3:D1.*

$$ BISTRO 🍴 **Jadis.** There's something very grown-up about the cooking of young chef Guillaume Delage, which isn't so much of a surprise when you learn that he trained with the likes of Michel Bras, Frédéric Anton (of Le Pré Catelan), and Pierre Gagnaire. It's worth making your way to what seems like the middle of nowhere to taste his nostalgic bistro cooking with a modern touch: you might find pâté en croûte among the chef's suggestions, but there are also dishes like the shrimp with saté spices, creamed black rice, and spinach. The best value is the €38 set menu (€26 for lunch), with several choices for each course; tasting menu is €57. Though simple, the gray-and-burgundy dining room decorated with mirrors and vintage posters has charm. [$] *Average main: €20* ✉ *208 rue de la Croix-Nivert, 15e, Around the Eiffel Tower* ☎ *01–45–57–73–20* 🌐 *www.bistrotjadisparis.com* ✍ *Reservations essential* ⊙ *Closed weekends, 3 wks in Aug., 1 wk at Christmas* [M] *Convention, Porte de Versailles* ✥ *3:B6.*

$ BISTRO 🍴 **Le Café Constant.** Parisians are a nostalgic bunch, which explains the popularity of this down-to-earth venue from esteemed chef Christian Constant. This is a relatively humble bistro with cream-color walls, red banquettes, and wooden tables, and you'll often see Constant himself perched at the bar at the end of lunch service. The menu reads like a French cookbook from the 1970s—who cooks veal *cordon bleu* these days?—but with Constant overseeing the kitchen, the dishes taste even better than back in the day. There's delicious and creamy lentil soup with morsels of foie gras, and the artichoke salad comes with fresh—not bottled or frozen—hearts. A towering *vacherin* (meringue layered with ice cream) might bring this delightfully retro meal to a close. On weekdays there is a bargain lunch menu for €16 (two courses) or €23 (three courses). [$] *Average main: €16* ✉ *139 rue St-Dominique, 7e, Around the Eiffel Tower* ☎ *01–47–53–73–34* 🌐 *www.cafeconstant.com* ✍ *Reservations not accepted* [M] *Métro École Militaire, Métro or RER: Pont de l'Alma* ✥ *3:D2.*

14

$$$$ MODERN FRENCH

🍴 **Le Jules Verne.** Alain Ducasse doesn't set his sights low, so it was no real surprise when he took over this prestigious dining room on the second floor of the Eiffel Tower and had designer Patrick Jouin give the room a neo-futuristic look in shades of brown. Sauces and pastries are prepared in a kitchen below the Champ de Mars before being whisked up the elevator to the kitchen, which is overseen by young chef Pascal Féraud. Most accessible is the €90 lunch menu (weekdays only), which brings you à la carte dishes in slightly smaller portions. Spend more (about €175 to €210 per person without drinks) and you'll be entitled to more lavish dishes such as lobster with celery root and black truffle, and fricassee of Bresse chicken with crayfish. For dessert the kitchen reinterprets French classics, as in an unsinkable pink grapefruit soufflé with grapefruit sorbet. Book months ahead or try your luck at the last minute. [$] *Average main: €77* ✉ *Tour Eiffel, south pillar, Av. Gustave Eiffel, 7e, Around the Eiffel Tower* ☎ *01–45–55–61–44* 🌐 *www.lejulesverne-paris.com* ✍ *Reservations essential* 👔 *Jacket and tie* [M] *Bir-Hakeim* ✣ *3:C2.*

$$ MODERN FRENCH FAMILY

🍴 **Le Troquet.** A quiet residential street shelters one of the best-value bistros around: prix-fixe menus start at €30 at lunch and rise to €41 for a six-course tasting menu (there is also à la carte), but it's the quality, not quantity, that counts. Chef Marc Mouton sends out a changing roster of dishes from the Basque and Béarn regions of southwestern France, and a typical meal might include vegetable soup with foie gras and cream, panfried scallops in crab sauce or *axoa de veau* (a Basque veal sauté), and a vanilla soufflé with cherry jam. Béarn red wine fills the glasses and happy regulars fill the dining room. [$] *Average main: €22* ✉ *21 rue François-Bonvin, 15e, Around the Eiffel Tower* ☎ *01–45–66–89–00* ⏲ *Closed Sun., Mon., 3 wks in Aug., 1 wk in May, and 1 wk at Christmas* [M] *Ségur* ✣ *3:E5.*

$$$ MODERN FRENCH

🍴 **Le Violon d'Ingres.** Following in the footsteps of Joël Robuchon and Alain Senderens, Christian Constant gave up the Michelin star chase in favor of relatively accessible prices and a packed dining room (book at least a week ahead). And with Grégory Gbiorczyk in charge of the kitchen here, Constant can dash among his four restaurants on this street, making sure the hordes are happy. Why wouldn't they be? The food is sophisticated and the atmosphere is lively; you can even find signature dishes like the almond-crusted sea bass with rémoulade sauce (a buttery caper sauce), alongside game and scallops (in season), and comforting desserts like *pots de crème* and chocolate tart. The food is still heavy on the butter, but with wines starting at around €25 (and a €47 lunch menu on weekdays) this is a wonderful place for a classic yet informal French meal. [$] *Average main: €32* ✉ *135 rue St-Dominique, 7e, Around the Eiffel Tower* ☎ *01–45–55–15–05* 🌐 *www.leviolondingres.com* ✍ *Reservations essential* [M] *École Militaire* ✣ *3:D2.*

$ MODERN FRENCH

🍴 **Les Cocottes de Christian Constant.** Chef Christian Constant has an unfailing sense of how Parisians want to eat these days, as proved by his third addition to his mini restaurant empire near the Eiffel Tower. At Les Cocottes he's shifted the normally leisurely bistro experience into high gear, which allows him to keep prices moderate. Seated at a long counter on slightly uncomfortable stools that discourage lingering, diners can mix and match from a menu of soups, salads, *cocottes* (dishes served in cast-iron pots), *verrines* (starters presented in tapas-style glasses), and comforting desserts, all made from fresh, seasonal ingredients. Bonus: lunch and dinner are served seven days a week. [$] *Average main: €17* ✉ *135 rue St-Dominique, 7e, Around the Eiffel Tower* ☎ *01–45–50–10–31* 🌐 *www.maisonconstant.com* [M] *École Militaire, Métro or RER: Pont de l'Alma* ✥ *3:D2.*

$$$$ FRENCH FUSION Fodor's Choice ★

🍴 **Restaurant David Toutain.** Though it lasted barely two years, the sheer virtuosity and daring of David Toutain's cooking at Agapé Substance electrified Paris foodies. The youthful Toutain is often called a prodigy, a status applied sparingly in Paris but in this case well deserved. Although his approach may be exasperatingly conceptual for some, others find his earthy, surprising, and inspired concoctions utterly thrilling. Each dish is a lesson in contrasts of temperature, texture, and flavor, as well as a feat of composition: briny oysters, Brussels sprouts, and foie gras in a warm potato consommé; creamy raw oysters with tart kiwi and yuzu; crispy pork chips alongside velvety smoked potato puree. Toutain has a particular soft spot for root vegetables and truffles (there are two all-truffle menus going for €158 and €210), which he sprinkles liberally throughout dishes like salsify broth with lardo and black truffle. The €42 lunch menu is a great way to sample a unique and challenging cuisine that changes daily. [$] *Average main: €40* ✉ *29 rue Surcouf, 7e, Around the Eiffel Tower* ☎ *01–45–50–11–10* 🌐 *www.davidtoutain.com* ✍ *Reservations essential* 🕓 *Closed weekends* [M] *Invalides, La Tour-Maubourg* ✥ *3:E1.*

INVALIDES

$ CAFÉ FAMILY

🍴 **Café Coutume.** A lofty space near the Musée Rodin and the Bon Marché makes this the perfect pit stop between museum-going and shopping. Look for healthy salads, sandwiches, snacks, desserts, and a sublime cup of any kind of coffee that takes your fancy. The sourced artisanal beans are freshly and lovingly roasted on the premises. [$] *Average main: €6* ✉ *47 rue de Babylone, 7e, Invalides* ☎ *01–45–51–50–47* 🌐 *www.coutumecafe.com* ✍ *Reservations not accepted* [M] *Saint-François Xavier, Sèvres-Babylone* ✥ *3:G3.*

$$$ BISTRO

🍴 **D'Chez Eux.** The red-checked tablecloths and jovial maître d'hôtel at this authentic southwestern French bistro near the École Militaire might seem like a tourist cliché—until you realize that the boisterous dining room is just as popular with food-loving locals and French politicians as it is with foreigners. The best way to start a meal here is with the "chariot" of starters, everything from lentil salad to ratatouille; just point to the ones you want. Classics among the main courses are duck confit with sautéed garlic potatoes, cassoulet, and game dishes in winter. Everything is hearty and delicious, if not especially refined—don't miss the gooey help-yourself chocolate mousse. Best value is the *tradition gourmande* set menu for €34, which brings you the hors d'oeuvres spread, a main course, and three desserts (you can try them all). [$] *Average main: €28* ✉ *2 av. de Lowendal, 7e, Invalides* ☎ *01–47–05–52–55* 🌐 *www.chezeux.com* 🕓 *Closed Aug.* [M] *Varenne, École Militaire* ✥ *3:E3.*

14

CLOSE UP

French Restaurant Types

Bistro: The broadest category, a bistro can be a simple, relaxed restaurant serving traditional fare, one of the new "bistronomic" eateries, or a chic hot spot where dinner costs more than €50 per person. The bistro menu is fairly limited and usually changes with the season.

Brasserie: More informal than a bistro, the brasserie is large, lively, and always has a bar. Ideal for relatively quick meals, it often specializes in Alsatian fare, like *choucroute garnie* (a mixed meat dish with sauerkraut and potatoes) or seafood platters. With flexible hours (usually open all day and well into the night) and diverse menus, brasseries are an excellent choice if you're traveling with kids.

Café: Often an informal neighborhood hangout, the café may also be a showplace attracting a well-heeled crowd. A limited menu of sandwiches and simple dishes is usually available throughout the day. Beware of the prices: a half bottle of mineral water can cost €5 or more.

French Fusion: The French Fusion restaurant has discernable influences of French cuisine and the cuisine of one other region or country.

Haute French: Ambitious and expensive, the Haute French restaurant is helmed by a pedigreed chef who prepares multicourse meals to be remembered.

Modern French: Although not necessarily superexpensive or pretentious, the Modern French restaurant boasts a creative menu showcasing a variety of culinary influences.

Wine Bar: A fairly recent phenomenon, the wine bar serves more than the usual three or four wines by the glass—often with an emphasis on natural wines—along with traditional charcuterie or cheese, small dishes, or, more often nowadays, a full gourmet meal.

$$$$ ✕ **Il Vino.** It might seem audacious to present hungry diners with noth-
FRENCH FUSION ing more than a wine list, but the gamble is paying off for Enrico Ber-
nardo at his wine-centric restaurant with a branch in Courchevel, in
the French Alps. This charismatic Italian left the George V to oversee
a dining room where food plays second fiddle (in status, not quality).
The hip decor—plum-color banquettes, body-hugging white chairs, a
few high tables—attracts a mostly young clientele that's happy to play
the game by ordering one of the blind, multicourse tasting menus. The
€95 menu, with four dishes and four wines, is a good compromise that
might bring you a white Mâcon with saffron risotto, crisp Malvasia
with crabmeat and black radish, a full-bodied red from Puglia with
Provençal-style lamb, sherrylike *vin jaune* d'Arbois with aged Comté
cheese, and sweet Jurançon with berry crumble. You can also order
individual wine-food combinations à la carte or pick a bottle straight
from the cellar and ask for a meal to match. $ *Average main: €40* ⊠ *13
bd. de la Tour-Maubourg, 7e, Invalides* ☎ *01-44-11-72-00* ⊕ *www.
ilvinobyenricobernardo.com* ⌖ *Reservations essential* ☉ *Closed Sun.
and Mon. No lunch Sat.* Ⓜ *Invalides* ⊕ *3:F1.*

$$$$ ✕ **L'Ami Jean.** If you love Yves Camdeborde's southwestern France–
BASQUE inflected cooking at Le Comptoir but can't get a table for dinner, head
to this tavernlike Basque restaurant run by his longtime second-in-
command, Stéphane Jégo. Jégo's style is remarkably similar to Camdeborde's because he uses the same suppliers and shares his knack for
injecting basic ingredients with sophistication reminiscent of haute cuisine. You can go hearty with Spanish *piquillo* peppers stuffed with salt-
cod paste or *poulet basquaise* (chicken stewed with peppers), or lighter
with seasonal dishes that change weekly. The restaurant is popular with
rugby fans (a sport beloved of Basques), who create a festive mood.
Reserve at least a week ahead for dinner. $ *Average main: €39* ⊠ *27 rue
Malar, 7e, Invalides* ☎ *01-47-05-86-89* ⊕ *www.lamijean.fr* ⌖ *Reservations essential* ☉ *Closed Sun., Mon., and Aug.* Ⓜ *Invalides* ⊕ *3:E1.*

$$$$ ✕ **L'Arpège.** Breton-born Alain Passard, one of the most respected chefs
MODERN FRENCH in Paris, famously shocked the French culinary world by declaring that
Fodor's Choice he was bored with meat. Though his vegetarianism is more theoretical
★ than practical—L'Arpège still caters to fish and poultry eaters—he does
cultivate his own vegetables outside Paris, which are then zipped into
the city by high-speed train. His dishes elevate the humblest vegetables
to sublime heights: salt-roasted beets with aged balsamic vinegar, leeks
with black truffles, black radishes, and *cardon,* a kind of thistle related
to the artichoke, with Parmigiano-Reggiano. Seafood dishes such as
turbot cooked at a low temperature for three hours or lobster braised
in vin *jaune* from the Jura are also extraordinary—as are the prices. A
€135 lunch menu, while still pricey, gives access to this revered cuisine.
The understated decor places the emphasis firmly on the food, but try
to avoid the gloomy cellar room. $ *Average main: €100* ⊠ *84 rue de
Varenne, 7e, Invalides* ☎ *01-47-05-09-06* ⊕ *www.alain-passard.com*
☉ *Closed weekends* Ⓜ *Varenne* ⊕ *3:G2.*

$$$ ✕ **La Table d'Aki.** Did the stars align during our meal, or could it be that
MODERN FRENCH La Table d'Aki actually *is* the most perfect restaurant in Paris? Set in
Fodor's Choice a quiet, aristocratic *quartier* near the Musée Rodin, its pale celadon
★ walls, crisp white linen, and restrained lighting add up to a simple

14

VEGETARIAN PARIS

Vegetarianism was so uncommon in Paris that star chef Alain Passard caused a sensation when he declared a few years ago that he was bored with red meat and would be focusing on vegetables and fish. True to his word, Passard established a small farm outside Paris where he grows heirloom vegetables that are whizzed to his restaurant **L'Arpège** (⊠ *84 rue Varenne* ☎ *01–45–51–47–33*) by high-speed train. Customers pay the price; a simple yet sensational beet dish costs €45. Though Paris is hardly a vegetarian paradise, Passard's initiative seems to have rubbed off on other chefs in the 7e. **Le Violon d'Ingres** (⊠ *135 rue St-Dominique* ☎ *01–45–55–15–05*) and **L'Atelier de Joël Robuchon** (⊠ *5 rue Montalembert* ☎ *01–42–22–56–56*) both cater, with imagination, to vegetarians.

elegance, all the better to highlight chef Akihiro Horikoshi's thrilling cuisine centered on the sea. Amazingly Horikoshi works all alone in an open kitchen while 16 lucky diners await the next course, dishes like plump langoustine shimmering in a velvety shallot-fennel sauce, or delicate medallions of sole in a mellow red wine and leek reduction—all of such lush simplicity. In the hands of another chef, the attempt to create these feasts alone would be an act of hubris, but chef Horikoshi is only guilty of making more unrepentant fans: some have even been known to order all four entrées or toast the chef repeatedly with their postdinner cognac, and all practically genuflecting their way out the door. $ *Average main: €32* ⊠ *49 rue Vaneau, 7e, Invalides* ☎ *01–45–44–43–48* ⌲ *Reservations essential* ⦾ *Closed Sun., Mon., 2 wks in Feb., and Aug.* Ⓜ *Saint Francis-Xavier* ✚ *3:G3.*

$$$$ ✕ **Thoumieux.** Former Crillon chef Jean-François Piège and Thierry
BRASSERIE   Costes of the fashionable brasserie clan that created Café Marly and Le Georges are behind the revival of this old-world bistro. The space has thankfully preserved much of its vintage character with globe lights and etched mirrors. Despite its location in the sedate 7e arrondissement, this has quickly become the place to be seen, with food that's a good notch above brasserie fare. A juicy Angus beef hamburger comes with a superfluous shower of Parmesan and ultra skinny fries, while the more sophisticated slow-cooked salmon is accompanied by vegetables from star market gardener Joël Thiébault. For dessert, try the piping-hot churros with chocolate sauce. The new *restaurant gastronomique* upstairs is ever so chic and a good bit pricier, yet proffers an experience commensurate with the top bistros in town (a €139 set menu at lunch and dinner and a €99 three-course menu at lunch that includes two glasses of wine; closed in August). Reservations are taken exactly six days ahead. $ *Average main: €40* ⊠ *79 rue St-Dominique, 7e, Invalides* ☎ *01–47–05–49–75* ⊕ *www.thoumieux.fr* ⌲ *Reservations essential* Ⓜ *La Tour-Maubourg* ✚ *3:E1.*

TROCADÉRO

$$$$
FRENCH FUSION
Fodor's Choice
★

✕ **Hiramatsu.** In this Art Deco dining room near Trocadéro, Yoshiaki Ito continues his variations on the subtly Japanese-inspired French cuisine of restaurant namesake Hiroyuki Hiramatsu, who still sometimes works the kitchen. Luxury ingredients feature prominently in dishes such as thin slices of lamb with onion jam and thyme-and-truffle-spiked jus, or an unusual pot-au-feu of oysters with foie gras and black truffle. For dessert, a mille-feuille of caramelized apples comes with rosemary sorbet. Helpful sommeliers will guide you through the staggering wine list, with more than 1,000 different bottles to choose from. There's no way to get away cheaply, so save this for a special occasion, when you might be tempted to order a carte blanche menu for €115 (lunch menus at €48). $ *Average main: €50* ✉ *52 rue de Longchamp, 16e, Trocadéro* ☎ *01–56–81–08–80* ⊕ *www.hiramatsu.co.jp/fr* ⚞ *Reservations essential* ⊘ *Closed weekends, Aug., and 1 wk at Christmas* Ⓜ *Trocadéro* ✛ *1:B6.*

$$$$
MODERN FRENCH
Fodor's Choice
★

✕ **L'Abeille.** The name refers to Napoléon's imperial emblem, the bee (the building once housed his grand-nephew), but also pays homage to Philippe Labbé, one of France's distinguished chefs. Everything, from the dove-gray decor to the sparkling silver, speaks of quiet elegance—all the better to highlight a masterful cuisine: "harlequin" of yellow, red, and white beets with a ginger-tinged yogurt and aloe vera emulsion; Breton langoustine in a cinnamon-perfumed gelée, with grapefruit pulp and a ginger- and Tahitian vanilla–infused mayonnaise; lightly caramelized scallops in an ethereal cloud of white chocolate foam; tender fillet of wild duck with a tart-sweet apricot reduction. Desserts are subtle and surprising, like the apple Reinette, paired with fennel and candied lemon zest. For cuisine of this quality, the €210, seven-course tasting menu at dinner is not outlandish. Service is friendly, discrete, devoid of snobbery, and includes all the flourishes that make a dining experience unforgettable, from the first flute of champagne to the parting gift of—what else?—a jar of honey. $ *Average main: €100* ✉ *Paris Shangri-La Hotel, 10 av. d'Iéna, 16e, Trocadéro* ☎ *01–53–67–19–90* ⊕ *www. shangri-la.com* ⚞ *Reservations essential* ⊘ *Closed Sun. and Mon. No lunch.* Ⓜ *Iéna* ✛ *1:B6.*

$$$$
MODERN FRENCH
Fodor's Choice
★

✕ **L'Astrance.** Pascal Barbot rose to fame thanks to his restaurant's amazing-value food and casual atmosphere, but after the passage of several years, Astrance has become resolutely haute, with prices to match. There's no à la carte; you can choose from a lunch menu for €70, a seasonal menu for €150, or the full tasting menu for €230 (this is what most people come for)—the latter two are available at lunch and dinner. His dishes often draw on Asian ingredients, as in grilled lamb with miso-lacquered eggplant and a palate-cleansing white sorbet spiked with chili pepper and lemongrass. Each menu also comes at a (considerably) higher price with wines to match each course. Barbot's cooking has such an ethereal quality that it's worth the considerable effort of booking a table—you should start trying at least two months in advance. $ *Average main: €120* ✉ *4 rue Beethoven, 16e, Trocadéro* ☎ *01–40–50–84–40* ⚞ *Reservations essential* ⊘ *Closed Sat.–Mon., 1 wk in early Nov., and all of Aug.* Ⓜ *Passy* ✛ *1:B6.*

14

$$ BISTRO 🍴 **La Table Lauriston.** Serge Barbey has developed a winning formula in his chic bistro near the Trocadéro: top-notch ingredients, simply prepared and generously served. To start, you can't go wrong with his silky foie gras *au torchon*—the liver is poached in a flavorful bouillon—or one of the seasonal salads, such as white asparagus in herb vinaigrette; his trademark dish, a gargantuan rib steak, is big enough to silence even the hungriest Texan. Given the neighborhood you might expect a businesslike setting, but the dining room feels cheerful, with vividly colored walls and velvet-upholstered chairs, and there is a 16-seat terrace. Don't miss the giant *baba au rhum,* which the waiters will douse with a choice of three rums. [$] *Average main: €23* ✉ *129 rue de Lauriston, 16e, Trocadéro* ☎ *01–47–27–00–07* 🌐 *www.latablelauriston.com* ✍ *Reservations essential* 🕒 *Closed Sun., 3 wks in Aug., and 1 wk at Christmas. No lunch Sat.* [M] *Trocadéro* ✥ *1:A6.*

$$ BISTRO 🍴 **Le Petit Rétro.** Chic clientele (men in expensive suits at noon, well-dressed locals in the evening) frequent this little bistro with Art Nouveau tiles and bentwood furniture. You can't go wrong with the daily specials, which are written on a chalkboard presented by one of the friendly servers: perhaps crisp-skinned blood sausage with apple-and-honey sauce, *blanquette de veau,* and a crêpe mille-feuille with orange and Grand Marnier. Arrive with an appetite because the food is hearty. There are several prix-fixe menus to choose from, starting at €25 at lunch (two courses). [$] *Average main: €23* ✉ *5 rue Mesnil, 16e, Trocadéro* ☎ *01–44–05–06–05* 🌐 *www.petitretro.fr* 🕒 *Closed Sun. and 1 wk in Aug.* [M] *Victor-Hugo* ✥ *1:A5.*

THE CHAMPS-ÉLYSÉES

$$$ BISTRO 🍴 **Chez Savy.** Just off the glitzy Avenue Montaigne, Chez Savy occupies its own circa-1930s dimension, oblivious to the area's fashionization. The Art Deco cream-and-burgundy interior is blissfully intact (avoid the back room unless you're in a large group), and the waiters show not a trace of attitude. Fill up on rib-sticking specialties from the Aveyron region of central France—lentil salad with bacon, foie gras (prepared on the premises), perfectly charred lamb with feather-light shoestring frites, and pedigreed Charolais beef. Order a celebratory bottle of Mercurey with your meal and feel smug that you've found this place. À la carte prices are high, but there is a set menu for €31.60. [$] *Average main: €29* ✉ *23 rue Bayard, 8e, Champs-Élysées* ☎ *01–47–23–46–98* 🌐 *www.chezsavy.com* 🕒 *Closed weekends and Aug.* [M] *Franklin-D.-Roosevelt* ✥ *1:E5.*

$$$$ MODERN FRENCH 🍴 **Epicure.** After a rapid ascent at his own new-wave bistro, which led to his renown as one of the more inventive young chefs in Paris, Eric Frechon became head chef at the restaurant for three-star Bristol hotel, the home-away-from-home for billionaires and power brokers. Frechon creates masterworks—say, farmer's pork cooked "from head to foot" with truffle-enhanced crushed potatoes—that rarely stray far from the comfort-food tastes of bistro cuisine. The €130 lunch menu makes his cooking accessible not just to the palate but to many pocketbooks. No wonder his tables are so coveted. Though the two dining rooms are impeccable—an oval oak-paneled one for fall and winter and a

CLOSE UP

A Cheese Primer

Their cuisine might be getting lighter, but the French aren't ready to relinquish their cheese. Some restaurants present a single, lovingly selected slice, whereas the more prestigious restaurants wheel in a trolley of specimens aged on the premises. Cheese always comes after the main course and before—or instead of—dessert.

Among the best bistros for cheese are **Astier,** where a giant basket of oozy wonders is brought to the table, and **Le Comptoir,** where a dazzling cheese platter is part of the five-course prix-fixe dinner, or **Le Bistro Paul Bert,** where an overflowing cheese board is left on your table for you to help yourself. A few *bars à fromages* are springing up, too: devoted to cheese the way *bars à vins* are dedicated to wine. **Fromagerie Cantin** (✉ 12 rue du Champ de Mars ☎ 01–45–50–43–94 ⊕ www. cantin.fr) is a terrific example.

Armed with these phrases, you can wow the waiter and work your way through the most generous platter.

Avez-vous le Beaufort d'été? Do you have summer Beaufort?

Beaufort is similar to Gruyère, and the best Beaufort is made with milk produced in summer, when cows eat fresh grass. Aged Beaufort is even more reminiscent of a mountain hike.

Je voudrais un chèvre bien frais/ bien sec. I'd like a goat cheese that's nice and fresh/nice and dry.

France produces many goat cheeses, some so fresh they can be scooped with a spoon, some tough enough to use as doorstops. It's a matter of taste, but hard-core cheese eaters favor drier specimens, which stick to the roof of the mouth and have a frankly goaty aroma.

C'est un St-Marcellin de vache ou de chèvre? Is this St-Marcellin made with cow's or goat's milk?

St-Marcellin is a more original choice than ubiquitous *crottin de chèvre* (poetically named after goats' turds). Originally a goat cheese, today it's more often made with cow's milk. The best have an oozy center, though some like it dry as a hockey puck.

C'est un Brie de Meaux ou de Melun? Is this Brie from Meaux or Melun?

There are many kinds of Brie. Brie de Meaux is the best known, with a smooth flavor and runny center; the much rarer Brie de Melun is more pungent and saltier.

Je n'aime pas le Camembert industriel! I don't like industrial Camembert!

Camembert might be a national treasure, but most of it is industrial. Real Camembert has a white rind with rust-color streaks and a yellow center.

Avez-vous de la confiture pour accompagner ce brebis? Do you have any jam to go with this sheep's cheese?

In the Basque region berry jam is the traditional accompaniment for sharp sheep's-milk cheeses like Ossau-Iraty.

C'est la saison du Mont d'Or. It's Mont d'Or season.

This potent mountain cheese, also known as Vacherin, is produced only from September to March. It's so runny it's eaten with a spoon.

—Rosa Jackson

14

marble-floor pavilion overlooking the courtyard garden for spring and summer—they provide few clues to help the world-weary traveler determine which city this might be. Ⓢ *Average main: €110* ⊠ *Hôtel Bristol, 112 rue du Faubourg St-Honoré, 8e, Champs-Élysées* ☎ *01–53–43–43–00* ⊕ *www.lebristolparis.com* ⌂ *Reservations essential* ⋔ *Jacket and tie* Ⓜ *Miromesnil* ✢ *1:F4.*

$$$$
MODERN FRENCH
Fodor's Choice
★

✕ **Guy Savoy.** With dark African wood, rich leather, cream-color marble, and the chef's own art collection, Guy Savoy's luxury restaurant doesn't dwell on the past. Come here for a perfectly measured haute-cuisine experience, since Savoy's several bistros have not lured him away from the kitchen. The artichoke soup with black truffles, sea bass with spices, and veal kidneys in mustard-spiked jus reveal the magnitude of his talent, and his mille-feuille is an instant classic. If the waiters see you're relishing a dish, they won't hesitate to offer second helpings. Generous half portions allow you to graze your way through the menu—unless you choose a blowout feast for set menus ranging from €360 to €490 for the 18-course menu—and reasonably priced wines are available (though beware the cost of wines by the glass). The €170 "discovery" menu at noon or after 10:30 pm is a good way to sample some of this fine chef's inspired cooking. Best of all, the atmosphere is joyful, because Savoy knows that having fun is just as important as eating well. Ⓢ *Average main: €120* ⊠ *18 rue Troyon, 17e, Champs-Élysées* ☎ *01–43–80–40–61* ⊕ *www.guysavoy.com* ⌂ *Reservations essential* ⋔ *Jacket required* ⊗ *Closed Sun., Mon., Aug., and 1 wk at Christmas. No lunch Sat.* Ⓜ *Charles-de-Gaulle–Étoile* ✢ *1:C3.*

$$$$
JAPANESE

✕ **Kifune.** Some Japanese expats say you won't find anything closer to authentic Japanese cooking in Paris than the kitchen in Kifune. Sit at the bar to admire the sushi chef's lightning-quick skills or opt for a more intimate table. The crab-and-shrimp salad is a sublime starter, and the miso soup with clams is deeply flavored. To follow, you can't go wrong with the sashimi. A meal here will leave a dent in your wallet (though there is a €32 set menu at lunch), but for fans of Japanese cuisine, the meals are worth it. With only 20 seats it often turns away would-be customers, so be sure to book in advance. Ⓢ *Average main: €35* ⊠ *44 rue St-Ferdinand, 17e, Champs-Élysées* ☎ *01–45–72–11–19* ⌂ *Reservations essential* ⊗ *Closed Sun. and Mon., 3 wks in Aug., 1 wk in Dec., and 2 wks in May* Ⓜ *Argentine* ✢ *1:A3.*

$$$$
MODERN FRENCH

✕ **L'Arôme.** Eric Martins ran a popular bistro in the far reaches of the 15e arrondissement before opening this contemporary restaurant off the Champs-Élysées, and his background in haute cuisine—he worked at Ledoyen and Hélène Darroze, among others—makes this ambitious restaurant an easy transition. The chef, Thomas Boullaut, turns out seasonal dishes with a touch of finesse from the open kitchen: dishes like foie gras confit with rosemary-poached quince and wild rose jam, or scallops *à la plancha* with vanilla and spaghetti squash might be featured. There is no à la carte, and if the dinner menus seem steep at €89 and €79 (€149 with wine pairing), the lunch menu is a mere €69. Watch out for the pricey wines by the glass. Ⓢ *Average main: €45* ⊠ *3 rue St-Philippe du Roule, 8e, Champs-Élysées* ☎ *01–42–25–55–98* ⊕ *www.larome.fr* ⌂ *Reservations essential* ⊗ *Closed weekends and Aug.* Ⓜ *St-Philippe du Roule* ✢ *1:E4.*

$$ ╳ **L'Huîtrier.** If you have a single-minded craving for oysters, this is the
SEAFOOD place for you. The friendly owner will describe the many different kinds
available, and you can follow with any of several daily fish specials—
or opt for a full seafood platter for around €50. Mood lighting, blond
wood, and cream tones create a tranquil, stylish atmosphere. Ⓢ *Average
main: €24* ✉ *16 rue Saussier-Leroy, 17e, Champs-Élysées* ☎ *01–40–54–
83–44* ⊕ *www.huitrier.fr* ⊘ *Closed Aug.* Ⓜ *Ternes* ✛ *1:C2.*

$$$$ ╳ **La Cristal Room.** The success of this restaurant in the Baccarat museum-
MODERN FRENCH boutique stems not only from the stunning decor by Philippe Starck—
mirrors, patches of exposed-brick wall, and a black chandelier—but
also from the culinary stylings of chef Adrien Manac'h. The menu pro-
vides a taste of his ultrarefined style with dishes such as green asparagus
soup with a lemon-poached egg, and sole meunière with grapefruit and
an arugula flan. Plan on reserving a week or two ahead for dinner;
lunch requires little advance notice and is a reasonable €36. Ⓢ *Average
main: €42* ✉ *11 pl. des États-Unis, 16e, Champs-Élysées* ☎ *01–40–
22–11–10* ⊕ *www.baccarat.fr* ⟟ *Reservations essential* ⊘ *Closed Sun.*
Ⓜ *Kléber* ✛ *1:C5.*

$$$ ╳ **La Fermette Marbeuf.** Graced with one of the most mesmerizing Belle
BRASSERIE Époque rooms in town—accidentally rediscovered during renovations
in the 1970s—this is a favorite haunt of French celebrities, who adore
the sunflowers, peacocks, and dragonflies of the Art Nouveau mosaic.
The menu rolls out updated classics: try the snails in puff pastry, beef
fillet with pepper sauce, and the Grand Marnier soufflé—but ignore
the limited-choice €29 prix fixe unless you're on a budget: the options
are a notch below what you get à la carte. Popular with tourists and
businesspeople at lunch, La Fermette becomes truly animated around
9 pm. Ⓢ *Average main: €28* ✉ *5 rue Marbeuf, 8e, Champs-Élysées*
☎ *01–53–23–08–00* ⊕ *www.fermettemarbeuf.com* Ⓜ *Franklin-D.-
Roosevelt* ✛ *1:D5.*

$$$$ ╳ **La Table de Lancaster.** Operated by one of the most enduring families
MODERN FRENCH in French gastronomy (the Troisgros clan has run a world-famous restaurant in Roanne for three generations), this stylish boutique-hotel
restaurant is the perfect setting for stellar cosmopolitan cuisine; try
to sit in the gorgeous Asian-inspired courtyard with its red walls and
bamboo. Often drawing on humble ingredients such as eel or pigs'
ears, the food reveals fascinating flavor and texture contrasts, like silky
sardines on crunchy melba toast or tangy frogs' legs in tamarind; the
salmon with sorrel sauce is a classic Troisgros dish. There is also a six-
course menu for €135. Don't miss the desserts, such as not one but
two slices of sugar tart, with grapefruit slices for contrast. On Sunday
there's a special €65 lunch menu (€48 for kids). Ⓢ *Average main: €50*
✉ *Hotel Lancaster, 7 rue de Berri, 8e, Champs-Élysées* ☎ *01–40–76–
40–18* ⊕ *www.hotel-lancaster.fr* ⟟ *Reservations essential* ⊘ *No lunch
Sat.* Ⓜ *George V* ✛ *1:D4.*

$$$$ ╳ **Le Cinq.** Eric Briffard is not the most famous chef in Paris but he *is*
MODERN FRENCH one of the best, as proved by his smooth transition into the role of head
Fodor's Choice chef in one of the city's most deluxe dining rooms. You'll find all the
★ luxury products you might expect—lobster, truffles, game in season—
but treated with a light touch that often draws on Asian ingredients

14

such as wasabi or cassia bark. A perfect example is his abalone, a rare shellfish prized by sushi chefs, prepared several ways: raw in a tartare, bathed in a creamy chicken bouillon, meunière-style in watercress sauce, and perched atop a bed of gingered kabocha squash. Desserts are ethereal and service is unfailingly thoughtful: really, the only problem with a meal here is that it has to end. Oh, and that it costs a small fortune—thankfully there is an €110 prix fixe at lunch. $ *Average main: €110* ✉ *Hôtel Four Seasons George V, 31 av. George V, 8e, Champs-Élysées* ☎ *01–49–52–70–00* ⊕ *www.fourseasons.com/paris* ⌁ *Reservations essential* ⌂ *Jacket and tie* Ⓜ *George V* ✣ *1:D5.*

$$$$

MODERN FRENCH

✕ **Ledoyen.** Tucked away in the quiet gardens flanking the Champs-Élysées, Ledoyen is a slightly faded study in the grandiose style of Napoléon III. Breton chef Christian Le Squer's menu is a treat, whether you opt for the lunchtime €120 prix fixe or the €250 tasting extravaganza (€350 with matching wines). He uses flawless ingredients, as showcased in *les coquillages* (shellfish), a delicious dish of herb risotto topped with lobster, langoustines, scallops, and grilled ham. The turbot with truffled mashed potatoes is excellent, too, and don't skip the superlative cheese trolley. $ *Average main: €120* ✉ *1 av. Dutuit, on Carré des Champs-Élysées, 8e, Champs-Élysées* ☎ *01–53–05–10–01* ⌁ *Reservations essential* ⌂ *Jacket required* ⊙ *Closed weekends and Aug.* Ⓜ *Concorde, Champs-Élysées–Clemenceau* ✣ *1:F6.*

$$

BISTRO

✕ **Le Hide.** Hide Kobayashi, known as "Koba," is one of several Japanese chefs in Paris who trained with some of the biggest names in French cuisine before opening their own restaurants. With stints at Lenôtre, the Louis XV in Monaco, and Joël Robuchon under his belt, Koba had the brilliant idea of opening a great-value bistro near the Arc de Triomphe (the three-course prix fixe is €32.50). Not surprisingly, this little dining room with cream-color walls and red banquettes became instantly popular with locals as well as visiting Japanese and Americans who follow the food scene. Generosity is the key to the cooking here, which steers clear of haute cuisine flourishes: both the monkfish fricassee with anchovy-rich tapenade and a classic veal kidney in mustard sauce, for instance, come with a heap of mashed potatoes. For dessert try the stunning *île flottante* (floating island), made with oven-baked meringue. Wines by the glass start at €4.50—unheard-of in this area. $ *Average main: €20* ✉ *10 rue du Général Lanzerac, 8e, Champs-Élysées* ☎ *01–45–74–15–81* ⊕ *www.lehide.fr* ⌁ *Reservations essential* ⊙ *Closed Sun. and 2 wks in Aug. No lunch Sat.* Ⓜ *Charles de Gaulle–Étoile* ✣ *1:B3.*

$$

BISTRO

✕ **Le Petit Verdot du 17e.** Sandwich bars might be threatening the traditional two-hour lunch, but that doesn't stop this old-fashioned neighborhood bistro with its painted facade and wine-theme dining room from flourishing. Businessmen loosen their neckties to feast on homemade pâté, plate-engulfing steak for two, or guinea hen with cabbage, along with one of 40 or so small-producer wines. $ *Average main: €18* ✉ *9 rue Fourcroy, 17e, Champs-Élysées* ☎ *01–42–27–47–42* ⊕ *www.le-petit-verdot.com* ⊙ *Closed Sun. and Mon.* Ⓜ *Charles-de-Gaulle–Étoile* ✣ *1:C2.*

$$$

MODERN FRENCH

✕ **Mini Palais.** Inside the Grand Palais, Mini Palais has gotten it smashingly right. With silvery ceilings, dark wood, and faux classical marble, it's among Paris's most stylish dining rooms, but the menu—designed by superchef Eric Frechon of Le Bristol and executed by protegé Stephane d'Aboville—is the real draw. The *burger de magret et foie gras,* a flavorful mélange of tender duckling breast and duck foie gras drizzled with truffled *jus* on a buttery brioche bun underscores what's best about this place: a thoroughly modern cuisine with an old-fashioned extravagance. For a summer meal or a cocktail, the majestically pillared terrace overlooking Pont d'Alexandre III must be the most beautiful in Paris. What's more, it's open nonstop from 10 am till 2 am, an oasis in a neighborhood short on conveniences. [$] *Average main: €25* ✉ *3 av. Winston Churchill, 8e, Champs-Élysées* ☎ *01–42–56–42–42* 🌐 *www.minipalais.com* ✍ *Reservations essential* [M] *Champs-Élysées-Clemenceau* ✣ *1:F6.*

$$$$ MODERN FRENCH Fodor's Choice ★

🍴 **Pierre Gagnaire.** If you want to venture to the frontier of contemporary luxe cooking—and if money is no object—dinner here is a must. Chef Pierre Gagnaire's work is at once intellectual and poetic, often blending three or four unexpected tastes and textures in a single dish. Just taking in the menu requires concentration (ask the waiters for help), so complex are the multiline descriptions about the dishes' six or seven ingredients. The Grand Dessert, a seven-dessert marathon, will leave you breathless, though it's not as overwhelming as it sounds. The businesslike gray-and-wood dining room feels refreshingly informal, especially at lunch, but it also lacks the grandeur expected at this level. The uninspiring prix-fixe lunch (€115) and occasional ill-judged dishes (Gagnaire is a big risk taker, but also one of France's top chefs) linger as drawbacks, and prices keep shooting skyward, so Pierre Gagnaire is an experience best saved for the financial elite. [$] *Average main: €110* ✉ *6 rue de Balzac, 8e, Champs-Élysées* ☎ *01–58–36–12–50* 🌐 *www.pierre-gagnaire.com* ✍ *Reservations essential* ⏲ *Closed weekends, Aug., and at Christmas* [M] *Charles-de-Gaulle–Étoile* ✣ *1:D4.*

$$$ SEAFOOD Fodor's Choice ★

🍴 **Rech.** Having restored the historic Paris bistros Aux Lyonnais and Benoît to their former glory, star chef Alain Ducasse turned his piercing attention to this seafood brasserie founded in 1925. His wisdom lies in knowing what not to change: the original Art Deco chairs in the main floor dining room; seafood shucker Malec, who has been a fixture on this chic stretch of sidewalk since 1982; and the XL éclair (it's supersize) that's drawn in locals for decades. Original owner Auguste Rech believed in serving a limited selection of high-quality products—a principle that suits Ducasse perfectly—and legendary chef Jacques Maximin is now in the kitchen, turning out Med-inspired dishes such as tomato cream with crayfish and fresh almonds or Niçoise-style sea bass with thyme fritters. Save room for the whole farmer's Camembert, another Rech tradition. A great-value €36 menu is available at lunch; the dinner menu is €54. [$] *Average main: €32* ✉ *62 av. des Ternes, 17e, Champs-Élysées* ☎ *01–45–72–29–47* 🌐 *www.restaurant-rech.fr* ✍ *Reservations essential* ⏲ *Closed Sun., Mon., late July–late Aug., and 1 wk at Christmas* [M] *Ternes* ✣ *1:B3.*

$$$$ MODERN FRENCH

🍴 **Taillevent.** Perhaps the most traditional—for many diners this is only high praise—of all Paris luxury restaurants, this grande dame basks in renewed freshness under brilliant chef Alain Solivérès, who draws inspiration from the Basque country, Bordeaux, and Languedoc for his daily menu. Traditional dishes such as scallops meunière are matched with contemporary choices like a splendid spelt risotto with truffles and frogs' legs or panfried duck liver with caramelized fruits and vegetables. One of the 19th-century paneled salons has been turned into a winter garden, and contemporary paintings adorn the walls. The service is flawless, and the exemplary wine list is well priced. All in all, a meal here comes as close to the classic haute-cuisine experience as you can find in Paris. There's an €102 lunch menu and special wine "degustation" evenings, pairing food with exceptional wines from their legendary cave for €180. $ *Average main: €110* ⊠ *15 rue Lamennais, 8e, Champs-Élysées* ☎ *01–44–95–15–01* ⊕ *www.taillevent.com* ⌂ *Reservations essential* 🎩 *Jacket and tie* ⊘ *Closed weekends and Aug.* Ⓜ *Charles-de-Gaulle–Étoile* ✥ *1:D4.*

AROUND THE LOUVRE

FAUBOURG ST-HONORÉ

$$

MODERN FRENCH

Fodor's Choice

★

✕ **La Régalade St. Honoré.** When Bruno Doucet bought the original La Régalade from bistro-wizard Yves Camdeborde, some feared the end of an era. How wrong they were. While Doucet kept some of what made the old dining room so popular (country terrine, wine values, convivial atmosphere), he had a few tricks under his toque, creating a brilliantly successful haute-cuisine-meets-comfort-food destination with dishes like earthy morel mushrooms in a frothy cream for a starter, followed by the chef's signature succulent caramelized pork belly over tender Puy lentils, and a perfectly cooked fillet of cod, crispy on the outside and buttery within, served in a rich shrimp bouillon. For dessert, don't skip the updated take on *grand-mère*'s creamy rice pudding or the house Grand Marnier soufflé. With an excellent price-to-value ratio (€35 for the prix-fixe menu at lunch and dinner), this chic bistro and its elder sister in the 14e have evolved into staples for Paris gastronomes. $ *Average main: €24* ⊠ *123 rue Saint-Honoré, 1er, Faubourg St-Honoré* ☎ *01–42–21–92–40* ⌂ *Reservations essential* ⊘ *Closed weekends, Aug.* Ⓜ *Louvre-Rivoli* ✥ *4:C1* $ *Average main: €24* ⊠ *49 av. Jean Moulin, 14e, Montparnasse* ☎ *01–45–45–68–58* ⌂ *Reservations essential* ⊘ *Closed weekends, Aug., 1 wk at Christmas. No lunch Mon.* Ⓜ *Alesia, Porte d'Orleans* ✥ *4:C1.*

$$$$

BISTRO

✕ **Restaurant du Palais-Royal.** This stylish modern bistro decorated in jewel tones serves food to match its stunning location under the arcades of the Palais-Royal, facing its magnificent gardens. Sole, scallops, and risotto—including a dramatic black squid-ink and lobster version, or an all-green vegetarian one—are beautifully prepared, but juicy beef fillet with *pommes Pont Neuf* (thick-cut frites), and pedigreed chicken with potato puree are also popular with expense-account lunchers. Finish with an airy mille-feuille that changes with the seasons—berries in summer, chestnuts in winter—or a decadent *baba* doused with rum. Book in advance, especially in summer, when the terrace tables are hotly sought after. $ *Average main: €35* ⊠ *Jardins du Palais-Royal, 110 Galerie Valois, 1er, Faubourg St-Honoré* ☎ *01–40–20–00–27* ⊕ *www. restaurantdupalaisroyal.com* ⌂ *Reservations essential* ⊘ *Closed Sun. and Mon.* Ⓜ *Palais-Royal* ✥ *2:B6.*

CLOSE UP

Museum Dining

Most Paris museums offer a passable café, but sometimes a top-notch lunch, teatime, or even dinner is just the thing after a few hours of museum going. For a good meal in a superb environment, these spots can't be beat, even if you don't buy a ticket.

Musée Jacquemart-André Café: Housed in the mansion's original dining room—with marble-topped tables, painted ceilings, and murals—the excellent salads and daily *plat du jour* make this lovely café a favorite with Parisian ladies who lunch, whether they've seen the exhibit or not. Wonderful for teatime or a copious prix-fixe brunch on weekends. ✉ *158 bd. Haussmann, 8e* ☎ *01–45–62–11–59* 🌐 *musee-jacquemart-andre.com* [M] *Miromesnil.*

Les Arts Décoratifs, Le Saut Loup: The menu here reflects the decor—elegant and contemporary. A sleek upstairs lounge has great views of the Eiffel Tower and the Louvre, and the outdoor terrace, part of the Tuilerie gardens, is one of the nicest in Paris. Best for a snack or afternoon tea. Museum entrance not necessary, but a slight discount is offered on prix-fixe menus with a ticket. ✉ *107 Rue de Rivoli, 1er* ☎ *01–42–25–49–55* [M] *Palais-Royal.*

Musée du Quai Branly, Les Ombres: The magnificent glass-ceilinged dining room, designed by museum architect Jean Nouvel, is perched atop the museum and boasts a *gastronomic* restaurant with some of the best views of Paris and the Eiffel Tower. Good prix-fixe deals on lunch, dinner, and teatime and a roomy outdoor terrace. ✉ *27 Quai Branly, 7e* ☎ *01–47–53–68–00* 🌐 *lesombres-restaurant.com* [M] *Alma-Marceau.*

Musee d'Orsay: A classified historic monument, the soaring ceilings, chandeliers, gilding, and murals are part of the original train station's dining room. Open for lunch every day, and dinner on Thursday, the classic French fare is punctuated by a special dish inspired by the museum program. ✉ *1 rue de la Légion d'Honneur, 7e* ☎ *01–45–49–47–03* 🌐 *musee-orsay.fr* [M] *Solférino.*

14

LES HALLES

$$ BRASSERIE 🍴 **Au Pied de Cochon.** One of the few remnants of Les Halles's raucous all-night past is this brasserie, which has been open every day since 1946. Now run by the Frères Blanc group, it still draws both a French and a foreign crowd with round-the-clock hours and trademark traditional fare such as seafood platters, breaded pigs' trotters, beer-braised pork knuckle with sauerkraut, and cheese-crusted onion soup. It's perfect stick-to-your-rib fare for a winter's day or to finish off a bar crawl. The dining room, with its white tablecloths and little piggy details, feels resolutely cheerful, and it's open 24/7. [$] *Average main: €21* ✉ *6 rue Coquillière, 1er, Les Halles* ☎ *01–40–13–77–00* 🌐 *www.pieddecochon.com* [M] *Les Halles* ✥ *2:C6.*

$$$ BISTRO Fodor's Choice ★ 🍴 **Frenchie.** The prodigiously talented Grégory Marchand worked with Jamie Oliver in London before opening this brick-and-stone-walled bistro on a pedestrian street near Rue Montorgueil. Word of mouth and bloggers quickly made this one of the most packed bistros in town, with tables booked two months in advance, despite two seatings each

evening. Marchand owes a large part of his success to the great-value €48 three-course menu at dinner (prix fixe only)—boldly flavored dishes such as calamari gazpacho with squash blossoms, and melt-in-the-mouth braised lamb with roasted eggplant and spinach are excellent options. Service can be, shall we say, a tad brusque, but for some that's a small price to pay for food this good. If you can't get a reservation, nearby Frenchie Bar à Vins will fix you right up. $ *Average main: €29* ⊠ *5 rue du Nil, 2e, Les Halles* ☎ *01–40–39–96–19* ⊕ *www.frenchie-restaurant.com* ⌲ *Reservations essential* ⊙ *Closed weekends, 2 wks in Aug., and 10 days at Christmas. No lunch* Ⓜ *Sentier* ✛ *2:D5.*

$
WINE BAR
Fodor's Choice
★

✕ **Frenchie Bar à Vins.** If this weren't one of Paris's outstanding wine bars, the wait, attitude, and metal tractor seats might be a deterrent. Yet wine lovers would be hard pressed to find a better venue for sampling a great list of French wines, many natural, and inspired selections from Italy and Spain—all sold by the bottle or glass, with superb cuisine to match. Feast on masterful small dishes like the "coleslaw" of citrusy calamari and carrot, black-olive coulis and sprinkling of pine nuts; bresaola with apple, spicy mizuna leaves, and dollops of creamy horseradish; a wedge of Stilton served atop a paste of speculoos biscuits, with poached pear and smoked walnuts. Because getting a reservation at the restaurant across the street is nearly impossible, this is an excellent alternative. ■ **TIP→ Get here five minutes before opening time for a choice table.** $ *Average main: €17* ⊠ *6 rue du Nil, 2e, Les Halles* ☎ *No phone* ⌲ *Reservations not accepted* ⊙ *Closed weekends. No lunch.* Ⓜ *Sentier* ✛ *2:D5.*

$
MODERN FRENCH
FAMILY

✕ **Frenchie To Go.** The third outpost in Frenchie's Rue du Nil empire, Frenchie To Go, capitalizes on three of the latest Paris food trends: breakfast, fast food, and takeaway, but with a spin that's totally Frenchie. The hotdogs and tasty pastrami (almost unheard of in Paris) are meticulously sourced, as is pretty much everything else—Brittany lobster for the lobster rolls and line-caught hake for the scrumptious fish-and-chips. A cheerful modern space invites lingering if you're lucky enough to snag a table—more likely for breakfast (which is served all day) or during the off hours, when a cup of hot chocolate, a homemade ginger beer, or a good cup of coffee and a doughnut are just the thing. The price-to-value quotient is excellent. $ *Average main: €10* ⊠ *9 rue du Nil, 2e, Les Halles* ☎ *01–40–39–96–19* ⊕ *www.frenchietogo.com* ⌲ *Reservations not accepted* ⊙ *Closed Sun.* Ⓜ *Sentier* ✛ *2:D5.*

$$
WINE BAR

✕ **La Robe et le Palais.** Come here for the more than 120 French wines served *au compteur* (according to the amount consumed), and a good selection of bistro-style food in a congenial atmosphere for lunch or dinner. Although a tad pricier than other *bistrot à vins*, the food is reliably good. $ *Average main: €20* ⊠ *13 rue des Lavandières-Ste-Opportune, 1er, Les Halles* ☎ *01–45–08–07–41* ⊕ *www.larobeetlepalais.com* ⊙ *Closed Sun.* Ⓜ *Châtelet Les Halles* ✛ *4:D1.*

$$$
MODERN FRENCH

✕ **Le Georges.** One of those rooftop show-stopping venues so popular in Paris, Le Georges preens atop the Centre Georges Pompidou, accessed by its own entrance to the left of the main doors. The staff is as streamlined and angular as the furniture, and about as responsive. Come snappily dressed or you may be relegated to something resembling a dentist's waiting room. Part of the Costes brothers' empire, the establishment trots out fashionable dishes such as sesame-crusted tuna and coriander-spiced beef fillet flambéed with cognac. It's all considerably less dazzling than the view, except for the suitably decadent desserts (indulge in the Cracker's cheesecake with yogurt sorbet). $ *Average main: €29* ⊠ *Centre Pompidou, 6th fl., 19 rue Beaubourg, 4e, Les Halles* ☎ *01–44–78–47–99* ⊕ *www.beaumarly.com* ⚓ *Reservations essential* ⊗ *Closed Tues.* Ⓜ *Rambuteau* ✛ *4:E1.*

$$$$
FRENCH FUSION
Fodor'sChoice
★

✕ **Yam'Tcha.** Adeline Grattard's little bistro has become so popular that tables are snapped up several weeks ahead, which is no surprise when you learn that she worked in the kitchens of L'Astrance before spending time in Hong Kong, where she picked up many of her techniques and ingredients. Inspired by Chinese cooking, many of her dishes rely on brilliant flavor combinations and very precise cooking. A signature dish is the roasted Challans duck (a cross between wild and domestic) with Sichuan-style eggplant: two elements that create magic together. Adeline's husband Chi Wa acts as a tea sommelier, introducing diners to earthy or grassy flavors that complement the food (Yam'Tcha means "to eat small steamed dishes while sipping tea"), though alcohol is also available. Menus are prix fixe only (€100 at lunch and dinner), but the €60 "discovery" lunch menu is a nice introduction. $ *Average main: €100* ⊠ *4 rue Sauval, 1er, Les Halles* ☎ *01–40–26–08–07* ⊕ *www. yamtcha.com* ⚓ *Reservations essential* ⊗ *Closed Sun. and Mon., Tues. dinner only; closed Aug. and Christmas* Ⓜ *Louvre–Rivoli or Les Halles* ✛ *2:C6.*

14

LOUVRE/TUILERIES

$$$
CAFÉ

✕ **Café Marly.** Run by the Costes brothers, this café overlooking the main courtyard of the Louvre and I.M. Pei's glass pyramid is one of the more stylish places in Paris to meet for a drink or a coffee, whether in the stunning jewel-toned dining rooms with their molded ceilings or on the Louvre's long, sheltered terrace. Regular café service shuts down during meal hours, when fashion-conscious folks dig into Asian-inspired salads and pseudo-Italian pasta dishes. $ *Average main: €30* ⊠ *Cour Napoléon du Louvre, enter from Louvre courtyard, 93 rue de Rivoli, 1er, Louvre/Tuileries* ☎ *01–49–26–06–60* ⊕ *www.beaumarly. com* Ⓜ *Palais-Royal* ✛ *4:B1.*

$$$
BISTRO

✕ **Chez Georges.** If you were to ask Parisian bankers, aristocrats, or antiques dealers to name their favorite bistro for a three-hour weekday lunch, many would choose Georges. The traditional fare, described in authentically indecipherable handwriting, is very good—chicken-liver terrine, curly endive salad with bacon and a poached egg, steak with béarnaise—and the atmosphere is better, compensating for the steep prices. In the dining room, a white-clothed stretch of tables lines the mirrored walls, and attentive waiters sweep efficiently up and down. Order one of the wines indicated in colored ink on the menu and you can drink as much or as little of it as you want (and be charged accordingly); there's also another wine list with grander bottles. $ *Average main: €30* ⊠ *1 rue du Mail, 2e, Louvre/Tuileries* ☎ *01–42–60–07–11* ⊗ *Closed weekends, Aug., 1 wk at Christmas* Ⓜ *Sentier* ✛ *2:C5.*

$$$
BISTRO
Fodor's Choice
★

✕ **L'Ardoise.** A minuscule storefront, decorated with enlargements of old sepia postcards of Paris, L'Ardoise is a model of the kind of contemporary bistros making waves in Paris. Chef Pierre Jay's first-rate three-course dinner menu for €36 tempts with such original dishes as mushroom and foie gras ravioli with smoked duck; farmer's pork with porcini mushrooms; and red mullet with creole sauce (you can also order à la carte, but it's less of a bargain). Just as enticing are the desserts, such as a superb *feuillantine au citron*—caramelized pastry leaves filled with lemon cream and lemon slices—and a boozy baba au rhum. With friendly waiters and a small but well-chosen wine list, L'Ardoise would be perfect if it weren't so popular (meaning noisy and crowded). Ⓢ *Average main: €27* ⊠ *28 rue du Mont Thabor, 1er, Louvre/Tuileries* ☎ *01–42–96–28–18* ⊕ *www.lardoise-paris.com* ⌂ *Reservations essential* ⊘ *No lunch Sun.* Ⓜ *Concorde* ✛ *1:H6.*

$$
BISTRO

✕ **La Bourse ou La Vie.** If you've been dreaming of the perfect steak frites in Paris, head for this eccentric little place run by a former architect in partnership with two loyal clients. The chairs in this cheery yellow-and-red dining room appear to have been salvaged from a theater, but they pair nicely with founder Patrice Tatard's theatrical streak. There's no questioning the threesome's enthusiasm for their new vocation when you taste the steak in its trademark creamy, peppercorn-studded sauce, accompanied by hand-cut french fries cooked to crisp perfection. Aside from a whole veal kidney with mustard sauce, there's little else on the menu. Ⓢ *Average main: €19* ⊠ *12 rue Vivienne, 2e, Louvre/Tuileries* ☎ *01–42–60–08–83* ⊘ *Closed Sun. and Aug. No lunch Sat.* Ⓜ *Bourse* ✛ *2:C5.*

$$$$
MODERN FRENCH

✕ **Le Grand Véfour.** Victor Hugo could stride in and still recognize this restaurant, which was in his day, as now, a contender for the title of most beautiful restaurant in Paris. Originally built in 1784, it has welcomed everyone from Napoléon to Colette to Jean Cocteau under its mirrored ceiling, and amid the early-19th-century glass paintings of goddesses and muses that create an air of restrained seduction. The rich and fashionable gather here to enjoy chef Guy Martin's unique blend of sophistication and rusticity, as seen in dishes such as frogs' legs with sorrel sauce, and oxtail *parmentier* (a kind of shepherd's pie) with truffles. There's an outstanding cheese trolley, and for dessert try the house specialty, *palet aux noisettes* (meringue cake with chocolate mousse, hazelnuts, and salted caramel ice cream). Prices are as extravagant as the decor, but there is a €98 lunch menu. Ⓢ *Average main: €120* ⊠ *17 rue de Beaujolais, 1er, Louvre/Tuileries* ☎ *01–42–96–56–27* ⊕ *www. grand-vefour.com* ⌂ *Reservations essential* ⊘ *Closed weekends, Aug., and Christmas holidays* Ⓜ *Palais-Royal* ✛ *2:B5.*

$$
BISTRO

✕ **Les Fines Gueules.** Invest in good ingredients and most of the work is done: that's the principle of this wine bar–bistro that's developed a loyal following. If you're not on first-name terms with food personalities like butcher Hugo Desnoyer, market gardener Joël Thiébault, and sausage-maker Thierry Daniel, you need only know that these are the crème de la crème of suppliers. Owner Arnaud Bradol wisely treats their products simply, often serving them raw alongside a salad or sautéed potatoes: the steak tartare with mesclun salad dressed in truffle oil is unparalleled.

Beyond the tiny cafélike area downstairs is a staircase leading to a cozy upstairs dining room, which is invariably lively. In keeping with the theme, wines are organic or natural and many are available by the glass. [$] *Average main: €19* ✉ *43 rue Croix des Petits Champs, 1er, Louvre/Tuileries* ☎ *01–42–61–35–41* 🌐 *www.lesfinesgueules.fr* ✍ *Reservations essential* [M] *Palais-Royal* ✥ *2:C6.*

$$$ MODERN FRENCH 🍴 **Macéo.** With a reasonably priced set menu at €39, this is an ideal spot for a relaxed meal after the Louvre. Natural light streams through the restaurant, and a broad, curved staircase leads to a spacious upstairs salon. It's also a hit with vegetarians: chef Gunther Janicot whips up a meatless prix-fixe menu with two starter and two main course options—perhaps summer vegetables with mimolette cheese, followed by mini-pasta with wild mushrooms, herbs, and artichoke (though his efforts can be hit-or-miss). Meat lovers might sink their teeth into farmer's lamb with confit vegetables and mousseline potatoes. The wine list spotlights little-known producers alongside the big names—as befits this sister restaurant to Willi's Wine Bar. [$] *Average main: €28* ✉ *15 rue des Petits-Champs, 1er, Louvre/Tuileries* ☎ *01–42–97–53–85* 🌐 *www.maceorestaurant.com* 🕒 *Closed Sun. and 3 wks in Aug. No lunch Sat.* [M] *Palais-Royal* ✥ *2:B5.*

$$$$ MODERN FRENCH Fodor's Choice ★ 🍴 **Spring.** The private party atmosphere in this intimate, elegantly modern space may be exuberance at having finally snagged a table, but most likely it's chef Daniel Rose's inspired—often resplendent—cuisine. Though firmly rooted in technique, Rose sets himself the task of improvising two different menus each day, one for lunch and one for dinner, from whatever strikes his fancy that morning. His insistence on fresh, top-quality ingredients sourced from every corner of France is evident in dishes that are both refined and deeply satisfying: you might have an updated *parmentier* with a velvety layer of deboned pig's foot topped with lemon-infused whipped potatoes or buttery venison with tart-sweet candied kumquat. For dessert, a sublime combo of whiskey-and-vanilla-infused pineapple, crunchy toasted coconut biscuits, and lime-zest-sprinkled vanilla ice cream. A four-course dinner menu will run you €84. The 17th-century vaulted dining room is an intimate spot yet can accommodate larger groups. [$] *Average main: €45* ✉ *6 rue Bailleul, 1er, Louvre/Tuileries* ☎ *01–45–96–05–72* 🌐 *www.springparis.fr* ✍ *Reservations essential* 🕒 *Closed Sun. and Mon. No lunch.* [M] *Louvre-Rivoli* ✥ *4:C1.*

$ CAFÉ Fodor's Choice ★ 🍴 **Télescope.** This warm, elegant space near the Palais Royal gardens is the perfect spot to savor an expertly prepared cup of coffee accompanied by just the right gourmet sweet. Strike up a conversation with the passionate barista and you may end up sampling several of the velvety artisanal brews from carefully sourced beans hand roasted by the owners. Here, true love and coffee go hand in hand. [$] *Average main: €6* ✉ *5 rue Villedo, 1e, Louvre/Tuileries* ☎ *01–42–61–33–14* 🌐 *www.telescopecafe.com* ✍ *Reservations not accepted* 🕒 *Weekdays 8:30–5, Sat. 9:30–6:30, closed Sun.* [M] *Palais Royal–Musée du Louvre; Pyramides* ✥ *2:B6.*

$ WINE BAR 🍴 **Verjus Bar à Vins.** On an atmospheric street behind the Palais Royal gardens, this tiny wine bar is the latest endeavor of the American couple behind the wildly popular (and now defunct) Hidden Kitchen. A dozen customers perch on metal stools at a narrow bar to enjoy a small but choice selection of wines by the glass and some very good nibbles, like crisp buttermilk chicken, succulent Basque pork belly, or the excellent house-smoked salmon. Although not a substitute for dinner—portions are miniscule, with three to five bite-size morsels—for a drink and a nosh on your way to or from somewhere else, including the excellent restaurant upstairs, it's ideal. The most plentiful dish is an assortment of artisanal cheeses, and the scrumptious butterscotch pudding flecked with toffee and topped with crème Chantilly is a toothsome finale. Open weekdays only for lunch (sandwiches, salads) and evening tapas. [$] *Average main: €9* ✉ *47 rue Montpensier, 1e, Louvre/Tuileries* ☎ *01–42–97–54–40* 🌐 *verjusparis.com* ✍ *Reservations not accepted* 🕒 *Closed weekends* [M] *Palais-Royal–Musée du Louvre* ✥ *2:B6.*

$$ MODERN FRENCH 🍴 **Willi's Wine Bar.** More a restaurant than a wine bar, this British-owned spot is a stylish haunt for Parisian and visiting gourmands who might stop in for a glass of wine at the oak bar or settle into the wood-beamed dining room. The selection of reinvented classic dishes changes daily and might include roast cod with artichokes and asparagus in spring, venison in wine sauce with roast pears and celery-root chips in fall, and mango candied with orange and served with vanilla cream in winter. Chef François Yon has been in the kitchen for 20 years, ensuring a consistency that isn't always reflected in the service. The restaurant is prix-fixe only, but you can order appetizers at the bar. The list of about 250 wines reflects co-owner Mark Williamson's passion for the Rhône Valley and Spanish sherries. [$] *Average main: €20* ✉ *13 rue des Petits-Champs, 1er, Louvre/Tuileries* ☎ *01–42–61–05–09* 🌐 *www.williswinebar.com* 🕒 *Closed Sun. and 2 wks in Aug.* [M] *Bourse* ✥ *2:B5.*

$ JAPANESE 🍴 **Zen.** There's no shortage of Japanese restaurants around the Louvre, but this one is a cut above much of the competition. The white-and-lime-green space feels refreshingly bright and modern, and you can perch at one of the curvy counters for a quick bite or settle in at a table. The menu has something for every taste, from warming ramen soups (part of a €12 lunch menu that includes five pork dumplings) to sushi and sashimi prepared with particular care. The donburi—rice topped with meat or fish—and the Japanese curry with breaded pork or shrimp are also very good. A sign of the chef's pride in his food is that he offers cooking classes some Sundays (in French). [$] *Average main: €17* ✉ *8 rue de l'Echelle, 1er, Louvre/Tuileries* ☎ *01–42–61–93–99* 🕒 *Closed 10 days in mid-Aug.* [M] *Pyramides or Palais-Royal* ✥ *2:B6.*

OPÉRA/GRANDS BOULEVARDS

$$$ BISTRO 🍴 **Aux Lyonnais.** With a passion for the old-fashioned bistro, Alain Ducasse resurrected this 1890s gem by appointing a terrific young chef to oversee the short, frequently changing, and reliably delicious menu of Lyonnais specialties. Dandelion salad with crisp potatoes, bacon, and a poached egg; watercress soup poured over parsleyed frogs' legs; and fluffy *quenelles de brochet* (pike-perch dumplings) show he is no bistro dilettante. The decor hews to tradition, too, with a zinc bar, an antique coffee machine, and original turn-of-the-20th-century woodwork.

There's a limited-choice lunch menu for €32, but the cacophonous dining room is jammed with traders from nearby Bourse. Tables turn relatively quickly, so despite the gorgeous setting this is not a spot for a romantic meal. $ *Average main: €26* ✉ *32 rue St-Marc, 2e, Opéra/ Grands Boulevards* ☎ *01–42–96–65–04* ⊕ *www.auxlyonnais.com* ⚖ *Reservations essential* ⊗ *Closed Sun., Mon., and 3 wks in Aug. No lunch Sat.* Ⓜ *Bourse* ✛ *2:B4.*

$ ✕ **Chartier.** This classic *bouillon* (a term referring to the Parisian soup
BISTRO   restaurants popular among workers in the early 20th century) is a
FAMILY   part of the Gérard Joulie group of bistros and brasseries, which discreetly updated the menu without changing the fundamentals. People come here more for the bonhomie and the stunning 1896 interior than the cooking, which could be politely described as unambitious—then again, where else can you find a plate of foie gras for €7? This cavernous restaurant—the only original fin-de-siécle *bouillon* to remain true to its mission of serving cheap, sustaining food to the masses— enjoys a huge following, including one regular who has come for lunch nearly every day since 1946. You may find yourself sharing a table with strangers as you study the old-fashioned menu of such standards as pot-au-feu and blanquette de veau. $ *Average main: €12* ✉ *7 rue du Faubourg-Montmartre, 9e, Opéra/Grands Boulevards* ☎ *01–47–70– 86–29* ⊕ *www.restaurant-chartier.com* ⚖ *Reservations not accepted* Ⓜ *Montmartre* ✛ *2:C4.*

$$ ✕ **Chez Casimir.** Thierry Breton's bright, easygoing bistro is popular with
BISTRO   polished Parisian professionals, for whom it serves as a sort of canteen—why cook when you can eat this well so affordably? The €32 dinner menu (€24 for two courses at lunch) covers lentil soup with fresh croutons, braised endive and andouille salad, and roast lamb on a bed of Paimpol beans, and there are 12 cheeses to choose from. Good, if not exceptional, desserts include *pain perdu,* a dessert version of French toast—here it's topped with a roasted pear or whole cherries. Drop in at lunchtime on the weekend for the great-value €28 buffet. There is no à la carte. $ *Average main: €18* ✉ *6 rue de Belzunce, 10e, Opéra/Grands Boulevards* ☎ *01–48–78–28–80* ⊗ *No dinner weekends* Ⓜ *Gare du Nord* ✛ *2:E2.*

$$ ✕ **Drouant.** Best known for the literary prizes awarded here since 1914,
MODERN FRENCH   Drouant has shed its dusty image to become a forward-thinking res-
FAMILY   taurant. The man behind the transformation is Alsatian chef Antoine Westermann, who runs the hit bistro Mon Vieil Ami on Ile St-Louis. At Drouant the menu is more playful, revisiting the French hors d'oeuvres tradition with starters that come as a series of four plates. Diners can pick from themes such as French classics (like a deconstructed leek salad) or convincing mini-takes on Thai and Moroccan dishes. Main courses similarly encourage grazing, with accompaniments in little cast-iron pots and white porcelain dishes. Even desserts take the form of several tasting plates. Pace yourself, since portions are generous and the cost of a meal quickly adds up. This is the place to bring adventurous young eaters, thanks to the €15 children's menu. The revamped dining room is bright and cheery, though the designer has gone slightly over-board with the custard-yellow paint and fabrics. $ *Average main: €19*

✉ 16–18 pl. Gaillon, 2e, Opéra/Grand Boulevards ☎ 01–42–65–15–16 🌐 www.drouant.com ⏲ Open 7 days a wk [M] Pyramides ⊕ 2:B5.

$$$ BISTRO

🍴 **Goupil le Bistro.** The best Paris bistros emit an air of quiet confidence, and this is certainly the case with Goupil, a triumph despite its out-of-the-way location not far from the Porte Maillot conference center. The dining room attracts dark suits at lunch and a festive crowd in the evenings, with a few well-informed English-speakers sprinkled into the mix. The tiny open kitchen works miracles with seasonal ingredients, transforming mackerel into luxury food (on buttery puff pastry with mustard sauce) and panfrying monkfish to perfection with artichokes and chanterelles. Friendly waiters are happy to suggest wines by the glass. [$] *Average main: €26 ✉ 4 rue Claude Debussy, 17e, Opéra/Grands Boulevards ☎ 01–45–74–83–25 ✍ Reservations essential ⏲ Closed weekends and 3 wks in Aug. [M] Porte de Champerret ⊕ 1:B1.*

$ JAPANESE

🍴 **Higuma.** When it comes to steaming bowls of noodles, this no-frills dining room divided into three sections beats its many neighboring competitors. Behind the counter—an entertaining spot for solo diners—cooks toil over giant flames, tossing strips of meat and quick-fried vegetables, then ladling noodles and broth into giant bowls. A choice of *formules* (fixed price menu options) allows you to pair various soups and stir-fried noodle dishes with six delicious *gyoza* (Japanese dumplings), and the stir-fried dishes are excellent, too. Don't expect much in the way of service, but it's hard to find a more generous meal in Paris at this price. There is a more subdued annex (without the open kitchen) at 163 rue St-Honoré, near the Louvre. [$] *Average main: €14 ✉ 32 bis rue Ste-Anne, 1er, Opéra/Grands Boulevards ☎ 01–47–03–38–59 [M] Pyramides ⊕ 2:B5.*

$$$ MODERN FRENCH

🍴 **Julien.** Famed for its 1879 decor—think Art Nouveau stained glass and *La Bohème*–style street lamps hung with vintage hats—this Belle Époque dazzler in the up-and-coming neighborhood near Gare de l'Est certainly lives up to its oft-quoted moniker, "the poor man's Maxim's." Look for smoked salmon, stuffed roast lamb, cassoulet, and, to finish, profiteroles or the *coupe Julien* (ice cream with cherries). The scene here is lots of fun, and the restaurant has a strong following with the fashion crowd, so it's mobbed during the biannual fashion and fabric shows. Food is served until midnight, and there are various prix-fixe menus that start at €34.50 for a main course with a dessert and a glass of wine. [$] *Average main: €25 ✉ 16 rue du Faubourg St-Denis, 10e, Opéra/Grands Boulevards ☎ 01–47–70–12–06 🌐 www.julienparis.com [M] Strasbourg St-Denis ⊕ 2:E4.*

$$ BRASSERIE Fodor's Choice ★

🍴 **Lazare.** With so many of Paris's fabled brasseries becoming parts of upscale chains, the news that award-winning chef Eric Frenchon (Epicure at Le Bristol and Mini Palais) was opening his own place at the St-Lazare train station was met with a mix of curiosity and joy. Bright and loft-like, dazzling Lazare riffs on familiar brasserie themes—think marble-top tables, globe lights, chalkboard menus, and mosaic floors. Unsurprisingly, Frenchon's take on classic brasserie fare is flawless. Meat dishes, like slow-cooked lamb with lemon confit and olives, or crispy grilled pork on a bed of turnip kraut, are tender and comforting (just like *grand-mère* used to make). Fish dishes, like scallops with truffles, salmon with lentils, and the superb quenelles also exceed expectations. And Frenchon doesn't forget the classics: steak tartare, escargots, and charcuterie make memorable appearances. It's open all day, as you'd expect in a busy train station, and reservations for lunch or dinner are a must. [$] *Average main: €22* ✉ *108 rue Saint-Lazare, 8e, Opéra/Grands Boulevards* ☎ *01–45–23–42–06* 🌐 *www.lazare-paris.fr* ✍ *Reservations essential* [M] *St-Lazare* ✥ *1:H3.*

$$$ BRASSERIE 🍴 **Le Vaudeville.** Part of the Flo group of historic brasseries, Le Vaudeville tends to fill with journalists, bankers, and locals *d'un certain âge* who come for the good-value assortment of prix-fixe menus, starting at €26, and highly professional service. Shellfish, house-smoked salmon, foie gras with raisins, slow-braised lamb, and desserts like the floating island topped with pralines are particularly enticing. Enjoy the graceful 1920s decor—almost the entire interior of this intimate dining room is done in real or faux marble—and lively dining until 1 am on weeknights, midnight on Friday and Saturday. [$] *Average main: €25* ✉ *29 rue Vivienne, 2e, Opéra/Grands Boulevards* ☎ *01–40–20–04–62* 🌐 *www.vaudevilleparis.com* [M] *Bourse* ✥ *2:C5.*

$$$ WINE BAR 🍴 **Racines.** The secret of the deceptively simple yet hearty food served here is top-quality ingredients and expert preparation. The wines are all natural—sulfite-free, hand-harvested, and unfiltered—so it's a great place to try out unusual, hard-to-find wines. The old tile floors, wood tables, and location in the atmospheric Passage des Panoramas, Paris's oldest covered arcade, only add to the ambiance. It's packed at mealtimes, so be sure to reserve. [$] *Average main: €26* ✉ *8 passage des Panoramas, 2e, Opéra/Grands Boulevards* ☎ *01–40–13–06–41* ✍ *Reservations essential* 🕒 *Closed weekends, last 3 wks Aug., and at Christmas* [M] *Grands Boulevards, La Bourse* ✥ *2:C4.*

$$$ MODERN FRENCH 🍴 **Saturne.** It's no surprise that chef Sven Chartier, a veteran of famous produce-centric restaurants L'Arpege and Racines, would focus his restaurant around seasonal, locally sourced veggies, along with the freshest seafood and pedigreed meats. The luminous dining room, with a huge central skylight, pale wood, and industrial details, is as contemporary and devoid of ostentation as the food. Dishes tend to be fresh and minimally cooked, featuring unusual pairings of vegetables and greens—tender baby scallops served with slivered radish, tiny watercress leaves, crisp raw mushrooms, and shallot; or fillet of mackerel drizzled with arugula pesto, a tiny dollop of uni, a sprinkling of mustard seed and piquant purslane—that are sophisticated almost to the point of cerebral. Desserts are equally original, and a superb roster of natural wines insures that diners who care to broaden their horizons won't be disappointed. Open for lunch and dinner weekdays. Prix fixe only. [$] *Average main: €30* ✉ *17 rue Notre-Dame des Victoires, 2e, Opéra/Grands Boulevards* ☎ *01–42–60–31–90* ✍ *Reservations essential* 🕒 *Closed weekends* [M] *Bourse* ✥ *2:C5.*

$$$$ MODERN FRENCH 🍴 **Senderens.** Iconic chef Alain Senderens waited until retirement age to make a rebellious statement against the all-powerful Michelin inspectors, "giving back" the three stars he had held for 28 years and renaming his restaurant (it was Lucas Carton). He also updated the decor, juxtaposing curvy, white, new furnishings, against the splendid Art

Nouveau interior. The fusion menu spans the globe, though Senderens also, happily, reintroduces the occasional Lucas Carton signature dish such as polenta with truffles in winter. Senderens takes his passion for food-and-drink matches to extremes, suggesting a glass of wine, whiskey, sherry, or even punch to accompany each dish. Hours are longer than the usual Paris restaurants, so you can enjoy a late lunch or linger as long as you like. Upstairs, Le Passage Bar serves tapas-style dishes for less than €38 a plate, or €44 for four small courses. [$] *Average main: €38* ✉ *9 pl. de la Madeleine, 8e, Opéra/Grands Boulevards* ☎ *01–42–65–22–90* 🌐 *www.senderens.fr* ⏲ *Closed 3 wks in Aug. and Christmas holidays* [M] *Madeleine* ✥ *1:H5.*

$$ BISTRO Fodor's Choice ★ 🍴 **Terroir Parisien–Palais Brongniart.** Yannick Alleno's departure from Le Meurice, where he'd earned three Michelin stars, stunned the culinary world. He had chaffed under the star system's onerous demands, and that turns out to be good news for diners. Alleno's newest endeavor, which opened in late 2013, is set in a warm, modern space under the Paris Bourse, the city's stock exchange. His dishes achieve an ephemeral balance, allowing top-notch ingredients to shine through while combining flavors and textures in unexpected and delightful ways. Delicate roasted leeks are sprinkled with eggs, shallots, chives, and wispy sprigs of chervil. A perfectly prepared steak with crispy matchstick fries and tender boudin blanc sausage with truffled celery root puree are comfort food at its very best. Desserts like a velvety chocolate tart with a layer of salted caramel or a roasted apple filled with raspberry jam are not to be missed. There's also a "rillette bar," where you can take out traditional French charcuterie: *rillettes de lapin* (rabbit terrine) and *pâté de campagne* (country terrine). A big plus here is the welcoming, helpful service. [$] *Average main: €22* ✉ *28 pl. de la Bourse, 2e, Opéra/Grands Boulevards* ☎ *01–83–92–20–30* 🌐 *www.yannick-alleno.com/restaurant/paris-terroir-parisien-palais-brongniart* ✍ *Reservations essential* ⏲ *Closed Sun.* [M] *Bourse* ✥ *2:C5.*

MONTMARTRE

$ CAFÉ FAMILY Fodor's Choice ★ 🍴 **Bal Café.** Set in a bright, modern space on a tiny street at the lower reaches of Montmartre, the hugely popular Bal Café caters to a diverse clientele that comes for the great coffee, excellent food, lively and diverse crowd, and the art gallery/bookstore. Weekend brunch is an event, with artists, hipsters, expats, and young families enthusiastically enjoying all of the above. British-French inspired cuisine with far-flung influences (like kedgeree, a Scottish-Indian rice and smoked haddock dish); tender pancakes, fried eggs with ham and roasted tomatoes, and buttery scones with jam represent some the best comfort food in town. There are also excellent salads and gourmet sandwiches and an awesome cup of coffee, whatever your pleasure. In warmer weather the outdoor terrace is a boon. [$] *Average main: €12* ✉ *6 impasse de la Défense, 18e, Montmartre* ☎ *01–44–70–75–51* 🌐 *www.le-bal.fr* ✍ *Reservations essential* ⏲ *Closed Mon. and Tues. No dinner Fri.–Wed.* [M] *Place de Clichy* ✥ *2:A1.*

$$ BISTRO 🍴 **Bistrot des Deux Théâtres.** This theater-lover's bistro with red-velour banquettes, black-and-white photos of actors, and a giant oil painting

depicting celebrities, is always packed, and with good reason. The great-value prix-fixe menu for €39 (there's no à la carte) includes three courses, a bottle of unpretentious wine, and coffee. This isn't a place for modest eaters, so have foie gras or escargots to start, a meaty main such as the crackly crusted rack of lamb, and a potent baba au rhum or rustic lemon meringue tart for dessert. Waiters are jokey, English-speaking, and efficient. $ *Average main: €22* ✉ *18 rue Blanche, 9e, Montmartre* ☎ *01–45–26–41–43* ⊕ *www.bistrocie.fr* ♿ *Reservations essential* Ⓜ *Trinité* ✛ *2:A2.*

$$$ ✕ **Guilo Guilo.** Already a star in Kyoto, Eiichi Edakuni created a sensa-
JAPANESE tion with his first Parisian restaurant, where 20 diners seated around the black bar can watch him at work each night. The €45 set menu is a bargain given the quality and sophistication of the food: it changes every month, but you might come across dishes such as sea bream and Wagyu beef on shiso leaves with ponzu sauce, or the chef's signature foie gras sushi, an idea that could easily fall flat but instead soars. If you can afford it, complement your meal with exceptional sakes by the glass, one of which is sparkling. Beware: The first seating gets very rushed; reserve the 9:30 seating if you want to linger. $ *Average main: €25* ✉ *8 rue Garreau, 18e, Montmartre* ☎ *01–42–54–23–92* ♿ *Reservations essential* ☽ *Closed Mon. No lunch.* Ⓜ *Abbesses* ✛ *2:B1.*

$$$ ✕ **La Mascotte.** Though everyone talks about the "new Montmartre,"
BRASSERIE exemplified by a wave of chic residents and throbbingly cool cafés and bars, it's good to know that the old Montmartre is alive and well at the untrendy-and-proud-of-it Mascotte. This old-fashioned café-brasserie—which dates from 1889, the same year that saw the opening of the Tour Eiffel and the Moulin Rouge—is where you can find neighborhood fixtures such as the drag queen Michou (of the nearby club Chez Michou), who always wears blue. Loyalists come for the seafood platters, the excellent steak tartare, the warming *potée auvergnate* (pork stew) in winter, and the gossip around the *comptoir* (bar) up front. There is a two-course lunch menu for €29 and nonstop service seven days a week. $ *Average main: €26* ✉ *52 rue des Abbesses, 18e, Montmartre* ☎ *01–46–06–28–15* ⊕ *www.la-mascotte-montmartre.com* Ⓜ *Abbesses* ✛ *2:B1.*

$$ ✕ **Le Miroir.** Residents of Montmartre are breathing a sigh of relief: they
BISTRO no longer have to leave the neighborhood to find a good-value bistro.
FAMILY Run by a trio who honed their skills at Lavinia, La Tour d'Argent, and Aux Lyonnais, this red-and-gray bistro with a glass roof at the back serves just the kind of sophisticated comfort food everyone hopes to find in Paris. A meal might start with a plate of *cochonailles* (pâté, cured sausage, and deboned pig's trotter with onion jam) or perhaps a salad of whelks and white beans, before hearty main courses such as a stunning beef rib for two with sautéed potatoes or duck breast with chanterelle mushrooms and a slice of panfried foie gras. To finish, it's hard to choose between the aged Beaufort cheese or the vanilla pot de crème, served with shortbread and chocolate *financiers* (almond cakes). $ *Average main: €21* ✉ *94 rue des Martyrs, 18e, Montmartre* ☎ *01–46–06–50–73* ♿ *Reservations essential* ☽ *Closed Sun., Mon., and 3 wks in Aug.* Ⓜ *Abbesses* ✛ *2:B1.*

14

$ 🍴 **Rose Bakery.** On a street lined with French food shops selling produce,
BRITISH FAMILY fish, bread, and cheeses, this British-run café-restaurant might easily go unnoticed—if it weren't for the frequent line out the door. Whitewashed walls, naive art, and concrete floors provide the decor, and organic producers supply the ingredients for food so fresh and tasty it draws crowds to feast on fresh juices, salads, soups, and hot dishes, such as delicious risotto, followed by carrot cake, sticky toffee pudding, or lemon tarts. The nostalgic can buy homemade granola, British marmalade, or baked beans to take home. Rose Bakery also has branches at 30 rue Debelleyme in the Marais and a spot in the Bastille, inside the Galerie Maison Rouge, at 10 boulevard de la Bastille. Weekend brunch is popular, so plan to arrive early. [$] *Average main: €15* ✉ *46 rue des Martyrs, 9e, Montmartre* ☎ *01–42–82–12–80* ✍ *Reservations not accepted* ⏲ *Closed Mon. and 2 wks in Aug. No dinner* [M] *Notre-Dame-de-Lorette* ✥ *2:C2.*

MARAIS

$$ 🍴 **Au Bourguignon du Marais.** The handsome, contemporary look of this
BISTRO Marais bistro and wine bar is the perfect backdrop for traditional fare and excellent Burgundies served by the glass and bottle. Unusual for Paris, food is served nonstop from noon to 11 pm, and you can drop by just for a glass of wine in the afternoon. Always on the menu are Burgundian classics such as *jambon persillé* (ham in parsleyed aspic jelly), escargots, and beef bourguignonne. More up-to-date picks include a cèpe-mushroom velouté with poached oysters, though the fancier dishes are generally less successful. The terrace is busy in warmer months. [$] *Average main: €22* ✉ *52 rue François-Miron, 3e, Marais* ☎ *01–48–87–15–40* ⏲ *Closed Sun. and Mon., 3 wks in Aug., and 2 wks in Feb.* [M] *St-Paul* ✥ *4:F2.*

$$$$ 🍴 **Benoît.** Without changing the vintage 1912 setting, superchef Alain
BISTRO Ducasse and Thierry de la Brosse of L'Ami Louis have subtly improved the menu here, with dishes such as marinated salmon, frogs' legs in a morel-mushroom cream sauce, and an outstanding cassoulet served in a cast-iron pot. Eric Azoug keeps the kitchen running smoothly, and the waiters are charm incarnate. It's a splurge to be here, so go all the way and top off your meal with the caramelized tarte tatin or a rum-doused baba. [$] *Average main: €35* ✉ *20 rue St-Martin, 4e, Marais* ☎ *01–42–72–25–76* 🌐 *www.benoit-paris.com* ⏲ *Closed Aug. and 1 wk in Feb.* [M] *Châtelet* ✥ *4:D1.*

$ 🍴 **Breizh Café.** Eating a crêpe in Paris might seem a bit clichéd, until
FRENCH FAMILY Fodor's Choice ★ you venture into this modern offshoot of a Breton crêperie. The pale-wood, almost Japanese-style decor is refreshing, but what really makes the difference are the ingredients—farmers' eggs, unpasteurized Gruyère, shiitake mushrooms, Valrhona chocolate, homemade caramel, and extraordinary butter from Breton dairy farmer Jean-Yves Bordier. You'll find all the classics among the galettes (buckwheat crêpes), but it's worth choosing something more adventurous like the *cancalaise* (traditionally smoked herring, potato, crème fraîche, and herring roe). You might also slurp a few Cancale oysters, a rarity in Paris, and try one of the 20 artisanal ciders on offer. The nonstop serving hours from noon

to 11 pm can be a lifesaver if you're shopping in the Marais. Weekends are hectic, so be sure to reserve. $ *Average main: €12* ✉ *109 rue Vieille du Temple, 3e, Marais* ☎ *01–42–72–13–77* ⊕ *www.breizhcafe.com* 🍴 *Reservations essential* ⊘ *Closed Mon., Tues., and Aug.* Ⓜ *St-Sébastien-Froissart* ✛ *4:F1.*

$ ✗ **Bubar.** In summer look for the hip crowd spilling out the front of
WINE BAR this signless wine bar in the Marais. It's named for Jean-Louis, the bartender (*bubar* or *barbu* is French slang for "bearded"). The wine menu—with many selections available by the glass—features French wines and small-batch vintages from South Africa, Chile, and Argentina. Try the small dishes and some lovely *tartines* (toasted bread with various toppings) or bring in whatever noshes suite your fancy from the neighborhood, the owner encourages it! $ *Average main: €12* ✉ *3 rue des Tournelles, 4e, Marais* ☎ *01–40–29–97–72* ⊘ *Open 7 days a wk, 7 pm–2 am* Ⓜ *Bastille* ✛ *4:G2.*

$ ✗ **Café des Musées.** Warm and authentic, this bustling little bistro offers
BISTRO a convivial slice of Parisian life—and excellent value. Here traditional French bistro fare is adapted to a modern audience, and the best choices are the old tried-and-trues: hand-cut *tartare de boeuf*; rare entrecôte served with a side of golden-crisp frites and homemade béarnaise; and the classic *parmentier* with pheasant instead of the usual ground beef. Portions are ample, but save room for dessert: old-style favorites like *diplomate aux cherises*, a rum-soaked, cherry-laden sponge cake, or the terrine de chocolate with crème Anglaise are not to be missed. Fixed menus are a bargain at €15 for lunch and €25 for dinner. $ *Average main: €16* ✉ *49 rue de Turenne, 3e, Marais* ☎ *01–42–72–96–17* 🍴 *Reservations essential* ⊘ *Closed Aug., 1 wk in Jan.* Ⓜ *St-Paul* ✛ *4:G1.*

$ ✗ **Cantine Merci.** Deep inside the city's latest concept store, whose pro-
MODERN FRENCH ceeds go to charities for women in India and Madagascar, lurks the perfect spot for a quick and healthy lunch between bouts of shopping. The brief menu of soups, salads, risottos, and a daily hot dish is more than slightly reminiscent of another city lunch spot, Rose Bakery—salads such as fava beans with radish and lemon wedges or melon, cherry tomato, and arugula are bright, lively, and crunchy, and you can order a freshly squeezed juice or iced tea with fresh mint to wash it all down. Delicious, homey desserts might include cherry clafoutis or raspberry and pistachio crumble. $ *Average main: €16* ✉ *111 bd. Beaumarchais, 3e, Marais* ☎ *01–42–77–79–28* ⊕ *www.merci-merci.com* ⊘ *Closed Sun. No dinner* Ⓜ *St-Sébastien-Froissart* ✛ *4:G1.*

$$$ ✗ **Chez Julien.** This charming vintage bistro next to the Seine was easy to
BISTRO overlook until the Costes Brothers—famous for stylish brasseries such as Café Marly and Georges—worked their magic on it. With a terrace that extends across the cobbled pedestrian street and a few modish touches in the turn-of-the-20th-century dining room that was once a boulangerie, Chez Julien is now one of the Marais's hippest spots. The steep prices for rather ordinary food reflect this transformation, so you might decide to skip the starters, linger over a thick steak with crisp shoestring fries or roast farmer's chicken with baby potatoes, then head into the Marais for ice cream or gelato. $ *Average main: €30* ✉ *1 rue du Pont Louis-Philippe, 4e, Marais* ☎ *01–42–78–31–64* 🍴 *Reservations essential* ⊘ *No lunch Sun. and Mon.* Ⓜ *Pont Marie* ✛ *4:E2.*

14

$ MIDDLE EASTERN

🍴 **Chez Marianne.** You'll know you've found Marianne's when you see the line of people reading the bits of wisdom and poetry painted across the windows. This restaurant-deli serves Middle Eastern and Jewish specialties like hummus, fried eggplant, soul-warming chopped liver which you can match with one of the affordable wines or a steaming glass of sweetened mint tea. The sampler platter lets you try four, five, or six items—even the smallest plate is a feast, to be enjoyed on the scenic stone terrace overlooking the church and the Seine on warm days. Falafel sandwiches are available at the takeout window. [$] *Average main: €14* ✉ *2 rue des Hospitalières-St-Gervais, 4e, Marais* ☎ *01–42–72–18–86* [M] *St-Paul* ✣ *4:F2.*

$ CAFÉ Fodor'sChoice ★

🍴 **La Caféothèque.** Paris's first and most famous coffee bar, founded by former Guatemalan Ambassador to France Gloria Montenegro, La Caféothèque is where the city's initial wave of baristas came to worship and train. With three spacious rooms, any coffee preparation under the sun, and a daily special brew chosen from among dozens of varieties of meticulously sourced beans from plantations around the globe, this place is a Paris institution. [$] *Average main: €4* ✉ *52 rue de l'Hotel de Ville, 4e, Marais* ☎ *01–53–01–83–84* 🌐 *www.lacafeotheque.com* [M] *Pont-Marie, Saint-Paul* ✣ *4:E2.*

$$ BISTRO

🍴 **L'Ambassade d'Auvergne.** A rare authentic Parisian bistro that refuses to change, the Ambassade claims one of the city's great restaurant characters: the maître d' Francis Panek, with his handlebar mustache and gravelly voice. Settle into the dining room in this ancient Marais house to try rich dishes from the Auvergne, a sparsely populated region in central France. Lighter dishes such as turbot with fennel are available, but it would be missing the point not to indulge in a heaping serving of the superb lentils in goose fat with bacon or the Salers beef in red wine sauce with *aligot* (mashed potatoes with cheese). You might want to loosen your belt for the astonishingly dense chocolate mousse, served in a giant bowl that allows you to decide the quantity. The Auvergnat wines come with appetizing descriptions, but don't expect anything remarkable from this (justifiably) obscure wine region. A three-course, €32 menu covers all the important bases. [$] *Average main: €20* ✉ *22 rue du Grenier St-Lazare, 3e, Marais* ☎ *01–42–72–31–22* 🌐 *www.ambassade-auvergne.com* [M] *Rambuteau* ✣ *4:E1.*

$ MIDDLE EASTERN FAMILY

🍴 **L'As du Fallafel.** Look no further than the fantastic falafel stands on the pedestrian Rue de Rosiers for some of the cheapest and tastiest meals in Paris. L'As (the Ace) is widely considered the best of the bunch, which accounts for the lunchtime line that extends down the street. A falafel sandwich costs €5 to go, €7.50 in the dining room, and comes heaped with grilled eggplant, cabbage, hummus, tahini, and hot sauce. The *shawarma* (grilled, skewered meat) sandwich, made with chicken or lamb, is also one of the finest in town. Though takeout is popular, it can be more fun (and not as messy) to eat off a plastic plate in one of the two frenzied dining rooms. Fresh lemonade is the falafel's best match. [$] *Average main: €10* ✉ *34 rue des Rosiers, 4e, Marais* ☎ *01–48–87–63–60* ⏲ *Closed Sat. No dinner Fri.* [M] *St-Paul* ✣ *4:F2.*

TARTE TATIN

A development in the land of the long lunch is the new focus on fast food. No, not those pernicious chains found the world over, but one-of-a-kind eateries, often associated with a well-known bistro or wine bar, where you can grab a sandwich at a small table or to go when a full day of sightseeing doesn't allow for lingering over a many-course lunch. These three standouts are the newest examples of a trend that's caught on like wildfire. **L'Epicerie le Verre Volé** (✉ *54 rue la Folie Méricourt* ☎ *01–48–05–36–55*), an offshoot of the beloved cave à manger, offers cheese, olive oil, charcuterie, and lovingly prepared gourmet sandwiches. **Verjus Bar à Vins** (✉ *5 rue Montpensier* ☎ *01–42–97–54–40*), behind the Palais Royal gardens, offers superb sandwiches and some toothsome salads, including one with shaved Brussels sprouts, fennel, dill, and red onions. **Frenchie To Go** (✉ *9 rue du Nil* ☎ *01–40–39–96–19*) serves a tempting array of breakfast noshes, such as scones, sticky buns, and smoked bacon on English muffins. Stop in for a pastrami on rye, classic fish-and-chips, or something a little more unusual, like a French take on the lobster roll. And don't say no to dessert.

14

EASTERN PARIS

BASTILLE/NATION

$$$$
BISTRO
✕ **Au Trou Gascon.** This elegant establishment off Place Daumesnil—well off-the-beaten tourist track but worth the trip—is overseen by celebrated chef Alain Dutournier while his wife runs the dining room, which combines contemporary furnishings and beautiful ceiling moldings. Dutournier does a refined take on the cuisine of Gascony—a region renowned for its ham, foie gras, lamb, and duck. Most popular with the regulars are the surprisingly light cassoulet (all the meats are grilled before going into the pot) with big white Tarbais beans and a superb duck or goose confit. There is an ethereal dessert of raspberries, ice cream, and meringue. Prices are steep but there is a limited-choice lunch menu for €42 and a five-course tasting menu at dinner for €62. With some 1,100 wines and 130 Armagnacs to choose from, this is the place to splurge on vintage. Ⓢ *Average main: €37* ✉ *40 rue Taine, 12e, Bastille/Nation* ☎ *01–43–44–34–26* ⊕ *www.autrougascon.com* ⊙ *Closed weekends, Aug., and 1 wk at Christmas* Ⓜ *Daumesnil* ✚ *4:H4.*

$
WINE BAR
✕ **Bistrot Mélac.** In the same family since 1938, this wine bar is named after the jolly second-generation owner who harvests grapes from the vine outside and bottles his own wines. Cheese is hacked from a giant hunk of Cantal, and much of the hearty bistro fare hearkens back to the Aveyron, a notable gastronomic region of France whence the Mélac family proudly hails. Ⓢ *Average main: €17* ✉ *42 rue Léon-Frot, 11e, Bastille/Nation* ☎ *01–43–70–59–27* ⊕ *bistrot-melac.fr* ⊙ *Closed Sun., Mon., and 2 wks in Aug.* Ⓜ *Charonne* ✚ *4:H2.*

$$
BRASSERIE
FAMILY
✕ **Bofinger.** One of the oldest, loveliest, and most popular brasseries in Paris has improved in recent years, so stake out one of the tables dressed in crisp white linen under the glowing Art Nouveau glass cupola and

enjoy classic brasserie fare: stick to trademark dishes such as the sea-food, choucroute, steak tartare, or smoked haddock with spinach, as the seasonal specials can be hit-or-miss. Take advantage of the prix-fixe menus for €29.90 (two courses) and €36.50 (three courses) and all-day service beginning at noon on Sunday. $ *Average main: €21* ⊠ *5–7 rue de la Bastille, 4e, Bastille/Nation* ☎ *01–42–72–87–82* ⊕ *www. bofingerparis.com* Ⓜ *Bastille* ✛ *4:H2.*

$$$ ✕ **Café Français.** Recently expanded and reopened by Gilbert and Thierry
BRASSERIE   Costes's hip Beaumarly group, Café Français is one of Paris's largest bar-restaurant-clubs and a welcome contrast to the Bastille's somewhat tatty café scene. This luxe design-lover's paradise—created by sought-after designer India Mahdavi and graphic design team M/M—has a vast terrace with panoramic views of Place de la Bastille, an oasis of red and blue leather banquettes, black-and-white marble floors, mirrors, and gilded embellishments. With Michelin-starred chef Jean-FranÃois PieÃge at the helm, classics like steak tartare and steak with sauce béarnaise are several steps above your average brasserie fare. All this adds up to one of Paris's chic new places to eat, see, and be seen. $ *Average main: €28* ⊠ *1 place de la Bastille, 4e, Bastille/Nation* ☎ *01–40–29–04–02* ⊕ *www.cafe-francais.fr* ⚑ *Reservations essential* Ⓜ *Bastille* ✛ *4:H3.*

$ ✕ **Jacques Genin Salon de Thé.** Master chocolatier-pâtissièr Jacques
FRENCH   Genin deserves the legion d'honneur for his efforts to restore great
Fodor's Choice   traditional French pastries to their classic form, particularly the august
★   mille-feuille. Genin's stripped-down version disposes with the usual bells and whistles—fresh fruit, custard, chocolate—to achieve a scin-tillating clarity: layers of lightly caramelized *pâte feuilletée*, a buttery puff pastry, and an ethereal, barely sweet pastry cream in either vanilla, caramel, or praline. The glorious pastries in this tearoom, chocolate boutique, and pastry shop (probably the most beautiful in Paris, by the way) are no longer available for takeaway, but are assembled to order to be eaten fresh on the premises. Along with a cup of Genin's bitter-sweet hot chocolate, well, you get the picture. Oh, yes, and then there are the chocolates, some of Paris's finest. $ *Average main: €8* ⊠ *133 rue de Turenne, 3e, Bastille/Nation* ☎ *01–45–77–29–01* ⊕ *jacquesgenin.fr* ☾ *Closed Mon.* Ⓜ *Filles du Calvaire* ✛ *2:G6.*

$$ ✕ **La Gazzetta.** This bistro epitomizes what makes Paris such an exciting
BISTRO   culinary hub right now: a talented young chef serving inventive, market-driven food at an offbeat location. Chef Petter Nilsson began cooking in his native Sweden and honed his skills in Provence; both figure in the kind of dishes that have made this a foodie hot spot, where fish—often lightly cooked or smoked—and regional meats (like Pyrenees lamb) are featured. It's a set menu (one starter, one main, one dessert), and whether it's a velvety spinach pesto in a spelt risotto or a silky puree of celeriac with grilled eel, veggies are never just sidekicks. The Art Deco dining room and old-style zinc bar are especially atmospheric at din-nertime when the lights are low; the three-course €19 lunch menu is a steal. $ *Average main: €23* ⊠ *29 rue de Cotte, 12e, Bastille/Nation* ☎ *01–43–47–47–05* ⊕ *www.lagazzetta.fr* ⚑ *Reservations essential* ☾ *Closed Sun., Mon., and Aug.* Ⓜ *Ledru Rollin* ✛ *4:H3.*

$ WINE BAR

🍴 **Le Baron Bouge.** Formerly Le Baron *Rouge*, this proletarian wine bar near the Place d'Aligre market is a throwback to another era, with a few tables and giant barrels along the walls for filling and refilling your take-home bottles. A fun time to come is Sunday morning (yes, morning) when it's packed with locals who have just been to the market or on a winter's day when oysters are shucked and slurped curbside. [$] *Average main: €11* ✉ *1 rue Théophile Roussel, 12e, Bastille/Nation* ☎ *01–43–43–14–32* ⏲ *Closed Mon.* [M] *Ledru-Rollin* ✣ *4:H3.*

$$ BISTRO Fodor's Choice ★

🍴 **Le Bistrot Paul Bert.** Faded 1930s decor: check. Boisterous crowd: check. Thick steak with real frites: check. Good value: check. The Paul Bert delivers everything you could want from a traditional Paris bistro, so it's no wonder its two dining rooms fill every night with a cosmopolitan crowd. Some are from the neighborhood, others have done their bistro research, but they've all come for the balance of ingredients that makes for a feel-good experience every time. The impressively stocked wine cellar helps, as does the cheese cart, the laid-back yet efficient staff, and hearty dishes such as monkfish with white beans and duck with pears. The reasonable prix fixe is three courses for €38, or you can order à la carte. If you're looking for an inexpensive wine, choose from the chalkboard rather than the wine list. [$] *Average main: €24* ✉ *18 rue Paul Bert, 11e, Bastille/Nation* ☎ *01–43–72–24–01* ✍ *Reservations essential* ⏲ *Closed Sun., Mon., and Aug.* [M] *Rue des Boulets* ✣ *4:H3.*

$$ BISTRO

🍴 **Le Repaire de Cartouche.** In this split-level, dark-wood bistro between Bastille and République, chef Rodolphe Paquin applies a disciplined creativity to earthy French regional dishes. The menu changes regularly, but typical options are a salad of haricots verts topped with tender slices of squid; scallops on a bed of diced pumpkin; juicy lamb with white beans; game dishes in winter; and old-fashioned desserts like baked custard with tiny shell-shaped madeleines. In keeping with cost-conscious times, there is a bargain three-course lunch menu for €19 that doesn't skimp on ingredients—expect the likes of homemade pâté to start, followed by fried red mullet or hanger steak with french fries, and chocolate tart. The wine list is very good, too, with some bargain selections from small producers. [$] *Average main: €24* ✉ *99 rue Amelot, 11e, Bastille/Nation* ☎ *01–47–00–25–86* ✍ *Reservations essential* ⏲ *Closed Sun., Mon., and Aug.* [M] *Filles du Calvaire* ✣ *4:G1.*

$$$ ITALIAN

🍴 **Sardegna a Tavola.** Paris might have more Italian restaurants than you can shake a noodle at, but few smack of authenticity like this out-of-the-way Sardinian spot with peppers, braids of garlic, and cured hams hanging from the ceiling. Dishes are listed in Sardinian with French translation—*malloredus* is a gnocchi-like pasta; Sardinian ravioli are stuffed with cheese and mint. Perhaps best of all are the clams in a spicy broth with tiny pasta and the orange-scented prawns with tagliatelle, though the choice of dishes changes with the seasons and the chef's imagination. [$] *Average main: €32* ✉ *1 rue de Cotte, 12e, Bastille/Nation* ☎ *01–44–75–03–28* ⏲ *Closed Sun. and Aug. No lunch Mon.* [M] *Ledru-Rollin* ✣ *4:H4.*

$$ BISTRO

🍴 **Septime.** This is the kind of bistro we'd all love in our neighborhood—good food and a convivial atmosphere where diners crane to admire each other's plates. Bertrand Grébaut, the affable young chef, can often

14

be found chatting away with guests in the cacophonous dining room. In a neighborhood where excellent bistro fare is ridiculously plentiful—thanks to several talented young chefs who've set up shop here in the last few years—this spot stands out. Seasonal ingredients, inventive pairings, excellent natural wines, plus dishes like creamy gnochetti in an orange rind–flecked Gouda sauce sprinkled with coriander flowers; tender fillet of Landes hen in a mustard-peanut sauce, with braised endive and cabbage perfumed with lemon; and fresh white asparagus with raspberries and blanched almonds, are sophisticated and satisfying. The €28 weekday lunch menu is a good place to begin. $ *Average main: €20* ⊠ *80 rue de Charonne, 11e, Bastille/Nation* ☎ *01–43–67–38–29* ⊕ *www.septime-charonne.fr* ⌂ *Reservations essential* ⊙ *Closed weekends. No lunch Mon.* Ⓜ *Ledru Rollin, Charonne* ✛ *4:H3.*

$$$

MODERN
ARGENTINE

✕ **Unico.** An architect and a photographer, both Parisians born in Argentina, teamed up to open one of Bastille's hottest restaurants—literally hot, too, since the Argentinean meat served here is grilled over charcoal—and good-looking young locals pile into the orange-tiled, vintage 1970s dining room or the covered terrace to soak up the party vibe. Whichever cut of beef you choose (the ultimate being *lomo,* or fillet), it's so melt-in-your-mouth that the sauces served on the side seem almost superfluous. Dessert probably won't be necessary, but banana in dulce de leche could satisfy the strongest sweet craving. If there's a wait for a table, head across the street to the eponymous *cave à vin* for an Argentine apèro and appetizer. $ *Average main: €26* ⊠ *15 rue Paul-Bert, 11e, Bastille/Nation* ☎ *01–43–67–68–08* ⊕ *www.resto-unico.com* ⊙ *Closed Sun., 2 wks in Aug., and Christmas. No lunch Mon.* Ⓜ *Faidherbe-Chaligny* ✛ *4:H3.*

BELLEVILLE

$$

BISTRO
FAMILY
Fodor'sChoice
★

✕ **Le Baratin.** This place has been around for more than 20 years, but that hasn't stopped it from recently becoming one of the most fashionable out-of-the-way bistros in Paris. The key to its success is the combination of inventive yet comforting cooking by Argentinean-born chef Raquel Carena and a lovingly selected list of organic and natural wines from small producers, courtesy of her partner Philippe Pinoteau. He might seem brusque at first, but show an interest and he opens up like a vintage wine. Chef Carena learned the art of making bouillons from none other than star Breton chef Olivier Roellinger, and uses them to bring out the best in any ingredient from fish to foie gras. $ *Average main: €23* ⊠ *3 rue Jouye Rouve, 20e, Ménilmontant* ☎ *01–43–67–68–08* ⌂ *Reservations essential* ⊙ *No lunch Sat., closed Sun., Mon., and Aug.* Ⓜ *Pyrénées, Belleville* ✛ *2:H3.*

$$

BISTRO
Fodor'sChoice
★

✕ **Le Chapeau Melon.** A real neighborhood find, this quirky little *cave* and wine bar is run with imagination, flair, and zero pretension. Dishes like salmon *cru* drizzled with grass-green Provençal olive oil and soy sauce, served alongside slices of tart green apple; a nutty velouté of shiitake mushrooms with a tiny dollop of crème fraiche, or calamari served in its ink with flecks of vanilla are the happy result of whatever inspires owner-chef-wine aficionado Olivier Camus that day. Wine here is a serious affair, and interested diners are met with enthusiastic annotations (and copious samplings) of the wines of the day listed on the blackboard. To get a real feel for this convivial neighborhood come to the 6 pm happy hour, for homemade terrine, artisanal charcuterie, and an excellent glass of wine. Ⓢ *Average main: €22* ✉ *92 rue Rebeval, 19e, Belleville* ☎ *01–42–02–68–60* ⚭ *Reservations essential* ◷ *Closed Mon. and Tues. No lunch* Ⓜ *Pyrénées* ✛ *2:H3.*

CANAL ST-MARTIN

$$
MODERN FRENCH
✕ **Abri.** This tiny storefront restaurant's well-deserved popularity has much to do with chef Katsuaki Okiyama's fresh and imaginative food, the friendly servers, and great prices. A veteran of Taillevent and Robuchon, Okiyama works from a small open kitchen behind a zinc bar, putting forth skillfully prepared dishes, like lemon-marinated mackerel topped with micro-thin slices of beet with honey vinaigrette, succulent duck breast with vegetables au jus, or a scrumptious pumpkin soup with fragrant coffee cream. With food this good, and prices to match (€25 at lunch, €40 for a four-course dinner) be sure to reserve early. Ⓢ *Average main: €22* ✉ *92 rue du Faubourg-Poissonnière, 10e, Canal St-Martin* ☎ *01–83–97–00–00* ⚭ *Reservations essential* ◷ *Closed Sun. and Mon.* Ⓜ *Poissonnière, Cadet* ✛ *2:D3.*

$
VIETNAMESE
✕ **Dong Huong.** Dong Huong isn't a secret, but you wouldn't find it by accident. These two undecorated dining rooms on a Belleville side street are where the local Chinese and Vietnamese come for a reassuring bowl of *pho* (noodle soup) or plate of grilled lemongrass-scented meat with rice. Spicy, peanut-y *saté* soup is a favorite, and at this price (€7) you can also spring for a plate of crunchy imperial rolls, to be wrapped in accompanying lettuce and mint. Try one of the lurid nonalcoholic drinks; they're surprisingly tasty. Ⓢ *Average main: €11* ✉ *14 rue Louis-Bonnet, 11e, Canal St-Martin* ☎ *01–13–57–18–88* ◷ *Closed Tues. and 3 wks in Aug.* Ⓜ *Belleville* ✛ *2:H4.*

$
CAFÉ
FAMILY
✕ **Holybelly.** A new and welcome addition to the Canal St-Martin area, this spacious, modern coffee bar caters to Paris's blossoming breakfast scene with a menu of classics: homemade granola, pancakes topped with fruit, and eggs and bacon served up all day long, accompanied by hearty sandwiches, healthy salads (with kale!), and sinful desserts. And, of course, there's the wonderful coffee—all you'd expect from baristas trained in the ways of the good brew. Ⓢ *Average main: €12* ✉ *19 rue Lucien Sampaix, 10e, Canal St-Martin* ☎ *09–73–60–13–64* ⚭ *Reservations not accepted* Ⓜ *Jacques Bonsergent* ✛ *2:F4.*

$
WINE BAR
✕ **Jeanne A.** This six-table épicerie-bistro-wine bar-traiteur on a pretty cobbled street is just the thing for an uncomplicated lunch, dinner, or afternoon snack. Next door to the popular old-style bistro Astier, and run by the same owner, it's the kind of place where you can follow your pleasure—whether that's just a great glass of wine and a plate of charcuterie and/or cheese you're hungering for, or a full meal, the classic French fare is always excellent. Tasty rotisserie chicken is served daily, along with another main, like *gigot d'agneau*, rabbit, or duck fresh from the kitchen next door, along with a creamy potato gratin, side salad, or soup of the day, with a dense almond financier for dessert. All this for under €17 for a two-course lunch and €27 for a three-course dinner. *Pas mal!* The big table is great for groups of five or more. You can also take anything out for later delectation. Ⓢ *Average main: €14* ✉ *42 rue*

Jean-Pierre-Timbaud, 11e, Oberkampf ☎ *01–43–55–09–49* ⚱ *Reservations not accepted* ⊘ *Closed Aug.* Ⓜ *Parmentier, Oberkampf* ✛ *2:H5.*

$$$$
MODERN FRENCH

✕ **Le Chateaubriand.** A chef who once presented a single, peeled apple pip (really) on a plate (at the museum restaurant Le Transversal outside Paris) has no ordinary approach to food. Self-taught Basque cook Inaki Aizpitarte is undeniably provocative, but he gets away with it because (a) he's young and extremely cool and (b) he has an uncanny sense of which unexpected ingredients go together, as in a combination of oysters and lime zest in chicken stock. The €60 set dinner menu is modern and deconstructed, and the vintage dining room buzzes with an artsy, black-dressed crowd. Open for dinner only. Ⓢ *Average main: €40* ✉ *129 av. Parmentier, 11e, Canal St-Martin* ☎ *01–43–57–45–95* ⊕ *www.lechateaubriand.net* ⚱ *Reservations essential* ⊘ *Closed Sun. and Mon. No lunch.* Ⓜ *Goncourt* ✛ *2:H6.*

$$
WINE BAR

✕ **Le Dauphin.** Avant-garde chef Inaki Aizpatarte has struck again, transforming (with a little help from Rem Koolhaas) a dowdy little café two doors from his acclaimed Le Chateaubriand into a sleek, if chilly, all-marble watering hole for late-night cuisinistas. Honing his ever-iconoclastic take on tapas, the dishes served here—along with a thoughtful selection of natural wines—are a great way to get an idea of what all the fuss is about. Offerings like sweetly delicate crabmeat punctuated with tart marinated radish and avocado puree, or a well-prepared lemon sole drizzled with hazelnut butter highlight what this chef can do with quality ingredients. Dishes are small, well-priced, and meant to be shared to maximize exposure to the food. Ⓢ *Average main: €20* ✉ *131 av. Parmentier, 11e, Canal St-Martin* ☎ *01–55–28–78–88* ⊕ *www.restaurantledauphin.net* ⚱ *Reservations essential* ⊘ *Closed Sun., Mon. and 1 wk Christmas. No lunch Sat.* Ⓜ *Parmentier* ✛ *2:H5.*

$$
BISTRO

✕ **Le Galopin.** Across from a pretty square on the border of two up-and-coming neighborhoods, this open, light-drenched spot, run by brothers Maxime and Romain Teschenko (the former a veteran of Inaki Aizpitarte's Chateaubriand and the latter Top Chef 2010) is one of Paris's better bistros. While the brothers adhere to a tried-and-true formula—meticulously sourced produce, natural wines, open kitchen—they've managed to make it very much their own. Dishes are small wonders of texture and flavor, like velvety Basque pork with razor-thin slices of cauliflower, briny olives, and crunchy pumpkinseeds; or crisp-moist sea bass with spring-fresh asparagus and mint. A great choice for diners eager to experience what this scene's all about in a hip, off-the-beaten-path locale. Ⓢ *Average main: €20* ✉ *34 rue Sainte-Marthe, 10e, Canal St-Martin* ☎ *01–42–06–05–03* ⊕ *www.le-galopin.com* ⚱ *Reservations essential* ⊘ *Closed Sun. and Mon. No lunch* Ⓜ *Goncourt, Belleville, Colonel Fabien* ✛ *2:H3.*

$$
WINE BAR

✕ **Le Verre Volé.** Cyril Bordarier blazed a path with this small bar à vins, which quickly became the ticket for hipsters seeking out exceptional, good-value natural wines with food to match. Nowadays you're as likely to be seated next to a table of American tourists or expats as a bunch of French wine aficionados. This is not so much due to the chic factor as to Bordarier's insistence on top-quality products. Wines are mostly organic, the charcuterie hails from top artisan producers, and the variety of small dishes alongside a few hearty main courses works just as well for lunch on the fly as for a leisurely dinner. This is a popular spot, so reserve ahead. [$] *Average main: €23* ✉ *67 rue de Lancry, 10e, Canal St-Martin* ☎ *01–48–03–17–34* 🌐 *www.leverrevole.fr* ✍ *Reservations essential* [M] *République* ✥ *2:G4.*

$$ BISTRO 🍴 **Philou.** On a quiet street between Canal St-Martin and the historic Hôpital Saint-Louis, few places could be more pleasant than a sidewalk table at this most welcome addition to Paris's thriving bistro scene. On a cool day the red banquettes and Ingo Maurer chandelier cast a cozy glow, all the better to enjoy a hearty, well-priced selection of dishes, like slices of foie gras served atop crème de lentilles and sprinkled with garlicky croutons, ham clafoutis with girolle mushrooms, or a rosy beef entrecôte with roasted baby Yukon gold potatoes and mushrooms *de Paris*. In springtime, fat white asparagus is nicely paired with salty smoked haddock and spring peas. A wine list replete with well-chosen natural wines plus the reasonable €27 tasting menu at lunch and €34 at dinner make it one of more popular tables in town, so reserve ahead. [$] *Average main: €22* ✉ *12 av. Richerand, 10e, Canal St-Martin* ☎ *01–42–38–00–13* ✍ *Reservations essential* 🕓 *Closed Sun. and Mon.* [M] *Jacques Bonsergent* ✥ *2:G4.*

$ CAFÉ 🍴 **Ten Belles.** Canal St-Martin's first seriously good coffee bar, Ten Belles is where pedigreed baristas cater to a hip crowd of connoisseurs of the good brew. Sandwiches, soups, and an irresistable assortment of snacks and sweets all come from the ladies at the Bal Café. [$] *Average main: €6* ✉ *10 rue de la Grange aux Belles, 10e, Canal St-Martin* ☎ *01–42–40–90–78* ✍ *Reservations not accepted* 🕓 *No dinner* [M] *Jacques Bonsergent, République* ✥ *2:G4.*

$ BAKERY 🍴 **Véronique Mauclerc.** To really know Paris is to know her great boulangeries, a tradition in free fall since the advent of that notorious cricket bat, the industrial baguette. Thankfully there's an ever-growing group of bakers carrying the flame, literally. Véronique Mauclerc, one of the best, makes her breads, classic viennoiserie (croissants, turnovers, pain au chocolat), and savory tarts on the premises in a traditional wood-fired oven using only organic flour and natural ferments for leavening. As if this weren't enough, her pastries are a triumph. The fine traditional Paris Brest—a slightly sweet, hazelnut cream–filled pâte à choux sprinkled with slivered almonds—sells out quickly, as do the excellent mini chocolate cakes and fruit strudels. Although out of the way, being two steps from the lovely Buttes Chaumont makes it picnic perfect. There's another branch on 11 rue Poncelet. [$] *Average main: €5* ✉ *83 Rue de Crimée, 19e, Buttes-Chaumont* ☎ *01–42–40–64–55* [M] *Botzaris* ✥ *2:H1.*

PÈRE LACHAISE

$$ BISTRO 🍴 **La Boulangerie.** In a former bakery spruced up with a bread-theme mural, this bistro within the shabby-chic neighborhood of Ménilmontant dishes up a great-value two-course lunch menu for €15. Dinner is a still-reasonable €36, and the quality of the ingredients is admirable, even if the cooking can be inconsistent. Expect seasonal dishes like squash soup with spice-bread croutons, pot-roasted veal with root vegetables, and *cannelés* (eggy, caramelized cakes) with jasmine ice

14

cream made on the premises. If you're exploring the area around Père Lachaise, you'd have a hard time finding a better French eatery. $ *Average main: €19* ⊠ *15 rue des Panoyaux, 20e, Père Lachaise* ☎ *01–43–58–45–45* ⊕ *www.laboulangerie-bistrot.fr* ⌕ *Reservations essential* ⊙ *Closed Sun., 1 wk in July, 3 wks in Aug., and 1 wk at Christmas. No lunch Sat. and Mon.* Ⓜ *Ménilmontant* ✛ *2:H5.*

RÉPUBLIQUE

$$
BISTRO
FAMILY

✕ **Astier.** There are three good reasons to go to Astier: the generous cheese platter plunked on your table atop a help-yourself wicker tray, the exceptional wine cellar with bottles dating back to the 1970s, and the French bistro fare (even if portions seem to have diminished over the years). Dishes like marinated herring with warm potato salad, sausage with lentils, and baba au rhum are classics on the frequently changing set menu for €35, which includes a selection of no less than 20 cheeses. The vintage 1950s wood-panel dining room attracts plenty of locals and remains a fairly sure bet in the area, especially because it's open every day. $ *Average main: €21* ⊠ *44 rue Jean-Pierre Timbaud, 11e, République* ☎ *01–43–57–16–35* ⊕ *www.restaurant-astier.com* ⌕ *Reservations essential* Ⓜ *Parmentier* ✛ *2:H5.*

$
WINE BAR

✕ **Au Passage.** This *bistrot à vins* has the lived-in look of a longtime neighborhood favorite—which it was until two veterans of the raging Paris wine bar scene reinvented the place, keeping the laid-back atmosphere and adding a serious foodie menu that quickly became one of the best deals in town. For lunch on Thursday and Friday, the two-course €18 *menu du marché* offers a choice of meat or fish, and at dinner the menu shifts to a blackboard selection of small €4 to €8 tapas dishes—including several house-made pâtés, fresh tomato or beet salad, a superb seafood carpaccio, and artisanal charcuterie and cheeses. Four or more diners can hack away at a crispy-succulent roasted lamb haunch. The excellent wine list features plenty of natural wines. It's a diverse and lively crowd of happy diners who know they've found a very good thing. $ *Average main: €15* ⊠ *1 bis, Passage Saint-Sébastien, 11e, République* ☎ *01–43–55–07–52* ⌕ *Reservations essential* ⊙ *Closed Sun. No lunch Sat.–Wed.* Ⓜ *Saint Ambroise; Saint Sebastien Froissart; Richard Lenoir* ✛ *2:H6.*

$$
MOROCCAN

✕ **Chez Omar.** It's no longer the only trendy North African restaurant in town, but during fashion week you still might see top models with legs like gazelles touching up their lipstick in front of the vintage mirrors here—though that doesn't stop them from digging into huge platters of couscous with grilled skewered lamb or spicy *merguez* sausage. Whatever you choose, wash it down with robust, fruity Algerian or Moroccan wine. Proprietor Omar Guerida speaks English and is famously friendly to all. The setting is that of a beautifully faded French bistro, complete with elbow-to-elbow seating, so be prepared to overhear your neighbors' conversations. $ *Average main: €19* ⊠ *47 rue de Bretagne, 3e, République* ☎ *01–42–72–36–26* ⌕ *Reservations not accepted* ▭ *No credit cards* ⊙ *No lunch Sun.* Ⓜ *Temple, République* ✛ *2:F6.*

$
MOROCCAN

✕ **Le Martel.** Of the scads of neighborhood couscous joints in Paris, a few have become fashionable thanks to their host's magnetic personality and their stylish setting—and this converted bistro ranks among the more recent of that set. It's crowded, but the clientele of fashion designers, photographers, models, and media folk are as cool as it gets in this up-and-coming quartier. Everyone digs in to a mix of French standbys (such as artichokes with vinaigrette) and more exotic fare like lamb tagine with almonds, prunes, and dried apricots. $ *Average main: €18* ⊠ *3 rue Martel, 10e, République* ☎ *01–47–70–67–56* ⊘ *Closed Sun. and 2 wks in Aug. No lunch Sat.* Ⓜ *Château d'Eau* ✛ *2:E4.*

LATIN QUARTER

$$$ ╳**Fogòn St-Julien.** The most ambitious Spanish restaurant in Paris, this
SPANISH spot occupies an airy Seine-side space, avoiding tapas-bar clichés. The seasonal all-tapas menu, at €55 per person, is the most creative choice, but that would mean missing out on the seven different takes on paella that are available daily: perhaps saffron with seafood (which could be a bit more generous), inky squid, vegetable, or Valencia-style with rabbit, chicken, and vegetables. Finish up with custardy crème Catalan and a glass of muscatel. $ *Average main: €27* ⊠ *45 quai des Grands-Augustins, 6e, Latin Quarter* ☎ *01–43–54–31–33* ⊕ *www.fogon.fr* ⌄*Reservations essential* ⊘ *Closed Mon., 2 wks in Aug.–Sept., and 1 wk in Jan. No lunch weekdays* Ⓜ *St-Michel* ✛ *4:C2.*

$$$ ╳**Itinéraires.** Having paid his dues in the tiny kitchen of Le Temps au
BISTRO Temps near the Bastille, Lyonnais chef Sylvain Sendra is now happily ensconced in the spacious former premises of the noted Chez Toutoune. The once faded surroundings have been revitalized with taupe walls, a long *table d'hôtes* (shared table), and a bar for solo meals or tapas-style snacks. Sendra's cooking, meanwhile, is as inspired as ever. Menu highlights include a tart of foie gras, duck confit, and nutmeg, cod poached in a vegetable and sage bouillon; and a deconstructed lemon tart with a touch of celery. There's a good wine list with some reasonable bottles and a well-conceived selection of wines by the glass to pair with the meal. Prices run the gamut from a €32 two-course lunch to an €85 degustation menu at dinner. $ *Average main: €26* ⊠ *5 rue de Pontoise, 5e, Latin Quarter* ☎ *01–46–33–60–11* ⊕ *www.restaurantitineraires. com* ⌄ *Reservations essential* ⊘ *Closed Sun., Mon., and Aug. No lunch Sat.* Ⓜ *Maubert-Mutualité* ✛ *4:E4.*

$$ ╳**L'Avant-Goût.** Christophe Beaufront belongs to a generation of gifted
BISTRO bistro chefs who have rejected the pressure-cooker world of haute cui-
FAMILY sine in favor of something more personal and democratic. The result: delighted and loyal customers. There's a lunch menu for €14.50 (soup, main course, glass of wine, and coffee), and the three-course dinner prix-fixe costs €33. Typical of his market-inspired cooking is his signature pot-au-feu *de cochon aux épices,* in which spiced pork stands in for the usual beef, and the bouillon is served separately. Homemade desserts and a good-value wine list round off a satisfying experience. Children get an especially warm welcome here. Drop into his *épicerie* across the street to browse the wine selection or order dinner to go, complete with a returnable cast-iron pot. $ *Average main: €20* ⊠ *26 rue Bobillot, 13e, La Butte aux Cailles* ☎ *01–53–80–24–00* ⊕ *www. lavantgout.com* ⌄ *Reservations essential* ⊘ *Closed Sun. and Mon.* Ⓜ *Place d'Italie* ✛ *4:G6.*

14

$$
BISTRO

✕ **L'Ourcine.** Sylvain Danière knows just what it takes to open a wildly popular bistro: choose an obscure location in a residential neighborhood, decorate it simply but cheerfully, work extremely hard, set competitive prices (€34 for three courses at dinner, €26 for two courses at lunch), and constantly reinvent your menu. The real key ingredient is talent, though, and Danière has plenty of it, as demonstrated by his updated duckling *au sang* (in blood sauce) with celery-root puree, and a popular *crémeux au chocolat* (chocolate pudding) to finish things off. Locals mingle with well-informed tourists from Texas or Toulouse in the red-and-cream dining room, and you can watch the chef hard at work in his small kitchen. $ *Average main: €19* ✉ *92 rue Broca, 13e, Latin Quarter* ☎ *01–47–07–13–65* ⊘ *Closed Sun., Mon., 3 wks in Aug., and 1 wk in Feb.* Ⓜ *Les Gobelins* ✛ *4:G6.*

$$$$
MODERN FRENCH

✕ **La Tour d'Argent.** La Tour d'Argent has had a rocky time in recent years with the death of owner Claude Terrail, but chef Laurent Delarbre has found his footing, and there's no denying the splendor of the setting overlooking the Seine. If you don't want to splash out on dinner, treat yourself to the three-course lunch menu for a reduced price of €75; this entitles you to succulent slices of one of the restaurant's numbered ducks (the great duck slaughter began in 1919 and is now well past the millionth mallard, as your numbered certificate will attest). Don't be too daunted by the vast wine list—with the aid of the sommelier you can splurge a little (about €85) and perhaps taste a rare vintage Burgundy from the extraordinary cellars, which survived World War II. $ *Average main: €95* ✉ *15–17 quai de la Tournelle, 5e, Latin Quarter* ☎ *01–43–54–23–31* ⊕ *www.latourdargent.com* ⚐ *Reservations essential* 🎩 *Jacket and tie* ⊘ *Closed Sun., Mon., and Aug.* Ⓜ *Cardinal Lemoine* ✛ *4:E4.*

$$$$
BISTRO

✕ **Lapérouse.** Émile Zola, George Sand, and Victor Hugo were regulars here, and the restaurant's mirrors still bear diamond scratches from the days when mistresses would double-check their jewels' value. It's hard not to fall in love with this storied 17th-century Seine-side town house with a warren of woodwork-graced salons. Christophe Guilbert's cuisine seeks a balance between traditional and modern, often drawing on Mediterranean inspirations. For a truly intimate meal, reserve one of the legendary private *salons* where anything can happen (and probably has). You can also sample the restaurant's magic at lunch, when a bargain prix-fixe menu is served for €45 in both the main dining room and the private salons. $ *Average main: €45* ✉ *51 quai des Grands Augustins, 6e, Latin Quarter* ☎ *01–43–26–68–04* ⊕ *www.laperouse.fr* ⚐ *Reservations essential* ⊘ *Closed Sun. and Aug. No lunch Sat.* Ⓜ *St-Michel* ✛ *4:C2.*

$$
BRASSERIE
FAMILY

✕ **Le Balzar.** Regulars grumble about the uneven cooking at Le Balzar, but they continue to come back because they can't resist the waiters' wry humor and the dining room's amazing people-watching possibilities (you can also drop in for a drink on the terrace). The restaurant attracts politicians, writers, tourists, and local eccentrics—and remains one of the city's classic brasseries: the perfect stop before or after a film in a local art-house cinema. Don't expect miracles from the kitchen, but stick to evergreens like snails in garlic butter, onion soup, pan-fried veal liver with sautéed potatoes, and baba au rhum for dessert.

PARIS CAFÉ CULTURE

The café capital of the world is making room for the new barista cafés sweeping cities across the globe. For discerning coffee lovers this is good news indeed. Scattered throughout Paris's most compelling neighborhoods, most of the new cafés have a character all their own and, alongside superb gastronomic coffee, offer a selection of top-notch snacks or even meals.

Here are some of the very best:

Bal Café. This modern café has top barista talent and superb food. It's great for weekend brunch on the lively terrace. ⊠ 16 Impasse de la Défense, 18e, Montmartre ☎ 01-44-70-75-51.

Café Coutume. Near the Musée Rodin and the Bon Marché, this lofty space is perfect for a quick pick-me-up. Lovingly sourced beans are roasted on the premises. ⊠ 47 rue du Babylone, 7e, Invalides ☎ 01-45-51-50-47 ⊕ www.coutumecafe.com.

Holybelly. This canalside café serves up any kind of coffee you desire—filtered, flat white, foamy cappucino, and a wicked good *chocolat chaud* to accompany some yummy nibbles and hearty breakfast fare. ⊠ 19 rue Lucien Sampaix, 10e, Canal St-Martin ☎ 09-73-60-13-64

La Caféothèque. The grand dame of them all, Paris's coffee revolution began here. ⊠ 52 rue de l'Hôtel de Ville, 4e, Marais ☎ 01-53-01-83-84.

Télescope. This comely café in a quiet spot near the Palais-Royal gardens serves a scintillating brew from house-roasted beans, along with gourmet snacks. ⊠ 5 rue Villedo, 1er, Louvre ☎ 06-82-63-72-74 ⊕ www.telescopecafe.com.

Ten Belles. First on the scene at the Canal St-Martin, where pedigreed baristas give it their all, plus fabulous snacks from the ladies at the Bal Café. ⊠ 10 rue de la Grange aux Belles, 10e, Canal St-Martin ☎ 01-42-40-90-78.

14

Night owls congregate for the €25.50 menu, after 10 pm. $ *Average main:* €22 ⊠ 49 rue des Écoles, 5e, Latin Quarter ☎ 01-43-54-13-67 ⊕ www.brasseriebalzar.com ⚒ Reservations essential Ⓜ Cluny–La Sorbonne ✛ 4:C4.

$$$ ✕ **Le Buisson Ardent.** This charming Quartier Latin bistro with wood-
BISTRO work and murals dating from 1925 is always packed and boisterous. A glance at chef Arnaud Vansanten's €38 set menu—a bargain €27 at lunch for three courses—makes it easy to understand why. Dishes such as chestnut soup with spice bread, squid with chorizo and creamy quinoa, and quince Tatin (upside-down tart) with mascarpone and pink pralines put a fresh twist on French classics, and service is reliably courteous. Bread is made on the premises, and if you don't finish your bottle of wine you can take it with you to savor the last drops. $ *Average main:* €26 ⊠ 25 rue Jussieu, 5e, Latin Quarter ☎ 01-43-54-93-02 ⊕ www.lebuissonardent.fr ⚒ Reservations essential ⊘ No dinner Sun. Ⓜ Jussieu ✛ 4:E4.

$$ ✕ **Le Pré Verre.** Chef Philippe Delacourcelle knows his cassia bark from
MODERN FRENCH his cinnamon thanks to a long stint in Asia. He opened this lively bistro with its purple-gray walls and photos of jazz musicians to showcase his

culinary style, rejuvenating archetypal French dishes with Asian and Mediterranean spices. His bargain prix-fixe menus (€13.90 at lunch, €30.50 at dinner) change constantly, but his trademark spiced suckling pig with crisp cabbage is always a winner, as is his rhubarb compote with gingered white-chocolate mousse. Ask for advice in selecting wine from a list that highlights small producers. Ⓢ *Average main: €19* ✉ *8 rue Thénard, 5e, Latin Quarter* ☎ *01–43–54–59–47* ⊕ *www.lepreverre.com* ⌕ *Reservations essential* ⊙ *Closed Sun., Mon., and 1 wk at Christmas* Ⓜ *Maubert-Mutualité* ✥ *4:D4.*

$$
WINE BAR
✕ **Les Papilles.** Part wineshop and épicerie, part restaurant, Les Papilles has a winning formula—pick any bottle off the well-stocked shelf and pay a €7 corkage fee to drink it with your meal. You can also savor one of several superb wines by the glass at your table or around the classic zinc bar. The superb set menu—made with top-notch, seasonal ingredients—usually begins with a luscious *velouté*, a velvety soup served from a large tureen, and proceeds with a hearty-yet-tender meat dish alongside perfectly cooked vegetables—well worth spending a little extra time for lunch or dinner. Ⓢ *Average main: €18* ✉ *30 rue Gay-Lussac, 5e, Latin Quarter* ☎ *01–43–25–20–79* ⊕ *www.lespapillesparis. fr* ⌕ *Reservations essential* ⊙ *Closed Sun., Mon., last wk of July and 2 wks in Aug.* Ⓜ *Cluny–La Sorbonne* ✥ *4:C5.*

$$
BISTRO
✕ **Ribouldingue.** Find offal off-putting? Off-cuts take pride of place on the prix-fixe menu (€28 at lunch, €34 at dinner), but don't let that stop you from trying this bistro near the ancient St-Julien-le-Pauvre church. You can avoid odd animal bits completely, if you must, and still have an excellent meal—opt for dishes like marinated salmon or veal rib with fingerling potatoes—or go out on a limb with the *tétine de vache* (thin breaded and fried slices of cow's udder) and *groin de cochon* (the tip of a pig's snout). This adventurous menu is the brainchild of Nadège Varigny, daughter of a Lyonnais butcher (*quel surprise*). Veal kidney with potato gratin is a house classic, and there are always three fish dishes. Don't miss the unusual desserts, like tangy ewe's-milk ice cream. Ⓢ *Average main: €21* ✉ *10 rue St-Julien-le-Pauvre, 5e, Latin Quarter* ☎ *01–46–33–98–80* ⊕ *www.ribouldingue-restaurant.fr* ⊙ *Closed Sun., Mon., and Aug.* Ⓜ *St-Michel* ✥ *4:D3.*

$$$$
ECLECTIC
✕ **Sola.** Chef Hiroki Yoshitake was schooled in the kitchens of famed innovators Pascal Barbot of Astrance and William Ledeuil of Ze Kitchen Galerie before striking out on his own. Dishes like miso-lacquered foie gras, served with toasted pain de mie, or sake-glazed suckling pig—perfectly crisp on the outside and melting inside—pair traditional Japanese and French ingredients to wondrous effect. Plates are artfully arranged with a sprinkling of piquant shiso leaves or jewel-like roasted vegetables to please the eye and the palate. Costing €48, the three-course set lunch menu offers a choice of fish or meat and finishes with Fukano Hirobu's stunning confections. Shoes stay on in the tranquil half-timbered dining room upstairs, but the vaulted room downstairs is totally traditional—and one of the loveliest in Paris. Ⓢ *Average main: €35* ✉ *12 Rue de l'Hôtel Colbert, 5e, Latin Quarter* ☎ *01–43–29–59–04* ⊕ *restaurant-sola.com* ⌕ *Reservations essential* ⊙ *Closed Sun. and Mon.* Ⓜ *Maubert Mutualié* ✥ *4:D3.*

$$$$ MODERN FRENCH Fodor's Choice ★ 🍴 **Ze Kitchen Galerie.** William Ledeuil made his name at the popular Les Bouquinistes before opening this contemporary bistro in a loftlike space. The name might not be inspired, but the cooking shows creativity and a sense of fun: from a deliberately deconstructed menu featuring raw fish, soups, pastas, and *à la plancha* (grilled) plates, consider the roast and confit duck with a tamarind-and-sesame condiment and foie gras, or lobster with mussels, white beans, and Thai herbs. A tireless experimenter, Ledeuil buys heirloom vegetables direct from farmers and tracks down herbs and spices in Asian supermarkets. The menu changes monthly, and there are several different prix-fixe options at lunch, starting at €40. [$] *Average main: €39* ✉ *4 rue des Grands-Augustins, 6e, Latin Quarter* ☎ *01–44–32–00–32* 🌐 *www.zekitchengalerie.fr* ✍ *Reservations essential* ⏲ *Closed Sun. No lunch Sat.* [M] *St-Michel* ✣ *4:C2.*

14

CHINATOWN

$ CHINESE FAMILY 🍴 **La Chine Massena.** With wonderfully overwrought rooms that seem draped in a whole restaurant-supply catalog's worth of Asiana (plus four monitors showing the very latest in Hong Kong music videos), this is a fun place. Not only is the pan-Asian food good and moderately priced, but the restaurant itself has lots of entertainment value—wedding parties often provide a free floor show, and on weekends Asian disco follows variety shows. Steamed dumplings, lacquered duck, and the fish and seafood you'll see swimming in the tanks are specialties, and the oyster bar serves heaping seafood platters. For the best value come at noon on weekdays for the bargain lunch menus, starting at €13, or drop in for dim sum on weekends. [$] *Average main: €13* ✉ *Centre Commercial Massena, 13 pl. de Vénétie, 13e, Chinatown* ☎ *01–45–83–98–88* 🌐 *www.chinemassena.fr* [M] *Porte de Choisy* ✣ *4:G6.*

$ VIETNAMESE 🍴 **Le Bambou.** The line outside this restaurant anytime after 7 pm is a sure sign that something exciting is going on in the kitchen. Its small dining room is crowded and noisy, and service is more than brisk—the only thing missing is an eject button on your seat—but it's well worth it for some of the cheapest and most authentic Vietnamese food in town. If you find yourself in doubt about how to eat some of the dishes that involve wrapping meat and herbs in transparent rice paper or lettuce leaves, just spy on the regulars, many of them Vietnamese. Otherwise, go for one of the huge bowls of soup: tripe is popular, though there are plenty of other meat and seafood variations. [$] *Average main: €11* ✉ *70 rue Baudincourt, 13e, Chinatown* ☎ *01–45–70–91–75* ⏲ *Closed Mon. and 3 wks in Aug.* [M] *Tolbiac or Olympiades* ✣ *4:G6.*

ST-GERMAIN-DES-PRÉS

$$$ BRASSERIE 🍴 **Alcazar.** When Sir Terence Conran opened this impressive 300-seat restaurant, he promised to reinvent the Parisian brasserie, and he's come close. Alcazar's mezzanine bar is famed for its DJ, and with its slick decor and skylight roof, it feels more like London than the Rive Gauche. The kitchen may have started out rather uncertain of what it wanted to accomplish, but the food is now resolutely French with the occasional Mediterranean touch, plus the house classic fish-and-chips. Prices are reasonable: lunch menus start at €22, while a dinner menu is €43. The

chef seems to have found his groove with dishes such as salmon-and-ginger tataki and veal braised with morels. For dessert, it's hard to pass up the profiteroles, mille-feuille, or baba au rhum. Sunday brunch is popular, and the restaurant is now the Paris venue for the TV show *Top Chef*. $ *Average main: €26* ⊠ *62 rue Mazarine, 6e, St-Germain-des-Prés* ☎ *01–53–10–19–99* ⊕ *www.alcazar.fr* Ⓜ *Odéon* ✛ *4:B2*.

$

WINE BAR

✕ **Au Sauvignon.** Edge your way in among the students and lively tipplers at this homey, old-fashioned spot—one of Paris's oldest wine bars—with antique tiles and a covered terrace. The basic menu, which includes several small dishes, like charcuterie, terrine, or regional cheeses, makes ordering the right glass a breeze. $ *Average main: €15* ⊠ *80 rue des Sts-Pères, 7e, St-Germain-des-Prés* ☎ *01–45–48–49–02* ⊙ *Closed mid-July–mid-Aug.* Ⓜ *Sèvres-Babylone* ✛ *4:A3*.

$$

BISTRO

✕ **Boucherie Roulière.** If it's steak you're craving, put your faith in Jean-Luc Roulière, a fifth-generation butcher who opened this long, narrow bistro near St-Sulpice church. Partner Franck Pinturier is from the Auvergne region, which is also known for its melt-in-the-mouth meat, so start with truffle-scented ravioli or a rich marrow bone before indulging in a generous slab of Limousin or Salers beef, excellent veal kidney, or, for the meat-shy, perhaps lobster or sea bass. The minimalist cream-and-brown dining room with checkerboard floor tiles and black-and-white photos on the walls keeps the focus on the food, and waiters are of the professional Parisian breed. $ *Average main: €21* ⊠ *24 rue des Canettes, 5e, St-Germain-des-Prés* ☎ *01–43–26–25–70* ⊙ *Closed Mon. and Aug.* Ⓜ *Mabillon* ✛ *4:B3*.

$$

CAFÉ

✕ **Café de Flore.** Picasso, Chagall, Sartre, and de Beauvoir, attracted by the luxury of a heated café, worked and wrote here in the early 20th century. Today you'll find more tourists than intellectuals, and prices are hardly aimed at struggling artists, but the outdoor terrace is great for people-watching and popular with Parisians. The service is brisk and the food is fine, but nothing special. $ *Average main: €22* ⊠ *172 bd. St-Germain, 6e, St-Germain-des-Prés* ☎ *01–45–48–55–26* ⊕ *www.cafedeflore.fr* Ⓜ *St-Germain-des-Pres* ✛ *4:A3*.

$

BISTRO

✕ **Eggs & Co.** With a cheerfully bright and tiny, wood-beamed dining room—there's more space in the loftlike upstairs—this spot is devoted to the egg in all its forms, and whether you like yours baked with smoked salmon, whisked into an omelet with truffle shavings, or beaten into fluffy pancakes, there will be something for you on the blackboard menu. It's perfect for a late breakfast or light lunch on weekdays (it opens at 10 am), though rather mobbed for weekend brunch (10 to 6 pm). $ *Average main: €12* ⊠ *11 rue Bernard Palissy, 6e, St-Germain-des-Prés* ☎ *01–45–44–02–52* ⊕ *www.eggsandco.fr* Ⓜ *St-Germain-des-Prés* ✛ *4:A3*.

$$$$

MODERN FRENCH

✕ **Gaya Rive Gauche.** If you can't fathom paying upward of €200 per person to taste the cooking of Pierre Gagnaire (the city's most avant-garde chef) at his eponymous restaurant, book a table at his fashionable fish restaurant. At Gaya Rive Gauche, Gagnaire uses seafood as a palette for his creative impulses: expect small portions of artfully presented food, as in a seafood gelée encircled by white beans and draped with Spanish ham, or cod "petals" in a martini glass with soba noodles, mango, and grapefruit. Don't miss the desserts, one of Gagnaire's great strengths. Aim for the main-floor room, with its fish-scale wall, natural lighting, and bar for solo diners. $ *Average main: €33* ⊠ *44 rue du Bac, 7e, St-Germain-des-Prés* ☎ *01–45–44–73–73* ⊕ *www.pierre-gagnaire. com* ⚲ *Reservations essential* ⊗ *Closed Sun. No lunch in Aug.* Ⓜ *Rue du Bac* ✛ *3:H2.*

$$$$ ✕ **Hélène Darroze.** The most celebrated female chef in Paris is now cook-
MODERN FRENCH ing at the Connaught in London, but her St-Germain dining room is an exclusive setting for her sophisticated take on southwestern French food. Darroze's intriguingly modern touch comes through in such dishes as a sublime duck foie gras confit served with an exotic-fruit chutney or a blowout of roast wild duck stuffed with foie gras and truffles. At its best, the food lives up to the very high prices, but for a sampling with-out the wallet shock, her €35 seven-course tapas lunch menu, including a glass of wine, is one of the best deals in town. $ *Average main: €85* ⊠ *4 rue d'Assas, 6e, St-Germain-des-Prés* ☎ *01–42–22–00–11* ⊕ *www. helenedarroze.com* ⚲ *Reservations essential* ⊗ *Closed Sun. and Mon.* Ⓜ *Sèvres-Babylone* ✛ *4:A4.*

$$ ✕ **Huîtrerie Régis.** When the oysters are this fresh, who needs anything
SEAFOOD else? That's the philosophy of this bright 14-seat restaurant with crisp white tablecloths and pleasant service, popular with the area's glitterati. If you find yourself puzzling over the relative merits of *fines de claires, spéciales,* and *pousses en claires,* you can always go with the €27 prix fixe that includes a glass of Charentais, a dozen No. 3 (medium) oys-ters, and coffee—or ask the knowledgeable waiters for advice. You can supplement this simplest of meals with shrimp and perhaps a slice of freshly made fruit pie. Because of the lack of space, there's a minimum order of a dozen oysters per person. $ *Average main: €24* ⊠ *3 rue de Montfaucon, 6e, St-Germain-des-Prés* ☎ *01–44–41–10–07* ⊕ *www. huitrerieregis.com* ⊗ *Closed Mon. and mid-July to end of Sept.* Ⓜ *Ma-billon* ✛ *4:B3.*

$$$$ ✕ **Josephine Chez Dumonet.** Theater types, politicos, and locals fill the
BISTRO moleskin banquettes of this venerable bistro, where the frosted-glass lamps and amber walls put everyone in a good light. Unlike most bis-tros, Josephine caters to the indecisive, since generous half portions allow you to graze your way through the temptingly retro menu. Try the excellent boeuf bourguignonne, roasted saddle of lamb with artichokes, top-notch steak tartare prepared table-side, or anything with truffles in season; game is also a specialty in fall and winter. For dessert, choose between a mille-feuille big enough to serve three and a Grand Marnier soufflé that simply refuses to sink, even with prodding. The wine list, like the food, is outstanding if expensive. $ *Average main: €34* ⊠ *117 rue du Cherche-Midi, 6e, St-Germain-des-Prés* ☎ *01–45–48–52–40* ⚲ *Reservations essential* ⊗ *Closed weekends* Ⓜ *Duroc* ✛ *3:G5.*

$$$ ✕ **KGB.** After extravagant success with his Asian-infused cuisine at Ze
MODERN FRENCH Kitchen Galerie, master-chef William Ledeuil extended his artistry to annex KGB (Kitchen Galerie Bis) just down the street, this time with a different focus and gentler prices. For starters, the "zors-d'oeuvres" of two-, four-, or six mini-dishes—think cubes of foie gras *mi-cuit* (half-cooked) in duck consommé, tender pork wontons in coconut milk

14

with a hint of galanga—allow for a deeper exploration of what makes Ledeuil's cooking so alluring. Main courses, like roasted monkfish with a prune-lemongrass relish or the superb braised veal cheek in teriyaki jus, showcase his wizardry. Top it all off with a banana cappucino with caramel glaze and coconut sorbet. At €35, the three-course lunch menu is a bargain in this neighborhood. [$] *Average main: €29* ✉ *25 rue des Grands Augustins, 6e, St-Germain-des-Prés* ☎ *01–46–33–00–85* 🌐 *kitchengaleriebis.com* ✍ *Reservations essential* 🕓 *Closed Sun., Mon., and Aug.* [M] *Odéon, St-Michel* ✥ *4:C3.*

$$$$ MODERN FRENCH 🍴 **L'Atelier de Joël Robuchon.** Worldwide phenomenon Joël Robuchon retired from the restaurant business for several years before opening this red-and-black-lacquer space with a bento-box-meets-tapas aesthetic. High seats surround two U-shape bars, and this novel plan encourages neighbors to share recommendations and opinions. Robuchon's devoted kitchen staff whip up small plates for grazing (€19 to €75) as well as full portions, which can turn out to be the better bargain. Highlights from the oft-changing menu have included an intense tomato jelly topped with avocado puree and the thin-crusted mackerel tart, although his inauthentic (but who's complaining?) take on carbonara with cream and Alsatian bacon, and the *merlan* Colbert (fried herb butter) remain signature dishes. Reservations are taken for the first sittings only at lunch and dinner. [$] *Average main: €36* ✉ *5 rue Montalembert, 7e, St-Germain-des-Prés* ☎ *01–42–22–56–56* 🌐 *www.joel-robuchon.net* [M] *Rue du Bac* ✥ *4:A2.*

$$$ BISTRO FAMILY 🍴 **L'Epigramme.** Great bistro food is not so hard to find in Paris, but only rarely does it come in a comfortable setting. At L'Epigramme, the striped orange-and-yellow chairs are softly padded, there's space between you and your neighbors, and a big glass pane lets in plenty of light from the courtyard. Chef Karine Camcian has an almost magical touch with meat: try her stuffed suckling pig with turnip choucroute, or seared slices of pink lamb with root vegetables in a glossy reduced sauce. In winter the eleborate game dish *lièvre à la royale* (hare stuffed with goose or duck liver and cooked in wine) sometimes makes an appearance. Desserts are not quite as inspired, so try to take a peek at the plates coming out of the kitchen before making your choice. [$] *Average main: €25* ✉ *9 rue de l'Eperon, 6e, St-Germain-des-Prés* ☎ *01–44–41–00–09* ✍ *Reservations essential* 🕓 *Closed Sun., Mon., 3 wks in Aug., and 1 wk at Christmas* [M] *Odéon* ✥ *4:C3.*

$$ BISTRO 🍴 **La Bastide Odéon.** The open kitchen of this popular Provençal bistro near the Jardin du Luxembourg allows you to watch the cooks at work, and chef Hugues Germany demonstrates a creative hand with Mediterranean cuisine. Expect unusual dishes such as aged Spanish ham with a grilled pepper pipérade and artichokes; mushroom-and-pea risotto with arugula; and duck breast with orange sauce, date puree, polenta, and wild asparagus. To finish things off, try the pear poached with lemon and saffron, served with a fromage blanc sorbet. Unusual for Paris, an entire section of the menu is devoted to vegetarian dishes. [$] *Average main: €22* ✉ *7 rue Corneille, 6e, St-Germain-des-Prés* ☎ *01–43–26–03–65* 🌐 *www.bastideodeon.com* [M] *Odéon; RER: Luxembourg* ✥ *4:C4.*

$$ ✕ **La Ferrandaise.** Portraits of cows adorn the stone walls of this bistro
BISTRO near the Luxembourg Gardens, hinting at the kitchen's penchant for
meaty cooking (Ferrandaise is a breed of cattle). Still, there's some-
thing for every taste on the market-inspired menu, which always lists
three meat and three fish mains. Dill-marinated salmon with sweet
mustard sauce is a typical starter, and a thick, milk-fed veal chop might
come with a squash pancake and spinach. The dining room buzzes
with locals who appreciate the good-value €35 prix fixe—there is no à
la carte—and the brilliant bento box–style €16 lunch menu, in which
three courses are served all at once. $ *Average main: €24* ⊠ *8 rue
de Vaugirard, 6e, St-Germain-des-Prés* ☎ *01–43–26–36–36* ⊕ *www.
laferrandaise.com* ⊙ *Closed Sun. and 3 wks in Aug. No lunch Mon.
and Sat.* Ⓜ *Odéon; RER: Luxembourg* ✛ *4:C4.*

$$ ✕ **Le Bouillon Racine.** Originally a *bouillon*—one of the Parisian soup res-
BRASSERIE taurants popular at the turn of the 20th century—this two-story restau-
rant is now a lushly renovated Belle Époque haven with a casual setting
downstairs and a lavish room upstairs. The menu changes seasonally:
lamb knuckle with licorice, wild boar *parmentier* (like a shepherd's pie,
with mashed potatoes on top and meat underneath), and roast suckling pig are warming winter dishes. For dessert, dig into crème brûlée
with maple syrup or the *café liégois* (coffee-flavored custard topped
with whipped cream), which comes in a jug. If you're on a budget, try
the set menus ranging from €30.90 to €41.90. This is a good place to
keep in mind for a late lunch or an early dinner, since it serves nonstop
from noon until 11 pm. You can also drop in for a Belgian waffle and
hot chocolate in the afternoon. $ *Average main: €22* ⊠ *3 rue Racine,
6e, St-Germain-des-Prés* ☎ *01–44–32–15–60* ⊕ *www.bouillon-racine.
com* Ⓜ *Odéon* ✛ *4:C4.*

$$ ✕ **Le Comptoir du Relais Saint-Germain.** Run by legendary bistro chef Yves
BISTRO Camdeborde, this tiny Art Deco hotel restaurant is booked up well in
advance for the single dinner sitting that features a five-course, €65 set
menu of haute-cuisine food. On weekdays from noon to 6 and week-
ends until 10, a brasserie menu is served; reservations are not accepted,
resulting in long lines and brisk, sometimes shockingly rude, service.
Start with charcuterie or pâté, then choose from open-faced sandwiches
like a smoked salmon–and–comté cheese croque monsieur, gourmet sal-
ads, and a variety of hot dishes such as braised beef cheek, roast tuna,
and Camdeborde's famed deboned and breaded pig's trotter. If you
don't mind bus fumes, sidewalk tables make for prime people-watch-
ing in summer. Camdeborde also runs neighboring Avant Comptoir, a
minuscule stand-up zinc bar with hanging hams and sausages where you
can score a superb plate of charcuterie and an inky glass of Morgon.
Quality crêpes and sandwiches are still served from the window out
front. $ *Average main: €22* ⊠ *9 carrefour de l'Odéon, 6e, St-Germain-
des-Prés* ☎ *01–44–27–07–50* ⊕ *www.hotel-paris-relais-saint-germain.
com* Ⓜ *Odéon* ✛ *4:B3.*

$$$$ ✕ **Les Bouquinistes.** Showcasing the talents of Guy Savoy protégé Sté-
BISTRO phane Perraud, this is the star chef Savoy's most popular "baby bistro,"
frequented by art dealers from the nearby galleries and the occasional
bouquiniste (bookseller) from the quais across the street. Expect to

hear more English than French in the cheery, contemporary dining room with its closely packed tables looking out onto the Seine, but the sophisticated seasonal cuisine—such as snails and mussels with gnocchi, followed by British Hereford beef with squash-stuffed rigatoni and a caramel crème brûlée—is as authentic as you could hope for. The €31 *menu du marché* (back from the market) lunch menu seems less imaginative than the pricier à la carte options—though it does include three courses and a glass of wine. The wine list is extensive, with 180 wines and 12 champagnes. [$] *Average main: €37* ✉ *53 quai des Grands-Augustins, 6e, St-Germain-des-Prés* ☎ *01–43–25–45–94* 🌐 *www.lesbouquinistes.com* 🕓 *Closed Aug.* [M] *St-Michel* ✥ *4:C2.*

$$$ BISTRO Fodor's Choice ★ 🍴 **Semilla.** The duo behind the popular neighborhood bistro Fish and the excellent La Dernière Goutte wine shop have poured their significant expertise into this laid-back new bistro in the heart of tony Saint Germain des Prés. Its sophisticated cuisine, superb wines by the bottle or glass, and total lack of pretension has quickly made Semilla the toast of the town. A lively open kitchen produces a menu of plentiful dishes either raw, roasted, baked, or steamed, with choices that will thrill both carnivores and herbivores. Velvety chestnut soup, lentil croquettes with a light curry emulsion, beet carpaccio, and the excellent marinated salmon are good choices to start, followed by roasted coquilles Saint Jacques with Jerusalem artichoke puree or venison served with celery root and quince. There are also plenty of bistro classics to choose from, like beef tartare or côte de boeuf with roasted potatoes and a fine sauce bordelaise, and it's open Sunday. [$] *Average main: €25* ✉ *54 Rue de Seine, 6e, St-Germain-des-Prés* ☎ *01–43–54–34–50* ✍ *Reservations essential* [M] *Odéon, St-Germain-des-Prés* ✥ *4:B3.*

$$$ JAPANESE 🍴 **Yen.** If you're having what is known in French as a *crise de foie* (liver crisis), the result of overindulging in rich food, this chic Japanese noodle house with a summer terrace and a VIP room upstairs is the perfect antidote. The blond-wood walls soothe the senses, the staff is happy to explain proper slurping technique, and the *soba* (buckwheat noodles), served in soup or with a restorative broth for dipping, will give you the courage to face another round of caramelized foie gras. The soba noodles are made fresh on the premises every day, showing Parisians that there is more to Japanese cuisine than sushi. Desserts come from Sadaharu Aoki, famous for green-tea *millefeuilles*. Prices are sobering, but various set menus are available for €38.50 at lunch or €68 at dinner. [$] *Average main: €31* ✉ *22 rue St-Benoît, 6e, St-Germain-des-Prés* ☎ *01–45–44–11–18* 🕓 *Closed Sun. and 2 wks in Aug.* [M] *St-Germain-des-Prés* ✥ *4:A2.*

MONTPARNASSE

$$$ BISTRO 🍴 **L'Assiette.** David Rathgeber spent 12 years working for Alain Ducasse as chef of Aux Lyonnais and then Benoît before taking over this landmark restaurant, where he has created his own menu and welcomed a devoted clientele. Expect bourgeois classics with a subtle modern touch, perhaps white tuna steak with spinach, lemon, capers, and croutons, and crème caramel with salted butter—all executed with the precision you would expect of a Ducasse veteran. The excellent two-course

lunch menu is a bargain at €23. Each month, the tea "tasting ateliers" span the globe via the world's great teas, pairing these grand cru's with French cuisine. $ *Average main: €27* ✉ *181 rue du Château, 14e, Montparnasse* ☎ *01–43–22–64–86* ⊕ *www.restaurant-lassiette. com* ☾ *Closed Mon., Tues., Aug., and 1 wk at Christmas* Ⓜ *Pernety, Mouton-Duvernet* ✛ *3:H6.*

$$
BISTRO

✕ **La Cerisaie.** Cyril Lalanne belongs to a breed of young chefs who like to cook for a privileged few. If you can nab a seat in this unremarkable yellow-and-red dining room (be sure to call ahead), you'll be rewarded with food whose attention to detail restores your faith in humanity. Foie gras makes several appearances on the chalkboard menu, since Lalanne is from southwest France, but you can also find freshly caught fish and perhaps farmer's pork from Gascony, a rarity in Paris. Lalanne does his own variation on baba au rhum—with Armagnac, another nod to his native region—and the wine list is strong on southwestern French bottles. $ *Average main: €18* ✉ *70 bd. Edgar Quinet, 14e, Montparnasse* ☎ *01 43 20 98 98* ⊕ *rrestaurantlacerisaie.pagesperso-orange.fr* ⚒ *Reservations essential* ☾ *Closed weekends, mid-July–mid-Aug., and 1 wk at Christmas* Ⓜ *Edgar Quinet* ✛ *4:A6.*

$$$
BRASSERIE
FAMILY

✕ **La Coupole.** This world-renowned cavernous spot with Art Deco murals practically defines the term *brasserie*. It's been popular since Jean-Paul Sartre and Simone de Beauvoir were regulars, and it's still great fun. Today it attracts a mix of bourgeois families, tourists, and lone diners treating themselves to a dozen oysters. Recent additions to the classic brasserie menu are a tart of caramelized apple and panfried foie gras, beef fillet flambéed with cognac before your eyes, and profiteroles made with Valrhona chocolate. You usually can't make reservations after 8 or 8:30, so be prepared for a wait at the bar. $ *Average main: €26* ✉ *102 bd. du Montparnasse, 14e, Montparnasse* ☎ *01–43–20–14–20* ⊕ *www.lacoupole-paris.com* Ⓜ *Vavin* ✛ *4:A6.*

$
MODERN FRENCH
FAMILY

✕ **La Crêperie Josselin.** With lacey curtains, beamed ceilings, and murals, this is the closest you'll get to an authentic Breton crêperie without heading to the coast. Tuck into a hearty buckwheat galette, perfectly crisped on the edges and filled with, perhaps, a classic combo of country ham, egg, cheese, and mushrooms accompanied by a pitcher of refreshing dry Breton cider. For dessert, the traditional crêpe filled with crème *chataigne* (chestnut) or the sublime *caramel au beurre salé* (salted caramel) is not to be missed. With a two-course lunch *formule* with beverage for €11, this is a great place for a quick, satisfying, and thoroughly

BRINY BLISS

Ever since the first trains from Brittany brought oyster-loving settlers to Montparnasse, the neighborhood has had a proud seafood tradition. The best oysters come from Normandy, Brittany, or Marennes-Oléron on the Atlantic coast. The knobbly shelled *creuses* are more common than the rounder *plates*, which are beloved by connoisseurs. Oysters can be dressed with vinegar and shallots, but a squeeze of lemon—or nothing at all—is probably the best accompaniment. Scoop the raw oyster from its shell with a small fork, slurp the juice, and chew a little before swallowing the taste of the sea.

14

French meal. Extra bonus: the kids will love it. [$] *Average main: €10* ✉ *67 rue du Montparnasse, 14e, Montparnasse* ☎ *01–43–20–93–50* 💳 *No credit cards* 🕒 *Closed Mon., Aug., and 1 wk in Jan.* [M] *Vavin, Edgar Quinet* ✥ *3:H6.*

$$$$ BRASSERIE 🍴 **Le Dôme.** Now a fancy fish brasserie serving seafood delivered fresh from Normandy every day, this restaurant began as a dingy meeting place for exiled artists and intellectuals like Lenin and Picasso. Try the sole meunière or the bouillabaisse, the ingredients of which are on display in their raw form in the restaurant's sparkling fish shop next door. You can still drop by the covered terrace for a cup of coffee or a drink. [$] *Average main: €36* ✉ *108 bd. Montparnasse, 14e, Montparnasse* ☎ *01–43–35–25–81* 🕒 *Closed Sun. and Mon. in July and Aug.* [M] *Vavin* ✥ *4:A6.*

$$ BISTRO 🍴 **Le Timbre.** Working in a tiny open kitchen, Manchester native Chris Wright could teach many a French chef a thing or two about *cuisine française.* He uses only the finest suppliers to produce a constantly changing seasonal menu that keeps the locals coming back: in fall you might sample the *cochon noir de Bigorre* (a pedigreed pig from southwest France) with marinated red cabbage, or blood sausage with french fries. The signature mille-feuille is spectacular, but try not to miss *le vrai et le faux fromage* (literally "the real and the fake cheese"): perhaps a two-year-old British cheddar juxtaposed with a farmer's goat cheese from the Ardèche. (The joke is that the English cheese is the "real" cheese and the French cheese is fake—although French people might read it the other way.) [$] *Average main: €19* ✉ *3 rue Ste-Beuve, 6e, Montparnasse* ☎ *01–45–49–10–40* 🌐 *www.restaurantletimbre.com* ✍ *Reservations essential* 🕒 *Closed Sun., Mon., mid-July–mid-Aug., and 10 days at Christmas* [M] *Vavin* ✥ *4:A5.*

WESTERN PARIS

$$$$ MODERN FRENCH 🍴 **Le Pré Catelan.** Live a Belle Époque fantasy by dining beneath the chestnut trees on the terrace of this fanciful landmark *pavilion* in the Bois de Boulogne. Each of chef Frédéric Anton's dishes is a variation on a theme, such as *l'os à moelle:* bone marrow prepared two ways, one peppered and the other stuffed with porcini and cabbage, both braised in a concentrated meat jus. For a taste of the good life at a (relatively) gentle price, order the €105 lunch menu and soak up the opulent surroundings along with service that's as polished as the silverware. [$] *Average main: €120* ✉ *Rte. de Suresnes, 16e, Western Paris* ☎ *01–44–14–41–14* 🌐 *www.restaurant-precatelan.com* ✍ *Reservations essential* 👔 *Jacket and tie* 🕒 *Closed Sun. and Mon., 2 wks in Feb., 3 wks in Aug., and 1 wk in late Oct.–early Nov.* [M] *Porte Dauphine* ✥ *1:A3.*

WHERE TO EAT
AND STAY IN PARIS

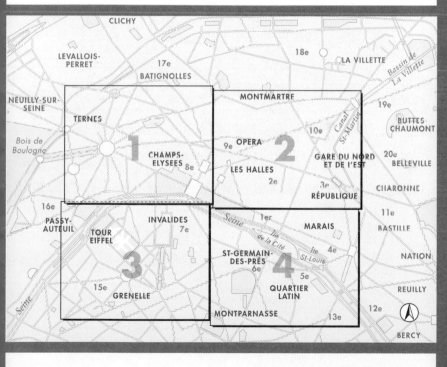

KEY	
□	Hotels
■	Restaurants
■	Restaurant in Hotel
Ⓜ	Métro Stations

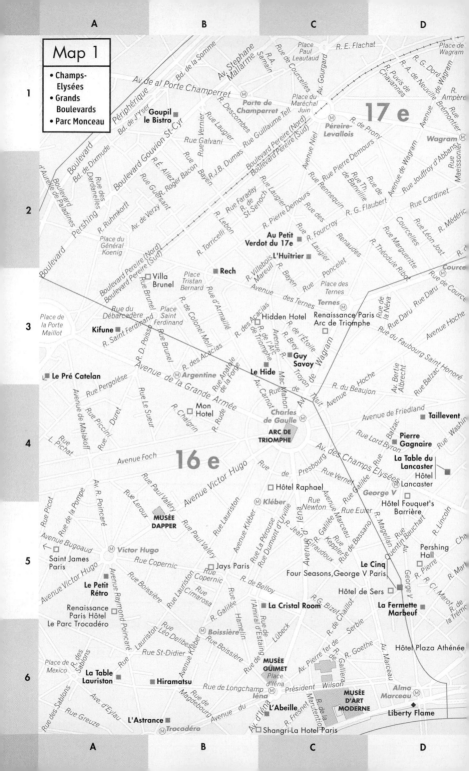

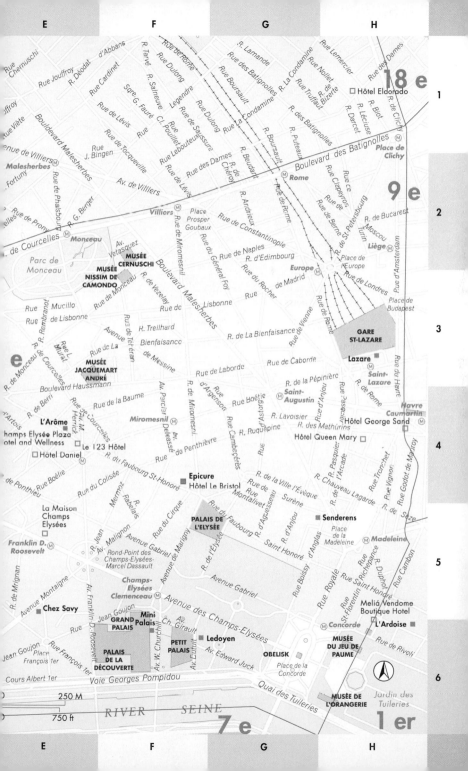

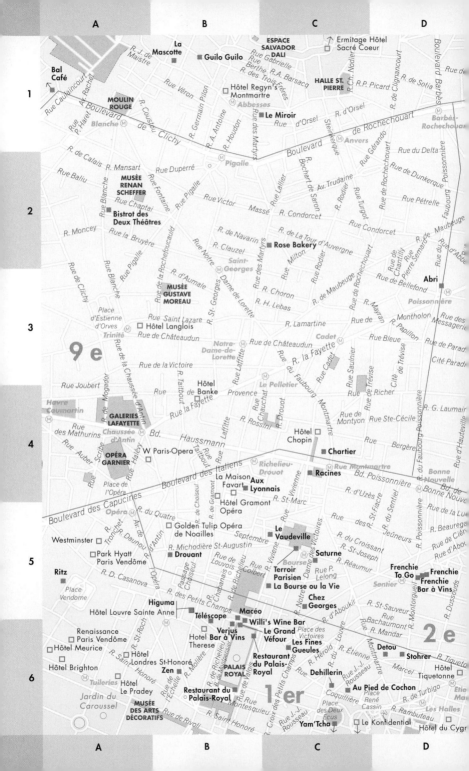

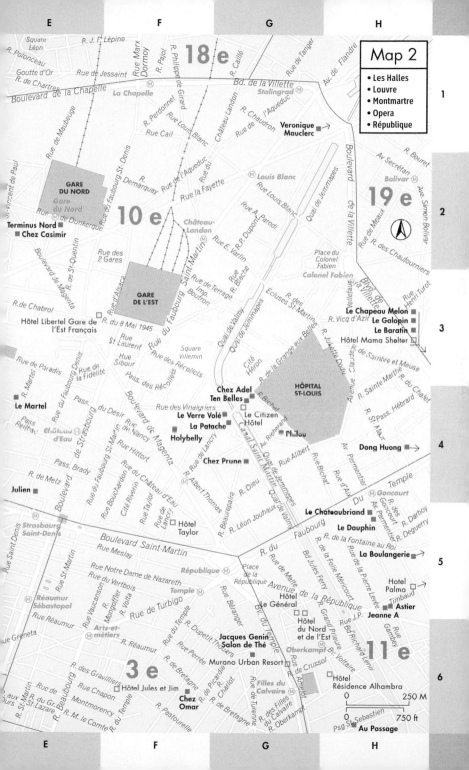

Map 2

- Les Halles
- Louvre
- Montmartre
- Opera
- République

18e
10e
19e
11e
3e

Square Léon
R. J. F. Lépine
Rue Marx Dormoy
R. Pajol
Rue Philippe de Girard
R. Caillé
Rue de Tanger
Av. de Flandre
R. Polonceau
Goutte d'Or
R. de Chartres
Rue de Jessaint
Boulevard de la Chapelle
La Chapelle
Bd. de la Villette
Stalingrad
Av Secrétan
R. Bouret
Bolívar
Ave. Simon Bolivar

R. Perdonnet
Rue Louis Blanc
Château Landon
R. Chaudron
Rue de l'Aqueduc
Rue Cail
Rue de Maubeuge
Rue du Faubourg St.-Denis
R. Demarquay
Rue de l'Aqueduc
Rue du Aqueduc
Rue de la Fayette
Veronique Mauclerc →
Boulevard de la Villette

R. St.-Vincent de Paul
GARE DU NORD
Gare du Nord
R. de Dunkerque
Louis Blanc
Rue Louis Blanc
R. A. Parodi
R. des Chaufourniers
Av Simon Bolivar

■ **Terminus Nord**
■ **Chez Casimir**
Boulevard de Magenta
R. de St.-Quentin
Rue des 2 Gares
Château-Landon
Rue E. Varlin
R. P. Dupont
Place du Colonel Fabien
Colonel Fabien

R. de Chabrol
GARE DE L'EST
Rue d'Alsace
Rue de Terrage
Imp. Boufron
R. Bacfer
Bd. de la Villette
R. Henri Turot

Hôtel Libertel Gare de l'Est Français
R. du 8 Mai 1945
Rue St Laurent
Rue Sibour
Rue des Écluses St.-Martin
R. des Écluses St.-Martin
R. Vicq d'Azir
Le Chapeau Melon ■
Le Galopin ■
Le Baratin ■
Hôtel Mama Shelter □

Rue de Paradis
Rue du Faubourg Denis
Rue de la Fidélité
Square Villemin
Rue des Récollets
Cité Héron
R. de la Grange aux Belles
Av. Juliette Dodu
R. de Sambre et Meuse

■ **Le Martel**
Pass. Reilhac
Pass. du Désir
Boulevard de Strasbourg
R. St.-Martin
Rue de Nancy
Rue Hittorf
Quai de Valmy
R. Bichat
HÔPITAL ST.-LOUIS
R. Ste. Marthe
R. du Chalet
Pass. Hébrard

Château d'Eau
Pass. Brady
R. de Metz
Rue du Château d'Eau
Cité Riverin
Chez Adel
Ten Belles ■
R. Bichat
Le Verre Volé ■
La Patache ■
Le Citizen Hôtel
Holybelly
Philou ■
Av. Richerand
R. St. Maur
Av. Parmentier

■ **Julien**
Rue Taylor
R. de Lancry
Chez Prune ■
R. Albert Thomas
R. Dieu
Quai de Jemmapes
Quai de Valmy
R. Alibert
R. Bichat
Dong Huong →

Strasbourg Saint-Denis
Rue Léon Jouhaux
R. Beaurepaire
Du Temple
Goncourt
Av. Parmentier
R. Darboy
R. Deguerry

R. St.-Martin
Hôtel Taylor
Boulevard Saint-Martin
Le Châteaubriand ■
Av. de la République
R. des Goncourt
Le Dauphin ■
R. de la Fontaine au Roi
La Boulangerie →

Rue Meslay
Rue Notre Dame de Nazareth
République
Place de la République
Avenue de la République
Bd Jules Ferry
Bd de la Folie Méricourt
Rue de la Pierre Levée
Hotel Palma □ →
R. Timbaud

Réaumur Sébastopol
Rue Réaumur
Rue du Vertbois
R. Volta
Temple
Rue de Turbigo
R. du Temple
Rue de Malte
Hôtel **Le Général**
Grand Prieuré
J.P. Timbaud
Astier ■
Jeanne A ■
R. Gambey

Arts-et-métiers
R. Réaumur
R. Mongoffier
Rue Vaucanson
R. Dupetit Thouars
Jacques Genin Salon de Thé
Hôtel du Nord et de l'Est
Oberkampf
Bd. Voltaire
R. J.P. Timbaud
Bd Richard Lenoir

Rue des Gravilliers
Rue Chapon
R. de Bretagne
R. Perrée
Murano Urban Resort
R. de Crussol
11e
Hôtel **Résidence Alhambra** □

R. de Montmorency
Hôtel Jules et Jim □
R. de Picardie
R. Charlot
R. de Bretagne
Filles du Calvaire
R. des Filles du Calvaire
R. Oberkampf
0 _____ 250 M

aux Ours St.-Martin
R. du Gr. Lazare
R. M. le Comte
Chez Omar
R. Pastourelle
R. de Turenne
Psg St Sébastien
0 _____ 750 ft
Au Passage ■

E   F   G   H
1 2 3 4 5 6

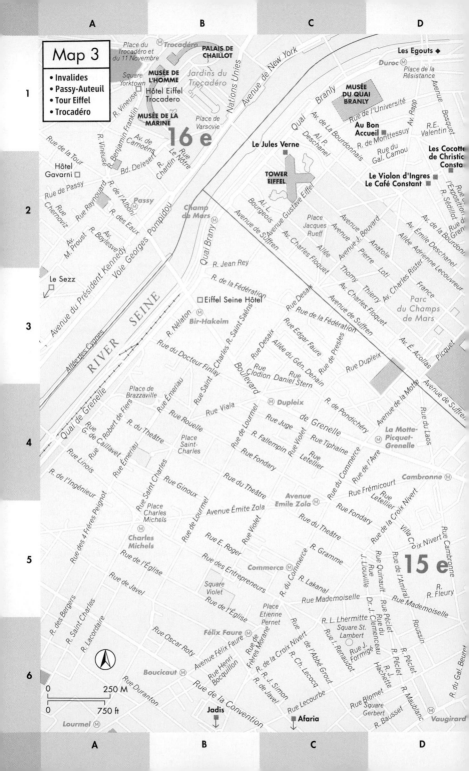

Map 3

- Invalides
- Passy-Auteuil
- Tour Eiffel
- Trocadéro

0 — 250 M
0 — 750 ft

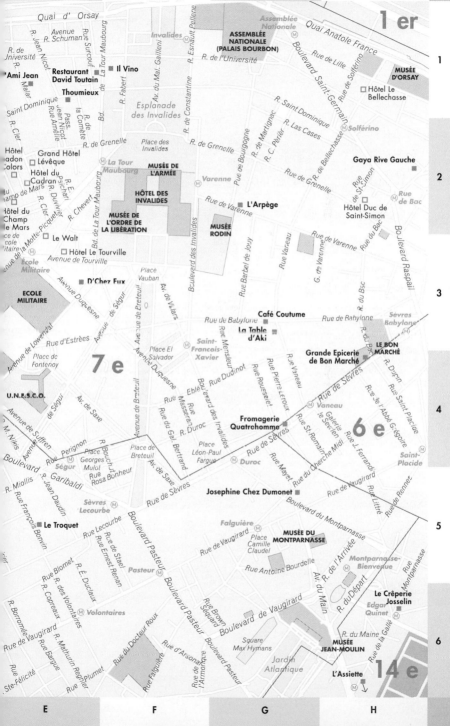

E   **F**   **G**   **H**

Quai d' Orsay

Assemblée Nationale

Quai Anatole France

1 er

Avenue R. Schuman

R. Surcouf

Rue Fabert

Invalides

ASSEMBLÉE NATIONALE (PALAIS BOURBON)

Boulevard Saint-Germain

Rue de Lille

Rue de Solférino

1

R. de Jean Nicot

R. de Université

R. Esnault Pelterie

R. de l'Université

Av. du Mal. Galliéni

R. de Constantine

MUSÉE D'ORSAY

Malar

Ami Jean

Restaurant David Toutain

Il Vino

Hôtel Le Bellechasse

Saint Dominique

Thoumieux

de la Tour Maubourg

R. Saint Dominique

R. de Martignac

R. Las Cases

R. C. Périèr

Solférino

R. de Grenelle

R. Cler

R. de la Comète

Pass. Jean Nicot

Esplanade des Invalides

R. de Grenelle

Rue de Bourgogne

Rue de Bellechasse

Gaya Rive Gauche

2

Hôtel adon Colors

Grand Hôtel Lévêque

La Tour Maubourg

Place des Invalides

MUSÉE DE L'ARMÉE

Varenne

Rue de Grenelle

Rue de St-Simon

Rue de Bac

Hôtel du Cadran

R. E. Psichari

R. Duvivier

R. Chevert

Bd. de La Tour Maubourg

HÔTEL DES INVALIDES

Hôtel Duc de Saint-Simon

amp de Mars

L'Arpège

Rue du Bac

ôtel du Champ e Mars

R. Cler

MUSÉE DE L'ORDRE DE LA LIBÉRATION

Rue de Varenne

MUSÉE RODIN

Rue de Varenne

Boulevard Raspail

ce de cole itaire

enue de la Motte-Picquet

Le Walt

Hôtel Le Tourville

Avenue de Tourville

Rue Barbet de Jouy

Rue Vaneau

G. de Varenne

École Militaire

Boulevard des Invalides

Place Vauban

ECOLE MILITAIRE

Avenue Duquesne

Avenue de Ségur

Av. de Breteuil

Av. de Vilars

D'Chez Eux

Rue de Babylone

Café Coutume

Rue de Babylone

Rue du Bac

Sèvres Babylone

3

Rue d'Estrées

La Table d'Aki

Place de Fontenoy

Avenue de Lowendal

7 e

Avenue de Ségur

Avenue Duquesne

Place El Salvador

Saint-François-Xavier

Rue Mensieur

Grande Epicerie de Bon Marché

LE BON MARCHÉ

Rue Dupin

Rue de l'Abbé G.-égoire

U.N.E.S.C.O.

Avenue de Saxe

Avenue de Breteuil

Rue Eblé

Boulevard des Invalides

Rue Dudinot

Rue Pierre Leroux

Rue Rousselet

Rue Vaneau

Rue de Sèvres

Galerie le Sevien

Rue Saint Placide

6 e

4

Avenue de Suffren

M. Nikis

Rue Masseran

Rue Duroc

Fromagerie Quatrehomma

Rue St-Romaine

Rue du Cherche Midi

Rue J. Ferrandi

Saint-Placide

Boulevard Garibaldi

Rue Perignon

Av. Bouchut

Place Georges Mulot

Place de Breteuil

Place Léon-Paul Fargue

Duroc

Rue de Sèvres

Rue Mayet

R. Miollis

R. Jean Daudin

Rue Rosa Bonheur

Av. de Saxe

Rue du Gal. Bertrand

Josephine Chez Dumonet

Rue de Vaugirard

Rue Littré

Rue de Rennes

R. François Bonvin

Sèvres Lecourbe

Rue de Sèvres

Boulevard du Montparnasse

5

Le Troquet

Rue Lecourbe

Rue de Staël

Rue Ernest Renan

Boulevard Pasteur

Falguière

Rue de Vaugirard

Place Camille Claudel

MUSÉE DU MONTPARNASSE

Av. de R. de l'Arrivée

Montparnasse-Bienvenue

Boulevard du Montparnasse

Rue Blomet

R. E. Duclaux

R. des Volontaires

Pasteur

Rue Antoine Bourdelle

Av. du Maine

Rue du Départ

Edgar Quinet

Le Crêperie Josselin

6

R. Borromée

R. Mathurin Regnier

Volontaires

Boulevard Pasteur

Rue Brown Séquard

Boulevard de Vaugirard

Rue de la Gaîté

Rue Montparnasse

Rue de Vaugirard

Rue du Docteur Roux

Rue d'Arsonvale

Boulevard Pasteur

Square Max Hymans

MUSÉE JEAN-MOULIN

R. du Maine

R. Copreaux

R. Bargue

Ste-Félicité

Rue Plumet

Rue Falguière

Rue de l'Armonique

Jardin Atlantique

L'Assiette

14 e

E   **F**   **G**   **H**

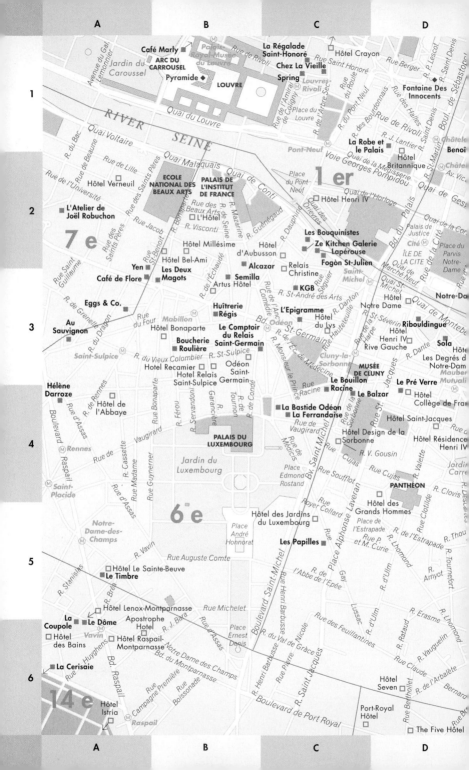

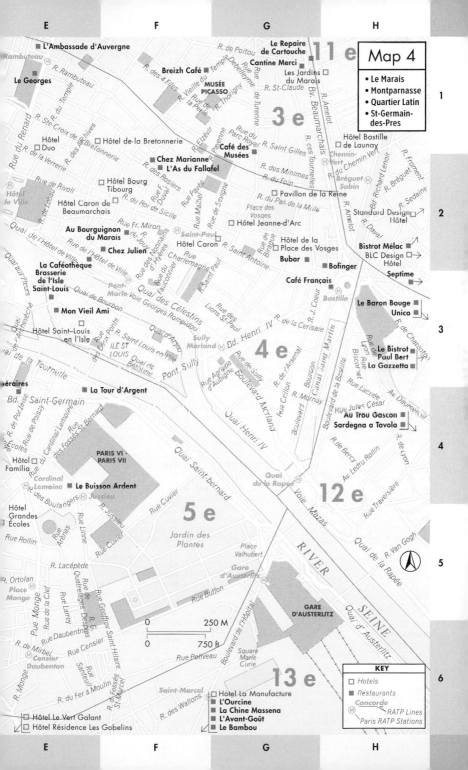

WHERE TO STAY

Updated by
Victoria Tang

If your Parisian fantasy involves romantic evenings in a historic hotel, awaking to the aroma of freshly baked croissants and café au lait, here's some good news: you need not be French aristocracy to make your dreams come true. With more than 2,000 hotels, the City of Light gives visitors stylish options in all price ranges, and a place with historic charm is practically a given.

In terms of location and price, there are more hotels on the *Rive Droite* (the Right Bank) offering formal luxury with premium service than on the *Rive Gauche* (the Left Bank), where the hotels are frequently smaller and richer in old-fashioned charm. The Rive Droite's 1er, 8e, and 16e arrondissements are still the most exclusive, and the prices there reflect that. Some of these palatial hotels charge more than €750 a night for standard rooms. Due to ongoing renovations at three major landmark luxury hotels, the Hôtel Ritz, Hôtel de Crillon, and Hôtel Plaza Athénée, other worthy establishments are strutting their premium stuff. Less-expensive alternatives on the Rive Droite can be found in the fashionable Marais quarter (3e and 4e arrondissements). The hotbed of chic hotels on the Rive Gauche is the 6e arrondissement; choices get cheaper in the 5e and 7e. Some excellent budget deals can be found slightly off the beaten track in the 9e, 10e, 13e, and 20e arrondissements. Wherever possible, in the more expensive neighborhoods we've located budget hotels—check out the handful of budget-priced sleeps in the shadow of Notre-Dame, St-Germain-des-Prés, and the Louvre.

As for the environment inside your room, change has been in the air—literally. Enforcement of the no-smoking law is not always perfect, but at least now you'll have a valid complaint if your room smells like stale smoke. Amenities have improved, with virtually every hotel now equipped with cable TV (meaning CNN and BBC news in English)—often high-definition screens, minibars, in-room safes, and wireless Internet access (though not always free). Another recent change is the increasing availability of air-conditioning in both hotels and restaurants—a godsend in the *canicules* (dog days) of July and August.

WHERE SHOULD I STAY?

	NEIGHBORHOOD VIBE	PROS	CONS
St-Germain and Montparnasse (6e, 14e, 15e)	The center of café culture and the emblem of the Rive Gauche. The mood is leisurely; attractions are easy to access.	A safe, historic area with chic fashion boutiques, famous cafés and brasseries, and lovely side streets; lively all day.	Overdeveloped. Noisy along the main streets; the busy commercial area around the Tour Montparnasse is void of charm.
The Latin Quarter (5e, 6e)	The historic student quarter of the Rive Gauche. Full of narrow, winding streets and major parks and monuments such as the Panthéon.	Plenty of cheap eats and sleeps, discount book and music shops, and noteworthy open-air markets; safe area for walks day and night.	Touristy. No métro stations around the Panthéon; student pubs can be noisy in summer; hotel rooms tend to be smaller.
Marais and Bastille (3e, 4e, 11e)	Museums, quaint shops, and laid-back bistros line the narrow streets of the Marais, home to Jewish and gay communities. Farther east are ethnic eats and edgy stores.	Generally excellent shopping, sightseeing, dining, and nightlife in the active Marais; bargains aplenty at Bastille hotels; several boutique designer hotels in both areas.	Overcrowded. Marais's narrow sidewalks are always packed, and rooms don't come cheap; always noisy around the gritty boulevards of Place de la Bastille and Nation.
Montmartre and northeast Paris (18e, 19e, 20e)	The Rive Droite's hilltop district is known for winding streets leading from the racy Pigalle district to the stark-white Sacré-Coeur Basilica.	Amazing views of Paris; romantic cobblestone streets; easy access to Roissy-Charles de Gaulle airport; authentic Parisian neighborhoods.	Inconvenient. Steep staircases are challenging; few métro stations; Pigalle and Barbès area raunchy and unsafe, especially late at night.
Champs-Élysées and Western Paris (8e, 16e, 17e)	The Triangle D'Or (Golden Triangle) and famous avenue are lively 24/7 with nightclubs, cinemas, and shops, all aimed at the moneyed jet set.	Home to most of the city's famous palace-like hotels and haute couture boutiques with no shortage of luxurious rooms and designer goods.	Super expensive. The sky-high prices of this neighborhood, along with its Times Square tendencies, lure pickpockets.
Around the Eiffel Tower (7e, 15e)	The impressive Eiffel Tower and verdant Champs de Mars sit next to the Seine River.	The safe, quiet, and relatively inexpensive Rive Gauche area of Paris has picture-perfect views at every turn.	Residential. With few shops and restaurants, this district is quiet at night; long distances between métro stations.
Louvre, Les Halles, Ile de la Cité (1er, 2e, 8e)	The central district around the Tuileries, Louvre, and Place de la Concorde is known for sightseeing and shopping; Les Halles is a buzzing commercial hub.	Convenient for getting around Paris on foot, bus, or métro. Safe, attractive district close to the Seine and shops of all types.	Noisy. The main artery of Rue de Rivoli is loud with traffic during the day; restaurants cater to tourists; a pickpocket's mecca.
Opéra and Grands Boulevards (9e, 10e)	The historic district centered around the Garnier Opera House and Bourse (Stock Exchange) is a popular district for its lively streets and important sites.	Perfect for walking tours, the area has unique Parisian finds, distinct neighborhoods like Belleville, and les Grands Magasins (department stores)	Crowded. Tourists and locals keep districts full of pietons, cars, buses, trucks, taxis, and scooters; be extra alert in areas near major train stations.

15

One thing that hasn't changed, however, is the lack of elbow room. Indoor spaces—from bed and bathrooms to elevators—may feel cramped to those not used to life on a European scale. If you're looking for enough room to spread out multiple suitcases, book a suite in one of the city's luxurious palace-like hotels.

PLANNING

APARTMENT RENTALS
See the Apartment Rentals box on p. 277.

BREAKFAST
Almost all Parisian hotels charge extra for breakfast, with per-person prices ranging from €8 to more than €50. So if you decide to eat elsewhere, inform the staff so breakfast won't be charged to your bill. Continental breakfast—coffee, baguette, croissant, jam, and butter—is sometimes included in the hotel rate. This is noted as *breakfast*, in the meal plan section of each review.

CHECKING IN
Typical check-in and check-out times are 2 pm and noon, respectively, although some properties allow check-in as early as noon and require check-out as early as 10 am. Many flights from North America arrive early in the morning, but having to wait six hours for a room after arriving jet-lagged at 8 am isn't the ideal way to start a vacation. Alert the hotel of your early arrival; while you may not be able to get into your room, you may be able to arrange for baggage storage, especially at the larger establishments.

CHILDREN
Most hotels in Paris allow children under the age of 12 to stay in their parents' room at no charge. Hotel rooms are often on the small side, unable to accommodate cots or cribs, so inquire about connecting rooms, suites, and floors with strategically placed doors to create private corridors for larger families and groups.

HOTEL FEATURES
Unless stated in the review, hotels have elevators, and all guest rooms have air-conditioning, TV, telephone, and a private bathroom. In France the first floor is the floor above the ground floor (*rez-de-chaussée*). The number of rooms listed at the end of each review reflects those with private bathrooms (which means they have a shower or a tub, but not necessarily both). Tubs don't always have fixed curtains or shower-heads; how the French rinse themselves with the handheld nozzle without flooding the entire bathroom remains a cultural mystery. It's rare to find moderately priced places that expect guests to share toilets or bathrooms, but be sure you know what facilities you are getting when you book a budget hotel.

HOTEL QUALITY
Note that the quality of accommodations can vary from room to room. If you don't like the room you're given, ask to see another. The French star ratings can be misleading: official stars are granted for specific

amenities and services rather than for ambience, style, or overall comfort, so you may find that a two-star hotel eclipses a three-star establishment. Many hotels prefer to remain "under-starred" for tax reasons.

LODGING STRATEGY

Where should we stay? With hundreds of Paris hotels, it may seem like a daunting question. But don't worry—our expert writers and editors have done most of the legwork. The 100-plus selections here represent the best and newest properties this city has to offer. Scan "Best Bets" on the following pages for top recommendations by price and experience. Or find a review quickly in the listings, which are arranged by arrondissement and then alphabetically.

RESERVATIONS

Make reservations as far in advance as possible, especially for May, June, September, and October. Calling directly works, but email may be the easiest way to make contact, because hotel staff members are more likely to read English than understand it over the phone. Specify arrival and departure dates, room size (single or double), room type (standard, deluxe, or suite), the number of people in your party, and whether you want a bathroom with a shower or bathtub (or both). Double check if breakfast, Internet, and taxes are included. Ask if a deposit is required, and what happens if you cancel. Always request a confirmation number to verify your reservation upon arrival.

WHAT IT COSTS

Often a hotel in a certain price category will have a few less expensive rooms; it's worth asking. In the off-season—late July, August, November, early December, and late January—rates can be considerably lower. Inquire about specials and weekend deals, and whether there are better rates if you're staying a week or longer. There's a nominal city *taxe de séjour* ranging between €0.50 and €1.80 per person, per night, based on the hotel's star rating. Sometimes this tax is included in the room price, sometimes not.

If you're staying in Paris for more than just a few days, you might want to look into the increasingly popular option of renting an apartment. Not only does this often save in nightly costs, but with your own kitchen you can cook some of your own meals. *Prices in the reviews are the lowest cost of a standard double room in high season.*

USING THE MAPS

Throughout the chapter, you'll see mapping symbols and coordinates (such as ✛ 3:F2) after property names or reviews. To locate the property on a map, turn to the Paris Dining and Lodging Atlas at the end of the Where to Eat chapter. The first number after the ✛ symbol indicates the map number. Following that is the property's coordinate on the map grid.

BEST BETS FOR PARIS LODGING

Fodor's offers a selective listing of high-quality lodging experiences at every price range, from the best budget options to the most sophisticated grande-dame hotel. *Below are our top recommendations by price and experience.*

Les Jardins du Marais, p. 283
Park Hyatt Paris Vendôme, p. 281
Renaissance Paris Arc de Triomphe, p. 275
Renaissance Paris Vendôme, p. 279

HISTORIC

Hôtel de la Place des Vosges, p. 282
Hôtel Odéon Saint-Germain, p. 289
Hôtel Raphael, p. 274
Pavillon de la Reine, p. 283

Fodor's Choice ★

Four Seasons Hôtel George V Paris, p. 273
Hôtel Familia, p. 286
Hôtel Jules & Jim, p. 283
Hôtel Meurice, p. 278
Hôtel Plaza Athénée, p. 274
Le Citizen Hôtel, p. 284
Park Hyatt Paris Vendôme, p. 281
Shangri-La Hotel Paris, p. 273
W Paris-Opéra, p. 281

$$$

Apostrophe Hotel, p. 290
Hôtel Duc de Saint-Simon, p. 289
Hôtel Jules & Jim, p. 283
Hôtel Langlois, p. 280
Hôtel Relais Saint-Sulpice, p. 290
Hotel Seven, p. 287

$$$$

Four Seasons Hôtel George V Paris, p. 273
Hidden Hotel, p. 273
Hôtel d'Aubusson, p. 288
Hôtel Le Pradey, p. 277
Hôtel Meurice, p. 278
Hôtel Odéon Saint-Germain, p. 289
Hôtel Plaza Athénée p. 274
Hôtel Recamier, p. 289
Hôtel Thérèse, p. 278
Hôtel Verneuil, p. 290
La Maison Favart, p. 280
Le Citizen Hôtel, p. 284

Park Hyatt Paris Vendôme, p. 281
Saint James Paris, p. 292
Shangri-La Hotel Paris, p. 273
W Paris-Opéra, p. 281

By Experience

BEST DESIGN

The Five Hôtel, p. 285
Hôtel Jules & Jim, p. 283
Hotel Seven, p. 287
La Maison Champs Elysées, p. 275
Hôtel Le Bellechasse, p. 272

BEST VIEWS

Champs-Élysées Plaza Hotel and Wellness, p. 273
Hôtel Brighton, p. 276
Hôtel Meurice, p. 278
Shangri-La Hotel Paris, p. 273

BUSINESS TRAVEL

Four Seasons Hôtel George V Paris, p. 273
Hôtel Lancaster, p. 274

By Price

$

Hôtel du Champ de Mars, p. 272
Hôtel Familia, p. 286
Hotel Résidence Les Gobelins, p. 287
Hôtel Tiquetonne, p. 276
Port-Royal Hôtel, p. 288

$$

Hôtel Mama Shelter, p. 283
Hôtel Taylor p. 284

MOST CENTRAL

Hôtel Britannique, p. 276
Hôtel Fouquet's Barrière, p. 274
Hôtel Henri IV, p. 271
Hôtel Le Bristol, p. 274
Hôtel Le Pradey, p. 277

MOST CHARMING

Hôtel d'Aubusson, p. 288
Hôtel Notre Dame, p. 287
Les Jardins du Luxembourg, p. 288

MOST ROMANTIC

Hôtel Daniel, p. 273
Hôtel Recamier, p. 289
Hotel Seven, p. 287
Hôtel Verneuil, p. 290
L'Hôtel, p. 290
Le Konfidentiel, p. 278

HOTEL REVIEWS

In alphabetical order by neighborhood.
For expanded hotel reviews, visit Fodors.com.

THE ISLANDS

ILE DE LA CITÉ

$ HOTEL **Hôtel Henri IV.** This 17th-century building, which once housed King Henri IV's printing presses, offers few comforts or amenities, but you'll be hard-pressed to find a more central hotel for this price. **Pros:** very quiet; top rooms have balconies; basic breakfast included. **Cons:** steep stairs in poor condition and no elevator; few services or amenities; phone reservations only. [$] *Rooms from: €83* ✉ *25 pl. Dauphine, 1er, Ile de la Cité* ☎ *01–43–54–44–53* 🌐 *www.henri4hotel.fr* 🛏 *15 rooms, 14 with bath* 🍴 *Breakfast* [M] *Cité, St-Michel, Pont Neuf* ✥ *4:C2.*

ILE ST-LOUIS

$$$ HOTEL **Hôtel Saint-Louis en L'Isle.** The location on the exceptionally charming Ile St-Louis is the real draw of this five-story hotel, which retains many of its original 17th-century stone walls and wooden beams. **Pros:** romantic location; ancient architectural details; friendly staff. **Cons:** location is a bit far from the sights; métro stations are not so convenient; small rooms. [$] *Rooms from: €195* ✉ *75 rue St-Louis-en-l'Ile, 4e, Ile St-Louis* ☎ *01–46–34–04–80* 🌐 *www.saintlouisenlisle.com* 🛏 *20 rooms* 🍴 *Breakfast* [M] *Pont Marie* ✥ *4:E3.*

AROUND THE EIFFEL TOWER

$$$ HOTEL FAMILY **Eiffel Seine Hôtel.** This tiny boutique hotel minutes from the Eiffel Tower mixes contemporary amenities and designer furnishings with Art Nouveau flourishes. **Pros:** very close to the Eiffel Tower and Champs de Mars; easy métro access; air-conditioned rooms. **Cons:** long walk from the center of town; minimal space in standard rooms; street noise in some rooms facing river. [$] *Rooms from: €185* ✉ *3 bd. de Grenelle, 15e, Around the Eiffel Tower* ☎ *01–45–78–14–81* 🌐 *www.eiffelseine.com* 🛏 *45 rooms* 🍴 *Breakfast* [M] *Bir Hakeim* ✥ *3:B3.*

$$ HOTEL FAMILY **Grand Hôtel Lévêque.** Sandwiched between casual cafés, this unobtrusive budget hotel is easy to miss, but its prime location shouldn't be overlooked—the Eiffel Tower and Champs de Mars are around the corner, and one of the city's finest street markets is literally outside the front door. **Pros:** in quiet residential district; some rooms have balconies with Eiffel Tower views; free Wi-Fi. **Cons:** air-conditioning only from June to September; faded decor. [$] *Rooms from: €160* ✉ *29 rue Cler, 7e, Around the Eiffel Tower* ☎ *01–47–05–49–15* 🌐 *www.hotel-leveque.com* 🛏 *50 rooms, 45 with bath* 🍴 *No meals* [M] *École Militaire* ✥ *3:E2.*

$$$ HOTEL **Hôtel du Cadran.** With its display of customized sweets for sale by trendy chocolatier Christopher Roussel, the lobby of the Cadran looks more like a modern chocolate shop. **Pros:** easy walk to Eiffel Tower and Les Invalides; free Wi-Fi; friendly reception staff. **Cons:** small rooms; premium prices for district; no restaurant or gym. [$] *Rooms from: €224*

✉ *10 rue du Champ de Mars, 7e, Around the Eiffel Tower* ☎ *01–40– 62–67–00* ⊕ *www.cadranhotel.com* ⮡ *40 rooms, 1 suite* ⦿ *Breakfast* Ⓜ *École Militaire* ✛ *3:E2.*

$ ⛨ **Hôtel du Champ de Mars.** Around the corner from picturesque Rue
HOTEL Cler, this charming, affordable hotel welcomes guests with a Provence-inspired lobby and huge picture windows overlooking a quiet street. **Pros:** good value; walking distance to Eiffel Tower, Les Invalides, and Rodin Museum; free Wi-Fi. **Cons:** small rooms compared to larger hotels; no air-conditioning; inconsistent service. $ *Rooms from: €120* ✉ *7 rue du Champ de Mars, 7e, Around the Eiffel Tower* ☎ *01–45– 51–52–30* ⊕ *www.hotelduchampdemars.com* ⮡ *25 rooms* ⦿ *Breakfast* Ⓜ *École Militaire* ✛ *3:E2.*

$$$$ ⛨ **Hôtel Eiffel Trocadéro.** A curious blend of Second Empire and Rococo
HOTEL styling awaits guests in this hotel on a quiet corner just off Place Trocadéro. **Pros:** views of Eiffel Tower from upper floors; upscale residential district convenient to métro; organic breakfast buffet. **Cons:** no full-service restaurant; long walk to center of town; basic rooms feel cramped. $ *Rooms from: €300* ✉ *35 rue Benjamin Franklin, Around the Eiffel Tower* ☎ *01–53–70–17–70* ⊕ *www.hoteleiffeltrocadero.com* ⮡ *16 rooms, 1 suite* ⦿ *Breakfast* Ⓜ *Trocadéro* ✛ *3:A1.*

$$$$ ⛨ **Hôtel Le Bellechasse.** If you like eclectic modern interior design, this
HOTEL tiny boutique hotel right around the corner from the popular Musée d'Orsay is a good choice for its access to the major sites. **Pros:** central location near top museums; one-of-a-kind style; helpful staff. **Cons:** pricey rates; street-facing rooms can be noisy; open bathrooms lack privacy. $ *Rooms from: €390* ✉ *8 rue de Bellechasse, 7e, Around the Eiffel Tower* ☎ *01–45–50–22–31* ⊕ *www.lebellechasse.com* ⮡ *33 rooms, 1 suite* ⦿ *Breakfast* Ⓜ *Solferino* ✛ *3:H1.*

$$$$ ⛨ **Hôtel Le Tourville.** This cozy, contemporary haven near the Eiffel
HOTEL Tower, Champs de Mars, and Invalides is a comfortable base for exploring Paris. **Pros:** convenient location near métro; friendly service; soundproof windows. **Cons:** standard rooms are small; air-conditioning only during summer months; no restaurant. $ *Rooms from: €295* ✉ *16 av. de Tourville, 7e, Around the Eiffel Tower* ☎ *01–47–05–62–62* ⊕ *www. hoteltourville.com* ⮡ *27 rooms, 3 suites* Ⓜ *École Militaire* ✛ *3:E3.*

$$$$ ⛨ **Hotel Valadon Colors.** Sharing facilities with its sister hotel a few steps
HOTEL away, the Hotel Valadon is a bold experiment in contemporary chic design that appeals to urban creative types. **Pros:** candy-colored rooms; large closets and windows; convenient to Rue Cler, Eiffel Tower, and Les Invalides. **Cons:** check in at Hotel Cadran; lacks traditional Parisian charm; petite bathrooms. $ *Rooms from: €270* ✉ *16 rue Valadon, Around the Eiffel Tower* ☎ *01–47–53–89–85* ⊕ *www.hotelvaladon.com* ⮡ *12 suites* ⦿ *Breakfast* Ⓜ *École Militaire* ✛ *3:E2.*

$$$$ ⛨ **Le Walt.** The convenient location stands out at this boutique hotel in
HOTEL the chic district between the Eiffel Tower and Les Invalides. **Pros:** great location; friendly staff; free Wi-Fi. **Cons:** on a busy street; no hotel restaurant; some complaints about noisy doors in hallways. $ *Rooms from: €290* ✉ *37 av. de la Motte Picquet, 7e, Around the Eiffel Tower* ☎ *01–45–51–55–83* ⊕ *www.lewaltparis.com* ⮡ *25 rooms* ⦿ *Breakfast* Ⓜ *École Militaire* ✛ *3:E3.*

$$$$ HOTEL Fodor's Choice ★ 🏨 **Shangri-La Hotel Paris.** French elegance at its best, this impressively restored 19th-century mansion gazing across the Seine at the Eiffel Tower was once the stately home of Prince Roland Bonaparte, grand-nephew of the emperor himself. **Pros:** close to the métro and luxury shopping; varied culinary options for all tastes; exceptional suites. **Cons:** astronomically high rates; pool only open until 9 pm; some obstructed views. [$] *Rooms from: €1000* ✉ *10 av. Iéna, 16e, Around the Eiffel Tower* ☎ *01–53–67–19–98* 🌐 *www.shangri-la.com* 🛏 *65 rooms, 36 suites* [M] *Iéna* ✥ *1:C6.*

CHAMPS-ÉLYSÉES

$$$$ HOTEL 🏨 **Champs-Élysées Plaza Hotel and Wellness.** Discreet, contemporary elegance sums up this graciously renovated seven-story town house steps from the hustle-and-bustle of the Champs-Élysées. **Pros:** extremely comfortable and elegant rooms; friendly, attentive service; central location. **Cons:** small spa; gym only has five machines; limited breakfast buffet. [$] *Rooms from: €400* ✉ *35 rue de Berri, 8e, Champs-Élysées* ☎ *01–53–53–20–20* 🌐 *www.champs-elysees-plaza.com* 🛏 *35 rooms and suites* 🍴 *Breakfast* [M] *St-Philippe-du-Roule, George V* ✥ *1:E4.*

$$$$ HOTEL FAMILY Fodor's Choice ★ 🏨 **Four Seasons Hôtel George V Paris.** The George V is as poised and polished as the day it opened in 1928—the original plaster detailing and 17th-century tapestries have been restored, the bas reliefs regilded, and the marble-floor mosaics rebuilt tile by tile. **Pros:** privileged address near top boutiques; courtyard dining in summer; indoor swimming pool. **Cons:** several blocks from the nearest métro; extra charge for Wi-Fi; lacks the intimacy of smaller boutique hotels. [$] *Rooms from: €1000* ✉ *31 av. George V, 8e, Champs-Élysées* ☎ *01–49–52–70–00, 800/332–3442 in U.S.* 🌐 *www.fourseasons.com/paris* 🛏 *184 rooms, 60 suites* 🍴 *Breakfast* [M] *George V* ✥ *1:D5.*

$$$$ HOTEL 🏨 **Hidden Hotel.** The rough-hewn wood facade heralds the eco-friendly theme of this under-the-radar boutique hotel a block from the Arc de Triomphe, and the interior follows through with handcrafted glass, wood, stone, and ceramic decor. **Pros:** a block from main métro line and Champs-Élysées; organic toiletries in recycled packaging; free Wi-Fi. **Cons:** rooms on the small side; open-plan bathrooms offer little privacy; separate entrance and breakfast area for some rooms isn't intimate. [$] *Rooms from: €270* ✉ *28 rue de l'Arc de Triomphe, 17e, Champs-Élysées* ☎ *01–40–55–03–57* 🌐 *www.hidden-hotel.com* 🛏 *33 rooms, 2 suites* 🍴 *Breakfast* [M] *Ternes* ✥ *1:B3.*

$$$$ HOTEL 🏨 **Hôtel Daniel.** A contemporary antidote to the minimalist trend, the Daniel is decorated in rich fabrics and antique furnishings from France, North Africa, and the Far East. **Pros:** intimate, homestyle atmosphere; close to the Champs-Élysées. **Cons:** across from a noisy bar; no fitness center; inconsistent customer service. [$] *Rooms from: €420* ✉ *8 rue Frédéric Bastiat, 8e, Champs-Élysées* ☎ *01–42–56–17–00* 🌐 *www.hoteldanielparis.com* 🛏 *24 rooms, 2 suites* 🍴 *No meals* [M] *St-Philippe-du-Roule* ✥ *1:E4.*

$$$$ HOTEL 🏨 **Hôtel de Sers.** Built for the Marquis de Sers with a horse-drawn carriage entrance, inner courtyard, expansive salons, and monumental staircase, this beautiful structure was transformed into a hotel in 1935.

15

Pros: convenient central location in Triangle D'Or; many dining options nearby; soothing Turkish bath and fitness room. **Cons:** basic rooms not so spacious; no formal spa; on the expensive side. $ *Rooms from: €500* ✉ *41 av. Pierre 1er de Serbie, 8e, Triangle d'Or* ☎ *01–53–23–75–75* ⊕ *www.hoteldesers-paris.fr* ⤳ *45 rooms, 7 suites* ⍾◎ *Breakfast* Ⓜ *Alma-Marceau, George V* ✛ *1:D5.*

$$$$ 🛏 **Hôtel Fouquet's Barrière.** Steps away from one of the world's most
HOTEL   famous streets, this luxury hotel adjacent to the legendary Fouquet's Brasserie at the corner of the Champs-Élysées and Avenue George V is recognizable by its uniformed valets, parked sports cars, and elegant Haussmanien entryway. **Pros:** many rooms overlook the Champs-Élysées; métro very close; beautiful spa and fitness center. **Cons:** very expensive prices; bar can get overcrowded; corporate events give the place a business hotel feel. $ *Rooms from: €690* ✉ *46 av. George V, 8e, Champs-Élysées* ☎ *01–40–69–60–00* ⊕ *www.fouquets-barriere.com* ⤳ *81 rooms, 33 suites* ⍾◎ *Breakfast* Ⓜ *George V* ✛ *1:D4.*

$$$$ 🛏 **Hôtel Lancaster.** Once a Spanish nobleman's town house, this luxurious
HOTEL   retreat dating from 1889 dazzles with its elegant decor, lush courtyard, and international restaurant led by Chef Julien Roucheteau. **Pros:** steps away from the Champs-Élysées and five minutes from métro; excellent seasonal menus at La Table du Lancaster; Sunday brunch with organic farm products. **Cons:** size of rooms varies greatly; pricey room service; decor look tired. $ *Rooms from: €670* ✉ *7 rue de Berri, 8e, Champs-Élysées* ☎ *01–40–76–40–76, 877/757–2747 in U.S.* ⊕ *www.hotel-lancaster.fr* ⤳ *43 rooms, 14 suites* ⍾◎ *Breakfast* Ⓜ *George V* ✛ *1:D4.*

$$$$ 🛏 **Hôtel Le Bristol.** The historic Bristol ranks among Paris's most exclusive
HOTEL   hotels and has numerous accolades to prove it—and it's even hit the big
FAMILY   screen, featured in Woody Allen's *Midnight in Paris.* **Pros:** teak-and-glass indoor pool with solarium; located on luxury shopping street; full-service spa with landscaped terrace. **Cons:** a few blocks from the nearest métro; old-fashioned atmosphere may not be for everyone; very expensive rates. $ *Rooms from: €1000* ✉ *112 rue du Faubourg St-Honoré, 8e, Champs-Élysées* ☎ *01–53–43–43–00* ⊕ *www.lebristolparis.com* ⤳ *96 rooms, 92 suites* ⍾◎ *No meals* Ⓜ *Miromesnil* ✛ *1:F4.*

$$$$ 🛏 **Hôtel Plaza Athénée.** "Superlative" sums up the overall impression of
HOTEL   this glamorous landmark hotel on one of the most expensive avenues
FAMILY   in Paris, treated to a top-to-bottom facelift in 2014. **Pros:** Eiffel Tower
Fodor'sChoice views; special attention to children; Dior Institute spa. **Cons:** vast dif-
★   ference in style of rooms; easy to feel anonymous in such a large hotel; exorbitant prices. $ *Rooms from: €1100* ✉ *25 av. Montaigne, 8e, Champs-Élysées* ☎ *01–53–67–66–65, 866/732–1106 in U.S.* ⊕ *www.dorchestercollection.com/fr/paris/hotel-plaza-athenee-paris* ⤳ *194 rooms, 46 suites* ⍾◎ *Breakfast* Ⓜ *Alma-Marceau* ✛ *1:D6.*

$$$$ 🛏 **Hôtel Raphael.** This discreet palace-like hotel was built in 1925 to
HOTEL   cater to travelers spending a season in Paris, so every space is gen-
FAMILY   erously sized for long, lavish stays. **Pros:** a block from the Champs-Élysées and Arc de Triomphe; rooftop garden terrace; intimate hotel bar frequented by locals. **Cons:** decor that can feel worn and dowdy; some soundproofing issues; neighborhood has a majestic yet cold atmosphere. $ *Rooms from: €670* ✉ *17 av. Kléber, 16e, Champs-Élysées*

☎ *01–53–64–32–00* ⊕ *www.raphael-hotel.com* ⟿ *53 rooms, 39 suites* ⊢◯⊣ *Breakfast* Ⓜ *Kléber* ✛ *1:C4.*

$$$$ ⊞ **Jays Paris.** Built in the mid-19th century, this discreet mansion with
HOTEL just five suites has a perfect location between the Champs-Élysées and the Eiffel Tower. **Pros:** personalized service; three rooms can be connected for families; handy kitchenettes. **Cons:** business district off main avenues lacks charm; modern breakfast room contrasts starkly with historic style; no elevator or accommodations for those with limited mobility. Ⓢ *Rooms from: €490* ✉ *6 rue Copernic, 16e, Champs-Élysées* ☎ *01–47–04–16–16* ⊕ *www.jays-paris.com* ⟿ *5 suites* ⊢◯⊣ *Breakfast* Ⓜ *Boissière* ✛ *1:B5.*

$$$$ ⊞ **La Maison Champs Elysées.** A 10-minute walk from the city's most
HOTEL famous avenue, this hotel in the heart of the Golden Triangle lures an art-minded crowd with an eclectic twist on a historical Haussmanian *belle demeure.* **Pros:** convenient location close to métro; on quiet street; unique decor. **Cons:** tired conditions in some rooms; no fitness center; not good for families. Ⓢ *Rooms from: €300* ✉ *8 rue Jean Goujon, Triangle d'Or* ☎ *01–40–74–64–65* ⊕ *www.lamaisonchampselysees. com* ⟿ *40 rooms and 17 suites* ⊢◯⊣ *Breakfast* Ⓜ *Franklin D. Roosevelt* ✛ *1:E5.*

$$$ ⊞ **Le 123 Hôtel.** Italian marble, exposed brick, rough concrete, and sleek
HOTEL wood mix with leather, feathers, Swarovski crystals, and fiber-optic fairy lights to give this boutique hotel a genuinely eclectic atmosphere. **Pros:** chic decor; near luxury shopping; hotel bar open daily. **Cons:** service can be impolite; no on-site restaurant; some rooms quite small for the price. Ⓢ *Rooms from: €330* ✉ *123 rue du Faubourg St-Honoré, 8e, Champs-Élysées* ☎ *01–53–89–01–23* ⊕ *www.astotel.com/hotel-le123-elysees-paris.php* ⟿ *41 rooms* ⊢◯⊣ *Breakfast* Ⓜ *Saint-Philippe du Roule, Franklin D. Roosevelt* ✛ *1:F4.*

$$$$ ⊞ **Mon Hotel.** The contemporary design, modern comforts, and close
HOTEL proximity to the Arc de Triomphe and Champs-Élysées—a 10-minute walk away—are big draws at this stylish boutique hotel. **Pros:** unique contemporary styling; convenient to the métro; quiet residential street. **Cons:** some rooms have limited closet space; no extra beds for children; breakfast costs extra. Ⓢ *Rooms from: €390* ✉ *1 rue Argentine, 16e, Champs-Élysées* ☎ *01–45–02–76–76* ⊕ *www.monhotel.fr* ⟿ *36 rooms* ⊢◯⊣ *No meals* Ⓜ *Argentine* ✛ *1:B4.*

$$$$ ⊞ **Pershing Hall.** Built in the 18th century for French aristocracy and
HOTEL once serving as the American Legion Hall, this boutique hotel is a must-stay address for the dressed-in-black pack. **Pros:** prime shopping and nightlife district; excellent Sunday brunch buffet; free Wi-Fi throughout hotel. **Cons:** bar noise can be heard in some rooms; inconsistent service. Ⓢ *Rooms from: €486* ✉ *49 rue Pierre-Charron, 8e, Champs-Élysées* ☎ *01–58–36–58–00* ⊕ *www.pershinghall.com* ⟿ *20 rooms, 6 suites* ⊢◯⊣ *Breakfast* Ⓜ *George V, Franklin D. Roosevelt* ✛ *1:D5.*

$$$$ ⊞ **Renaissance Paris Arc de Triomphe.** This American-style hotel catering
HOTEL to corporate executives is located in a predominantly business district between the Arc de Triomphe and Place des Ternes. **Pros:** walking distance to Champs-Élysées and métro; spacious rooms; good discounts with Marriott points. **Cons:** neighborhood lacks character; filled with

business conferences; rather unfriendly service. $ *Rooms from:* €460 ✉ *39 av. de Wagram, 17e, Champs-Élysées* ☎ *01–55–37–55–37* ⊕ *www. marriott.fr/hotels/travel/parwg-renaissance-paris-arc-de-triomphe-hotel* 🛏 *84 rooms, 17 suites* ⦿ *Breakfast* Ⓜ *Ternes* ✥ *1:C3.*

$$$
HOTEL
FAMILY

🏨 **Villa Brunel.** On a quiet corner, this small 19th-century building between the Arc de Triomphe and Porte Maillot is an exceptional deal if you don't mind the less-than-convenient location. **Pros:** suites good for families; quiet location; close to Palais Congrès and RER/métro access. **Cons:** a bit off the beaten track; too far to walk to most attractions; small bathrooms. $ *Rooms from:* €240 ✉ *46 rue Brunel, 17e, Champs-Élysées* ☎ *01–45–74–74–51* ⊕ *www.villabrunel.com* 🛏 *32 rooms* ⦿ *Breakfast* Ⓜ *Porte Maillot, Argentine* ✥ *1:B3.*

AROUND THE LOUVRE

LES HALLES

$$$
HOTEL

🏨 **Hôtel Britannique.** Open since 1861 and a stone's throw from the Louvre, the romantic Britannique blends courteous English service with old-fashioned French elegance near the banks of the Seine. **Pros:** on calm side street; less than a block from the métro/RER station; excellent service from friendly staff. **Cons:** small rooms; soundproofing could be better. $ *Rooms from:* €229 ✉ *20 av. Victoria, 1er, Les Halles* ☎ *01–42–33–74–59* ⊕ *www.hotel-britannique.fr* 🛏 *39 rooms, 1 suite* ⦿ *Breakfast* Ⓜ *Châtelet* ✥ *4:D1.*

$$
HOTEL

🏨 **Hôtel du Cygne.** Passed down from mother to daughter, "the Swan" is decorated with homey touches like hand-sewn curtains, country quilts, and interesting flea market finds. **Pros:** small but comfortable rooms; central location on a pedestrian street; good value. **Cons:** old building with small rooms; no elevator; intimidating area after dark. $ *Rooms from:* €122 ✉ *3 rue du Cygne, 1er, Les Halles* ☎ *01–42–60–14–16* ⊕ *www.hotelducygne.fr* 🛏 *18 rooms* ⦿ *Breakfast* Ⓜ *Étienne Marcel, Les Halles* ✥ *2:D6.*

$
HOTEL

🏨 **Hôtel Tiquetonne.** Just off the market street of Rue Montorgueil and a short walk from Les Halles, this is one of the least expensive hotels in the city center. **Pros:** cheap rooms in the center of town; in trendy shopping and nightlife area; some views onto Sacre Coeur. **Cons:** minimal service and no amenities; noise from the street; decor feels outdated. $ *Rooms from:* €65 ✉ *6 rue Tiquetonne, 2e, Les Halles* ☎ *01–42–36–94–58* ⊕ *www.hoteltiquetonne.fr* 🛏 *45 rooms, 33 with bath* ⦿ *No meals* Ⓜ *Étienne Marcel* ✥ *2:D6.*

LOUVRE/TUILERIES

$$$$
HOTEL
FAMILY

🏨 **Hôtel Brighton.** A few of the city's most prestigious hotels face the Tuileries or Place de la Concorde, but the 19th-century Brighton occupies the same prime real estate and offers a privileged stay for a fraction of the price. **Pros:** convenient central location; friendly service; breakfast buffet (free for kids under 12). **Cons:** some areas in need of repair; variable quality in decor between rooms; no restaurant for lunch or dinner. $ *Rooms from:* €260 ✉ *218 rue de Rivoli, 1er, Louvre/Tuileries* ☎ *01–47–03–61–61* ⊕ *www.paris-hotel-brighton.com* 🛏 *61 rooms* ⦿ *Breakfast* Ⓜ *Tuileries* ✥ *2:A6.*

CLOSE UP

Apartment Rentals

Many Fodorites rent apartments in Paris because they favor extra space plus that special feeling of living like a local. Rentals can also offer savings, especially for groups.

Check out the **Paris Tourism Office** website (🌐 *www.parisinfo.com*) for reputable agency listings. Policies differ, but you can expect a minimum required stay from three to seven days; a refundable deposit payable on arrival; possibly an agency fee; and maid and linen service. A great website with unbiased ratings of agencies and listing services is **Paris Apartment Info** (🌐 *www.paris-apartment-info.com*).

The following is a list of property hunters, good-value residence hotels, and apartment services: **Cattalan Johnson** (☎ *01–45–74–87–77* 🌐 *www.cattalanjohnson.com*) is an established French fee-based real estate agent highly specialized in rental properties for more than 20 years. The multilingual staff has a city-wide inventory of furnished apartments available for one month to a few years. **Citadines Résidences Hôtelières** (☎ *08–25–33–33–32* 🌐 *www.citadines.fr*) is a chain of apartment-style hotel accommodations. They're somewhat generic, but offer many services and good value for short stays. **Home Rental** (☎ *01–78–76–59–14* 🌐 *www.home-rental.com*) has been in business since 1992 and rents furnished studios to six-bedrooms with a one-week minimum stay, short or long term. No agency fees, maid service, cable, and wireless Internet are included. **Lodgis Paris** (☎ *01–70–39–11–11* 🌐 *www.lodgis.com*) has one of the largest selections in Paris; however, the agency fee makes it cheaper per diem to rent for more than one week. **Paris Attitude** (☎ *01–42–96–31–46* 🌐 *www.parisattitude.com*) offers a large selection of furnished rentals of studios to five bedrooms from a week to a year. **Paris Vacation Apartments** (☎ *06–63–60–67–14* 🌐 *www.parisvacationapartments.com*) specializes in luxury rentals, with all-inclusive prices by the week. Agencies based in the United States can also help you find an apartment in Paris: **Rendez-vous à Paris** (✉ *rendezvousaparis@club-internet.fr* 🌐 *www.rendez-vousaparis.com*) has just a few properties, but all are in prime locations and are top quality at a reasonable price. **Rentals in Paris** (☎ *516/874–0474* ✉ *abby@rentals-paris.com* 🌐 *www.rentals-in-paris.com*) has two-dozen centrally located rentals with all-inclusive weekly rates and last-minute special offers.

15

$$$ HOTEL 🏨 **Hôtel Crayon.** Managed by artists, this hotel near the Louvre and Palais-Royal distinguishes itself with an eclectic pop-art decor—expect an unusual canvas of local and international guests that's just as colorful. **Pros:** bright decor; very friendly staff; central location. **Cons:** small bathrooms; basement breakfast area; lobby lounge lacks any coziness and warmth. [$] *Rooms from: €225* ✉ *25 rue du Bouloi, 1er, Louvre/Tuileries* ☎ *01–42–36–54–19* 🌐 *www.hotelcrayon.com* 🛏 *24 rooms* 🍴 *Breakfast* [M] *Louvre* ✥ *4:C1.*

$$$$ HOTEL 🏨 **Hôtel Le Pradey.** Offering Michel Cluizel chocolates and Fragonard toiletries, this compact boutique hotel near the Tuileries has a luxe feel. **Pros:** choice of copious breakfast buffet or quick coffee and croissant; designer touches throughout; double doors for soundproofing in suites. **Cons:** smaller rooms lack closet space; rooms vary greatly in style; nondescript entry and lackluster service results in lukewarm welcome. [$] *Rooms from: €370* ✉ *5 rue St-Roch, 1e, Louvre/Tuileries* ☎ *01–42–60–31–70* 🌐 *www.lepradey.com* 🛏 *21 rooms, 7 suites* 🍴 *Breakfast* [M] *Tuileries* ✣ *2:A6.*

$$ HOTEL **Hôtel Londres St-Honoré.** Smack-dab in the center of Paris, this no-frills hotel across from a 17th-century church gets points for its location—shops, restaurants, and points of interest are literally steps away. **Pros:** within walking distance of major sites; friendly service; free Wi-Fi. **Cons:** small beds with worn decor; tiny elevator doesn't go to ground floor; extremely narrow staircase. [$] *Rooms from: €149* ✉ *13 rue St-Roch, 1er, Louvre/Tuileries* ☎ *01–42–60–15–62* 🌐 *www.hotellondresssthonore-paris.com* 🛏 *24 rooms, 4 suites* 🍴 *Breakfast* [M] *Pyramides* ✣ *2:A6.*

$$ HOTEL **Hôtel Louvre Sainte Anne.** Walk to many major sites from this small, low-key property located between the Opéra and Louvre. **Pros:** convenient location; free Wi-Fi; helpful reception. **Cons:** very small rooms and dull decor; district can feel very un-Parisian; subterranean breakfast area slightly claustrophic. [$] *Rooms from: €175* ✉ *32 rue Ste-Anne, 1er, Louvre/Tuileries* ☎ *01–40–20–02–35* 🌐 *www.louvre-ste-anne.fr* 🛏 *20 rooms* 🍴 *Breakfast* [M] *Pyramides* ✣ *2:B5.*

$$$$ HOTEL FAMILY Fodor's Choice ★ **Hôtel Meurice.** Since 1835, the Meurice has welcomed royalty and celebrities from the Duchess of Windsor to Salvador Dalí—who both resided in the *grande dame* establishment—and Paris's first palace hotel continues to please with service, style, and views. **Pros:** stunning art and architecture; views over the Tuileries gardens; central location convenient to métro and major sites. **Cons:** popularity makes the public areas not very discreet; inconsistent front desk service at times inattentive; *très expensive.* [$] *Rooms from: €720* ✉ *228 rue de Rivoli, 1er, Louvre/Tuileries* ☎ *01–44–58–10–09* 🌐 *www.lemeurice.com* 🛏 *118 rooms, 42 suites* 🍴 *No meals* [M] *Tuileries, Concorde* ✣ *2:A6.*

$$$$ HOTEL **Hôtel Thérèse.** Tucked away from the traffic and crowds of Avenue de l'Opéra, Hotel Thérèse, named after the wife of Louis XIV, is a stone's throw from regal sites like the Louvre, Palais Royal, and the historic Comédie Française theater. **Pros:** excellent location on quiet street; free Wi-Fi; breakfast can be served in room. **Cons:** rooms are relatively small for price; breakfast area located in basement; no restaurant or gym. [$] *Rooms from: €330* ✉ *5/7 rue Thérèse, 1er, Louvre/Tuileries* ☎ *01–42–96–10–01* 🌐 *www.hoteltherese.com* 🛏 *42 rooms* 🍴 *No meals* [M] *Pyramides* ✣ *2:B6.*

$$$$ HOTEL **Le Konfidentiel.** Sleep beneath the pre-guillotined head of Marie-Antoinette or amid the turmoil of the French Revolution in one of the six individually themed rooms. **Pros:** next to the Louvre; comfortable rooms; good restaurant. **Cons:** can feel a bit enclosed; no tubs in bathrooms; unreliable Wi-Fi. [$] *Rooms from: €379* ✉ *64 rue de l'Arbre Sec, 1er, Louvre/Tuileries* ☎ *01–55–34–40–40* 🌐 *www.konfidentiel-paris.com* 🛏 *6 suites* 🍴 *Breakfast* [M] *Louvre–Rivoli* ✣ *2:C6.*

$$$$ **Meliá Vendome Boutique Hotel.** In a prestigious quarter a few minutes
HOTEL from the Jardin des Tuileries, Place de la Concorde, Opéra Garnier,
and the Louvre, the Meliá Vendome has handsome and spacious rooms
in attractive contemporary tones that exude an understated elegance.
Pros: outstanding location in the city center; near world-class shopping; elegant, immaculate rooms. **Cons:** expensive breakfast; no spa
or pool; in-room cooling system unreliable. $ *Rooms from: €350* ⊠ *8
rue Cambon, 1e, Louvre/Tuileries* ☎ *01–44–77–54–00* ⊕ *www.melia.
com/en/hotels/france/paris/melia-vendome-boutique-hotel/index.html*
↘ *78 rooms, 5 suites* ⦿ *Breakfast* Ⓜ *Concorde, Madeleine* ✛ *1:H5.*

$$$$ **Renaissance Paris Vendôme.** Hiding behind a classic 19th-century
HOTEL facade is a fresh, contemporary hotel with subtle 1930s influences.
FAMILY **Pros:** posh location; trendy restaurant; full-service spa and fitness
room. **Cons:** lacks authentic French character; public lounges noisy
at times; packed with business groups. $ *Rooms from: €620* ⊠ *4 rue
du Mont Thabor, 1er, Louvre/Tuileries* ☎ *01–40–20–20–00* ⊕ *www.
renaissanceparisvendome.com* ↘ *82 rooms, 15 suites* ⦿ *Breakfast*
Ⓜ *Tuileries* ✛ *2:A6.*

$$$$ **Ritz.** Ever since César Ritz opened the doors of his hotel in 1898, the
FAMILY mere name of this venerable institution in one of Paris's most exclusive
spots has become synonymous with luxury. **Pros:** spacious swimming
pool; superlative selection of bars and restaurants; top-notch service.
Cons: easy to get lost in the vast hotel; paparazzi magnet; astronomical
prices. $ *Rooms from: €1000* ⊠ *15 pl. Vendôme, 1er, Louvre/Tuile-
ries* ☎ *01–43–16–30–30* ⊕ *www.ritzparis.com* ↘ *105 rooms, 56 suites*
⦿ *No meals* Ⓜ *Opéra* ✛ *2:A5.*

OPÉRA/GRANDS BOULEVARDS

$$$$ **Golden Tulip Opera de Noailles.** With a nod to the work of postmodern
HOTEL designers like Putman and Starck, this stylish boutique hotel is both
contemporary and cozy. **Pros:** 15- to 20-minute walk to the Louvre
and Opéra; a block from the airport bus; free Wi-Fi. **Cons:** no interesting views; some bathrooms in need of renovation; small elevator.
$ *Rooms from: €319* ⊠ *9 rue de Michodière, 2e, Opéra/Grands Bou-
levards* ☎ *01–47–42–92–90* ⊕ *www.hoteldenoailles.com* ↘ *56 rooms*
⦿ *Breakfast* Ⓜ *Opéra* ✛ *2:B5.*

$$$$ **Hôtel Banke.** In a stately bank building dating from the early 20th
HOTEL century, this interesting hotel lies in the heart of the Opéra district,
which is full of shops and theaters. **Pros:** great location; excellent service; free Internet access. **Cons:** pricey restaurant; cramped gym; several blocks from the nearest métro. $ *Rooms from: €280* ⊠ *20 rue
LaFayette, 9e, Opéra/Grands Boulevards* ☎ *01–55–33–22–05* ⊕ *www.
derbyhotels.com/banke-hotel-paris* ↘ *76 rooms, 18 suites* ⦿ *No meals*
Ⓜ *Opéra* ✛ *2:B4.*

$ **Hôtel Chopin.** A unique mainstay of the district, the Chopin recalls
HOTEL its 1846 birth date with a creaky-floored lobby and aged woodwork.
Pros: special location; close to major métro station; great nightlife
district. **Cons:** thin walls; single rooms are very small; few amenities.
$ *Rooms from: €94* ⊠ *10 bd. Montmartre, 46 passage Jouffroy, 9e,*

15

Opéra/Grands Boulevards ☎ *01–47–70–58–10* ⊕ *www.hotelchopin.fr*
🛏 *36 rooms* ⊙⏐ *Breakfast* Ⓜ *Grands Boulevards* ⊹ *2:C4.*

$$$ 🛎 **Hôtel George Sand.** This family-run hotel, where the 19th-century
HOTEL writer George Sand once lived, feels fresh and modern while preserving
some of its original architectural details. **Pros:** near two famous depart-
ment stores; historic atmosphere; simple but comfortable rooms. **Cons:**
noisy street; can hear métro rumble on lower floors; some rooms are
quite small. Ⓢ *Rooms from: €250* ⊠ *26 rue des Mathurins, 9e, Opéra/
Grands Boulevards* ☎ *01–47–42–63–47* ⊕ *www.hotelgeorgesand.com*
🛏 *20 rooms* ⊙⏐ *Breakfast* Ⓜ *Havre Caumartin* ⊹ *1:H4.*

$$ 🛎 **Hôtel Gramont Opéra.** Near the Opéra Garnier and some of the city's
HOTEL best department stores, this family-owned boutique hotel has lots of
little extras that make it a great value. **Pros:** good breakfast buffet
with eggs to order; personalized and professional service; connecting
rooms for families. **Cons:** singles have no desk; small bathrooms; elevator doesn't go to top floor rooms. Ⓢ *Rooms from: €145* ⊠ *22 rue
Gramont, 2e, Opéra/Grands Boulevards* ☎ *01–42–96–85–90* ⊕ *www.
hotel-gramont-opera.com* 🛏 *22 rooms, 3 suites* ⊙⏐ *Breakfast* Ⓜ *Quatre-
Septembre* ⊹ *2:B4.*

$$$ 🛎 **Hôtel Langlois.** After starring in the 2002 film *The Truth About Char-
HOTEL lie*, this darling hotel gained a reputation as one of the most atmospheric
budget sleeps in the city. **Pros:** excellent views from the top floor; close
to department stores and Opéra Garnier; historic decor. **Cons:** noisy
street; off the beaten path; some sagging furniture and worn fabrics.
Ⓢ *Rooms from: €190* ⊠ *63 rue St-Lazare, 9e, Opéra/Grands Boule-
vards* ☎ *01–48–74–78–24* ⊕ *www.hotel-langlois.com* 🛏 *24 rooms, 3
suites* ⊙⏐ *Breakfast* Ⓜ *Trinité* ⊹ *2:A3.*

$$$ 🛎 **Hôtel Queen Mary.** Although showing its age, this cozy hotel is well sit-
HOTEL uated near high-end shopping and the city's famous department stores.
Pros: close to Place de la Madeleine; extra-attentive service; pretty
garden. **Cons:** some rooms are claustrophobic; those on the ground
floor and facing the street can be noisy; decor can feel somewhat old-
fashioned. Ⓢ *Rooms from: €202* ⊠ *9 rue Greffulhe, 8e, Opéra/Grands
Boulevards* ☎ *01–42–66–40–50* ⊕ *www.hotelqueenmary.com* 🛏 *36
rooms, 1 suite* ⊙⏐ *Breakfast* Ⓜ *Madeleine, St-Lazare, Havre–Caumartin* ⊹ *1:H4.*

$$$$ 🛎 **Hôtel Westminster.** On one of the most prestigious streets in Paris,
HOTEL between the Opéra and Place Vendôme, this mid-19th-century inn happily retains its old-world feel. **Pros:** prestigious location near major
sights; soothing steam room; popular jazz bar. **Cons:** a bit old-fashioned; some rooms overlook an airshaft; poor bathroom plumbing.
Ⓢ *Rooms from: €320* ⊠ *13 rue de la Paix, 2e, Opéra/Grands Boulevards* ☎ *01–42–61–57–46* ⊕ *www.warwickwestminsteropera.com*
🛏 *80 rooms, 22 suites* ⊙⏐ *Breakfast* Ⓜ *Opéra* ⊹ *2:A5.*

$$$$ 🛎 **La Maison Favart.** An atmospheric indoor pool, relaxing sauna, and
HOTEL around-the-clock concierge are some of the reasons this jewel-box hotel
is fast becoming a popular choice for travelers. **Pros:** lovely rooms and
interior design; spacious bathrooms; central location within walking
distance of the sights. **Cons:** high demand for best rooms; impractical
use of space in some rooms and bathrooms; no spa. Ⓢ *Rooms from:*

€300 ✉ *5 rue de Marivaux, 2e, Opéra/Grands Boulevards* 🖀 *01–42–97–59–83* ⊕ *www.lamaisonfavart.com* 🗗 *37 rooms* ⚐ *Breakfast* Ⓜ *Quatre-Septembre* ✛ *2:B4.*

$$$$ 🖼 **Park Hyatt Paris Vendôme.** Understated luxury with a contemporary
HOTEL Zen vibe differentiates this Hyatt from its more classic neighbors
Fodor's Choice between Place Vendôme and Opéra Garnier. **Pros:** stylish urban chic
★ design; the latest technology; don't-miss restaurants. **Cons:** as part of
the Hyatt chain, it can feel anonymous; many corporate events held on-
site; very expensive room rates. Ⓢ *Rooms from: €830* ✉ *3–5 rue de la
Paix, 2e, Opéra/Grands Boulevards* 🖀 *01–58–71–12–34* ⊕ *www.paris.
vendome.hyatt.com* 🗗 *132 rooms, 36 suites* ⚐ *Breakfast* Ⓜ *Concorde,
Opéra* ✛ *2:A5.*

$$$$ 🖼 **W Paris-Opéra.** Located near the Opéra Garnier, this 91-room hotel—
HOTEL the first W in France—feels part Moulin Rouge, part art gallery, with
Fodor's Choice cheeky and irreverent touches strewn throughout. **Pros:** coveted loca-
★ tion in historic 19th-century building; excellent restaurant; cutting-edge
rooms with comfortable beds. **Cons:** fee for Wi-Fi; rooms and public
spaces feel claustrophobic; light switches are confusing. Ⓢ *Rooms from:
€450* ✉ *4 rue Meyerbeer, 9e, Opéra/Grands Boulevards* 🖀 *01–77–48–
91–94* ⊕ *www.wparisopera.com* 🗗 *85 rooms, 6 suites* ⚐ *No meals*
Ⓜ *Chaussée d'Antin-La Fayette* ✛ *2:A4.*

15

MONTMARTRE

$ 🖼 **Ermitage Hôtel Sucré Coeur.** It's definitely a hike from the nearest
HOTEL métro station, but this family-run hotel in a Napoléon III–era building has a friendly vibe and is filled with mirrored armoires, elegant
chandeliers, and other antiques. **Pros:** charming Parisian neighborhood; quiet district; warm welcome from the staff. **Cons:** no online
reservations; no credit cards accepted; no facilities. Ⓢ *Rooms from:
€105* ✉ *24 rue Lamarck, 18e, Montmartre* 🖀 *01–42–64–79–22* ⊕ *www.
ermitagesacrecoeur.fr* 🗗 *11 rooms* ▬ *No credit cards* ⚐ *Breakfast*
Ⓜ *Lamarck-Caulaincourt* ✛ *2:H4.*

$ 🖼 **Hôtel Eldorado.** The unpretentious Hôtel Eldorado, just west of Mont-
HOTEL martre, is perfect for those who are happy lying low without room
phones, satellite TVs, or an elevator. **Pros:** eclectic character; artsy clientele; free Wi-Fi. **Cons:** far from the city center; few amenities; courtyard
can be noisy in summer. Ⓢ *Rooms from: €85* ✉ *18 rue des Dames, 17e,
Montmartre* 🖀 *01–45–22–35–21* ⊕ *www.eldoradohotel.fr* 🗗 *33 rooms,
23 with bath* ⚐ *Breakfast* Ⓜ *Place de Clichy* ✛ *1:H1.*

$$ 🖼 **Hôtel Regyn's Montmartre.** Many travelers book a room in the tiny
HOTEL Hôtel Regyn's Montmartre for its proximity to Place des Abbesses, one
of the most well-known spots in the city thanks to the movie *Amélie.*
Pros: métro station right outside; great views over Paris; atmospheric
locale. **Cons:** no air-conditioning; some street noise; carpets and bath-
rooms need upgrades. Ⓢ *Rooms from: €125* ✉ *18 pl. des Abbesses, 18e,
Montmartre* 🖀 *01–42–54–45–21* ⊕ *www.hotel-regyns-paris.com* 🗗 *22
rooms* ⚐ *Breakfast* Ⓜ *Abbesses* ✛ *2:B1.*

THE MARAIS

$$$ HOTEL 🏨 **Hôtel Bourg Tibourg.** Scented candles and subdued lighting announce the blend of romance and contemplation designer-du-jour Jacques Garcia brought to the Hôtel Bourg Tibourg. **Pros:** in the heart of the trendy Marais; moderate prices; great nightlife district. **Cons:** rooms are small, poorly lit, and ill equipped for those with large suitcases; no hotel restaurant; lounge area gets crowded. [$] *Rooms from: €250* ✉ *19 rue Bourg Tibourg, 4e, Marais* ☎ *01–42–78–47–39* 🌐 *www.hotelbourgtibourg.com* 🛏 *29 rooms, 1 suite* 🍴 *Breakfast* [M] *Hôtel de Ville* ⊕ *4:E2.*

$$$ HOTEL 🏨 **Hôtel Caron.** On a relatively quiet side street, this contemporary boutique bed-and-breakfast may be petite, but many thoughtful extras make it as accommodating as bigger hotels. **Pros:** excellent location in center of Paris; friendly staff; great amenities. **Cons:** only enough room for small suitcases; no hotel restaurant or bar; tight space in bathrooms. [$] *Rooms from: €245* ✉ *3 rue Caron, Marais* ☎ *01–40–29–02–94* 🌐 *www.hotelcaron.com* 🛏 *18 rooms* 🍴 *Breakfast* [M] *St-Paul* ⊕ *4:G2.*

$$ HOTEL 🏨 **Hôtel Caron de Beaumarchais.** For that traditional French feeling, book a room at this intimate, affordable, romantic hotel—the theme is the work of former next-door neighbor Pierre-Augustin Caron de Beaumarchais, a supplier of military aid to American revolutionaries and the playwright who penned *The Marriage of Figaro* and *The Barber of Seville.* **Pros:** cozy Parisian decor of yesteryear; breakfast in bed served until noon; excellent location within easy walking distance of major monuments. **Cons:** small rooms with few amenities; busy street of bars and cafés can be noisy; may feel old-fashioned for younger crowd. [$] *Rooms from: €165* ✉ *12 rue Vieille-du-Temple, 4e, Marais* ☎ *01–42–72–34–12* 🌐 *www.carondebeaumarchais.com* 🛏 *19 rooms* 🍴 *Breakfast* [M] *Hôtel de Ville* ⊕ *4:F2.*

$$$ HOTEL 🏨 **Hôtel de la Bretonnerie.** In a 17th-century *hôtel particulier* (town house) on a side street in the Marais, this small hotel with exposed wooden beams and traditional styling sits a few minutes from the Centre Pompidou and the numerous bars and cafés of Rue Vieille du Temple. **Pros:** typical Parisian character; moderate prices; free Wi-Fi access. **Cons:** quality and size of the rooms vary greatly; no air-conditioning; rooms facing street can be noisy. [$] *Rooms from: €212* ✉ *22 rue Ste-Croix-de-la-Bretonnerie, 4e, Marais* ☎ *01–48–87–77–63* 🌐 *www.bretonnerie.com* 🛏 *22 rooms, 7 suites* 🍴 *Breakfast* [M] *Hôtel de Ville* ⊕ *4:E1.*

$$ HOTEL 🏨 **Hôtel de la Place des Vosges.** Despite a Lilliputian elevator that doesn't serve all floors, this small, simple hotel just off 17th-century Place des Vosges draws a loyal clientele. **Pros:** excellent location near famous sights and public transportation; traditional ambience; reasonable rates. **Cons:** no air-conditioning; most rooms are very small; street-facing rooms can be noisy. [$] *Rooms from: €140* ✉ *12 rue de Birague, 4e, Marais* ☎ *01–42–72–60–46* 🌐 *www.hotelplacedesvosges.com* 🛏 *16 rooms* 🍴 *Breakfast* [M] *Bastille* ⊕ *4:G2.*

$$$$ HOTEL 🏨 **Hôtel Duo.** For this hotel in the heart of the trendy Marais district, architect Jean Philippe Nuel was commissioned to bring things up to date with bold colors and dramatic lighting; some rooms still have the original 16th-century beams, but the overall feel is casual urban chic.

Pros: central location near shops and cafés; walking distance to major monuments; good amenities. **Cons:** noisy neighborhood; service not always delivered with a smile; small standard rooms and bathrooms. [$] *Rooms from: €290* ✉ *11 rue du Temple, 4e, Marais* ☎ *01–42–72–72–22* 🌐 *www.duo-paris.com* 🛏 *58 rooms* 🍴 *Breakfast* [M] *Hôtel de Ville* ✥ *4:E1.*

$ HOTEL 🏨 **Hôtel Jeanne-d'Arc.** This hotel is prized for its unbeatable location off tranquil Place du Marché Ste-Catherine, one of the city's lesser-known pedestrian squares. **Pros:** charming street close to major attractions; good value for the Marais; lots of drinking and dining options nearby. **Cons:** noisy garbage trucks and late-night revelers on the square after midnight; dreary decor; no air-conditioning. [$] *Rooms from: €110* ✉ *3 rue de Jarente, 4e, Marais* ☎ *01–48–87–62–11* 🌐 *www.hoteljeannedarc.com* 🛏 *35 rooms* [M] *St-Paul* ✥ *4:G2.*

$$$ HOTEL Fodor's Choice ★ 🏨 **Hôtel Jules & Jim.** In the less-traveled corner of the trendy Marais district, this contemporary boutique hotel feels almost like an art gallery. **Pros:** bright and modern; stylish design; close to public transportation. **Cons:** the small "Jules" rooms are best for those traveling light or staying just one night; no restaurant. [$] *Rooms from: €220* ✉ *11 rue des Gravilliers, 3e, Marais* ☎ *01–42–78–10–01* 🌐 *www.hoteljulesetjim.com* 🛏 *21 rooms, 2 duplexes* 🍴 *Breakfast* [M] *Arts-et-Métiers* ✥ *2:F6.*

$$$$ HOTEL 🏨 **Pavillon de la Reine.** Hidden off regal Place des Vosges behind a stunning garden courtyard, this enchanting château has gigantic beams, chunky stone pillars, and a weathered fireplace that speaks to its 1612 origins. **Pros:** historic character; quiet setting; soothing spa treatments. **Cons:** expensive for the area and the size of the rooms; the nearest métro is a few blocks away; no uniform theme in interior design. [$] *Rooms from: €440* ✉ *28 pl. des Vosges, 3e, Marais* ☎ *01–40–29–19–19, 800/447–7462 in U.S.* 🌐 *www.pavillon-de-la-reine.com* 🛏 *31 rooms, 23 suites* 🍴 *Breakfast* [M] *Bastille, St-Paul* ✥ *4:G2.*

EASTERN PARIS

BASTILLE

$$$ HOTEL 🏨 **Hôtel Bastille de Launay.** The no-frills decor might seem spartan at first, but this boutique hotel also offers some creature comforts, modern amenities like free Wi-Fi, and a perfect location a few blocks from regal Place des Vosges. **Pros:** homey proportions; attentive service; reasonably spacious for the neighborhood. **Cons:** tiny elevator; some rooms small; basic bathrooms. [$] *Rooms from: €190* ✉ *42 rue Amelot, 11e, Bastille* ☎ *01–47–00–88–11* 🌐 *www.bastilledelaunay-hotel-paris.com* 🛏 *36 rooms* 🍴 *Breakfast* [M] *Chemin Vert* ✥ *4:H1.*

$$ HOTEL 🏨 **Hôtel Mama Shelter.** Close to Père Lachaise in the up-and-coming 20th arrondissement, this large hotel has a fun and funky interior designed by Philippe Starck. **Pros:** trendy design without designer prices; cool vibe; entertainment center in each room. **Cons:** in remote part of Paris; nearby club can be noisy. [$] *Rooms from: €159* ✉ *109 rue de Bagnolet, 20e, Bastille* ☎ *01–43–48–48–48* 🌐 *www.mamashelter.com* 🛏 *172 rooms* 🍴 *No meals* [M] *Gambetta* ✥ *2:H3.*

$$$$ HOTEL 🏨 **Les Jardins du Marais.** Behind an unassuming facade on a narrow street, this rambling hotel's nine historic buildings (including Gustave

Eiffel's old workshop) surround a spacious sculpture-garden courtyard. **Pros:** historic building; easy walk to the Marais and Bastille; lovely courtyard. **Cons:** often booked by groups; some rooms have a pillar in the center and look worn. $ *Rooms from: €269* ☒ *74 rue Amelot, 11e, Bastille* ☎ *01–40–21–20–00* ⊕ *www.homeplazza.com* ⇨ *205 rooms, 58 suites* ❍ *Breakfast* Ⓜ *St-Sébastien-Froissart* ✛ *4:H1*.

$$ **⊞ Standard Design Hôtel.** For an ultra-contemporary hotel in the hipster
HOTEL corner of the Bastille district, the Standard Design is anything but standard. **Pros:** friendly service; personalized gift packs; funky shopping and nightlife district. **Cons:** street noise; some rooms very small; interior design lacks traditional Parisian charm. $ *Rooms from: €175* ☒ *29 rue des Taillandiers, 11e, Bastille* ☎ *01–48–05–30–97* ⊕ *www.standard-design-hotel-paris.com* ⇨ *36 rooms* ❍ *Breakfast* Ⓜ *Bastille* ✛ *4:H2*.

CANAL ST-MARTIN

$$ **⊞ Hôtel Taylor.** Tucked away on a tiny one-way street between Répub-
HOTEL lique and Canal St-Martin, the Hôtel Taylor offers spacious rooms at an affordable price in the edgy 10e arrondissement. **Pros:** close to the métro; Wi-Fi available; breakfast can be served in your room. **Cons:** bathrooms need refurbishment; street can seem intimidating at night; some rooms in need of renovation. $ *Rooms from: €136* ☒ *6 rue Taylor, 10e, Canal St-Martin* ☎ *01–42–40–11–01* ⊕ *www.paris-hotel-taylor.com* ⇨ *37 rooms* ❍ *Breakfast* Ⓜ *République* ✛ *2:F5*.

$$$$ **⊞ Le Citizen Hôtel.** Boasting direct views over historic Canal St-Martin
HOTEL and a setting close to the Marais, Le Citizen features a minimalist-chic
Fodor'sChoice decor, high-tech touches like loaner iPads, and a cool East-Paris vibe.
★ **Pros:** trendy neighborhood; cool perks; friendly, attentive staff. **Cons:** smallest rooms are best for one person or short stays; noisy street; about 20 minutes by métro from the main attractions. $ *Rooms from: €269* ☒ *96 quai de Jemmapes, 10e, Canal St-Martin* ☎ *01–83–62–55–50* ⊕ *www.lecitizenhotel.com* ⇨ *12 rooms* ❍ *Breakfast* Ⓜ *Jacques-Bonsergent* ✛ *2:G4*.

RÉPUBLIQUE

$$ **⊞ Hotel du Nord et de L'Est.** A sign of the times, the venerable Hotel du
HOTEL Nord et de l'Est near Place de la Republique is equipped with an iPad terminal that can take room service requests, arrange wake-up calls, or provide information about Paris sites. **Pros:** handy address; accommodates families; reasonable rates. **Cons:** neighborhood can be noisy; uninspired decor; basic bathrooms. $ *Rooms from: €135* ☒ *49 rue de Malte, République* ☎ *01–47–00–71–70* ⊕ *www.hotel-nord-est.com* ⇨ *45 rooms* ❍ *Breakfast* Ⓜ *République* ✛ *2:G6*.

$$ **⊞ Hôtel Libertel Gare de l'Est Français.** This Haussmann-era hotel facing
HOTEL historic Gare de l'Est is two blocks from Gare du Nord and the popular Canal St-Martin district. **Pros:** convenient for Eurostar travelers; smoke-free establishment; friendly multilingual staff. **Cons:** noisy street; unattractive neighborhood; pricey breakfast. $ *Rooms from: €150* ☒ *13 rue du 8 Mai 1945, 10e, République* ☎ *01–40–35–94–14* ⊕ *www.hotelfrancais.com* ⇨ *70 rooms* ❍ *No meals* Ⓜ *Gare de l'Est* ✛ *2:E3*.

$ **⊞ Hôtel Palma.** Down the street from Père Lachaise Cemetery, this off-
HOTEL the-beaten-path hotel may be far from the action, but the métro is steps

away and connects quickly and efficiently to the heart of the city. **Pros:** a block from Place de Gambetta; breakfast served in room; inexpensive rates. **Cons:** far from city center; lacks Parisian charm. $ *Rooms from: €100* ⊠ *Angle 2 rue des Gâtines, 77 av. Gambetta, 20e, République* ☎ *01–46–36–13–65* ⊕ *www.paris-hotel-palma.com* ⮑ *32 rooms* Ⓜ *Gambetta* ✣ *2:H5.*

$$
HOTEL
🛏 **Hôtel Résidence Alhambra.** The gleaming white facade, enclosed garden, and flower-filled window boxes brighten this hotel in a lesser-known neighborhood between the Marais and Rue Oberkampf. **Pros:** popular nightlife district; friendly service; inexpensive rates. **Cons:** small doubles with dated decor; long walk to the center of town; no air-conditioning. $ *Rooms from: €130* ⊠ *13 rue de Malte, 11e, République* ☎ *01–47–00–35–52* ⊕ *www.hotelalhambra.fr* ⮑ *58 rooms* ⦿ *Breakfast* Ⓜ *Oberkampf* ✣ *2:H6.*

$$$
HOTEL
🛏 **Le Général Hôtel.** Designer Jean-Philippe Nuel applied his sleek styling to Le Général, one of Paris's first low-budget/high-design hotels. **Pros:** friendly service; smart design; in popular nightlife district. **Cons:** noisy neighborhood; not within easy walking distance of major tourist attractions; basic breakfast. $ *Rooms from: €240* ⊠ *5–7 rue Rampon, 11e, République* ☎ *01–47–00–41–57* ⊕ *www.legeneralhotel.com* ⮑ *43 rooms, 3 suites* ⦿ *Breakfast* Ⓜ *République; Oberkampf* ✣ *2.G5.*

15

LATIN QUARTER

$$$
HOTEL
🛏 **The Five Hôtel.** Small is beautiful at this design hotel on a quiet street near the Rue Mouffetard market and the Latin Quarter. **Pros:** unique design; personalized welcome; quiet side street. **Cons:** most rooms are too small for excessive baggage; the nearest métro is a 15 minute walk; most rooms only have showers. $ *Rooms from: €225* ⊠ *3 rue Flatters, 5e, Latin Quarter* ☎ *01–43–31–74–21* ⊕ *www.thefivehotel.com* ⮑ *24 rooms* ⦿ *Breakfast* Ⓜ *Gobelins* ✣ *4:D6.*

$
HOTEL
🛏 **Hôtel Collège de France.** Exposed stone walls, wooden beams, and medieval artwork echo the style of the Musée Cluny, two blocks from this charming family-run hotel. **Pros:** walking distance to major Rive Gauche sights; free Wi-Fi; ceiling fans. **Cons:** big difference between renovated and unrenovated rooms; thin walls between rooms; no air-conditioning. $ *Rooms from: €115* ⊠ *7 rue Thénard, 5e, Latin Quarter* ☎ *01–43–26–78–36* ⊕ *www.hotelcdf.com* ⮑ *29 rooms* ⦿ *Breakfast* Ⓜ *Maubert-Mutualité, St-Michel–Cluny–La Sorbonne* ✣ *4:D4.*

$$
HOTEL
🛏 **Hôtel des Grandes Écoles.** Distributed among a trio of three-story buildings, Madame Le Floch's rooms have a distinct grandmotherly vibe because of their flowery wallpaper and lace bedspreads, but they're downright spacious for this part of Paris. **Pros:** close to Latin Quarter nightlife spots; lovely courtyard; good value. **Cons:** uphill walk from the métro; some noisy rooms; few amenities. $ *Rooms from: €150* ⊠ *75 rue du Cardinal Lemoine, 5e, Latin Quarter* ☎ *01–43–26–79–23* ⊕ *www.hotel-grandes-ecoles.com* ⮑ *51 rooms* ⦿ *Breakfast* Ⓜ *Cardinal Lemoine* ✣ *4:E5.*

$$$$
HOTEL
🛏 **Hôtel des Grands Hommes.** The "great men" this hotel honors with its name rest in peace within the towering Panthéon monument across the street. **Pros:** major Latin Quarter sights within walking distance;

comfortable and attractive rooms. **Cons:** closest métro is a 10-minute walk; neighborhood can be loud after dark; high price for this area. $ *Rooms from: €266* ⊠ *17 pl. du Panthéon, 5e, Latin Quarter* ☎ *01– 46–34–19–60* ⊕ *www.hoteldesgrandshommes.com* ⌕ *31 rooms* ⧉ *No meals* Ⓜ *RER: Luxembourg* ✛ *4:D4.*

$$$$ 🎌 **Hotel Design de la Sorbonne.** For what French students pay to study
HOTEL   at the Sorbonne (tuition is inexpensive), you can stay a few nights next door at this swanky design hotel—recently renovations brought a bigger lobby, designer rooms, a high-tech sound system, a new breakfast area, and free Wi-Fi access throughout the hotel. **Pros:** centrally located; fun decor; attentive service. **Cons:** tiny rooms for the price; small breakfast room; trendy design lacks traditional French flavors. $ *Rooms from: €320* ⊠ *6 rue Victor Cousin, 5e, Latin Quarter* ☎ *01–43–54–01–52* ⊕ *www.hotelsorbonne.com* ⌕ *38 rooms* ⧉ *Breakfast* Ⓜ *Cluny–La Sorbonne* ✛ *4:C4.*

$$ 🎌 **Hôtel du Lys.** To jump into an inexpensive Parisian fantasy, just climb
HOTEL   the stairway to your room in this former 17th-century royal residence. **Pros:** central location on a quiet side street; historic character; free Wi-Fi. **Cons:** old-fashioned decor; perfunctory service, no air-conditioning or elevator. $ *Rooms from: €165* ⊠ *23 rue Serpente, 6e, Latin Quarter* ☎ *01–43–26–97–57* ⊕ *www.hoteldulys.com* ⌕ *22 rooms* ⧉ *Breakfast* Ⓜ *St-Michel, Odéon* ✛ *4:C3.*

$ 🎌 **Hôtel Familia.** Owners Eric and Sylvie Gaucheron continue to update
HOTEL   and improve this popular budget hotel—they've added custom-made
FAMILY   wood furniture from Brittany, antique tapestries and prints, and lovely
Fodor's Choice   carpeting. **Pros:** attentive, friendly service; great value; lots of charac-
★   ter. **Cons:** on a busy street; some rooms are small; some noise between rooms. $ *Rooms from: €120* ⊠ *11 rue des Écoles, 5e, Latin Quarter* ☎ *01–43–54–55–27* ⊕ *www.familiahotel.com* ⌕ *30 rooms* ⧉ *Breakfast* Ⓜ *Cardinal Lemoine* ✛ *4:E4.*

$$$ 🎌 **Hôtel Henri IV Rive Gauche.** About 50 paces from Notre-Dame and
HOTEL   the Seine, this elegant hotel has identical, impeccable rooms with beige
FAMILY   and rose linens and framed prints of architectural drawings. **Pros:** comfortable decor; central location close to major sights and RER station; friendly reception staff. **Cons:** on a busy street full of late-night bars; single rooms are small; furnishings showing their age. $ *Rooms from: €230* ⊠ *9 rue St-Jacques, 5e, Latin Quarter* ☎ *01–46–33–20–20* ⊕ *www.henri-paris-hotel.com* ⌕ *23 rooms* ⧉ *Breakfast* Ⓜ *St-Michel* ✛ *4:D3.*

$$$ 🎌 **Hôtel La Manufacture.** Just behind Place d'Italie and a short stroll from
HOTEL   both the Jardin des Plantes and Rue Mouffetard, La Manufacture's lesser-known location makes you feel like a *vrai* (real) Parisian. **Pros:** easy access to major métro and bus lines; safe nontouristy district; bright breakfast room. **Cons:** street noise; a long stroll to the center of Paris; small rooms. $ *Rooms from: €180* ⊠ *8 rue Philippe de Champagne, 13e, Latin Quarter* ☎ *01–45–35–45–25* ⊕ *www.hotel-la-manufacture. com* ⌕ *57 rooms* ⧉ *Breakfast* Ⓜ *Place d'Italie* ✛ *4:G6.*

$$ 🎌 **Hôtel Le Vert Galant.** In a little-known neighborhood west of Place
HOTEL   d'Italie you'll find the welcoming Madame Laborde, the proprietress
FAMILY   of this plain but proper hotel that encloses a peaceful green garden.

Pros: quiet location; kitchenettes in some rooms; safe residential district. **Cons:** not very central; no air-conditioning; some noise between rooms. Ⓢ *Rooms from: €140* ✉ *43 rue Croulebarbe, 13e, Latin Quarter* ☎ *01–44–08–83–50* ⊕ *www.vertgalant.com* ➽ *15 rooms* ⦿ *Breakfast* Ⓜ *Les Gobelins* ✛ *4:E6.*

$$ 🖭 **Hotel Les Degrés de Notre-Dame.** On a quiet lane a few yards from
HOTEL   the Seine, this diminutive budget hotel is lovingly decorated with the owner's flea-market finds. **Pros:** breakfast included; attractive location in quiet part of Latin Quarter; close to public transport. **Cons:** street noise; no air-conditioning or elevator. Ⓢ *Rooms from: €170* ✉ *10 rue des Grands Degrés, 5e, Latin Quarter* ☎ *01–55–42–88–88* ⊕ *www. lesdegreshotel.com* ➽ *10 rooms* ⦿ *Breakfast* Ⓜ *Maubert Mutualité* ✛ *4:D3.*

$$$$ 🖭 **Hôtel Notre Dame.** If you love the quirky and eclectic fashions of
HOTEL   Christian Lacroix and don't mind hauling your bags up some steps, this unique boutique hotel overlooking Notre Dame may be for you. **Pros:** decor by Christian Lacroix; views of the river; comfortable beds. **Cons:** stairs can be tricky with large bags; no minibars; some noise from busy street. Ⓢ *Rooms from: €280* ✉ *1 quai Saint-Michel, Latin Quarter* ☎ *01–43–54–20–43* ⊕ *www.hotelnotredameparis.com* ➽ *26 rooms* ⦿ *Breakfast* Ⓜ *St-Michel* ✛ *4:D3.*

$$$$ 🖭 **Hôtel Résidence Henri IV.** This small hotel on a quiet cul-de-sac is per-
HOTEL   fect for travelers—especially those with children—who need a home
FAMILY   base where they can kick back, make their own meals, and feel at home. **Pros:** handy kitchenettes; close to Latin Quarter attractions; charming interior decor. **Cons:** closest métro is a few blocks away; some rooms on the small side; decor a bit dated. Ⓢ *Rooms from: €260* ✉ *50 rue des Bernadins, 5e, Latin Quarter* ☎ *01–44–41–31–81* ⊕ *www. residencehenri4.com* ➽ *8 rooms, 5 apartments* ⦿ *Breakfast* Ⓜ *Maubert-Mutualité* ✛ *4:D4.*

$ 🖭 **Hotel Résidence Les Gobelins.** Simple furnishings and sunny colors
HOTEL   warm up this small hotel, located on a quiet side street between Place d'Italie and the Latin Quarter. **Pros:** close to major métro and bus lines; friendly owners; near shops and cafés. **Cons:** 20-minute walk to the center of Paris; basic decor; no air-conditioning. Ⓢ *Rooms from: €118* ✉ *9 rue des Gobelins, 13e, Latin Quarter* ☎ *01–47–07–26–90* ⊕ *www. hotelgobelins.com* ➽ *32 rooms* ⦿ *Breakfast* Ⓜ *Les Gobelins* ✛ *4:E6.*

$$$ 🖭 **Hôtel Saint Jacques.** Nearly every wall in this Latin Quarter hotel is
HOTEL   bedecked with faux-marble and trompe-l'oeil murals. **Pros:** unique Parisian decor; close to Latin Quarter sights; free Wi-Fi. **Cons:** busy street makes it noisy in summer; thin walls between rooms; decor needs refurbishment. Ⓢ *Rooms from: €216* ✉ *35 rue des Écoles, 5e, Latin Quarter* ☎ *01–44–07–45–45* ⊕ *www.hotel-saintjacques.com* ➽ *38 rooms* Ⓜ *Maubert-Mutualité* ✛ *4:D4.*

$$$ 🖭 **Hotel Seven.** The "seven" refers to the level of heaven you'll find at this
HOTEL   extraordinary boutique hotel, where a team of designers and artists has created seven magnificent suites with imaginative themes like Alice in Wonderland, James Bond, and Marie-Antoinette. **Pros:** fun design elements; copious breakfast buffet; quiet location near Mouffetard market street. **Cons:** small closets; several blocks to closest métro; expensive

15

room rates for so few amenities. $ *Rooms from: €250* ✉ *20 rue Berthollet, 5e, Latin Quarter* ☎ *01–43–31–47–52* ⊕ *www.sevenhotelparis.com* ⇄ *28 rooms, 7 suites* Ⓜ *Censier-Daubentin* ✣ *4:D6.*

$$$ 🛏 **Les Jardins du Luxembourg.** Blessed with a personable staff and a warm
HOTEL ambience, this hotel on a calm cul-de-sac puts you just a block away
from the Jardin du Luxembourg. **Pros:** on a quiet street close to major
attractions and transportation; hot buffet breakfast; relaxing sauna.
Cons: extra charge for Wi-Fi; some very small rooms; air-conditioning
not very strong. $ *Rooms from: €195* ✉ *5 impasse Royer-Collard, 5e,
Latin Quarter* ☎ *01–40–46–08–88* ⊕ *www.les-jardins-du-luxembourg.
com* ⇄ *26 rooms* 🍴 *Breakfast* Ⓜ *RER: Luxembourg* ✣ *4:C5.*

$ 🛏 **Port-Royal Hôtel.** The sparkling rooms and extra-helpful staff at the
HOTEL Port-Royal are well above average for hotels in this price range. **Pros:**
excellent value for the money; attentive service; close to two major markets. **Cons:** not very central; on a busy street; no room air-conditioning
or Wi-Fi. $ *Rooms from: €93* ✉ *8 bd. de Port-Royal, 5e, Latin Quarter*
☎ *01–43–31–70–06* ⊕ *www.port-royal-hotel.fr* ⇄ *46 rooms, 20 with
bath* ▭ *No credit cards* 🍴 *Breakfast* Ⓜ *Les Gobelins* ✣ *4:C6.*

ST-GERMAIN-DES-PRÉS

$$$$ 🛏 **Artus Hôtel.** One of the best things about this comfortable six-story
HOTEL hotel is that it's smack in the middle of Rue de Buci in the lively St-
FAMILY Germain-des-Prés district. **Pros:** attentive service and helpful concierge;
excellent location on a market street; kid-friendly vibe. **Cons:** rooms are
small and dated for the price; neighborhood is quite busy; service not
a forté. $ *Rooms from: €295* ✉ *34 rue de Buci, 6e, St-Germain-des-
Prés* ☎ *01–43–29–07–20* ⊕ *www.artushotel.com* ⇄ *25 rooms, 2 suites*
🍴 *Breakfast* Ⓜ *Mabillon* ✣ *4:B3.*

$$$$ 🛏 **Hôtel Bel-Ami.** A short stroll from famous Café de Flore, the Bel-
HOTEL Ami hides its past as an 18th-century textile factory behind low-slung
furnishings, computer stations, and flat-screen TVs. **Pros:** central St-
Germain-des-Prés location; feels completely up to date; spacious fitness
center and spa. **Cons:** some guests report loud noise between rooms;
some small rooms in lower price category; not suitable for families
with younger kids. $ *Rooms from: €500* ✉ *7–11 rue St-Benoît, 6e,
St-Germain-des-Prés* ☎ *01–42–61–53–53* ⊕ *www.hotel-bel-ami.com*
⇄ *113 rooms, 2 suites* Ⓜ *St-Germain-des-Prés* ✣ *4:B2.*

$$$ 🛏 **Hôtel Bonaparte.** The service, amenities, and *petit déjeuner* (break-
HOTEL fast) may be far from luxurious at this unpretentious family-run hotel,
FAMILY but the location in the heart of St-Germain is fabulous. **Pros:** upscale
shopping neighborhood; large rooms for the Rive Gauche; welcoming
to families. **Cons:** outdated decor; minuscule elevator big enough for
only one person; showers lack curtains. $ *Rooms from: €180* ✉ *61
rue Bonaparte, 6e, St-Germain-des-Prés* ☎ *01–43–26–97–37* ⊕ *www.
hotelbonaparte.fr* ⇄ *29 rooms* 🍴 *Breakfast* Ⓜ *St-Sulpice* ✣ *4:B3.*

$$$$ 🛏 **Hôtel d'Aubusson.** The showpiece at this 17th-century town house in
HOTEL the heart of St-Germain-des-Prés is the stunning front lobby, spanned
FAMILY by massive beams and a gigantic stone fireplace reminiscent of French
aristocratic homes of yore. **Pros:** central location near shops and a
market street; spacious rooms; staff greets you warmly. **Cons:** some of

the newer rooms lack character; busy street and bar can be noisy; very touristy. [$] *Rooms from: €405* ✉ *33 rue Dauphine, 6e, St-Germain-des-Prés* ☎ *01–43–29–43–43* 🌐 *www.hoteldaubusson.com* 🛏 *49 rooms* 🍴 *Breakfast* [M] *Odéon* ✥ *4:C2.*

$$$ HOTEL 🏨 **Hôtel de l'Abbaye.** An 18th-century convent, this compact hotel on a tranquil side street near St-Sulpice welcomes you with a cobblestone ante-courtyard. **Pros:** tranquil setting; upscale neighborhood; good value packages. **Cons:** rooms differ greatly in size and style; some bathrooms are quite small, with handheld showerheads; old-fashioned decor a bit somber. [$] *Rooms from: €280* ✉ *10 rue Cassette, 6e, St-Germain-des-Prés* ☎ *01–45–44–38–11* 🌐 *www.hotel-abbaye.com* 🛏 *26 rooms, 8 suites* 🍴 *Breakfast* [M] *St Sulpice* ✥ *4:A4.*

$$$ HOTEL 🏨 **Hôtel Duc de Saint-Simon.** For pure French flavor, including rooms decorated in floral chintz, head to this intimate hotel in a hidden location between Boulevard St-Germain and Rue de Bac. **Pros:** upscale neighborhood close to St-Germain-des-Prés; historic character; friendly service. **Cons:** rooms in the annex are smaller and have no elevator; cramped bathrooms; no room service. [$] *Rooms from: €250* ✉ *14 rue St-Simon, 7e, St-Germain-des-Prés* ☎ *01–44–39–20–20* 🌐 *www.hotelducdesaintsimon.com* 🛏 *29 rooms, 5 suites* 🍴 *Breakfast* [M] *Rue du Bac* ✥ *3:H2.*

15

$$$ HOTEL 🏨 **Hôtel Millésime.** The beautiful stone archway of this 17th-century city mansion in St-Germain-des-Prés was the original entrance to the Saint Germain Abbey—as you enter, you'll feel transported to the sunny south of France. **Pros:** upscale shopping nearby; young, friendly staff; plenty of atmosphere. **Cons:** ground-floor rooms can be noisy; smoke from courtyard when windows are open; some furnishings need repair. [$] *Rooms from: €250* ✉ *15 rue Jacob, 6e, St-Germain-des-Prés* ☎ *01–44–07–97–97* 🌐 *www.millesimehotel.com* 🛏 *20 rooms, 1 suite* 🍴 *Breakfast* [M] *St-Germain-des-Prés* ✥ *4:B2.*

$$$$ HOTEL 🏨 **Hôtel Odéon Saint-Germain.** Exposed stone walls and original wooden beams give this 16th-century building typical Rive Gauche character, and designer Jacques Garcia's generous use of striped taffeta curtains, velvet upholstery, and plush carpeting imbues it with the distinct luxury of St-Germain-des-Prés. **Pros:** free Internet; luxuriously appointed rooms; in an upscale shopping district near Jardin Luxembourg. **Cons:** small rooms a challenge for those with extra-large suitcases; tiny elevator; prices high for room size and average service. [$] *Rooms from: €265* ✉ *13 rue St-Sulpice, 6e, St-Germain-des-Prés* ☎ *01–43–25–70–11* 🌐 *www.paris-hotel-odeon.com* 🛏 *22 rooms, 5 junior suites* 🍴 *Breakfast* [M] *Odéon* ✥ *4:B3.*

$$$$ HOTEL 🏨 **Hôtel Recamier.** This discreet boutique hotel in a quiet corner overlooking the Eglise St-Sulpice is perfect if you're seeking a romantic and cozy hideaway in the St-Germain-des-Près district. **Pros:** peaceful garden courtyard; free Wi-Fi and computer station; well-appointed bathrooms. **Cons:** small closets and bathrooms; room service only until 11 pm; no fitness area, spa, or restaurant; some interior details already look worn. [$] *Rooms from: €270* ✉ *3 bis, pl. St-Sulpice, St-Germain-des-Prés* ☎ *01–43–26–04–89* 🌐 *www.hotelrecamier.com* 🛏 *24 rooms* 🍴 *Breakfast* [M] *Mabillon* ✥ *4:B3.*

$$$ :: **Hôtel Relais Saint-Sulpice.** Sandwiched between St-Sulpice and the Jar-
HOTEL din du Luxembourg, this little hotel wins accolades for its location.
Pros: chic location; close to two métro stations; bright breakfast room
and courtyard. **Cons:** some smallish rooms; noise from the street on
weekend evenings; poorly designed lighting. $ *Rooms from: €200* ⊠ *3
rue Garancière, 6e, St-Germain-des-Prés* ☎ *01–46–33–99–00* ⊕ *www.
relais-saint-sulpice.com* ⇄ *26 rooms* ⦿ *Breakfast* Ⓜ *St-Germain-des-
Prés, St-Sulpice* ✛ *4:B3.*

$$$$ :: **Hotel Verneuil.** Steps away from the Museé d'Orsay and the Louvre
sits an intimate and tastefully decorated boutique hotel in the heart of
St. Germain. **Pros:** nicely renovated rooms; near-it-all location on Left
Bank; welcoming service. **Cons:** sometimes touristy; no restaurant; no
gym or spa. $ *Rooms from: €290* ⊠ *8 rue de Verneuil, 7e, St-Germain-
des-Prés* ☎ *01–42–61–40–38* ⊕ *www.hotel-verneuil-saint-germain.com*
⇄ *26 rooms* ⦿ *Breakfast* ✛ *4:A2.*

$$$$ :: **L'Hôtel.** There's something just a bit naughty in the air at this eccen-
HOTEL tric and opulent boutique hotel. **Pros:** luxurious decor; elegant bar and
restaurant; walking distance to the Museé d'Orsay and the Louvre.
Cons: some rooms are very small for the price; closest métro station
is a few blocks away; eclectic decoration seems mismatched. $ *Rooms
from: €295* ⊠ *13 rue des Beaux-Arts, 6e, St-Germain-des-Prés* ☎ *01–
44–41–99–00* ⊕ *www.l-hotel.com* ⇄ *16 rooms, 4 suites* ⦿ *Breakfast*
Ⓜ *St-Germain-des-Prés* ✛ *4:B2.*

$$$$ :: **Relais Christine.** On a quiet street on the Left Bank, this exquisite *hotel
HOTEL de charme* dates back to the 13th century as a former abbey of the
Grands-Augustins and has an impressive stone courtyard and interior
garden. **Pros:** quiet address; close to the Latin Quarter action; historic
character. **Cons:** thin walls in some rooms; no on-site restaurant; a
bit touristy. $ *Rooms from: €400* ⊠ *3 rue Christine, 6e, St-Germain-
des-Prés* ☎ *01–40–51–60–80, 800/525–4800 in U.S.* ⊕ *www.relais-
christine.com* ⇄ *33 rooms, 18 suites* ⦿ *Breakfast* Ⓜ *Odéon* ✛ *4:C2.*

MONTPARNASSE

$$$ :: **Apostrophe Hotel.** Those enamored of the artistic and literary history
HOTEL of Paris's Left Bank will appreciate this whimsical family-run hotel
between Montparnasse and Luxembourg Gardens. **Pros:** very friendly
multilingual staff; quiet street in charming neighborhood; close to
métro. **Cons:** limited closet space; little privacy with bathrooms opening up directly to rooms; no restaurant or bar. $ *Rooms from: €230*
⊠ *3 rue de Chevreuse, 6e, Montparnasse* ☎ *01–56–54–31–31* ⊕ *www.
apostrophe-hotel.com* ⇄ *16 rooms* ⦿ *Breakfast* Ⓜ *Vavin* ✛ *4:A6.*

$ :: **Hôtel des Bains.** In a charming neighborhood close to Jardin du Lux-
HOTEL embourg and St-Germain-des-Prés, this hidden budget find has tastefully
decorated rooms and excellent prices. **Pros:** relaxing garden courtyard;
great rates; typical Parisian character. **Cons:** streets can be noisy; some
rooms and bathrooms very small and worn. $ *Rooms from: €103*
⊠ *33 rue Delambre, 14e, Montparnasse* ☎ *01–43–20–85–27* ⊕ *www.
hotel-des-bains-montparnasse.com* ⇄ *34 rooms, 8 suites* ⦿ *Breakfast*
Ⓜ *Vavin, Edgar Quinet* ✛ *4:A6.*

$$ HOTEL 🏨 **Hôtel Istria.** This small, family-run hotel on a quiet side street was a Montparnasse artists' hangout in the '20s and '30s. **Pros:** close to major métro and train stations; quiet courtyard-facing rooms. **Cons:** no air-conditioning; some rooms very small; not centrally located. [$] *Rooms from: €130* ✉ *29 rue Campagne-Première, 14e, Montparnasse* ☎ *01–43–20–91–82* 🚪 *26 rooms* 🍴 *Breakfast* [M] *Raspail* ⊕ *4:A6.*

$$$ HOTEL 🏨 **Hôtel Le Sainte-Beuve.** On a tranquil street between the Jardin du Luxembourg and Montparnasse's cafés and brasseries sits this pleasant six-story hotel. **Pros:** stylish decor; good location without the tourist crowds; close to major métro lines. **Cons:** 20-minute walk to the Latin Quarter or St-Germain-des-Prés; small rooms and elevator; unremarkable service. [$] *Rooms from: €222* ✉ *9 rue Ste-Beuve, 6e, Montparnasse* ☎ *01–45–48–20–07* 🌐 *www.hotelsaintebeuve.com* 🚪 *21 rooms, 1 suite* [M] *Vavin* ⊕ *4:A5.*

$$$ HOTEL 🏨 **Hôtel Lenox-Montparnasse.** On a street lined with fish restaurants, this six-story hotel gets points for its proximity to the Jardin du Luxembourg and good-value amenities like free Wi-Fi access. **Pros:** lively district close to Montparnasse and St-Germain-des-Prés; well-stocked honesty bar; friendly multilingual staff. **Cons:** standard rooms are small; noisy street; attracts business clientele. [$] *Rooms from: €300* ✉ *15 rue Delambre, 14e, Montparnasse* ☎ *01–43–35–34–50* 🌐 *www.paris-hotel-lenox.com* 🚪 *46 rooms, 6 suites* 🍴 *Breakfast* [M] *Vavin* ⊕ *4:A5.*

$$ HOTEL 🏨 **Hôtel Raspail Montparnasse.** Montparnasse was the art capital of the world in the '20s and '30s, and this affordable hotel captures some of that spirit by naming its rooms after some of the illustrious neighborhood stars—Picasso, Chagall, and Modigliani. **Pros:** convenient to métro and bus; many markets and cafés nearby; friendly staff. **Cons:** traffic noise; some rooms small with stale cigarette smoke odor; dated interiors with worn fabrics. [$] *Rooms from: €170* ✉ *203 bd. Raspail, 14e, Montparnasse* ☎ *01–43–20–62–86* 🌐 *www.hotelraspailmontparnasse.com* 🚪 *38 rooms* 🍴 *Breakfast* [M] *Vavin* ⊕ *4:A6.*

WESTERN PARIS

$$$ HOTEL 🏨 **BLC Design Hotel.** In the young and trendy area between Bastille and Nation, the BLC pays homage to everything *blanc,* hence the name. **Pros:** cool, contemporary interior; free Wi-Fi access; good location in a lively neighborhood. **Cons:** small spaces; renovations needed in some bathrooms; expensive rates. [$] *Rooms from: €210* ✉ *4 rue Richard Lenoir, 11e, Oberkampf* ☎ *01–40–09–60–16* 🌐 *www.blcdesign-hotel-paris.com* 🚪 *29 rooms* 🍴 *Breakfast* [M] *Charonne, Ledru Rollin* ⊕ *4:H2.*

$$$ HOTEL 🏨 **Hôtel Gavarni.** Considering the traditional, almost old-fashioned Parisian decor, you may be surprised to learn that this lodging, located in a chic residential neighborhood, is one of the city's first certified eco-friendly hotels. **Pros:** organic breakfast; charming neighborhood; friendly welcome. **Cons:** a few blocks to the nearest métro; standard rooms and bathrooms quite small; few amenities. [$] *Rooms from: €210* ✉ *5 rue Gavarni, 16e, Passy, Western Paris* ☎ *01–45–24–52–82* 🌐 *www.gavarni.com* 🚪 *21 rooms, 4 suites* 🍴 *Breakfast* ⊕ *3:A2.*

$$$$ HOTEL 🏨 **Le Sezz.** Created by French furniture designer Christophe Pillet in a chic residential district of Paris, Le Sezz mixes rough stone walls with

splashes of tomato red and mustard yellow for the ultimate bachelor pad feel. **Pros:** trendy designer decor; huge bathtubs; quiet location. **Cons:** close to Eiffel Tower but not much else; services are limited for a hotel in this price range; breakfast area feels cold and somber. [$] *Rooms from: €290* ✉ *6 av. Frémiet, 16e, Passy-Auteuil* ☎ *01–56–75–26–26* 🌐 *www.paris.hotelsezz.com* 🛏 *13 rooms, 13 suites* 🍴 *Breakfast* [M] *Passy* ✥ *3:A3.*

$$$$ HOTEL FAMILY 🏨 **Renaissance Paris Hôtel Le Parc Trocadéro.** This spacious and historic urban retreat in an upscale neighborhood, now part of the Marriott chain, was once the home of Alfred Nobel (whose would go on to establish the famous peace prize). **Pros:** near métro stations; 24-hour fitness center and room service; complimentary breakfast. **Cons:** hosts large groups; long walk from center of Paris; service and housekeeping could be better. [$] *Rooms from: €500* ✉ *55–59 rue Raymond-Poincaré, 16e, Trocadéro* ☎ *01–44–05–66–66* 🌐 *www.marriott.com/hotels/travel/parsp-renaissance-paris-le-parc-trocadero-hotel* 🛏 *122 rooms* 🍴 *Breakfast* [M] *Trocadéro* ✥ *1:A5.*

$$$$ HOTEL 🏨 **Saint James Paris.** Beyond a stone gateway you'll pass a beautiful fountain on your way into a grand foyer—this renovated 19th-century mansion feels like a countryside château nested in the heart of the busy metropolis. **Pros:** beautiful decor and spacious rooms; generous breakfast served in-room; wellness spa. **Cons:** expensive rates; residential area quiet at night; entrance may be difficult to find. [$] *Rooms from: €370* ✉ *43 av. Bugeaud, 16e, Western Paris* ☎ *01–44–05–81–81* 🌐 *www.saint-james-paris.com* 🛏 *48 rooms* 🍴 *Breakfast* [M] *Porte Dauphine, Victor Hugo, Rue de la Pompe* ✥ *1:A5.*

SHOPPING

Updated by Jennifer Ditsler-Ladonne

Nothing, but nothing, can push you into the current of Parisian life faster than a few hours of shopping. Follow the lead of locals, who slow to a crawl as their eyes lock on a tempting display. Window-shopping is one of this city's greatest spectator sports; the French call it *lèche-vitrine*— literally, "licking the windows"—which is fitting because many of the displays look good enough to eat.

Store owners here play to sophisticated audiences with voracious appetites for everything from spangly flagship stores to minimalist boutiques to under-the-radar spots in 19th-century glass-roofed passages. Parisians know that shopping isn't about the kill, it's about the chase: walking down cobblestone streets looking for items they didn't know they wanted, they're casual yet quick to pounce. They like being seduced by a clever display and relish the performance elements of browsing. Watching them shop can be almost as much fun as shopping yourself.

And nowhere is the infamous Parisian "attitude" more palpable than in the realm of fine shopping—the more *haute* the more hauteur.

Parisians are a proud bunch, and they value decorum. So dress to impress—and remember your manners. You must say *bonjour* upon entering a shop and *merci, au revoir* when leaving, even if it's to no one in particular. Think of it more as announcing your coming and going. Beyond this, protocol becomes less prescribed and more a matter of good judgment. If a salesperson is hovering, there's a reason; let him or her help you. To avoid icy stares once and for all, confidence and politeness go a long way.

As for what to buy, the sky's the limit in terms of choices. If your funds aren't limitless, however, take comfort in knowing that treasures can be found on a budget. And if you do decide to indulge, what better place to make that once-in-a-blue-moon splurge? When you get home and friends ask where you got those to-die-for shoes, with a shrug you'll casually say, "These? Oh . . . I bought them in Paris."

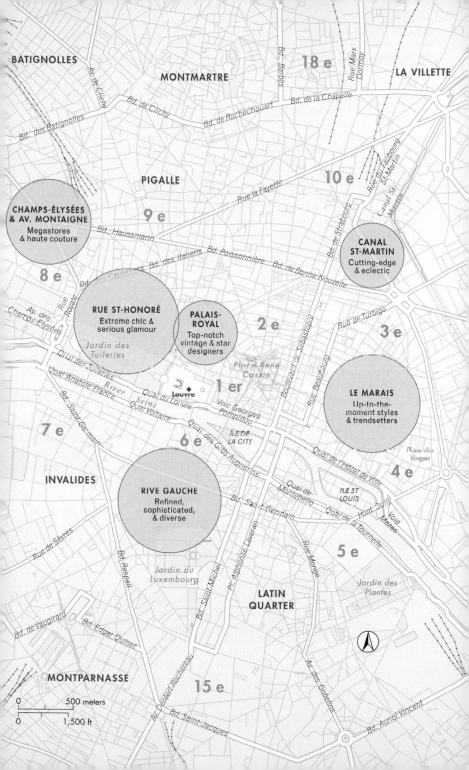

BATIGNOLLES

Av. de Clichy

Bd. de Clichy

Bd. des Batignolles

MONTMARTRE

Bd. Barbès

18 e

Rue Marx Dormoy

LA VILLETTE

Bd. de Rochechouart

Bd. de la Chapelle

PIGALLE

Rue la Fayette

10 e

Rue du Faubourg St-Martin

Canal St-Martin

CHAMPS-ÉLYSÉES & AV. MONTAIGNE
Megastores & haute couture

9 e

Bd. Haussmann

Bd. des Capucines

Bd. des Italiens

Bd. Poissonnière

Bd. de Bonne Nouvelle

Bd. de Strasbourg

CANAL ST-MARTIN
Cutting-edge & eclectic

8 e

Rue Royale

Av. des Champs-Élysées

RUE ST-HONORÉ
Extreme chic & serious glamour

Jardin des Tuileries

PALAIS-ROYAL
Top-notch vintage & star designers

2 e

Rue de Turbigo

3 e

Quai des Tuileries

River Seine

Quai du Louvre

Quai Voltaire

🦁 ♦ ○

Louvre

1 er

Place René Cassin

Boulevard de Sébastopol

Rue Beaubourg

LE MARAIS
Up-to-the-moment styles & trendsetters

Bd. Saint-Germain

Quai Anatole France

Voie Georges Pompidou

7 e

Quai des Grands Augustins

ÎLE DE LA CITÉ

6 e

Quai de l'Hôtel de Ville

Place des Vosges

INVALIDES

Quai de Montebello

ÎLE ST LOUIS

Voie Mazas

Pont Sully

4 e

RIVE GAUCHE
Refined, sophisticated, & diverse

Bd. Saint-Germain

Quai de la Tournelle

Rue de Sèvres

Pl. Alphonse Laveran

Rue Monge

5 e

Bd. Raspail

Jardin du Luxembourg

Bd. Saint-Michel

LATIN QUARTER

Jardin des Plantes

Bd. de Vaugirard

Bd. Edgar Quinet

Av. des Gobelins

MONTPARNASSE

15 e

Av. Denfert-Rochereau

Bd. Saint-Jacques

Bd. Auriol Vincent

0 — 500 meters
0 — 1,500 ft

PLANNING

BOOKS

The scenic open-air *bouquinistes* bookstalls along the Seine are stacked with secondhand volumes (mostly in French), prints, and souvenirs. French-language bookshops—specializing in art, film, literature, and philosophy—can be found in the scholarly Latin Quarter and the publishing district, St-Germain-des-Prés.

HOW TO DO DUTY-FREE

A value-added tax (or T.V.A.) of 20% is imposed on most consumer goods; and the rate can be as high as 33% for certain luxury items. To qualify for a refund, you must have bought more than €175 of goods in the same store on the same day, and have stayed three months or less in the EU at the time of purchase. In 2014, the new PABLO reimbursement system was introduced: now, instead of lengthy paper forms, retailers provide computer-generated ones with a barcode and the PABLO logo, which must be scanned in the airport at a designated PABLO terminal before you check in for your outbound flight. Refunds are processed more quickly, and funds are directly credited to your credit card or bank account.

FOOD MARKETS

The city's open-air food markets attract the entire spectrum of Paris society, from the splendid matron with her minuscule dog in tow, to the mustachioed regular picking up his daily baguette. Although some markets are busier than others, there's not one in Paris that doesn't captivate the senses. Each season has its delicacies: *fraises des bois* (wild strawberries) and tender asparagus in spring, squash blossoms and fragrant herbs in summer, saffron-tinted chanterelles in autumn, bergamot oranges in late winter. Year-round you can find pungent *lait cru* (unpasteurized) cheeses, charcuterie, and unfarmed game and fish. Many of the better-known open-air markets are in areas you'd visit for sightseeing. To get a list of market days in your area, ask your concierge or check the markets section on the website ⊕ *www.paris.fr/marches*.

If you're unused to the metric system, it may be helpful to know that *une livre* is French for a pound; *une demi-livre* is a half pound. For cheese or meats, *un morceau* will get you a piece, *une tranche* a slice.

Most markets are open from 8 am to 1 pm three days a week year-round (usually the weekend and one weekday, but never Monday) on a rotating basis.

STORE HOURS

Store hours can be tricky in Paris. Aside from department stores, which keep slightly longer hours and usually shut their doors late on Thursday, shops tend to open around 10 am and close around 7 pm. It's not unusual to find a "back at 3" sign taped on the doors of smaller boutiques at lunchtime. Plan to do most of your foraging between Tuesday and Saturday, as the majority of shops, including department stores, are closed Sunday and some on Monday as well. You can find areas—particularly the Marais and tourist-oriented Champs-Élysées—where stores are open on Sunday. However, if you're making a special trip somewhere, always call ahead to check hours.

BEST BETS FOR PARIS SHOPPING

With thousands of shops to choose from, how will you decide where to go? Below you'll find some of Fodor's writers' and editors' favorites to help you get started. You can also search by category within each neighborhood for noteworthy shops and peruse the previous pages for spotlights on specific neighborhoods.

BEST WOMENSWEAR

Azzedine Alaïa, p. 321
Chloé, p. 305
French Trotters, p. 322
Isabel Marant, p. 326
Le Bon Marché, p. 332
Spree, p. 319
Vanessa Bruno, p. 308

BEST MENSWEAR

A.P.C., p. 331
BHV, p. 314
French Trotters, p. 322
Galeries Lafayette, p. 316
L'Eclaireur, p. 322
Le Bon Marché, p. 332

BEST SHOES

Avril Gau, p. 336
Galeries Lafayette, p. 316
Le Bon Marché, p. 332
Pierre Hardy, p. 312
Roger Vivier, p. 313
Tila March, p. 337

BEST TRENDSETTING STYLE

Colette, p. 305
COS, p. 322
Isabel Marant, p. 326
L'Eclaireur, p. 322
Maison Martin Margiela p. 307
Surface to Air, p. 324

BEST BARGAIN HUNTING

A.P.C., p. 331
Jamin Puech Inventaire, p. 329
L'Habilleur, p. 320
Le Dépôt Vente Luxe, p. 300
Monoprix, p. 315
Zadig & Voltaire Stock, p. 320

BEST FOR BEAUTY

Anne Sémonin, p. 313
Au Printemps, p. 316
By Terry, p. 304
Galeries Lafayette, p. 316
Make Up For Ever, p. 316
Shu Uemura, p. 330

BEST VINTAGE

Didier Ludot, p. 306
La Jolie Garde-Robe, p. 322
Pretty Box, p. 323
Vintage Clothing Paris, p. 324

BEST HIGH FASHION

Azzedine Alaïa, p. 321
Chloé, p. 305
Hermès, p. 312
Loris Azzaro, p. 307
Saint Laurent, p. 308
Stella McCartney, p. 308

BEST LINGERIE

Alice Cadolle, p. 311
Chantal Thomass, p. 311
Fifi Chachnil, p. 311
Sabbia Rosa, p. 336

BEST PERFUME

Annick Goutal, p. 304
Editions de Parfums Frédéric Malle, p. 330
Guerlain, p. 298
L'Artisan Parfumeur, p. 321

Les Salons du Palais-Royal Serge Lutens, p. 304
Nose, p. 313

BEST JEWELRY

Adelline, p. 335
Agatha, p. 335
Dinh Van, p. 318
Médecine Douce, p. 328
Yves Gratas, p. 325

BEST HANDBAGS

Avril Gau, p. 336
Goyard, p. 311
Hermès, p. 312
Jérôme Dreyfuss, p. 336
Renaud Pellegrino, p. 312
Tila March, p. 337

BEST FOR THE WHOLE FAMILY

Agnès b, p. 313
BHV, p. 314
Eric Bompard, p. 316
Galeries Lafayette, p. 316
Le Bon Marché, p. 332
Monoprix, p. 315

BEST BOOKSTORES

Artazart, p. 327
La Hune, p. 331
Librairie Galignani p. 304
Shakespeare & Company, p. 329
Taschen, p. 331

16

SHOPPING IN PARIS

Reviews are alphabetical by neighborhood.

CHAMPS-ÉLYSÉES

Step into your Chanel suit, gird your loins, and plunge into Paris's most desirable (and most daunting) hunting grounds, where royals, jet-setters, starlets, and other glitterati converge in pursuit of the high life. This elegant triangle—bordered by avenues Montaigne, Georges V, and Champs-Élysées, with Rue François 1er in between—is home to almost all the luxury Goliaths with a few lesser worthies added in.

BEAUTY

Guerlain. Guerlain has long resided at this opulent address, a fitting home for Paris's first—and most famous—perfumer. Still the only Paris outlet for legendary perfumes like Shalimar and L'Heure Blue, it has added several new signature scents (including Myrrhe et Délires and Cuir Beluga). A perfume "fountain" allows for personalized bottles in several sizes to be filled on demand. Or, for a mere €30,000, a customized scent can be blended just for you. Also here are makeup, scented candles, and a spa featuring their much-adored skin-care line. ⊠ *68 av. des Champs-Élysées, 8e, Champs-Élysées* ☎ *01–45–62–52–57* ⊕ *www. guerlain.com* Ⓜ *Franklin-D.-Roosevelt.*

Parfums de Nicolaï. This perfumerie is run by a member of the Guerlain family: Patricia de Nicolaï. Children's, women's, and men's scents are on offer (including some unisex), as are sprays for the home and fragrant candles. ⊠ *69 av. Raymond Poincaré, 16e, Champs-Élysées* ☎ *01–47–55–90–44* ⊕ *www.pnicolai.com* Ⓜ *Victor-Hugo.*

CHILDREN'S CLOTHING

Fodor'sChoice
★ **Bonpoint.** Bonpoint is for the prince or princess in your life (royalty *does* shop here). Yes, prices are high, but the quality is exceptional. The mini-duds couldn't be more stylish (or adorable) with items such as a perfect emerald-green hand-smocked silk dress, a mini leopard-print jacket, or a midnight-blue velvet suit for Little Lord Fauntleroy. ⊠ *64 av. Raymond Poincaré, 16e, Champs-Élysées* ☎ *01–47–27–60–81* ⊕ *www.bonpoint.com* Ⓜ *Trocadéro* ⊠ *15 rue Royale, 8e, Louvre/Tuileries* ☎ *01–47–42–52–63* Ⓜ *Madeleine.*

Petit Bateau. Petit Bateau provides a fundamental part of the classic French wardrobe from cradle to teen and beyond. The signature T-shirt—cut close to the body, with smallish shoulders—works equally well with school uniforms or vintage Chanel. High-grade cotton clothes follow designs that haven't changed in decades (think onesies and pajamas for newborns, underwear sets, and dresses with tiny straps for summer); however, lines in cotton-silk or cotton-cashmere and popular partnerships with designers like Christian Lacroix mean there's now even more in store. Stock up: if you can find this brand back home, the prices are sure to be higher. ⊠ *116 av. des Champs-Élysées, 8e, Champs-Élysées* ☎ *01–40–74–02–03* ⊕ *www.petit-bateau.fr* Ⓜ *George V.*

CLOTHING

Fodor'sChoice ★ **Balenciaga.** This venerable Paris fashion house was completely revamped under the brilliant Nicolas Ghesquière, whose singular vision electrified the runway world. With his abrupt departure in late 2012, American wunderkind Alexander Wang took charge. Today the young designer's structured-yet-feminine and freshly appealing designs consistently reaffirm his stellar fashion credentials. ✉ *10 av. George V, 8e, Champs-Élysées* ☎ *01–47–20–21–11* ⊕ *www.balenciaga.com* Ⓜ *Alma-Marceau.*

SUPER SHOPPING TIP

Galeries Lafayette and Au Printemps each offer 10%-off discount cards to foreign visitors. Some things, usually designer clothing and sale items, are excluded. To get one, go to the welcome desk on the main floor of either store. Remember to bring a passport or driver's license.

Fodor'sChoice ★ **Céline.** Reinvigorated by Michael Kors in the late 1990s, Céline got another much-needed jolt when Phoebe Philo arrived in 2009 and began drawing raves from critics for her focused approach. Philo's characteristically refined tailoring and minute attention to detail underlie the seeming simplicity of her styles, which veer from flowing pants and long, unstructured jackets to streamlined swing skirts and python tops. Along with the ready-to-wear, Céline's hugely popular two-toned totes and luxurious bags are beloved by Paris's fashion elite. ✉ *24 rue François 1er, 8e, Champs-Élysées* ☎ *01–40–70–07–03* ⊕ *www.celine.com* Ⓜ *Franklin-D.-Roosevelt.*

Chanel. Elegant, modern looks, with sex appeal and lasting value are Chanel's stock in trade. Although the spectacular Avenue Montaigne flagship takes shoppers' breath away, the heart of this revered fashion house—now helmed by Karl Lagerfeld—is still the boutique at 31 rue Cambon, where Chanel once perched high up on the mirrored staircase watching audience reactions to her collection debuts. Great investments include all of Coco's favorites: the perfectly tailored suit, a lean soigné dress, or a quilted bag with a gold chain. ✉ *42 av. Montaigne, 8e, Champs-Élysées* ☎ *01–47–23–74–12* ⊕ *www.chanel.com* Ⓜ *Franklin-D.-Roosevelt.*

Fodor'sChoice ★ **Christian Dior.** Raf Simons's back-to-glamorous looks have revivified this legendary label. Since taking the helm in 2012, following John Galliano's inglorious fall from grace, Simons has taken an architectural approach to ready-to-wear, playing with volume and contrasting geometric forms with fluid, dimensional fabrics (sometimes pierced or transparent). His meticulously styled clothes and steadfast vision have consistently elated the fashion press. ✉ *30 av. Montaigne, 8e, Champs-Élysées* ☎ *01–40–73–73–73* ⊕ *www.dior.com* Ⓜ *Franklin-D.-Roosevelt.*

Dolce & Gabbana. Dolce & Gabbana offers a sexy, young-Italian-widow vibe with a side of moody boyfriend. Svelte silk dresses, sharply tailored suits, and plunging necklines are made for drama. Women's clothes are at the Avenue Montaigne location; men's are at 3 rue Faubourg St-Honoré. ✉ *54 av. Montaigne, 8e, Champs Élysées* ☎ *01–42–25–68–78* ⊕ *www.dolcegabbana.com* Ⓜ *Alma-Marceau.*

16

Jean-Paul Gaultier. Jean-Paul Gaultier first made headlines by engineering that celebrated corset with the ironic iconic breasts for Madonna but now sends fashion editors into ecstasies with his sumptuous haute-couture creations. Designer Philippe Starck spun an *Alice in Wonderland* fantasy for the boutique, with quilted cream walls and Murano mirrors. Make no mistake, though, it's all about the clothes. ✉ *44 av. George V, 8e, Champs-Élysées* ☎ *01–44–43–00–44* ⊕ *www.jeanpaulgaultier. com* Ⓜ *George V.*

Le66. Finding just the right totally chic, totally black anything is a breeze here. This up-to-the-second concept store, comprised of three boutiques on two levels (including shoes, jewelry, accessories, and men's), lines up all the top names that you know, along with those that you may not but should. Diffusion lines of the major labels mingle with Acne, Kenzo, Helmut Lang, Azzaro, Alexander Wang, Dolfie, and nearly 200 others, all hand-picked to ensure fabulousness. If pressed for time, it's a good bet for all-around satisfaction. ✉ *66 av. des Champs-Élysées, 8e, Champs-Élysées* ☎ *01–53–53–33–80* ⊕ *www.le66.fr* Ⓜ *Franklin-D.-Roosevelt.*

Le Dépôt Vente Luxe. This beautiful high-end consignment shop carries barely worn (and sometimes never worn) designer ready-to-wear from big names, including Chanel, Dior, Hermès, Gucci, Vuitton, and Prada. Few can pass up one of last season's outfits at one-third the price, or forgo browsing the vast selection of furs, bags, belts, scarves, shoes, and costume jewelry (and menswear). The exceptional stock justifies the hike you'll have to make to the 17e. Alternatively, you can visit Le Dépôt Vente Luxe's second location at 14 rue de la Tour—it's smaller but still sublime. ✉ *109 rue de Courcelles, 17e, Champs-Élysées* ☎ *01–40–53–80–82* ⊕ *www.depot-vente-paris.fr* Ⓜ *Wagram.*

Marni. Marni started out as a little Italian label that created a quirky take on the classics, employing retro-ish prints and colors (think citron-yellow or seaweed-green) and funky fabrics (such as rubberized cotton and filmy silks). Now it has evolved into a major player on the edgy fashion scene. Each season has something new to say—whether it's an inventive take on bold ethnic prints, ingenious knits, or eloquent color schemes. Sought-after shoes and jewelry never make it to sale time. ✉ *57 av. Montaigne, 8e, Champs-Élysées* ☎ *01–56–88–08–08* ⊕ *www. marni.com* Ⓜ *Franklin-D.-Roosevelt.*

Nina Ricci. Nina Ricci appeals to the leather-and-lace sensibility in surprising ways; that is, the lace might be in leather. Creative director Peter Copping provides archly feminine elements (picture bows, ruffles, perforated leather, pastel silks, delicate florals, and frothy colors, along with sensuous lingerie touches), and the label's airy white-on-white Avenue Montaigne boutique is one of Paris's dreamiest. ✉ *39 av. Montaigne, 8e, Champs-Élysées* ☎ *01–83–97–71–71* ⊕ *www.ninaricci.com* Ⓜ *Franklin-D.-Roosevelt.*

Paul & Joe. Paul & Joe is designer Sophie Albou's eclectic, girlish blend of modern trends. There's a retro feel to the diaphanous blouses, A-line jackets with matching short shorts, and swingy felt coats. In summer she'll mix in a little hippie chic. The secondary line, Paul & Joe Sister—with a decidedly younger clientele—brings a slouchy, casual edge to the line. ✉ *2 av. Montaigne, 8e, Champs-Élysées* ☎ *01–47–20–57–50* ⊕ *www.paulandjoe.com* Ⓜ *Alma-Marceau.*

Prada. Prada spins gold out of fashion straw. Knee-length skirts, peacock colors, cardigan sweaters, geometric prints: the waiting lists cross continents. Shoes, bags, and other accessories for men and women perennially become cult items. ✉ *10 av. Montaigne, 8e, Champs-Élysées* ☎ *01–53–23–99–40* ⊕ *www.prada.com* Ⓜ *Alma-Marceau.*

Réciproque. Paris's largest, most exclusive consignment store carries everything from furs and jewelry to evening gowns and lingerie. Almost any coveted designer you can think of is represented, and the savings are significant; but prices aren't as cheap as you might expect, and there's not much in the way of service or space. The six shops that comprise Réciproque (individually dedicated to women's clothing, menswear, accessories, and the like) are clustered together on Rue de la Pompe; all are closed Sunday and Monday. ✉ *89, 92, 93, 95, 97, and 101 rue de la Pompe, 16e, Champs-Élysées* ☎ *01–47–04–30–28* ⊕ *www.reciproque. fr* Ⓜ *Rue de la Pompe.*

HOME DECOR

Laguiole. This is France's most famous brand of knives; designers like Philippe Starck and Sonia Rykiel have created special models for the company. ✉ *29 rue Boissy d'Anglas, 8e, Champs-Élysées* ☎ *01–40–06–09–75* ⊕ *www.forge-2-laguiole.fr* Ⓜ *Concorde.*

Maison de Baccarat. This museum and crystal store was once the home of Marie-Laure de Noailles, known as the Countess of Bizarre. Philippe Starck revamped the space with his signature cleverness—yes, that's a chandelier floating in an aquarium and, yes, that crystal arm sprouting from the wall alludes to Jean Cocteau (a friend of Noailles). Follow the red carpet to the jewelry room, where crystal baubles hang from bronze figurines, and to the immense table stacked with crystal items for the home. ✉ *11 pl. des États-Unis, 16e, Champs-Élysée* ☎ *01–40–22–11–00* ⊕ *www.baccarat.com* Ⓜ *Trocadéro.*

JEWELRY AND ACCESSORIES

Dior Joaillerie. Dior Joaillerie got a big dollop of wit and panache when it signed on young designer Victoire de Castellane to create Dior's first line of fine jewelry. She does oversize rings, hoop earrings, and bracelets swinging with diamonds, and—lest you forget the amped-up spirit at Dior house—white-gold death's-head cufflinks. ✉ *28 av. Montaigne, 8e, Champs-Élysées* ☎ *01–47–23–52–39* ⊕ *www.dior.com* Ⓜ *Franklin-D.-Roosevelt.*

SHOES, HANDBAGS, AND LEATHER GOODS

Berluti. Berluti has been making exquisite and expensive men's shoes for more than a century. "Nothing is too beautiful for feet" is Olga Berluti's motto; she even exposes her creations to the moonlight to give them an extra-special patina. One model is named after Andy Warhol; other famous clients of the past include the Duke of Windsor, Fred Astaire, and James Joyce. ✉ *26 rue Marbeuf, 8e, Champs-Élysées* ☎ *01–53–93–97–97* ⊕ *www.berluti.com* Ⓜ *Franklin-D.-Roosevelt.*

16

Giuseppe Zanotti Design. Every pair of shoes here is fetish worthy, if not downright dangerous. Mile-high spike heels, buckle stilettos, slinky python booties, and jewel-encrusted black-satin pumps beg to be noticed. More toned-down models, like over-the-knee leather flats, and even sneakers, can be had, too. ⊠ *12 av. Montaigne, 8e, Champs-Élysées* ☎ *01–47–20–07–85* ⊕ *www.giuseppezanottidesign. com* Ⓜ *Franklin-D.-Roosevelt.*

Jimmy Choo. This is the place for vampy stilettos, strappy flats, and butch biker boots. Recent *Belle de Jour* inspired kitten heels are a nice respite from the famous mile-high styles that put Choo on the map. Beautiful bags, clutches, and small leather items in animal print, reptile, and metallics are deservedly popular. ⊠ *34 av. Montaigne, 8e, Champs-Élysées* ☎ *01–47–23–03–39* ⊕ *www.jimmychoo.com* Ⓜ *Franklin-D.-Roosevelt.*

Fodor'sChoice
★
Louis Vuitton. Louis Vuitton has spawned a voracious fan base from Texas to Tokyo with its mix of classic leather goods and saucy revamped versions orchestrated by Marc Jacobs. Jacobs's collaborations with the likes of Japanese artist Takashi Murakami and, more recently, Yayoi Kusama have become instant collectibles and knockoffables. With Jacobs's departure in late 2013, all eyes are on this jewel in the luxury giant LVMH's crown. ⊠ *101 av. des Champs-Élysées, 8e, Champs-Élysées* ☎ *01–53–57–52–00* ⊕ *www.louisvuitton.com* Ⓜ *George V.*

Robert Clergerie. Robert Clergerie knows that shoes make the woman. Styles combine visionary design, first-rate craftsmanship, and wearability with rare staying power. Plus, they're still a relative bargain on this side of the Atlantic. ⊠ *18 av. Victor Hugo, 16e, Champs-Élysées* ☎ *01–45–01–81–30* ⊕ *www.robertclergerie.com* Ⓜ *Charles de Gaulle–Étoile.*

SPAS

Villa Thalgo. Dip into the pools at Villa Thalgo to experience the benefits of a *spa marin* (literally, sea spa) in the heart of Paris. Take advantage of its aquagym, fitness room, and hammams (€100, half-day pass), or opt for an Aquazen massage with warm water balloons to de-stress your sore spots (€110, 50 minutes). ⊠ *8 av. Raymond Poincaré, 16e, Trocadéro* ☎ *01–45–62–00–20* ⊕ *www.villathalgo.com* Ⓜ *Trocadéro.*

AROUND THE LOUVRE

The flagship stores of big luxury brands rub elbows here with independent boutiques and concept stores notable for their fashion cachet. The fabulous Rue St-Honoré—a bastion of Parisian chic—is the area's retail spine, but the Marché St-Honoré and the Faubourg provide tempting detours. Whatever you do, don't miss the gorgeous Palais-Royal gardens, where flashy fashion stars mix with the discrete purveyors of handmade gloves.

FAUBOURG ST-HONORÉ

ANTIQUES AND COLLECTIBLES

Astier de Villatte. Come here for tongue-in-chic interpretations of 18th-century table settings and furniture; live out your Baroque or Empire fancies with milk-white china sets and lots of mahogany. Moody candles and incense complete the atmosphere. ⊠ *173 rue St-Honoré,*

Notable Neighborhoods, Select Streets

Paris's legendary shopping destinations draw people from the world over, but perhaps a deeper allure lies in lesser-known attractions: the city harbors scores of hidden neighborhoods and shopping streets—some well traveled, others just emerging. Each has a distinct style that reflects the character of the particular quarter. Here are a few of Paris's most satisfying and *très branché* (very trendy) enclaves.

Rue Keller, Rue Charonne (11e). These streets are a haven for young clothing designers. Stylish housewares, jewelry, and art galleries augment the appeal. Start at the end of Rue Keller where it intersects with Rue de la Roquette: walk the length of this short street, then make a right onto Rue Charonne and meander all the way to Rue du Faubourg St-Antoine.

Rue Oberkampf (11e). At the outer edge of the Marais, this street is well known among youthful fashionistas for its eclectic atmosphere and bohemian flavor. High-end jewelry and of-the-minute boutiques are clustered amid stylish wine bars and comfy cafés.

Rue des Abbesses, Rue des Martyrs (18e and 9e). In the shadow of lofty Sacré-Coeur, Rue des Abbesses is studded with shops focused on anything from vintage jewelry and unique clothing to antiques and upscale gardening tools. Turn onto Rue des Martyrs and discover a burgeoning scene, with hot boutiques scattered among inviting cafés, and superb gourmet shops.

Rues Étienne Marcel, du Jour, du Louvre, and Montmartre (2e). Just around the corner from teeming Les Halles, this area is jam-packed with big names (like Yohji Yamamoto and Agnès b), but it also boasts a multitude of smaller boutiques (such as Shine) that are popular with hip young Parisians.

Rue du Bac (7e). After browsing at Le Bon Marché turn the corner at the Grand Epicerie and stroll down this most bountiful of shopping streets. Old and well established, it's where the Paris *beau monde* finds everything from elegant linens and home furnishings to any item of apparel a grownup or child could possibly want.

Rue Vavin (6e). One of Paris's epicenters for outfitting those hopelessly chic Parisian children, this street is lined with boutiques for tots. If you have the kids in tow, follow up with a pony ride at the Luxembourg Gardens (weekends and Wednesday afternoon only). Jewelry stores, clothing stores, and Jean-Paul Hévin (one of Paris's top chocolatiers) give adults plenty to love, too.

Rue Pont Louis Philippe (4e). Known for a plethora of elegant paper and stationery shops, the street also has boutiques selling antiques, musical instruments, artisan jewelry, and classy clothing. It's a great spot for window-shopping en route from the Marais to Ile St-Louis.

Rue Francois Miron (from St-Paul métro to Place St-Gervais, 4e). Many overlook this lovely street at the Marais's Seine-side fringes, but there's plenty to make a wander worthwhile. Parisians in the know head here for spices, top-notch designs for the home, antiques, jewelry, pretty cafés, and much more. Bonus: Two of the oldest houses in Paris are here; they're the medieval half-timbered ones.

16

1er, Louvre/Tuileries ☎ *01–42–60–74–13* ⊕ *www.astierdevillatte.com* Ⓜ *Tuileries.*

BEAUTY

Annick Goutal. Annick Goutal sells its own line of signature scents, which come packaged in gilded gauze purses. Gardenia, Passion, Petite Chérie, and l'Eau d'Hadrien are perennial favorites. ✉ *14 rue de Castiglione, 1er, Louvre/Tuileries* ☎ *01–42–60–52–82* ⊕ *www.annickgoutal.com* Ⓜ *Concorde.*

By Terry. This small, refined store is the brainchild of Terry de Gunzburg, Yves Saint Laurent's former director of makeup, whose brand of ready-to-wear cosmetics is a favorite of French actresses and socialites. Upstairs, specialists create what de Gunzburg calls *haute couleur*: exclusive made-to-measure makeup tailored for each client (it's very expensive; book far in advance). ✉ *36 Galerie Véro-Dodat, 1er, Louvre/Tuileries* ☎ *01–44–76–00–76* ⊕ *www.byterry.com* Ⓜ *Palais-Royal, Louvre.*

Jovoy. Representing 80 artisanal perfumers, Jovoy is not only Paris's largest independent purveyor of fragrances, but also the world's. Owner François Hénin can often be found in the shop expounding on the unique qualities and fascinating histories of the fragrances, some of which date back hundreds of years. Many are exclusive to the boutique. The shop also carries fragrances for the home and a range of beautifully packaged scented candles. ✉ *4 rue de Castiglione, 1er, Louvre/Tuileries* ☎ *01–40–20–06–19* ⊕ *www.jovoyparis.com* Ⓜ *Tuileries, Concorde.*

Fodor's Choice ★ **Les Salons du Palais-Royal Serge Lutens.** Every year Shiseido's creative genius, Serge Lutens, dreams up two new fragrances, which are then sold exclusively in this boutique. Each is compellingly original, from the strong *somptueux* scents (often with musk and amber notes) to intense florals (Rose de Nuit). Bottles can be etched and personalized for sumptuous gifts. ✉ *Jardins du Palais-Royal, 142 Galerie de Valois, 1er, Louvre/Tuileries* ☎ *01–49–27–09–09* ⊕ *www.sergelutens.com* Ⓜ *Palais-Royal.*

BOOKS AND STATIONERY

Librarie Galignani. Dating back to 1520s Venice, this venerable bookstore opened in Paris in 1801 and was the first to specialize in English language books. Its present location, across from the Tuileries Garden on Rue de Rivoli, opened in 1856, and the wood bookshelves, creaking floors, and hushed interior provide the perfect atmosphere for perusing Paris's best collection of contemporary and classic greats in English and French, plus a huge selection of gorgeous art books. ✉ *224 rue de Rivoli, 1e, Louvre/Tuileries* ☎ *01–42–60–76–07* ⊕ *www.galignani.com* Ⓜ *Tuileries.*

W. H. Smith. This bookseller carries a multitude of travel and language books, cookbooks, plus fiction for adults and children. It also has the best selection of foreign magazines and newspapers in Paris (which you're allowed to flip through without interruption—many magazine dealers in France aren't so kind). ✉ *248 rue de Rivoli, 1er, Louvre/Tuileries* ☎ *01–44–77–88–99* ⊕ *www.whsmith.fr* Ⓜ *Concorde.*

CLOTHING

& Other Stories. H&M's latest up-market "style-lab" covers all the major fashion bases while appealing to women of different tastes and ages. Unlike the minimalist COS—another H&M spawn—& Other Stories offers the kind of *au courant* looks and well-made basics that are

beloved by urban sophisticates who wouldn't be caught dead buying the parent brand but still want style on a budget. The shoe collection downstairs is a serious draw all on its own. Accessories, lingerie, and makeup are also available. ✉ *277 rue Saint-Honoré, 1er, Faubourg St-Honoré* ☎ *01–53–32–85–05* ⊕ *www.stories.com* Ⓜ *Concorde.*

Fodor's Choice ★ Acne Studios. This Stockholm-based design collective initially gained a large and loyal following among both sexes for its super-comfortable, flattering (and pricey) jeans. These days Acne Studios is also known for full-length asymmetric silk or leather dresses, cutting-edge suits, chic sportswear, plus shoes and accessories—all exhibiting the brand's underplayed cool. ✉ *124 Galerie de Valois, 1er, Louvre/Tuileries* ☎ *01–42–60–16–62* ⊕ *www.shop.acnestudios.com* Ⓜ *Palais Royal–Musée du Louvre.*

Alberta Ferretti. Sheer, flowing, and structured by turns, these super-feminine creations seek to enchant—and succeed. Sexy silk dresses mine past fashion tropes and make them new: the flapperish gold-beaded mini dress is a case in point. The well-loved (and more gently priced) diffusion line, Philosophy, is here, too, along with shoes, bags, and accessories. ✉ *418 rue St-Honoré, 8e, Louvre/Tuileries* ☎ *01–42–60–14–97* ⊕ *www.albertaferretti.com* Ⓜ *Madeleine/Concorde.*

Fodor's Choice ★ Chloé. Much like the clothes it sells, Chloé's new flagship boutique is softly feminine and modern without being stark. Housed in an 18th-century mansion, its creamy marble floors, gold sconces, and walls in the brand's signature rosy beige are the perfect backdrop for designer Clair Waight Keller's beautifully tailored yet fluid designs. Visitors are met with the kind of sincere attention that is all but extinct in most high-end Paris shops. Whether it's for a handbag or a whole new wardrobe, VIP rooms and professional stylists are available to assist anyone who calls for an appointment. ✉ *253 rue St-Honoré, 1e, Louvre/Tuileries* ☎ *01–47–23–00–08* ⊕ *www.chloe.com* Ⓜ *Franklin-D.-Roosevelt.*

Claudie Pierlot. This designer is deservedly lauded for her smart, urban clothes that unite youthful chic with solid designs; they also successfully transition over several seasons. The irresistible combination of classic looks, good tailoring, and affordability keeps loyal fans coming back year after year. ✉ *1 rue du 29 Juillet, 1er, Louvre/Tuileries* ☎ *01–42–60–01–19* ⊕ *www.claudiepierlot.com* Ⓜ *Étienne Marcel.*

Colette. This is *the* place for ridiculously cool fashion. So the staff barely deigns to make eye contact—who cares! There are ultramodern trinkets and trifles of all kinds: from Lego-link alarm clocks to snappy iPad cases, the latest out-there CDs, and tongue-in-chic sportswear—and

16

that's just on the ground floor. The first floor has wearable wares from every internationally known and unknown designer with street cred. The basement has a water bar (because that's what models eat), plus a small restaurant that's good for a quick bite. ✉ *213 rue St-Honoré, 1er, Louvre/Tuileries* ☎ *01–55–35–33–90* ⊕ *www. colette.fr* Ⓜ *Tuileries.*

Costume National. Costume National is all about sharp styling and unerring sophistication. Ennio Capasa's flawlessly cut suits confer high-powered status, and teensy dresses with plunging necklines shoot for unabashed allure. Shoes and accessories are surprisingly versatile. ✉ *5 rue Cambon, 1er, Louvre/Tuileries* ☎ *01–40–15–04–13* ⊕ *www. costumenational.com* Ⓜ *Tuileries.*

> ### TOP PARIS SHOPPING EXPERIENCES
>
> **Visiting Le Bon Marché.** The city's chicest and oldest department store is a great first stop for an overview of the current season's pieces from all the top designers.
>
> **Shopping at the food markets.** Year-round and in any weather, the city's open-air food markets are an integral part of daily Parisian life.
>
> **The Marais.** This is one of Paris's most charming places to stroll and shop, with tons of local boutiques and French-owned chains, along cobblestone streets.

Cotélac. Cotélac gives feminine shapes a bohemian edge in earthy tones from azure to deep aubergine. The figure-skimming and frillier separates beg to be layered. ✉ *284 rue St-Honoré, 1er, Louvre/Tuileries* ☎ *01–47–03–21–14* ⊕ *www.cotelac.fr* Ⓜ *Tuileries.*

Damir Doma. The fashion press consistently lauds these fluid, unconstrained, yet rigorously constructed clothes for men and women. A cut-wool cape cascades to the floor, a grass-green evening gown ripples like water, crisp cotton blouses and slouchy silk trousers remain stylish season after season. The beautiful modern-Baroque boutique also houses the diffusion line, Silent, along with sleek accessories. ✉ *54 rue du Faubourg St-Honoré, 8e, Louvre/Tuileries* ☎ *01–45–27–09–30* ⊕ *www.damirdoma.com* Ⓜ *Concorde.*

Didier Ludot. The incredibly charming Didier Ludot inspired a fervent craze for vintage couture, and riffling through his racks of French-made pieces from the '20s to the '80s can yield wonderful Chanel suits, Balenciaga dresses, and Hermès scarves. Ludot has two boutiques in Galerie Montpensier: No. 20 houses his amazing vintage couture collection, while No. 24 has vintage ready-to-wear and accessories. Across the gardens, at No. 125 Galerie de Valois, La Petite Robe Noire sells his own vintage-inspired black dresses as well as his coffee-table book— which is aptly titled *The Little Black Dress.* ✉ *Jardins du Palais-Royal, 20–24 Galerie Montpensier, 1er, Louvre/Tuileries* ☎ *01–42–96–06–56* ⊕ *www.didierludot.fr* Ⓜ *Palais-Royal.*

Gabrielle Geppert. Gabrielle Geppert carries only the big guys—Chanel, Hermès, YSL, Vuitton—and what's here is exactly what Gabrielle likes: from a 1950s-era fully sequined cape and '60s jet-beaded minidress to an '80s number right at home under the disco ball. Geppert's personal line of shades, handbags, and jewelry is at the teensy boutique at No. 34. ✉ *31–34 Galerie de Montpensier, 1er, Louvre/Tuileries* ☎ *01–42–61–53–52* ⊕ *www.gabriellegeppert.com* Ⓜ *Palais Royal–Musée du Louvre.*

Jérôme L'Huillier. L'Huillier cut his teeth at the ateliers of Balmain and Givenchy, and it shows. A wizard with silk in all its iterations (the joyously colored prints are L'Huillier's own designs), you can find lively, sexy new interpretations of the wrap dress, along with rainbow-hue blouses, sexy empire-waist dresses, and velvet trench coats in jewel colors. ✉ *138–139 Galerie de Valois, 1er, Louvre/Tuileries* ☎ *01–49–26–07–07* ⊕ *www.jeromelhuillier.com* Ⓜ *Palais Royal–Musée du Louvre.*

Loris Azzaro. Azzaro is a master of the dramatic dress: floor-length columns with jeweled collars and sheer gowns with strategically placed sequins. When he saw his 1970s designs, now collector's items, worn by stars like Nicole Kidman and Liz Hurley, he decided to update his best sellers. ✉ *65 rue de Faubourg St-Honoré, 8e, Louvre/Tuileries* ☎ *01–42–66–92–98* ⊕ *www.azzaro-couture.com* Ⓜ *Concorde.*

Lucien Pellat-Finet. Lucien Pellat-Finet does cashmere that shakes up the traditional world of cable knits: here, sweaters for men, women, and children come in punchy colors and cheeky motifs. A psychedelic marijuana leaf may bounce across a sky-blue crewneck; a crystal-outlined skull could grin from a sleeveless top. The cashmere is wonderfully soft—and the prices are accordingly high. ✉ *231 rue Saint Honoré, 1er, Louvre/Tuileries* ☎ *01–42–22–22–77* Ⓜ *Tuileries.*

Maison Martin Margiela. This famously elusive Belgian designer has earned a devoted following for his avant-garde styling and for his innovative technique, from spiraling seams to deconstructed shirts. Women's fashion is sold at 25 rue de Montpensier, menswear at No. 23 (Passage Potier). ■TIP➔ **Look for Ligne 6—Margiela's cool, secondary line of more casual (and less expensive) clothes for women—in his store at 22 place du Marché Saint-Honoré.** ✉ *23 and 25 rue de Montpensier, 1er, Louvre/Tuileries* ☎ *01–40–15–07–55* ⊕ *www.maisonmartinmargiela.fr* Ⓜ *Palais-Royal.*

Maje. Maje brings a certain ease to looking great. The designs are original, up-to-the-moment, and not wildly expensive—that's why the popular label has expanded exponentially. Seasonal collections include minis in every form: sequined, flouncy, leather; lean, peg-leg trousers in denim and leather; and some of the best outerwear around. ✉ *267 rue St-Honore, 2e, Louvre/Tuileries* ☎ *01–42–96–84–93* ⊕ *www.maje.com* Ⓜ *Palais Royal–Musée du Louvre.*

Marc Jacobs. Marc Jacobs remains the darling of American style with his singular take on 20th-century American classics—from flapper-style (big flowers, unstructured lines, drop waists, flounces) to 1960s prom (empire waists, copious tulle) with a bit of motorcycle chic thrown in. Metallics appear in most every collection, as do breezy, feminine fabrics and lots of layers. Ready-to-wear is at Palais Royal. The secondary line, Marc by Marc Jacobs, is sold in his eponymous store at 19 place du Marché St-Honoré. Men's wear and accessories are at both.

✉ *56–62 Galerie de Montpensier, 1e, Louvre/Tuileries* ☎ *01–55–35–02–60* ⊕ *www.marcjacobs.com* Ⓜ *Palais Royal–Musée du Louvre.*

Miu Miu. This St-Honoré boutique dispenses with the designer's Modernist ethos in favor of a neo-Baroque sensibility—and it influences everything from the velvet wallpaper to, perhaps, a lavish pair of ruby slippers. Although the shoes and accessories scream glitz, the clothes still have a sleek refinement, with the designer's notorious tension between minimalism and opulence. ✉ *219 rue St-Honoré, 1er, Louvre/Tuileries* ☎ *01–58–62–53–20* ⊕ *www.miumiu.com* Ⓜ *Tuileries.*

Rick Owens. Rick Owens expertly finessed the jump from L.A. rockstar chic to Paris offbeat elegance. Lately defined more by glamour than grunge, his lush fabrics and asymmetrical designs have evolved to a new level of artistry—and wearability. Owens still loves a paradox (shrouding while revealing), and mixes high luxury with a bit of the tooth and the claw. You'll also find shoes, furs, jewely, and accessories. ✉ *130–133 Galerie de Valois, 1er, Louvre/Tuileries* ☎ *01–40–20–42–52* ⊕ *www.rickowens.eu* Ⓜ *Palais Royal–Musée du Louvre.*

Saint Laurent. Yves Saint Laurent revolutionized women's wear in the 1970s, putting pants in couture shows for the first time. His safari jackets, "le smoking" suits, Russian-boho collections, and tailored *Belle de Jour* suits are considered fashion landmarks—so his are big shoes to fill. Hedi Slimane, successor to the controversial Stefano Pilati in 2012, has managed to stir things up in his brief tenure, renaming the brand and nose-tweaking fashion journalists. Despite the controversy, there's no doubt he's returned the brand to its roots, drawing praise for his inspired collections. The menswear shop, at No. 32 rue du Faubourg St-Honoré, features new and sleekly beautiful riffs on Saint Laurent's classic satin-lapel tuxes. ✉ *38 and 32 rue du Faubourg St-Honoré, 8e, Louvre/Tuileries* ☎ *01–42–65–74–59* ⊕ *www.ysl.com* Ⓜ *Concorde.*

Stella McCartney. Stella McCartney has an uncanny knack for knowing what women want. Since launching her own label in 2001, she has steadily built on her success. Season after season, McCartney channels the prevailing mood into innovative takes on classics like the boyfriend blazer, the silk sheath, and the cigarette jean. The clothes flatter real women, and the steep prices can be justified by their staying power (and the fact that nothing was killed in the making). ✉ *114–121 Galerie de Valois, 1er, Louvre/Tuileries* ☎ *01–47–03–03–80* ⊕ *www.stellamccartney.com* Ⓜ *Palais Royal–Musée du Louvre.*

Tara Jarmon. Tara Jarmon has her bases covered when it comes to that coveted French élan: sleek designs, excellent quality, luxe fabrics, and prices well within the stratosphere. With styles that vie with the high-profile designers, and accessories to match, this label is fast becoming the chic Parisian's wardrobe essential. ✉ *400 rue St-Honoré, 1er, Louvre/Tuileries* ☎ *01–40–15–02–13* ⊕ *www.tarajarmon.com* Ⓜ *Concorde.*

Vanessa Bruno. Vanessa Bruno stirs up a new brew of feminine dressing: some androgynous pieces (skinny pants) plus delicacy (filmy tops) with a dash of whimsy (lace insets). Separates are coveted for their sleek styling, gorgeous colors, and unerring sexiness. Wardrobe staples include perfectly proportioned cotton tops and sophisticated dresses. Athé, the

CLOSE UP

Jardin du Palais Royal

Paris's secret oasis no more. With the arrival of Marc Jacobs, Rick Owens, and Stella McCartney, the palace and gardens of the Jardin du Palais-Royal officially join the ranks of fashion hot spots. Not that it ever lacked allure; those in the know have come here for fabulous shoes, artisanal perfumes, and vintage haute couture for years. Shopping in Paris is no common experience, but shopping at the Palais-Royal—under its neat rows of lime and chestnut trees and vaulted arcades—is almost worship.

Entering the gardens from Rue St-Honoré, you'll see the Colonnes de Buren, a series of sculpted columns, covering the first inner courtyard. Galerie de Montpensier is the long arcade to your left; Galerie de Valois flanks the gardens to your right.

GALERIE DE VALOIS

No. 156: **Pierre Hardy:** head-turning heels that tantalize while they flatter, with some of Paris's best bags to match (☎ 01–42–60–59–75).

No. 142: **Les Salons du Palais-Royal Serge Lutens:** perfumes and exclusive scents from the titular "nose" par excellence are sold in this jewel-like boutique (☎ 01–49–27–09–09).

No. 138–139: **Jérôme l'Huillier:** color-saturated silks in sexy, mod styles, with sleek new takes on the wrap dress (☎ 01–49–26–07–07).

No. 130–133: **Rick Owens:** over-the-top rock-star glamour with an avant-garde edge, he makes serious fashion waves worldwide (☎ 01–40–20–42–52).

No. 128–129: **Maison Fabre:** proving that practice makes perfect, it's been crafting some of the most beautiful

gloves in the world since 1924 (☎ 01–42–60–75–88).

No. 124: **Acne Studios:** Swedish design for men and women who demand it all—style, fit, comfort, and plenty of cool (☎ 01–42–60–16–62).

No. 114–121: **Stella McCartney:** McCartney has A-List cred, and her wearable-yet-sexy separates are a must in any well-appointed wardrobe (☎ 01–47–03–03–80).

GALERIE DE MONTPENSIER

No. 56–62: **Marc Jacobs:** from flapper to prom queen to motorcycle moll—iconic American style updated (☎ 01–55–35–02–60).

No. 31: **Gabrielle Geppert:** vintage haute couture at its best: why buy a knockoff when you can have the original? Bags, jewelry, and sunglasses, too (☎ 01–42–61–53–52).

No. 20–24: **Didier Ludot:** vintage French couture from the '20s to the '80s; plus his personal take on the little black dress across the gardens at 125 Galerie de Valois (☎ 01–42–96–06–56).

16

diffusion line, flies off the racks, so if you see something you love, grab it. Bruno's shoes and accessories are the cherry on the cake: her ultrapopular sequin-striped totes inspired an army of knockoffs. ✉ *12 rue de Castiglione, 1er, Louvre/Tuileries* ☎ *01–42–61–44–60* ⊕ *www. vanessabruno.com* Ⓜ *Pyramides.*

Ventilo. Ventilo brings cool ethnic style to the city. Where else can you find a bright-fuchsia silk-velvet bolero jacket with sequin appliqué or a modern Mongol leather coat lined in fur? There's also room for classics to mix and match, such as handmade wool turtlenecks and a pleated raincoat that fit perfectly. ✉ *27 bis, rue du Louvre, 2e, Louvre/Tuileries* ☎ *01–44–76–82–95* ⊕ *www.ventilo.fr* Ⓜ *Louvre.*

Veronique Leroy. Veronique Leroy highlights a woman's silhouette while paying close attention to details like open seam work and perfect draping. Slinky silk-jersey dresses, form-flattering sweaters in dusky hues, and lacy dresses with come-hither necklines help explain her current darling-of-the-fashion-world status. ✉ *10 rue d'Alger, 1er, Louvre/Tuileries* ☎ *01–49–26–93–59* ⊕ *www.veroniqueleroy.com* Ⓜ *Tuileries.*

FOOD AND TREATS

Jean-Paul Hévin. Forty masterful varieties of chocolate and some of the best pastries in Paris earned Jean-Paul Hévin his world-class chocolatier status. Devotees will be pleased to know that there's also an outpost near the Luxembourg Gardens at 3 rue Vavin. ✉ *231 rue St-Honoré, 1er, Louvre/Tuileries* ☎ *01–55–35–35–96* ⊕ *www.jeanpaulhevin.com* Ⓜ *Louvre/Tuileries.*

Ladurée. Founded in 1862, Ladurée oozes period atmosphere—even at the big Champs-Élysées branch (No. 75)—but nothing beats the original tearoom on Rue Royale, with its pint-size tables and frescoed ceiling. Ladurée claims a familial link to the invention of the *macaron*, and appropriately there's a fabulous selection of these lighter-than-air cookies. Classic flavors include pistachio, salted caramel, and coffee; others, like violet–black currant, chestnut, and lime-basil, are available seasonally. When you've worked your way through the *macaron* menu, try a cup of their famously rich hot chocolate with a flaky mille-feuille. ■**TIP**➔ Ladurée's stylish boxes alone are worth the purchase; filled with sweet treats, they make memorable gifts. ✉ *16 rue Royale, 8e, Louvre/Tuileries* ☎ *01–42–60–21–79* ⊕ *www.laduree.com* Ⓜ *Madeleine.*

HOME DECOR

E. Dehillerin. E. Dehillerin has been around since 1820. Never mind the creaky stairs; the huge range of professional cookware in enamel, stainless steel, or fiery copper is gorgeous. Julia Child was a regular. ✉ *18–20 rue Coquillière, 1er, Louvre/Tuileries* ☎ *01–42–36–53–13* ⊕ *www.e-dehillerin.fr* Ⓜ *Les Halles.*

Gien. Gien has been making fine china since 1821. The faience spans traditional designs—such as those inspired by Italian majolica, blue-and-white delftware, and French toile—as well as contemporary looks. ✉ *18 rue de l'Arcade, 8e, Louvre/Tuileries* ☎ *01–42–66–52–32* ⊕ *www. gien.com* Ⓜ *Madeleine.*

La Chalcographie du Louvre. More than 13,000 prints from the Louvre's collection can be had at the museum's own print shop for a relatively minor investment. The most popular images are in stock, easy to view, and can walk right out with you. ✉ *Louvre museum store, 1er, Louvre/Tuileries* ☎ *01–40–20–59–35* ⊕ *www.chalcographiedulouvre.com* Ⓜ *Palais-Royal–Musée du Louvre.*

JEWELRY AND ACCESSORIES

Fodor'sChoice **Cartier.** Cartier flashes its jewels at more than half a dozen boutiques in
★ the city. Longtime favorites such as the Trinity rings and Tank watches compete for attention with the newer Panthère, Love, and Caresse d'Orchidées collections. ✉ *23 pl. Vendôme, 1er, Louvre/Tuileries* ☎ *01–44–55–32–20* ⊕ *www.cartier.fr* Ⓜ *Tuileries, Concorde.*

Dary's. This wonderful, family-run cavern teeming with artists, actors, models, and jewelry lovers offers an Ali Baba–ish shopping experience. You'll need to take your time though, because the walls are filled with row upon row of antique jewels from every era, more modern second-hand jewelry, and drawer upon drawer of vintage one-of-a-kinds. ✉ *362 rue St-Honoré, 1er, Louvre/Tuileries* ☎ *01–42–60–95–23* Ⓜ *Tuileries.*

LINGERIE

Fodor'sChoice **Alice Cadolle.** Alice Cadolle, which has been selling lingerie to Parisians
★ since 1889, offers some of the city's most sumptuous couture undergarments. Ready-to-wear bras, corsets, and sleepwear fill the Rue Cambon boutique; made-to-measure service is provided at 255 rue St-Honoré. ✉ *4 rue Cambon, 1er, Louvre/Tuileries* ☎ *01 42 60 94 22* ⊕ *www.cadolle.com* Ⓜ *Concorde.*

Fodor'sChoice **Chantal Thomass.** The legendary lingerie diva is back with a *Pillow Talk–*
★ meets–Louis XIV–inspired boutique. This is French naughtiness at its best, striking the perfect balance between playful and seductive. Sheer silk negligees edged in Chantilly lace and lascivious bra-and-corset sets punctuate the signature line. ✉ *211 rue St-Honoré, 1er, Louvre/Tuileries* ☎ *01 42 60 40 56* ⊕ *www.chantalthomass.fr* Ⓜ *Tuileries.*

Fifi Chachnil. Fifi Chachnil girls are real boudoir babes, with a fondness for quilted-satin bed jackets and lingerie in candy-land colors. The look is cheerfully sexy, with checkered push-up bras, frilled white knickers, and peach-satin corsets. ✉ *231 rue St-Honoré, 1er, Louvre/Tuileries* ☎ *01–42–61–21–83* ⊕ *fifichachnil.com* Ⓜ *Tuileries.*

SHOES, HANDBAGS, AND LEATHER GOODS

Causse. Causse dates back to a time when the quality of the gloves said it all. Supple python or cherry-lacquered lambskin may not have been the rage in 1892 when this eminent glove maker was founded, but its 100-plus years in the business add up to unparalleled style and fit. ✉ *12 rue de Castiglione, 1er, Louvre/Tuileries* ☎ *01–49–26–91–43* ⊕ *www.causse-gantier.fr* Ⓜ *Tuileries.*

Goyard. These colorful totes are the choice of royals, blue bloods, and the like (clients have included Sir Arthur Conan Doyle, Gregory Peck, and the Duke and Duchess of Windsor). Parisians swear by their durability and longevity; they're copious enough for a mile-long baguette, and durable enough for a magnum of champagne. What's more, they easily transition into ultrachic beach or diaper bags. ✉ *233 rue*

16

St-Honoré, 1er, Louvre/Tuileries ☎ *01–42–60–57–04* ⊕ *www.goyard. com* Ⓜ *Tuileries.*

Hermès. The go-to for those who prefer their logo discrete yet still crave instant recognition, Hermès was established as a saddlery in 1837; then went on to create the eternally chic Kelly (named for Grace Kelly) and Birkin (named for Jane Birkin) handbags. The silk scarves are legendary for their rich colors and intricate designs, which change yearly. Other accessories are also extremely covetable: enamel bracelets, dashing silk-twill ties, and small leather goods. During semiannual sales, in January and July, prices are slashed up to 50%, and the crowds line up for blocks. ✉ *24 rue du Faubourg St-Honoré, 8e, Louvre/Tuileries* ☎ *01–40–17–47–17* ⊕ *www.hermes.com* Ⓜ *Concorde.*

Lancaster. A household name in France for 100 years, Lancaster has a reputation for style and craftsmanship. Its bags are chic and sporty, with an emphasis on practicality; and all the classic models are available in this new spaceship-modern boutique. Look for the popular cross-body Versailles bag (it's made of patent leather or soft cowhide and comes in a rainbow of colors), along with exclusive designs sold only here, some in genuine reptile. ✉ *422 rue St-Honoré, 1er, Louvre/Tuileries* ☎ *01–42–28–88–88* ⊕ *www.lancaster-paris.com.*

Maison Fabre. Until you've eased into an exquisite pair of gloves handcrafted by Fabre, you probably haven't experienced the sensation of having a second skin far superior to your own. Founded in 1924, this is one of Paris's historic *gantiers*. Styles range from classic to haute: picture elbow-length croc leather, coyote-fur mittens, and peccary driving gloves. ✉ *128–129 Galerie de Valois, 1er, Louvre/Tuileries* ☎ *01–42–60–75–88* ⊕ *www.maisonfabre.com* Ⓜ *Palais Royal–Musée du Louvre.*

Moynat. Designed to evoke a wheel, as in "we're going places, baby," this gleaming boutique showcases the new Moynat, while evoking the brand's 19th- and early 20th-century glory days, when Pauline Moynat was the queen of luggage design. Women's bags are sleek, expertly engineered, and exceedingly beautiful (the reversible leather tote in either bone/coral or mocha/taupe is an instant classic). Men's briefcases are convex on one side to avoid bumping legs: an ingenious design that harkens back to the advent of automobile travel, when Moynat's trunks were curved to hug a car roof. Crocodile bags, silk scarves, and a thriving bespoke service are cherries on the cake. ✉ *348 rue Saint Honoré, 1er, Louvre/Tuileries* ☎ *01–47–03–83–90* ⊕ *moynat.com* Ⓜ *Tuileries.*

Pierre Hardy. Pierre Hardy completes the triumvirate (with Vivier and Louboutin) of anointed Paris shoe designers. Armed with a pedigree—Dior, Hermès, Balenciaga—Hardy opened his own boutique in 2003 and made serious waves. Luxe bags are ever popular and the shoes are unmistakable: sky-scraping platforms and wedges or demure kitten heels double as sculpture with breathtaking details. His sensational bags became instant classics. ✉ *Palais Royal Gardens, 156 Galerie de Valois, 1er, Louvre/Tuileries* ☎ *01–42–60–59–75* ⊕ *www.pierrehardy. com* Ⓜ *Palais Royal–Musée du Louvre.*

Fodor'sChoice ★ **Renaud Pellegrino.** Just steps away from the Palais Royal, Renaud Pellegrino is a black-book address for style icons like Catherine Deneuve and Paloma Picasso, who eschew status labels in favor of individuality and staying power. A black lace-over-leather bag or an azure tote with tiny silver grommets brings glamour to daytime looks, and a Mondrian-esque patchwork of a silk-satin adds magnificence to eveningwear. ✉ *149 rue St-Honoré, 1er, Louvre/Tuileries* ☎ *01–42–61–75–32* ⊕ *www.renaudpellegrino.com* Ⓜ *Palais Royal–Musée du Louvre.*

Roger Vivier. Known for decades for his Pilgrim-buckle shoes and inventive heels, Roger Vivier's name is being resurrected through the creativity of über-Parisienne Inès de la Fressange and the expertise of shoe designer Bruno Frisoni. The results are easily some of the best shoes in town: leather boots that mold to the calf perfectly, towering rhinestone-encrusted or feathered platforms for evening, and vertiginous crocodile pumps. ✉ *29 rue du Faubourg St-Honoré, 8e, Louvre/Tuileries* ☎ *01–53–43–00–85* ⊕ *www.rogervivier.com* Ⓜ *Concorde.*

SHOPPING GALLERIES
Galerie Véro-Dodat. Galerie Véro-Dodat was built in 1826. At what is now the Café de l'Époque, just at the gallery's entrance, the French writer Gérard de Nerval took his last drink before heading to Châtelet to hang himself. The glass-ceilinged gallery has painted medallions and copper pillars and shops selling contemporary art, instruments, and leather goods. It's best known, though, for its antiques stores. ✉ *19 rue Jean-Jacques Rousseau, 1er, Louvre/Tuileries* Ⓜ *Louvre.*

LES HALLES
BEAUTY
Anne Sémonin. Anne Sémonin sells skin-care products made out of seaweed and trace elements, as well as essential oils that are popular with fashion models. ✉ *2 rue des Petits-Champs, 2e, Les Halles* ☎ *01–42–60–94–66* ⊕ *www.annesemonin.com* Ⓜ *Palais-Royal.*

Nose. This new concept store set out to help tackle the dilemma of finding just the right perfume by offering a personalized service to help identify your ideal fragrance. A bilingual specialist takes you through a seven-step diagnostic to identify your olfactive profile . . . then the smelling begins. With all there is to choose from, one never leaves unsatisfied. You may also browse hard-to-find lines of luxe body lotions, face serums, bath gels, scented candles, and yummy laundry soaps. ■**TIP→** Fans can keep up with promotions and in-store events via the monthly "noseletter." ✉ *20 rue Bachaumont, 2e, Les Halles* ☎ *01–40–26–46–03* ⊕ *www.nose.fr* Ⓜ *Etienne-Marcel.*

CLOTHING
Agnès b. Agnès b embodies the quintessential French approach to easy but stylish dressing. There are many branches, and the clothes are also sold in department stores, but for the fullest range go to Rue du Jour, where Agnès takes up much of the street (women's and children's wear is at No. 6, menswear at No. 3). For women, classics include sleek black-leather jackets, flattering black jersey separates, and trademark wide-stripe T-shirts. Children love the two-tone T-shirts proclaiming their age. And the stormy-gray velour or corduroy suits you see on those slouchy, scarf-clad men? Agnès b. ✉ *3 and 6 rue du Jour, 1er, Les Halles* ☎ *01–42–33–04–13* ⊕ *europe.agnesb.com* Ⓜ *Châtelet–Les Halles.*

16

Et Vous Stock. This is a great alternative to the regular boutiques because the clothes are still very much in style and are 50% off. You'd never know you were in a stock store if you walked in off the street. There are accessories, too. ⊠ *17 rue Turbigo, 2e, Les Halles* ☎ *01–40–13–04–12* Ⓜ *Étienne Marcel.*

G-Star Store. This is a haven for fans of raw denim. It, uniquely, stocks the designs of the Dutch-based label G-Star, whose highly desirable jeans have replaced Levi's as the ones to be seen in. There are also military-inspired clothing, bags, and T-shirts. ⊠ *46 rue Étienne Marcel, 2e, Les Halles* ☎ *01–42–21–44–33* ⊕ *www.g-star.com* Ⓜ *Étienne Marcel.*

Yohji Yamamoto. Yohji Yamamoto made his name in the 1980s as a master of the drape, fold, and twist. The design legend favors predominantly black clothes that are both functional and edgy. A canny fashion investment, these pieces never go out of style. You'll find ready-to-wear for men and women at the Louvre boutique, along with the Y's casual line. ⊠ *25 rue du Louvre, 1er, Les Halles* ☎ *01–42–21–42–93* ⊕ *www. yohjiyamamoto.co.jp* Ⓜ *Étienne Marcel.*

DEPARTMENT STORES

BHV. BHV, short for Bazar de l'Hôtel de Ville, houses an enormous basement hardware store that sells everything from doorknobs to cement mixers and has to be seen to be believed. The fashion offerings for men, women, and kids have been totally revamped, with many of the top labels and a fabulous, not-too-crowded lingerie department on the second floor. But BHV is most noteworthy for its huge selection of high-quality household goods, home-decor material, electronics, and office supplies. If you're looking for typically French household items (those heavy, gold-rimmed café sets, gorgeous French linen, or Savon de Marseille), this is your ticket. The extensive men's store is across the street at 36 rue de la Verrerie. ⊠ *52–64 rue de Rivoli, 4e, Les Halles* ☎ *09–77–40–14–00* Ⓜ *Hôtel de Ville.*

FNAC. Parisians flock to this high profile French "cultural" department store for the huge selection of music and books, as well as photo, TV, and audio equipment. ⊠ *Forum des Halles, 1er, Les Halles* ☎ *01–40–41–40–00* ⊕ *www.fnac.com* Ⓜ *Les Halles* ⊠ *74 av. des Champs-Élysées, 8e, Champs-Élysées* ☎ *01–53–53–64–64* Ⓜ *Franklin-D.-Roosevelt.*

HOME DECOR

A. Simon. This is where Parisian chefs come for their kitchen needs—from plates and glasses to pans and wooden spoons. The quality is excellent and the prices reasonable. ⊠ *48 rue Montmartre, 2e, Les Halles* ☎ *01–42–33–71–65* Ⓜ *Étienne Marcel.*

LINGERIE

Princesse Tam Tam. Princesse Tam Tam is the go-to for affordable and beguiling bra-and-panty sets that combine sex appeal and playfulness. Designed for mileage as much as allure, the softer-than-soft cotton wrap tops and nighties, lace-edged silk tap pants, camisoles, slips, and adorable separates for the boudoir are comfortable *and* comely. ⊠ *5 rue Montmartre, 1er, Les Halles* ☎ *01–45–08–50–69* ⊕ *www. princessetamtam.com* Ⓜ *Les Halles.*

MARKETS

Rue Montorgueil. This old-fashioned market street has evolved into a chic Bobo zone; its stalls now thrive amid stylish cafés and the oldest oyster counter in Paris. ✉ *1er, Les Halles* Ⓜ *Châtelet–Les Halles.*

SHOES, HANDBAGS, AND LEATHER GOODS

Christian Louboutin. These shoes carry their own red carpet with them, thanks to their trademark crimson soles. Whether tasseled, embroidered, or strappy, in Charvet silk or shiny patent leather, the heels are always perfectly balanced. No wonder they set off such legendary legs as Tina Turner's and Gwyneth Paltrow's. ✉ *19 rue Jean-Jacques Rousseau, 1er, Les Halles* ☎ *01–42–36–53–66* ⊕ *www.christianlouboutin. com* Ⓜ *Palais-Royal.*

SHOPPING GALLERIES

Passage du Grand-Cerf. Passage du Grand-Cerf has regained the interest of Parisians. La Parisette, a small boudoir-pink space at No. 1, sells fun accessories, and Marci Noum, at No. 4, riffs on street fashion. Silk bracelets, crystals, and charms can be nabbed at Eric & Lydie and Satellite. ✉ *145 rue St-Denis, 2e, Les Halles* Ⓜ *Étienne Marcel.*

SPAS

Spa Nuxe. Spa Nuxe is a hip spa by the creators of Nuxe skin-care products. The ancient cellar with arched corridors has cozy treatment rooms. Try the *rêverie orientale*: a two-and-a-half-hour hammam, body scrub, and detoxifying wrap, plus massage (€220). There is a second branch in the Printemps department store and another in the Hotel Square in the 16th arrondissement. ✉ *32-34 rue Montorgueil, 1er, Les Halles* ☎ *01–42–36–65–65* ⊕ *www.nuxe.com* Ⓜ *Les Halles.*

OPÉRA/GRANDS BOULEVARDS

From the venerable old boutiques on Rue de la Paix to Paris's great grands magasins on Boulevard Haussmann (namely Galeries Lafayette and Au Printemps), there's no shortage of shopping opportunities here. Once you add in the area's elegant covered passages and the storied Drouot auction house, there is enough to keep you busy for a weekend, if not an entire week.

ANTIQUES AND COLLECTIBLES

Drouot auction house. This world-famous auction house draws all the top dealers as well as savvy novices and those who just love the chase. You can find advance information on all auctions online with catalogs detailing the objects on offer. ✉ *9 rue Drouot, 9e, Opéra/Grands Boulevards* ☎ *01–48–00–20–20* ⊕ *www.drouot.com* Ⓜ *Richelieu Drouot.*

BARGAIN SHOPPING

Monoprix. With branches throughout the city, this is *the* French dime store par excellence, stocking everyday items like French cosmetics, groceries, toys, typing paper, kitchen wares, and more. It also has a line of stylish, inexpensive, basic wearables for the whole family—particularly adorable kids clothes—and isn't a bad place to stock up on French chocolate, jams, or *confit de canard* at reasonable prices. ✉ *21 av. de l'Opéra, 1er, Opéra/Grands Boulevards* ☎ *01–42–61–78–08* ⊕ *www. monoprix.fr* Ⓜ *Opéra.*

16

BEAUTY

Make Up For Ever. Poised at the back of a courtyard, this store is a must-stop for makeup artists, models, actresses, and divas of all stripes. The riotous color selection includes hundreds of hues for foundation, eye shadow, powder, and lipstick. ⊠ *5 rue de la Boétie, 8e, Opéra/Grands Boulevards* ☎ *01–53–05–93–31* ⊕ *www.make upforever.fr* Ⓜ *St-Augustin.*

CLOTHING

Anouschka. Anouschka has set up shop in her apartment (by appointment only, Monday to Saturday) and has rack upon rack of vintage clothing dating from the 1930s to the '80s. It's the perfect place to find a '50s cocktail dress in mint condition or a mod jacket for him. A former model herself, she calls this a "designer laboratory," and teams from top fashion houses often pop by looking for inspiration. ⊠ *6 av. du Coq, 9e, Opéra/Grands Boulevards* ☎ *01–48–74–37–00* Ⓜ *St-Lazare, Trinité.*

Charvet. Charvet is the Parisian equivalent of a Savile Row tailor. It's a conservative, aristocratic institution famed for made-to-measure shirts, exquisite ties, and accessories; for garbing John F. Kennedy, Charles de Gaulle, and the Duke of Windsor; and for its regal address. Although the exquisite silk ties, in hundreds of colors and patterns, and custom-made shirts for men are the biggest draw, refined pieces for women and girls, as well as adorable miniatures for boys, round out the collection. ⊠ *28 pl. Vendôme, 1er, Opéra/Grands Boulevards* ☎ *01–42–60–30–70* ⊕ *www.charvet.com* Ⓜ *Opéra.*

Eric Bompard. Eric Bompard provides stylish Parisians with luxury cashmeres in every color, style, and weight; yarns range from light as a feather to a hefty 50-ply for the jaunty caps. The store caters to men and women (there are some kids' models, too). Styles are updated seasonally yet tend toward the classic. ⊠ *75 bd. Haussmann, 8e, Opéra/Grands Boulevards* ☎ *01–42–68–00–73* ⊕ *www.eric-bompard.com* Ⓜ *Miromesnil.*

DEPARTMENT STORES

Au Printemps. Au Printemps is actually three major stores: Printemps de la Maison (home furnishings) on four refurbished floors, Printemps de l'Homme (menswear—six floors of it), and the brilliant Printemps de la Mode (fashion, fashion, fashion), which has everything from cutting-edge to teeny bopper. Be sure to check out the beauty area, with the Nuxe spa, hairdressers, and seemingly every beauty product known to woman under one roof. ⊠ *64 bd. Haussmann, 9e, Opéra/Grands Boulevards* ☎ *01–42–82–50–00* ⊕ *www.printemps.com* Ⓜ *Havre Caumartin, Opéra; RER: Auber.*

Galeries Lafayette. Galeries Lafayette is one of those places that you wander into unawares, leaving hours later a poorer and humbler person.

Inside its flagship building at 40 boulevard Haussmann, a Belle Époque stained-glass dome caps the world's largest perfumery. The store bulges with thousands of designers, and free 25-minute fashion shows are held Friday at 3 pm in the upstairs café to showcase their wares (reservations are a must: call ☎01–42–82–30–25 or email ✉fashionshow@ galerieslafayette.com). Another big draw is the comestibles department, stocked with everything from herbed goat cheese to Iranian caviar. Just across the street at 35 boulevard Haussmann is Galeries Lafayette Maison, which focuses on goods for the fashionable home. ■TIP→ The Montparnasse branch is a pale shadow of the Boulevard Haussmann behemoths. ✉35–40 bd. Haussmann, 9e, Opéra/Grands Boulevards ☎01–42–82–34–56 ⊕ www.galerieslafayette.com Ⓜ Chaussée d'Antin, Opéra, Havre Caumartin.

FOOD AND TREATS

À la Mère de Famille. This enchanting shop is well versed in French regional specialties as well as old-fashioned bonbons, sugar candy, and more. ✉35 rue du Faubourg-Montmartre, 9e, Opéra/Grands Boulevards ☎01–47–70–83–69 ⊕ www.lameredefamille.com Ⓜ Cadet.

Fauchon. Fauchon remains the most iconic of Parisian food stores. It's expanding globally, but the flagship is still behind the Madeleine church. Established in 1886, it sells renowned pâté, honey, jelly, tea, and private-label champagne. Expats come for hard-to-find foreign foods (U.S. pancake mix, British lemon curd); those with a sweet tooth make a beeline to the pâtisserie for airy, ganache-filled macarons. There's a café for a quick bite. Prices can be eye-popping—marzipan fruit for €95 a pound? ✉26 pl. de la Madeleine, 8e, Opéra/Grands Boulevards ☎01–70–39–38–00 ⊕ www.fauchon.com Ⓜ Madeleine.

Hédiard. Hédiard, established in 1854, was famous in the 19th century for its high-quality imported spices. These—along with rare teas and beautifully packaged house brands of jam, mustard, and cookies—continue to make excellent gifts. ✉21 pl. de la Madeleine, 8e, Opéra/Grands Boulevards ☎01–43–12–88–88 ⊕ www.hediard.fr Ⓜ Madeleine.

HOME DECOR

Christofle. Christofle, founded in 1830, has fulfilled all kinds of silver wishes, from a silver service for the Orient Express to a gigantic silver bed. Come for timeless table settings, vases, jewelry boxes, and more. ✉24 rue de la Paix, 2e, Opéra/Grands Boulevards ☎01–42–65–62–43 ⊕ www.christofle.com Ⓜ Opéra.

JEWELRY AND ACCESSORIES

Alexandre Reza. One of Paris's most exclusive jewelers, Alexandre Reza is first and foremost a gemologist. He travels the world looking for the finest stones and then works them into stunning pieces, many of which are replicas of jewels of historical importance. ✉21 pl. Vendôme, 1er, Opéra/Grands Boulevards ☎01–42–61–51–21 ⊕ www.alexandrereza.com Ⓜ Opéra.

Chanel Jewelry. Chanel Jewelry feeds off the iconic design elements of the pearl-draped designer: witness the quilting (reimagined for gold rings), camellias (now brooches), and shooting stars (used for her first

16

jewelry collection in 1932, now appearing as diamond rings). ⊠ *18 pl. Vendôme, 1er, Opéra/Grands Boulevards* ☎ *01–40–98–55–55* ⊕ *www. chanel.com* Ⓜ *Tuileries, Opéra.*

Dinh Van. Dinh Van, just around the corner from Place Vendôme's titan jewelers, thumbs its nose at in-your-face opulence. The look here is refreshingly spare. Best sellers include a hammered gold orb necklace and leather-cord bracelets joined with geometric shapes in white or yellow gold, some with pavé diamonds. ⊠ *16 rue de la Paix, 2e, Opéra/Grands Boulevards* ☎ *01–42–61–74–49* ⊕ *www.dinhvan.com* Ⓜ *Opéra.*

MARKETS

Rue Lévis. This market, near Parc Monceau, has Alsatian specialties and a terrific cheese shop. It's closed Sunday afternoon and Monday. ⊠ *17e, Parc Monceau* Ⓜ *Villiers.*

SHOPPING GALLERIES

Fodor's Choice
★ **Galerie Vivienne.** Galerie Vivienne, between the Bourse and the Palais-Royal, is home to a range of interesting luxury shops as well as a lovely tearoom (A Priori Thé) and a terrific wineshop (Cave Legrand Filles et Fils). Don't leave without checking out the Jean-Paul Gaultier boutique at 6 rue Vivienne. ⊠ *4 rue des Petits-Champs, 2e, Opéra/Grands Boulevards* ⊕ *www.galerie-vivienne.com* Ⓜ *Bourse.*

Passage des Panoramas. Passage des Panoramas, opened in 1799, is the oldest extant arcade and has become a foodie paradise, with no less than five major gourmet destinations. ⊠ *11 bd. Montmartre, 2e, Opéra/ Grands Boulevards* Ⓜ *Opéra, Grands Boulevards.*

Passage Jouffroy. Passage Jouffroy is full of shops selling toys, Oriental furnishings, and cinema books and posters. Pain D'épices, at No. 29, has dollhouse decor. ⊠ *12 bd. Montmartre, 9e, Opéra/Grands Boulevards* Ⓜ *Grands Boulevards.*

Passage Verdeau. Passage Verdeau, across from Passage Jouffroy, has shops carrying antique cameras, comic books, and engravings. Au Bonheur des Dames, at No. 8, has all things embroidery. ⊠ *4–6 rue de la Grange Batelière, 9e, Opéra/Grands Boulevards* Ⓜ *Grands Boulevards.*

TOYS

Pain d'Epices. This shop has anything you can imagine for the French home (and garden) in miniature, including Lilliputian croissants, wine decanters, and minuscule instruments in their cases. Build-it-yourself dollhouses include a 17th-century town house and a boulangerie storefront. Upstairs are do-it-yourself teddy-bear kits and classic toys. ⊠ *29 Passage Jouffroy, 9e, Opéra/Grands Boulevards* ☎ *01–47–70–08–68* ⊕ *www.paindepices.fr* Ⓜ *Grands Boulevards.*

FAMILY
Fodor's Choice
★ **Village JouéClub.** Le Passage des Princes—one of the city's historic covered *passages*—is home to Paris's most comprehensive toy store. Part of a large French chain, the two-level Village JouéClub carries all the usual suspects (Barbie, Disney, Hello Kitty, and the like) plus the better traditional European brands, including Vilac, Moulin Roty, and L'Atelier du Bois. It's made up of more than 10 "shops," each of which is dedicated to a different age group or toy genre. You'll find virtually

every kind of plaything here, so be prepared to linger. ✉ *5 bd. des Italiens, 2e, Opéra/Grands Boulevards* ☎ *01–53–45–41–41* ⊕ *www. joueclub.fr* Ⓜ *Richelieu–Drouot.*

WINE

Lavinia. Lavinia has the largest selection of wine in one spot in Europe—more than 6,000 wines and spirits from all over the world, ranging from the simple to the sublime. On-site there are expert English-speaking sommeliers to help you sort it all out, as well as a wine-tasting bar, a bookshop, and a restaurant. ✉ *3–5 bd. de la Madeleine, 1er, Opéra/Grands Boulevards* ☎ *01–42–97–20–20* ⊕ *www.lavinia.fr* Ⓜ *St-Augustin.*

Les Caves Augé. Les Caves Augé, one of the best wine shops in Paris since 1850, is just the ticket, whether you're looking for a rare vintage, a select Bordeaux, or a seductive champagne for a tête-à-tête. English-speaking Marc Sibard is a well-known aficionado and an affable adviser. ✉ *116 bd. Haussmann, 8e, Opéra/Grands Boulevards* ☎ *01–45–22–16–97* ⊕ *www.cavesauge.com* Ⓜ *St-Augustin.*

MONTMARTRE

16

To avoid an uphill climb, the Abbesses métro stop on Rue de la Vieuville is a good starting point for serious shoppers. From here, descend picturesque Rue des Martyrs all the way down to Notre Dame de Lorette: the route promises a cornucopia of captivating boutiques that sell everything from chic antiques and offbeat fashion to gourmet food.

CLOTHING

A.P.C. Stock. A.P.C. opened its surplus store steps away from Sacré-Coeur. No need to wait for the sales; funky classics can be found here for a whopping 50% off. ✉ *20 rue André del Sarte, 18e, Montmartre* ☎ *01–42–62–10–88* ⊕ *www.apc.fr* Ⓜ *Château Rouge.*

Spree. When Spree first opened, its mission was to give young designers a venue; it has since branched out to include fashion elites like Margiela, Isabel Marant, Comme des Garçons, and Tsumori Chisato. The expertly chosen inventory seems almost curated. A great selection of accessories and jewelry, along with cool furniture and a revolving exhibition of artwork by local artists, complete the gallery feel. ✉ *16 rue la Vieuville, 18e, Montmartre* ☎ *01–42–23–41–40* ⊕ *www.spree.fr* Ⓜ *Abesses.*

FOOD AND TREATS

À l'Étoile d'Or. This quintessential candy shop will delight children of all ages—not to mention chocoholics, as it stocks some famously hard-to-find brands (like Bernachon, from Lyon). Dedicated to French confections, it's a walk back in time, with classic sweets from every Gallic region. Although a tad out of the way, it is worth the trip. ✉ *30 rue Pierre Fontaine, 9e, Montmartre* ☎ *01–48–74–59–55* Ⓜ *Pigalle.*

MARKETS

Fodor'sChoice ★ **Marché aux Puces St-Ouen** (*Clignancourt*). This picturesque market on Paris's northern boundary—open Saturday to Monday, from 9 to 6—still attracts crowds, but its once-unbeatable prices are now a relic. Packed with antiques booths and *brocante* stalls, the century-old, miles-long labyrinth has been undergoing a mild renaissance, with new vintage shops drawing buzz from fashion fans and new destination eateries (including Philippe Starck's hugely chic Ma Cocotte) attracting a hip Paris contingent. That means you can arrive early to pick up the best loot, then linger over an excellent meal or apèro. Be warned—if there's one place in Paris where you need to know how to bargain, this is it! ■ TIP→ If you're arriving by métro, walk under the overpass and take the first left at Rue de Rosiers to reach the center of the market. Note that stands selling dodgy odds and ends (think designer knockoffs and questionable gadgets) set up around the overpass. These blocks are crowded and gritty; be careful with your valuables. ⊠ *18e, Montmartre* ⊕ *www.marcheauxpuces-saintouen.com* Ⓜ *Porte de Clignancourt.*

THE MARAIS

The Marais has stolen the show as the city's hippest shopping destination—and for sheer volume it can't be beat. Rue des Francs Bourgeois and Rue Vieille de Temple form the central retail axis from which the upper and lower Marais branch out. The newest frontier is its northeastern edge (the haut Marais), which is known for ultrastylish boutiques, vintage stores, and design ateliers.

ANTIQUES AND COLLECTIBLES

Village St-Paul. This clutch of streets, in the beautiful historic netherworld tucked between the fringes of the Marais and the banks of the Seine, has many antique shops. ⊠ *Enter from Rue St-Paul, 4e, Marais* ⊕ *www.levillagesaintpaul.com* Ⓜ *St-Paul.*

BARGAIN SHOPPING

L'Habilleur. L'Habilleur is a favorite with the fashion press and anyone looking for a deal. For women there's a great selection from designers like Firma, Roberto Collina, and Giorgio Brato. Men can find elegant suits from Paul Smith at slashed prices. ⊠ *44 rue de Poitou, 3e, Marais* ☎ *01–48–87–77–12* ⊕ *lhabilleur.fr* Ⓜ *St-Sébastien Froissart.*

Fodor's Choice ★ **Merci.** The world's most gorgeous charity shop was put together by the founders of the luxury kid's line, Bonpoint. Everything here is high-concept (the designer fashions, furniture, antiques, jewelry, and housewares have been plucked straight from top-tier designers), and it's all offered at a discount. Five percent of the proceeds are earmarked to aid disadvantaged children in Madagascar. The store's three cafés make lingering among Paris's fashion elite a pleasure. ⊠ *111 bd. Beaumarchais, 3e, Marais* ☎ *01–42–77–00–33* ⊕ *www.merci-merci.com* Ⓜ *St-Sebastien Froissart.*

Zadig & Voltaire Stock. Here you'll find new unsold stock from last season. There's a great selection of beautiful cashmere sweaters, silk slip dresses, rocker jeans, and leather jackets, all in their signature luscious colors for 30%–70% off. ⊠ *22 rue Bourg Tibourg, 4e, Marais* ☎ *01–44–59–39–62* ⊕ *www.zadig-et-voltaire.com* Ⓜ *Hôtel de Ville.*

BEAUTY

L'Artisan Parfumeur. L'Artisan Parfumeur is known for its own brand of scents for the home plus perfumes with names like Mûre et Musc (Blackberry and Musk). It also carries sumptuous shower gels and body lotions in the popular fragrances. ⊠ *32 rue du Bourg Tibourg, 4e, Marais* ☎ *01–48–04–55–66* ⊕ *www.artisanparfumeur.com* Ⓜ *Hôtel de Ville.*

BOOKS AND STATIONERY

Comptoir de l'Image. This is where designers John Galliano, Marc Jacobs, and Emanuel Ungaro stock up on old copies of *Vogue, Harper's Bazaar,* and *The Face.* You'll also find trendy magazines like *Dutch, Purple,* and *Spoon;* designer catalogs from the past; and rare photo books. ⊠ *44 rue de Sévigné, 3e, Marais* ☎ *01–42–72–03–92* Ⓜ *St-Paul.*

CHILDREN'S CLOTHING

Bonton. Bonton takes the prize for most-coveted duds among those who like to think of children as fashion accessories. (Moms may find some useful wardrobe pointers, too.) Sassy separates in saturated colors layer beautifully, look amazing, and manage to be perfectly kid-friendly. Bonton sells toys and furniture, too. ⊠ *5 bd. des Filles du Calvaire, 3e, Marais* ☎ *01–53–63–14–41* ⊕ *www.bonton.fr* Ⓜ *Filles du Calvaire.*

CLOTHING

AB33. AB33 is like a sleek boudoir—complete with comfy chair and scented candles—and the clothes here are unabashedly feminine. Separates in luxury fabrics from top designers, irresistible silk lingerie, dainty jewelry, and a selection of accessories celebrate that certain French *je ne sais quoi.* ⊠ *33 rue Charlot, 3e, Marais* ☎ *01–42–71–02–82* ⊕ *ab33. fr* Ⓜ *Filles du Calvaire.*

Abou d'Abi Bazar. A one-stop outfitter, Abou d'Abi Bazar organizes its collection of up-to-the-moment designers on color-coordinated racks that highlight the asymmetrical design of this opulent boutique. Artsy and bohemian all at once, there is plenty to covet here, from frothy Isabel Marant silk-organza blouses to sumptuous cashmere-blend tunics and satin shirtwaist dresses. Reasonably priced picks make it a desirable destination. ⊠ *125 rue Vieille du Temple, 3e, Marais* ☎ *01–42–71–13–26* ⊕ *www.aboudabibazar.com* Ⓜ *Filles du Calvaire.*

Fodor's Choice ★ **Azzedine Alaïa.** Darling of the fashion set, thanks to his perfectly proportioned "king of cling" dresses, Alaïa is considered a master at his game. You don't have to be under 20 to look good in his garments; Tina Turner wears them well, as does every other beautiful woman with the courage and the curves. His boutique/workshop/apartment is covered with artwork by Julian Schnabel and is not the kind of place you casually wander into out of curiosity: the sales staff immediately makes you feel awkward in that distinctive Parisian way. ■TIP→ Think $3,500 is too much for a dress? The Alaïa stock store (same building, different entrance) takes 50% off last season's styles, samples, and gently worn catwalk items. Access it at 18 rue de la Verrerie. ⊠ *7 rue de Moussy, 4e, Marais* ☎ *01–42–72–19–19* ⊕ *www.alaia.fr* Ⓜ *Hôtel de Ville.*

Comptoir des Cotonniers. Comfortable, affordable, *au courant* clothes make this chain popular. Its reputation is built on smart, wearable styles

16

that stress ease over fussiness. Separates in natural fibers—cotton, silk, and cashmere blends—can be light and breezy or cozy and warm, but are always soft, flattering, and in a range of beautiful colors. Styles for moms and daughters ages four and up. ⊠ *33 rue des Francs-Bourgeois, 4e, Marais* ☎ *01–42–76–95–33* ⊕ *www.comptoirdescotonniers. com* Ⓜ *St-Paul.*

COS. COS—which stands for Collection of Style—is the H&M group's answer to fashion sophisticates, who flock here in droves for high-concept, minimalist design with serious attention to quality tailoring and fabrics at a reasonable price. Classic accessories and shoes look more expensive than they are. ⊠ *4 rue des Rosiers, 4e, Marais* ☎ *01–44–54– 37–70* ⊕ *www.cosstores.com* Ⓜ *St-Paul.*

Et Vous. Et Vous takes its cue from the catwalk, turning out affordable, extremely well-cut clothing: pants (low waist/slim hip), knee-skimming skirts, chunky sweaters, and classic work wear with individual details. ⊠ *17 rue de Sévigné, 4e, Marais* ☎ *01–44–54–94–14* Ⓜ *St-Paul.*

Free 'P' Star. Don't let the chaos at Free 'P' Star discourage you—there's gold in them there bins. Determined seekers on a budget can reap heady rewards, at least according to the young hipsters who flock here for anything from a floor-sweeping peasant skirt to a cropped chinchilla cape. ■TIP→ A second Marais branch—at 61 rue de la Verrerie—is equally stuffed to the gills. Happy hunting! ⊠ *8 rue Sainte Croix de la Bretonnerie, 4e, Marais* ☎ *01–42–76–03–72* ⊕ *www.freepstar.com* Ⓜ *Hôtel de Ville.*

FrenchTrotters. The flagship store features an understated collection of contemporary French-made classic clothes and accessories for men and women that emphasize quality fabrics, style, and cut over trendiness. You'll also find a handpicked collection of exclusive collaborations with cutting-edge French brands (like sleek leather-and-suede booties by Avril Gau for FrenchTrotters), as well as FrenchTrotters namesake label, and a limited selection of housewares for chic Parisian apartments. ⊠ *128 rue Vieille du Temple, 3e, Marais* ☎ *01–44–61–00–14* ⊕ *www.frenchtrotters.fr* Ⓜ *Saint-Sébastien Froissart, Filles du Calvaire.*

L'Eclaireur. This Rue de Sevigné boutique is Paris's touchstone for edgy, up-to-the-second styles. L'Eclaireur's knack for uncovering new talent and championing established visionaries is legendary—no surprise after 30 years in the business. Hard-to-find geniuses, like leather wizard Isaac Sellam and British prodigy Paul Harnden, cohabit with luxe labels such as Ann Demeulemeester, Haider Ackermann, and Lanvin. ■TIP→ There's a second Marais outpost at 12 rue Mahler. ⊠ *40 rue de Sevigné, 3e, Marais* ☎ *01–48–87–10–22* ⊕ *www.leclaireur.com* Ⓜ *St-Paul.*

La Jolie Garde-Robe. Could that minutely pleated, full-length black organdy gown prominently displayed front and center really be a genuine, circa 1955 Madame Grès couture gown? Yes! And a steal at $2,000. There's plenty more to tempt you at this pretty boutique, specializing in ready-to-wear and designer styles from the '30s to the '80s. While the collection isn't huge, it's chosen with a connoisseur's eye. ⊠ *15 rue Commines, 3e, Marais* ☎ *01–42–72–13–90* Ⓜ *Filles du Calvaire.*

Majestic Filatures. Wearing a Majestic cashmere-cotton blend T-shirt, dress, cardigan, or blazer is like spending the day cocooned in your favorite jammies. Fans have been known to buy five pairs of the silky soft leggings in one go, just to be sure never to run out. The fact that you'll look totally stylish is just gilding the lily. ⊠ *7 rue des Francs Bourgeois, 4e, Marais* ☎ *01–57–40–62–34* ⊕ *www.majesticfilatures. com* Ⓜ *St-Paul.*

Paule Ka. Paule Ka has that movie-star glamour down pat: for daytime, perfectly cut silk, belted shirtdresses with matching coats; for evening, gemstone-studded gowns and furs. Both Hepburns (Audrey *and* Katherine) could have made this their second home. ⊠ *20 rue Malher, 4e, Marais* ☎ *01–40–29–96–03* ⊕ *www.pauleka.com* Ⓜ *St-Paul.*

Pretty Box. The owners of Pretty Box have scoured Europe for unique pieces from the '20s through the '80s. Women love the super-stylish belts, shoes, and bags—many in reptile—sold here for a fraction of what they'd cost new, along with an eccentric selection of cool separates and Betty Page-era lingerie. The men's collection includes vintage French military coats and riotously patterned '70s Pierre Cardin shirts. ⊠ *46 rue de Saintonge, 3e, Marais* ☎ *01–48–04–81–71* Ⓜ *Saint-Sébastien.*

Fodor'sChoice ★ **Ra.** Straight out of fashion forward Antwerp, the high-concept Ra boutique is part fashion laboratory part symbolist salon, where the line between outfit and costume blur in the most delightful ways. Mainstays, like Juun J, Rodart, and Gareth Pugh, mingle with an ever-changing roster of avant-garde newcomers—Meadham Kirchhoff, Rad Hourani, and shoe designer Iris Van Herpen among them—who like to shake things up with whimsy, humor, and more than a little madness. Expect outrageous accessories and a choice selection of vintage, too. ⊠ *14 rue de la Corderie, 3e, Marais* ☎ *01–42–74–04–07* ⊕ *www.ra13.be* Ⓜ *Republique.*

16

Samy Chalon. Samy Chalon brings hand-knits into the 21st century with inspired shapes and colors. Updates on the classics are never bulky and ever flattering. Come for form-fitting cashmeres, long mohair wrap coats in deep crimson or indigo, along with light-as-air skirts, and summer dresses made from vintage designer silk scarves. ⊠ *24 rue Charlot, 3e, Marais* ☎ *01–44–59–39–16* ⊕ *samy-chalon.lexception.com* Ⓜ *Filles du Calvaire.*

Shine. Even in its trendy Marais location, this boutique lives up to its name. Retro and übermodern, it deals in only the sharper edge of chic (with a clientele to match): Marc by Marc Jacobs, Alexander Wang, Carven, and Equipment, plus accessories. ⊠ *15 rue de Poitou, 3e, Marais* ☎ *01–48–05–80–10* Ⓜ *Filles du Calvaire.*

Studio W. If you're nostalgic for the days of Studio 54, sashay over to Studio W, where a rare Loris Azzaro gold-chain top or a plunging Guy Laroche beaded couture dress in crimson mousseline have Liza and Bianca written all over them. With plenty of jewelry, shoes, bags, and even gloves to match, this elegant boutique is a must-see for fashion divas who don't mind spending a little more for sublimity. ⊠ *21 rue du Pont aux Choux, 3e, Marais* ☎ *01–44–78–05–02* Ⓜ *St.-Sébastien Froissart.*

Surface to Air. Promoting itself as a style lab and art gallery rather than a straight-on boutique, Surface to Air has become the hipster's label of choice. The focus here is on cool, understated design with an air of counterculture chic. Women's separates range from metallic jeans to asymmetrical minidresses, along with cool shoes and accessories; menswear includes enigmatic T-shirts, streamlined jeans, and cropped leather jackets. ⊠ *108 rue Vieille du Temple, 3e, Marais* ☎ *01–44–61–76–27* ⊕ *www.surfacetoair.com* Ⓜ *St-Sébastien-Froissart.*

Swildens. Swildens pioneered the haut Marais and has since gained an ardent following of street-smart twenty- and thirtysomethings who insist as much on comfort as they do on cool. Slouchy separates in natural fibers and fetching colors are punctuated by pieces in leather and shearling, along with belted cardigans and long, drapey sweaters that can be worn almost year-round. The clothes accomplish that rare feat of being both of-the-moment and timeless. ⊠ *22 rue de Poitou, 3e, Marais* ☎ *01–42–71–19–12* ⊕ *www.swildens.fr* Ⓜ *St-Sébastien Froissart.*

Vintage Clothing Paris. It's worth a detour to the Marais's outer limits to visit Vintage Clothing Paris, where the racks read like an A-list of designer greats—Yves Saint Laurent, Hermès, Balman, Valentino, Lagerfeld, Mugler, just to name a few. Brigitte Petit's minimalist shop is the fashion insider's go-to spot for rare pieces that stand out in a crowd, like a circa 1985 Alaia suede skirt with peek-a-boo grommets and a jaunty Yves Saint Laurent Epoch Russe hooded cape. ⊠ *10 rue de Crussol, 11e, Marais* ☎ *01–48–07–16–40* ⊕ *www.vintageclothingparis. com* Ⓜ *Filles du Calvaire, Oberkampf.*

Zadig & Voltaire. Zadig & Voltaire rocks the young fashionistas, offering street wear at its best: racy camisoles, cashmere sweaters in gorgeous colors, cropped leather jackets, and form-fitting pants to cosset those tiny French derrieres. ⊠ *42 rue des Francs Bourgeois, 3e, Marais* ☎ *01–44–54–00–60* ⊕ *www.zadig-et-voltaire.com* Ⓜ *St-Paul.*

FOOD AND TREATS

Izraël. Izraël is not called the "*épicerie du monde*" for nothing. It's the one-stop shop for any spice under the sun, plus those hard-to-find items you'd otherwise spend days tracking down. Overflowing bins of every variety of candied fruit, nuts, beans, olives, pickles, and preserved fish and the perfume of exotic spices give this tiny shop the air of an exotic bazaar. You'll also find all manner of canned goods, candies, rare spirits, and baking necessities. ⊠ *30 rue François Miron, 4e, Marais* ☎ *01–42–72–66–23* Ⓜ *St-Paul.*

Jacques Genin. Pared down to the essentials, Genin offers the essence of great chocolate: not too sweet, with handpicked seasonal ingredients for the velvety ganaches. ⊠ *133 rue de Turenne, 3e, Marais* ☎ *01–45–77–29–01* ⊕ *jacquesgenin.fr* Ⓜ *Filles du Calvaire, Oberkampf.*

Le Palais des Thés. Le Palais des Thés is a comprehensive experience— white tea, green tea, black tea, tea from China, Japan, Indonesia, South America, and more. Try one of the flavored teas such as Hammam, a traditional Turkish recipe with date pulp, orange flower, rose, and red berries. ⊠ *64 rue Vieille du Temple, 3e, Marais* ☎ *01–48–87–80–60* ⊕ *www.palaisdesthes.com* Ⓜ *St-Paul.*

Mariage Frères. Mariage Frères, with its colonial *charme* and wooden counters, has 100-plus years of tea purveying behind it. Choose from more than 450 blends from 32 countries, not to mention teapots, teacups, books, and tea-flavor biscuits and candies. High tea and light lunches are served here and at several other Paris locations. ✉ *30 rue du Bourg-Tibourg, 4e, Marais* ☎ *01–42–72–28–11* ⊕ *www.mariagefreres.com* Ⓜ *Hôtel de Ville.*

Meert. The first Paris offshoot of the famous patisserie and tea salon in Lille (one of France's oldest) specializes in the *gauffre*, a delicate waffle handmade in the original 19th-century molds and wrapped in gilt-paper packages. Native to Belgium and northern France, Meert's version is treasured for its light cream center perfumed with Madagascar vanilla. There are also chocolates, pastries, and flavored *guimauves*, the airy French marshmallows. ✉ *16 rue Elzévir, 3e, Marais* ☎ *01–49–96–56–90* ⊕ *www.meert.fr* Ⓜ *St. Paul.*

HOME DECOR
Kitchen Bazaar. This shop gleams with an astonishing array of culinary essentials for the novice and professional. Don't be surprised if you're struck by the urge to replace every utensil in your kitchen with these cool, contemporary designs. ✉ *4 rue de Bretagne, 3e, Marais* ☎ *01–44–78–97–04* ⊕ *www.kitchenbazaar.fr* Ⓜ *Filles du Calvaire.*

Muji. Muji runs on the concept of *kanketsu,* or simplicity, and the resulting streamlined designs are all the rage in Europe. Must-haves include a collection of mini-necessities—travel essentials, wee office gizmos, purse-size accoutrements, plus the best notebooks and pens around. They're so useful and adorable you'll want them all. ✉ *47 rue des Francs Bourgeois, 4e, Marais* ☎ *01–49–96–41–41* ⊕ *www.muji.eu* Ⓜ *St-Paul.*

Sentou. Sentou knocked the Parisian world over the head with its fresh designs. Avant-garde furniture, rugs, and a variety of home accessories line the cool showroom. Look for the April Vase (old test tubes linked together to form different shapes) or the oblong suspended crystal vases and arty tableware. ✉ *29 rue Francois Miron, 4e, Marais* ☎ *01–42–78–50–60* ⊕ *www.sentou.fr* Ⓜ *St-Paul.*

Van der Straeten. Paris designer Hervé van der Straeten started out creating jewelry for Saint Laurent and Lacroix, designed a perfume bottle for Christian Dior, and then moved on to making rather Baroque and often wacky furniture. In his loft gallery-cum-showroom, furniture, lighting, jewelry, and startling mirrors are on display. ✉ *11 rue Ferdinand Duval, 4e, Marais* ☎ *01–42–78–99–99* ⊕ *www.vanderstraeten.fr* Ⓜ *St-Paul.*

JEWELRY AND ACCESSORIES
Fodor'sChoice ★ **Yves Gratas.** Yves Gratas has a knack for pairing gems of varying sizes, brilliance, and texture, allowing each stone to influence the design. Whether it's a spectacular necklace of sapphire beads to be worn long or doubled, or a simple agate sphere tipped in gold and dangling like a tiny planet, these stellar jewels feel like one organic whole. ✉ *9 rue Oberkampf, 11e, Marais* ☎ *01–49–29–00–53* ⊕ *yvesgratas.com* Ⓜ *Filles du Calvaire, Oberkampf.*

16

SHOES, HANDBAGS, AND LEATHER GOODS

K. Jacques. K. Jacques has shod everyone from Brigitte Bardot to Drew Barrymore. The famous St-Tropez–based maker of strappy leather-soled flats has migrated to the big time while still keeping designs classic and comfortable. From gladiator-style to lightweight cork platforms, metallics to neutrals, these are perennial favorites. ⊠ *16 rue Pavée, 4e, Marais* ☎ *01–40–27–03–57* ⊕ *www.kjacques.fr* Ⓜ *St-Paul.*

Miguel Lobato. This is a sweet little boutique with accessories for the woman who wants it all. Beautiful high heels by Balenciaga, Chloé, and Pierre Hardy and fabulous bags by Martin Margiela, Jil Sander, and Proenza Schouler are just a start. ⊠ *6 rue Malher, 4e, Marais* ☎ *01–48–87–68–14* ⊕ *www.lobato-paris.com* Ⓜ *St-Paul.*

SPAS

Nickel. Nickel is the place for him, specializing in men's products and body treatments. Attack *poignées d'amour* (love handles) with a 50-minute massage (€74), or try the express 30-minute back massage (€42). ⊠ *48 rue des Francs-Bourgeois, 4e, Marais* ☎ *01–42–77–41–10* Ⓜ *St-Paul.*

EASTERN PARIS

"Off the beaten track" aptly describes the up-and-coming neighborhoods of Eastern Paris, which are dotted with galleries, vintage shops, and funky boutiques. Low-key cool reigns here, so you won't encounter the high-wattage, high-profile designers that vie for attention elsewhere. Instead, local hipster shops ensure a few choice finds that will be seen on you and only you.

BASTILLE/NATION

CLOTHING

Isabel Marant. This rising design star is a honeypot of bohemian rockstar style. Her separates skim the body without constricting: layered miniskirts, loose peek-a-boo sweaters ready to slip from a shoulder, and super fox-fur jackets in lurid colors. Look for the secondary line, Étoile, for a less expensive take. ⊠ *16 rue de Charonne, 11e, Bastille/ Nation* ☎ *01–49–29–71–55* ⊕ *www.isabelmarant.com* Ⓜ *Ledru-Rollin.*

MARKETS

Marché Bastille. Paris's largest market is as much an event as a place to shop. Blocks of specialized stalls—including ones devoted to rare wines, regional cheeses, game, seafood, and flowers—cater to scores of Parisian chefs and epicures. Open Sunday 7 am–3 pm. ⊠ *Bd. Richard Lenoir, between rues Amelot and Saint-Sabin, 11e, Bastille/Nation* Ⓜ *Ledru-Rollin.*

Marché d'Aligre. Arguably the most locally authentic market, Marché d'Aligre is open until 1 every day except Monday. Don't miss the covered hall on Place d'Aligre, where you can stop by a unique olive-oil boutique for bulk and prebottled oils from top producers. ⊠ *Rue d'Aligre, 12e, Bastille/Nation* Ⓜ *Ledru-Rollin.*

SHOES, HANDBAGS, AND LEATHER GOODS

Fodor's Choice
★ **Philippe Roucou.** By turns bold and dainty, these exquisitely constructed vintage-inspired bags are some of the yummiest in Paris. A python-and-calf tote is demure in storm gray: in ice blue it's a statement. Day bags in myriad shapes and sizes are always stylish; for evening, ingenious faceted clutches come in a range of colors and skins, with a sexy signature version chained to a python wristband. Other leather accessories (like iPad cases and wallets) and whimsical Polaroid-print silk scarves are also available. ⊠ *30 rue de Charonne, 11e, Bastille/Nation* ☎ *01–49–29–97–35* ⊕ *www.philipperoucou.com* Ⓜ *Ledru-Rollin, Bastille.*

CANAL ST-MARTIN

BOOKS AND STATIONERY

Fodor's Choice
★ **Artazart.** The best design bookstore in France carries tomes on everything from architecture to tattoo art: there are sections dedicated to photography, fashion, graphic art, typography, illustration, package design, color, and more. ⊠ *83 Quay de Valmy, 10e, Canal St-Martin* ☎ *01–40–40–24–00* ⊕ *www.artazart.com* Ⓜ *République.*

CLOTHING

Antoine & Lili. This bright, fuchsia-colored store is packed with an international assortment of eclectic objects and items from Antoine & Lili's own clothing line. There's an ethnic rummage-sale feel, with old Asian posters, small lanterns, and basket upon basket of inexpensive doodads, baubles, and trinkets for sale. The clothing itself has simple lines, and there are always plenty of raw silk pieces to pick from. ⊠ *95 quai de Valmy, 10e, Canal St-Martin* ☎ *01–40–37–41–55* ⊕ *www.antoineetlili. com* Ⓜ *Jacques Bonsergent.*

Boutique Renhsen. This boutique is popular for its jeans, which are slender and ultraflattering. But those in the know also come for stylish separates in natural fibers (many are from the fetching French label Sessùn), and a range of must-have accessories, including Patricia Blanchet's sensational booties in cherry-red patent, metallic black, or glittery fuchsia leather. ⊠ *22 rue Beaurepaire, 10e, Canal St-Martin* ☎ *01–48–04–01–01* ⊕ *www.renhsen.com* Ⓜ *République.*

Des Petits Hauts. Des Petits Hauts charmed its way into the local fashion idiom with chic yet beguilingly feminine styles. Fabrics are soft, and styles are casual with a tiny golden star sewn into each garment for good luck. ⊠ *21 rue Beaurepaire, 10e, Canal St-Martin* ☎ *01–40–40–95–47* ⊕ *www.despetitshauts.com* Ⓜ *République.*

Liza Korn. Liza Korn is that rare designer who seems to do it all and do it well. Whether it's rock 'n' roll (grommeted leather baseball jackets), asymmetry (slant-necked minidresses), or classic (tailored blazers over stovepipe trousers), she raises the bar on eclecticism. Her togs for stylish tots are refreshingly childlike, and her home and baby linens are simply beautiful. ⊠ *19 rue Beaurepaire, 10e, Canal St-Martin* ☎ *01–42–01–36–02* ⊕ *www.liza-korn.com* Ⓜ *République.*

DEPARTMENT STORES

Bazar Éthic. Bazar Éthic may be a "department store" that believes in eco-friendly, ethical commerce, but that doesn't mean it can't have fun. Smart contemporary design is found in everything from candles and

16

Browsing through Canal-St Martin's iconoclastic boutiques allows you to savor the slower pace of life, especially around the bridges and small cobblestone streets.

pillows to leather-alternative bags and deconstructed scarves. Luscious Tibetan cashmere sweaters for women and adorable kids clothes are both à la mode *and* virtuous. ⊠ *25 rue Beaurepaire, 10e, Canal St-Martin* ☎ *01–42–00–15–73* ⊕ *www.bazarethic.com* Ⓜ *République.*

HOME DECOR
Idé Co. Idé Co. offers small items for the home in a riot of color. But you'll also find fabulous rubber jewelry and funky stuff for kids big and small. ⊠ *19 rue Beaurepaire, 10e, Canal St-Martin* ☎ *01–42–01–00–11* ⊕ *www.idecoparis.com* Ⓜ *République.*

JEWELRY AND ACCESSORIES
Médecine Douce. Médecine Douce proffers sculptural pieces that combine leather, suede, rhinestones, sheered agate, or resin with whimsical themes. The wildly popular lariat necklace can be looped and dangled according to your mood du jour. ⊠ *10 rue de Marseille, 10e, Canal St-Martin* ☎ *01–48–03–57–28* ⊕ *www.bijouxmedecinedouce. com* Ⓜ *République.*

Viveka Bergström. Viveka Bergström leads the ranks of designers who thumb their noses at the pretensions of traditional costume jewelry— these baubles just want to have fun! Whether it's a bracelet of gigantic rhinestones, a ring of fluorescent pink resin, or a pair of floating angel wings on a necklace, each piece has an acute sense of style while not taking itself too seriously. ⊠ *23 rue de la Grange aux Belles, 10e, Canal St-Martin* ☎ *01–40–03–04–92* ⊕ *viveka-bergstrom.blogspot.fr* Ⓜ *République.*

SHOES, HANDBAGS, AND LEATHER GOODS
Jamin Puech Inventaire. These are last season's models, but no one will guess; savings are 30% to 60%. ✉ *61 rue d'Hauteville, 10e, Canal St-Martin* ☎ *01–40–22–08–32* ⊕ *www.jamin-puech.com* Ⓜ *Poisonnière.*

LATIN QUARTER

Considering this fabled *quartier* is home to the Sorbonne and historically one of Paris's intellectual-bohemian centers, it's not surprising that it has a rich selection of bookstores— not just for students but for collectors and bargain hunters, too. Gastronomes, meanwhile, flock in to shop at the outstanding charcuteries and fromageries along Rue Mouffetard.

BOOKS AND STATIONERY
Abbey Bookshop. Paris's Canadian bookstore has books on Canadian history as well as new and secondhand Québécois and English-language novels. The Canadian Club of Paris also organizes regular poetry readings and literary conferences here. ✉ *29 rue de la Parcheminerie, 5e, Latin Quarter* ☎ *01–46–33–16–24* ⊕ *abbeybookshop.wordpress.com* Ⓜ *Cluny–La Sorbonne.*

16

Shakespeare & Company. This sentimental Rive Gauche favorite is named after the bookstore whose American owner, Sylvia Beach, first published James Joyce's *Ulysses.* Nowadays it specializes in expat literature. Although the eccentric and beloved owner, George Whitman, passed away in 2011, his daughter Sylvia has taken up the torch. You can still count on a couple of characters lurking in the stacks, a sometimes spaccy staff, the latest titles from British presses, and hidden secondhand treasures in the odd corners and crannies. Poets give readings upstairs on Monday at 8 pm; there is also music and special workshops. ✉ *37 rue de la Bûcherie, 5e, Latin Quarter* ☎ *01–43–25–40–93* ⊕ *shakespeareandcompany.com* Ⓜ *St-Michel.*

HOME DECOR
Avant-Scène. Avant-Scène is good for original, poetic furniture. Owner Elisabeth Delacarte commissions limited-edition pieces from artists like Mark Brazier-Jones, Franck Evennou, Elizabeth Garouste, and Hubert Le Gall. ✉ *4 pl. de l'Odéon, 6e, Latin Quarter* ☎ *01–46–33–12–40* ⊕ *www.avantscene.fr* Ⓜ *Odéon.*

Le Monde Sauvage. Le Monde Sauvage is a must-visit for home accessories. Expect reversible silk bedspreads in rich colors, velvet throws, hand-quilted bed linens, silk floor cushions, colorful rugs, and the best selection of hand-embroidered curtains in silk, cotton, linen, or velvet. ✉ *11 rue de l'Odéon, 6e, Latin Quarter* ☎ *01–43–25–60–34* ⊕ *www.lemondesauvage.com* Ⓜ *Odéon.*

JEWELRY AND ACCESSORIES
Peggy Kingg. The minimalist accessories designed by former architect Peggy Huynh Kinh include understated totes, shoulder bags, wallets, and belts in the highest-quality leather, as well as a line of picnic bags and elegant office-oriented pieces. Look for them at her streamlined boutique—and recently re-branded—Peggy Kingg boutique. ✉ *9 rue Coëtlogon, 6e, Latin Quarter* ☎ *01–42–84–83–84* Ⓜ *St-Sulpice.*

MARKETS

Rue Mouffetard. This market, near the Jardin des Plantes, reflects its multicultural neighborhood: vibrant, with a laid-back feel that still smacks of old Paris. It's best on weekends. ✉ *5e, Latin Quarter* Ⓜ *Place Monge.*

ST-GERMAIN-DES-PRÉS

Ever since Yves Saint Laurent arrived in the 1960s, the Rive Gauche has been synonymous with iconoclastic style. Trendsetting stores line a jumble of streets in the 6e arrondissement, and exciting boutiques await between Place de l'Odéon and Église St-Sulpice. In the 7e arrondissement, don't miss Rue du Bac and that jewel of a department store, Le Bon Marché.

ANTIQUES AND COLLECTIBLES

Fodor'sChoice **Carré Rive Gauche.** Carré Rive Gauche is where you'll unearth museum-
★ quality pieces. Head to the streets between Rue du Bac, Rue de l'Université, Rue de Lille, and Rue des Sts-Pères to find more than 100 associated shops, marked with a small, blue square banner on their storefronts. ✉ *Between St-Germain-des-Prés and Musée d'Orsay, 6e, St-Germain-des-Prés* ⊕ *www.carrerivegauche.com* Ⓜ *St-Germain-des-Prés, Rue du Bac.*

Fodor'sChoice **Deyrolle.** This fascinating 19th-century taxidermist has long been a stop
★ for curiosity seekers. A 2008 fire destroyed what was left of the original shop, but it has been lavishly restored and remains a cabinet of curiosities par excellence. Create your own box of butterflies or metallic beetles from scores of bug-filled drawers or just enjoy the menagerie that includes stuffed zebras, monkeys, lions, bears, and more. Also in stock: collectible shells, corals, and crustaceans, plus a generous library of books and posters that once graced every French schoolroom. There is a new line of cool wallpaper murals, too. ✉ *46 rue du Bac, 7e, St-Germain-des-Prés* ☎ *01–42–22–30–07* ⊕ *www.deyrolle.com* Ⓜ *Rue du Bac.*

BEAUTY

Editions de Parfums Frédéric Malle. This perfumerie is based on a simple concept: take the nine most famous noses in France and have them edit singular perfumes. The result? Exceptional, highly concentrated fragrances. Le Parfum de Thérèse, for example, was created by famous Dior nose Edmond Roudnitska for his wife. Monsieur Malle has devised high-tech ways to keep each smelling session unadulterated. At the Rue de Grenelle store, individual scents are released in glass columns—just stick your head in and sniff. A second boutique at 40 avenue Victor Hugo has a glass-fronted "wall of scents," which mists the air with a selected fragrance at the push of a button. ✉ *37 rue de Grenelle, 7e, St-Germain-des-Prés* ☎ *01–42–22–76–40* ⊕ *www.fredericmalle.com* Ⓜ *Rue du Bac.*

Shu Uemura. Shu Uemura has enhanced those whose faces are their fortune for decades. Models swear by the cleansing oil; free samples are proffered. A huge range of colors, every makeup brush imaginable, and the no-pinch eyelash curler keep fans coming back. ✉ *176 bd. St-Germain, 6e, St-Germain-des-Prés* ☎ *01–45–48–02–55* ⊕ *www.shuuemura.fr* Ⓜ *St-Germain-des-Prés.*

BOOKS AND STATIONERY

La Hune. Poised between the Café de Flore and Les Deux Magots, La Hune is a landmark for intellectuals. French literature is downstairs, but the main attraction is the comprehensive collection of international books on art and architecture upstairs. You can hang out until midnight with all the other genius-insomniacs. ✉ *16-18 rue de l'Abbaye, 6e, St-Germain-des-Prés* ☎ *01–45–48–35–85* Ⓜ *St-Germain-des-Prés.*

Taschen. Perfect for night owls, Taschen is open until midnight on Friday and Saturday. The Starck-designed shelves and desks hold glam titles on photography, fine art, design, fashion, and fetishes. ✉ *2 rue de Buci, 6e, St-Germain-des-Prés* ☎ *01–40–51–79–22* ⊕ *www.taschen.com* Ⓜ *Mabillon.*

CHILDREN'S CLOTHING

Alice à Paris. Alice à Paris stocks inventive, stylish, affordable and, above all, kid-proof clothing. These adorable outfits, for children from birth to 14 years old, are functional takes on classic styles in durable cottons and woolens. ✉ *9 rue de l'Odeon, 6e, St-Germain-des-Prés* ☎ *01–42–22–53–89* ⊕ *www.aliceaparis.com* Ⓜ *St-Placide* ✉ *64 rue Condorcet, 9e, Montmartre* ☎ *01–48–78–17–31* Ⓜ *Pigalle.*

Baghère. Baghère is a favorite of movie-star moms. Designer Sylvie Loussiers's meticulous care with fabrics and cuts ensures supremely elegant clothing for kids from birth to age 4. Whether a charming pair of topstitched overalls with dainty shell buttons, a tiny cashmere cardigan, or a winsome dress in charming Liberty print cotton, each piece is of heirloom quality. ✉ *17 rue de Tournon, 6e, St-Germain-des-Prés* ☎ *01–43–29–37–21* ⊕ *www.baghere.com* Ⓜ *Odéon.*

Pom d'Api. Pom d'Api lines up footwear for babies and preteens in quality leathers and vivid colors. Expect well-made, eye-catching fashion—bright fuchsia sneakers and leopard suede boots, as well as classic Mary Janes in shades of silver, pink, and gold. There are also utility boots for boys and sturdy rain gear. ✉ *28 rue du Four, 6e, St-Germain-des-Prés* ☎ *01–45–48–39–31* ⊕ *www.pomdapi.fr* Ⓜ *St-Germain-des-Prés.*

CLOTHING

Antik Batik. Antik Batik has a wonderful line of ethnically inspired clothes. There are rows of beaded and sequined dresses, Chinese silk tunics, short fur jackets and fur-lined anoraks, flowing organza separates, and some of Paris's most popular sandals and giant scarves. The store carries maxi-versions for mothers-to-be, plus adorable mini-versions for girls ages 2 to 14. ✉ *26 rue St-Sulpice, 6e, St-Germain-des-Prés* ☎ *01–44–07–68–53* Ⓜ *Odéon, Marais.*

A.P.C. A.P.C. may be antiflash and minimal, but a knowing eye can always pick out their jeans in a crowd. The clothes here are rigorously well-made and worth the investment in lasting style. Prime wardrobe pieces include dark indigo and black denim, zip-up cardigans, peacoats, and streamlined ankle boots. ✉ *38 rue Madame, 6e, St-Germain-des-Prés* ☎ *01–42–22–12–77* Ⓜ *St-Sulpice.*

Fodor's Choice ★ **Carven.** Ever since Guillaume Henry assumed the role of artistic director in 2010, Carven has been steadily rising into the fashion stratosphere, with each new show garnering rave reviews. Inspired by the true-to-life movie heroines of Chabrol and Cassavetes, Henry injects the line with a vibrant sex appeal that's smart and classy. Meticulous tailoring applied to up-to-the-minute silhouettes, daring designs (that are still wearable), and a fondness for mixing luxe fabrics with artsy prints and surprising colors: it all adds up to couture quality at half the price. ⊠ *34 rue St-Sulpice, St-Germain-des-Prés* ☎ *01–44–61–02–07* Ⓜ *Saint-Sulpice, Odéon.*

Karl Lagerfeld. Karl Lagerfeld's own chiseled profile is a key design element in his new Saint-Germain flagship store. Inside, look for two new lines: Lagerfeld, featuring "everyday" clothes for the urban man, and Karl Lagerfeld Paris (KLP), a ready-to-wear collection for men and women. The latter line is aimed at fashion conscious twenty- and thirtysomethings who want to strut their stuff (think body-slimming jackets, lace-inset tops, hot pants, and skin-tight jeans, mostly in black, white, and gray). The store also stocks eyewear, accessories, bags, shoes, fragrances, and—you guessed it—Lagerfeld's signature fingerless leather gloves. ⊠ *194 bd. St-Germain, 7e, St-Germain-des-Prés* ☎ *01–42–22–74–99* ⊕ *www.karl.com* Ⓜ *Rue du Bac.*

Sonia Rykiel. Sonia Rykiel has been designing insouciant knitwear since the 1960s. Sweaters drape and cling by turns and her color combinations (she's partial to stripes) are lovely. Opulent silks, furs, accessories dotted with rhinestones, and soft leather bags punctuate the collection. Sonia by Sonia Rykiel, the secondary line, is playful, smart, and targets a slightly younger crowd. ⊠ *175 bd. St-Germain, 6e, St-Germain-des-Prés* ☎ *01–49–54–60–60* Ⓜ *St-Germain-des-Prés.*

DEPARTMENT STORES

Fodor's Choice
★
Le Bon Marché. Founded in 1852, Le Bon Marché has emerged as the city's chicest department store. Long a hunting ground for linens and other home items, the store got a face-lift that brought fashion to the fore. The ground floor sets out makeup, perfume, and accessories; this is where celebs duck in for essentials while everyone pretends not to recognize them. Upstairs, do laps through labels chichi (Givenchy, Stella McCartney, Lanvin) and überhip (Martin Margiela, Comme des Garçons, Ann Demeulemeester). The newly refurbished menswear department, under the moniker Balthazar, has now consumed the entire basement level and keeps pace with designers like Saint Laurent and Paul Smith. Zip across the second floor walkway to the mode section (above the next-door *épicerie*): home to streetwise designers and edgy secondary lines, it also has a funky café. French favorites include Athé by Vanessa Bruno, Zadig & Voltaire, Tsumori Chisato, Isabel Marant's Étoile line, and Helmut Lang jeans. Best of all, this department store isn't nearly as crowded as those near the Opéra. Don't miss the spectacularly renovated La Grande Épicerie and Cave (wineshop) next door: it's the haute couture of grocery stores. Artisanal jams, olive oils, and much more make great gifts, and the luscious pastries, fruit, and huge selection of prepared foods beg to be chosen for a snack. ⊠ *24 rue de Sèvres, 7e, St-Germain-des-Prés* ☎ *01–44–39–80–00* ⊕ *www. lebonmarche.com* Ⓜ *Sèvres-Babylone.*

FOOD AND TREATS

Christian Constant. Christian Constant is deservedly praised for his exquisite ganaches, perfumed with jasmine, ylang-ylang, or verveine. ⊠ *37 rue d'Assas, 6e, St-Placide* ☎ *01–53–63–15–15* ⊕ *www.christianconstant. fr* Ⓜ *St-Placide.*

Debauve & Gallais. The two former chemists who founded Debauve & Gallais in 1800 became the royal chocolate purveyors and were famed for their "health chocolates," made with almond milk. Test the benefits yourself with ganache, truffles, or *pistols* (flavored dark-chocolate disks). ⊠ *30 rue des Sts-Pères, 7e, St-Germain-des-Prés* ☎ *01–45–48– 54–67* Ⓜ *St-Germain-des-Prés.*

Henri Le Roux. Henri Le Roux, originator of the renowned *caramel au beurre salé*, pairs a Breton pedigree with Japanese flair. Brilliant confections result. ⊠ *1 rue de Bourbon le Château, 6e, St-Germain-des-Prés* ☎ *02–97–50–06–83* ⊕ *www.chocolatleroux.com* Ⓜ *St Germain des Prés* ⊠ *24 rue des Martyrs, 9e, St-Germain-des-Prés* ☎ *01–82–28–49–83* ⊕ *www.chocolatleroux.com* Ⓜ *Notre-Dame-de-Lorette, Saint Georges.*

Jean-Charles Rouchoux. Rouchoux makes three superb collections: the Ephemeral, with fresh fruit; Made-to-Measure, with animals and figurines; and the Permanent Collection of everyday favorites. ⊠ *16 rue d'Assas, 6e, St-Placide* ☎ *01–42–84–29–45* ⊕ *www.jcrochoux.com* Ⓜ *Rennes.*

La Maison du Chocolat. This is chocolate's gold standard. The silky ganaches are renowned for subtlety and flavor. ⊠ *19 rue de Sevre, 6e, St-Germain-des-Prés* ☎ *01–45–44–20–40* ⊕ *www.lamaisonduchocolat.fr* Ⓜ *Sèvres-Babylone* ⊠ *8 bd. de la Madeleine, 9e, Louvre/Tuileries* ☎ *01– 47–42–86–52* ⊕ *www.lamaisonduchocolat.fr* Ⓜ *Madeleine* ⊠ *225 rue du Faubourg St-Honoré, 8e, Louvre/Tuileries* ☎ *01–42–27–39–44* ⊕ *www.lamaisonduchocolat.fr* Ⓜ *Ternes.*

Patrick Roger. Paris's bad-boy chocolatier likes to shock with provocative shapes and wicked humor. Everything is sinfully good. ⊠ *108 bd. St-Germain, 6e, St-Germain-des-Prés* ☎ *01–43–29–38–42* ⊕ *www. patrickroger.com* Ⓜ *Odéon* ⊠ *3 Place de la Madeleine, 8e, Louvre/ Tuileries* ☎ *01-42-65-24-47* ⊕ *www.patrickroger.com.*

Pierre Hermé. Hermé may be Paris's most renowned pâtissier. Sample the peerless cakes and cookies, or savor the chocolate delights (classic varieties, like the dark-chocolate and orange-rind batons, are perennial favorites). ■TIP➔ Hermé offers a scrumptious, zesty lemon pound cake preboxed and dense enough to survive the trip home. Maybe. ⊠ *72 rue Bonaparte, 6e, St-Germain-des-Prés* ☎ *01–43–54–47–77* ⊕ *www. pierreherme.com* Ⓜ *Odéon* ⊠ *4 rue Cambon, 1er, Louvre/Tuileries* ☎ *01–58–62–43–17* ⊕ *www.pierreherme.com* Ⓜ *Concorde* ⊠ *185 rue de Vaugirard, 15e, Montparnasse* ☎ *01–47–83–29–72* ⊕ *www. pierreherme.com* Ⓜ *Pasteur.*

Pierre Marcolini. Pierre Marcolini proves it's all in the bean with his specialty *saveurs du monde* collection, made with a single cacao from a single location, such as Madagascar or Ecuador. ⊠ *89 rue de Seine, 6e, St-Germain-des-Prés* ☎ *01–44–07–39–07* ⊕ *www.marcolini.com* Ⓜ *Mabillon.*

16

The interior of the Galeries Lafayette department store—especially the ceiling—almost outshines the fabulous merchandise.

Richart. How do I love thee? The ways are too numerous to count. Inspired chocolates dazzle the eye and elevate the palate. ✉ *258 bd. St-Germain, 6e, St-Germain-des-Prés* ☎ *01–56–81–16–10* ⊕ *www. chocolats-richart.com* Ⓜ *St Germain des Prés* ✉ *27 rue Bonaparte, 6e, St-Germain-des-Prés* ☎ *01–56–81–16–10* ⊕ *www.chocolats-richart. com.*

Tomat's. Tucked into a courtyard, this luxe épicerie carries the full line of Huilerie Artisanale J. Leblanc et Fils oil—15 varieties pressed the old-fashioned way, with a big stone wheel, from olives, hazelnuts, pistachios, or grape seeds. You can also buy aged vinegars, *fleur de sel* (unprocessed sea salt), foie gras, and other regional French delicacies, plus the tools to serve them with. ✉ *12 rue Jacob, 6e, St-Germain-des-Prés* ☎ *01–44–07–36–58* ⊕ *www.huile-leblanc.com* Ⓜ *Mabillon, Saint Germain des Prés.*

HOME DECOR

Alexandre Biaggi. Alexandre Biaggi specializes in 20th-century Art Deco and also commissions designs from such talented designers as Patrick Naggar and Hervé van der Straeten. ✉ *14 rue de Seine, 6e, St-Germain-des-Prés* ☎ *01–44–07–34–73* Ⓜ *St-Germain-des-Prés.*

Catherine Memmi. This trendsetter in pared-down, tastefully hued housewares also sells lamps, furniture, and home accessories. ✉ *11 rue St-Sulpice, 6e, St-Germain-des-Prés* ☎ *01–44–07–02–02* ⊕ *www. catherinememmi.com* Ⓜ *St-Sulpice.*

Fodor'sChoice ★ **Cire Trudon.** Cire Trudon has illuminated the great palaces and churches of Paris since the 1700s. Nowadays it provides the atmosphere for tony restaurants and exclusive soirees. The all-vegetal, atmospherically scented candles come in elegant black glass, pillars of all sizes, or busts of clients past—like Napoléon and Marie-Antoinette. ⊠ *78 rue de Seine, 6e, St-Germain-des-Prés* ☎ *01–43–26–46–50* ⊕ *www.ciretrudon.com* Ⓜ *Odéon.*

Conran Shop. This is the brainchild of British entrepreneur Terence Conran. The shop carries expensive contemporary furniture, beautiful bed linens, and items for every other room in the house—all marked by a balance of utility with not-too-sober style. Conran makes even shower curtains fun. ⊠ *117 rue du Bac, 7e, St-Germain-des-Prés* ☎ *01–42–84– 10–01* Ⓜ *Sèvres-Babylone.*

Fodor'sChoice
★
Diptyque. A Paris mainstay since 1961, Diptyque's flagship shop is famous for its candles, eaux de toilette, and body fragrances in a huge range of sophisticated scents like myrrh, fig tree, wisteria, and quince. They're delightful but not cheap; the candles, for instance, cost nearly $1 per hour of burn time. ⊠ *34 bd. St-Germain, 5e, St-Germain-des-Prés* ☎ *01–43–26–77–44* Ⓜ *Maubert–Mutualité.*

R&Y Augousti. R&Y Augousti are two Paris-based designers who make furniture and objects for the home from nacre, ostrich, palm wood, and parchment. Also for sale are their hand-tooled leather bags and wallets. ⊠ *103 rue du Bac, 7e, St-Germain-des-Prés* ☎ *01–42–22–22–21* Ⓜ *Sèvres-Babylone.*

Fodor'sChoice
★
Zuber. Have you always wanted to imitate the grand homes of Paris? Here's your chance. Zuber has operated nonstop for more than two centuries as the world's oldest producer of prestige hand-printed wallpapers, renowned for their magnificent panoramic scenes. Warning: with only one scene produced per year, the wait can be nearly a decade long. Opulent Restoration-era wallpapers (including metallics, silks, velvets, and pressed leather) make modern statements and can be purchased in 32-foot rolls for slightly less than a king's ransom. ⊠ *3 rue des Saints-Pères, 6e, St-Germain-des-Prés* ☎ *01–42–77–95–91* ⊕ *www.zuber.fr* Ⓜ *St-Germain-des-Prés.*

JEWELRY AND ACCESSORIES

Adelline. Entering this jewelry shop is like landing in Ali Baba's cave: each piece is more gorgeous than the last, and the bounty of beautiful shapes and styles satisfies a large range of tastes (and budgets). Cabochon rings can be pebble-size or rocklike, jeweled cuffs sport diamonds in a web of gold, and simple cord-and-gem bracelets cannot fail to make a statement. ⊠ *54 rue Jacob, 6e, St-Germain-des-Prés* ☎ *01–47–03–07– 18* ⊕ *www.adelline.com* Ⓜ *St-Germain-des-Prés.*

Agatha. This chain is the perfect place to buy a moderately priced piece of fun jewelry. Agatha's line of earrings, rings, hair accessories, bracelets, necklaces, watches, brooches, and pendants is ultrapopular with Parisians. Styles change quickly, but classics include charm bracelets and fine gold necklaces with whimsical pendants. ⊠ *45 rue Bonaparte, 6e, St-Germain-des-Prés* ☎ *01–46–33–20–00* ⊕ *www. agatha.fr* Ⓜ *St-Germain-des-Prés.*

Alexandra Sojfer. Alexandra Sojfer, the proprietress, is the queen of walking sticks. The late president François Mitterrand bought his at this tiny shop—open since 1834—which also has an amazing range of umbrellas.

16

✉ *218 bd. St-Germain, 7e, St-Germain-des-Prés* ☎ *01–42–22–17–02* Ⓜ *Rue du Bac.*

Arthus-Bertrand. Arthus-Bertrand, which dates back to 1803, has glass showcases full of designer jewelry and numerous objects to celebrate births. ✉ *54 rue Bonaparte, 6e, St-Germain-des-Prés* ☎ *01–49–54–72– 10* Ⓜ *St-Germain-des-Prés.*

Marie Mercié. Marie Mercié—one of Paris's most fashionable milliners, and one of its last—makes charming hats for every season. Her raffish straw models are masterworks. Husband Anthony Peto, who makes men's headgear, has a store at 56 rue Tiquetonne. ✉ *23 rue St-Sulpice, 6e, St-Germain-des-Prés* ☎ *01–43–26–45–83* ⊕ *www.mariemercie.com* Ⓜ *Mabillon, St-Sulpice.*

LINGERIE

Fodor's Choice **Sabbia Rosa.** You could easily walk straight past this discreet, boudoir- ★ like boutique. It is, however, one of the world's finest lingerie stores and the place where actresses Catherine Deneuve and Isabelle Adjani (along with others who might not want to reveal their errand) buy superb French silks. ✉ *71–73 rue des Sts-Pères, 6e, St-Germain-des-Prés* ☎ *01–45–48–88–37* Ⓜ *St-Germain-des-Prés.*

MARKETS

Boulevard Raspail. Boulevard Raspail, between Rue du Cherche-Midi and Rue de Rennes, is the city's major *marché biologique,* or organic market, bursting with produce, fish, and eco-friendly products every Sunday. The market is also open on Tuesday and Friday with nonor-ganic products. ✉ *6e, St-Germain-des-Prés* Ⓜ *Rennes.*

Rue de Buci. Vendors at this market often tempt you with tastes of their wares: slices of sausage, slivers of peaches. It's closed Sunday afternoon and Monday. ✉ *6e, St-Germain-des-Prés* Ⓜ *Odéon.*

SHOES, HANDBAGS, AND LEATHER GOODS

Fodor's Choice **Avril Gau.** After designing a dozen collections for Chanel, Gau struck ★ out on her own, opening her neo-Baroque boutique on charming Rue des Quatre Vents. Gau takes her inspiration from glamorous French movie icons, dreaming up styles that are elegant and sexy without being trashy. Sleek pumps, wedge booties, ballerina flats, and riding boots (all in the finest quality calf, reptile and lambskin) are as classy as they come. Bags share the spotlight, with updated riffs on the classics. ✉ *17 rue des Quatre Vents, 6e, St-Germain-des-Prés* ☎ *01–43–29–49–04* ⊕ *www.avrilgau.com* Ⓜ *Odéon.*

Fodor's Choice **Jamin Puech.** Jamin Puech thinks of its bags not just as a necessity, but ★ as jewelry. Nothing's plain Jane here. Beaded bags swing from thin link chains; fringes flutter from dark embossed-leather totes; and small evening purses are covered with shells, oversize sequins, or hand-dyed crochet. The collections fluctuate with the seasons but never fail to be whimsical, imaginative, and highly coveted. ✉ *43 rue Madame, 6e, St-Germain-des-Prés* ☎ *01–45–48–14–85* ⊕ *www.jamin-puech.com* Ⓜ *St-Sulpice.*

Fodor's Choice **Jérôme Dreyfuss.** The newest star in the city's handbag universe has cap- ★ tivated *le tout Paris* with his artsy take on hobo, Birkin, and messenger bags. Unique styles (like the twee-mini) are impossibly cute, and you'll be glad you took out that second mortgage just to tote around a luxe matte-python model. A new line of gorgeous, high-heeled footwear is equally chic. ✉ *4 rue Jacob, 6e, St-Germain-des-Prés* ☎ *01–43–54–70– 93* ⊕ *www.jerome-dreyfuss.com* Ⓜ *St-Germain-des-Prés.*

Michel Perry Collector. Whimsy, humor, and high-chic collide at this colorful boutique devoted to Perry's imaginative footwear. From the adorable strappy sandals sporting metallic pythons to the brilliantly hued platform laceups and booties, the shoes here are bound to turn heads. ✉ *42 rue de Grenelle, 7e, St-Germain-des-Prés* ☎ *01–42–84–12–45* ⊕ *www. michelperry.com* Ⓜ *Rue du Bac.*

Fodor's Choice ★ **Tila March.** Fame came quickly to this ex-fashion editor, whose wildly successful first handbag collection was snatched up by celebs such as Sienna Miller, Kirsten Dunst, and Scarlett Johansson. March uses velvety nubuck in a range of saturated colors—aubergine, olive, brick, taupe, and more—along with sleek matte crocodile to craft everything from large totes (like her handy Daisy bag) to tiny evening bags. With sleekly sophisticated shoes to match, it's not just a boutique—it's a destination. ✉ *24 rue Saint Sulpice, 6e, St-Germain-des-Prés* ☎ *01–43– 26–69–20* ⊕ *www.tilamarch.com* Ⓜ *Odéon, Saint Sulpice.*

WINE

Fodor's Choice ★ **La Dernière Goutte.** This inviting *cave* (literally winestore or wine cellar) focuses on wines by small French producers. Each is handpicked by the owner, along with a choice selection of estate champagnes, Armagnac, and the classic Vieille Prune (plum brandy). The friendly English-speaking staff makes browsing a pleasure. Don't miss the Saturday afternoon tastings with the winemakers. ✉ *6 rue de Bourbon le Château, 6e, St-Germain-des-Prés* ☎ *01–46–29–11–62* Ⓜ *Odéon.*

Ryst-Dupeyron. Ryst-Dupeyron specializes in fine wines and liquors, with port, calvados, and Armagnacs that date from 1878. Looking for a great gift idea? Find a bottle from the year of a friend's birth and have it labeled with your friend's name. Personalized bottles can be ordered and delivered on the same day. ✉ *79 rue du Bac, 7e, St-Germain-des-Prés* ☎ *01–45–48–80–93* Ⓜ *Rue du Bac.*

MONTPARNASSE

The legendary Rue d'Alessia alone lands this neighborhood on the Paris shopping radar. If you're willing to dig a little, a thrilling afternoon can be had seeking out the many bargains here—from steeply discounted designer clothes, shoes, and accessories to housewares and kids togs. Just roll up your sleeves and dive in.

BARGAIN SHOPPING

Rue d'Alésia. Rue d'Alésia, in the 14e arrondissement, is the main place to find shops selling last season's fashions at a discount. Be forewarned: most of the outlets are much more downscale than their elegant sister shops; dressing rooms are not always provided. ✉ *14e, Montparnasse* Ⓜ *Alésia.*

MARKETS

Porte de Vanves. This smaller flea market, on the southern side of the city, is a hit with the fashion and design set. It specializes in easily portable items (like textiles or clothing) and collectible objects that include books, posters, postcards, and glassware. With tables sprawling along both sides of the sidewalk, there's an extravagant selection—just be sure to bargain. ■TIP➜ It's open on weekends from 8 to 1, but come early for the real deals: good stuff goes fast, and stalls are liable to pack up before noon. ⊠ *14e, Montparnasse* Ⓜ *Porte de Vanves.*

NIGHTLIFE

Updated
by Jennifer
Ditsler-Ladonne

You haven't seen the City of Light until you've seen the city at night. Throngs pour into popular streets, filling the air with the melody of engaged conversation and clinking glasses. This is when locals let down their hair and reveal their true bonhomie, laughing and dancing, flirting and talking. Parisians love to savor life together: they dine out, drink endless espressos, offer innumerable toasts, and are often so reluctant to separate that they party all night.

Parisians go out weekends and weeknights, late and early. They tend to frequent the same places once they've found spots they like: it could be a wine bar, corner café, or hip music club, and you can often find a welcoming "the gang's all here" atmosphere. A wise way to spend an evening is to pick an area in a neighborhood that interests you, then give yourself time to browse. Parisians also love to bar-hop, and the energy shifts throughout the evening, so be prepared to follow the crowds all night.

PLANNING

GETTING PAST THE BOUNCER

It shouldn't surprise any nightlife lover that the more *branché* (literally, "plugged-in" or trendy) the spot, the knottier the door-entry issue will be. Most bars aren't a problem, but when it comes to clubbing, don't assume you're going to get in just because you show up. This is particularly true at the hot spots near the Champs-Élysées. Although a limo at your disposal and global fame aren't essential to pass muster, you absolutely must have a cocky yet somehow simultaneously polite attitude and look fabulous. Having a high female quotient in your party definitely helps (models are a particular plus). Solo men—or, worse, groups of men—are going to have a tougher time, unless they are high rollers and have reserved a table (bottle purchase *obligatoire*).

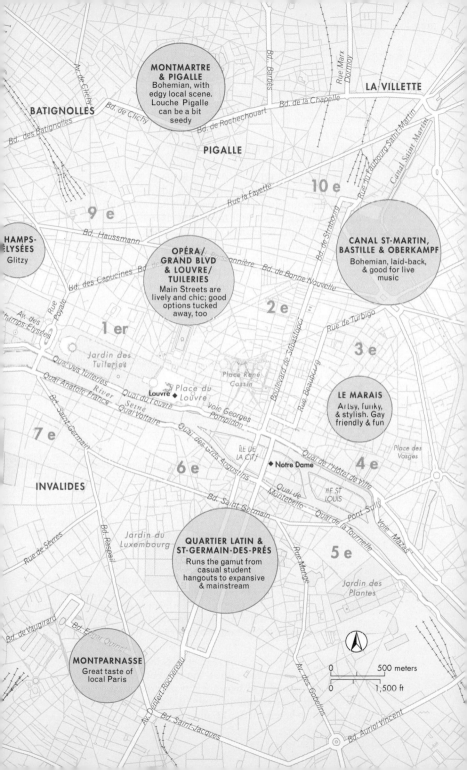

BATIGNOLLES

MONTMARTRE & PIGALLE
Bohemian, with edgy local scene. Louche Pigalle can be a bit seedy

LA VILLETTE

PIGALLE

Rue la Fayette

10 e

9 e

Bd. Haussmann

CANAL ST-MARTIN, BASTILLE & OBERKAMPF
Bohemian, laid-back, & good for live music

HAMPS-ÉLYSÉES
Glitzy

OPÉRA/ GRAND BLVD & LOUVRE/ TUILERIES
Main Streets are lively and chic; good options tucked away, too

Bd. de Bonne Nouvelle

2 e

Rue de Turbigo

1 er

3 e

Jardin des Tuileries

Place René Cassin

LE MARAIS
Artsy, funky, & stylish. Gay friendly & fun

Quai des Tuileries

Quai du Louvre
Louvre ♦ Place du Louvre

Voie Georges Pompidou

Quai Anatole France

River Seine
Quai Voltaire

Place des Vosges

7 e

Bd. Saint-Germain

Quai des Grands Augustins

ÎLE DE LA CITÉ

Quai de l'Hôtel de ville

4 e

6 e
♦ Notre Dame

INVALIDES

Quai de Montebello

ÎLE ST LOUIS

Bd. Saint Germain

Pont Sully

Voie Mazas

Jardin du Luxembourg

QUARTIER LATIN & ST-GERMAIN-DES-PRÉS
Runs the gamut from casual student hangouts to expansive & mainstream

Quai de la Tournelle

Rue Monge

5 e

Jardin des Plantes

MONTPARNASSE
Great taste of local Paris

| 0 | | | 500 meters |
| 0 | | 1,500 ft |

HOURS

Bars tend to stay open until between midnight and 2 am, with no specific last call. Clubs often stay open until 4 am, and many until dawn. If you want to hit bars at a relatively quiet hour, go for an aperitif around 6 pm. Many places offer drink specials at this time, and it's also when Parisians congregate to make late-night plans. Many bars charge slightly higher prices after 10.

LATE-NIGHT TRANSPORTATION

The last métro runs until 1 am Sunday through Thursday; there is service, however, on Friday and Saturday until 2 am. After that, you can try a cab, but it can be extremely difficult to find one in the wee hours. Taxi stands are plagued with long lines for few cabs, and even calling one on weekends can be a frustrating exercise. Another alternative is the Noctilien, the sometimes rowdy night-bus system. If you stay within biking distance of chosen destinations, Vélib' is an option, too—though after a few champagnes it may be better to do like the Parisians and just stay out until the métro starts running again at 5:30 am *(see the Travel Smart Paris chapter for more on your late-night options)*.

TABLE SERVICE

Some bars have table service; at others (designated by "Service au Bar" signs), you must fetch your own drinks.

WHAT TO WEAR

Parisians are stylish, so if you want to blend in (and get into clubs), dress up. Men, you can wear your jeans—designer jeans, that is—but leave the sneakers at your hotel and try adding a blazer. Ladies, dressing up doesn't necessarily mean a dress and heels—Parisian girls manage to look like a million bucks in jeans and a chic top.

BARS

Paris bars run the gamut from the toniest hotel lounge to the tiniest neighborhood *troquet,* where old timers gather for a chat over their morning *petit blanc.*

Hotel bars are the aristocrats of the genre. Some mix historic pedigrees with a hushed elegance, while others go for a modern, edgy luxe. A few represent the chicest spots in Paris. But breathtaking prices and the fickle Parisian fashion pack ensure that only the latest, highly hyped bars regularly draw in locals.

Cocktail bars, on the other hand, have been steadily gaining in popularity, edging their way into the sophisticated bar scene that was once the domain of a handful of hotels and eminent watering holes. Although most cocktail bars offer anything from craft beer to champagne, the real focus is a fresh take on mixed drinks. Many have reintroduced happy hour.

Wine bars are different from regular bars in that they also serve food—from simple snacks (like cheese and charcuterie) to full-fledged meals, along with handpicked wines, often natural or *biodynamique.* Wine bars usually keep mealtime hours and close earlier than full-fledged bars—somewhere between 11 and midnight.

CABARETS

Paris's cabarets range from vintage venues once haunted by Picasso and Piaf to those sinful showplaces where *tableaux vivants* offer acres of bare female flesh. Some of these places, like the Lido, are more Vegas than the petticoat vision re-created by Hollywood in Baz Luhrmann's *Moulin Rouge*—but the rebirth of burlesque is making some of the old-school venues more popular. Although you can dine at many cabarets, food isn't the attraction. Prices range from about €50 (admission plus one drink) to more than €175 (dinner plus show) and can go as high as €300 for the works. Liberated parents take note: admission to the Lido is free for children between the ages of 4 and 12.

CLUBS

Paris's hyped *boîtes de nuit*—more often referred to as simply *boîtes* (nightclubs)—tend to be expensive and exclusive. If you're friends with a regular or you've modeled in *Vogue,* you'll have an easier time getting through the door. Cover charges at some spots push the €20 range, with drinks at the bar starting at €10 for a beer. Others are free to enter, but getting past the doorman can still be problematic. Locals looking to dance generally stick to the smaller clubs, where the cover ranges from free (usually on slower weekdays) to €15, and the emphasis is on the music and upbeat atmosphere. Club popularity depends on the night or event, as Parisians are more loyal to certain DJs than venues and often hit two or three spots before ending up at one of the many after-parties, which can last until noon the next day.

17

GAY AND LESBIAN BARS AND CLUBS

These bars and clubs—mostly concentrated in the Marais and Les Halles—include some of the hippest addresses in the city. Keep in mind, however, that many of these spots fall in and out of favor at lightning speed. The best way to find out what's hot is by perusing the gay and lesbian magazine *Têtu* (available at newsstands and online at ⊕ *www. tetu.com*) or *2X,* the free "agenda" that can be found in any of the venues listed here. Paris's gay, lesbian, bi, and trans tourist office (⊕ *www. centrelgbtparis.org*) is another good resource, as is the civic-run nightlife website (⊕ *www.parisnightlife.fr/en*).

PUBS

Pubs wooing English-speaking clients with selections of British and Irish beers are becoming increasingly popular with Parisians. They're also good places to watch an important soccer match or find reasonably priced food at off hours.

NIGHTLIFE IN PARIS

Reviews are alphabetical by neighborhood.

CHAMPS-ÉLYSÉES

As the sun sets, Paris's most elegant neighborhood comes to life. Join the fashionistas for a *coupe de champagne* in an opulent hotel bar, spend a night clubbing with the international jet set, or indulge in a bit of over-the-top French "culture" at a cabaret.

BARS

Apicius. Apicius offers sublime elegance mere steps from the Champs-Élysées. Wander through the luxe front garden and château restaurant to the sleekly modern black bar where couture cocktails are concocted to suit any cultured taste. Closed weekends. ⊠ *20 rue d'Artois, 8e, Champs-Élysées* ☎ *01–43–80–19–66* ⊕ *www.restaurant-apicius.com* ⊗ *Closed weekends and month of Aug.* Ⓜ *George V.*

Bar Metropolitan. This cozy spot in the Radisson Blu Hotel seats 25 at most and has one of the best bar views of the Eiffel Tower. It also serves luscious champagne cocktails dreamed up by the head bartender, who is only too happy to practice his English on you. ⊠ *10 pl. de Mexico, 16e, Champs-Élysées* ☎ *01–56–90–40–04* ⊕ *www.radissonblu.fr* Ⓜ *Trocadéro.*

Blind Bar, Maison Champs Elysées. This romantic spot in the ultrachic Maison Champs Elysées offers a wood fire in winter and a quiet terrace in warmer months. Its impressive range of champagnes and impeccable cocktails is well worth the stellar prices. The separate all-black cigar bar is one of the remaining few in Paris. ⊠ *8 rue Jean Goujon, 8e, Champs-Élysées* ☎ *01–40–74–64–65* ⊕ *www.lamaisonchampselysees. com* Ⓜ *Franklin D. Roosevelt, Champs-Elysées–Clémenceau.*

Buddha Bar. While it may be past its prime with Parisians, visitors can't seem to get enough of the high-camp towering gold Buddha that holds court over this bar's giant palm fronds, red satin walls, and colorful chinoiserie. A themed dining room serves pan-Asian fare. ⊠ *8 rue Boissy d'Anglas, 8e, Champs-Élysées* ☎ *01–53–05–90–00* ⊕ *www.buddhabar. com* Ⓜ *Concorde.*

English Bar. You might find diplomats and other dignitaries discussing state affairs at this rich red den of masculinity in L'Hôtel Raphael, a stone's throw from the Arc de Triomphe. ∎TIP➜ **The hotel's Rooftop Bar, a well-guarded Parisian secret, was voted the best bar in Europe in recent years.** ⊠ *17 av. Kleber, 16e, Champs-Élysée* ☎ *01–53–64–32–00* ⊕ *www.raphael-hotel.com* Ⓜ *Kleber, Charles de Gaulle–Etoile.*

Flûte Bar. A Paris offshoot of the original Flûte bar in New York, the romantic Flûte L'Etoile is just off the Champs in the chic 17th. In a country where you might expect to find champagne bars on every corner, it's one of only a handful that serve a serious selection by the glass or bottle. ⊠ *19 rue de l'Étoile, 17e, Champs-Élysées* ☎ *01–45–72–10–14* Ⓜ *Ternes.*

Hotel Daniel. A quiet haven off the Champs-Élysées? Doesn't exist, you say? At Hotel Daniel you can install yourself on an overstuffed silk couch or divan and sip a flute of champagne while having a quiet conversation until late into the night. Really. ⊠ *8 rue Frédéric Bastiat, 8e, Champs-Élysées* ☎ *01–42–56–17–00* ⊕ *www.hoteldanielparis.com* Ⓜ *Saint-Philippe du Roule.*

Hôtel Plaza Athénée. This hotel bar *par excellence* is bound to be better than ever—if such a thing were possible—when it emerges from a major makeover, spearheaded by Philippe Starck protégé Patrick Jouin. The reopening is expected to take place in the second half of 2014. ⊠ *25 av. Montaigne, 8e, Champs-Élysées* ☎ *01–53–67–66–00* ⊕ *www.plaza-athenee-paris.com* Ⓜ *Alma–Marceau.*

Le Bar. The Shangri-La Hotel's popular bar serves cocktails with a signature Asian touch. La Bauhinia, the hotel's restaurant, has well-attended Tuesday jazz nights. ⊠ *10 av. d'Iéna, 16e, Champs-Élysées* ☎ *01–53–67–19–98* ⊕ *www.shangri-la.com* Ⓜ *Iéna.*

Le Bar at George V. An ultraluxe, clubby hideaway in the Four Seasons Hotel, Le Bar at George V is perfect for star-gazing from the plush wine-red armchairs, cognac in hand. Its charm still lures the glitterati, especially during fashion weeks. Be sure to notice the hotel's signature—and stunning—flower arrangements. ⊠ *31 av. George V, 8e, Champs-Élysées* ☎ *01–49–52–70–00* ⊕ *www.fourseasons.com/paris/dining/lounges/le_bar* Ⓜ *George V.*

Fodor'sChoice
★
Le Bar du Bristol. This splendid spot apparently isn't satisfied with its usual clientele of the rich and powerful. Now it's vying for the impossibly hip, too. Along with the stellar cocktails, exceptional wines, and tapas by superchef Eric Frechon, Le Bar hosts art appreciation programs on weekdays between 9 and 10:30, and chic Paris DJs heat up the scene between 9:30 and 2 am, Thursday to Saturday. ■ **TIP➔** Try the famous Crazy Horse cocktail or their signature Dolce Vita with raspberry puree and champagne. ⊠ *112 rue du Faubourg St-Honoré, 8e, Champs-Élysées* ☎ *01–53–43–43–00* ⊕ *www.lebristolparis.com* Ⓜ *Miromesnil.*

No Comment. This nightclub, housed in a former swinger's club, boasts that it has retained the libertine vibe without the libertine ways. Only the trendiest seem to go—and get in. ⊠ *36 rue de Ponthieu, 8e, Champs-Élysées* ☎ *01–43–59–23–95* Ⓜ *Saint-Philippe-du-Roule.*

Pershing Hall. Pershing Hall has an überstylish lounge with muted colors and minimalist lines, plus an enormous "vertical garden" in the simply stunning indoor courtyard. The chic ambience and hip lounge music make this a popular neighborhood nightspot; starting at 10 pm there's a DJ. ■ **TIP➔** Try the signature Lalique cocktail—it comes in an actual Lalique crystal glass. ⊠ *49 rue Pierre Charron, 8e, Champs-Élysées* ☎ *01–58–36–58–00* ⊕ *www.pershinghall.com* Ⓜ *George V.*

Publicis Drugstore. Open daily until 2 am, this bustling, phantasmagorical, multilevel, bar-brasserie-hipster shop is just across the street from the Arc de Triomphe. ⊠ *133 av. des Champs-Élysées, 8e, Champs-Élysées* ☎ *01–44–43–79–00* ⊕ *www.publicisdrugstore.com* Ⓜ *Charles de Gaulle–Étoile.*

17

Fodor's Choice   ★   **Saint James Club Paris.** Like a library room out of *Harry Potter*, the bar at the Saint James Club Paris—complete with 5,000 leather-bound volumes and a cozy fireplace—is studiously inviting. It's very French, and open to nonmembers only after 7 pm or during Sunday brunch. The owners are a venerable old Bordeaux family; accordingly, you'll find a respectable selection of champagnes and wines. ✉ *43 av. Bugeaud, 16e, Bois de Boulogne* ☎ *01–44–05–81–82* ⊕ *www.saintjamesclub.com* Ⓜ *Porte Dauphine.*

CABARET

Fodor's Choice   ★   **Crazy Horse.** This world-renowned cabaret has elevated the striptease to an art form. Founded in 1951, it's famous for gorgeous dancers and naughty routines characterized by lots of humor and very little clothing. What garments there are have been dazzlingly designed by the likes of Louboutin and Alaïa and shed by top divas (including Dita von Teese). ✉ *12 av. George V, 8e, Champs-Élysées* ☎ *01–47–23–32–32* ⊕ *www. lecrazyhorseparis.com* Ⓜ *Alma-Marceau.*

Lido. The glamorous supercalifragilisticexpialidelicious Blubell Girls (picture feathers, spangles, boas, and lots of skin) are the stars here. Lido owners claim that no show this side of Vegas rivals theirs for special effects. ✉ *116 bis, av. des Champs-Élysées, 8e, Champs-Élysées* ☎ *01–40–76–56–10* ⊕ *www.lido.fr* Ⓜ *George V.*

CLUBS

Black Calavados. Known as "BC" to its trendsetting devotees, Black Calavados is a sleek bar where the party starts late (don't bother coming before 1 am) and lasts until morning. Ring the buzzer out front for the doorman to assess your worth—this is a celebrity hangout. Inside, try the Black Kiss, a shot of black vodka served on ice with sugar-cube lips. ■TIP→ If all else fails, head upstairs to the smaller but equally sexy Blitz tequila bar. ✉ *40 av. Pierre 1er de Serbie, 8e, Champs-Élysées* ☎ *01–47–20–77–77* Ⓜ *Alma–Marceau, George V.*

Le Baron. Formerly a seedy "hostess" bar, Le Baron didn't bother to update its decadent cabaret decor (red banquettes, mirror ball, and baronial top-hat sign) when it opened in 2004—and it didn't need to. Models, musicians, and Oscar winners party until morning while indulging in the bar's classic cocktail: a mix of red fruits, champagne, and vodka called the Baron Deluxe. It's notoriously difficult to get in. ✉ *6 av. Marceau, 8e, Champs-Élysées* ☎ *01–47–20–04–01* Ⓜ *Alma–Marceau.*

Queen. This mythic gay club of the '90s is not quite as monumental as it once was, but it still packs 'em in and the doors are still difficult to get through, especially—inevitably—on weekends. Proudly hosting a fantastic roster of top DJs, it's known for its campy soirées. These days it attracts a gay-straight mix of international partygoers eager to dance on podiums. ✉ *102 av. des Champs-Élysées, 8e, Champs-Élysées* ☎ *01–53–89–08–90* ⊕ *www.queen.fr* Ⓜ *George V.*

Fodor's Choice   ★   **Showcase.** Under the golden Pont Alexandre, Showcase takes the gold medal for best location. Inside, a long bar, two VIP sections, and a stage that hosts a diverse range of talented acts and DJs makes this a mandatory stop on any night of clubbing. ■TIP→ Reserve ahead for the best seating. ✉ *Pont Alexandre III, Port des Champs-Élysées, 8e,*

Champs-Élysées ☎ *01–45–61–25–43* ⊕ *www.showcase.fr* Ⓜ *Champs-Élysées–Clemenceau, Invalides.*

JAZZ CLUBS

Jazz Club Etoile. This moody club at the Méridien Hotel hosts a roster of top-billed international musicians in a classy set of rooms. Check out the Sunday afternoon jazz brunch buffet and the interior garden. ✉ *Méridien Hotel, 81 bd. Gouvion–St-Cyr, 17e, Bois de Boulogne* ☎ *01–40–68–30–42* Ⓜ *Porte Maillot.*

AROUND THE LOUVRE

The cocktail craze has taken off in this atmospheric neighborhood, where dusky speakeasies and cozy hotel bars provide the perfect prelude to an evening of jazz or dancing 'til dawn at hip all-night clubs.

LES HALLES

BARS

Fodor's Choice ★ **Ballroom du Beef Club.** Unmarked black door, basement setting, pressed tin ceilings, atmospheric lighting—did anyone say speakeasy? All this and luscious concoctions draw a sophisticated crowd that appreciates the extra touches that make this cocktail bar a standout. ✉ *58 rue Jean-Jacques-Rousseau, 1e, Les Halles* ☎ *09–54–37–13–65* Ⓜ *Les Halles, Palais Royal–Musée du Louvre.*

Chacha Club. Behind a nondescript facade you'll find a 1930s-style bar-club-restaurant arranged like a private home, with a series of rooms on three floors—including a special smoking lounge—and lots of corners where the casually stylish cool cats of Paris get cozy until the wee hours. ✉ *47 rue Berger, 1er, Les Halles* ☎ *01 40 13 12 12* ⊕ *www.chachaclub.fr* Ⓜ *Louvre–Rivoli.*

Experimental Cocktail Club. Fashioned as a speakeasy on a tiny brick-paved street, the Experimental Cocktail Club seems like it should be lighted by gas lamps. The show is all about the *alcool*; colorful, innovative cocktails like the Lemon Drop are mixed with aplomb by friendly (and attractive) bartenders. By 11 pm it's packed with a diverse mix of locals, professionals, and fashionistas, who occasionally dress up like characters from a Toulouse-Lautrec painting on special costume nights. ✉ *37 rue Saint-Sauveur, 2e, Les Halles* ☎ *01–45–08–88–09* Ⓜ *Réamur–Sébastopol.*

Jefrey's. The custom DJ'd music track, the love seats, and the inventive cocktails make this a sophisticated and easy choice for an intimate evening in good company and stylish surroundings. Great for return customers, Jefrey's lets you keep your bottle stored on the shelf, with your name on it, for next time. ✉ *14 rue Saint-Sauveur, 2e, Les Halles* ☎ *01–42–33–60–77* ⊕ *www.jefreys.fr* Ⓜ *Étienne Marcel.*

Le Café Noir. Parisians from *bobos* (bourgeois-bohemians) to *pompiers* (fire fighters) are lured to Le Café Noir's elegantly worn digs. In addition to cool drinks and friendly staff, the place features a pipe-smoking papier-mâché fish and a vintage leopard-print-covered motorbike. (The restaurant with the same name is unrelated.) ✉ *65 rue Montmartre, 2e, Les Halles* ☎ *01–40–39–07–36* Ⓜ *Étienne Marcel.*

17

GAY AND LESBIAN BARS AND CLUBS

Banana Café. Banana Café draws a trendy, scantily clad mixed crowd and offers show tunes in the cellar, where dancing on tables is the norm. A very happy happy hour lasts from 6 to 11 pm to prime the audience for the incomparable banana "go-go boys" nightly show—ooh la la! ✉ *13 rue de la Ferronnerie, 1er, Les Halles* ☎ *01–42–33–35–31* ⊕ *www.bananacafeparis.com* Ⓜ *Châtelet–Les Halles.*

Bar d'Art/Le Duplex. Young tortured-artist types flock here to enjoy the frequent art exhibitions, alternative music, and mood-inspiring ambient lighting. ✉ *25 rue Michel-Le-Comte, 3e, Les Halles* ☎ *01–42–72–80–86* ⊕ *www.duplex-bar.com* Ⓜ *Rambuteau.*

Le Dépôt. Le Dépôt is a cruising bar, club, and the largest back room in Europe. The ever-popular Gay Tea Dance spices up Sunday afternoon. ✉ *10 rue aux Ours, 3e, Les Halles* ☎ *01–44–54–96–96* ⊕ *www.ledepot-paris.com* Ⓜ *Étienne Marcel.*

JAZZ CLUBS

Duc des Lombards. Located in a famously bopping neighborhood, the Duc's cozy interior and top-class jazz acts make it one Paris's most popular small venues. ■TIP→ It's best to purchase advance tickets online (go to bons plans for discounted tickets). ✉ *42 rue des Lombards, 1er, Les Halles* ☎ *01–42–33–22–88* ⊕ *www.ducdeslombards.com* Ⓜ *Châtelet–Les Halles.*

Le Sunset-Sunside. This two-part club hosts French and American jazz musicians: the Sunside upstairs is devoted mostly to acoustic jazz, while the Sunset downstairs features everything from electronic jazz, fusion, and groove to classic and swing. Jam sessions have been known to last well into the wee hours. ✉ *60 rue des Lombards, 1er, Les Halles* ☎ *01–40–26–46–60* ⊕ *www.sunset-sunside.com* Ⓜ *Châtelet–Les Halles.*

LOUVRE

BARS

Bar 8. Since this monolithic marble bar at the Mandarin Oriental Hotel opened its doors, it has been the "in" game in town. There's an extensive champagne menu, and the terrace is especially busy during fashion weeks. ✉ *251 rue Saint-Honoré, 1e, Louvre/Tuileries* ☎ *01–70–98–78–88* ⊕ *www.mandarinoriental.com* Ⓜ *Concorde, Tuileries.*

Bar 228. Hôtel Meurice converted its ground-floor Fontainebleau library into the intimate Bar 228, with wood paneling and huge murals depicting the royal hunting forests of Fontainebleau. Its loyal fashion crowd is continually wooed by Philippe Starck's decor updates and lubricated with the bar's famous Bellinis. ■TIP→ Try the Meurice Millennium cocktail, made with champagne, rose liqueur, and Cointreau. ✉ *228 rue de Rivoli, 1er, Louvre* ☎ *01–44–58–10–66* ⊕ *www.lemeurice.com* Ⓜ *Tuileries.*

The Hemingway Bar & the Ritz Bar. Literature lovers, cocktail connoisseurs and other drink-swilling devotees drew a collective sigh when the iconic Hemingway Bar & the Ritz Bar were shuttered—along with the rest of the Ritz—when the hotel closed for a top-to-bottom makeover in 2012. It's expected that libations will started being poured again in late 2014 or early 2015. Watch for the big reveal: this is one of the most hotly anticipated facelifts in Paris. ✉ *15 pl. Vendôme, 1er, Louvre/Tuileries* ⊕ *www.ritzparis.com* Ⓜ *Opéra.*

Hôtel Costes. Despite years on the scene, Hôtel Costes still draws big names—and not just during fashion weeks. Expect to cross paths with anyone from Rihanna to Orlando Bloom, as long as you make it past the chilly greeting of the statuesque hostess. Dressing to kill is strongly advised, especially for newcomers; otherwise, expect all the tables to be suddenly reserved. ✉ *239 rue St-Honoré, 1er, Louvre* ☎ *01–42–44– 50–25* ⊕ *hotelcostes.com* Ⓜ *Tuileries.*

L'Assaggio Bar. At this bar, in Chanel's old neighborhood, you can order tea and *macarons* until midnight—in addition to cocktails. ✉ *33–37 rue Cambon, 1e, Louvre/Tuileries* ☎ *01 44 58 44 58* ⊕ *www.castille.com* Ⓜ *Concorde, Madeleine.*

Le Bar O d'Oro Ïto. Slip into a sinuous banquette at Hôtel O's intimate, stylish bar while you still can. It's an undiscovered gem, ideal for savoring a choice selection of ambrosial cocktails. ∎**TIP➜ The Cointreau Fizz—a blend of ginger soda, lemon, and Cointreau, with a split vanilla bean and a hint of rose—is as classy as they come.** ✉ *19 rue Herold, 1e, Around the Louvre* ☎ *01–42–36–04–02* ⊕ *www.hotel-o-paris.com* Ⓜ *Palais Royal–Musée du Louvre, Sentier, Les Halles.*

Le Fumoir. Le Fumoir is an oh-so-reliably ultrachic charmer across from the Louvre, where fashionable neighborhood gallery owners and young professionals meet for late-afternoon wine, early-evening cocktails, or dinner. It features a super-stocked bar in the front, an ample multilingual library in the back, and chessboards for the clientele to use while sipping martinis. ✉ *6 rue de l'Amiral-Coligny, 1er, Louvre* ☎ *01–42– 92–00–24* ⊕ *www.lefumoir.com* Ⓜ *Louvre.*

CLUBS

Kong. Kong is glorious not only for its panoramic skyline views, but for its exquisite manga-inspired decor, the top-shelf DJs for weekend dancing, and its kooky, disco-ball-and-kid-sumo-adorned bathrooms. ✉ *1 rue du Pont-Neuf, 1er, Louvre* ☎ *01–40–39–09–00* ⊕ *www.kong. fr* Ⓜ *Pont-Neuf.*

VIP Room. Although it's no longer on the Champs Élysées, this temple of bling still attracts hot DJs, beautiful people, and VIPs! Check the website for the latest soirée: usually R&B/hip-hop/top 40 crowd pleasers. There's a gift shop, a ground floor café, and a pricey Italian restaurant on the top floor. Dress to impress. ✉ *188 bis rue de Rivoli, 1er, Louvre* ☎ *01–58–36–46–00* ⊕ *www.viproom.fr* Ⓜ *Palais-Royal.*

GAY CLUBS

Club 18. This elegant spot (the oldest gay club in Paris) takes gay pride to the heart of the Louvre district on the weekends. Club 18 boasts a well-earned reputation as a "friendly party scene." ✉ *18 rue de Beaujolais, 1er, Louvre* ☎ *01–42–97–52–13* ⊕ *www.club18.fr* Ⓜ *Palais-Royal.*

17

The Paris Cocktail Scene

The cocktail bar is undergoing a renaissance in Paris. In fact, classy concoctions haven't been served up with such flair since the days when the Bloody Mary and the Sidecar were introduced at fabled Harry's Bar and martinis were the drink du jour at the Ritz Hotel's Hemingway Bar (the writers and aristocrats who assembled at the latter included the bar's notoriously thirsty namesake).

The new cocktail bars run the gamut from dauntingly elegant hotel lounges to designer dives, and they attract a diverse crowd willing to shell out anywhere from €10 to €26 a pop. Once called barmen, the new curators of cocktails are "mixologists," and the best of the lot garner fame and a following among devoted enthusiasts. Drinks are crafted, ingredients are sourced, the booze is barrel-aged or infused, syrups are house-made, and the ice is artisanal. Many also serve excellent food.

Opening hours tend to be perfect for an *apéro* (six-o'clock-ish), and closing hours are later than the average Paris bar (around 2 am) except for hotel bars, which close as early as 11 pm. Here are a few standouts:

Le Bar O d'Ora Ïto (Hotel O): Sip custom cocktails in a bar that's as sleek and stylish as the hotel that houses it.

Glass: Party to the DJ beats at this shrine to urban cool—complete with microbrews and a frozen drinks machine.

Dirty Dick: The newest destination cocktail club combines retro tiki-lounge cheekiness with a serious selection of rum.

La Conserverie: High-low loft style, a congenial atmosphere, and superlative drinks draw the cocktail cognoscenti.

Le Mary Celeste: Hipsters come for Happy Hour oysters—then stay to linger over craft cocktails and natural wines.

Little Red Door: This tiny trendsetter with atmosphere to spare serves sophisticated choices behind its eponymous door.

Playtime Cocktails (Artus Hotel): Expect an intimate Mad Men vibe with banquettes, and classy classic cocktails.

L'Entrée des Artistes: It's too moody and dark to read the drinks menu, so just point your finger—it's all good.

Ballroom du Beef Club: An unmarked door, a dim interior, and upholstered loveseats add to the speakeasy ambience.

Prescription Cocktail Club: Lively and louche, it's just what the doctor ordered—if your doctor is Dorothy Parker.

OPÉRA/GRANDS BOULEVARDS

An assortment of well-established British-Irish pubs and clubs bring an Anglo-inflected nuance to this many-faceted neighborhood that bustles by day and empties out at night.

BARS

Barramundi. The city's nouveau-riche chill to electro-lounge tunes and world music here, drinking in Barramundi's cool golden ambience as they sip cold tropical drinks at the long copper bar. ✉ *3 rue Taitbout, 9e, Opéra/ Grands Boulevards* ☎ *01–47– 70–21–21* ⊕ *www.barramundi.fr* Ⓜ *Richelieu–Drouot.*

Corcoran's Irish Pub. This roomy pub, with several locations in central Paris, has an ample menu, a gorgeous bar, plus old-timey photos and quotations on the walls—such as "He who opens his mouth most is the one who opens his purse least." Conversation turns to dancing at night with a regulated guy-to-girl ratio, so men shouldn't try coming alone. ✉ *23 bd. Poissonière, 2e, Opéra/Grands Boulevards* ☎ *01–40–39–00–16* ⊕ *www.corcoransirishpub.fr* Ⓜ *Grands Boulevards.*

Delaville Café. With its huge, heated sidewalk terrace, Belle Époque mosaic-tile bar, graffitied walls, and swishy lounge, Delaville Café boasts a funky Baroque ambience. Hot Paris DJs ignite the scene Thursday to Saturday, so arrive early on weekends if you want a seat. ✉ *34 bd. Bonne Nouvelle, 10e, Opéra/Grands Boulevards* ☎ *01–48–24–48–09* ⊕ *delavillecafe.com* Ⓜ *Bonne Nouvelle, Grands Boulevards.*

Duke's Bar. A favorite not only for its prestigious location between Opéra and Place Vendôme, but also for its worn leather chairs and English private club feel, the Westminster Hotel's bar offers drinks like the "James Bond" and "Duke's Martini." At times you get the feeling that Mr. Hercule Poirot is lurking just behind that wingback chair. ✉ *13 rue de la Paix, 2e, Opéra/Grands Boulevards* ☎ *01–42–61–55–11* ⊕ *www. hotel-westminster-opera-paris.fr* Ⓜ *Opéra.*

Harry's Bar. Also known as Harry's New York Bar, this cozy, wood-paneled hangout decorated with dusty college pennants is popular with expats and American-loving French people who welcome the ghosts of Ernest Hemingway and F. Scott Fitzgerald, who drank himself unconscious here. Founded in 1911, Gershwin composed "An American in Paris" in the piano bar downstairs and the Bloody Mary is said to have originated on-site. ✉ *5 rue Daunou, 2e, Opéra/Grands Boulevards* ☎ *01–42–61–71–14* ⊕ *www.harrys-bar.fr* Ⓜ *Opéra.*

Kitty O'Shea's. This ever-popular Irish pub near Place Vendôme attracts both a posh after-work crowd and salt-of-the-earth types. Authentic trimmings—including stained glass and Gaelic street signs—are decor

---

APERITIFS

For aperitifs French style, try a *pastis*—anise-flavored liquor such as Pernod or Ricard that turns cloudy when water is added. Ask for *"un petit jaune, s'il vous plait."* A *pineau* is cognac and fruity grape juice. The *kir* (white wine with a dash of black-currant syrup) is a popular drink, too; a *kir royale* is made with champagne.

La Fée Verte. Absinthe—the vivid green, once-outlawed liquor— has made a comeback around town. Try a taste at La Fée Verte in the Bastille area. The food is good here, too. ✉ *108 rue de la Roquette, 11e, Bastille* ☎ *01–43– 72–31–24* Ⓜ *Charonne.*

17

CLOSE UP

Jazz Clubs

The French fell hard for jazz during World War I, but the real *coup de foudre*—literally "lightning bolt" or figuratively "love at first sight"—came after the war when Yank sax man Sidney Bechet and 19-year-old song-and-dance vamp Josephine Baker of St. Louis joined a European tour of the Revue Nègre musical. Baker, or the "Black Venus that haunted Baudelaire," as she was known by French critics, instantly became the sweetheart of Paris. Note: A larger-than-life picture of Baker wearing only a smile, a string of pearls, and a thigh-high skirt today adorns a wall of historic photographs along the platform of the Tuileries métro.

By 1934 France had created its own impressive claim to jazz fame, the all-string Quintette du Hot Club de France, which featured Gypsy guitarist Django Reinhardt and his partner, violinist Stéphane Grappelli. They, in turn, influenced string players from country musicians to Carlos Santana. Reinhardt performed throughout much of World War II in the underground French jazz scene. In the 1950s Paris grew to become a major destination of the bebop diaspora, and expat jazz musicians including Bechet, Bud Powell, and Dexter Gordon played the venues along with such jazz greats as Dizzy Gillespie, Charlie Parker, and Miles Davis. France embraced the evolving jazz sound that many Americans were still struggling to accept and provided a worshipful welcome to musicians battling discrimination at home. In Paris, Davis said, he was "treated like a human being."

WANT A NIGHT OF JAZZ?
The French obsession with jazz continues to this day, and travelers seeking a quintessential Parisian experience have the opportunity to hear jazz artists from all over the world nearly any night of the week. Aficionados can choose from traditional jazz to the latest experimental efforts, in clubs ranging from casual to chichi, sedate to hopping. Many venues present a wide spectrum of music. A good option is the double club on Rue des Lombards near Les Halles: Le Sunside specializes in more traditional jazz, and its downstairs sister, Le Sunset, features edgier options.

Music generally begins after 9 pm, so plan accordingly. You can dine at some of the clubs, including Le Petit Journal Montparnasse, or in the Hotel Méridien on the Champs-Élysées, which houses the classy Jazz Club Etoile.

As everywhere else in the city, the French folks at the clubs tend to dress more stylishly than the average traveler with a limited wardrobe, but they're generally a tolerant bunch—particularly in venues frequented by students and in the heart of tourist areas (like Caveau de la Huchette, a hot cellar dance club across the river from Notre-Dame). Keep in mind, though, that the French are serious about their jazz: with a few exceptions, the audience is generally focused and quiet during performances.

Recognizable names to watch for include expat Yank flute and sax man Bobby Rangell and singer Sara Lazarus, and much-loved French musicians like the pianists Alain Jean-Marie and Pierre de Bethman, sax man Didier Malherbe, and Olivier Ker Ourio on the harmonica. You might want to check out a jazz style you're

less likely to find at home, though, like the latest iteration of Gypsy musette (a distinctive, swing-infused interpretation of old Paris dance music) presented by virtuosos like accordionist Richard Galliano, violinist Didier Lockwood, and the guitar-picking Ferre brothers, Boulou and Elios. Look for them inside Duc des Lombards on Rue des Lombards. Alternatively, you can head to New Morning, on Rue des Petites-Ecuries—it's the top spot for experimental and avant-garde jazz.

The best place to find out what's playing and even purchase tickets is at ⊕ *www.infoconcert.com* or on club websites, some of which offer English versions. *Pariscope, Jazz Magazine,* and *Jazz Hot,* available at newsstands, have listings in English and French. Reservations can be critical, especially for leading U.S. jazz musicians.

Entrance charges are rarely more than €20 and often less. Some venues have free jam sessions, depending on the night, so check listings. Drink prices can be sky-high, but most table staff won't harass budget-conscious customers nursing a single drink.

Another way to experience a variety of top-quality jazz is by attending world-renowned Paris festivals that run from early spring through September, including the **Banlieues Bleues** (☏ *01–49–22–10–10* ⊕ *www. banlieuesbleues.org*), the **Paris Jazz Festival** (☏ *01–48–72–32–97* ⊕ *www. parisjazzfestival.fr*), and the **Villette Jazz Festival** (☏ *01–44–84–44–84* ⊕ *www.citedelamusique.fr*).

17

highlights. A restaurant serves pub standards like fish-and-chips, and rugby games are shown on the big screen in season. ■TIP→ Check the website for guest DJs and concert info. ✉ *10 rue des Capucines, 2e, Opéra/Grands Boulevards* ☎ *01–40–15–00–30* ⊕ *www.kittyosheas.com* Ⓜ *Opéra.*

Fodor'sChoice **La Conserverie.** La Conserverie is a rustic-elegant loft space with exposed ductwork, Aubusson tapestries, comfy sofas, and glass-bottle chandeliers. Skillfully crafted

> **DID YOU KNOW?**
>
> **Café des Deux Moulins.** If you're looking to pay homage to the French hit film *Amélie* in Montmartre (you aren't the only one), stop in at Café des Deux Moulins, a watering hole with a copper-topped bar where much of the film was shot. ✉ *15 rue Lepic, 18e, Montmartre* ☎ *01–42–54–90–50* Ⓜ *Blanche, Abesses.*

cocktails—for those on and off the wagon—and reliably good food keep the crowd convivial. A smaller downstairs space accommodates romantics. ■TIP→ Reserve ahead to be sure of a table. ✉ *37 bis, rue du Sentier, 2e, Opéra/Grands Boulevards* ☎ *01–40–26–14–94* ⊕ *www.laconserveriebar.com* Ⓜ *Bonne Nouvelle, Sentier.*

Le Bar Long. At the Royal Monceau's innovative bar your mixologist will fix your drink right next to you at the illuminated, Philippe Stark–designed bar. The collection of glasses on the walls isn't just decoration—you may choose which to drink from. A light tapas menu is served between 6 and 11 pm. ✉ *37 av. Hoche, 8e, Opéra/Grands Boulevards* ☎ *01–42–99–88–00* ⊕ *www.leroyalmonceau.com* Ⓜ *Ternes.*

Le Truskel. What looks, sounds and feels like an English pub but kicks booty like a punk club? Le Truskel, whose basement showcases gigs by the globe's hottest new alternative acts, while a loud, happy Parisian rocker crowd staggers around the roomy bar. ✉ *12 rue Feydeau, 2e, Opéra/Grands Boulevards* ☎ *01–40–26–59–97* ⊕ *www.truskel.com* Ⓜ *Bourse.*

CABARET

Le Limonaire. This old-world-style wine-and-*chanson* bistro oozes Parisian charm. It serves food until 10 pm Tuesday–Sunday before giving way to the singing of traditional French songs of "expression," with musical accompaniment *bien sûr*. There's no entrance fee; musicians pass the hat. ✉ *18 cité Bergère, 9e, Opéra/Grands Boulevards* ☎ *01–45–23–33–33* ⊕ *limonaire.free.fr* Ⓜ *Grands Boulevards.*

CLUBS

Le Rex. This temple of techno and house is popular with students and open Wednesday through Sunday. One of France's most famous DJs, Laurent Garnier, is sometimes at the turntables. ✉ *5 bd. Poissonnière, 2e, Opéra/Grands Boulevards* ☎ *01–42–36–10–96* ⊕ *www.rexclub.com* Ⓜ *Grands Boulevards.*

Silencio. David Lynch named his nightclub after a reference in his Oscar hit, *Mulholland Drive*. Silencio, which hosts concerts, films, and other performances, is open only to members and their guests until midnight; after that everyone is allowed. Guest DJs spin until 4 am on weeknights, 6 am on Friday and Saturday. ✉ *142 rue Montmartre, 2e,*

Opéra/Grands Boulevards ☎*01–40–13–12–33* ⊕*www.silencio-club. com* Ⓜ *Bourse, Sentier.*

JAZZ CLUBS

Fodor'sChoice **New Morning.** At New Morning—the premier spot for serious fans of
★ avant-garde jazz, folk, and world music—the look is spartan, the mood reverential. ✉ *7 rue des Petites-Ecuries, 10e, Opéra/Grands Boulevards* ☎*01–45–23–51–41* ⊕ *www.newmorning.com* Ⓜ *Château d'Eau.*

MONTMARTRE

Vestiges of this *quartier*'s absinthe-tinged heyday, immortalized by Toulouse-Lautrec and Renoir, still endure in the cabarets and clubs that extend from the heights of Montmartre down to louche Pigalle's newly vibrant cocktail bar and dance scene.

BARS

Café la Fourmi. One of Pigalle's trendiest addresses, Café la Fourmi has a funky, spacious bar-café where cool locals party. ✉ *74 rue des Martyrs, 18e, Montmartre* ☎*01–42–64–70–35* Ⓜ *Pigalle.*

Fodor'sChoice **Dirty Dick.** An updated version of the classic tiki lounge, this stylish
★ option in a newly hip neighborhood comes complete with lurid lighting, life-size totems, and retro rattan furniture. All the exotic drinks you'd expect at a Polynesian beach hut (or '60s motel lounge) are here—including fruity cocktails, a range of rums, and punchbowls with names like Amazombie. ✉ *10 rue Frochot, 9e, Montmartre* ☎*01–48–78–74–58* Ⓜ *Pigalle.*

Fodor'sChoice **Glass.** Masquerading as a dive in Pigalle's rapidly gentrifying red-light
★ district, this dark, candlelighted space is actually a shrine to urban cool. Hipsters party to a DJ while knocking back sophisticated cocktails, artisanal beers, and frosty margaritas from the frozen drinks machine. It might also be the only place in Paris to find a boilermaker (a beer and a shot). Gourmet hot dogs help fuel the late-night party scene. ✉ *9 rue Frochot, 9e, Montmartre* ☎*06–25–16–72–17* ⊕ *www.glassparis. com* Ⓜ *Pigalle.*

Le Rendez-Vous des Amis. This makes an intriguing midway breather if you climb the hill of Montmartre by foot. Le Rendez-Vous des Amis has a jovial staff, eclectic music, and a century's worth of previous patrons immortalized in photos. ✉ *23 rue Gabrielle, 18e, Montmartre* ☎*01–46–06–01–60* Ⓜ *Abbesses.*

Le Sancerre. Café by day, Le Sancerre turns into an essential watering hole for Montmartrois and artists at night, with Belgian beers on tap and an impressive list of cocktails. Locals love its traditional old-school vibe. ✉ *35 rue des Abbesses, 18e, Montmartre* ☎*01–42–58–08–20* Ⓜ *Abbesses.*

CABARET

Fodor'sChoice **Au Lapin Agile.** An authentic survivor from the 19th century, Au Lapin
★ Agile considers itself the doyen of cabarets. Founded in 1860, it inhabits the same modest house that was a favorite subject of painter Maurice Utrillo. It became the home-away-from-home for Braque, Modigliani, Apollinaire, and Picasso—who once paid for a meal with one of his

17

paintings, then promptly exited and painted another that he named after this place. There are no topless dancers; this is a genuine French cabaret with songs, poetry, and humor (in French) in a publike setting. Entry is €28. ✉ *22 rue des Saules, 18e, Montmartre* ☎ *01–46–06–85–87* ⊕ *www.au-lapin-agile.com* Ⓜ *Lamarck–Caulaincourt.*

Michou. The always-decked-out-in-blue owner, Michou, presents an over-the-top show here. It features *tranformiste* men on stage in extravagant drag, performing with high camp for a radically different cabaret experience. Dinner shows are €110 and €140, or you can watch from the bar for €40, which includes a drink. ✉ *80 rue des Martyrs, 18e, Montmartre* ☎ *01–46–06–16–04* ⊕ *michou.com* Ⓜ *Pigalle.*

Moulin Rouge. When it opened in 1889, the Moulin Rouge lured Parisians of all social stripes—including, of course, the famous Toulouse-Lautrec, who immortalized the venue and its dancers in his paintings. Although shows are no longer quite so exotic (no elephants or donkey rides for the ladies), you will still see the incomparable French cancan. It's the highlight of what is now a classy version of a Vegas-y revue, starring 100 dancers, acrobats, ventriloquists, and contortionists, and more than 1,000 costumes. Dinner starts at 7, revues at 9 and 11 (arrive 30 minutes early). Men are expected to wear a jacket and tie. Prices range from €99 for just a revue to €210 for a luxe dinner and a show. ✉ *82 bd. de Clichy, 18e, Montmartre* ☎ *01–53–09–82–82* ⊕ *www.moulinrouge. fr* Ⓜ *Blanche.*

CLUBS

Le Folie's Pigalle. Decorated like a '30s-era bordello, this former cabaret cultivates a decadent ambience, with music that ranges from house and techno to R&B and electro. After-parties hop on Sunday morning. ✉ *11 pl. Pigalle, 9e, Pigalle* ☎ *01–48–78–55–25* Ⓜ *Pigalle.*

GAY AND LESBIAN BARS AND CLUBS

Chez Moune. Chez Moune is the former lesbian cabaret now run by the same team as Le Baron (expect the same strict door policy), with regular DJs and aftershow parties that keep the devoted dancing until dawn. ✉ *54 rue Jean-Baptiste Pigalle, 9e, Pigalle* ☎ *01–45–26–64–64* Ⓜ *Pigalle.*

THE MARAIS

A first-class shopping destination by day, by night this superchic neighborhood draws a diverse and trendy crowd for its branché cocktail bars and Paris's most vibrant gay and lesbian scene.

BARS

Andy Wahloo. Andy Wahloo has a hip crowd and an Andy Warhol-meets-*Casablanca* decor. Fans of the ginger-rum Wahloo *spéciales* relax on oversize paint-can stools beneath high-kitsch silk-screened Moroccan coffee ads, and listen to funky Arabic Raï remixes. Dancing to DJs starts later in the night. ✉ *69 rue des Gravilliers, 3e, Marais* ☎ *01–42–71–20–38* ⊕ *andywahloo-bar.com* Ⓜ *Arts et Métiers.*

Auld Alliance. Auld Alliance has Scottish shields on the walls, and the bar staff dresses in kilts for special events. There are more than 120 whiskeys, Scottish beer, soccer, and rugby on TV, and sometimes live music.

✉ *80 rue François Miron, 4e, Marais* ☎ *01–48–04–30–40* ⊕ *www. theauldalliance.com* Ⓜ *St-Paul.*

Bar at the Hotel Jules & Jim. The look here is something between a chic contemporary Paris apartment and a low-key lounge. Enjoy a cocktail over a good book from the bar library, or relax with a smooth drink in front of the outdoor fireplace. ✉ *11 rue des Gravilliers, 3e, Marais* ☎ *01–44–54–13–13* ⊕ *www.hoteljulesetjim.com* Ⓜ *Arts et Métiers, Rambuteau.*

Fodor's Choice ★ **Candelaria.** If a muscled man bars your way, just whisper the magic word: cocktail. Then traverse the tiny Mexican taqueria (the best in Paris) through an unmarked door and into a crowded, steamy room where the tang of tequila hangs in the air. You've found one of Paris's hip hideaways. ✉ *52 rue de Saintonge, 3e, Marais* ☎ *01–42–74–41–28* ⊕ *www.candelariaparis.com* Ⓜ *Filles du Calvaire.*

Grazie. Equal parts cocktail bar and gourmet pizzeria, this stylish offspring of the übercool concept store Merci promises top-quality libations and stone-oven-baked pizza. The decor is industrial-rustic, with pressed-tin ceilings and a corrugated iron bar, all enhanced by mood lighting. It's jam-packed with neighborhood hipsters, so reservations are a must. ✉ *91 bd. Beaumarchais, 3e, Marais* ☎ *01–42–78–11–96* ⊕ *www.graziegrazie.fr* Ⓜ *Saint-Sébastien–Froissart.*

La Belle Hortense. La Belle Hortense is heaven for anyone who ever wished they had a book in a bar (or a drink in a bookstore). The *bar littéraire* is the infamous spot where gal-about-town Catherine M. launched her *vie sexuelle* that became a bawdy bestseller. ✉ *31 rue Vielle-du-Temple, 4e, Marais* ☎ *01–48–04–74–60* Ⓜ *St-Paul.*

La Perle. La Perle is a bustling, buzzy Marais masterpiece, where straights, gays, and lesbians of all types come to mingle. The crowd makes this place interesting, not the neon lights, diner-style seats, or stripped-down decor. It continues to pack in some of the city's fashion movers and shakers from midafternoon on. ✉ *78 rue Vielle-du-Temple, 3e, Marais* ☎ *01–42–72–69–93* ⊕ *cafelaperle.com* Ⓜ *Chemin-Vert.*

Fodor's Choice ★ **Le Mary Celeste.** Half-price oysters at happy hour (5–7 pm) aren't the only reason this refreshingly unpretentious cocktail bar has been wildly popular since debuting in 2013. One of a trilogy of superhip watering holes (including Candelaria and Glass) opened by a trio of expat restaurateurs, its craft cocktails, microbrews, natural wines, and standout tapas menu deliver the goods and then some. ■ TIP→ **If you're planning to dine, reserve ahead online.** ✉ *1 rue Commines, 3e, Marais* ⊕ *www. lemaryceleste.com* Ⓜ *Saint-Sébastien–Froissart.*

Le Trésor. Le Trésor is lively and sophisticated, with mismatched Baroque furnishings in a large space and a chill vibe on a tiny street that's a tad separate from the sometimes madding crowd of the Marais. ✉ *7 rue du Trésor, 4e, Marais* ☎ *01–42–71–35–17* Ⓜ *St-Paul.*

Little Red Door. Behind the red door, you'll discover a dark, cozy lounge that has style, sophistication, and atmosphere without the attitude. Deftly crafted cocktails—supplemented by artisanal beers and well-chosen wines by the glass (the last of which aren't always easy to come

17

by in a cocktail bar)—can be enjoyed from a cushy velour barstool or cubbyhole alcove. ⊠ *60 rue Charlot, 3e, Marais* ☎ *01–42–71–19–32* ⊕ *www.lrdparis.com* Ⓜ *Filles du Calvert.*

Max y Jeremy. An almost-too-cool crowd can be found in Max y Jeremy's red emberlike interior, drinking cocktails and eating the sultry bite-sized *pintxos* of Basque country. There's a distinct party atmosphere here, which can spill into the street, especially in summer. ⊠ *6 rue Dupuis, 3e, Marais* ☎ *01–42–78–00–68* ⊕ *www.maxyjeremy.com* Ⓜ *Temple.*

Fodor's Choice ★ **Sherry Butt.** On a quiet street close to the Bastille, Sherry Butt's relaxed loft-like atmosphere, imaginative drinks, whisky flights, and tasty bar menu draw a cool crowd that appreciates meticulously crafted cocktails. On weekends a DJ spins to a lively crowd. ⊠ *20 rue Beautreillis, 4e, Marais* ☎ *09–83–38–47–80* ⊕ *www.sherrybuttparis.com* Ⓜ *Bastille, Sully–Morland.*

GAY AND LESBIAN BARS AND CLUBS

3W Kafé. 3W, as in "Women With Women," is a pillar of the lesbian scene. ⊠ *8 rue des Ecouffes, 4e, Marais* ☎ *01–48–87–39–26* Ⓜ *St-Paul.*

Café Cox. "Le Cox" is a prime gay pickup joint. Behind the frosted glass windows of the fire-engine-red hotspot, men appraise the talent. The café is known for its Thursday DJ night, and Sunday happy hour—from 6–2 am—is always a rollicking good time. ⊠ *15 rue des Archives, 4e, Marais* ☎ *01–42–72–08–00* ⊕ *www.cox.fr* Ⓜ *Hôtel de Ville.*

Open Café. Open Café is a relaxed, packed Marais favorite with a disco-café vibe. Drawing everyone from suits to punks, it's less of a gay meat market than neighboring Café Cox. ⊠ *17 rue des Archives, 4e, Marais* ☎ *01–42–72–26–18* ⊕ *www.opencafe.fr* Ⓜ *Hôtel de Ville.*

Raidd Bar. Raidd Bar is popular and friendly, with a darker downstairs bar and potent drinks. The men are hot, and so is the steamy shower show presented after 11 pm—not for timid voyeurs. ⊠ *23 rue du Temple, 3e, Marais* ☎ *0142770488* ⊕ *www.raiddbar.com* Ⓜ *Hôtel de Ville, St-Paul.*

So What!. So What! is a happening lesbian bar in the heart of the gay district that welcomes all comers (including small groups of men). The DJ in the tiny basement cooks on Friday and Saturday nights. ⊠ *30 rue du Roi de Sicile, 4e, Marais* Ⓜ *St-Paul.*

Tango. Tango has carefully safeguarded its dance-hall origins and lures a friendly mixed crowd of gays, lesbians, and "open minded" heteros. Late-night music is mostly French and American pop, but the DJ plays classic *chanson*s (French torch songs) before midnight—so arrive early to waltz and swing! ⊠ *13 rue au Maire, 3e, Marais* ☎ *01–42–72–17–78* ⊕ *www.boite-a-frissons.fr* Ⓜ *Arts et Métiers.*

EASTERN PARIS

Young and hip—from the colorful cafés and bars surrounding Place de la Bastille to the newly chic 20e arrondissement, with Oberkampf's artsy cocktail clubs and Canal St-Martin's trendy watering holes in between—there's enough here for a week of stellar nights out.

BASTILLE/NATION

BARS

Bar Sans Nom. In the increasing hubbub of the Bastille, the warm, red decor of this cozy getaway exudes a sultry glow, and hip lounge music adds to the charm. A flaming Kucaracha shot will turn up the heat. ✉ *49 rue de Lappe, 11e, Bastille* ☎ *01–48–05–59–36* Ⓜ *Bastille.*

Barrio Latino. Barrio Latino rocks the rafters for adventurers who love to indulge in Latin cultures from Brazilian to Cuban in the middle of Paris. The quirky four-story hacienda-resto, two dance bars, and top-floor nightclub fuel the devoted who shake to salsa and samba beats all night. The pricey €20 weekend entrance fee includes a drink. ✉ *46–48 rue du Faubourg St-Antoine, 12e, Bastille* ☎ *01–55–78–84–75* ⊕ *www. barrio-latino.com* Ⓜ *Bastille.*

WORD OF MOUTH

"Go to an old, rowdy jazz club such as Caveau de la Huchette, pay 10 euros to the guy in the tiny ticket window because you can already hear how good the music is . . . enter the 'caveau,' an ancient stone room with vaulted ceilings . . . and watch the trombonist fill his cheeks. Fantastique." —dekoder

CLUBS

Le Balajo. A casual dance club in an old ballroom, Le Balajo has been around since 1936. Latin groove, funk, and R&B disco are the standards, with old-style musette Sunday afternoon, salsa on Tuesday and Thursday nights, and rock on Wednesday. Saturday is ladies' night with a half-price entrance charge. ✉ *9 rue de Lappe, 11e, Bastille* ☎ *01–47–00–07–87* ⊕ *www.balajo.fr* Ⓜ *Bastille.*

BERCY/TOLBIAC

BARS

Folie en Tête. Folie en Tête, or "Lunacy in the Head," is a former mainstay of Paris's '70s punk scene. The comfortable interior is decorated with percussion instruments, comic books, and old skis. It's known for world music and jazz, not to mention the traffic light in the toilet that lets you know when it's safe to enter. ✉ *33 rue de la Butte aux Cailles, 13e, Bercy/Tolbiac* ☎ *01–45–80–65–99* ⊕ *lafolieentete.wix.com/lesite* Ⓜ *Corvisart, Place d'Italie.*

CLUBS

Le Batofar. An old tugboat refitted as a hip (yet reasonably priced) bar and concert venue, Le Batofar plays eclectic music, from live world-beat to electronic and techno. ◼ TIP→ **(Stylish) sneakers are recommended on the slippery deck.** ✉ *Port de la Gare, 13e, Bercy/Tolbiac* ☎ *01–53–60–17–00* ⊕ *www.batofar.org* Ⓜ *Bibliothèque.*

Le Djoon. This is not the place to stand around. Le Djoon attracts a devoted dance crowd, and DJs (inspired by the '80s New York house scene) mix Afro, disco, and funk. It's a taxi ride away from everywhere, but a fun diversion from the normally cramped clubs. Open Friday and Saturday from 11:30 to 5 am, Thursday from 6:30 to 1 am. ✉ *22 bd. Vincent Auriol, 13e, Bercy/Tolbiac* ☎ *01–45–70–83–49* ⊕ *www.djoon. com* Ⓜ *Quai de la Gare.*

17

CANAL ST-MARTIN

BARS

Chez Prune. Epitomizing the effortless cool of this arty neighborhood, Chez Prune is a lively golden getaway. It offers the designers, architects, and journalists who gather here a prime terrace for gazing out at the arched footbridges and funkier locals of Canal St-Martin. ⊠ *36 rue Beaurepaire, 10e, Canal St-Martin* ☎ *01–42–41–30–47* Ⓜ *Republique, Jacques Bonsergent.*

Hôtel du Nord. Hôtel du Nord—which starred in the classic Marcel Carné film of the same name—has been spiffed up but still maintains its cool with a vibrant lounge-bar (and restaurant) scene in the buzz-worthy Canal St-Martin district. ⊠ *102 quai de Jemmapes, 10e, Canal St-Martin* ☎ *01–40–40–78–78* ⊕ *www.hoteldunord.org* Ⓜ *Goncourt.*

La Patache. Among the bars and eateries lining Rue Lancry, you'll find La Patache. It has a wide selection of wines and a retro-inspired ambience fueled by a jukebox and candlelight that illuminates the vintage photos on the wall. ⊠ *60 rue Lancry, 10e, Canal St-Martin* ☎ *01–42–08–14–35* Ⓜ *Jacques-Bonsergent.*

CLUBS

La Java. The spot where Piaf and Chevalier made their names, La Java has reinvented itself as a dance club with rock–pop and soul music. It also hosts inexpensive performances by up-and-coming bands. ⊠ *105 rue du Faubourg du Temple, 10e, Canal St-Martin* ☎ *01–42–02–20–52* ⊕ *www.la-java.fr* Ⓜ *Belleville, Goncourt.*

Le Gibus. Le Gibus is one of Paris's most famous music venues. More than 6,500 concerts (put on by the likes of Iggy Pop, The Clash, and The Police) have packed in fans for 30-plus years. Today the Gibus's cellars are *the* place for trance, techno, and especially hip-hop. ⊠ *18 rue du Faubourg du Temple, 11e, Canal St-Martin* ☎ *01–47–00–78–88* ⊕ *www.gibus.fr* Ⓜ *République.*

OBERKAMPF

BARS

Café Charbon. Neighborhood bohos are seduced by Café Charbon's warm wooden Belle Époque charm and floor-to-soaring-ceiling mirrors. The attached Nouveau Casino offers cutting-edge live performances. ⊠ *109 rue Oberkampf, 11e, Oberkampf* ☎ *01–43–57–55–13* Ⓜ *Rue St-Maur, Parmentier.*

Favela Chic. This popular Latin cocktail bar took the scene early, forging Oberkampf's hip reputation. Back behind courtyard gates you'll find caipirinhas and mojitos, guest DJs presenting an eclectic mix of samba, soul, and hip-hop, and a nonstop dance scene. ⊠ *18 rue du Faubourg du Temple, 11e, Oberkampf* ☎ *01–40–21–38–14* ⊕ *favelachic. com* Ⓜ *République.*

L'Entrée des Artistes. Veterans of some of Paris's best new-generation cocktail clubs, the bar talent here strikes out with a few rarified options that will please both amateurs and aficionados. Small, dark, and in the hip Oberkampf area, the bar feels more like an atmospheric neighborhood joint than a magnet for trendy bar crawlers. Some very good nibbles and a skillful wine selection are just icing on the cake. ⊠ *8 rue*

Crussol, 11e, Oberkampf ☎*09–50–99–67–11* Ⓜ *Filles du Calvaire, Oberkampf.*

CLUBS

Le Nouveau Casino. Le Nouveau Casino is a concert hall and club tucked behind the Café Charbon. Pop and rock concerts prevail during the week, with revelry on Friday and Saturday from midnight until dawn. Electronic, house, disco, and techno DJs are the standard. ✉ *109 rue Oberkampf, 11e, Oberkampf* ☎*01–43–57–57–40* ⊕ *www. nouveaucasino.net* Ⓜ *Parmentier.*

Pop-In. On a back street just off Boulevard Beaumarchais (which links the Bastille to République), this dark, hard-partying boho playhouse has a pronounced English-rocker feel. ✉ *105 rue Amelot, 4e, Oberkampf* ☎*01–48–05–56–11* ⊕ *popin.fr* Ⓜ *St-Sebastien-Froissart.*

PÈRE-LACHAISE

BARS

Flèche d'Or. A bastion of rock concerts and other musical performances, this venue is just across the street from Mama Shelter, in a neighborhood some like to call the Brooklyn of Paris. ✉ *102 bis rue Bagnolet, 20e, Père Lachaise* ☎*01–44–64–01–02* ⊕ *www.flechedor.fr* Ⓜ *Alexandre Dumas.*

Mama Shelter. Hip Parisians make the pilgrimage to visit the Island Bar at this hotel, the happeningest spot around. Beautiful people flock in for solid cocktails, foosball, and even an adjacent pizza bar. It's always packed, but lines will be out the door on Saturday, when DJs and other international artists perform. ✉ *109 rue de Bagnolet, 20e, Père Lachaise* ☎*01–43 18–48–48* ⊕ *www.mamashelter.com* Ⓜ *Alexandre Dumas.*

CABARET

Le Bellevilloise. This multiuse exhibition space in a hip, up-and-coming neighborhood functions as a bar, dance club, restaurant, and performance venue, with concerts, and burlesque shows. ✉ *19-21 rue Boyer, 20e, Belleville* ☎*01–46–36–07–07* ⊕ *www.labellevilloise.com* Ⓜ *Gambetta, Ménilmontant.*

17

LATIN QUARTER

The smoke may have cleared from the jazz clubs in the city's historically bohemian quarter, but the atmosphere's still hot—or cool, depending on how you look at it.

BARS

Curio Parlor. Hidden away on a quiet street at the eastern end of the Latin Quarter, this low-lit speakeasy was created by the team from the Experimental Cocktail Club. It serves that establishment's same creative libations in an Art Deco setting, complete with emerald velour, curtained niches, and taxidermied animals. ■TIP→ Regular Japanese whiskey tastings are offered in the lower level bar. ✉ *16 rue des Bernadins, 5e, Latin Quarter* ☎*01–44–07–12–47* ⊕ *www.curioparlor.com* Ⓜ *Maubert–Mutualité.*

Delmas. This bar-café-resto attracts a buzzing student crowd with its comfy leather couches, exposed brick walls, trompe l'oeil bookcases, and diner-style food. ⊠ *2 pl. de la Contrescarpe, 5e, Latin Quarter* ☎ *01–43–26–51–26* ⊕ *www.cafedelmasparis.com* Ⓜ *Cardinal Lemoine.*

Polly Maggoo. This convivial hangout is legendary as the student rioters' unofficial HQ during the May '68 uprising and is named after the satirical French art-house movie about a supermodel. Weekends are wild, with drinks at the wacky tile bar and live Latino music that keeps the party thumping until morning. ⊠ *3–5 rue du Petit Pont, 5e, Latin Quarter* ☎ *01–46–33–33–64* Ⓜ *St-Michel.*

CABARET

Paradis Latin. Occupying a building that's attributed to Gustav Eiffel, Paradis Latin peppers its quirky show with acrobatics and eye-popping lighting effects, making this the liveliest and trendiest cabaret on the Left Bank. ⊠ *28 rue du Cardinal Lemoine, 5e, Latin Quarter* ☎ *01–43–25–28–28* ⊕ *www.paradislatin.com* Ⓜ *Cardinal Lemoine.*

JAZZ CLUBS

Caveau de la Huchette. Caveau de la Huchette is one of the few surviving cellar clubs from the 1940s. It boasts the "best boppers" in the city, and packs 'em in for swing dancing and Dixieland tunes. It's a killer jazz spot for everyone but claustrophobics. The music continues till dawn Thursday to Saturday. ⊠ *5 rue de la Huchette, 5e, Latin Quarter* ☎ *01–43–26–65–05* ⊕ *www.caveaudelahuchette.fr* Ⓜ *St-Michel.*

ST-GERMAIN-DES-PRÉS

Exclusivity is the theme in the Bobo (bourgeois-bohème) left bank, where "private" clubs draw celebs and fashionistas, and stylish cocktail bars cater to an urbane mix of students, gallerists, expats, and urban sophisticates.

BARS

Alcazar. Alcazar is Sir Terence Conran's makeover of a 17th-century Parisian *jeu de paume* court that features a stylish mezzanine-level bar under a greenhouse-glass roof. DJs and "sound designers" spin mixes into the wee hours every night of the week. ⊠ *62 rue Mazarine, 6e, St-Germain-des-Prés* ☎ *01–53–10–19–99* ⊕ *www.alcazar.fr* Ⓜ *Odéon.*

Bar du Marché. Bar du Marché is a local legend where waiters wearing red overalls and revolutionary "Gavroche" hats serve drinks every day of the week (they demonstrate particular zeal around happy hour). With bottles of wine at about €25, it draws a quintessential Left Bank mix of expat locals, fashion-house interns, and even some professional rugby players. Sit outside on the terrace and enjoy the prime corner location. ⊠ *75 rue de Seine, 6e, St-Germain-des-Prés* ☎ *01–43–26–55–15* Ⓜ *Mabillon, Odéon.*

Chez Georges. Chez Georges has been serving red wine, pastis, and beer for the past 60-odd years in pretty much the same *caveau* that still packs in devotees today. Older students and locals fill sofas and crowd around tiny tables glowing with candles in the cellar bar before grinding to pulsing world music all night. ⊠ *11 rue de Canettes, 6e, St-Germain-des-Prés* ☎ *01–43–26–79–15* Ⓜ *Mabillon.*

Compagnie des Vins Surnaturels. After jump-starting the Paris cocktail bar scene, the partners behind Experimental Cocktail Club and the Ballroom du Beef Club apply the same winning formula to this hybrid wine bar-nightclub. Plush surroundings, an extensive wine list, and upscale nibbles draw a crowd of hip young Parisians who can hone their wine-tasting skills on classics in every price range. Natural wine aficionados get thee to a wine bar; though solid, the wine list does not deliver as promised. ✉ *7 rue Lobineau, 6e, St-Germain-des-Prés* ☎ *06–14–76–81– 08* ⊕ *compagniedesvinssurnaturels.com* Ⓜ *Odéon, Mabillon.*

L'Hôtel. L'Hôtel's hushed Baroque bar is the perfect place for a discreet rendezvous. Designed in typically jaw-dropping Jacques Garcia style, the hideaway has a photo of a louche Keanu Reeves on the wall and evokes the decadent spirit of one-time resident Oscar Wilde. ✉ *13 rue des Beaux-Arts, 6e, St-Germain-des-Prés* ☎ *01–44–41–99–00* ⊕ *www.l-hotel.com* Ⓜ *St-Germain-des-Prés.*

Playtime Cocktails. The banquettes and throw pillow may mislead, but at this snug little hotel bar "playtime" means choose according to suit (namely clubs, diamonds, hearts, or spades). Veteran barman Emeric Aguillar, who learned his trade at the Dorcester and the Royal Monceau, skillfully executes a clever cocktail menu that reads like a deck of cards. Happy hour starts at 6. ✉ *34 rue Buci, 6e, St-Germain-des-Prés* ☎ *01– 43–29–07–20* ⊕ *www.artushotel.com* Ⓜ *Odéon, St-Germain-des-Prés.*

Prescription Cocktail Club. This club is brought to you by the owners of popular cocktails bars in London, New York, and Paris—including the Ballroom du Beef Club and the Experimental Cocktail Club. So rest assured: the atmosphere will be stylish (think upholstered chairs, dim lighting, and vintage touches), the crowd hip, and the drinks tasty. Located in the fashionable Saint-Germain-des-Prés, it's a good after-shopping *apéro* or dinner option. ✉ *23 rue Mazarine, 6e, St-Germain-des-Prés* ☎ *01–46–34–67–73* ⊕ *www.prescriptioncocktailclub.com* Ⓜ *Odéon.*

CLUBS

Jane Club. The Jane Club is tucked beneath the popular bar-resto Alcazar, in a vaulted stone cellar that was Jim Morrison's hangout back in the '70s when the Whiskey-a-Go-Go was located here. It's now a welcoming dance club with state-of-the-art sound, lighting, and guest DJs. You'll hear vintage disco, funk, groove, and salsa (the last of these on Sunday night, with classes that start at 3:30 pm). ✉ *62 rue Mazarine, 6e, St-Germain-des-Prés* ☎ *01–55–42–22–01* ⊕ *www.janeclub.fr* Ⓜ *Odéon.*

Le Montana. It's notoriously difficult to get past the doorman at Le Montana: a sleek St-Germain club owned by French nightlife king André (Le Baron). A Studio 54 vibe, Vincent Darré decor, and enormous cocktails make it popular among models, actors, artists, and Parisian playboys. ✉ *28 rue St-Benoît, 6e, St-Germain-des-Prés* ☎ *01–44–39–71–00* Ⓜ *St-Germain-des-Prés, Mabillon.*

MONTPARNASSE

Immortalized in the 1920s by the likes of F. Scott Fitzgerald and Pablo Picasso, the cafés and bars in this quiet corner of the city still radiate atmosphere. Whether sipping a sidecar at Hemingway's beloved La Closerie des Lilas or slurping oysters at one of the quarter's storied brasseries, you can't help but fall under Paris's spell here.

BARS

La Closerie des Lilas. La Closerie's swank "American-style" bar lets you drink in the swirling action of the adjacent restaurant and brasserie at a piano bar adorned with plaques honoring former habitués like Man Ray, Jean-Paul Sartre, Samuel Beckett, and Ernest Hemingway, who talks of "the Lilas" in *A Moveable Feast.* ✉ *171 bd. du Montparnasse, 6e, Montparnasse* ☎ *01–40–51–34–50* ⊕ *www.closeriedeslilas. fr* Ⓜ *Montparnasse.*

Le Rosebud. Step through the Art Nouveau front door of Jean-Paul Sartre's one-time haunt and you're instantly immersed in the dark, moody, fourth dimension of Old Montparnasse, where white-jacketed servers and red-lacquered tables transport you into the past. ✉ *11 bis, rue Delambre, 14e, Montparnasse* ☎ *01–43–35–38–54* Ⓜ *Vavin.*

CLUBS

Le Red Light. Le Red Light's two giant dance floors draw a casual, mixed crowd. Friday and Saturday, from midnight until dawn, expect mainly house and electronic music played by big-name international DJs. ✉ *34 rue du Départ, 15e, Montparnasse* ☎ *01–42–79–94–53* ⊕ *www. leredlight.com* Ⓜ *Montparnasse–Bienvenüe.*

JAZZ CLUBS

Le Petit Journal Montparnasse. Le Petit Journal Montparnasse has long attracted the greats in French and international jazz, with a focus on big band music. Dinner is served from 8 pm to 1:00 am. A second Le Petit Journal location (at 71 bd. St-Michel in the Latin Quarter) specializes in Dixieland tunes. ✉ *13 rue du Commandant-Mouchotte, 14e, Montparnasse* ☎ *01–43–21–56–70* ⊕ *petitjournalmontparnasse.com* Ⓜ *Montparnasse–Bienvenüe.*

PERFORMING ARTS

Updated
by Jennifer
Ditsler-Ladonne

The performing-arts scene in Paris runs the gamut from high-brow to lowbrow, cheap (or free) to break-the-bank expensive. Venues are indoors and outdoors, opulent or spartan, and dress codes vary accordingly. Regardless of the performance you choose, it's unlikely to be like anything you've seen before. Parisians have an audacious sense of artistic adventure and a stunning eye for scene and staging. An added bonus in this city of classic beauty is that many of the venues themselves—from the opulent interiors of the Opéra Garnier and the Opéra Royal de Versailles to the Art Deco splendor of the Théâtre des Champs-Élysées—are a feast for the eyes.

One thing that sets Paris apart in the arts world is the active participation of the Ministry of Culture, which sponsors numerous concert halls and theaters, like the Comédie Française, which tend to present less commercial, though artistically captivating, productions. Other theaters, like the Théâtre de Marigny and Palais de Chaillot, are known for sold-out shows and decade-long production runs.

Most performances are in French, although you can find English theater productions. English-language movies are often presented undubbed, with subtitles. Of course, you don't need to speak the language to enjoy opera, classical music, dance, or the circus.

PLANNING

FESTIVALS
The music and theater season generally runs from September to June, but summer is packed with all sorts of performing arts festivals.

Orangerie du Parc de Bagatelle. The annual Chopin and Solosit Festivals are highlights at the picturesque Orangerie in Parc de Bagatelle, one of Paris's most beautiful gardens. Concerts are held mid-June through September. Check the France Festivals website for specific concerts and dates. ⊠ *Parc de Bagatelle, Allée de Longchamp, 16e, Bois de Boulogne* ☎ *01–45–00–22–19* ⊕ *www.francefestivals. com* ⊠ *Free; €5.50 special exhibits; €15 concerts* ⊘ *Daily* Ⓜ *Porte Maillot, then Bus 244.*

Parc Floral. Free outdoor classical concerts lure fans to the Parc Floral of the Bois de Vincennes on August and September weekends at 4 (entrance to the park is €5). This is also the spot that hosts the Paris Jazz Festival each weekend in summer. ⊠ *12e, Bois de Vincennes* ☎ *01–54–95–20–20* ⊕ *www.parcfloraldeparis.com* Ⓜ *Château de Vincennes.*

Quartier d'Été. The Quartier d'Été festival in July and August, held throughout Paris, attracts international stars of dance, classical music, and jazz. ☎ *01–44–94–98–00* ⊕ *www.quartierdete.com.*

Rock-en-Seine. Rock-en-Seine is a three-day rock festival held every August on the outskirts of Paris. It's one of the largest of its kind in France; past headliners include My Chemical Romance, Arcade Fire, and the Foo Fighters. ⊠ *Domaine National de St-Cloud, Parc de St-Cloud, Saint-Cloud* ⊕ *www.rockenseine.com* Ⓜ *Boulogne-Pont de Saint-Cloud.*

Villette Jazz Festival. The annual Villette Jazz Festival is held at the Cité de la Musique in Parc de La Villette and other venues around Paris in late August and early September. Check the website for detailed information. ⊠ *211 av. Jean Jaurès, 20e, La Villette* ☎ *01–40–03–75–75* ⊕ *www.villette.com* Ⓜ *Porte de Pantin.*

TICKET PRICES AND DISCOUNTS

As anywhere it's best to buy tickets in advance.

Events range in price from about €5 for standing room at the Opéra Bastille or €7 for a circus performance to upward of €200 for an elaborate National Opéra production. Most performances, however, are in the €15–€25 range. Discounts are often available for limited-visibility seats or for students and senior citizens. Movies cost about €6–€11, but many cinemas have reduced rates for matinees or for people under a certain age (18 or 26, depending on the cinema).

Le Kiosque Théâtre. Half-price tickets for same-day theater performances are available at Le Kiosque Théâtre's Madeleine location. See the website for information on outlets in Montparnasse and Place des Ternes. ⊠ *Across from 15 pl. de la Madeleine, 8e, Opéra/Grands Boulevards* ⊕ *www.kiosquetheatre.com* ⊘ *Tues.–Sat. 12:30–8, Sun. 12:30–4; closed Mon.* Ⓜ *Madeleine.*

18

Half-price tickets are also available at many theaters during the first week of each new show's run, and inexpensive tickets are often available at the last minute.

WORD OF MOUTH

"If you're interested in the Garnier opera house you might want to see a performance. There's a wide variety of ticket prices including cheap ones. Usually it's ballets at the Garnier but they do operas there occasionally as well as musical concerts." —Apres_Londee

FNAC. FNAC sells tickets in stores and online. It has more than two-dozen sales outlets in the city, including one on the Champs-Élysées. ⊠ *Galerie du Claridge, 74 av. des Champs-Elysées, 8e, Champs-Élysées* ☎ *08–25–02–00–20 €0.15 per min* ⊕ *www.fnactickets.com* ☉ *Mon.–Sat. 10 am–11:45 pm, Sun. noon–11:45* Ⓜ *George V.*

WHERE TO GET INFO

Detailed entertainment listings in French can be found in the weekly magazines *Pariscope* and *L'Officiel des Spectacles*, available at newsstands and in bookstores; in the Wednesday entertainment insert *Figaroscope,* in the *Figaro* newspaper (⊕ *scope.lefigaro.fr/theatres-spectacles*); and in the weekly *À Nous Paris*, distributed free in the métro. The webzine *Paris Voice* (⊕ *www.parisvoice.com*) offers superb highlights in English. Most performing arts venues also have their own websites, and many include listings as well as other helpful information in English.

The website of the Paris Tourist Office (⊕ *www.parisinfo.com*) has theater and music listings in English.

ARTS CENTERS

Le Lucernaire. Le Lucernaire wins a standing ovation as far as cultural centers are concerned. With two theaters (eight performances a night), three movie screens, an art gallery, a bookstore, a lively restaurant-bar, and the equally lively surrounding neighborhood of Vavin, it caters to young intellectuals. ⊠ *53 rue Notre-Dame-des-Champs, 6e, Montparnasse* ☎ *01–45–44–57–34* ⊕ *www.lucernaire.fr* Ⓜ *Notre-Dame-des-Champs.*

Fodor's Choice ★ **Opéra Garnier.** Opéra Garnier—the magnificent, magical former haunt of the Phantom of the Opera, painter Edgar Degas, and any number of legendary opera stars—still hosts performances of the Opéra de Paris, along with a fuller calendar of dance performances (the theater is the official home of the Ballet de l'Opéra National de Paris). The grandest opera productions are usually mounted at the Opéra de la Bastille, whereas the Garnier now presents smaller-scale works such as Mozart's *La Clemenza di Tito* and *Così Fan Tutte.* Gorgeous and intimate though the Garnier is, its tiara-shape theater means that many seats have limited visibility, so it's best to ask specifically what the sight lines are when booking ("partial view" in French is *visibilité partielle*). ■ TIP→ The cheaper seats are often those with partial views. Seats generally go on sale at the box office a month before any given show, earlier by phone and online; you must appear in person to buy the cheapest tickets. Last-minute discount tickets, if available, are offered 15 minutes prior to a performance for senior citizens and anyone under 28. The box office is

The Frank Gehry–designed Cinémathèque Française presents an ever-changing range of films and exhibitions.

open 10–4:30 daily (until 5:30 mid-July through August), but you should get in line up to two hours in advance. Venue visits (€10) and guided tours in English (€12.50) are available and can be reserved online; see the website for details. ⊠ *Pl. de l'Opéra, 9e, Opéra/Grands Boulevards* ☎ *08–92–89–90–90 €0.34 per min* ⊕ *www.operadeparis.fr* Ⓜ *Opéra.*

Fodor's Choice
★

Opéra Royal de Versailles. The Royal Opera of Versailles, the most lavish opera house in France (and perhaps in all of Europe) hosts an impressive yearly calendar of major operas, ballets, recitals, and musical theater by world-class French and international performers. The intimate 652-seat structure has excellent acoustics and provides an ideal setting for works by big name composers, with an emphasis on the Baroque and classical periods. Finished in 1770—just in time for the marriage ceremonies of the young dauphin (later King Louis XVI) and 14-year-old Marie-Antoinette—the structure's stunning neoclassical decor is crafted entirely of gilded and faux-marbled wood. A regular program of smaller concerts is also held in the splendid Hall of Mirrors (Galerie des Glaces) and at the Royal Chapel, where recitals might feature a 300-year-old royal organ. Although it's recommended to buy tickets online one to two months in advance (up to six months ahead for star performers), they can be purchased at the box office on the day of the performance. ■ TIP➔ There are no bad seats at the Royal Opera, so instead of spending upward of €100 on a ticket, you can get away with something a bit less pricey. For the Hall of Mirrors, you may not see much in the cheap seats, but the sound will still be glorious. ⊠ *Place d'Armes, Versailles* ⟐ *By commuter train (SNCF) from Paris Gare Montparnasse or Paris*

Gare Saint Lazare to Gare de Versailles ☎ *01–30–83–75–05* ⊕ *www. chateauversailles-spectacles.fr* Ⓜ *RER C, Chateau de Versailles.*

Théâtre des Champs-Élysées. Théâtre des Champs-Élysées was the scene of 1913's infamous Battle of the Rite of Spring, when police had to be called in after the audience ripped up seats in outrage at Stravinsky's *Le Sacre du Printemps* and Nijinsky's choreography. Today it is elegantly restored and worthy of a visit if only for the architecture (it's one of Paris's most striking examples of Art Deco). The theater also hosts first-rate opera and dance performances, along with jazz, world music, orchestral, and chamber concerts. ⊠ *15 av. Montaigne, 8e, Champs-Élysées* ☎ *01–49–52–50–50* ⊕ *www.theatrechampselysees.fr* Ⓜ *Alma-Marceau.*

CIRCUS

Italian Antonio Franconi helped launch the first Cirque Olympique (considered the start of the modern circus) in Paris in 1783, and the French have been hooked ever since. Circus acts are cherished as high art in Paris—for all ages. The city boasts a 19th-century permanent circus theater and sprouts tents in every major park to present spectacles from the sublime to the quirky.

Circus Arts at the Parc de la Villette. Circus Arts at the Parc de la Villette features an *Espace Chapiteaux*: a high-tech circus-tent complex that hosts entertaining innovators, including students from the National Circus Arts Center. It focuses on contemporary performance art—not to be missed by "new circus" fans. ⊠ *211 av. Jean-Jaurès, 20e, La Villette* ☎ *01–40–03–75–75* ⊕ *www.villette.com* Ⓜ *Porte de Pantin.*

Cirque d'Hiver Bouglione. Cirque d'Hiver Bouglione brings together two famous circus institutions: the beautiful Cirque d'Hiver hall, constructed in 1852, and the Bouglione troupe, known for its rousing assembly of acrobats, jugglers, clowns, trapeze artists, tigers, and housecats that leap through rings of fire. ⊠ *110 rue Amelot, 11e, République* ☎ *01–47–00–28–81* ⊕ *www.cirquedhiver.com* Ⓜ *Filles du Calvaire.*

Cirque National Alexis Gruss. Cirque National Alexis Gruss, founded in 1854, remains an avowedly old-fashioned production with showy horseback riders, trapeze artists, and clowns. It runs mid-October through mid-March, with performances on Saturday, Sunday, and Wednesday. ⊠ *Av. de l'Hippodrome, 16e, Bois de Boulogne* ☎ *01–45–01–71–26* ⊕ *www.alexis-gruss.com* Ⓜ *Ranelagh.*

FAMILY

Fodor'sChoice
★

Théâtre Équestre Zingaro. Ready for a variation on the circus theme? If you're lucky enough to be visiting during the two months Zingaro performs at home (usually in late fall), you'll have the chance to witness a truly unique spectacle. Since 1984, France's foremost horse whisperer, who goes by the name of Bartabas, has created captivating equestrian shows that mix theater, dance, music and poetry. The 500-seat theater-in-the-round on the outskirts of Paris is part of a gypsy caravan, where trainers and their families, 45 horses, and Bartabas himself live and work. The horses perform in close proximity to the audience in astonishing displays of choreography and acrobatic skill. Shrouded in mystery, Bartabas has taken his inspiration from eclectic sources (including Japanese Butoh dance, shamanism, Gypsy music, Baroque liturgy, and the Mexican Day of the Dead). The results are utterly original. ■TIP➔ If you can't make it for Zingaro, there is a consolation prize: in 2003, Bartabas created the Académie du Spectacle Équestre at the royal stables of Versailles (Grandes Écuries), where audiences can view a twice-daily display on weekends and certain weekdays. ✉ *176 avenue Jean Jaurès, Aubervilliers* ☎ *01–39–02–62–75* ⊕ *www.bartabas. fr* Ⓜ *Fort d'Aubervilliers.*

CONCERTS

There's something majestic about listening to classical music under the airy roof of a medieval church, where many free or almost-free lunchtime and evening concerts are performed. Check weekly listings and flyers posted at the churches for information.

Museums also host classical concerts; tickets are usually sold separately from admission. The Auditorium du Louvre presents chamber music, string quartets, and a special series of promising new musicians on Thursday; the Musée de Cluny stages medieval music concerts between September and June, including the *l'Heure Musicale* (tickets €6) on Sunday at 4 and Monday at 12:30; and the Musée d'Orsay often offers small-scale concerts in the lower-level auditorium.

Cité de la Musique. Cité de la Musique presents a varied program of classical, experimental, and world-music concerts in a postmodern setting. ✉ *Parc de La Villette, 221 av. Jean-Jaurès, 19e, La Villette* ☎ *01–44–84–44–84* ⊕ *www.citedelamusique.fr* Ⓜ *Porte de Pantin.*

IRCAM. IRCAM organizes contemporary and classical music concerts, as well as dance and other modern art performances, in its own theater and at the Centre Pompidou next door. Tickets start at only €14. ✉ *1 pl. Igor Stravinsky, 4o, Beaubourg/Les Halles* ☎ *01 44 78 48 43* ⊕ *www. ircam.fr* Ⓜ *Châtelet, Les Halles, Hôtel de Ville.*

Fodor's Choice ★ **L'Olympia.** Paris's legendary music hall hosts an eclectic roster of performances that covers such far-flung genres as gospel, jazz, French *chanson*, and rock. Edith Piaf rose to fame after a series of Olympia concerts and Jeff Buckley's famous *Live at the Olympia* was recorded here. Now everyone from Leonard Cohen to Lady Gaga is in on the action. ✉ *28 bd. des Cappuccines, 9e, Opéra* ☎ *08–92–68–33–68* €0.34 *per min* ⊕ *en.olympiahall.com* Ⓜ *Madeleine, Opéra.*

Fodor's Choice ★ **La Cigale.** What these walls have seen! Artists like Maurice Chevalier and Arletty were once a staple of this small concert hall in the storied Pigalle neighborhood before cabaret and vaudeville moved in. Today it's one of Paris's top pop and contemporary music venues, featuring such acts as Adele and Coldplay. ✉ *120 bd. de Rochechouart, 18e, Pigalle* ☎ *01–49–25–89–99* ⊕ *www.lacigale.fr* Ⓜ *Pigalle, Anvers.*

Fodor's Choice ★ **Salle Cortot.** Salle Cortot is an acoustic jewel built by Auguste Perret in 1918. At the time he promised to construct "a hall that sounds like a Stradivarious." Jazz and classical concerts are held here. ■TIP➔ Free student recitals are offered at 12:30 on Tuesday and Thursday from

18

October to April. ⊠ *78 rue Cardinet, 17e, Parc Monceau* ☏ *01–47–63–47–48* ⊕ *www.ecolenormalecortot.com* Ⓜ *Malesherbes.*

Salle Gaveau. Salle Gaveau is a perfectly appointed gold-and-white hall with 1,200 seats, remarkable acoustics, and a distinctly Parisian allure. It hosts chamber music, piano, and vocal recitals. ⊠ *45-47 rue la Boétie, 8e, Champs-Élysées* ☏ *01–49–53–05–07* ⊕ *www.sallegaveau.com* Ⓜ *Miromesnil.*

Salle Pleyel. Salle Pleyel's packed concert calendar—covering everything from jazz to Mozart—features international stars like Lionel Hampton and directors of the New York Philharmonic and the London Symphony Orchestra, plus repeat performances by the Orchestre de Paris. ⊠ *252 rue du Faubourg-St-Honoré, 8e, Concorde* ☏ *01–42–56–13–13* ⊕ *www.sallepleyel.fr* Ⓜ *Ternes.*

OPERA

Opéra Comique. Opéra Comique is a gem of an opera house whose reputation was forged by its former director, enfant terrible Jérôme Savary. As well as staging operettas, the hall hosts modern dance, classical concerts, and vocal recitals. Tickets usually range from €6 to €50 and can be purchased at the theater, online, or by phone. ⊠ *5 rue Favart, 2e, Opéra/Grands Boulevards* ☏ *08–25–01–01–23 € 0.15 per min* ⊕ *www. opera-comique.com* Ⓜ *Richelieu Drouot.*

Opéra de la Bastille. Opéra de la Bastille, the mammoth ultramodern facility designed by architect Carlos Ott and built in 1989, long ago took over the role of Paris's main opera house from the Opéra Garnier (although both operate under the same Opéra de Paris umbrella). Like the building, performances tend to be on the avant-garde side—you're as likely to see a contemporary adaptation of *La Bohème* as you are to hear Kafka set to music. Tickets for Opéra de Paris productions range from €5 to €200 and generally go on sale at the box office a month before shows, earlier by phone and online. The opera season usually runs September through July, and the box office is open Monday–Saturday 11–6:30. ■ TIP➜ You can buy tickets (€12) for guided tours of the opera house at the box office. ⊠ *Pl. de la Bastille, 12e, Bastille/Nation* ☏ *08–92–89–90–90 €0.34 per min, 01–40–01–19–70 Tours* ⊕ *www. operadeparis.fr* Ⓜ *Bastille.*

Théâtre du Châtelet. Also known as Théâtre Musical de Paris, this venue stages some of the finest opera productions in the city and regularly attracts international divas like Cecilia Bartoli and Anne-Sofie von Otter. It also hosts classical concerts, dance performances, Broadway musicals, and the occasional play. ⊠ *Pl. du Châtelet, 1er, Beaubourg/Les Halles* ☏ *01–40–28–28–40* ⊕ *www.chatelet-theatre.com* Ⓜ *Châtelet.*

DANCE

Classical ballet takes the stage in Paris in places as varied as the historic Opéra Garnier and the Grand Palais. More avant-garde or up-and-coming choreographers tend to show their works off in the smaller performance spaces of the Bastille and the Marais, and in theaters in nearby suburbs. And of course there's the Centre National de Danse.

Centre National de la Danse. After being sidelined by politics and budget problems for a decade, this dance center opened in a former administrative center of the Pantin suburb of Paris. The space is dedicated to supporting professional dancers, with classes, rehearsal studios, and a multimedia dance library. A regular program of performances, expositions, and conferences is also open to the public. ⊠ *1 rue Victor Hugo, Pantin* ☎ *01–41–83–98–98* ⊕ *www.cnd.fr* Ⓜ *Hoche; RER: Pantin.*

PUPPET SHOWS

On most Wednesday, Saturday, and Sunday afternoons, the Guignol—the French equivalent of Punch and Judy—can be seen launching their hilarious puppet battles in most of Paris's larger parks. Look for performance spaces called *Théâtre de Marionnettes.* Entrance is usually about €3.50–€5; performances are in French.

Maison des Arts de Créteil. This popular dance venue just outside Paris often attracts top-notch international and French companies, such as Blanca Li, Bill T. Jones, and the cutting-edge annual EXIT Festival. ⊠ *Pl. Salvador Allende, Creteil* ☎ *01–45–13–19–19* ⊕ *www.maccreteil.com* Ⓜ *Créteil-Préfecture.*

Théâtre de la Bastille. Théâtre de la Bastille merits mention as an example of the innovative activity in the Bastille area; it has an enviable record as a launch pad for tomorrow's modern-dance stars. ⊠ *76 rue de la Roquette, 11e, Bastille/Nation* ☎ *01–43–57–42–14* ⊕ *www.theatre-bastille.com* Ⓜ *Bastille.*

Théâtre de la Cité Internationale. Théâtre de la Cité Internationale is a complex of three theaters in the heart of the Cité Internationale Universitaire de Paris, an international student residence community and park. It hosts young avant-garde companies. ⊠ *17 bd. Jourdan, 14e, Parc Montsouris* ☎ *01–43–13–50–50* ⊕ *www.theatredelacite.com* Ⓜ *RER: Cité Universitaire.*

Théâtre de la Ville. Théâtre de la Ville is *the* top spot for contemporary dance. Troupes like Anne-Teresa de Keersmaeker's Rosas company are presented here. Book early; shows sell out quickly. ⊠ *2 pl. du Châtelet, 4e, Beaubourg/Les Halles* ☎ *01–42–74–22–77* ⊕ *www.theatredelaville-paris.com* Ⓜ *Châtelet.*

FILM

The French call films the *septième art* (seventh art) and discuss the latest releases with the same intensity as they do gallery openings or theatrical debuts. Most theaters run English-language films undubbed, with subtitles, which are indicated with v.o., meaning *version originale*; films that are dubbed are v.f. (*version française*). First-run cinemas are clustered around the principal tourist areas, such as the Champs-Élysées, Boulevard des Italiens near the Opéra, Bastille, Châtelet, and Odéon. For listings online check ⊕ *www.allocine.fr* or ⊕ *www.offi.fr/cinema.*

Cinéma des Cinéastes. Cinéma des Cinéastes shows previews of feature films, as well as documentaries, films for kids, short films, and rarely shown movies; it's in an old cabaret transformed into a movie house and wine bar. ✉ *7 av. de Clichy, 17e, Montmartre* ☎ *08–92–68–97–17 €0.34 per min* ⊕ *www.cinema-des-cineastes.fr* Ⓜ *Place de Clichy.*

Fodor's Choice ★ **Cinémathèque Française.** Cinémathèque Française is a mecca for cinephiles brought up on Federico Fellini, Igmar Bergman, and Alain Resnais. Its spectacular home—in the former American Center, designed by Frank Gehry—includes elaborate museum exhibitions as well as four cinemas and a video library. ✉ *51 rue de Bercy, 12e, Bercy* ☎ *01–71–19–33–33* ⊕ *www.cinematheque.fr* Ⓜ *Bercy.*

La Géode. La Géode screens wide-angle Omnimax films—including kid-friendly documentaries—on a gigantic spherical surface. ✉ *Cité des Sciences et de l'Industrie, Parc de La Villette, 26 av. Corentin-Cariou, 19e, La Villette* ☎ *01–40–05–79–99* ⊕ *www.lageode.fr* Ⓜ *Porte de La Villette.*

Fodor's Choice ★ **La Pagode.** La Pagode—where else but Paris would you find movies screened in an antique pagoda? A Far Eastern fantasy, this structure was built in 1896 as a ballroom for the wife of the owner of Le Bon Marché department store. In the 1970s it was slated for demolition but saved by a grassroots wave of support spearheaded by director Louis Malle. Though the fare is standard, the surroundings are enchanting. Come early for tea in the garden (summer only). ✉ *57 rue de Babylone, 7e, Invalides* ☎ *01–45–55–48–48* Ⓜ *St-François-Xavier.*

Le Balzac. Le Balzac often presents directors' talks before film screenings and features concerts as well as live music for silent classics. ✉ *1 rue Balzac, 8e, Champs-Élysées* ☎ *01–45–61–10–60* ⊕ *www.cinemabalzac. com* Ⓜ *George V.*

Le Desperado. Le Desperado specializes in American classics and cult films for only €8! ✉ *23 rue des Écoles, 5e, Latin Quarter* ☎ *01–43–25–72–07* Ⓜ *Maubert–Mutualité.*

Le Forum des Images. Le Forum des Images organizes thematic viewings in six state-of-the-art screening rooms, often presenting directors or a film expert for discussion beforehand. Archival films and videos, workshops, and lectures are also on the schedule here. Entry starts at €5; €8 for festivals. ✉ *Forum des Halles, Porte St-Eustache entrance, 2 rue du Cinéma, 1er, Beaubourg/Les Halles* ☎ *01–44–76–63–00* ⊕ *www. forumdesimages.fr* ☾ *Weekdays 12:30–11:30, weekends 2–11:30* Ⓜ *Les Halles.*

Fodor's Choice ★ **Le Louxor.** The newly reopened Art Deco Louxor was lavishly restored to its 1921 Egyptian-themed splendor as part of Paris's ongoing urban rehabilitation project. Now the city's grandest cinema, it is gorgeously appointed—all in rich ochre with jewel-toned velvet seating—and shows a roster of contemporary international art films. ■**TIP→ Have a drink at the top-floor bar or balcony for spectacular views of the neighborhood and Sacré Coeur.** ✉ *170 bd. Magenta, 10e, Invalides* ☎ *01–44–63–96–96* ⊕ *www.cinemalouxor.fr* Ⓜ *Barbès–Rochechouart.*

MK2 Bibliothèque. MK2 Bibliothèque is a slick, 14-*salle* cineplex in the shadow of Mitterrand's National Library with trademark scarlet-red chairs—they fit two people without a divider, so the experience is sort of like watching a movie at home on your couch. The site also has two restaurants, plus shops selling gifts and DVDs. ✉ *128–162 av. de France, 13e, Bibliothèque* ☎ *08–92–69–84–84 €0.34 per min* ⊕ *www. mk2.com* Ⓜ *Quai de la Gare, Bibliothèque.*

Parc de La Villette. Parc de La Villette shows free open-air movies in July and August. Most people take along a picnic. You can rent deck chairs and blankets by the entrance. ✉ *Prairie du Triangle at Parc de La Villette, 221 av. Jean-Jaurès, 19e, La Villette* ☎ *01–40–03–75–75* ⊕ *www. villette.com* Ⓜ *Porte de Pantin, Porte de La Villette.*

St-André-des-Arts. St-André-des-Arts, one of a number of popular cinemas near the Sorbonne, is also one of the best cinemas in Paris. It hosts an annual festival devoted to a single director, such as Bergman or Tarkovski. ✉ *30 rue St-André-des-Arts, 6e, Latin Quarter* ☎ *01–43–26–48–18* ⊕ *cinesaintandre.fr* Ⓜ *St-Michel.*

UGC Ciné-Cité Bercy. UGC Ciné-Cité Bercy is a mammoth 18-screen complex in the Bercy Village shopping area. For sound and seating, it's one of the best. ✉ *2 cour St-Emilion, 12e, Bercy* ☎ *08–92–70–00–00 €0.34 per min* ⊕ *www.ugc.fr* Ⓜ *Cour St-Emilion.*

THEATER

A number of theaters line the Grands Boulevards between the Opéra and République, but there is no Paris equivalent of Broadway or the West End. Shows are mostly in French, with a few notable exceptions listed here. English-language theater groups playing in various venues throughout Paris and its suburbs include the **International Players** (⊕ *www.internationalplayers.co.uk*). Broadway-scale singing-and-dancing musicals are generally staged at either the Palais des Sports or the Palais des Congrès.

Ateliers Berthier. Ateliers Berthier is the outlying atelier for the more illustrious Théâtre de l'Odéon. Its location in the 17e is a bit off the beaten path; the upside is that on Tuesday and Saturday it often has 3 pm matinees in addition to the 8 pm show. ✉ *1 rue André Suarès, 17e, Parc Monceau* ☎ *01–44–85–40–00* ⊕ *www.theatre-odeon.eu* Ⓜ *Porte de Clichy.*

Café de la Gare. Café de la Gare offers a fun opportunity to experience a particularly Parisian form of theater, the *café-théâtre*—part satire, part variety revue, jazzed up with slapstick humor and performed in a café salon. ■**TIP**➔ **You'll need a good grasp of French slang and current events to keep up with the jokes.** ✉ *41 rue du Temple, 4e, Marais* ☎ *01–42–78–52–51* ⊕ *www.cdlg.org* Ⓜ *Hôtel de Ville.*

Casino de Paris. Casino de Paris—once a favorite of the immortal Serge Gainsbourg—has a horseshoe balcony, a cramped but cozy music-hall feel, and performances by everyone from Dora the Explorer to the Scissor Sisters. This is where Josephine Baker performed in the early '30s with her leopard Chiquita. ✉ *16 rue de Clichy, 9e, Opéra/Grands Boulevards* ☎ *08–92–69–89–26 €0.34 per min* ⊕ *www.casinodeparis. fr* Ⓜ *Trinité.*

Comédie des Champs-Élysées. Comédie des Champs-Élysées offers intriguing productions in its small theater, next door to the larger Théâtre des Champs-Élysées. ⊠ *15 av. Montaigne, 8e, Champs-Élysées* ☎ *01–53–23–99–19* ⊕ *www.comediedeschampselysees.com* Ⓜ *Alma-Marceau.*

Fodor's Choice **Comédie Française.** Comédie Française, founded in 1680, is the most hal-
★ lowed institution in French theater. It specializes in splendid classical French plays by the likes of Racine, Molière, and Marivaux. ■ TIP➜ Buy tickets at the box office, by telephone, or online. If the theater is sold out, the Salle Richelieu offers steeply discounted last-minute tickets an hour before the performance. ⊠ *Salle Richelieu, Pl. Colette, 1er, Louvre* ☎ *08–25–10–16–80 €0.15 per min* ⊕ *www.comedie-francaise. fr* Ⓜ *Palais-Royal–Musée du Louvre.*

La Cartoucherie. This multi-theater complex in a former munitions factory lures cast and spectators into an intimate theatrical world. Go early for a simple meal; actors often help serve "in character." Detailed information for each venue is available at the website. ⊠ *Route du Champ de manoeuvre, 12e, Bois de Vincennes* ☎ *01–43–74–24–08 Théâtre du Soleil, 01–43–74–99–61 Théâtre de l'Aquarium, 01–43–28–36–36 Théâtre de la Tempête, 01–48–08–39–74 Théâtre de l'Epée de Bois* ⊕ *www.cartoucherie.fr* Ⓜ *Château de Vincennes, then shuttle bus or Bus 112.*

Le Manoir de Paris. Let yourself be enchanted—and frightened—as talented performers bring Paris legends to life. When you walk through this mansion, the history of the Bloody Baker, the Phantom of the Opera, and Catherine de Medici's hired assassin are acted out—on you! ■ TIP➜ If you're in Paris during Halloween, this is just about the best game in town. ⊠ *18 rue de Paradis, 10e, Eastern Paris* ☎ *06–70–89–35–87* ⊕ *www.lemanoirdeparis.fr* Ⓜ *Chateau d'Eau.*

Odéon–Théâtre de l'Europe. Odéon–Théâtre de l'Europe was once home to the Comédie Française. This venue focuses on pan-European theater, offering a variety of European-language productions for no more than €36. ⊠ *Pl. de l'Odéon, 6e, St-Germain-des-Prés* ☎ *01–44–85–40–00* ⊕ *www.theatre-odeon.eu* Ⓜ *Odéon.*

Théâtre Darius Milhaud. Théâtre Darius Milhaud stages classics by Camus and Baudelaire, as well as occasional productions in English and shows for children. ⊠ *80 allée Darius Milhaud, 19e, La Villette* ☎ *01–42–01–92–26* ⊕ *www.theatredariusmilhaud.fr* Ⓜ *Porte de Pantin.*

Théâtre de la Huchette. Théâtre de la Huchette is a tiny Rive Gauche theater that has been staging the titanic Romanian-French writer Ionesco's *The Bald Soprano* and *The Lesson* since 1957. Other productions are on view, too. (The box office is open Monday–Saturday 5 pm–9 pm.) ⊠ *23 rue de la Huchette, 5e, Latin Quarter* ☎ *01–43–26–38–99* ⊕ *www.theatre-huchette.com* Ⓜ *St-Michel.*

Théâtre de la Renaissance. This theater was put on the map by Belle Époque superstar Sarah Bernhardt (she was the manager from 1893 to 1899). Big French stars often perform here. ⊠ *20 bd. St-Martin, 10e, Opéra/Grands Boulevards* ☎ *01–42–02–47–35* ⊕ *www.theatre delarenaissance.com* Ⓜ *Strasbourg–St-Denis.*

18

Théâtre des Abbesses. Théâtre des Abbesses, part of the Théâtre de la Ville, is a 400-seat venue in Montmartre. It features lesser-known acts and up-and-coming choreographers, who often make it onto the program in the Théâtre de la Ville the following year. ✉ *31 rue des Abbesses, 18e, Montmartre* ☎ *01–42–74–22–77* ⊕ *www.theatredelaville-paris. com* Ⓜ *Abbesses.*

Théâtre des Bouffes du Nord. Théâtre des Bouffes du Nord is the wonderfully atmospheric, slightly decrepit home of English director Peter Brook, who regularly delights with his quirky experimental productions in French and, sometimes, English. ✉ *37 bis, bd. de la Chapelle, 10e, Stalingrad/La Chapelle* ☎ *01–46–07–34–50* ⊕ *www.bouffesdunord. com* Ⓜ *La Chapelle.*

Théâtre du Palais-Royal. Théâtre du Palais-Royal is a sumptuous 750-seat, Italian-style theater bedecked in gold and purple. Located in the former residence of Cardinal Richelieu, it stages comedies, adaptations of American productions (like *The Vagina Monologues*), and children's theater. ✉ *38 rue Montpensier, 1er, Louvre* ☎ *01–42–97–40–00* ⊕ *theatrepalaisroyal.com* Ⓜ *Palais-Royal.*

Théâtre Marigny. When it reopens in late 2014, a newly renovated Théâtre Marigny will again offer top-flight theater, often with a big-name French star topping the bill. ✉ *Carré Marigny, 8e, Champs-Élysées* ☎ *01–53–96–70–30* ⊕ *www.theatremarigny.fr* Ⓜ *Champs-Élysées–Clemenceau.*

Théâtre Mogador. Théâtre Mogador, one of Paris's most sumptuous theaters, features musicals and other productions with a pronounced popular appeal (think *Mamma Mia!*). ✉ *25 rue de Mogador, 9e, Opéra/ Grands Boulevards* ☎ *01–53–32–32–32* ⊕ *www.stage-entertainment. fr* Ⓜ *Trinité.*

Théâtre National de Chaillot. Théâtre National de Chaillot, housed in an imposing neoclassic building overlooking the Eiffel Tower, has two theaters dedicated to experimental, world and avant-garde drama, dance and music or a mix of all three. Major names in dance—like the Ballet Royal de Suède and William Forsythe's company—also visit regularly. There are programs for children, too. ✉ *1 pl. du Trocadéro, 16e, Trocadéro/Tour Eiffel* ☎ *01–53–65–30–00* ⊕ *theatre-chaillot.fr* Ⓜ *Trocadéro.*

SIDE TRIPS FROM PARIS

With Versailles, Disneyland Paris, and Chartres

Updated
by Jennifer
Ditsler-Ladonne
With so much to see in Paris, it may seem hard to justify a
side trip. But just outside the city lies the rest of the fabled
region known as Ile-de-France: there, along with gorgeous
countryside and quiet towns, you can find spectacular Versailles, the immense Chartres cathedral, and a little region
unto itself where a mouse named Mickey is king.

Plan to spend an entire day (at least) at **Versailles,** perusing the manicured
gardens that make up one of the largest parks in Europe, and touring
the palace, which includes the Hall of Mirrors and Marie-Antoinette's
private retreat in an enclave of the royal park. The charming town of
Chartres is a lovely day or half-day outing from Paris. Its main attraction is Cathédrale de Chartres, an awe-inspiring Gothic church that
looms like a great fantasy ship on the horizon and is world renowned
for its stained-glass windows. **Disneyland Paris** arrived in 1992, but the
magic was slow to take effect. The resort opened with the uninspir-
ing name of EuroDisney and further baffled the French, for whom no
meal is complete without wine, with its ban on alcohol. After the ban
was lifted in the park's sit-down restaurants and the site's name was
changed, Disneyland Paris became France's leading tourist attraction,
drawing sellout crowds of Europeans seeking a kitschy glimpse of the
American Dream—and of American families stealing a day from their
museum schedule.

PLANNING

Traveling to Chartres, Disneyland Paris, and Versailles from Paris is
easy. Although each side trip is within an hour's drive, we *strongly* recommend taking the train from the city rather than renting a car. If Disneyland is your destination and you don't plan to visit Paris, there are
shuttle buses that will take you directly from the airports to the park.

The château of Versailles is closed Monday. Disneyland Paris gets
extremely crowded on summer weekends, so plan your trip during the
week, and early, if possible.

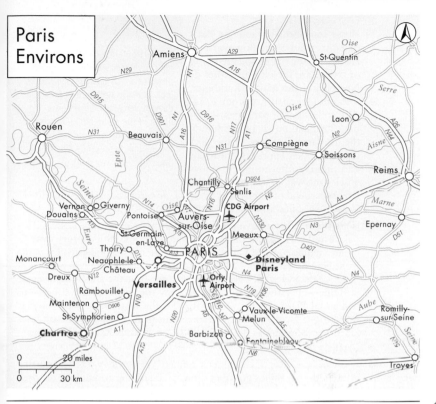

Paris
Environs

VERSAILLES

19

16 km (10 miles) west of Paris via A13.

Fodor's Choice
★

It's hard to tell which is larger at **Château de Versailles**—the world-famous château that housed Louis XIV and 20,000 of his courtiers or the mass of tour buses and visitors standing in front of it. The grandest palace in France remains one of the marvels of the world. But this edifice was not just home to the Sun King: it was also to be the new seat of the French government (from 1682 to 1789 and again from 1871 to 1879) and, by extension, the new French capital.

GETTING HERE

Versailles has three train stations, all reached from different stations in Paris (journey time 25–40 minutes). Versailles Rive Gauche provides the easiest access from Paris. The other two stations in Versailles are about a 10-minute walk from the château, although the municipal Bus B or a summertime shuttle service (use your métro ticket or pay a small fee in coins) can also deposit you at the front gates.

Visitor Information Versailles Tourist Office ✉ *2 bis av. de Paris* ☎ *01–39–24–88–88* ⊕ *www.versailles-tourisme.com.*

EXPLORING

> **DID YOU KNOW?**
>
> The 2012 French flick *Farewell, My Queen* (*Les Adieux à la Reine*) provides a raw upstairs-downstairs look at Marie-Antoinette's final days at Versailles. Based on a novel of the same name, it was shot largely on-site and captures the seldom seen grimy side of palace life—rats and all.

Musée Lambinet. Around the back of Notre-Dame, on Boulevard de la Reine (note the regimented lines of trees), are the elegant Hôtel de Neyret and the Musée Lambinet, a sumptuous mansion from 1751, with collections of paintings, weapons, fans, and porcelain (including the Madame du Barry "Rose"). A tearoom, open Thursday, Saturday, and Sunday afternoons, provides an elegant way to refresh after an intensive round of sightseeing. ✉ *54 bd. de la Reine* ☎ *01–39–50–30–32* 🌐 *www.versailles-tourisme.com* 🎟 *€4* 🕒 *Sat.–Thurs. 2–6.*

Nôtre-Dame. If you have any energy left after exploring Louis XIV's palace and park, a tour of Versailles—a textbook 18th-century town—offers a telling contrast between the majestic and the domestic. From the front gate of Versailles's palace turn left onto Rue de l'Independence-Américaine and walk over to Rue Carnot past the stately Écuries de la Reine—once the queen's stables, now the regional law courts—to octagonal Place Hoche. Down Rue Hoche to the left is the powerful Baroque facade of Notre-Dame, built from 1684 to 1686 by Jules Hardouin-Mansart as the parish church for Louis XIV's new town.

WHERE TO EAT

$$$ | MODERN FRENCH | Fodor's Choice ★

🍴 **L'Angelique.** Régis Douysset's refined yet unfussy French cuisine attracts the Versailles gourmet crowd. The dining room, in a restored 17th-century town house, is serene and comfortable, with white walls, wood-beam ceilings, dark wood paneling, and tasteful artwork—and the meals served here are among the best in town. A seasonally changing menu offers a good balance of seafood and game: a delicate perch fillet with spaghetti *de mer* (in a shellfish bouillon) or venison shoulder with grilled turnips and a spaetzle of girolle mushrooms. ■ **TIP→ Desserts alone are worth a Michelin star—the tart feuilletée, with candied peaches, cardamom, and peach sorbet is ethereal.** [$] *Average main: €31* ✉ *27 av. de Saint-Cloud* ☎ *01–30–84–98–85* 🌐 *www.langelique.fr* 🕒 *Closed Sun., Mon., 1 wk Christmas, 1 wk Feb., and 2 wks Aug.*

$$ | BISTRO

🍴 **Le Saint Julien.** It's not just convenience that draws a mix of locals, expats, and tourists to this pleasant corner bistro, close to the château in the old Saint Louis quarter. In terms of both decor and cuisine, Le Saint Julien mixes the traditional and the modern; hearty dishes like lamb confit and rabbit parmentier (a riff on the classic beef-and-potato casserole) are complemented by tender foie gras-stuffed ravioli or velvety mushroom soup. For lighter fare, the menu always includes a fish and a vegetarian dish. Helpings are generous, but try to leave room for an impressive cheese plate or one of the famously decadent desserts. [$] *Average main: €22* ✉ *6 rue Saint Julien* ☎ *01–39–50–00–97* 🌐 *www.lesaintjulien.fr* ✍ *Reservations essential* 🕒 *Closed Mon.*

$ MODERN FRENCH FAMILY Fodor's Choice ★ 🍴 **Lenôtre.** Set in the glamorous new Cour des Senteurs, this handsome café (a branch of the renowned Paris caterer-*pâtissier*) fills a much-needed gap in Versailles dining. The warm, English-speaking staff and well-priced, reliably good food—combined with a prime location amid elegant boutiques and beautiful gardens—make it a lovely choice at lunchtime, teatime, or just about any other time. The outdoor terrace is a fine spot on temperate days. **■TIP→ Don't miss the sublime jasmine-scented macaron, specially created for the Cour des Senteurs.** [$] *Average main: €12* ✉ *8 rue de la Chancellerie* ☎ *01–39–02–60–13* 🌐 *www.lenotre.com.*

WHERE TO STAY

For expanded hotel reviews, visit Fodors.com.

$ HOTEL 🏨 **Le Cheval Rouge.** Built in 1676, this unpretentious option is in a corner of the market square, close to the château and strongly recommended if you plan to explore the town on foot. **Pros:** great setting in town center; good value for Versailles. **Cons:** bland public areas; some rooms need renovating. [$] *Rooms from: €89* ✉ *18 rue André-Chénier* ☎ *01–39–50–03–03* 🌐 *www.chevalrougeversailles.fr* 🛏 *40 rooms* 🍽 *No meals.*

$$$$ HOTEL 🏨 **Trianon Palace Versailles.** Like a modern-day Versailles, this deluxe turn-of-the-20th-century hotel is a creamy white creation of imposing size, filled with soaring rooms (including the historic Salle Clemenceau, site of the 1919 Versailles Peace Conference). **Pros:** palatial glamour; wonderful setting right by château park; Gordon Ramsay's on-site restaurant. **Cons:** lacks a personal touch. [$] *Rooms from: €220* ✉ *1 bd. de la Reine* ☎ *01–30–84–50–00* 🌐 *www.trianonpalace.fr* 🛏 *176 rooms, 23 suites* 🍽 *No meals.*

NIGHTLIFE AND THE ARTS

Académie du Spectacle Equestre. On most weekends, horses and their riders perform to music in a dazzling hour-long show directed by the great equine choreographer Bartabas. It's held in the converted 17th-century Manège (riding school) at the Grandes Écuries, opposite the palace. Fodor's Travel Talk Forum readers rave about the spectacle. **■TIP→ If you can't make it, try catching a morning practice session.** ✉ *Av. Rockefeller* ☎ *01–39–02–07–14* 🌐 *www.bartabas.fr* ⏲ *Shows €25; morning practice €12.*

Centre de Musique Baroque. Baroque music concerts are presented in the château's Opéra Royal and chapel. 🌐 *www.cmbv.com.*

Fodor's Choice ★ **Opéra Royal de Château de Versailles.** One of the most beautiful opera houses in Europe was built for 14-year-old Marie-Antoinette on the occasion of her marriage to Louis XVI, and entering this extravagantly gilded performance hall from the hewn-stone passageway can literally take your breath away. But the beauty is not just skin deep—the intimate 700-seat venue is blessed with rich acoustics. Home to the Royal Opéra, it also hosts an impressive roster of orchestral and chamber concerts, as well as ballets. For music and dance lovers, this spot alone is well worth the quick trip from Paris. ✉ *Château de Versailles* ☎ *01–30–83–78–89* 🌐 *www.chateauversailles-spectacles.fr.*

Continued on page 393

GILT TRIP
A TOUR OF VERSAILLES

By Robert I.C. Fisher

Louis XIV's Hall of Mirrors

A two-century spree of indulgence in the finest bling-bling of the age by the consecutive reigns of three French kings produced two of the world's most historic artifacts: gloriously, the Palace of Versailles and, momentously, the French Revolution.

Less a monument than an entire world unto itself, Versailles is the king of palaces. The end result of 380 million francs, 36,000 laborers, and enough paintings, if laid end to end, to equal 7 miles of canvas, it was conceived as the ne plus ultra expression of monarchy by Louis XIV. As a child, the king had developed a hatred for Paris (where he had been imprisoned by a group of nobles known as the Frondeurs), so, when barely out of his teens, he cast his cantankerous royal eye in search of a new power base. Marshy, inhospitable Versailles was the stuff of his dreams. Down came dad's modest royal hunting lodge and up, up, and along went the minion-crushing, Baroque palace we see today.

Between 1661 and 1710, architects Louis Le Vau and Jules Hardouin Mansart designed everything his royal acquisitiveness could want, including a throne room devoted to Apollo, god of the sun (Louis was known as *le roi soleil*). Convinced that his might depended upon dominating French nobility, Louis XIV summoned thousands of grandees from their own far-flung châteaux to reside at his new seat of government. In doing so, however, he unwittingly triggered the downfall of the monarchy. Like an 18th-century Disneyland, Versailles kept its courtiers so richly entertained they all but forgot the murmurs of discontent brewing back home.

As Louis XV chillingly foretold, "After me, the deluge." The royal commune was therefore shocked—shocked!—by the appearance, on October 5, 1789, of a revolutionary mob from Paris ready to sack Versailles and imprison Louis XVI. So as you walk through this awesome monument to splendor and excess, give a thought to its historic companion: the French Revolution. A tour of Versailles's grand salons inextricably mixes pathos with glory.

CROWNING GLORIES: TOP SIGHTS OF VERSAILLES

Seducing their court with their self-assured approach to 17th- and 18th-century art and decoration, a trinity of French kings made Versailles into the most vainglorious of châteaux.

Versailles from the outside

Galerie des Glaces (Hall of Mirrors). Of all the rooms at Versailles, none matches the magnificence of the Galerie des Glaces (Hall of Mirrors). Begun by Mansart in 1678, this represents the acme of the Louis Quatorze (Louis-XIV) style. Measuring 240 feet long, 33 feet wide, and 40 feet high, it is ornamented with gilded candlesticks, crystal chandeliers, and a coved ceiling painted with Charles Le Brun's homage to Louis XIV's reign.

Detail of the ceiling

In Louis's day, the Galerie was laid with priceless carpets and filled with orange trees in silver pots. Nighttime galas were illuminated by 3,000 candles, their blaze doubled in the 17 gigantic mirrors that precisely echo the banner of windows along the west front. Lavish balls were once held here, and you can still get the full royal treatment at the Serenade Royale. This reenacts one of Louis XIV's grand soirées with dancers in period costumes. The 45-minute spectacle is held at 6:45 and 7:45 pm, from mid-June to September. (☎ €39, €27 ages 6–18 ⊕ www.chateauversailles-spectacles.fr ☎ 01–30–83–78–98).

Hall of Mirrors

The Grands Appartements (State Apartments). Virtual stages for ceremonies of court ritual and etiquette, Louis XIV's first-floor state salons were designed in the Baroque style on a biceps-flexing scale meant to one-up the lavish Vaux-le-Vicomte château recently built for Nicolas Fouquet, the king's finance minister.

Inside the Apollo Chamber

Flanking the Hall of Mirrors and retaining most of their bombastic Italianate Baroque decoration, the Salon de la Guerre (Salon of War) and the Salon de la Paix (Salon of Peace) are ornately decorated with gilt stucco, painted ceilings, and marble sculpture. Perhaps the most extravagant is the Salon d'Apollon (Apollo Chamber), the former throne room.

Hall of Battles

Appartements du Roi (King's Apartments). Completed in 1701 in the Louis-XIV style, the king's state and private chambers comprise a suite of 15 rooms set in a "U" around the east facade's Marble Court. Dead center across the sprawling cobbled forecourt is Louis XIV's bedchamber—he would awake and rise (just as the sun did, from the east) attended by members of his court and the public. Holding the king's chemise when he dressed soon became a more definitive reflection of status than the possession of an entire province. Nearby is Louis XV's magnificent Cabinet Intérieur (Office of the King), shining with gold and white boiseries; in the center is the most famous piece of furniture at Versailles, Louis XV's roll-top desk, crafted by Oeben and Riesener in 1769.

Louis XIV

King's Apartments

VINTAGE BOURBON

Versailles was built by three great kings of the Bourbon dynasty. Louis XIV (1638–1715) began its construction in 1661. After ruling for 72 years, Louis Quatorze was succeeded by his great grandson, Louis XV (1710–74), who added the Royal Opera and the Petit Trianon to the palace. Louis XVI (1754–93) came to the throne in 1774 and was forced out of Versailles in 1789, along with Marie Antoinette, both guillotined three years later.

Chambre de la Reine (Queen's Bedchamber). Probably the most opulent bedroom in the world, this was initially created for Marie Thérèse, first wife of Louis XIV, to be part of the Queen's Apartments. For Marie Antoinette, however, the entire room was glammed up with silk wall-hangings covered with Rococo motifs that reflect her love of flowers. Legend has it that the gardens directly beyond these windows were replanted daily so that the queen could enjoy a fresh assortment of blossoms each morning. The bed, decked out with white ostrich plumes *en panache*, was also redone for Louis XVI's queen. Nineteen royal children were born in this room.

Queen's Bedchamber

Petits Appartements (Small Apartments). As styles of decor changed, Louis XIV's successors felt out of sync with their architectural inheritance. Louis XV exchanged the heavy red-and-gilt of Italianate Baroque for lighter, pastel-hued Rococo. On the top floor of the palace, on the right side of the central portion, are the apartments Louis XV commissioned to escape the wearisome pomp of the first-floor rooms. Here, Madame de Pompadour, mistress of Louis XV and famous patroness of the Rococo style, introduced grace notes of intimacy and refinement. In so doing, she transformed the daunting royal apartments into places to live rather than pose.

Parc de Versailles. Even Bourbon kings needed respite from Versailles's endless maze, hence the creation of one of Europe's largest parks. The sublime 250-acre grounds (☎ 01–30–83–77–88 for guided tour) is the masterpiece of André Le Nôtre, presiding genius of 17th-century classical French landscaping. Le Nôtre was famous for his "green geometries": ordered fantasies of clipped yew trees, multicolored flower beds (called *parterres*), and perspectival allées cleverly punctuated with statuary, laid out between 1661 and 1668. The spatial effect is best admired from inside the palace, views about which Le Nôtre said, "Flowers can only be walked on by the eyes."

Ultimately, at the royal command, rivers were diverted—to flow into more than 600 fountains—and entire forests were imported to ornament the park, which is centered around the mile-long Grand Canal. As for the great fountains, their operation costs a fortune in these democratic days, and so they perform only on Saturday and Sunday afternoons (🕙 3:30–5:30) from mid-April through mid-October; admission to the park during this time is €8. The park is open daily 8 AM–8:30 PM.

LIGHTING UP THE SKY

The largest fountain at Versailles, the Bassin de Neptune, becomes a spectacle of rare grandeur during the Grandes Eaux Nocturnes, a light show to the strains of Baroque music, held Saturdays from the end of June through August at 9 pm, with fireworks at 11. Tickets are €23, €19 ages 6–17, and free for children under 6. ⊕ www.chateauversailles-spectacles.fr ☎ 01–30–83–78–98.

Dauphin's Apartments

Bassin de Neptune

Chapel and Opéra Royal: In the north wing of the château are three showpieces of the palace. The solemn white-and-gold Chapelle was completed in 1710—the king and queen attended daily mass here seated in gilt boxes. The Opéra Royal (Opera House), entirely constructed of wood painted to look like marble, was designed by Jacques-Ange Gabriel for Louis XV in 1770. Connecting the two, the 17th-century Galeries have exhibits retracing the château's history.

Opéra Royal

IN FOCUS GILT TRIP: A TOUR OF VERSAILLES

19

VERSAILLES: FIRST FLOOR, GARDENS & ADJACENT PARK

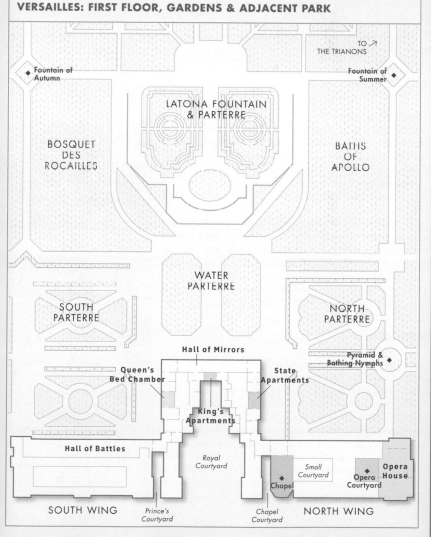

TO THE TRIANONS

Fountain of Autumn
Fountain of Summer

LATONA FOUNTAIN & PARTERRE

BOSQUET DES ROCAILLES

BATHS OF APOLLO

WATER PARTERRE

SOUTH PARTERRE

NORTH PARTERRE

Hall of Mirrors

Pyramid & Bathing Nymphs

Queen's Bed Chamber

State Apartments

King's Apartments

Hall of Battles

Royal Courtyard

Small Courtyard

Opera House

Opera Courtyard

Chapel

SOUTH WING

Prince's Courtyard

Chapel Courtyard

NORTH WING

LET THEM EAT CRÊPE: MARIE ANTOINETTE'S ROYAL LAIR

Was Marie Antoinette a luxury-mad butterfly flitting from ball to costume ball? Or was she a misunderstood queen who suffered a loveless marriage and became a prisoner of court etiquette at Versailles? Historians now believe the answer was the latter and point to her private retreats at Versailles as proof.

R.F.D. VERSAILLES?

Here, in the northwest part of the royal park, Marie Antoinette (1755–93) created a tiny universe of her own: her comparatively dainty mansion called Petit Trianon and its adjacent "farm," the relentlessly picturesque Hameau ("hamlet"). In a life that took her from royal cradle to throne of France to guillotine, her happiest days were spent at Trianon. For here she could live a life in the "simplest" possible way; here the queen could enter a salon and the game of cards would not stop; here women could wear simple gowns of muslin without a single jewel. Toinette only wanted to be queen of Trianon, not queen of France. And considering the horrible, chamber-pot-pungent, gossip-infested corridors of Versailles, you can almost understand why.

TEEN QUEEN

From the first, Maria-Antonia (her actual name) was ostracized as an outsider, "l'Autrichienne"—the Austrian "bitch." Upon arriving in France in 1770—at a mere 14 years of age—she was married to the Dauphin, the future King Louis XVI. But shamed by her initial failure to deliver a royal heir, she grew to hate overcrowded Versailles and escaped to the Petit Trianon. Built between 1763 and 1768 by Jacques-Ange Gabriel for Madame de Pompadour, this bijou palace was a radical statement: a royal residence designed to be casual and unassuming. Toinette refashioned the Trianon's interior in the sober Neoclassical style.

Hameau

Queen's House

Temple of Love

Petit Trianon

Marie Antoinette

19

"THE SIMPLE LIFE"

Just beyond Petit Trianon lay the storybook Hameau, a mock-Norman village inspired by the peasant-luxe, simple-life daydreams caught by Boucher on canvas and by Rousseau in literature. With its water mill, thatched-roof houses, pigeon loft, and vegetable plots, this make-believe farm village was run by Monsieur Valy-Busard, a farmer, and his wife, who often helped the queen—outfitted as a Dresden shepherdess with a Sèvres porcelain crook—tend her flock of perfumed sheep.

As if to destroy any last link with reality, the queen built nearby a jewel-box theater (open by appointment). Here she acted in little plays, sometimes essaying the role of a servant girl. Only the immediate royal family, about seven or so friends, and her personal servants were permitted entry; disastrously, the entire officialdom of Versailles society was shut out—a move that only served to infuriate courtiers. This is how fate and destiny close the circle. For it was here at Trianon that a page sent by Monsieur de Saint-Priest found Marie-Antoinette on October 5, 1789, to tell her that Paris was marching on an already half-deserted Versailles.

Was Marie Antoinette a political traitor to France whose execution was well merited? Or was she the ultimate fashion victim? For those who feel that this tragic queen spent—and shopped—her way into a revolution, a visit to her relatively modest Petit Trianon and Hameau should prove a revelation.

LES BEAUX TRIANONS

A mile from the château, the Grand Trianon was created by Hardouin Mansart in 1687 as a retreat for Louis XIV; it was restored in the early 19th century, with Empire-style salons. It's a memorable spot often missed by foot-weary tourists exhausted by the château, but well worth the effort. A special treat is Marie Antoinette's hideaway nearby, the Petit Trianon, presumably restored to how she left it before being forced to Paris by an angry mob of soon-to-be revolutionaries.

TAKING ON VERSAILLES (WITHOUT LOSING YOUR HEAD)

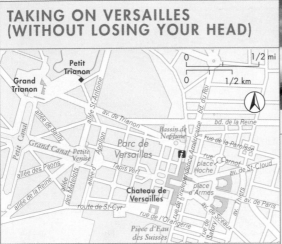

Statue of King Louis XIV

✉ Place d'Armes, Versailles

🌐 www.chateauversailles.fr

☎ 01-30-83-78-00

🎫 An €18 Passport, good for a day, gets you into almost all the sites, as well as temporary exhibits. Add €7 if you also want to see the Grand Eaux fountain show. Two-day Passports are €25. Kids under 18 are free.

If you only want to see the palace itself, tickets are €10. Admission to the Petit and Grand Trianons is €10.

🕙 The palace is open Apr.–Oct., Tues.–Sun. 9–6:30; Nov.–Mar., Tues.–Sun, 9–5:30. The Petit and Grand Trianons are open Apr.–Oct., Tues.–Sun. noon–6:30; Nov.–Mar., Tues.–Sun. 12–5:30. Gardens are open Apr.–Oct., daily 8 am–8:30 pm; Nov.–Mar., daily 8–6.

Ⓜ RER Line C from Paris to Versailles–Rive Gauche station (closest to the Palace) or Transilian trains from Paris's Gare St-Lazare to Versailles–Rive Droite and Gare Montparnasse to Versailles. Train tickets are €4.20.

TOURING THE PALACE

The army of 20,000 noblemen, servants, and sycophants who moved into Louis XIV's huge Château de Versailles is matched today by the battalion of 3 million visitors a year. You may be able to avoid the modern-day crowds if you arrive here at 9 AM and buy your ticket in advance at FNAC or SNCF or online. The main entrance is near the top of the courtyard to the right; there are different lines depending on tour, physical ability, and group status. Frequent English guided tours visit the private royal apartments. More detailed hour-long tours explore the opera house (now reopened after a spectacular renovation; book a tour or concert ticket online) or Marie Antoinette's private parlors. You can wander the grandest rooms—including the Hall of Mirrors—without a group tour. To figure out the system, pick up a brochure at the information office for details.

TOURING THE PARK

If the grandeur of the palace begins to overwhelm, the Parc de Versailles is the best place to come back down to earth. The distances of the park are vast—the Trianons themselves are more than a mile from the château—so you might want to climb aboard the train (🎫€6.80 round-trip ☎01-39-54-22-00), or rent a bike from Petite-Venise (🎫€6.50 per hr or €17 for 6 hrs ☎01-39-66-97-66). You can hire a rowboat on the Grand Canal (🎫€15 per hr) or drive to the Trianons and canal through the Grille de la Reine (🎫€5.50 per car).

SHOPPING

Aux Colonnes. A highly rated *confiserie* (candy shop), Aux Colonnes has a cornucopia of chocolates and candies. It's closed Monday. ⊠ *14 rue Hoche.*

Fodor'sChoice
★

La Cour des Senteurs. At the threshold of Versailles's old town, the beautiful new Cour des Senteurs—Courtyard of Fragrances—celebrates the town's status as the birthplace of the modern perfumer. The tiny **Maison des Parfums** charmingly recounts the history of perfume via a timeline and interactive displays, while the exquisite **Guerlain** boutique—only the second in the world after Paris—offers all the company's signature fragrances and cosmetics, plus a new jasmine-and-bergamot-based perfume you'll find only here. Couture glove maker **Maison Fabre** offers a limited-edition perfumed glove in honor of Marie-Antoinette, along with a line of stylish handmade gloves; and the fabled **Diptyque** boutique sells the scented candles, home fragrances, and perfumes that are beloved by chic Parisians. ⊠ *8 rue de la Chancellerie* ☎ *01–39–51–17– 21* ⊕ *www.parfumsetsenteurs.fr.*

Les Délices du Palais. Everyone heads here to pick up homemade pâté, cold cuts, cheese, salad, and other picnic essentials. It's closed Monday. ⊠ *4 rue du Maréchal-Foch.*

CHARTRES

39 km (24 miles) southwest of Rambouillet via N10 and A11, 88 km (55 miles) southwest of Paris.

If Versailles is the climax of French secular architecture, Chartres is its religious apogee. All the descriptive prose and poetry that have been lavished on this supreme cathedral can only begin to suggest the glory of its 12th- and 13th-century statuary and stained glass, somehow suffused with burning mysticism and a strange sense of the numinous. Chartres is more than a church—it's a nondenominational spiritual experience.

19

GETTING HERE

Both Transilien and main-line (Le Mans–bound) trains leave Paris's Gare Montparnasse for Chartres (50–70 mins, €15). The train station on place Pierre-Sémard puts you within walking distance of the cathedral.

Visitor Information Chartres Tourist Office ⊠ *Pl. de la Cathédrale* ☎ *02–37– 18–26–26* ⊕ *www.chartres-tourisme.com.*

EXPLORING

The whole town, with its old houses and quaint streets, is worth a leisurely exploration. From Rue du Pont-St-Hilaire there's an intriguing view of the rooftops below the cathedral. Ancient streets tumble down from the cathedral to the river, lined most weekends with *bouquinistes* selling old books and prints. Each year on August 15 pilgrims and tourists flock here for the Procession du Vœu de Louis XIII, a religious procession through the streets commemorating the French monarchy's vow to serve the Virgin Mary.

If you need an incentive to linger until dusk, "Chartres en Lumieres" (Chartres's festival of lights) provides it: 28 of the city's most revered monuments, including the glorious Notre-Dame Cathedral, are transformed into vivid light canvases.

Fodor's Choice **Cathédrale Notre-Dame** (*Chartres Cathedral*). Worship on the site of the
★ Cathédrale Notre-Dame, better known as Chartres Cathedral, goes back to before the Gallo-Roman period—the crypt contains a well that was the focus of druid ceremonies. In the late ninth century Charles II (aka "the Bald") presented Chartres with what was believed to be the tunic of the Virgin Mary, a precious relic that went on to attract hordes of pilgrims. The current cathedral, the sixth church on the spot, dates mainly from the 12th and 13th centuries and was erected after the previous building, dating from the 11th century, burned down in 1194. A well-chronicled outburst of religious fervor followed the discovery that the Virgin Mary's relic had miraculously survived unsinged. Motivated by this "miracle," princes and paupers, barons and bourgeoisie gave their money and their labor to build the new cathedral. Ladies of the manor came to help monks and peasants on the scaffolding in a tremendous resurgence of religious faith that followed the Second Crusade. Just 25 years were needed for Chartres Cathedral to rise again, and it has remained substantially unchanged ever since.

The lower half of the facade survives from the earlier Romanesque church: this can be seen most clearly in the use of round arches rather than pointed Gothic-style ones. The **Royal Portal** is richly sculpted with scenes from the life of Christ—these meticulously detailed figures are among the greatest created during the Middle Ages. The taller of the two spires (380 feet versus 350 feet) was erected at the start of the 16th century, after its predecessor was destroyed by fire; its fanciful Flamboyant intricacy contrasts sharply with the stumpy solemnity of its Romanesque counterpart (access €3, open daily 9:30–noon and 2–4:30). The **rose window** above the main portal dates from the 13th century, and the three windows below it contain some of the finest examples of 12th-century stained-glass artistry in all of France.

As spiritual as Chartres is, the cathedral also had its more-earthbound uses. Look closely and you can see that the main nave floor has a subtle slant. It was designed to provide drainage because this part of the church was often used as a "hostel" by thousands of overnighting pilgrims in medieval times.

Your eyes will need time to adjust to the somber interior. The reward is seeing the gemlike richness of the stained glass, with the famous deep Chartres blue predominating. The oldest window is arguably the most beautiful: **Notre-Dame de la Belle Verrière** (Our Lady of the Lovely Window), in the south choir. The cathedral's windows are gradually being cleaned—a lengthy, painstaking process—and the contrast with those still covered in the grime of centuries is staggering. ■ TIP→ It's worth taking a pair of binoculars along with you to pick out the details. If you wish to know more about stained-glass techniques and the motifs used, visit the small exhibit in the gallery opposite the north porch. Since 2008, the cathedral has been undergoing an ambitious €270-million

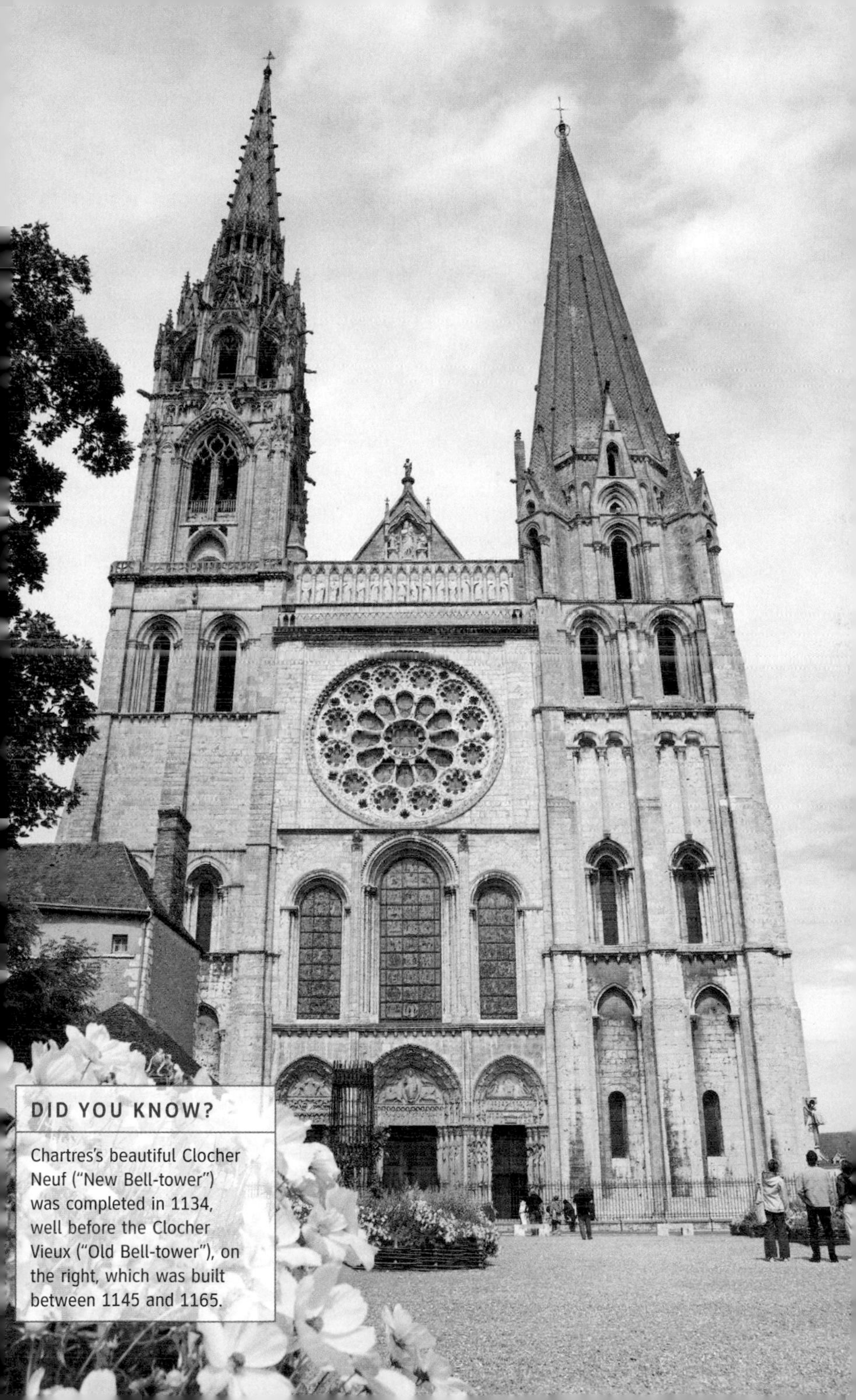

DID YOU KNOW?

Chartres's beautiful Clocher Neuf ("New Bell-tower") was completed in 1134, well before the Clocher Vieux ("Old Bell-tower"), on the right, which was built between 1145 and 1165.

renovation that will continue through 2015. To date, two major chapels (the chapels of the Martyrs and the Apostles) have been completely restored, as have the two bays of the nave and the lower choir and the transept windows. For those who remember these dark recesses before the restoration the transformation is nothing short of miraculous, with an estimated 160,000 square feet of original plasterwork now visible and many of the sublime details for which the cathedral is famous returned to their original 13th-century glory. For even more detail, try to arrange a tour (in English) with local institution Malcolm Miller, whose knowledge of the cathedral's history is formidable. (He leads tours twice a day Monday through Saturday, April–October, and once a day November–March at noon. You can contact him at ☎ *02–37–28–15–58* or at ✉ *millerchartres@aol.com.)* The vast black-and-white labyrinth on the floor of the nave is one of the few to have survived from the Middle Ages; the faithful were expected to travel along its entire length (some 300 yards) on their knees. Guided tours of the **Crypte** start from the Maison de la Crypte opposite the south porch. You can also see a fourth-century Gallo-Roman wall and some 12th-century wall paintings. ⌧ *16 cloître Notre-Dame* ☎ *02–37–21–75–02* 🌐 *www.chartres-tourisme.com* 🎟 *Crypt €3; tours €6.20* 🕒 *Cathedral daily 8:30–7:30. Guided tours of crypt Apr.–Oct., daily at 11, 2:15, 3:30, and 4:30; Nov.–Mar., daily at 11 and 4:15.*

Musée des Beaux-Arts (*Fine Arts Museum*). Just behind the famed cathedral, the town art museum is housed in a handsome 18th-century building that once served as the bishop's palace. Its varied collection includes Renaissance enamels, a portrait of Erasmus by Holbein, tapestries, armor, and some fine (mainly French) paintings from the 17th, 18th, and 19th centuries. There's also a room devoted to the forceful 20th-century landscapes of Maurice de Vlaminck, who lived in the region. ⌧ *29 cloître Notre-Dame* ☎ *02–37–90–45–80* 🎟 *€3.40* 🕒 *Wed. and Sat. 10–noon and 2–6, Sun. 2–5.*

WHERE TO EAT AND STAY

For expanded hotel reviews, visit Fodors.com.

$$$ FRENCH FUSION

🍴 **La Vieille Maison.** Just 100 yards from the cathedral, in a pretty 14th-century building with a flower-decked patio, this restaurant is a fine choice. Chef Bruno Letartre changes his menu regularly, often including such regional specialties as asparagus, rich duck pâté, and superb homemade foie gras, along with seafood and game in season. **■ TIP→ Prices, though justified, can be steep, but the "suggested" lunch menu (€29) served on summer weekdays is a good bet.** [$] *Average main: €31* ⌧ *5 rue au Lait* ☎ *02–37–34–10–67* 🌐 *www.lavieillemaison.fr* 🕒 *Closed Mon. and Tues.; no dinner Sun.*

$$ FRENCH

🍴 **Moulin de Ponceau.** Ask for a table with a view of the River Eure and the cathedral looming above at this 16th-century converted water mill. Better still, eat outside beneath a parasol on the stone terrace by the water's edge—an idyllic setting on sunny days. You can choose from a menu of French stalwarts that might include rabbit terrine, trout with almonds, and tarte tatin, or splurge on "la trilogie" of scallops, foie gras, and langoustine. [$] *Average main: €22* ⌧ *21 rue de la Tannerie* ☎ *02–37–35–30–05* 🌐 *www.moulindeponceau.fr* 🕒 *No dinner Sun.*

$$ 🖼 **Best Western Le Grand Monarque.** On Chartres's main square, not far
HOTEL from the cathedral, this converted coaching inn warmly evokes the 19th
century; many guest rooms are outfitted with brick walls, attractive
antiques, lush drapes, and modern bathrooms (the best are in a sepa-
rate turn-of-the-20th-century building overlooking a garden, while the
most atmospheric are tucked away in the attic). **Pros:** its old-fashioned
charm still works today; the spa and fitness center offers beauty treat-
ments and massage. **Cons:** best rooms are in an annex; uphill walk to
cathedral. $ *Rooms from: €139* ⊠ *22 pl. des Épars* ☎ *02–37–18–15–15*
⊕ *www.bw-grand-monarque.com* ⮑ *50 rooms, 5 suites* ◯ *No meals.*

$$$$ 🖼 **Château d'Esclimont.** One of France's most spectacular château-hotels
HOTEL lies northeast of Chartres in the town of St-Symphorien. **Pros:** the grand
Fodor'sChoice style of a country château; wonderful rural setting. **Cons:** service can
★ be pompous; off the beaten path and not easy to find. $ *Rooms from:*
€220 ⊠ *2 rue du Château-d'Esclimont, 24 km (15 miles) northeast of*
Chartres via N10/D18, St-Symphorien-le-Château ☎ *02–37–31–15–15*
⊕ *www.grandesetapes.fr* ⮑ *48 rooms, 4 suites* ◯ *No meals.*

DISNEYLAND PARIS

*68 km (40 miles) southwest of Pierrefonds via D335, D136, N330, and
A4; 38 km (24 miles) east of Paris via A4*

Disneyland Paris is probably not what you've traveled to France for.
But if you have a child in tow, the promise of a day here may get you
through an afternoon at Versailles or Chartres. Dyed-in-the-wool fans
will be curious to see how it has been molded to appeal to European
tastes. (Disney's "Imagineers" call it their most lovingly detailed park,
and it simultaneously feels both decidedly foreign and eerily familiar.)
Alternately, if you've never experienced this particular form of Disney
showmanship before, you may want to put in an appearance simply to
see what all the fuss is about.

19

GETTING HERE

Take the RER-A from central Paris (stations at Étoile, Auber, Les Halles,
Gare de Lyon, and Nation) to Marne-la-Vallée–Chessy—the gare there
is 100 yards from the Disneyland entrance; trains operate every 10–30
minutes, depending on the time of day (40 mins, €7.50). High-speed
TGV train service (⊕ *www.tgv.com*) links Disneyland to Lille, Lyon,
Brussels, and London (via Lille and the Channel Tunnel). Disneyland's
hotel complex also offers a shuttle bus service connecting it with the
Orly and Charles de Gaulle airports; in each case the trip takes about
45 minutes and tickets cost €20.

Visitor Information Disneyland Paris Reservations Office ☎ *01–60–30–60–
90, 407/939–7675 in U.S.* ⊕ *www.disneylandparis.com.*

EXPLORING

FAMILY **Disneyland Paris.** A slightly downsized version of its United States coun-
Fodor'sChoice terpart, Disneyland Paris is a spectacular sight created with an acute
★ attention to detail. Disney never had quite the following here as it did
Stateside, so when the park first opened, few turned up; Walt's vision,
however, eventually won them over. Today the place is jammed with

families from around the world reveling in the many splendors of the Disney universe.

Some of the rides can be a bit scary for little kids, but tots adore Alice's Maze, Peter Pan's Flight, and especially the whirling Mad Hatter's Tea-cups. Also getting high marks are the afternoon parades, which feature music, introductions in five languages, and huge floats swarming with all of Disney's most beloved characters—just make sure to stake your place along Main Street in advance for a good spot (check for posted times). There's a lot here, so pace yourself: kids can easily feel over-whelmed by the barrage of stimuli or frustrated by extra-long waits at the rides (also be aware that there are size restrictions for some). The older the children, the more they will enjoy Walt Disney Studios, a cinematically driven sister park, where many of the newer attractions can be found.

Disneyland Park, the original part of the complex, consists of five "lands": Main Street U.S.A., Frontierland, Adventureland, Fantasyl-and, and Discoveryland. The central theme of each is relentlessly echoed in everything from attractions to restaurant menus to souvenirs. The park is circled by a railroad, which stops three times along the perim-eter. **Main Street U.S.A.** goes under the railroad and past shops and restaurants toward the main plaza; Disney parades are held here every afternoon and, during holiday periods, every evening.

Top attractions at **Frontierland** are the chilling Phantom Manor, haunted by holographic spooks, and the thrilling runaway mine train of Big Thunder Mountain, a roller coaster that plunges wildly through floods and avalanches in a setting meant to evoke Utah's Monument Valley. Whiffs of Arabia, Africa, and the Caribbean give **Adventureland** its exotic cachet; the spicy meals and snacks served here rank among the best food in the park. Don't miss Pirates of the Caribbean, an excit-ing *mise-en-scène* populated by lifelike animatronic figures, or Indiana Jones and the Temple of Doom, a rapid-fire ride that recreates some of this hapless hero's most exciting moments.

Fantasyland charms the youngest parkgoers with familiar cartoon characters from such classic Disney films as *Snow White, Pinocchio, Dumbo, Alice in Wonderland,* and *Peter Pan.* The focal point of Fan-tasyland, and indeed Disneyland Paris, is Le Château de la Belle au Bois Dormant (Sleeping Beauty's Castle), a 140-foot, bubblegum-pink structure topped with 16 blue- and gold-tipped turrets. Its design was allegedly inspired by illustrations from a medieval Book of Hours—if so, it was by way of Beverly Hills. The castle's dungeon conceals a 2-ton scaly green dragon that rumbles in its sleep and occasionally rouses to roar—an impressive feat of engineering, producing an answering chorus of shrieks from younger children. **Discoveryland** is a high-tech, futuris-tic eye-popper. Robots on roller skates welcome you on your way to Star Tours, a pitching, plunging, sense-confounding ride based on the *Star Wars* films; and another robot, the staggeringly realistic 9-Eye, hosts a simulated space journey in Le Visionarium. Other top Discovery-land attractions include the Jules Verne–inspired Space Mountain Mis-sion 2, which pretends to catapult *exploronauts* on a rocket-boosted, comet-battered journey through the Milky Way; and Buzz Lightyear Laser Blast, which challenges kids to blast the villain Zurg with their own laser gun from a whirling star cruiser.

As you'd expect, Disneyland Paris has lots of dining options, ranging from snack bars and fast-food joints to five full-service restaurants—all with a distinguishing theme. If your child has his or her heart set on a specifically themed restaurant, say, Pirates of the Caribbean (a dark corsair's lair that looks over the titular ride) or the Auberge de Cendrillon (Cinderella's Inn, where the nasty stepmother and sisters themselves bustle through the aisles), make sure to make advance reservations in person or online. In addition, Walt Disney Studios, Disney Village, and Disney Hotels have restaurants open to the public. But since these are outside the park, it's not recommended that you waste time traveling to them for lunch. Disneyland Paris has relaxed its no-alcohol policy and now serves wine and beer in the park's sit-down restaurants, as well as in the hotels and restaurants outside the park.

Walt Disney Studios opened next to the Disneyland Park in 2002. It's divided into four "production zones." Beneath imposing entrance gates and a 100 foot water tower inspired by the one erected in 1939 at Disney Studios in Burbank, California, **Front Lot** contains shops, a restaurant, and a studio recreating the atmosphere of Sunset Boulevard. In **Animation Courtyard,** Disney artists demonstrate the various phases of character animation; Animagique brings to life scenes from *Pinocchio* and *The Lion King,* while the Genie from *Aladdin* pilots Flying Carpets over Agrabah. **Production Courtyard** hosts the Walt Disney Television Studios; Cinémagique, a special-effects tribute to U.S. and European cinema; and a behind-the-scenes Studio Tram tour of location sites, movie props, studio interiors, and costumes, ending with a visit to Catastrophe Canyon in the heart of a film shoot. **Back Lot** majors in stunts. At Armageddon Special Effects you can confront a flaming meteor shower aboard the Mir space station, then complete your visit at the giant outdoor arena with a Stunt Show Spectacular involving cars, motorbikes, and Jet Skis. The newest addition to Walt Disney Studios opens in the summer of 2014. Appropriately, it's a mini-land—complete with ride and restaurant—themed around the Paris-based Pixar flick *Ratatouille.* ⊠ *Marne-la-Vallée* ☎ *01–60–30–60–90* ⊕ *www.disneylandparis.com* ✉ *€81, or €169 for 3-day Passport; includes admission to all individual attractions within Disneyland or Walt Disney Studios; tickets for Walt Disney Studios are also valid for admission to Disneyland during last 3 opening hrs of same day* ⊗ *Disneyland mid-June–mid-Sept., daily 9 am–10 pm; mid-Sept.–Dec. 19 and Jan. 5–mid-June, weekdays 10–8, weekends 9–8; Dec. 20–Jan. 4, daily 9–8. Walt Disney Studios daily 10–6.*

19

WHERE TO STAY

For expanded hotel reviews, visit Fodors.com.

$$$$ 🏨 **Sequoia Lodge.** Ranging from superluxe to still-a-pretty-penny, Dis-
HOTEL neyland Paris has 5,000 rooms in five hotels, but your best bet on all counts may be the Sequoia Lodge—a grand recreation of an American mountain lodge, just a few minutes' walk from the theme park. **Pros:**

package deals include admission to theme park; cozy, secluded feel; great pools. **Cons:** restaurants a bit ho-hum; many rooms do not have lake view. $ *Rooms from: €300* ⊠ *Marne-la-Vallée* ☎ *01–60–30–60– 90, 407/939–7675 in U.S.* ⊕ *www.disneylandparis.com* ⇄ *1,020 rooms* ⦿| *No meals.*

NIGHTLIFE AND THE ARTS

Disney Village. Nocturnal entertainment outside the park centers on Disney Village, a vast pleasure mall designed by American architect Frank Gehry. Homesick kids who've had enough of *croque-monsieur* sandwiches will be happy to hear that vintage American-style restaurants—a diner, a deli, and a steak house among them—dominate the food scene here. ⊠ *Marne-la-Vallée.*

   Buffalo Bill's Wild West Show. Also in Disney Village is Buffalo Bill's Wild West Show, a two-hour dinner extravaganza with a menu of sausage, spare ribs, and chili. The entertainment component includes performances by a talented troupe of stunt riders, bronco busters, tribal dancers, and musicians; plus some 50 horses, a dozen buffalo, a bull, and an Annie Oakley–style sharpshooter, with a golden-maned "Buffalo Bill" as emcee. A re-creation of a show that dazzled Parisians 100 years ago, it's corny but great fun. ⊠ *Marne-la-Vallée* ☎ *01–60–45–71–00 for reservations* ⊠ *€59.90* ⊙ *Nightly at 6:30 and 9:30.*

UNDERSTANDING PARIS

Books and Movies

Vocabulary

BOOKS AND MOVIES

Books

Fiction. Think of writers in Paris, and the romanticized expat figures of the inter-war "lost generation" often come to mind: Ernest Hemingway (*The Sun Also Rises*), F. Scott Fitzgerald, Ezra Pound, and Gertrude Stein just to name a few. Further back in time are classics like Charles Dickens's *A Tale of Two Cities*, set during the Revolution, and Henry James's novels *The American* and *The Ambassadors*, both tales of Americans in Europe. The expats of World War II set the scene for future Americans in Paris: James Baldwin's life in the city in the 1950s informed novels such as *Giovanni's Room*, and the denizens of the so-called Beat Hotel (Allen Ginsberg, William Burroughs, and Henry Miller) squeezed in some writing among their less salubrious activities. The Canadian writer Mavis Gallant, who published many stories in *The New Yorker*, also began her tenure in Paris in the '50s; her collection *Paris Stories* is a delight.

Recent best sellers with a Paris setting include, of course, Dan Brown's *The Da Vinci Code*, as well as Diane Johnson's *Le Divorce* and *Le Mariage*, Anita Brookner's *Incidents in the Rue Laugier*, and Patrick Suskind's *Perfume: The Story of a Murderer*. Paul LaFarge's *Haussmann, or the Distinction* spins historical detail about the ambitious city planner into a fascinating period novel. Paula McLain's *The Paris Wife* imagines Hemingway's Paris from the perspective of his first wife, Hadley. For literary snacking, *Paris in Mind* pulls together excerpts from books by American authors.

For Children. Who doesn't remember Miss Clavel and her 12 young students in two straight lines? Ludwig Bemelmans' beloved *Madeleine* series about the namesake heroine is also illustrated with the author's drawings of Paris landmarks such as the Opéra and the Jardins du Luxembourg. *Eloise in Paris,* by Kay Thompson, also has illustrations, these by Hilary Knight (look for his take on Christian Dior). The *Anatole* books by Eve Titus are classics, starring a Gallic mouse. Playful, bright illustrations drive Maira Kalman's *Ooh-la-la (Max in Love)*; the singsong language, smattered with French, is perfect for reading aloud. Joan MacPhail Knight wrote a pair of books about an American girl visiting France in the late 1800s: *Charlotte in Giverny* and *Charlotte in Paris*.

History. Recent studies devoted to the capital include Philip Mansel's *Paris Between Empires: Monarchy and Revolution*; Jill Harsin's *Barricades: War on the Streets in Revolutionary Paris*; and Johannes Willms's *Paris: Capital of Europe*, which runs from the Revolution to the Belle Époque. Simon Schama's *Citizens* is a good introduction to the French Revolution. Alistair Horne's *Seven Ages of Paris* skips away from standard historical approaches, breaking the city's past into seven eras and putting a colorful spin on the Renaissance, the Revolution, Napoléon's Empire, and other periods.

Biographies and autobiographies of French luminaries and Paris residents can double as satisfying portraits of the capital during their subjects' lifetimes. Works on Baron Haussmann are especially rich, as the 19th-century prefect so utterly changed the face of the city. For a look at American expatriates in Paris between the wars, pick up *Sylvia Beach and the Lost Generation,* by Noel R. Fitch. Tyler Stovall's *Paris Noir: African-Americans in the City of Light* examines black American artists' affection for Paris during the 20th century; *Harlem in Montmartre*, by William A. Shack, homes in on expat jazz culture. Walter Benjamin's *The Arcades Project* uses the 19th century as a point of intersection for studies on advertising, Baudelaire, the Paris Commune, and other subjects.

Memoirs, Essays, and Observations. Ernest Hemingway's *A Moveable Feast,* the tale of his 1920s expat life in Paris as a struggling writer, grips from its opening lines. Gertrude Stein, one of Hemingway's friends, gave her own version of the era in *The Autobiography of Alice B. Toklas*. In *The Secret Paris of the '30s*, Brassaï put into words the scenes he captured in photographs. Joseph Roth gave an exile's point of view in *Report from a Parisian Paradise*. Art Buchwald's funny yet poignant *I'll Always Have Paris* moves from the postwar GI Bill days through his years as a journalist and adventurer. Stanley Karnow also drew on a reporter's past in *Paris in the Fifties*. Henry Miller's visceral autobiographical works such as *The Tropic of Cancer* reveal a grittier kind of expat life. Janet Flanner's incomparable *Paris Journals* chronicle the city from the 1940s through 1970, and no one has yet matched A.J. Liebling at table, as described in *Between Meals*.

More recent accounts by Americans living in Paris include Edmund White's *Our Paris: Sketches with Memory* (White is also the author of a brief but captivating wander through the city in *The Flâneur*), Alex Karmel's *A Corner in the Marais: Memoir of a Paris Neighborhood*, Thad Carhart's *The Piano Shop on the Left Bank*, and the very funny *Me Talk Pretty One Day*, by David Sedaris. Adam Gopnik, a *New Yorker* writer who lived in Paris in the 1990s, intersperses articles on larger French issues with descriptions of daily life with his wife and son in *Paris to the Moon*. Gopnik also edited the anthology *Americans in Paris*, a collection of observations by everyone from Thomas Jefferson to Cole Porter.

Works in Translation. Many landmarks of French literature have long been claimed as classics in English as well—Victor Hugo's great 19th-century novels, including *The Hunchback of Notre-Dame* and *Les Misérables*, spin elaborate descriptions of Paris. Other 19th-century masterpieces include Gustave Flaubert's *Sentimental Education*, set against the capital's 1848 uprisings, and Honoré de Balzac's *Human Comedy*, a series of dozens of novels, many set in Paris.

Marcel Proust's masterpiece *À la Recherche du Temps Perdu* (*In Search of Lost Time*) describes fin-de-siècle Paris's parks, glittering aristocratic salons, and dread during the Great War. Colette was another great chronicler of the Belle Époque; her short works include *Chéri* and the Claudine stories.

Simone de Beauvoir's *The Prime of Life*, the second book in her autobiographical trilogy, details her relationship with the existentialist philosopher Jean-Paul Sartre in the context of 1930s and '40s Paris, when the Rive Gauche cemented its modern bohemian reputation in its cafés and jazz clubs.

Movies

In English. In 2012, Woody Allen made what many consider to be his best recent film with his playful tribute to the city of love in *Midnight in Paris*. Before that in 2007, French actress Julie Delpy did a sweet cinematique tale of culture clash in *Two Days in Paris*, and Pixar Studios highlighted Paris' love of fine food in *Ratatouille*. Back in 2006, Sofia Coppola's lavish *Marie Antoinette* focused on the isolation and posh life of France's famous queen; it might not have been a box office hit, but it's an interesting take on life at Versailles. Previous to that, the film version of *The Da Vinci Code* (2006), starring Tom Hanks and Audrey Tautou, was talked about for months preceding its release, although some were disappointed. The heist film *Ronin* (1998) pairs Robert De Niro and Jean Reno with a hyperkinetic chase through the streets of Paris; and in *Frantic* (1987) Harrison Ford plays an American doctor visiting Paris when his wife disappears, and director Roman Polanski shoots the city to build suspense and dread. The Palais-Royal gets an equally tense treatment in the Audrey Hepburn–Cary Grant thriller *Charade* (1963); the 2002 remake, *The Truth About Charlie*, doesn't hold a candle to the original. In *Before Sunset* (2004), Ethan Hawke meets Julie Delpy in Paris in the sequel to *Before Sunrise*.

French Films. One of the biggest hits out of France was *Amélie* (2001), which follows a young woman determined to change people's lives. There's a love angle, *bien sûr,* and the neighborhood of Montmartre is practically a third hero, although Parisians sniffed that it was a sterilized version of the raffish quartier.

More recently, Marion Cotillard took home the Oscar for her portrayal of singer Édith Piaf in *La Vie en Rose* (2007), a performance all the more stunning by Cotillard's ability to bring Piaf to the screen in all stages of life.

Jean-Luc Godard's *Breathless* (1960) and François Truffaut's *The 400 Blows* (slang for "raising hell"; 1959) kicked off the New Wave cinema movement. Godard eschewed traditional movie narrative techniques, employing a loose style—including improvised dialogue and hand-held camera shots—for his story about a low-level crook (Jean-Paul Belmondo) and his girlfriend (Jean Seberg). Truffaut's film is a masterwork of innocence lost, a semiautobiographical story of a young boy banished to juvenile detention.

Catherine Deneuve is practically a film industry in and of herself. Her movies span the globe; those shot in Paris range from *Belle de Jour* (1967)—Luis Buñuel's study of erotic repression—to *Le Dernier Métro* (1980), a World War II drama.

Classic film noir and contemporary crime dramas are also highlights of French cinema: for a taste, rent *Rififi* (1955), with its excruciatingly tense 33-minute heist scene; *Le Samouraï* (1967), in which Alain Delon plays the ultimate cool assassin; or Robert Bresson's *Pickpocket* (1959). *La Casque d'Or* (1952) looks back to the underworld of the early 1900s, with Simone Signoret as the title irresistible blond. French director Luc Besson introduced a sly female action hero with *La Femme Nikita* (1990), in which Jean Reno chills as the creepy "cleaner" you don't want making house calls.

Filmed during the Occupation, *The Children of Paradise* (1945) became an allegory for the French spirit of resistance: the love story was set in 1840s Paris, thereby getting past the German censors. Other romantic films with memorable takes on Paris include *Cyrano de Bergerac* (1990), with Gérard Depardieu as the large-schnozzed hero; the comedy *When the Cat's Away* (1996); the talk-heavy films of Eric Rohmer; *Camille Claudel* (1988), about the affair between Rodin and fellow sculptor Claudel; and the gritty *The Lovers on the Bridge* (1999), the flaws balanced by the bravado of Juliette Binoche waterskiing on the Seine surrounded by fireworks. *The Red Balloon* (1956) is also a love story of a sort: a children's film of a boy and his faithful balloon.

Musicals. Love in the time of Toulouse-Lautrec? Elton John songs? Baz Luhrmann's *Moulin Rouge* (2001) whirls them together and wins through conviction rather than verisimilitude. John Huston's 1952 film of the same name is also well worth watching. Gene Kelly pursues Leslie Caron through postwar Paris in *An American in Paris* (1951); the Gershwin-fueled film includes a stunning 17-minute dance sequence. Caron reappears as the love interest—this time as a young girl in training to be a courtesan—in *Gigi* (1958). *Funny Face* (1957) stars Fred Astaire and Audrey Hepburn, and there's an unforgettable scene of Hepburn descending the staircase below the *Winged Victory* in the Louvre.

VOCABULARY

One of the trickiest French sounds to pronounce is the nasal final n sound (whether or not the n is actually the last letter of the word). You should try to pronounce it as a sort of nasal grunt—as in "huh." The vowel that precedes the n will govern the vowel sound of the word, and in this list we precede the final n with an h to remind you to be nasal.

Another problem sound is the ubiquitous but untransliterable eu, as in bleu (blue) or deux (two), and the very similar sound in je (I), ce (this), and de (of). The closest equivalent might be the vowel sound in "put," but rounded. The famous rolled r is a glottal sound. Consonants at the ends of words are usually silent; when the following word begins with a vowel, however, the two are run together by sounding the consonant. There are two forms of "you" in French: vous (formal and plural) and tu (a singular, personal form). When addressing an adult you don't know, vous is always best.

ENGLISH	FRENCH	PRONUNCIATION
BASICS		
Yes/no	Oui/non	wee/nohn
Please	S'il vous plaît	seel voo play
Thank you	Merci	mair-**see**
You're welcome	De rien	deh ree-**ehn**
Excuse me, sorry	Pardon	pahr-**don**
Good morning/ afternoon	Bonjour	bohn-**zhoor**
Good evening	Bonsoir	bohn-**swahr**
Good-bye	Au revoir	o ruh-**vwahr**
Mr. (Sir)	Monsieur	muh-**syuh**
Mrs. (Ma'am)	Madame	ma-**dam**
Miss	Mademoiselle	mad-mwa-**zel**
Pleased to meet you	Enchanté(e)	ohn-shahn-**tay**
How are you?	Comment allez-vous?	kuh-mahn-tahl-ay **voo**
Very well, thanks	Très bien, merci	tray bee-ehn, mair-**see**
And you?	Et vous?	ay voo?
NUMBERS		
one	un	uhn
two	deux	deuh
three	trois	twah

ENGLISH	FRENCH	PRONUNCIATION
four	quatre	**kaht**-ruh
five	cinq	sank
six	six	seess
seven	sept	set
eight	huit	wheat
nine	neuf	nuf
ten	dix	deess
eleven	onze	ohnz
twelve	douze	dooz
thirteen	treize	trehz
fourteen	quatorze	kah-**torz**
fifteen	quinze	kanz
sixteen	seize	sez
seventeen	dix-sept	deez-**set**
eighteen	dix-huit	deez-**wheat**
nineteen	dix-neuf	deez-**nuf**
twenty	vingt	vehn
twenty-one	vingt-et-un	vehnt-ay-**uhn**
thirty	trente	trahnt
forty	quarante	ka-**rahnt**
fifty	cinquante	sang-**kahnt**
sixty	soixante	swa-**sahnt**
seventy	soixante-dix	swa-sahnt-**deess**
eighty	quatre-vingts	kaht-ruh-**vehn**
ninety	quatre-vingt-dix	kaht-ruh-vehn-**deess**
one hundred	cent	sahn
one thousand	mille	meel

COLORS

black	noir	nwahr
blue	bleu	bleuh

ENGLISH	FRENCH	PRONUNCIATION
brown	brun/marron	bruhn/mar-**rohn**
green	vert	vair
orange	orange	o-**rahnj**
pink	rose	rose
red	rouge	rouge
violet	violette	vee-o-**let**
white	blanc	blahnk
yellow	jaune	zhone

DAYS OF THE WEEK

Sunday	dimanche	dee-**mahnsh**
Monday	lundi	luhn **dee**
Tuesday	mardi	mahr-**dee**
Wednesday	mercredi	mair-kruh-**dee**
Thursday	jeudi	zhuh **dee**
Friday	vendredi	vawn-druh-**dee**
Saturday	samedi	sahm-**dee**

MONTHS

January	janvier	zhahn-vee-**ay**
February	février	feh-vree-**ay**
March	mars	marce
April	avril	a-**vreel**
May	mai	meh
June	juin	zhwehn
July	juillet	zhwee-**ay**
August	août	ah-**oo**
September	septembre	sep-**tahm**-bruh
October	octobre	awk-**to**-bruh
November	novembre	no-**vahm**-bruh
December	décembre	day-**sahm**-bruh

ENGLISH	FRENCH	PRONUNCIATION

USEFUL PHRASES

Do you speak English?	Parlez-vous anglais?	par-lay **voo** ahn-**glay**
I don't speak . . .	Je ne parle pas . . .	zhuh nuh parl pah . . .
French	français	frahn-**say**
I don't understand	Je ne comprends pas	zhuh nuh kohm-**prahn** pah
I understand	Je comprends	zhuh kohm-**prahn**
I don't know	Je ne sais pas	zhuh nuh say **pah**
I'm American/ British	Je suis américain/ anglais	zhuh sweez a-may-ree-**kehn**/ ahn-**glay**
What's your name?	Comment vous appelez-vous?	ko-mahn vooz a-pell-ay-**voo**
My name is . . .	Je m'appelle . . .	zhuh ma-**pell** . . .
What time is it?	Quelle heure est-il?	kel air eh-**teel**
How?	Comment?	ko-**mahn**
When?	Quand?	kahn
Yesterday	Hier	yair
Today	Aujourd'hui	o-zhoor-**dwee**
Tomorrow	Demain	duh-**mehn**
Tonight	Ce soir	suh **swahr**
What?	Quoi?	kwah
What is it?	Qu'est-ce que c'est?	kess-kuh-**say**
Why?	Pourquoi?	poor-**kwa**
Who?	Qui?	kee
Where is . . .	Où est . . .	oo ay
the train station?	la gare?	la gar
the subway station?	la station de métro?	la sta-**syon** duh may-**tro**
the bus stop?	l'arrêt de bus?	la-ray duh booss
the post office?	la poste?	la post
the bank?	la banque?	la bahnk

ENGLISH	FRENCH	PRONUNCIATION
the . . . hotel?	l'hôtel . . .?	lo-**tel**
the store?	le magasin?	luh ma-ga-**zehn**
the cashier?	la caisse?	la **kess**
the . . . museum?	le musée . . .?	luh mew-**zay**
the hospital?	l'hôpital?	lo-pee-**tahl**
the elevator?	l'ascenseur?	la-sahn-**seuhr**
the telephone?	le téléphone?	luh tay-lay-**phone**
Where are the . . .	Où sont les . . .	oo sohn lay
restrooms?	toilettes?	twah-**let**
(men/women)	(hommes/femmes)	(**oh**-mm/**fah**-mm)
Here/there	Ici/là	ee-**see**/la
Left/right	A gauche/à droite	a goash/a draht
Straight ahead	Tout droit	too drwah
Is it near/far?	C'est près/loin?	say pray/lwehn
I'd like . . .	Je voudrais . . .	zhuh voo-**dray**
a room	une chambre	ewn **shahm**-bruh
the key	la clé	la clay
a newspaper	un journal	uhn zhoor-**nahl**
a stamp	un timbre	uhn **tam**-bruh
I'd like to buy . . .	Je voudrais acheter . . .	zhuh voo-**dray** **ahsh**-tay
cigarettes	des cigarettes	day see-ga-**ret**
matches	des allumettes	days a-loo-**met**
soap	du savon	dew sah-**vohn**
city map	un plan de ville	uhn plahn de **veel**
road map	une carte routière	ewn cart roo-tee-**air**
magazine	une revue	ewn reh-**vu**
envelopes	des enveloppes	dayz ahn-veh-**lope**
writing paper	du papier à lettres	dew pa-pee-**ay** a **let**-ruh
postcard	une carte postale	ewn cart pos-**tal**

ENGLISH	FRENCH	PRONUNCIATION
How much is it?	C'est combien?	say comb-bee-**ehn**
A little/a lot	Un peu/beaucoup	uhn peuh/bo-**koo**
More/less	Plus/moins	plu/mwehn
Enough/too (much)	Assez/trop	a-say/tro
I am ill/sick	Je suis malade	zhuh swee ma-**lahd**
Call a . . .	Appelez un . . .	a-play uhn
doctor	docteur	dohk-**tehr**
Help!	Au secours!	o suh-**koor**
Stop!	Arrêtez!	a-reh-**tay**
Fire!	Au feu!	o fuh
Caution!/Look out!	Attention!	a-tahn-see-**ohn**

DINING OUT

A bottle of . . .	une bouteille de . . .	ewn boo-**tay** duh
A cup of . . .	une tasse de . . .	ewn tass duh
A glass of . . .	un verre de . . .	uhn vair duh
Bill/check	l'addition	la-dee-see-**ohn**
Bread	du pain	dew panh
Breakfast	le petit-déjeuner	luh puh-**tee** day-zhuh-**nay**
Butter	du beurre	dew burr
Cheers!	A votre santé!	ah **vo**-truh sahn-**tay**
Cocktail/aperitif	un apéritif	uhn ah-pay-ree-**teef**
Dinner	le dîner	luh dee-**nay**
Dish of the day	le plat du jour	luh plah dew **zhoor**
Enjoy!	Bon appétit!	bohn a-pay-**tee**
Fixed-price menu	le menu	luh may-**new**
Fork	une fourchette	ewn four-**shet**
I am diabetic	Je suis diabétique	zhuh swee dee-ah-bay-**teek**
I am vegetarian	Je suis végétarien(ne)	zhuh swee vay-zhay-ta-ree-**en**

ENGLISH	FRENCH	PRONUNCIATION
I cannot eat . . .	Je ne peux pas manger de . . .	zhuh nuh puh pah mahn-**jay** deh
I'd like to order	Je voudrais commander	zhuh voo-**dray** ko-mahn-**day**
Is service/the tip included?	Est-ce que le service est compris?	ess kuh luh sair-**veess** ay comb-**pree**
It's good/bad	C'est bon/mauvais	say bohn/mo-**vay**
It's hot/cold	C'est chaud/froid	say sho/frwah
Knife	un couteau	uhn koo-**toe**
Lunch	le déjeuner	luh day-zhuh-**nay**
Menu	la carte	la cart
Napkin	une serviette	ewn sair-vee-**et**
Pepper	du poivre	dew **pwah**-vruh
Plate	une assiette	ewn a-see-**et**
Please give me . . .	Donnez-moi . . .	doe-nay-**mwah**
Salt	du sel	dew sell
Spoon	une cuillère	ewn kwee-**air**
Sugar	du sucre	dew **sook**-ruh
Waiter!/Waitress!	Monsieur!/Mademoiselle!	muh-**syuh**/mad-mwa-**zel**
Wine list	la carte des vins	la cart day vehn

MENU GUIDE

FRENCH	ENGLISH

GENERAL DINING

Entrée	Appetizer/Starter
Garniture au choix	Choice of vegetable side
Plat du jour	Dish of the day
Selon arrivage	When available
Supplément/En sus	Extra charge
Sur commande	Made to order

FRENCH	ENGLISH

PETIT DÉJEUNER (BREAKFAST)

Confiture	Jam
Miel	Honey
Oeuf à la coque	Boiled egg
Oeufs sur le plat	Fried eggs
Oeufs brouillés	Scrambled eggs
Tartine	Bread with butter

POISSONS/FRUITS DE MER (FISH/SEAFOOD)

Anchois	Anchovies
Bar	Bass
Brandade de morue	Creamed salt cod
Brochet	Pike
Cabillaud/Morue	Fresh cod
Calmar	Squid
Coquilles St-Jacques	Scallops
Crevettes	Shrimp
Daurade	Sea bream
Ecrevisses	Prawns/Crayfish
Harengs	Herring
Homard	Lobster
Huîtres	Oysters
Langoustine	Prawn/Lobster
Lotte	Monkfish
Moules	Mussels
Palourdes	Clams
Saumon	Salmon
Thon	Tuna
Truite	Trout

FRENCH	ENGLISH
VIANDE (MEAT)	
Agneau	Lamb
Boeuf	Beef
Boudin	Sausage
Boulettes de viande	Meatballs
Brochettes	Kebabs
Cassoulet	Casserole of white beans, meat
Cervelle	Brains
Chateaubriand	Double fillet steak
Choucroute garnie	Sausages with sauerkraut
Côtelettes	Chops
Côte/Côte de boeuf	Rib/T-bone steak
Cuisses de grenouilles	Frogs' legs
Entrecôte	Rib or rib eye steak
Épaule	Shoulder
Escalope	Cutlet
Foie	Liver
Gigot	Leg
Porc	Pork
Ris de veau	Veal sweetbreads
Rognons	Kidneys
Saucisses	Sausages
Selle	Saddle
Tournedos	Tenderloin of T-bone steak
Veau	Veal
METHODS OF PREPARATION	
A point	Medium
A l'étouffée	Stewed
Au four	Baked
Ballotine	Boned, stuffed, and rolled

FRENCH	ENGLISH
Bien cuit	Well-done
Bleu	Very rare
Frit	Fried
Grillé	Grilled
Rôti	Roast
Saignant	Rare

VOLAILLES/GIBIER (POULTRY/GAME)

Blanc de volaille	Chicken breast
Canard/Caneton	Duck/Duckling
Cerf/Chevreuil	Venison (red/roe)
Coq au vin	Chicken stewed in red wine
Dinde/Dindonneau	Turkey/Young turkey
Faisan	Pheasant
Lapin/Lièvre	Rabbit/Wild hare
Oie	Goose
Pintade/Pintadeau	Guinea fowl/Young guinea fowl
Poulet/Poussin	Chicken/Spring chicken

LÉGUMES (VEGETABLES)

Artichaut	Artichoke
Asperge	Asparagus
Aubergine	Eggplant
Carottes	Carrots
Champignons	Mushrooms
Chou-fleur	Cauliflower
Chou (rouge)	Cabbage (red)
Laitue	Lettuce
Oignons	Onions
Petits pois	Peas
Pomme de terre	Potato
Tomates	Tomatoes

FRENCH	ENGLISH

FRUITS/NOIX (FRUITS/NUTS)

Abricot	Apricot
Amandes	Almonds
Ananas	Pineapple
Cassis	Black currants
Cerises	Cherries
Citron/Citron vert	Lemon/Lime
Fraises	Strawberries
Framboises	Raspberries
Pamplemousse	Grapefruit
Pêche	Peach
Poire	Pear
Pomme	Apple
Prunes/Pruneaux	Plums/Prunes
Raisins/Raisins secs	Grapes/Raisins

DESSERTS

Coupe (glacée)	Sundae
Crème Chantilly	Whipped cream
Gâteau au chocolat	Chocolate cake
Glace	Ice cream
Tarte tatin	Caramelized apple tart
Tourte	Layer cake

DRINKS

A l'eau	With water
Avec des glaçons	On the rocks
Bière	Beer
Blonde/brune	Light/dark
Café noir/crème	Black coffee/with steamed milk
Chocolat chaud	Hot chocolate
Eau-de-vie	Brandy

FRENCH	ENGLISH
Eau minérale	Mineral water
Gazeuse/non gazeuse	Carbonated/still
Jus de . . .	. . . juice
Lait	Milk
Sec	Straight or dry
Thé	Tea
Au lait/au citron	With milk/lemon
Vin	Wine
Blanc	White
Doux	Sweet
Léger	Light
Brut	Very dry
Rouge	Red

TRAVEL SMART
PARIS

GETTING HERE AND AROUND

Addresses in Paris are fairly straight-forward: there's the number, the street name, and the zip code designating one of Paris's 20 *arrondissements* (districts); for instance, in Paris 75010, the last two digits "10" indicates that the address is in the 10e. The large 16e arrondissement has two numbers assigned to it: 75016 and 75116. *For the layout of Paris's arrondissements, see the What's Where map in the Experience chapter.*

The arrondissements are laid out in a spiral, beginning from the area around the Louvre (1er arrondissement), then moving clockwise through the Marais, the Latin Quarter, St-Germain, and then out from the city center to the outskirts to Ménilmontant/Père-Lachaise (20e arrondissement). Occasionally you may see an address with a number plus *bis*—for instance, 20 bis, rue Vavin. This indicates the next entrance or door down from 20 rue Vavin. Note that in France you enter a building on the ground floor, or *rez-de-chaussée* (RC or 0), and go up one floor to the first floor, or *premier étage*. General address terms used in this book are *av.* (avenue), *bd.* (boulevard), *carrefour* (crossway), *cours* (promenade), *passage* (passageway), *pl.* (place), *quai* (quay/wharf/pier), *rue* (street), and *sq.* (square).

▌ AIR TRAVEL

Flying time to Paris is 7 hours from New York, 9 hours from Chicago, and 11 hours from Los Angeles. Flying time from London to Paris is 1½ hours.

The French are notoriously stringent about security, particularly for international flights. Don't be surprised by the armed security officers patrolling the airports, and be prepared for very long check-in lines. Peak travel times in France are between mid-July and September, during the Christmas–New Year's holidays in late December and early January,

and during the February school break. Through these periods airports are especially crowded, so allow plenty of extra time. Never leave your baggage unattended, even for a moment. Unattended baggage is considered a security risk and may be destroyed.

Airline and Airport Links.com. Airline and Airport Links.com has links to many of the world's airlines and airports. ⊕ *www.airlineandairportlinks.com.*

Airline Security Issues Transportation Security Administration. The Transportation Security Administration has answers for almost any question that might come up. ⊕ *www.tsa.gov.*

AIRPORTS

The major airports are Charles de Gaulle (CDG, also known as Roissy), 26 km (16 miles) northeast of Paris, and Orly (ORY), 16 km (10 miles) south of Paris. Both are easily accessible from the city. Whether you take a car or bus to travel from Paris to the airport on your departure, always allot an extra hour because of the often horrendous traffic tie-ups in the airports themselves (especially in peak seasons and at peak times). Free light rail connections (Orlyval and CDGval) available between the major terminals are one option for avoiding some of the traffic mess, but still give yourself enough time to navigate through these busy airports. Check the Aéroports de Paris Live! function on the website (or smartphone application) for more up-to-date details and real-time news from the airports.

Airport Information Charles de Gaulle (*CDG*) ☎ *0033/1–70–36–39–50 outside of France* ⊕ *www.adp.fr.* **Charles de Gaulle/ Roissy and Orly** ☎ *3950 (press "0" for service in English) €0.34 per minute* ⊕ *www.adp.fr.*

GROUND TRANSPORTATION

By bus from CDG/Roissy: Roissybus, operated by the RATP (Paris Transit Authority), runs between Charles de Gaulle and the Opéra every 15 minutes from 6 am to 8:45 pm and then every 20 minutes until 11 pm; the cost is €10. The trip takes about 45 minutes in regular traffic, about 90 minutes in rush-hour traffic.

By shuttle from CDG/Roissy: The Air France shuttle service is a comfortable option to get to and from the city—you don't need to have flown the carrier to use it. Line 2 goes from the airport to Paris's Charles de Gaulle Étoile and Porte Maillot from 6 am to 11 pm. It leaves every 20 minutes (every half hour between 10 and 11 pm) and costs €17, which you can pay onboard. Line 4 goes to Montparnasse and the Gare de Lyon from 6 am to 10 pm. Buses run every 30 minutes and cost €16.50. Passengers arriving in Terminal 1 need to take Exit 34; Terminals 2A and 2C go to Exit C2; 2B and 2D take Exit B1; Terminals 2E and 2F, Exit 3. There's a 15% discount on any of these buses for parties of four or more.

A number of van companies, such as SuperShuttle Paris, serve both Charles de Gaulle and Orly airports. Prices are set so there are no surprises even if traffic is a snail-pace nightmare. To make a reservation, call or reserve online at least one week in advance and an air-conditioned van with a bilingual chauffeur will be waiting for you upon your arrival. Confirm the day before. These vans sometimes pick up more than one party, though, so you may have to share the shuttle with other passengers. Likewise, when taking people to the airport these shuttles usually pick up a couple of groups of passengers. This adds at least 20 minutes to the trip.

NAVIGATING PARIS

Paris is a walker's city, but public transportation is excellent when your feet get tired. The métro and bus systems are extensive and easy to use.

There are many landmarks in Paris to orient yourself by—churches, the Opéra, the Tour Eiffel, and so on. Choose one near your hotel, for example, and if you get lost, it'll be easy to get back on track.

As with any city that's not laid out in a numbered grid, it can be confusing to find what you're looking for—especially in a foreign language; don't hesitate to ask for help. Most people are happy to give assistance, especially if you try out some French (like *bonjour*).

By taxi from CDG/Roissy: Taxis are generally the least desirable mode of transportation into the city. If you're traveling at peak hours, journey times—and, by extension, prices—are unpredictable. At best, the ride takes 30 minutes, but it can be as long as an hour; fares can range from €50 to €70. Voyages & Business, a subsidiary of Taxis G7 (⇨ *see Train Travel, below*) offers a special shared taxi service between CDG and Paris that costs 40% less than a regular cab.

By train from CDG/Roissy: The least expensive way to get into Paris from CDG is the RER-B Line, the suburban express train, which runs from 5 am to 11 pm daily. There are two RER stations at CDG "RER B Aéroport Charles de Gaulle 1" for Terminals 1 (via CDGval) and 3 (via a covered walkway). "RER B Aéroport Charles de Gaulle 2" serves Terminal 2, accessible via walkways or by the free N1 shuttle. Trains to central Paris (Les Halles, Gare du Nord, St-Michel, Luxembourg) depart every 10–15 minutes. The fare (including métro connection) is €9.50, and journey time is usually about 35 minutes.

By bus from Orly: Air France buses run from Orly to Les Invalides, Charles de Gaulle Étoile, and Montparnasse every 20 minutes from 6 am to 11:40 pm. (You need not have flown on Air France to use this service.) The fare is €12, and journey time is between 45 and 60 minutes, depending on traffic. To find the bus, take Exit L if you've arrived in Orly South, or Exit D from Orly West. RATP's Orlybus is yet another option; buses leave every 15 minutes for the Denfert-Rochereau métro station in Montparnasse from Exit H in Orly South and Exit G in Orly West. The cost is €7.20. The cheapest bus is the RATP city bus 183, which shuttles you from Métro Porte de Choisy (Line 7) to Orly South for just €4, every 30 minutes from 5:30 am to midnight on weekdays (from 6 am on weekends). Travel time is approximately 50 minutes.

By taxi from Orly: You'll find taxi stands at Orly Sud (South) as you exit the baggage claim area at "M" and "L," and at Orly Ouest (West) by arrivals areas "H" and "I." A cab downtown will cost €40–€55 and take at least 25 minutes if traffic is light.

By train from Orly: The cheapest way to get into Paris by train is to take the shuttle bus from Exit F at Orly South or Exit G at Orly West to the station RER-C Pont de Rungis–Aéroport d'Orly into Paris. Trains to Paris leave every 15 minutes. The fare is €2.50 (Shuttle) plus €3.90 (RER), and journey time is about 35 minutes. Another slightly faster option is to take RATP's monorail service, Orlyval, which runs between the Antony RER-B station and Orly Airport daily every four to seven minutes from 6 am to 11 pm. Passengers arriving in the South Terminal should use Exit K; take Exit W if you've arrived in the West Terminal. The fare to downtown Paris is €11.30 and includes the RER transfer.

TRAVEL TO CENTRAL PARIS

From	CDG	Orly
Taxi	30 mins–60 mins; €50–€70	25 mins–45 mins; €40–€55
Bus	45 mins–90 mins; €10–€17	45 mins–60 mins; €4–€12
Airport Shuttle	1 hr–2 hrs; €16.50–€45	45 mins–90 mins; €25–€45
RER	35 mins–50 mins; €9.50	30 mins–35 mins; €6.40–€11.30

TRANSFERS BETWEEN AIRPORTS

To transfer between Paris's airports, there are several options. *See the "By Train" options above:* The RER-B travels from CDG to Orly with Paris in the middle, so to transfer, just stay on. Travel time is about 50–70 minutes and costs €19.65. The Air France Bus Line 3 also runs between the airports for €20 one-way, every 30 minutes, with between 50 and 75 minutes travel time. Taxis are available but expensive: from €60 to €80, depending on traffic.

Contacts Air France Bus ☎ 08–92–35–08–20 *(recorded information in English) €0.34 per min* ⊕ *www.cars-airfrance.com.* **Paris Airports Services** ☎ *01–55–98–10–80* ⊕ *www. parisairportservice.com.* **RATP (including Roissybus, Orlybus, Orlyval)** ☎ *3246 €0.34 per min* ⊕ *www.ratp.fr.* **SuperShuttle Paris** ☎ *08–11–70–78–12 €0.06 per min.* ⊕ *www. supershuttle.fr.*

FLIGHTS

As one of the premier destinations in the world, Paris is serviced by a great many international carriers and a surprisingly large number of U.S.-based airlines. Air France (which partners with Delta) is the French flag carrier and offers numerous direct flights (often several per day) between Paris's Charles de Gaulle Airport and New York City's JFK Airport; Newark, New Jersey; Washington's Dulles

Airport; and the cities of Boston, Philadelphia, Atlanta, Cincinnati, Miami, Chicago, Houston, Seattle, San Francisco, Los Angeles, Toronto, Montréal, and Mexico City. Most other North American cities are served through Air France's partnership with Delta via connecting flights. American-based carriers are usually less expensive, but offer, on the whole, fewer nonstop direct flights. United Airlines has nonstop flights to Paris from Chicago, New York, Washington, and San Francisco. American Airlines offers daily nonstop flights to Paris's Charles de Gaulle Airport from numerous cities, including New York City's JFK, Miami, Chicago, and Dallas/Fort Worth. In Canada, Air France and Air Canada are the leading choices for departures from Toronto and Montréal; in peak season departures are often daily. From London, Air France and British Airways offer up to 15 flights daily in peak season. In addition, direct routes link Manchester, Edinburgh, and Southampton with Paris. Ryanair, easyJet, CityJet, and Aer Lingus offer direct service from Paris to Dublin, Birmingham, London, Glasgow, Amsterdam, Zurich, Copenhagen, Madrid, Marrakech, Prague and Brussels, to name just a few destinations. Tickets are available online only and need to be booked well in advance to get the best prices—a one-way ticket from Paris to Dublin could cost a mere €45, for example. But with the low-cost airlines you must be mindful of auxiliary charges that could set you back €25 for a single piece of checked luggage.

Airline Contacts Air Canada ☎ 888/247–2262 in U.S. and Canada, 08-25-88-29-00 €0.15 per min ⊕ www.aircanada.com. **Air France** ☎ 800/237-2747 in U.S. and Canada, 3654 €0.34 per min ⊕ www.airfrance.com. **American Airlines** ☎ 800/433-7300 in U.S. and Canada, 08-26-460-950 €0.15 per min ⊕ www.aa.com. **Delta Airlines** ☎ 800/241-4141 in U.S. and Canada, 08-92-70-26-09 €0.34 per min ⊕ www.delta.com. **United Airlines** ☎ 800/864-8331 in U.S. and Canada, 01-71-23-03-35 ⊕ www.united.com.

Discount Airlines Aer Lingus ☎ 516/622–4222 in U.S., 800/474-7424 in Canada, 08-21-23-02-67 €0.12 per min ⊕ www.aerlingus.com. **CityJet** ☎ 800/237-2747 in U.S. and Canada, 3654 €0.34 per min ⊕ www.cityjet.com. **easyJet** ☎ 08-20-42-03-15 €0.12 per min ⊕ www.easyjet.com. **Ryanair** ☎ 08-92-78-02-10 €0.34 per min ⊕ www.ryanair.com.

Within Europe Air France ☎ 800/237-2747 in U.S. and Canada, 3654 €0.34 per minute ⊕ www.airfrance.com. **British Airways** ☎ 800/247-9297 in U.S. and Canada, 08-25-82-54-00 €0.15 per min ⊕ www.britishairways.com.

∎ BOAT TRAVEL

Ferries linking France and the United Kingdom cross the Channel in about 90 minutes; popular routes connect Boulogne and Folkestone, Le Havre, and Portsmouth, and—the most booked passage—Calais and Dover. DirectFerries.fr groups the websites for several operators to make reservations more streamlined. P&O European Ferries has 23 sailings a day between Dover and Calais; My Ferry Link also serves the route, with up to 16 sailings a day.

The driving distance from Calais to Paris is 290 km (180 miles). The fastest routes to Paris from each port are via N43, A26, and A1 from Calais and the Channel Tunnel; and via N1 from Boulogne.

Information DirectFerries.fr ☎ 08-92-23-08-58 €0.33 per min ⊕ www.directferries.fr. **My Ferry Link** ☎ 08-11-65-47-65 ⊕ www.myferrylink.com. **P&O European Ferries** ☎ 08-25-12-01-56 €0.15 per min ⊕ www.poferries.com.

∎ BUS TRAVEL

ARRIVING AND DEPARTING PARIS

The excellent national train service in France means that long-distance bus service in the country is practically nonexistent; regional buses are found where train service is spotty. Local bus information to the rare rural areas where trains do not have access can be obtained from the SNCF (⇨ *see Train Travel, below*).

The largest international operator is Eurolines France, whose main terminal is in the Parisian suburb of Bagnolet (a ½-hour métro ride from central Paris, at the end of métro Line 3). It runs to more than 1,500 cities in Europe.

You can take a bus (via ferry) to Paris from the United Kingdom; just be aware that what you save in money will almost certainly cost you in time—the bus trip takes about seven hours as opposed to three on the Eurostar train line (St-Pancras Station–Gare du Nord). In general, the price of a round-trip bus ticket is 50% less than that of a plane ticket and 25% less than that of a train ticket, so if you have the time and the energy, this is a good way to cut the cost of travel. Eurolines also offers a 15-day (€215–€355) or 30-day (€320–€465) pass if you're planning on doing the grand European tour. Ask about one of the Circle tours that leave from Paris (for example, via London, Amsterdam, then back to Paris again). Eurolines operates a service from London's Victoria Coach Station, via the Dover–Calais ferry, to Paris's Porte de Bagnolet. There's an 8 am departure that arrives in Paris at 4:30 pm, a 10 am departure that arrives at 8:05 pm, a noon departure that arrives at 8:45 pm, and a 1:30 pm departure that arrives at 10 pm, plus three overnight trips with departures at 9:30 pm, 10:30 pm, and 11:30 that pull into Paris between 7:45 am and 9 am. Fares are €60–€70 round-trip. Check the Eurolines website for special discounts or incentives, and avoid buying your ticket at the last minute, when prices are highest. Reservations for international bus trips are essential.

IN PARIS

With dedicated bus lanes now in place throughout the city—allowing buses and taxis to whiz past other traffic mired in tedious jams—taking the bus is an appealing option. Although nothing can beat the métro for speed, buses offer great city views, and the new ones are equipped with air-conditioning—a real perk on those sweltering August days.

Paris buses are green and white; the route number and destination are marked in front, major stopping places along the sides. Glass-covered bus shelters contain timetables and route maps; note that buses must be hailed at these larger bus shelters, as they service multiple lines and routes. Smaller stops are designated simply by a pole bearing bus numbers.

Today 59 bus routes run throughout Paris, reaching virtually every nook and cranny of the city. On weekdays and Saturday, buses run every 5 minutes; but you'll have to wait 15 to 20 minutes on Sunday and holidays. One ticket will take you anywhere within the city and is valid for one transfer within 90 minutes.

Most routes operate from 7 am to 8:30 pm; some continue until midnight. After midnight you must take either the métro or one of the Noctilien lines (indicated by a separate signal at bus stops). Using the same tickets as the métro and regular buses, Noctilien buses operate every 10–60 minutes (12:30 am–5:30 am) between Châtelet, major train stations, and various nearby suburbs; you can hail them at any point on their route.

A map of the bus system is on the flip side of every métro map, in all métro stations, and at all bus stops. Maps are also found in each bus; a free map is available at RER stations and tourist offices. A recorded message and onboard electronic display announce the name of the next stop. To get off, press one of the red buttons mounted on the silver poles that run the length of the bus, and the *arrêt demandé* (stop requested) light directly behind the driver will light up. Use the rear door to exit.

The Balabus—an orange-and-white public bus that runs on Sunday and holidays from 1:30 pm to 8:30 pm, April through September—gives an interesting

50-minute tour around the major sights. You can use your Paris-Visite or Mobilis pass (⇨ *Métro Travel*), or one to three bus tickets, depending on how far you ride. The route runs from La Défense to the Gare de Lyon.

The city also has expanded its tram system with the opening of three new lines: T-5 (St-Denis to Garges-Sarcelles); T-6 (Châtillon to Viroflay); and T-7 (Villejuif to Athis-Mons). T-8 (St-Denis to Épinay-Villetanuese) is due to launch by the end of 2014. Designed more to serve locals getting into and around the city, these lines operate in the suburbs, with T-3 trams running along Paris's entire southern edge. One ticket is good for the whole line.

Trams and buses take the same tickets as the métro. When buying tickets, your best bet is a *carnet* of 10 tickets, available for €13.70 at any métro station, or a single ticket, which can be bought onboard (exact change appreciated) for €1.70. If you have individual tickets or Paris-Visite passes, you should be prepared to validate your ticket in the gray machines at the entrance of the vehicle. Tickets can be bought onboard, in the métro, or in most bar–tabac stores displaying the lime green métro symbol above its street sign.

Bus Information Eurolines ☎ 08–92–89–90–91 €0.34 per min, 0033/141–862–421 from abroad ⊕ www.eurolines.fr, www.eurolines-pass.eu. **Noctilien** ⊕ vianavigo.com. **RATP** ☎ 3246 €0.34 per min ⊕ www.ratp.com.

■ CAR TRAVEL

We can't say it too many times: unless you have a special, compelling reason, do yourself a favor and **avoid driving in Paris.** But if you've decided to do it anyway, there are some things to know. France's roads are classified into five types; they are numbered and have letter prefixes: *A* (*autoroute*, expressways), *N* (*route nationale*), *D* (*route départmentale*), and the smaller *C* or *V*. There are excellent links between Paris and most French cities.

When trying to get around Ile-de-France, it's often difficult to avoid Paris—just try to steer clear of rush hours (7–9:30 and 4:30–7:30). A *péage* (toll) must be paid on most expressways outside Ile-de-France: the rate varies but can be steep. Certain booths allow you to pay with a credit card.

The major ring road encircling Paris is called the *périphérique,* with the *périphérique intérieur* going counterclockwise around the city, and the *périphérique extérieur,* or the outside ring, going clockwise; maximum speed is 70 kph (43 mph). Up to five lanes wide, the périphérique is a major highway from which 30 *portes* (gates) connect Paris to the major highways of France. The names of these highways function on the same principle as the métro, with the final destination as the determining point in the direction you must take.

Heading north, look for Porte de la Chapelle (direction Lille and Charles de Gaulle Airport); east, for Porte de Bagnolet (direction Metz and Nancy); south, for Porte d'Orléans (direction Lyon and Bordeaux); and west, for Porte d'Auteuil (direction Rouen and Chartres) or Porte de St-Cloud.

GASOLINE

There are gas stations throughout the city, but they can be difficult to spot; you will often find them in the underground tunnels that cross the city and in larger parking garages. Gas is expensive and prices vary enormously, ranging from about €1.60 to €2 per liter. If you're on your way out of Paris, save money by waiting until you've left the city to fill up. All gas stations accept credit cards.

PARKING

Finding parking in Paris is tough. Both meters and parking-ticket machines use parking cards (*cartes de stationnements–* "Paris Carte"), which you can purchase at any café posting the red tabac sign; they're sold in two denominations: €10 and €30. Parking in the capital costs €1 to

€3 per hour, depending on the arrondissement, and is payable Monday to Saturday from 9 am to 7 pm, with a 2-hour limit. Insert your card into the nearest meter (they do not accept coins), choose the approximate amount of time you expect to stay, and receive a green receipt. Place it on the dashboard on the passenger side, making sure the receipt is clearly visible to the meter patrol. Parking tickets are expensive, and there's no shortage of blue-uniformed parking police. Parking lots, indicated by a blue sign with a white "P", are usually underground and are generally expensive (charging around €2.50 per hour or €20 per day; outside of the city center you'll pay €10–€15 per day). One bright spot: you can park for free on Sunday, national holidays, and in certain residential areas in August. Parking meters with yellow circles indicate the free parking zone during August. Before walking away, double check that the car doors are locked and that any valuables are out of sight, either in the glove compartment or the trunk.

ROAD CONDITIONS

Chaotic traffic is a way of life in Paris. Some streets in the city center can seem impossibly narrow; street signs are often hard to spot; jaded city drivers often make erratic, last-minute maneuvers without signaling; and motorcycles often weave around traffic. Priority is given to drivers coming from the right, so watch for drivers barreling out of small streets on your right. When the speed limit is 30 kph (18.5 mph) cyclists can travel against traffic on one-way streets, so keep an eye open for them as well. Traffic lights are placed to the left and right of crosswalks, not above, so they may be blocked from view by vehicles ahead of you.

There are a few major roundabouts at the most congested intersections, notably at *L'Étoile* (around the Arc de Triomphe), Place de la Bastille, and Place de la Concorde. Watch oncoming cars carefully and stick to the outer lane to make your exit. The *périphériques* (ring roads) are generally easier to use, and the quays that parallel the Seine can be a downright pleasure to drive when there's no traffic. Electronic signs on the périphériques and highways post traffic conditions: *fluide* (clear) or *bouchon* (jammed).

Some important traffic terms and signs to note: *sortie* (exit), *sens unique* (one way), *stationnement interdite* (no parking), *impasse* (dead end). Blue rectangular signs indicate a highway; triangles carry illustrations of a particular traffic hazard; speed limits are indicated in a circle, with the maximum speed circled in red.

ROADSIDE EMERGENCIES

If your car breaks down on an expressway, pull your car as far off the road as quickly as you can, set your emergency indicators, and, if possible, take the emergency triangle from the car's trunk and put it at least 30 yards behind your car to warn oncoming traffic; then go to a roadside emergency telephone. These phones put you in direct contact with the police, automatically indicating your exact location, and are available every 3 km (2 miles). If you have a breakdown anywhere else, find the nearest garage or contact the police. There are also 24-hour assistance hotlines valid throughout France (available through rental agencies and supplied to you when you rent the car), but do not hesitate to call the police in case of any roadside emergency, for they are quick and reliable and the phone call is free.

Emergency Services Police ☎ *112, 17.*

RULES OF THE ROAD

You must always carry vehicle registration documents and your personal identification. The French police are entitled to stop you at will to verify your ID and your car—such spot checks are frequent, especially at peak holiday times. In France you drive on the right and give priority to drivers coming from the right (this rule is called *priorité à droite*).

The driver and all passengers in vehicles must wear seat belts, and children under 12 may not travel in the front seat.

Children under 10 need to be in a car seat or specific child-restraining device, always in the backseat. Speed limits are designated by the type of road you're driving on: 130 kph (80 mph) or 110 kph (70 mph) on expressways (*autoroutes*), 90 kph (55 mph) on divided roads (*routes nationales*), 50 kph (30 mph) on departmental roads (*routes*), and 35 kph (22 mph) in some cities and towns (*villes et villages*). These limits are reduced by 10 kph (6 mph) in rainy, snowy, and foggy conditions. Drivers are expected to know these limits, so signs are generally posted only when there are exceptions to these rules. Right-hand turns are not allowed on a red light.

The use of handheld cellular phones while driving is forbidden (even if you are only holding it); the penalty is a €135 fine. Alcohol laws have become quite tough—there is a 0.05% blood alcohol limit (a lower limit than in the United States).

▌ MÉTRO TRAVEL

Taking the métro is the most efficient way to get around Paris. Métro stations are recognizable either by a large yellow *M* within a circle or by the distinctive curly green Art Nouveau railings and archway bearing the full title (Métropolitain). *See the Métro map at the back of this book.*

Sixteen métro and five RER (Réseau Express Régional, or the Regional Express Network) lines crisscross Paris and the suburbs, and you are seldom more than 500 yards from the nearest station. The métro network connects at several points in Paris with the RER, the commuter trains that go from the city center to the suburbs. RER trains crossing Paris on their way from suburb to suburb can be great time-savers, because they make only a few stops in the city (you can use the same tickets for the métro and the RER within Paris).

It's essential to know the name of the last station on the line you take, as this name appears on all signs. A connection

(you can make as many as you like on one ticket) is called a *correspondance*. At junction stations, illuminated orange signs bearing the name of the line terminus appear over the correct corridors for each correspondance. Illuminated blue signs marked *sortie* indicate the station exit. Note that tickets are valid only inside the gates, or *limites*.

Access to métro and RER platforms is through an automatic ticket barrier. Slide your ticket in and pick it up as it pops out. **Keep your ticket during your journey**; you'll need it to leave the RER system and in case you run into any green-clad ticket inspectors, who will impose a hefty fine if you can't produce your ticket (they even accept credit cards!).

TICKET/PASS FOR ZONES 1 & 2	PRICE
Single Fare	€1.70 (purchased on bus, not valid for transfers)
Daily Mobilis Pass	€6.80
Paris-Visite One-Day Pass	€10.85
10-Ticket Carnet	€13.70
Paris-Visite Two-Day Pass	€17.65
Paris-Visite Three-Day Pass	€24.10
Paris-Visite Five-Day Pass	€34.70
Pass Navigo Découverte Weekly	€20.40
Pass Navigo Découverte Monthly	€67.10

Métro service starts at 5:30 am and continues until 1 am Sunday through Thursday, and until 2 am on Friday and Saturday, when the last train on each line reaches its terminus. Some lines and stations in Paris are a bit risky at night, in particular lines 2 and 13, and the mazelike stations at Les Halles and République. But in general, the métro is relatively safe throughout, providing you don't travel alone late at night or walk around with your wallet hanging out of your back pocket.

All métro tickets and passes are valid not only for the métro but also for all RER, tram, and bus travel within Paris. Métro tickets cost €1.70 each; a *carnet* (10 tickets for €13.70) is a better value. The *Carte Navigo* system is the monthly and weekly subscription plan, with reusable cards available at most ticket windows. Receive a Pass Navigo Découverte for €5 plus the subscription for weekly (€20.40, valid Monday–Sunday) or monthly (€67.10, beginning the first of the month) service. Be sure to immediately attach a passport-size photo and sign your name. This magnetic swipe card allows you to zoom through the turnstiles and can be kept for years; just recharge it at any purple kiosk in the métro stations. Visitors can also purchase the one-day (Mobilis) and two- to five-day (Paris-Visite) tickets for unlimited travel on the entire RATP (Paris transit authority) network: métro, RER, bus, tram, funicular (Montmartre), and Noctilien (the night bus, operated by Vianavigo). The Mobilis and Paris-Visite passes are valid starting any day of the week. Paris-Visite also gives you discounts on a few museums and attractions, too. Mobilis tickets cost €6.60. Paris-Visite is €10.85 (one day), €17.65 (two days), €24.10 (three days), and €34.70 (five days) for Paris only.

Métro Information Any RATP window in the métro sells tickets and provides maps. **RATP** ☎ *3246 €0.34 per min* ⊕ *www.ratp.fr.*

▌TAXI TRAVEL

Taxi rates are based on location and time. Daytime rates, denoted A (7 am–7 pm), within Paris are €0.96 per kilometer (½ mile), and nighttime rates, B, are €1.21 per kilometer. Suburban zones and airports, C, are €1.50 per kilometer. There's a basic hire charge of €2.50 for all rides, a €1 supplement per piece of luggage, and a €0.70 supplement if you're picked up at an SNCF (the French rail system) station.

Waiting time is charged at around €30 per hour. The easiest way to get a taxi is to ask your hotel or a restaurant to call one for you, or go to the nearest taxi stand (you can find one every couple of blocks)—they're marked by a square, dark blue sign with a white T in the middle. ▌**TIP→ People waiting for cabs often form a line, but will jump at any available taxi; be firm and don't let people cut in front of you.** A taxi is available when the entire sign is lighted green and taken when it's lighted red. They'll accept a fourth passenger for an average supplement of €3. It's customary to tip the driver about 10% (⇨ *Tipping in Essentials*).

Taxi Companies Central Taxi Parisien ☎ *08-25-56-03-20 €0.15 per min* ⊕ *www.central-taxi-parisien.com.* **Taxis Bleus** ☎ *08-91-70-10-10 €0.23 per min, 3609 €0.15 per min* ⊕ *www.taxis-bleus.com.* **Taxis G7** ☎ *01-41-27-66-99 for service in English, 3607 €0.15 per min* ⊕ *www.taxisg7.fr.*

▌TRAIN TRAVEL

The SNCF, France's rail system, is fast, punctual, comfortable, and comprehensive. There are various options: local trains, overnight trains with sleeping accommodations, and the high-speed TGV (or Trains à Grande Vitesse), which average 255 kph (160 mph) on the Lyon/southeast line and 320 kph (200 mph) on the Lille and Bordeaux/southwest lines.

The TGVs, the fastest way to get around the country, operate between Paris and Lille/Calais, Paris and Lyon/Switzerland/Provence, Paris and Angers/Nantes, Paris and Tours/Poitiers/Bordeaux, Paris and Brussels, and Paris and Amsterdam. As with other mainline trains, a small supplement may be assessed at peak hours.

Paris has six international rail stations: Gare du Nord (northern France, northern Europe, and England via Calais or Boulogne); Gare St-Lazare (Normandy, England via Dieppe); Gare de l'Est (Strasbourg, Luxembourg, Basel, and central Europe); Gare de Lyon (Lyon,

Marseille, Provence, Geneva, Italy); Gare d'Austerlitz (Loire Valley, southwest France, Spain); and Gare Montparnasse (Brittany, Aquitaine, TGV-Atlantique service to the west and south of France, Spain). Smoking is prohibited on all trains in France.

The country has two classes of train service: *première* (first class) or *deuxième* (second). First-class seats have 50% more legroom and nicer upholstery than those in second class, and the first-class cars tend to be quieter. First-class seats on the TGV have computer connections. First-class fares cost nearly twice as much as those for second-class seats.

Fares are cheaper if you avoid traveling at peak times (around holidays and weekends), purchase tickets at least 15 days in advance (look for the *billet Prem's*), or find your destination among the last-minute offers online every Tuesday.

You can call for train information or reserve tickets in any Paris station, irrespective of destination, and you can access the multilingual computerized schedule information network at any Paris station. You can also make reservations and buy your ticket while at the computer. Go to the Grandes Lignes counter for travel within France and to the Billets Internationaux desk if you're heading out of the country. Note that calling the SNCF's 08 number costs €0.34 per minute; to save this cost, go to the nearest station and make the reservations in person or visit the SNCF website.

If you plan to travel outside Paris by train, consider purchasing a France Rail Pass, which allows three days of unlimited train travel in a one-month period. If you travel solo, first class will run you $308 and second class is $250; you can add up to six days on this pass for $43 a day for first class, $34 a day for second class. For two people traveling together on a Saver Pass, the first-class cost is $370 per person, and in second class it's $219; additional days (up to six) cost $22 each

for first class, $31 each for second class. Other options include the France Rail 'n Drive Pass (combining rail and rental car).

France is one of 24 countries in which you can use EurailPasses, which provide unlimited first-class rail travel in all the participating countries for the duration of the pass. If you plan to rack up the miles, get a standard pass. These are available for 15 days ($823), 21 days ($1,061), one month ($1,305), two months ($1,841), and three months ($2,272). Another option is the Regional Pass, which covers rail travel in and between pairs of bordering countries over a two-month period. Unlike most Eurail passes, Regional Passes are available for first- or second-class travel. Costs begin at $439 (first class) and $374 (second class) for four days of travel; up to six extra days can be purchased.

In addition to standard EurailPasses, there are the Eurail Youthpass (for those under age 26, with second-class travel), the Eurail Saver Pass (which gives a discount for two or more people traveling together), the Eurail Flexipass (which allows a certain number of travel days within a set period), and the Euraildrive Pass (train and rental car). ■TIP➔ Remember that you must purchase your Eurail passes at home before leaving for France. You can purchase Eurail passes through the Eurail website as well as through travel agents.

Another option is to buy one of the discount rail passes available for sale only in France from SNCF. You can, for instance, save up to 50% by purchasing a Weekend Railcard.

Reduced fares are available if you're a senior citizen (over 60), for children under 12 and up to four accompanying adults, and if you're under 26.

If you purchase an individual ticket from SNCF in France and you're under 26, you automatically get a 25% reduction (a valid ID such as an ISIC card or your passport is necessary). If you're going to be using the train quite a bit during your stay in France and if you're under 27, consider buying the Carte 12–27 (€50), which offers unlimited 50% reductions for one year (provided that there's space available at that price; otherwise, you'll just get the standard 25% discount).

If you don't benefit from any of these reductions and you plan on traveling at least 200 km (132 miles) round-trip and don't mind staying over a Saturday night, look into the Découverte Séjour. This ticket gives you a 25% reduction.

■TIP→ A rail pass does not guarantee you a seat on the train you wish to ride. You need to book seats ahead even if you have a pass.

Seat reservations (available at a minimal fee) are required on TGVs and are a good idea on trains that may be crowded—particularly in summer and during holidays on popular routes. You also need a reservation for sleeping accommodations.

Train Information **Rail Europe** ☎ 800/622–8600 in U.S. and Canada, 847/916–1028 outside U.S. and Canada ⊕ www.raileurope. com. **SNCF** ☎ 3635 €0.34 per min ⊕ www. voyages-sncf.com. **TGV** ☎ 3635 €0.34 per min ⊕ www.tgv.com.

THE CHANNEL TUNNEL
Short of flying, taking the Channel Tunnel is the fastest way to cross the English Channel: 35 minutes from Folkestone to Calais, 60 minutes from motorway to motorway, or 2 hours and 15 minutes from London's St. Pancras Station to Paris's Gare du Nord, with stops in Lille, Calais, Ashford (U.K.), and Ebbsfleet (U.K.). The Belgian border is just a short drive northeast of Calais. High-speed Eurostar trains use the same tunnels to connect London's St. Pancras Station directly with Midi Station in Brussels in around two hours.

There's a vast range of prices for Eurostar—round-trip tickets range from €300 for first class (with access to the Philippe Starck–designed Première Class lounge and a three-course Raymond Blanc

meal) to €100 for second class, depending on when you travel. It's a good idea to make a reservation if you're traveling with your car on a Chunnel train; cars without reservations, if they can get on at all, are charged 20% extra.

Channel Tunnel Information **Eurostar** ☎ 08-92-35-35-39 €0.34 per min ⊕ www. eurostar.co.uk. **Eurotunnel** ☎ 08-10-63-03-04 ⊕ www.eurotunnel.com. **Rail Europe** ☎ 800/622-8600 in U.S. and Canada ⊕ www. raileurope.com.

▊ VÉLIB' BICYCLE TRAVEL

Cycling is a wonderful way to get a different view of Paris while working off all those extra calories you've consumed—and Vélib', a self-service bike-rental program launched by the city in 2007, makes it easy. More than 20,000 bikes are available 24/7 at some 1,800 docking stations citywide. To take advantage of the service, you must first buy a pass (one-day and seven-day versions can be purchased online for €1.70 and €8, respectively). Then you simply release a bike from any station, pedal away, and return it to any station when you're done. Individual rides lasting less than 30 minutes are free; for longer ones, minimal user fees apply. *See the "Bicycling in Paris" Close-Up box in Chapter 1 for details.*

Vélib' ☎ 01-30-79-79-30 ⊕ www.velib. paris.fr.

ESSENTIALS

▮ COMMUNICATIONS

INTERNET AND WI-FI

Getting online in Paris is rarely a problem because free and pay-as-you-go (via credit card) Wi-Fi service is available in most of the city's cafés, public spaces, and hotels through major service providers like Orange. Note that you may pick up a signal for "Free Wi-Fi," but this is the name of a French Internet provider and its network is open only to paying clients. Paris has made a big push in going wireless in recent years, so Wi-Fi (called WIFI) is now available in more than 260 public parks, squares and civic centers (like the Centre Pompidou) as well as many libraries. Access is free and unlimited for anyone, though network speed may not be as fast as you are used to back home. Cafés will usually have a WIFI sticker on their window if there is wireless available, but always verify before ordering a drink; McDonald's also has free Wi-Fi spaces (sometimes disabled during peak dining hours), as do the 50-odd Starbucks outlets. Many hotels have business services with Internet access or high-speed wireless access; and these days most accommodations offer in-room Wi-Fi as well, sometimes at an extra cost. A helpful website for finding Wi-Fi hotspots is ⊕ *www. journaldunet.com/wifi.* ▮TIP➜ You will need an adapter for your computer for the European-style plugs. If you're traveling with a laptop, carry a spare battery and adapter. Never plug your computer into any socket before asking about surge protection.

PHONES

The good news is that you can now make a direct-dial telephone call from virtually any point on earth. The bad news? You can't always do so cheaply. Calling from a hotel is almost always the most expensive option because hotels usually add huge surcharges to all calls, particularly international ones. Calling cards can keep costs low, but only if you buy them locally. And then there are mobile phones *(➪ below)*, which are sometimes more prevalent than landlines; as expensive as mobile phone calls can be, they are still usually a much cheaper option than calling from your hotel.

The country code for France is 33. The first two digits of French numbers are a prefix determined by zone: Paris and Ile-de-France, 01; the northwest, 02; the northeast, 03; the southeast, 04; and the southwest, 05. Pay close attention to numbers beginning with 08: some are toll-free—but not all (when you dial one with a fee attached, a recorded message will tell you how much it will cost to proceed with the call, usually around €0.34 per minute). Numbers beginning with 09, connected to DSL and Internet lines, are generally free when calling in France. Numbers that begin with 06 and 07 are reserved for cell phones.

Note that when dialing France from abroad, you should drop the initial 0 from the telephone number (all numbers listed in this book include the initial 0, which is used for calling *from within* France). To call a number in Paris from the United States, dial 00–33 plus the phone number, but minus the initial 0 listed for the specific number in Paris. In other words, the local number for the Louvre is 01–40–20–51–51. To call this number from New York City, dial 00–33–1–40–20–51–51. To call this number from within Paris, dial 01–40–20–51–51.

CALLING CARDS

Phone booths are disappearing one by one, almost daily, but the city is still required to maintain two for arrondissements with more than 1,000 people. So there are some in service if you're in a pinch, though most serve as makeshift homeless shelters and are rarely used by locals or tourists. French pay phones are operated by *télécartes* (phone cards), which you can buy from post offices, tabacs, and magazine kiosks. The ones you insert into pay phones have a "puce" microchip—a small copper square—that you can see on the card. There are several options; to be safe, request the *télécarte international,* which, despite its name, allows you to make either local or international calls for up to one year from purchase date and offers greatly reduced rates. Instructions are in English, and the cost is €9 for 60 units and €18 for 120 units. You may also request the simple *télécarte,* which allows you to make calls in France (the cost is €8 for 50 units, €15 for 120 units). You can use your credit card in much the same way as a télécarte, but there's a minimum €20 charge. You have 30 days after the first call on your credit card to use the €20 credit.

There are also international calling cards that work on any phone (including your hotel phone) because you dial a free number and punch in a code indicated on the back of the card; these do not have the puce microchip. Don't hesitate to invest in one if you plan on making calls from your hotel, as hotels often levy service charges and also have the most expensive rates.

CALLING OUTSIDE FRANCE

For prepaid cell phones bought in France, calls cost around €0.70 per minute to the United States and Canada, and nearly double that to the rest of the world, depending on the provider. Incoming calls, however, are usually at no cost. Foreign cell phones used in France to call Canada or the United States will generally be more costly depending on the provider, though texting international numbers on either foreign or French mobiles is generally cheaper. If you're planning on calling home from your cell once in France, it's best to check with your carrier to know your options. Most telecom operators in France offer an all-in-one service, with Internet, free local and international calls, and French TV, for an amazing monthly rate of about €35/month; hence, many landlines feature free international calling

to most countries. But if you're staying in a rental apartment with a phone, ask first before you start calling abroad.

To make a direct international call out of France, dial 00 and wait for the tone; then dial the country code (1 for the United States and Canada, 44 for the United Kingdom, 61 for Australia, and 64 for New Zealand) and the area code (minus any initial 0) and number.

To call with the help of an operator, dial the toll-free number 08–00–99–00 plus the last two digits of the country code. Dial 08–00–99–00–11 for the United States and Canada, 08–00–99–00–44 for England, and 08–00–99–00–61 for Australia.

Access Codes AT&T Direct ☎ *08–00–99–00– 11, 800/222–0300 in U.S. and Canada* ⊕ *www. att.com/esupport/traveler.jsp.* **MCI World- Phone** ☎ *08–00–99–00–19, 800/444–4444 in U.S. and Canada* ⊕ *consumer.mci.com/ international.* **Sprint International Access** ☎ *08–00–99–00–87, 888/211–4727 in U.S. and Canada.*

CALLING WITHIN FRANCE

For telephone information in France, you need to call one of the dozen or so six-digit *renseignement* numbers that begin with 118. (For Les Pages Jaunes—the French Yellow Pages—you dial 118–008.) The average price for one of these calls is about €1.50 per minute.

Since all local numbers in Paris and the Ile-de-France begin with a 01, you must dial the full 10-digit number, including the initial 0.

MOBILE PHONES

If you have a multiband phone (some countries use different frequencies than the United States) and your service provider uses the world-standard GSM network (as do T-Mobile, AT&T, and Verizon), you can probably use your phone abroad. Roaming fees can be steep, however: 99¢ a minute is considered reasonable. And overseas you normally pay the toll charges for incoming calls. It's almost always cheaper to send a text

LOCAL DO'S AND TABOOS

CUSTOMS OF THE COUNTRY

The French like to look at people (that's half the point of cafés and fashion), so you might as well get used to it—it's as natural here as breathing. They'll look at your shoes or your watch, check out what you're wearing or reading. What they will not do is maintain steady eye contact or smile. If a stranger of the opposite sex smiles at you, it's best to do as the French do and return only a blank look before turning away. If you smile back, you might find yourself in a Pepé Le Pew–type situation.

Visitors' exuberance—and accompanying loud voices—may cause discreet Parisians to raise their eyebrows or give a deep chesty sigh. They're not being rude, but they're telling you that they think you are. Be aware of your surroundings and lower your voice accordingly, especially in churches, museums, restaurants, theaters, cinemas, and the métro.

When entering and leaving a shop, greet and say good-bye to the staff. A simple *bonjour, monsieur/madame,* and *au revoir, merci* are considered a virtual necessity for politeness. Other basic pleasantries in French include *bonne journée* (have a nice day); *bonne soirée* (have a nice evening); *enchanté* (nice to meet you); *s'il vous plaît* (please); and *je vous en prie* (you're welcome). When asking for directions or other help, be sure to preface your request with a polite phrase such as *excusez-moi, madame/monsieur* (excuse me, ma'am/sir).

GREETINGS

When meeting someone for the first time, whether in a social or a professional setting, it's appropriate to shake hands. Other than that, the French like to kiss. For the Parisians, it's two *bisous,* which are more like air kisses with your cheeks touching lightly—don't actually smack your lips onto the person's face!

OUT ON THE TOWN

When visiting a French home, don't expect to be invited into the kitchen or taken on a house tour. The French have a very definite sense of personal space, and you'll be escorted to what are considered the guest areas. If you're invited to dinner, be sure to bring a gift, such as wine, flowers, or chocolates.

Table manners are often considered a litmus test of your character or upbringing. When dining out, note that the French fill wineglasses only half full—it's considered bad manners to fill it to the brim. They never serve themselves before serving the rest of the table. During a meal, keep both hands above the table, and keep your elbows off the table. Bread is broken, never cut, and is placed next to the plate, never on the plate. When slicing a cheese, don't cut off the point (or "nose"). Coffee or tea is ordered after dessert, not with dessert. (In fact, coffee and tea usually aren't ordered with any courses during meals, except breakfast.) Eating on the street is generally frowned on—though with the onslaught of Starbucks you can sometimes see people drinking coffee on the go.

LANGUAGE

One of the best ways to avoid being an Ugly American is to learn a bit of the local language. Parisians may appear prickly at first to English-speaking visitors, but it usually helps if you make an effort to speak some French. A simple, friendly *bonjour* will do, as will asking if the person you're greeting speaks English (*parlez-vous anglais?*). Be patient, and speak English slowly—but not loudly. *See the French Vocabulary and Menu Guide at the back of the book.* Need audio assistance? Click ⊕ *www.fodors.com/language/french* to hear more than 150 essential phrases.

message than to make a call, since text messages have a very low set fee (often less than 5¢).

If you just want to make local calls, consider buying a new SIM card (note that your provider may have to unlock your phone for you to use it) and a prepaid service plan in the destination. You'll then have a local number and can make local calls at local rates. If your trip is extensive, you could also simply buy a new cell phone in your destination, as the initial cost will be offset over time.

■TIP➜ If you travel internationally frequently, save one of your old mobile phones or buy a cheap one online; ask your cell-phone company to unlock it for you, and take it with you as a travel phone, buying a new SIM card with pay-as-you-go service in each destination.

Cell phones are called *portables,* and most Parisians have one. British standard cell phones work in Paris, but for North Americans only triband phones work. If you'd like to rent or buy a cell phone for your trip, reserve one at least four days prior to departure, as most companies will ship it to you before you travel. Cellular Abroad rents cell phones packaged with prepaid SIM cards that give you a French cell-phone number and calling rates. Mobal sells GSM phones (priced from $29) that will operate in 190 countries. Planetfone rents GSM phones, which can be used in more than 150 countries, but the per-minute rates are expensive. You can also buy a disposable "BIC" prepaid phone (available from tabacs, magazine kiosks, and some supermarkets) or a MobiKit pay-as-you-go phone from boutiques operated by major service providers (like Orange) if you want the best rates. Calls to the U.S. made with Le French Mobile—a service catering to English-speaking visitors in France—cost as little as €0.25 per minute but incoming calls are more expensive; it offers a range of plans without the obligation of long-term contracts.

Contacts Cellular Abroad ☎ 00800/36-23-33-33 in France, 800/287-5072 in U.S. and Canada ⊕ www.cellularabroad.com. **Le French Mobile** ⊕ www.lefrenchmobile.com. **Mobal** ☎ 888/888-9162 in U.S. and Canada ⊕ www.mobal.com. **Orange** ☎ 09-69-36-39-00 English helpline in France ⊕ www.orange.fr. **Planet Fone** ☎ 888/988-4777 in U.S. ⊕ www.planetfone.com.

▮ CUSTOMS AND DUTIES

You're always allowed to bring goods of a certain value back home without having to pay any duty or import tax. But there's a limit on the amount of tobacco and liquor you can return with duty-free, and some countries have separate limits for perfumes; for exact quotas, check with your customs department. The values of so-called duty-free goods are included in these amounts. When you shop abroad, save all your receipts, as customs inspectors may ask to see them as well as the items you purchased. If the total value of your goods is more than the duty-free limit, you'll have to pay a tax (most often a flat percentage) on the value of everything beyond that limit.

If you're coming from outside the European Union (EU), you may import the following duty-free: (1) 200 cigarettes or 100 cigars or 250 grams of tobacco; (2) 2 liters of wine and, in addition, (a) 1 liter of alcohol over 22% volume (most spirits) or (b) 2 liters of alcohol under 22% volume (fortified or sparkling wine) or (c) 4 more liters of table wine; (3) 50 milliliters of perfume and 250 milliliters of eau de toilette; (4) 200 grams of coffee, 100 grams of tea; and (5) other goods to the value of about €182 (€91 for ages 14 and under).

If you're arriving from an EU country, you may be required to declare all goods and prove that anything over the standard limit is for personal consumption. But there is no limit or customs tariff imposed on goods carried within the EU except on tobacco (800 cigarettes, 200 cigars, 1 kilogram of tobacco) and alcohol

(10 liters of spirits, 90 liters of wine, with a maximum of 60 liters of sparkling wine, 110 liters of beer).

PETS

Any pet coming to France must have recent rabies shots (no less than 21 days before departure), all standard vaccinations, and either a microchip or a tattoo applied before 2011. Be sure to have all paperwork on hand at the airport—including the bilingual "Certificat Vétérinaire vers l'UE" (EU veterinary certificate), as customs officials will inspect the animal in question. The form can be downloaded from the Animal and Plant Health Inspection Service website (⊕ *www.aphis.usda. gov*).

Information in Paris Direction des Douanes ☎ 08–11–20–44–44 *€0.06 per minute, 0033/01–72–40–78–50 from U.S.* ⊕ *www. douane.gouv.fr.*

U.S. Information U.S. Customs and Border Protection ⊕ *www.cbp.gov.*

■ ELECTRICITY

The electrical current in Paris is 220 volts, 50 cycles alternating current (AC); and electrical outlets take continental-type plugs, with two round prongs. So you may need to use both an adapter (which enables you to plug your appliance into the different style of socket) and a converter (which allows it to run on the different voltage). Most laptops and mobile phone chargers are dual voltage (i.e., they operate equally well on 110 and 220 volts), so require only an adapter. These days the same is true of many small appliances, though be wary of hair dryers. Always check labels and manufacturer instructions to be sure. Don't use 110-volt outlets marked "For Shavers Only" for high-wattage appliances such as hair dryers.

■ EMERGENCIES

The French National Health Care system has been organized to provide fully equipped, fully staffed hospitals within 30 minutes of every resident in Paris. A sign of a white cross in a blue box appears on all hospitals. This book does not list the major Paris hospitals, as the French government prefers that an emergency operator assign you the best and most convenient option. Note that if you're able to walk into a hospital emergency room by yourself, you are often considered "low priority," and the wait can be interminable (but nowhere near as long as at an ER stateside). So if time is of the essence, it's best to call 112—the French equivalent of 911. Be sure to check with your insurance company before going abroad to verify that you are covered for medical care in other countries.

In a less urgent situation, do what the French do and call SOS Doctor or SOS Dental services; like magic, in less than an hour a certified, experienced doctor or dentist arrives at the door, armed with an old leather case filled with the essentials for diagnosis and treatment (at an average cost of €65). The doctor or dentist may or may not be bilingual, but, at worst, will have a rudimentary understanding of English. This is a very helpful 24-hour service to use for common symptoms of benign illnesses that need to be treated quickly for comfort, such as high fever, toothache, or upset stomachs (which seem to have the unfortunate habit of announcing themselves late at night).

The American Hospital and the Institut Hospitalier Franco-Britannique (formerly the Hertford British Hospital) both have 24-hour emergency hotlines with bilingual doctors and nurses who can provide advice. For small problems, go to a pharmacy, marked by a green neon cross. Pharmacists are authorized to administer first aid and recommend over-the-counter drugs, and they can be very helpful in advising you in English or sending you to the nearest English-speaking pharmacist. Call the police (☎ *112 or 17*) if there has been a crime or an act of violence. On the street, some French phrases that may be needed in an emergency are *Au secours!* (Help!), *urgence* (emergency), *samu* (ambulance), *pompiers* (firemen), *poste de police* (police station), *médecin* (doctor), and *hôpital* (hospital). A hotline of note is SOS Help for English-language crisis information, open daily 3 pm–11 pm.

Doctor and Dentist Referrals SOS Dentaire ☎ *01-43-37-51-00*. **SOS Médecin** ☎ *01-47-07-77-77, 3624 €0.12 per min* ⊕ *www.sosmedecins.com.*

Foreign Embassies U.S. Embassy Consular Section ✉ *4 av. Gabriel, 8e* ☎ *01-43-12-22-22, appointments required (online form) except for lost or stolen passports and emergencies* ⊕ *france.usembassy.gov* Ⓜ *Concorde.*

General Emergency Contacts Ambulance ☎ *15.* **Fire Department** ☎ *18.* **General emergency services for police, fire, and ambulance (like 911)** ☎ *112.* **Police** ☎ *112, 17.*

Hospitals and Clinics The American Hospital ✉ *63 bd. Victor-Hugo, Neuilly-sur-Seine* ☎ *01-46-41-25-25* ⊕ *www.american-hospital.org.* **Institut Hospitalier Franco-Britannique** ✉ *3 rue Barbès, or 4 Rue Kléber, Levallois-Perret* ☎ *01-47-59-59-59* ⊕ *www.ihfb.org/en.*

Hotline SOS Help ☎ *01-46-21-46-46* ⊕ *www.soshelpline.org.*

Pharmacies Pharmacie des Arts. Pharmacie des Arts is open Monday–Saturday, 9 am–9 pm. ✉ *106 bd. Montparnasse, 14e* ☎ *01-43-35-44-88.* **Pharmacie Internationale.** Pharmacie Internationale is open daily, 8 am–1 am. ✉ *5 pl. Pigalle, 9e* ☎ *01-48-78-38-12* ⊕ *pharmacieinternationale.pharminfo.fr.* **Pharmacie Les Champs Dhéry.** Les Champs Dhéry is open all day, every day. ✉ *Galerie des Champs, 84 av. des Champs-Élysées, 8e* ☎ *01-45-62-02-41.* **Pharmacie Matignon.** Pharmacie Matignon is open 24/7. ✉ *1 av. Matignon, at Rond-Point*

des Champs-Élysées, 8e ☎ *01-43-59-86-55* ⊕ *www.pharmaciematignon.com.*

▌HOLIDAYS

With 11 national holidays (*jours feriés*) and five weeks of paid vacation, the French have their share of repose. In May there's a holiday nearly every week, so be prepared for stores, banks, and museums to shut their doors for days at a time. If a holiday falls on a Tuesday or Thursday, many businesses *font le pont* (make the bridge) and close on that Monday or Friday as well. Some exchange booths in tourist areas, small grocery stores, restaurants, cafés, and bakeries usually remain open. Bastille Day (July 14) is observed in true French form. Celebrations begin on the evening of the 13th, when city firefighters open the doors to their stations, often classed as historical monuments, to host their much-acclaimed all-night balls and finish the next day with the annual military parade and air show.

Note that these dates are for the calendar year 2015: January 1 (New Year's Day); April 5–April 6 (Easter Sunday–Monday); May 1 (Labor Day); May 8 (VE Day); May 29 (Ascension Day); June 9 (Pentecost Monday); July 14 (Bastille Day); August 15 (Assumption); November 1 (All Saints' Day); November 11 (Armistice); December 25 (Christmas).

▌HOURS OF OPERATION

On weekdays banks are open generally 9–5, with a lunchtime closure from 12:30–2 (note that the Banque de France is an exception, operating from 9:30–12:30 and 2–4); some banks are also open Saturday 9–5. In general, government offices and businesses are open 9–5. *See Mail, below, for post office hours.*

Most museums are closed one day a week—usually Monday or Tuesday—and on national holidays. Generally, museums and national monuments are open from 10 to 5 or 6. A few close for lunch (noon–2) and are open only in the afternoon on Sunday. Many of the large museums have one *nocturne* (nighttime) opening per week, when they are open until 9:30 or 10. Pharmacies are generally open Monday to Saturday 8:30–8. Nearby pharmacies that stay open late, for 24 hours, or Sunday, are listed on the door.

Generally, large shops are open from 9:30 or 10 to 7 or 8 Monday to Saturday and remain open through lunchtime. Many of the large department stores stay open later on Thursday, and laws passed in 2009 allow them to open on Sunday. Smaller shops and many supermarkets often open earlier (8 am) but take a lengthy lunch break (1–3) and generally close around 8 pm; small food shops are often open Sunday morning 9–1. There is typically a small corner grocery store that stays open late, usually until 11, if you're in a bind for basic necessities like diapers, bread, cheese, and fruit. Note that prices are substantially higher in such outlets than in the larger supermarkets. Not all stores stay open on Sunday, except in the Marais, where shops that stand side by side on Rue des Francs Bourgeois, from antiques dealers to chic little designers, open their doors to welcome hordes of Sunday browsers. The Bastille, the Quartier Latin, the Champs-Élysées, Ile St-Louis, and the Ile de la Cité also have shops that open Sunday.

▌ MAIL

Post offices, or PTT, are scattered throughout every arrondissement and are recognizable by a yellow "La Poste" sign. They're usually open weekdays 8–7, Saturday 8–noon. Airmail (*prioritaire*) letters or postcards usually take at least four days to reach North America. When shipping home antiques or art, request assistance from the dealer, who can usually handle the customs paperwork for you or recommend a licensed shipping company.

Airmail letters and postcards to the United States and Canada cost €0.98 for 20 grams, €1.78 for 50 grams, and €2.40 for 100 grams. Stamps can be bought in post offices and cafés displaying a red "Tabac" sign.

Post Office La Poste Main Office ⊠ *52 rue du Louvre, 1er* ☎ *3631, 08–10–82–18–21 international customer service (press 2 for English), €0.06 per min* ⊕ *www.laposte.fr* ⊙ *Mon.–Sat. 6 am–7:30 am, Sun. 6 am–10 am.*

SHIPPING PACKAGES

Sending overnight mail from Paris is relatively easy. Besides DHL, Federal Express, and UPS, the French post office has an overnight mail service called Chronopost that has special prepaid boxes for international use (and also boxes specifically made to mail wine). All agencies listed can be used as drop-off points, and all have information in English.

Express Services DHL ⊠ *23 rue Feydeau, 2e* ☎ *01–55–35–30–30, 08–20–20–25–25 customer service, €0.15 per min* ⊕ *www.dhl.com.* **Federal Express** ⊠ *63 bd. Haussmann, 8e* ☎ *01–40–85–56–60* ⊕ *www.fedex.com/fr.* **UPS** ⊠ *Office Depot, 168 rue du Faubourg St-Honore, 8e* ☎ *08–21–23–38–77 €0.12 per min* ⊕ *www.ups.com.*

▌ MONEY

Although a stay in Paris is far from cheap, you can find plenty of affordable places to eat and shop, particularly if you avoid the obvious tourist traps. Prices tend to reflect the standing of an area in the eyes of Parisians; the touristy area where value is most difficult to find is the 8e arrondissement, on and around the Champs-Élysées. Places where you can generally be certain to shop, eat, and stay without overpaying include the St-Michel/Sorbonne area on the Rive Gauche; the mazelike streets around Les Halles and Le Marais in central Paris; in Montparnasse south of the boulevard; and in the Bastille, République, and Belleville areas of eastern Paris.

In cafés, bars, and some restaurants you can save money by eating or drinking at the counter instead of sitting at a table. Two prices are listed—*au comptoir* (at the counter) and *à salle* (at a table)—and sometimes a third for the terrace. A cup of coffee, standing at a bar, costs from €1.50; if you sit, it will cost €2 to €7. A glass of beer costs from €2 standing and from €2.50 to €7 sitting; a soft drink costs between €2 and €5. A ham sandwich will cost between €3 and €6.

Expect to pay €7–€10 for a short taxi ride. Museum entry is usually between €7 and €12, though there are hours or days of the week when admission is reduced or free.

Prices throughout this guide are given for adults. Substantially reduced fees are almost always available for children, students, and senior citizens.

ATMS AND BANKS

Your own bank will probably charge a fee for using ATMs (*guichets*) abroad; the foreign bank you use may also charge a fee. Nevertheless, you can usually get a better exchange rate at an ATM than at a currency-exchange office. And extracting funds as you need them is a safer option than carrying around a large amount of cash. Be sure to know your withdrawal limit before taking out cash, and note that French ATMs sometimes restrict how much money you can take out.

Although ATMs are plentiful, you may have to hunt around for Cirrus and Plus locations (they can be looked up online at ⊕ *www.mastercard.ca/atm-locator.html* and ⊕ *www.visa.com/atmlocator*, respectively). Note, too, that you may have better luck with ATMs if you're using a credit card or debit card that is also a Visa or MasterCard rather than just your bank card.

The largest bank in France, BNP Paribas, has agreements with both Barclay's and Bank of America, among others, that allow no-fee withdrawals between affiliated ATMs. In these cases, a withdrawal of €20 would equal the direct exchange value in your home currency. Check with your local bank to see if it has an agreement with a French bank.

■ TIP➔ To get cash at ATMs in Paris, your PIN must be four digits long. If yours has five or more, remember to change it before you leave. If you're having trouble remembering your PIN, do not try more than twice, because at the third attempt the machine will eat your card, and you will have to go back the next morning to retrieve it.

CREDIT CARDS

It's a good idea to inform your credit-card company before you travel, especially if you're going abroad and don't travel internationally very often. Otherwise, the credit-card company might put a hold on your card owing to unusual activity—not a good thing halfway through your trip. Record all your credit-card numbers—as well as the phone numbers to call if your cards are lost or stolen—in a safe place (other than your wallet or purse!), so you're prepared should something go wrong. Both MasterCard and Visa have general numbers you can call if your card is lost, but you're better off calling the number of your issuing bank, since MasterCard and Visa generally just transfer you to your bank anyway; your bank's number is usually printed on your card.

If you plan to use your credit card for cash advances, you'll need to apply for a PIN at least two weeks before your trip. Although it's usually cheaper (and safer) to use a credit card abroad for large purchases (so you can cancel payments or be reimbursed if there's a problem), note that some credit-card companies *and* the banks that issue them add substantial percentages to all foreign transactions, whether they're in a foreign currency or not. Check on these fees before leaving home, so there won't be any surprises when you get the bill.

Also be warned that most non-European cards lack the puce microchip typically found in French credit cards. While waiters and store vendors will have no problem swiping your card, buying métro cards from a machine is impossible without a European card.

■ TIP→ Before you charge something, ask the merchant whether he or she plans to do a dynamic currency conversion (DCC). In such a transaction the credit-card processor (shop, restaurant, or hotel, not Visa or MasterCard) converts the currency and charges you in dollars. In most cases you'll pay the merchant a 3% fee for this service in addition to any credit-card company and issuing-bank foreign-transaction surcharges.

Reporting Lost Cards American Express ✉ *800/528-4800 in U.S. and Canada, 336/393-1111 collect from France* ⊕ *www. americanexpress.com.* **MasterCard** ✉ *800/627-8372 in U.S. and Canada, 08-00-90-13 87* ⊕ *www.mastercard.com.* **Visa** ✉ *800/847-2911 in U.S. and Canada, 08-00-90-11-79* ⊕ *www.visa.com.*

CURRENCY AND EXCHANGE

In 2002 the single European Union (EU) currency—the euro—became the official currency of the 12 (now 18) countries participating in the controversial European Monetary Union (with the notable exceptions of Great Britain, Denmark, and Sweden). The euro system has eight coins: 1 and 2 euros, plus 1, 2, 5, 10, 20, and 50 cents. All coins have one side that has the value of the euro on it, whereas the opposite side is adorned with each country's own unique national symbol. (Be aware that, because of their high nickel content, euro coins can pose problems for people with an allergic sensitivity to the metal.) There are also seven colorful notes: 5, 10, 20, 50, 100, 200, and 500 euros. Notes have the principal architectural styles from antiquity onward on one side and the map and the flag of Europe on the other and are the same for all countries. If you happen to have brought some rumpled old francs from home on this trip, you may as well frame them and

hang them on the wall for posterity, not prosperity: the Banque de France stopped exchanging francs in 2012.

At this writing, €1 equaled approximately US$1.38 and $1.52 Canadian.

The easiest way to get euros is through ATMs; you can find them in airports, train stations, and throughout the city. ATM rates are excellent because they are based on wholesale rates offered only by major banks but when possible it's best to use machines that are protected by a door and not directly on the street. ■ TIP→ It's a good idea to bring some euros with you from home so you don't have to wait in line at the airport. At exchange booths always confirm the rate with the teller before exchanging money. You won't do as well at exchange booths in airports or rail and bus stations, in hotels, in restaurants, or in stores. French banks only exchange the money of their own clients.

■ PACKING

You'll notice it right away: in Paris the women dress well to go shopping, to go to the cinema, to have a drink; the men look good when they're fixing their cars. Admittedly you may see them wearing sweats now, even when they're not doing something *sportif*—but we're not talking gray hoodies. Embroidered designs, quilted materials, animal prints, sparkles: leave it to the French to create a style that's comfy chic. If you want to blend in, don't wear shorts, traditional sweats, or sneakers. Good food in good settings especially deserves good clothing—not necessarily a suit and tie, but a long-sleeved shirt and pants for him, something nice for her.

Be sure to bring rain gear, a comfortable pair of walking shoes, and a sweater or shawl for cool churches and museums. You can never tell about the weather, so a small, foldable umbrella is a good idea. If you'd like to scrutinize the stained glass in churches, bring a pair of small binoculars. A small package of tissues is always a good idea for the occasional rustic

438 < **Travel Smart Paris**

bathroom in cafés, airports, and train stations. An additional note: if you're the kind of person who likes a washcloth in the bathroom, bring your own; they're not something you'll find in Paris hotels.

PASSPORTS AND VISAS

All citizens of Canada and the United States, even infants, need only a valid passport to enter France for stays of up to 90 days. If you lose your passport, call the nearest embassy or consulate and the local police immediately.

RESTROOMS

Use of public toilet facilities in cafés and bars is usually reserved for customers, so you may need to buy a little something first. Bathrooms are often downstairs and are unisex, which may mean walking by a men's urinal to reach the cubicle. Turkish-style toilets—holes in the ground with porcelain pads for your feet—are still found (though they are becoming scarcer). Stand as far away as possible when you press the flushing mechanism to avoid water damage to your shoes. In certain cafés the lights will not come on in the bathroom until the cubicle door is locked. These lights work on a three-minute timer to save electricity. Simply press the button again if the lights go out. Clean public toilets are available in fast-food chains, department stores, and public parks. The city also has 400 *sanisettes*, or public toilet units, located around the city. They are free and generally as proper as one could expect, because they self-clean after every use.

There are restroom attendants in train and métro stations and some of the nicer restaurants and clubs, so always bring some coins to the bathroom. Attendants in restaurants and clubs are in charge of cleaning the bathrooms and perhaps handing you a clean towel; slip some small change into the prominently placed saucer.

SAFETY

Paris is one of the safest big cities in the world, but—as in any big city—you should always be streetwise and alert. Certain neighborhoods are more seedy than dangerous, thanks to the night trade that goes on around Les Halles and St-Denis and on Boulevard Clichy in Pigalle. Some off-the-beaten-path neighborhoods (particularly the outlying suburban communities) may warrant extra precaution. When in doubt, stick to the boulevards and well-lighted, populated streets, but keep in mind that even the Champs-Élysées is a haven for pickpockets.

The métro is quite safe overall, though some lines and stations, in particular lines 2 and 13, get dodgy late at night. Try not to travel alone late at night, memorize the time of the last métro train to your station, ride in the first car by the conductor, and just use your common sense. If you're worried, spend the money on a taxi. Pickpocketing is the main problem, day or night. Be wary of anyone crowding you unnecessarily or distracting you. Pickpockets often work in groups; on the métro they usually strike just before a stop so that they can leap off the train as it pulls into the station. Be especially careful if taking the RER from Charles de Gaulle/Roissy airport into town; disoriented or jet-lagged travelers are vulnerable to sticky fingers.

Pickpockets often target laptop bags, so keep your valuables on your person. It's also wise to distribute your cash, credit cards, IDs, and other valuables between a deep front pocket, an inside jacket or vest pocket, and a hidden money pouch. Don't reach for the money pouch once you're in public.

A tremendous number of protest demonstrations are held in Paris—scarcely a week goes by without some kind of march or public gathering. Most are peaceful, but it's best to avoid them. The CRS (French riot police) carefully guard all major demonstrations, directing traffic and preventing violence. They are armed and use tear gas when and if they see fit.

Report any thefts or other problems to the police as soon as possible (note that *officiers* wear a badge indicating what languages they speak). There are three or four police stations in every arrondissement in Paris and one police station in every train station; go to the police station in the area where the event occurred. In the case of pickpocketing or other theft, the police will give you a Déclaration de Perte ou de Vol (receipt for theft or loss). Police reports must be made in person, and the process is helped along by the S.A.V.E. assistance system for foreign victims—a multilingual software program that files your complaint (and provides you with a receipt) in English. In the case of theft, valuables are usually unrecoverable, but identity documents have been known to resurface. You may need your receipt of theft or loss to replace stolen train or plane tickets, or passports; the receipts may also be useful for filing insurance claims.

Although women traveling alone sometimes encounter troublesome comments and the like, *dragueurs* (men who persistently profess their undying love to hapless female passersby) are a dying breed in this increasingly politically correct world. Note that smiling automatically out of politeness is not part of French culture and can be quickly misinterpreted. If you encounter a problem, don't be afraid to show your irritation. Completely ignoring the *dragueur* should be discouragement enough; if the hassling doesn't let up, don't hesitate to move quickly away.

■TIP➜ A few words of advice: Leave your jewelry at home, and make sure that smartphones and tablets stay out of sight. Don't talk to strangers. If someone approaches asking you to take a photo, sign a petition, or provide directions, just keep walking.

■ TAXES

Taxes must be included in affixed prices in France. Prices in restaurants and hotels must by law include taxes and service charges. ■TIP➜ If these appear as additional items on your bill, you should complain. There is, however, one exception: don't be shocked to find the taxe de séjour (tourist tax) on your hotel tab when you check out. Ranging from €0.20 to €1.50 per person per day, it is applied to all types of lodging. Even if you pre-paid your accommodation online through a third-party travel website, you'll still have to cough up the coins.

The standard rate of the V.A.T. (Value-Added Tax, known in France as T.V.A.) is now 20%, with luxury goods taxed at a higher rate (up to 33%) and restaurant food taxed at a lower one (10%). The V.A.T. for services (restaurants, theaters, etc.) is not refundable, but foreigners are often entitled to a V.A.T. refund on goods they buy. To be eligible for one, the item (or items) that you purchased must have been bought in a single day in a participating store (look for the "Tax-Free" sticker on the door) and must equal or exceed €175.01. ■TIP➜ As of January 1, 2014, there is a new procedure for obtaining this refund—the PABLO system. Participating retailers will provide you with a computer-generated PABLO Value-Added Tax (V.A.T.) refund form containing a barcode and the PABLO logo. You then scan the code before checking in at the airport for your outbound flight. The PABLO machines at CDG and Orly provide service in English and can credit the refunded amount directly to your bank account.

At the airport, be sure to have your passport, your ticket, and your PABLO form for items purchased. Scan the form's barcode and you'll receive a message "OK bordereau confirmé" ("OK, form approved"). An electronic confirmation will be sent directly to the retailer for your reimbursement to be processed.

Remember, this must be done BEFORE checking-in your luggage.

Global Blue is a Europe-wide service with 270,000 affiliated stores and more than 250 refund counters at major airports and border crossings. Its Tax Free Form is the most common cross-continent V.A.T. refund system (look for shops displaying the Global Blue Tax Free Shopping sign). The service issues refunds in the form of cash, check, or credit-card adjustment.

V.A.T. Refunds Global Blue ☎ *00800/32–11–11–11 in France* ⊕ *www.globalblue.com.*

▌TIME

The time difference between New York and Paris is six hours (so when it's 1 pm in New York, it's 7 pm in Paris). The time difference between London and Paris is one hour (so 1 pm in London is 2 pm in Paris).

The European format for abbreviating dates is day/month/year, so 7/5/06 means May 7, not July 5.

▌TIPPING

Bills in bars and restaurants must by law include service (despite what entrepreneurial servers may tell you), so tipping isn't required, but it is polite to round your bill with small change unless you're dissatisfied. The amount varies—from €0.20 for a beer to €1–€3 after a meal. In expensive restaurants it's common to leave an additional 5% on the table.

Tip taxi drivers and hairdressers 10% of the bill. In some theaters and hotels cloakroom attendants may expect nothing (watch for signs that say *pourboire interdit*—tipping forbidden); otherwise, give them €0.50.

If you stay more than two or three days in a hotel, leave something for the chambermaid—about €1–€2 per day. Expect to pay €1.50 (€0.75 in a moderately priced hotel) to the person who carries your bags or hails a taxi for you. In hotels providing room service, give €1–€2 to the waiter (unless breakfast is routinely served in your room). If the chambermaid does pressing or laundering for you, give her €1.50–€2 on top of the bill. If the concierge has been helpful, leave a tip of €5–€15 depending on the service.

Museum guides should get about 10% of the tour price after a guided tour. It's standard practice to tip long-distance bus drivers about €2 after an excursion.

TIPPING GUIDELINES FOR PARIS	
Bellhop	€1–€2, depending on the level of the hotel
Hotel Concierge	€5–€15 if he or she performs a service for you
Hotel Doorman	€1–€2 if he helps you get a cab
Hotel Maid	€1–€2 a day (either daily or at the end of your stay, in cash)
Hotel Room-Service Waiter	€1–€3 per delivery, even if a service charge has been added
Taxi Driver	10% is considered a good tip
Tour Guide	10% of the cost of the tour
Valet Parking Attendant	€1–€2, but only when you get your car
Waiter	Round up for small bills, €1–€3 for meals, 5% in expensive restaurants
Restroom Attendant	Restroom attendants in more expensive restaurants expect small change or €1

▌TOURS

Guided tours are a good option when you don't want to do it all yourself. And not all guided tours are an if-it's-Tuesday-this-must-be-Belgium experience. A knowledgeable guide can take you places that you might never discover on your own, and you may be pushed to see more than you would have otherwise. Tours aren't for everyone, but they can be just the thing for trips to places where making travel arrangements is difficult or time-consuming (particularly when you don't speak the language). Whenever you book a guided tour, find out what's included and what isn't. Also, in most cases prices in tour brochures don't include fees and taxes. And remember that you'll be expected to tip your guide (in cash) at the end of the tour.

BIKE AND SEGWAY TOURS

A number of companies organize bike tours around Paris and its environs (Versailles, Chantilly, and Fontainebleau); these tours always include bikes, helmets, and an English-speaking guide. Costs start at around €30 for a half day; reservations are recommended.

Fat Tire Bike Tours is the best-known anglophone group; in addition to a general orientation bike tour, it organizes a nighttime cycling trip that includes a boat cruise on the Seine. Paris à Vélo, C'est Sympa offers tours that take pedal pushers through the heart of Paris or around outlying arrondissements.

Information Fat Tire Bike Tours ✉ *24 rue Edgar Faure, 15e* ☎ *01-56-58-10-54, 866/614-6218 in U.S. and Canada* ⊕ *www. fattirebiketoursparis.com.* **Paris à Vélo, C'est Sympa** ✉ *22 rue Alphonse Baudin, 11e* ☎ *01-48-87-60-01* ⊕ *www.parisvelosympa. com.*

BOAT TOURS

Several boat tour companies operate Seine cruises that include sightseeing and, in some cases, dining; they generally last from one to three hours. *See the In-Focus on the Seine for more information.* Canauxrama organizes leisurely tours year-round in flat-bottom barges along the Canal St-Martin in eastern Paris. There are four daily departures from April to October (less during the rest of the year); trips last about 2½ hours and have live commentary in French and English. Reservations are required. Paris Canal runs 2½-hour trips with live bilingual commentary between the Musée d'Orsay and the Parc de La Villette from April to mid-November. Reservations are required.

WORD OF MOUTH

"We've been very confused on tipping in the cafés and restaurants. All the guidebooks we read (and many menus) say that service is included. However, whenever we get a bill, it only gives the food prices and TVA. When we ask if 'the service est compris'?, they say no, so we have been leaving tips. Are we double-tipping?" —beachgirl86

"Are you double-tipping? Absolutely. Service is included in the menu prices. As a general rule, if we're very happy with the service—or it's a place we go to often—we leave one or two euros." —PBProvence

Evenings year-round, Yachts de Paris organizes romantic 2½-hour "gourmand cruises" that include a three-course meal (about €200, drinks extra). Cruising the Seine on the Batobus is a convenient way to travel between all of the major sites along the river including Notre-Dame, the Louvre, and the Eiffel Tower. A ticket for one day of unlimited hop-on/hop-off travel costs €15.

Information Batobus ✉ *Port de la Bourdonnais, 7e* ☎ *08-25-05-01-01 €0.15 per min* ⊕ *www.batobus.com.* **Canauxrama** ✉ *13 quai de la Loire, 19e* ☎ *01-42-39-15-00* ⊕ *www. canauxrama.com.* **Paris Canal** ✉ *Paris Canal, Bassin de la Villette, 21 quai de la Loire, 19e* ☎ *01-42-40-96-97* ⊕ *www.pariscanal.com.* **Yachts de Paris** ✉ *Port Henri IV, 4e* ☎ *01-44-54-14-70* ⊕ *entreprises.yachtsdeparis.fr.*

BUS TOURS

Pariscityvision.com offers tours starting at €20. Buses are equipped with headsets that provide commentary in more than a dozen languages, and there are special recordings for children. Paris L'Open Tour runs tours in a London-style double-decker bus with English or French commentary again given via individual headsets. You can catch the bus at any of 50 pickup points; tickets cost €48 for one day, €55 for two days. More hop-on/hop-off tours aboard double-decker buses are available through Les Cars Rouges; these feature nine stops, and a ticket good for two consecutive days costs €31. Low-cost Foxity has two main departures, from Notre-Dame and Opera; a 90-minute outing with headphone commentary costs €17. By day or night, Foxity takes visitors around most of central Paris and offers rare handicap access. For an economical, commentary-free alternative, try a regular Parisian bus. The Montmartrobus (€1.70) runs from the Anvers métro station to the top of Montmartre's winding streets. The RATP's Balabus goes from Gare du Lyon to the Grand Arche de la Défense, passing by dozens of major sights on the way. The Balabus runs from April through September on Sunday and holidays; tickets are €1.70 each, with one to three tickets required, depending on how far you travel.

Information Foxity ⌧ 3 rue de la Chaussée d'Antin, 9e ☎ 01–40–17–09–22 ⊕ www.foxity. com. **Les Cars Rouge** ⌧ 17 quai de Grenelle, 15e ☎ 01–53–95–39–53 ⊕ www.carsrouges. com. **Paris L'OpenTour** ⌧ 13 rue Auber, 9e ☎ 01–42–66–56–56 ⊕ www.parislopentour. com. **RATP** ☎ 3246 €0.34 per min ⊕ www. ratp.fr.

MINIBUS AND CAR TOURS

Pariscityvision.com runs minibus excursions with a multilingual guide to places like Mont St-Michel and the Loire Valley (check the website for promos and prices). Paris Trip and Paris Major Limousine organize tours of Paris and environs by limousine, Mercedes, or minibus (for 4–15 passengers) for a minimum of four hours. Chauffeurs are bilingual. Prices range from €76 to €498, depending on the type of car and the distance covered. Another four-wheel option is 4 Roues sous 1 Parapluie: take an Unexpected Ride (90 minutes, €60) discovering Paris's best kept secrets in an old-school Citroën 2CV (France's answer to the Volkswagen Beetle), or try a quick motor tour around the Champs-Élysées (30 minutes, €20). With 20-odd options available in this iconic car, you can leave the driving to others and just enjoy being a tourist.

Information 4 Rues sous 1 Parapluie ⌧ 22 rue Bernard Dimey, 18e ☎ 08–00–80–06–31 ⊕ www.4roues-sous-1parapluie.com. **Paris Major Limousine** ⌧ 199 bld. Malesherbes, 17e ☎ 01–44–52–50–00 ⊕ www.1st-limousine-services.com. **Paris Trip** ⌧ 2 Cité de Pusy, 17e ☎ 01–56–79–05–23 ⊕ www.paris-trip.com. **Pariscityvision.com** ☎ 01–44–55–61–00 ⊕ www.pariscityvision.com.

SPECIAL-INTEREST AND WALKING TOURS

Has it been a while since Art History 101? Paris Muse can help guide you through the city's museums; with its staff of art historians (all native English-speakers) you can crack the Da Vinci code or gain a new understanding of hell in front of Rodin's sculpted gates. Rates range from €80 to €280, including museum admission.

If you'd like a bit of guidance flexing your own artistic muscles, take a themed photography tour with Paris Photo Tours. Run by Randy Harris, these relaxed excursions are perfect for first-time visitors and anyone hoping to improve their photographic skills.

Sign up with Chic Shopping Paris to smoothly navigate the city's retail scene. You can choose a set tour, such as Chic & Cheap (vintage–secondhand places) or Made in France (unique French products), or ask for an itinerary tailor-made to your interests. Tours start at €100.

Edible Paris, the brainchild of food writer Rosa Jackson, is a customized service for vacationing gastronomes. Submit a wish list of your interests and guidelines for your tastes, and you'll receive a personalized itinerary, maps, and restaurant reservations on request. Prices start around €125 per half day.

Paris by Mouth—the most popular English-language website about eating and drinking in the city—offers tasting tours led by local food writers. Small group tours, which run every day of the week, are available for two to six people (€95 per person). Private tours and larger group tours are available upon request; you can also add on a wine tasting, shared lunch, or baguette-making class.

Paris Walks offers a wide selection of tours, from neighborhood visits and museum jaunts to themed tours such as Writers of the Left Bank. The guides are knowledgeable, taking you into less trammeled streets and divulging interesting stories about even the most unprepossessing spots. A 2-hour group tour costs €12. For a more intimate experience, Context Paris offers specialized in-depth tours of the city's art and architecture led by English-speaking architects and art historians; tours aimed at foodie are also available. Prices range from about €70 per person for a 2½-hour group tour to €550 per party for a full day of custom touring (maximum five people).

Black Paris Tours explores the places made famous by African-American musicians, writers, artists, and political exiles. Options include a 5-hour walking-bus-métro tour (€110, lunch extra) that provides first-time visitors with a city orientation and a primer on the history of African-Americans in Paris.

Secrets of Paris offers personally designed walking tours throughout Paris's neighborhoods for solo travelers or families, adapting half-day or whole-day itineraries based on your specific requests and needs. Museum tours can be arranged, and local guides will also take you to surrounding areas including Chantilly, Versailles, and the flea markets.

A list of interesting walking tours is also available from the Centre des Monuments Nationaux, in the weekly magazine *Pariscope,* and in *L'Officiel des Spectacles,* which covers them under the heading *"Conférences"* (most are in French, unless otherwise noted). The magazines are available at the press kiosk.

If you are as interested in the locals as in the sights per se, you can't go wrong with Paris Greeters (Parisien d'un Jour).

English-speaking resident volunteers take groups of up to six visitors out for a stroll, providing an insider's look at Parisian life along the way. Best of all, the experience is free, though donations are always welcome.

Information **Black Paris Tours** ☎ *01–46–37–03–96, 972/325-8516 U.S. Office* ⊕ *www.blackparistour.com.* **Centre des monuments nationaux** ✉ *Bureau des Visites/Conférences, Hôtel de Sully, 62 rue St-Antoine, 4e* ☎ *01-44-61-21-00* ⊕ *www.monuments-nationaux.fr.* **Chic Shopping Paris** ☎ *09-77-19-77-85, 573/355-9777 U.S. Office* ⊕ *www.chicshoppingparis.com.* **Context Paris** ☎ *09-75-18-04-15, 800/691-6036 U.S. Office* ⊕ *www.contexttravel.com.* **Edible Paris** ⊕ *www.edible-paris.com.* **Paris by Mouth** ⊕ *www.parisbymouth.com.* **Paris Greeters** ⊕ *www.parisgreeters.fr.* **Paris Muse** ☎ *06-73-77-33-52* ⊕ *www.parismuse.com.* **Paris Photo Tours** ☎ *425/281-4649 U.S. office* ⊕ *www.parisphototours.com.* **Paris Walks** ✉ *12 passage Meunier, St-Denis* ☎ *01-48-09-21-40* ⊕ *www.paris-walks.com.* **Secrets of Paris** ☎ *01-71-20-42-27* ⊕ *www.secretsofparis.com.*

▌ VISITOR INFORMATION

The regional tourism board—with multiple Arrivals-level kiosks at both Charles de Gaulle and Orly airports—can provide you with maps, brochures, and more the moment you touch down. Once you're in Paris, you can turn to the civic tourist information office. The main one is centrally located on Rue des Pyramides (near the Opéra), and four branch offices are stationed at the city's most popular tourist sights. Most are open daily; the Gare de Lyon and Gare de l'Est branches, however, are open Monday through Saturday only. These tourism bureaus have friendly, efficient, multilingual staff. You can gather info on special events, local transit, hotels, tours, excursions, and discount passes. You can also purchase Museum Passes and the coveted passports for Versailles, which enable you to avoid additional lines at the château. Extra kiosks pop up in the summer by Notre-Dame, Hotel de Ville, the Champs-Élysées, and Bastille.

Local Tourism Information Office du Tourisme de la Ville de Paris Gare de l'Est ⊠ *Facing platforms 1 and 2, Pl. du 11 novembre 1918, 10e* ⊕ *www.parisinfo.com* Ⓜ *Gare de l'Est.* **Office du Tourisme de la Ville de Paris Anvers** ⊠ *Across from 72 bd. Rochechouart, 18e, Montmartre* ⊕ *www. parisinfo.com* Ⓜ *Anvers.* **Office du Tourisme de la Ville de Paris Gare du Lyon** ⊠ *Facing L & M lines, 20 bd. Diderot, 12e, Bastille/ Nation* ⊕ *www.parisinfo.com* Ⓜ *Gare du Lyon.* **Office du Tourisme de la Ville de Paris Gare du Nord** ⊠ *18 rue de Dunkerque, 10e, Stalingrad/La Chapelle* ⊕ *www.parisinfo.com* Ⓜ *Gare du Nord.* **Office du Tourisme de la Ville de Paris Pyramides** ⊠ *25 rue des Pyramides, 1er, Pyramides* ⊕ *www.parisinfo. com* Ⓜ *Pyramides.* **Visit Paris Region** ⊕ *www. visitparisregion.com.*

ONLINE RESOURCES

Besides the official tourist office websites ⊕ *en.parisinfo.com* and ⊕ *www. visitparisregion.com,* there are several other helpful government-sponsored sites. The Paris mayor's office site, ⊕ *www. paris.fr,* covers all kinds of public cultural attractions, student resources, parks, markets, and more. On the French Ministry of Culture's site, ⊕ *www.culture.fr,* you can search by theme (contemporary art, cinema, music, theater, etc.) or by region (Paris is in the Ile-de-France). The Réunion des Musées Nationaux (RMN), a consortium of public museums, hosts a group site for than 30 national institutions: ⊕ *www.rmn.fr.* Seventeen of these museums are in Paris proper, including the Louvre, the Musée Rodin, and the Musée d'Orsay. The site has visitor info and an exhibition calendar for current and upcoming shows.

A useful website for checking Paris addresses is the phone and address directory, Les Pages Jaunes (⊕ *www. pagesjaunes.fr*). Input a specific address, and you get not just a street map but a photo.

The team at Paris by Mouth (⊕ *parisby-mouth.com*) dishes on the local food scene with help from expat writers like Alexander Lobrano. Also check Lobrano's site (⊕ *www.hungryforparis.com*) for his latest dining reviews and favorite Paris food links. Social media giant Yelp (⊕ *www. yelp.fr*), which launched its French site in 2010, offers honest appraisals of eateries, stores, entertainment venues, and more from regular-Joe reviewers, in both English and French. Secrets of Paris (⊕ *www. secretsofparis.com*) is a free online newsletter with tips on dining, nightlife, accommodations, and sightseeing off the beaten path. Paris-Anglo.com (⊕ *www.paris-anglo.com*) includes directories of cooking schools, galleries, language classes, and more, plus a biweekly column on various *la vie parisienne* topics. Though not entirely dedicated to Paris, the journal *France Today* (⊕ *www.francetoday.com*) and *The Local* (⊕ *www.thelocal.fr*) often cover Paris-related news, arts events, and restaurants. And, of course, there are all sorts of Paris-related blogs that can be great sources of information and travel inspiration. Some of our faves are the Paris Blog (⊕ *www.theparisblog.com*), whose daily posts source from the sizable Parisian English-speaking blogosphere, covering every imaginable topic; Paris Daily Photo (⊕ *www.parisdailyphoto. com*), a fun blog with cool photos from around the city; and Do It in Paris (⊕ *www.doitinparis.com*), a bilingual site covering fashion, shopping, dining, and fun things to do in Paris. French Word-a-Day (⊕ *www.french-word-a-day.typepad. com*) is an engaging slice of life, with a vocabulary bonus.

INDEX

A

A.P.C. (shop), *319, 331*
A. Simon (shop), *314*
À la Mère de Famille (shop), *317*
À l'Étoile d'Or (shop), *319*
A Priori Thé ✕ , *79*
Abbey Bookshop, *329*
Abou d'Abi Bazar (shop), *321*
Abri ✕ , *239*
AB33 (shop), *321*
Acne Studio (shop), *305, 309*
Adelline (shop), *335*
Adventureland (Disneyland Paris), *398*
Afaria ✕ , *206–207*
After-hours dining, *205*
Agatha (shop), *335*
Agnès b (shop), *313*
Agoudas Hakehilos Synagogue, *137*
Air travel, *418–421*
Alberta Ferretti (shop), *305*
Alcazar ✕ , *247–248*
Alexandra Sojfer (shop), *335–336*
Alexandre Biaggi (shop), *334*
Alexandre Reza (shop), *317*
Alice Cadolle (shop), *311*
Alice à Paris (shop), *331*
American Church, *52, 55*
Amorino ✕ , *21, 39*
Ancien Cloître Quartier, *40, 42*
& Other Stories (shop), *305*
Angélina ✕ , *100*
Animation Courtyard (Disneyland Paris), *399*
Anne Sémonin (shop), *313*
Annick Goutal (shop), *304*
Anouschka (shop), *316*
Antik Batik (shop), *331*
Antoine & Lili (shop), *327*
Apartment rentals, *277*
Apostrophe Hotel ⬚ , *290*
Appartements du Roi (King's Apartments), *387*
Aquarium de Paris, *72*
Arc de Triomphe, *16, 21, 64, 67*
Arcades, *107*
Archives Nationales, *137–138*
Arènes de Lutèce (Lutetia Amphitheater), *162, 166–167*
Artazart (shop), *327*
Arthus-Berthand (shop), *336*
Arts centers, *368–370*

Artus Hôtel ⬚ , *288*
Astier ✕ , *242*
Astier de Villatte (shop), *302, 304*
ATMs and banks, *14, 436*
Au Bon Accueil ✕ , *207*
Au Bourguignon du Marais ✕ , *232*
Au Lapin Agile (cabaret), *114, 119, 355–356*
Au Passage ✕ , *242*
Au Pied de Cochon ✕ , *221*
Au Printemps (shop), *104–105, 299, 316*
Au Rocher de Cancale ✕ , *77*
Au Sauvignon ✕ , *248*
Au Trou Gascon ✕ , *235*
Aux Lyonnais ✕ , *226–227*
Avant-Scène (shop), *329*
Avenue des Champs-Élysées, *62, 66*
Avril Gau (shop), *336*
Azzedine Alaïa (shop), *321*

B

Baccarat Museum, *72*
Back Lot (Disneyland Paris), *399*
Backstage Café ✕ , *185*
Baghère (shop), *331*
Bal Café ✕ , *230, 245*
Balenciaga (shop), *299*
Ballroom du Beef Club, *347*
Bars. ⇨ See Nightlife
Basilique de St-Denis, *116*
Bastille district
  hotels, *267*
  nightlife, *359*
  restaurants, *235–238*
  shopping, *326–329*
Bateau-Lavoir (wash-barge), *114, 115*
Bazar Éthic (shop), *327–328*
Belleville, *144, 238–239*
Benoît ✕ , *232*
Bercy
  nightlife, *359*
  sightseeing, *145*
Berluti (shop), *301*
Berthillon ✕ , *21, 39*
BHV (shop), *314*
Bibliothèque National François Mitterrand, *145, 153–154*
Bibliothèque Nationale Richelieu, *86*
Bicycling, *30, 428, 441*

Bistrot des Deux Théâtres ✕ , *230–231*
Bistrot Mélac ✕ , *235*
BLC Design Hotel ⬚ , *291*
Boat and ferry travel, *421*
Boat tours, *21, 36, 50, 146, 392, 441*
Bofinger ✕ , *235–236*
Bois de Boulogne, *21, 194, 196*
Bois de Vincennes, *144, 154–155*
Bonpoint (shop), *298*
Bonton (shop), *321*
Books and movies about Paris, *402–404*
Botanical Gardens (Jardin des Plantes), *159, 162, 163, 165*
Boucherie Roulière ✕ , *248*
Boulevard de Clichy, *114*
Boulevard Raspail, *336*
Boulevard St-Germain, *171*
Boulevard St-Michel, *160*
Bourse du Commerce, *86*
Boutique Renhsen (shop), *327*
Brasserie de l'Isle Saint-Louis ✕ , *206*
Brasserie Lipp ✕ , *175*
Breizh Café ✕ , *232–233*
Bubar ✕ , *233*
Bus tours, *441–442*
Bus travel, *421–423*
Business hours, *14, 434–435*
  nightlife, *342*
  restaurants, *202*
  shops, *14, 296*
By Terry (shop), *304*

C

Cabarets. ⇨ See Nightlife
Café A ✕ , *143*
Café Antoine ✕ , *195*
Café Central ✕ , *51*
Café Coutume ✕ , *209, 245*
Café de Flore ✕ , *175, 248*
Café de la Mairie ✕ , *171*
Café de la Musique ✕ , *151*
Café de la Paix ✕ , *103*
Café des Deux Moulins, *354*
Café des Musées ✕ , *233*
Café du Marché ✕ , *51*
Café du Metro ✕ , *171*
Café Français ✕ , *236*
Café La Belle Férronnière ✕ , *63*
Café Marly ✕ , *223*

PHOTO CREDITS

Cover Photos: Front cover: Jon Arnold/awl-images [Description: Croissant and coffee in a café]. Back cover (from left to right): Tom Nance/iStockphoto; Madeleine Openshaw/Shutterstock; SOMATUS-CAN/Shutterstock. Spine: Ferenc Cegledi/Shutterstock. 1, Sam Gillespie/Alamy. 2, Jon Arnold/age fotostock. 5, SuperStock/age fotostock. Chapter 1: Experience: 8-9, Bildarchiv Monheim/age fotostock. 10-13 (all) and 16 (left), Joanne Rosensweig. 16 (top center), Bryan Busovicki/Shutterstock. 16 (bottom center), Bensliman/Shutterstock. 16 (top right), Jan Kranendonk/Shutterstock. 16 (bottom right), Ferenc Cegledi/Shutterstock. 17 (top left), wikipedia.org. 17 (bottom left), José Fuste Raga/age fotostock. 17 (top center), Jan Kranendonk/Shutterstock. 17 (bottom center), Joanne Rosensweig. 17 (right), travelstock44/Alamy. 18, Rob Knight/iStockphoto. 19 (left), Joanne Rosensweig. 19 (right), Steven Allan/iStockphoto. 20, Jan Kranendonk/Shutterstock. 21 (left), Photofrenetic/Alamy. 21 (right), Jochem Wijnands/age fotostock. 24, Francesco Dazzi/Shutterstock. 25 (left), Joanne Rosensweig.25 (right), alysta/Shutterstock. 26, hsinli wang/iStockphoto. 27 (left), Joanne Rosensweig. 27 (right), claude thibault/Alamy. 28, Joseph Cesare/wikipedia.org. 29 (left), Fpinault/wikipedia.org. 29 (right), Raphael Frey/wikipedia.org. 30, Pline/wikipedia.org. 31 (top), Paul Hahn/laif/Aurora Photos. 31 (bottom), SuperStock/age fotostock. 32, (top) Galina Barskaya/Shutterstock. 32 (bottom), Renand Visage/age fotostock. 33 (top left) Stevan Stratford/iStockphoto. 33 (top right), Robert Haines/Alamy. 33 (bottom), Paul Hahn/Laif/Aurora Photos. 34 (left), Renaud Visage/age fotostock. 34 (right), Carsten Madsen/iStockphoto. 35 (top left), xc/Shutterstock. 35 (top right), Mehdi Chebil/Alamy. 35 (bottom), Corbis. 36, Elena Elisseeva/Shutterstock. Chapter 2: The Islands: 37, Jonathan Larsen/Shutterstock. 39, ImageGap/Alamy. 40, ImageGap/Alamy. 43, SuperStock/age footstock. 45, Ewan Chesser/Shutterstock. 46, Fabien1309/wikipedia.org. 47, Renaud Visage/age fotostock. 48, (left), Frank Peterschroeder/Bilderberg/Aurora Photos.48, (right), ostill/Shutterstock. Chapter 3: Around the EIffel Tower: 49, Sean Nel/Shutterstock. 51, Patrick Hermans/Shutterstock. 52, Cristina CIOCHINA/Shutterstock. 53, tkachuk/Shutterstock. 56, Directphoto.org/Alamy. 58, and 59, (left), Directphoto.org/Alamy. Chapter 4: The Champs-Elysées: 61, Art Kowalsky/Alamy. 63, Clay McLachlan/Aurora Photos. 64, dalbera/Flickr. 65, fabio chironi/age fotostock. 67, Lazar Mihai-Bogdan/Shutterstock. 73, dalbera/Flickr. Chapter 5: Around the Louvre: 75, blickwinkel/Alamy. 77, Sylvain Grandadam/age fotostock. 78, David A. Barnes/Alamy. 80, Travel Pix Collection/age fotostock. 82, pandapaw/Shutterstock. 88-89, Fischer/Bilderberg/Aurora Photos. 89 (top), Public Domain. 90 (top left, top right, bottom left, bottom 2nd from left, bottom 3rd from left, and right), Public Domain. 90 (4th from left), Toño Labra/age fotostock. 91 (top left), Visual Arts Library (London)/Alamy. 91 (top right), SPC 5 James Cavalier, US Military/wikipedia. org. 91 (bottom left), Hideo Kurihara/Alamy. 91 (bottom 2nd from left), Directphoto.org/Alamy. 91 (bottom 3rd from left, bottom 4th from left, and bottom right), Public Domain. 92, Rough Guides/Alamy. 93 (top), Peter Horree/Alamy. 93 (2nd from top), Public Domain. 93 (3rd from top), Timothy McCarthy/Art Resource. 93 (bottom), INTERFOTO Pressebildagentur/Alamy. 94, PCL/Alamy. 95 (top), The Bridgeman Art Library. 95 (2nd from top), Toño Labra/age foto stock. 95 (3rd from top), legge/Alamy. 95 (bottom), Public Domain. 96, SuperStock/age fotostock. 97 (top, 2nd from top, and bottom), Public Domain. 97 (3rd from top), Hideo Kurihara/Alamy. Chapter 6: Les Grand Boulevards: 101, Kevin George/Alamy. 103, Tristan Deschamps/Alamy. 104, iStockphoto. Chapter 7: Montmartre: 111, Hemis/Alamy. 113, Matthew Berg heiser/Shutterstock. 114, Jon Arnold Images/Alamy. 117, rfx/SHutterstock. 120, L F File/Shutterstock. 121, Rough Guides/Alamy. Chapter 8: Le Marais: 123, Oliver Knight/Alamy. 125, Berndt Fischer/age fotostock. 126, David Jordan/age fotostock. 128-29, Marisa Allegra Williams/iStockphoto. 132, M & M Valledor/age fotostock. 136, tbkmedia.de/Alamy. 139, Timothy Ball/iStockphoto. Chapter 9: Eastern Paris: 141, Bob Handelman/Alamy. 143, Berndt Fischer/age fotostock. 144, f1 online/Alamy. 147, Boris Karpinski/ Alamy. 148, Alex Segre/Alamy. Chapter 10: The Latin Quarter: 157, Danita Delimont/Alamy. 159, AA World Travel Library/Alamy. 160, Renaud Visage/age fotostock. 161, adam eastland/Alamy. 164, Aschaf/Flickr. Chapter 11: St-Germain-des-Pres: 169, Robert Harding Picture Library Ltd/Alamy. 171, Robert Harding Picture Library Ltd/Alamy. 172, Ian Dagnall/Alamy. 173, David Noton Photography/Alamy. 176, Sylvain Grandadam/age fotostock. 178, Public Domain. 180, Mark Edward Smith/age fotostock. Chapter 12: Montparnasse: 183, Berndt Fischer/age fotostock. 185 and 186, Berndt Fischer/age fotostock. Chapter 13: Western Paris: 191, Eddie Gerald/Alamy. 193, Brian Yarvin/age fotostock. 194, tbkmedia.de/Alamy. 196, Directphoto.org/Alamy. Chapter 14: Where to Eat: 199, Directphoto.org/Alamy. 200, Dana Ward/Shutterstock. 210, P. Narayan/age fotostock. Chapter 15: Where to Stay: 265, Four Seasons Hotels and Resorts. 266, The Leading Hotels of the World. Chapter 16: Shopping: 293, Alex Segre / Alamy. 294, Croixboisee, Fodors.com member. 328, Robert Harding Picture Library Ltd/Alamy. 334, Walter Bibikow / age foto stock. Chapter 17: Nightlife: 339, Marco Cristofori/age fotostock. 340, cgo2/Flickr. 353, Linda Sole/Alamy. Chapter 18: Performing Arts: 365 and 366, Direct-

NOTES

NOTES

NOTES

NOTES

NOTES

NOTES

NOTES